The

International Critical Commentary

on the Holy Scriptures of the Old and New Testaments

UNDER THE EDITORSHIP OF

THE REV. CHARLES AUGUSTUS BRIGGS, D.D., D.LITT.
Edward Robinson Professor of Biblical Theology, Union Theological Seminary, New York;

THE REV. SAMUEL ROLLES DRIVER, D.D., D.LITT.
Regius Professor of Hebrew, Oxford;

THE REV. ALFRED PLUMMER, D.D.
Master of University College, Durham.

The International Critical Commentary

on the Holy Scriptures of the Old and New Testaments.

EDITORS' PREFACE.

THERE are now before the public many Commentaries, written by British and American divines, of a popular or homiletical character. *The Cambridge Bible for Schools*, the *Handbooks for Bible Classes and Private Students*, *The Speaker's Commentary*, *The Popular Commentary* (Schaff), *The Expositor's Bible*, and other similar series, have their special place and importance. But they do not enter into the field of Critical Biblical scholarship occupied by such series of Commentaries as the *Kurzgefasstes exegetisches Handbuch zum A. T.;* De Wette's *Kurzgefasstes exegetisches Handbuch zum N. T.;* Meyer's *Kritisch-exegetischer Kommentar;* Keil and Delitzsch's *Biblischer Commentar über das A. T.;* Lange's *Theologisch-homiletisches Bibelwerk;* Nowack's *Handkommentar zum A. T.;* Holtzmann's *Handkommentar zum N. T.* Several of these have been translated, edited, and in some cases enlarged and adapted, for the English-speaking public; others are in process of translation. But no corresponding series by British or American divines has hitherto been produced. The way has been prepared by special Commentaries by Cheyne, Ellicott, Kalisch, Lightfoot, Perowne, Westcott, and others; and the time has come, in the judgment of the projectors of this enterprise, when it is practicable to combine British and American scholars in the production of a critical, comprehensive

Commentary that will be abreast of modern biblical scholarship, and in a measure lead its van.

Messrs. Charles Scribner's Sons of New York, and Messrs. T. & T. Clark of Edinburgh, propose to publish such a series of Commentaries on the Old and New Testaments, under the editorship of Prof. C. A. Briggs, D.D., in America, and of Prof. S. R. Driver, D.D., for the Old Testament, and the Rev. Alfred Plummer, D.D., for the New Testament, in Great Britain.

The Commentaries will be international and inter-confessional, and will be free from polemical and ecclesiastical bias. They will be based upon a thorough critical study of the original texts of the Bible, and upon critical methods of interpretation. They are designed chiefly for students and clergymen, and will be written in a compact style. Each book will be preceded by an Introduction, stating the results of criticism upon it, and discussing impartially the questions still remaining open. The details of criticism will appear in their proper place in the body of the Commentary. Each section of the Text will be introduced with a paraphrase, or summary of contents. Technical details of textual and philological criticism will, as a rule, be kept distinct from matter of a more general character; and in the Old Testament the exegetical notes will be arranged, as far as possible, so as to be serviceable to students not acquainted with Hebrew. The History of Interpretation of the Books will be dealt with, when necessary, in the Introductions, with critical notices of the most important literature of the subject. Historical and Archæological questions, as well as questions of Biblical Theology, are included in the plan of the Commentaries, but not Practical or Homiletical Exegesis. The Volumes will constitute a uniform series

THE INTERNATIONAL CRITICAL COMMENTARY.

THE following eminent Scholars are engaged upon the Volumes named below :—

THE OLD TESTAMENT.

Genesis.	The Rev. T. K. CHEYNE, D.D., Oriel Professor of the Interpretation of Holy Scripture, University of Oxford.
Exodus.	The Rev. A. R. S. KENNEDY, D.D., Professor of Hebrew, University of Edinburgh.
Leviticus.	J. F. STENNING, M.A., Fellow of Wadham College, Oxford.
Numbers.	G. BUCHANAN GRAY, D.D., Professor of Hebrew, Mansfield College, Oxford. [*Now Ready.*
Deuteronomy.	The Rev. S. R. DRIVER, D.D., D.Litt., Regius Professor of Hebrew, Oxford. [*Now Ready.*
Joshua.	The Rev. GEORGE ADAM SMITH, D.D., LL.D., Professor of Hebrew, Free Church College, Glasgow.
Judges.	The Rev. GEORGE MOORE, D.D., Professor of Theology, Harvard University, Cambridge, Mass. [*Now Ready.*
Samuel.	The Rev. H. P. SMITH, D.D., Professor of Biblical History, Amherst College, Mass. [*Now Ready.*
Kings.	The Rev. FRANCIS BROWN, D.D., D.Litt., LL.D., Professor of Hebrew and Cognate Languages, Union Theological Seminary, New York City.
Chronicles.	The Rev. EDWARD L. CURTIS, D.D., Professor of Hebrew, Yale University, New Haven, Conn.
Ezra and Nehemiah.	The Rev. L. W. BATTEN, Ph.D., sometime Professor of Hebrew, P. E. Divinity School, Philadelphia, now Rector of St. Mark's Church, New York City.
Esther.	The Rev. L. B. PATON, Ph.D., Professor of Hebrew, Hartford Theological Seminary, Hartford, Conn.
Psalms.	The Rev. CHARLES A. BRIGGS, D.D., D.Litt., Edward Robinson Professor of Biblical Theology, Union Theological Seminary, New York.
Proverbs.	The Rev. C. H. TOY, D.D., LL.D., Professor of Hebrew, Harvard University, Cambridge, Massachusetts. [*Now Ready.*
Job.	The Rev. S. R. DRIVER, D.D., D.Litt., Regius Professor of Hebrew, Oxford.
Isaiah, Ch. 1–39.	The Rev. S. R. DRIVER, D.D., D Litt., Regius Professor of Hebrew, Oxford.
Isaiah, Ch. 40–66.	The late Rev. A. B. DAVIDSON, D.D., LL.D., sometime Professor of Hebrew, Free Church College, Edinburgh.
Jeremiah.	The Rev. A. F. KIRKPATRICK, D.D., Regius Professor of Hebrew, Cambridge, England.
Daniel.	The Rev. JOHN P. PETERS, Ph.D., D.D., sometime Professor of Hebrew, P. E. Divinity School, Philadelphia, now Rector of St. Michael's Church, New York City.
Amos and Hosea.	W. R. HARPER, Ph.D., LL.D., President of the University of Chicago, Illinois. [*In the Press.*
Micah to Malachi.	W. R. HARPER, Ph.D., LL.D., President of the University of Chicago, Illinois.

THE NEW TESTAMENT.

St. Matthew.	The Rev. WILLOUGHBY C. ALLEN, M.A., Fellow of Exeter College, Oxford.
St. Mark.	The late Rev. E. P. GOULD, D.D., sometime Professor of New Testament Literature, P. E. Divinity School, Philadelphia. [*Now Ready.*
St. Luke.	The Rev. ALFRED PLUMMER, D.D., sometime Master of University College, Durham. [*Now Ready.*
Harmony of the Gospels.	The Rev. WILLIAM SANDAY, D.D., LL.D., Lady Margaret Professor of Divinity, Oxford, and the Rev. WILLOUGHBY C. ALLEN, M.A., Fellow of Exeter College, Oxford.
Acts.	The Rev. FREDERICK H. CHASE, D.D., Fellow of Christ's College and Vice Chancellor, Cambridge, Eng.
Romans.	The Rev. WILLIAM SANDAY, D.D., LL.D., Lady Margaret Professor of Divinity and Canon of Christ Church, Oxford, and the Rev. A. C. HEADLAM, M.A., Fellow of All Souls' College, Oxford. [*Now Ready.*
Corinthians.	The Right Rev. ARCH. ROBERTSON, D.D., LL.D., Lord Bishop of Exeter.
Galatians.	The Rev. ERNEST D. BURTON, D.D., Professor of New Testament Literature, University of Chicago.
Ephesians and Colossians.	The Rev T. K. ABBOTT, B.D., D.Litt., sometime Professor of Biblical Greek, Trinity College, Dublin, now Librarian of the same. [*Now Ready.*
Philippians and Philemon.	The Rev. MARVIN R. VINCENT, D.D., Professor of Biblical Literature, Union Theological Seminary, New York City. [*Now Ready.*
Thessalonians.	The Rev. JAMES EVERETT FRAME, M.A., Asst. Professor in the New Testament Department, Union Theological Seminary, New York.
The Pastoral Epistles.	The Rev. WALTER LOCK, D.D., Warden of Keble College, and Professor of Exegesis, Oxford.
Hebrews.	The Rev. A. NAIRNE, M.A., Professor of Hebrew in King's College, London.
St. James.	The Rev JAMES H. ROPES, B.D., Bussey Professor of New Testament Criticism in Harvard University.
Peter and Jude.	The Rev. CHARLES BIGG, D.D., Regius Professor of Ecclesiastical History and Canon of Christ Church, Oxford. [*Now Ready.*
The Epistles of John.	The Rev. S. D. F. SALMOND, D.D., Principal and Professor of Systematic Theology, Free Church College, Aberdeen.
Revelation.	The Rev. ROBERT H. CHARLES, D.D., Professor of Biblical Greek in the University of Dublin.

Other engagements will be announced shortly.

NUMBERS

GEORGE BUCHANAN GRAY, M.A., D.D.

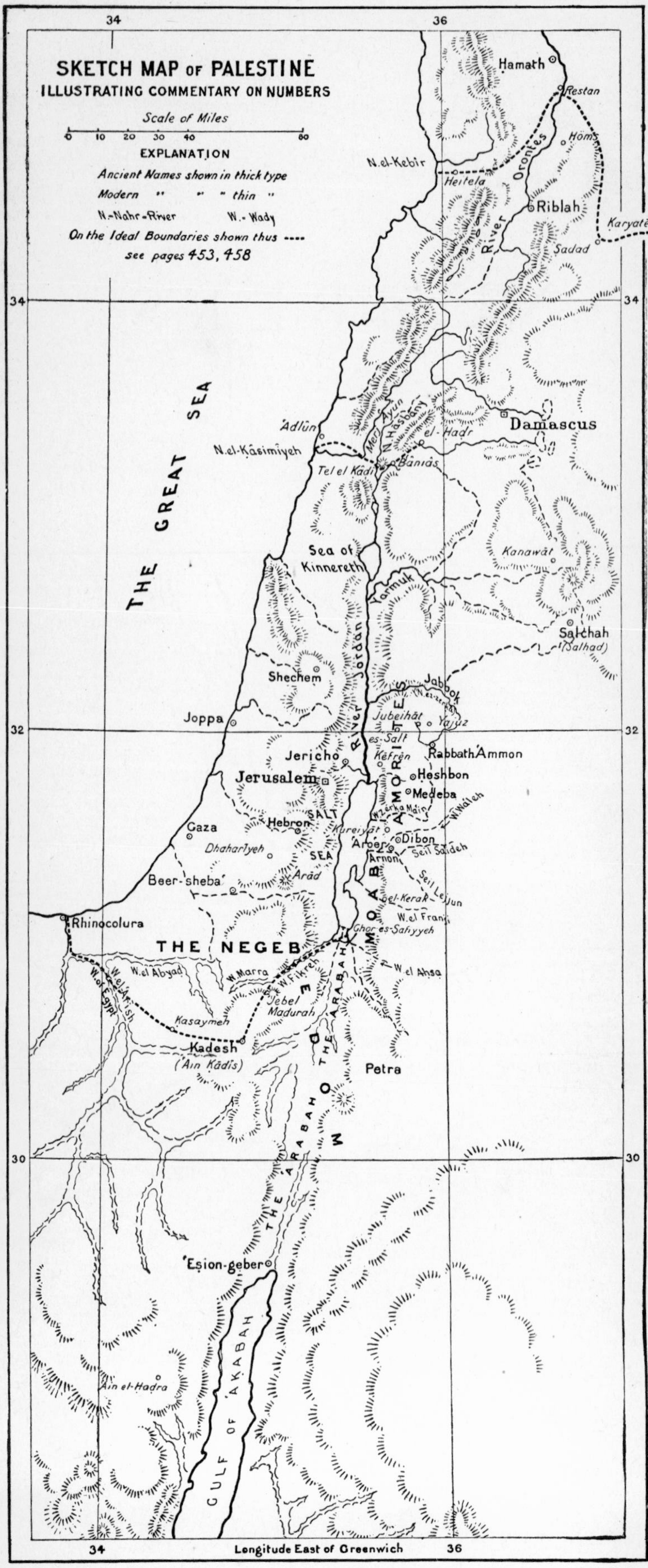
SKETCH MAP of PALESTINE
ILLUSTRATING COMMENTARY ON NUMBERS
Scale of Miles
0 10 20 30 40 80
EXPLANATION
Ancient Names shown in thick type
Modern " " " thin "
N.-Nahr-River W.-Wady
On the Ideal Boundaries shown thus ----
see pages 453, 458
34
36
32
30
THE GREAT SEA
Hamath
Restan
Homs
N.el-Kebir
Heitela
River Orontes
Riblah
Karyatên
Sadad
Damascus
Adlûn
N.el-Kâsimîyeh
Merj 'Ayûn
N.Hasbâny
el-Hadr
Tel el Kâdi
Bânias
Sea of Kinnereth
Kanawât
Yarmuk
Salchah
(Salhad)
Shechem
River Jordan
Jabbok
Jubeihât
Yajuz
Joppa
es-Salt
Jericho
Kefrên
Rabbath Ammon
Jerusalem
Heshbon
Medeba
AMORITES
SALT SEA
Hebron
W.Zerka Main
W.Waleh
Gaza
Kureiyât
Dibon
Aroer
Arnon
Seil Saideh
Dhaharîyeh
Arâd
Beer-sheba
Seil Lejjun
Seil Kerak
MOAB
W.el Franj
Rhinocolura
Ghor es-Safiyyeh
THE NEGEB
W.el Ahsa
W.el Abyad
W.Marra
W.Fikreh
EDOM
W.el-Arish
W.of Egypt
Jebel Madurah
Kasaymeh
Kadesh
('Ain Kâdîs)
Petra
THE ARABAH
Esion-geber
GULF OF 'AKABAH
'Ain el-Hadra
Longitude East of Greenwich

THE INTERNATIONAL CRITICAL COMMENTARY

A CRITICAL AND EXEGETICAL COMMENTARY ON NUMBERS

BY

GEORGE BUCHANAN GRAY, M.A., D.D.
PROFESSOR OF HEBREW AND OLD TESTAMENT EXEGESIS
IN MANSFIELD COLLEGE, OXFORD

NEW YORK
CHARLES SCRIBNER'S SONS
1903

PREFACE.

IT is five-and-thirty years since the English translation of Keil's Commentary on Numbers, which had been published in Germany five years before, appeared. Neither the *Speaker's Commentary*, nor any other English Commentary on the book published since, possesses any independent value. Keil's interpretation started from a standpoint which was at the time professedly, and recognised to be, conservative, and which the advance of scholarship in the interval has increasingly shown to be untenable. It is unnecessary to say more to indicate the need for a new English Commentary.

In Germany a second edition of Keil's work appeared in 1870, Dillmann's Commentary in 1886, and Strack's in 1894. To Dillmann the present writer is greatly indebted. But even since 1886 standpoints have changed, and knowledge on many special points has increased. It is the aim of the present Commentary to enable the reader to look at and interpret the Book of Numbers from these new standpoints in the light of the new, as well as of the old, knowledge.

Two new German Commentaries are announced as likely to appear shortly:* these, of course, have not been available for use in the preparation of the present volume.

* One in Nowack's *Handkommentar zum AT*, by Baentsch; the other in Marti's *Kurzer Hand-Commentar zum AT*, by Holzinger.

A few monographs on certain sections of the book have recently appeared, and Paterson's critical edition of the text was published in 1900; but in the main the new material for the interpretation of the book has had to be sought in more general works on Lexicography, Textual and Literary Criticism, Archæology, and Anthropology. Inscriptions and Monumental Evidence have cast less direct light on Numbers than on many of the books of the Old Testament. On the other hand, several sections of the book, when viewed from the standpoint of modern anthropological study, especially as represented in the works of Tylor and Frazer, gain greatly in intelligibility.

Many of the works to which the writer has been mainly indebted will be found in the List of Abbreviations (p. xvi); others, in the literature given at the beginning of several sections of the Commentary and in the footnotes. Special reference may be made here to the volume on Deuteronomy in the present series. In some parts the Books of Numbers and Deuteronomy are parallel; where this is the case, it has frequently seemed best to explain matters, which had been already fully discussed in the Commentary on Deuteronomy, briefly and with a reference to that work. Numbers is also closely related to Exodus and Leviticus; but the commentaries on these books have not yet appeared; certain matters not alluded to in Numbers should obviously find their full explanation in those works: in other cases it has been more difficult to decide where the fuller discussion should most naturally be given or sought; but I hope that I have been able to avoid both leaving too much to my fellow-contributors to this series, and unduly anticipating them in what it is for them to interpret.

In the transliteration of Proper Names I have followed in the main the practice of the editor of the series in his Commentary on Deuteronomy. But in the last eight years those who are likely to use this work have been becoming increasingly accustomed to the form *Yahweh*: I have therefore adopted it in preference to the non-form *Jehovah*, for it cannot come far short of representing the original pronunciation. The צ I have transliterated by ṣ, since ẓ, when comparison has to be made with the Arabic, is misleading; this necessitates substituting Ṣelopheḥad, Ṣoan, etc., for the familiar Zelophehad, Zoan, etc. Cross references under Z in the Index (in the case of words beginning with this letter) will, I hope, diminish any difficulty which this may occasion to some readers. The quantities of vowels I have in many cases not marked at every occurrence of the word, but only on the first occurrence, or where, for the sake of comparison, it was important.

The map, it is hoped, will prove a convenience in a volume which necessarily contains a number of geographical notes and discussions, and refers to places which cannot be found in any single existing and easily accessible map. To avoid the unfortunate confusion produced by the common practice of attaching Old Testament names to sites even when the identifications are at best very uncertain,* the ancient names have only been inserted when the identifications are free from all reasonable doubt; in other cases modern names, distinguished from the ancient by difference of type, have been used. Without overcrowding it would have been impossible to include all the sites (especially those East of Jordan) to which reference is made in the Commentary, but none that are essential to the understanding of the more important notes have been intentionally omitted.

I need not repeat or epitomise here what I have said in the Introduction on the religious value of Numbers. But

* This fault is very conspicuous in the otherwise convenient map of Palestine in Murray's *Handy Classical Maps*, edited by G. B. Grundy.

one thing I may add: Numbers is but part of a whole; and the value of the part can only be adequately judged when its connection with the whole is borne in mind. Still more true is this of individual sections of the book; in some of these we come across crude, or primitive, or very imperfect, religious ideas and sentiments; I have felt it my duty, no less in the interests of religion than of scholarship (and in so far as the goal of both is truth, their interests are the same), to indicate as fully and as faithfully as I could the crudeness and imperfections of these ideas as well as the finer and higher ideas that find their expression in other parts of the book. For the highest that the religion of Israel attained to can only be fully appreciated in the light of the lowest which it touched, sometimes wholly, sometimes partially, to transform and ennoble.

My last word must be one of the warmest gratitude for the unwearying attention with which Dr. Driver has read my book as it has been passing through the press, and for the numerous suggestions with which he has favoured me. It has not been always possible to utilise these suggestions as fully as I could have wished; to have done so would have involved overmuch rearrangement of the printed sheets; but even as it is, the work has been enriched in many places as a result of this help, which can only be duly appreciated by those who have received or given similar service. I must also thank the editors of the *Encyclopædia Biblica* for the favour of allowing me to see advance sheets of many articles in that work, including some in the forthcoming and concluding fourth volume.

G. BUCHANAN GRAY.

OXFORD, *January* 1903.

CONTENTS.

ADDENDA AND CORRIGENDA.

Pp. 45, 55. More interesting than any of the parallels to the ordeal of Jealousy which are cited in the Commentary, is the parallel afforded by the recently discovered laws of Ḫammurabbi (*c.* 2000 B.C.). In the law of Nu. 5, the ordeal and the oath of purgation are combined; in the law of Manu (cited on p. 45), they are alternative means of reaching the truth, but no rule is given as to the circumstances under which a particular alternative is to be adopted; in the Babylonian law the oath is provided for one case, the ordeal for another. Apparently, as the Rev. H. W. Robinson, of Pitlochry, in a written communication, expresses it, "the suspicion confined to the husband (and therefore self-originated) is dealt with by the more lenient test of a tribunal-oath; whilst outside suspicion requires the more severe treatment of the water ordeal." The relevant sections of the laws of Ḫammurabbi run as follows in Mr. Johns' translation (*The Oldest Code of Laws in the World*, Edin. 1903): "§ 131. If the wife of a man her husband has accused her, and she has not been caught in lying with another male, she shall swear by God and return to her house. § 132. If a wife of a man on account of another male has had the finger pointed at her, and has not been caught in lying with another male, for her husband she shall plunge into the holy river." The nature of the ordeal, which is here provided for, is clearly indicated in § 2: "If a man has put a spell upon a man, and has not justified himself, he upon whom the spell is laid shall go to the holy river, he shall plunge into the holy river, and if the holy river overcome him, he who wove the spell upon him shall take to himself his house. If the holy river makes that man to be innocent, and has saved him, he who laid the spell upon him shall be put to death. He who plunged into the holy river shall take to himself the house of him who wove the spell upon him."

P. 121, *top*. The second meaning of Cush (Cassites) would have been better described as highly probable than as "certain."

Pp. 299, 300. It is very difficult to find a rendering of הַמֹּשְׁלִים that does not imply either more or less than the actual evidence, which is scanty, warrants. "Ballad-singers," the rendering proposed long ago by J. J. S. Perowne (Smith's *DB*. ii. 584*a*), comes nearest to what is required, especially, perhaps, if we understand "ballad" chiefly of popular songs, treating (like the "border minstrelsy") in most cases of the defeat of foes, the deeds of famous warriors, and the like. We can only be guided by the nature of the one and only specimen (Nu. 21^{27-30}) that happens to be preserved of the poems actually sung or recited by these men, and by the use of משל. משל is a word of very wide meaning (p. 344 f.); but some of its meanings are clearly inapplicable in determining the meaning of הַמֹּשְׁלִים; the *m^eshālim* which these men recited were neither short pregnant sayings of the type found in 1 S. 24^{14}, nor artistic apothegms such as constitute the bulk of the Book of Proverbs (c. 10 ff.). Still, if משל became so widely applicable, it is necessary to allow for the probability that the poems whence the "ballad-singers" derived their name were not strictly limited to a single type. The usages of משל most directly serviceable in considering the type of poems recited by the "ballad-singers" are to be found in Is. 14^{4}, Mic. 2^{4}, Hab. 2^{6}. The *māshāl* of Is. 14^{4} is a triumphal song over the fall of the king of Babylon, Israel's great enemy; this *māshāl* may well have been modelled on the ancient *m^eshālîm* or "ballads," which used to be actually recited; many of these popular and often-repeated poems, it is only probable, still existed in and after the Exile, and were known to the author of Is. 14. Possibly, however, the *māshāl* in Is. 14 excels the ancient *m^eshālîm* in length, elaboration, and artistic skill as greatly as the dirges of Lamentations excel the earlier dirges cited in 2 S. $3^{33f.}$, Am. 5^{1}, and, so far as length and elaboration are concerned, the more famous dirge of David (2 S. $1^{17ff.}$). The use in Hab. 2^{6} is similar. The *māshāl* of Mic. $2^{4f.}$ is called a "lamentation" (נְהִי); it is not a triumphal poem; in spite of an obviously corrupt text (see Nowack's *Comm.*), it somewhat clearly bewails the calamities of Israel. Possibly, therefore, the "ballad-singers" may at times have worked on the emotions of their audience by other than triumphal and heroic songs. If a "lamentation" (נהי) might be termed a *māshāl*, might not also a *ḳînah* or dirge, such as that in Ezek. 19^{2-9}, with its correct allusions, be similarly classed? In any case it is hazardous to assume that the term *māshāl* could not have been applied to many poetical compositions which do not happen to be so termed in the OT.; but, if this be so, it is impossible to determine, with the scanty evidence available, the precise range of subjects which the "ballad-singers" treated, or the emotions to which they appealed. So far as the *character* of the poem is concerned, we should perhaps be justified in concluding (from a comparison with Nu. 21^{27-30}) that a *māshāl* was a poem dealing pre-eminently with war or defeat, but at the same time written in a less elevated strain than the triumphal odes of Ex. 15 and Jud. 5, and also probably treating the theme from a more *secular* point of view.

PRINCIPAL ABBREVIATIONS EMPLOYED.

1. Texts and Versions.

AV. . . . Authorised Version.
EV. . . . English Version.
MT. . . . The Massoretic Text (*i.e.* the vocalised text of the Hebrew Bible). Variants in the Hebrew codices have been cited from De Rossi, *Variæ Lectiones Vet. Test.*, vol. ii.
OT. . . . Old Testament.
RV. . . . Revised Version.
S . . . . The Samaritan recension of the Hebrew (unvocalised) text (ed. Blayney, Oxford, 1790).
𝔊 . . . . The Greek (LXX) Version of the Old Testament (ed. Swete, Cambridge, 1887–1894). The readings of the codices are, when necessary, distinguished thus:—$𝔊^{A}$ $𝔊^{B}$ (Alexandrian, Vatican, etc.); but $𝔊^{L}$ = Lucian's recension as edited by Lagarde (*Libr. Vet. Test. Græce*, Göttingen, 1883). The cursives have been (occasionally) cited from *Vet. Test. Græce, cum variis lectionibus*, ed. Holmes, Oxon. 1798.
ℌ . . . . Jewish recension of the Hebrew (unvocalised) text, *i.e.* the consonants of the ordinary Hebrew MSS. and printed Bibles.
𝔖 . . . . The Syriac Version (Peshiṭto).
𝔗 . . . . The Aramaic Versions or Targums. 𝔗 commonly stands in particular for the Targum of Onkelos, which, when necessary, is distinguished as $𝔗^{o}$; $𝔗^{Jer}$=the (so-called) Jerusalem Targum; $𝔗^{Jon}$= the Targum of Jonathan. These are cited from Walton's "Polyglott," vols. i. and iv.
𝔙 . . . . Vulgate.

2. Sources (see pp. xxix–xxxix).

D . . . . The Deuteronomist.
E . . . . The Elohistic narrative, or the Elohist.
H . . . . The Law of Holiness.

J . . . . The Yahwistic narrative, or the Yahwist.

JE . . . . The editor (or work of the editor) who combined J and E; also the narrative of J and E when these cannot be analysed.

P . . . . The work of the priestly school, or the (or a) priestly writer.

P^g . . . . The author of the History of Sacred Institutions, or his work (^{g}=groundwork; see p. xxxiii f.).

P^s . . . . Work of the priestly school later than P^g (^{s}= secondary).

P^x . . . . Work of the priestly school of uncertain (=^{x}) date, but in some cases probably *earlier* than P^g.

3. Authors' Names and Books.

[See also the literature cited at the beginning of several sections of the Commentary; the works thus given are, within the section, often cited by the author's name only.]

Addis . . . W. E. Addis, *The Documents of the Hexateuch*, vol. i. 1892; vol. ii. 1898. Vol. i. contains in consecutive form the work of JE; vol. ii. that of D and P; both volumes include introductions and critical notes.

Bacon . . . B. W. Bacon, *The Triple Tradition of the Exodus* (Hartford (U.S.A.), 1894).

A translation of Exodus and Numbers and the last chapters of Deuteronomy (exclusive of the detached laws) in which the work of J, E, and P, and editorial additions, etc., are distinguished by variations of type. In an appendix the main documents are given separately and consecutively. This work gives the results of the literary analysis in a most convenient form, and the critical discussions are often marked by much acuteness.

Barth (or Barth *NB*) J. Barth, *Die Nominalbildung in den Semitischen Sprachen*, Leipzig, 1894.

BDB. . . . *A Hebrew and English Lexicon of the Old Testament, based on the Lexicon and Thesaurus of Gesenius*, by F. Brown, C. A. Briggs, and S. R. Driver, Oxford, 1891 ff. (parts 1–10, reaching as far as קִיץ, now (Jan. 1903) published).

BN. . . . See Lagarde.

BR. . . . Edward Robinson, *Biblical Researches in Palestine* (references are to ed. 1, the pages of which are marked at the *foot* of the pages of ed. 2), London, 1841; *Later Bibl. Researches*, 1852. Ed. 2, 1856.

CH. . . . *The Hexateuch according to the Revised Version arranged in its constituent documents by Members of the Society of Historical Theology, Oxford, and edited, with introduction, notes, marginal references, and synoptical tables*, by J. E. Carpenter and G. Harford-Battersby (now G. Harford), London, 1900.

The introductory matter (with additions), the tables, and many of the notes have been republished under the title, *The Composition of the Hexateuch*, by J. E. Carpenter and G. Harford, London, 1902.

CH. followed by a numeral and symbol, such as 27^{JE}, 15^{D}, 35 , refers to the tables of words and phrases characteristic of JE, D, and P respectively given in this work on pp. 185–221 of vol. i. of the first edition, and pp. 384–425 of the second edition. The number without the symbol is often given when the context renders the citation of the letters unnecessary.

Che[yne] . . T. K. Cheyne.

CIS. . . . *Corpus Inscriptionum Semiticarum*, Paris, 1881 ff.

Corn. . . C. H. Cornill, *Einleitung in das alte Testament*, eds. 3 and 4, 1896.

COT. . . . *The Cuneiform Inscriptions and the OT.*; a translation (London, 1885), by O. C. Whitehouse. The second edition of *Die Keilinschriften und das alte Testament* (abbreviated *KAT.*), by Eb. Schrader. References are given to the pages of the 2nd German edition which are marked in the margin of the translation.

A third edition of the German work edited (and indeed entirely rewritten) by H. Zimmern and H. Winckler is now (Feb. 1903) complete.

Dav. . . . A. B. Davidson, *Hebrew Syntax* (Edin. 1894).

DB. . . . Dictionary of the Bible, and in particular *A Dictionary of the Bible*, edited by James Hastings (N. Y. 1898–1902).

Del. . . . Franz Delitzsch, or (before references to the Assyrian dictionary) Friedrich Delitzsch.

Di. . . . August Dillmann, *Numeri, Deuteronomium und Josua*, 1886 (rewritten on the basis of Knobel's Commentary [Kn.] on the same books, 1861).

Dr(iver). . . S. R. Driver.

(1) *A Treatise on the Use of the Tenses in Hebrew* (ed. 3, Oxford, 1892).

(2) *An Introduction to the Literature of the OT.* (abbreviated *L.O.T.*), cited according to the pagination of ed. 6 (N. Y., 1897), which is retained in subsequent editions.

b

EBi. . . . *Encyclopædia Biblica, a Critical Dictionary of the Bible*, edited by T. K. Cheyne and J. Sutherland Black (Lond. 1899 ff.).
Vols. i.–iii. at present published.

Ew. . . . Heinrich Ewald.

GB. . . . *The Golden Bough, a study in Magic and Religion*, by J. G. Frazer (ed. 2, London, 1900).

Ges. . . . Wilhelm Gesenius, *Thesaurus ling. hebr. et chald. Vet. Test.* (Leipzig, 1829–1853); the last part (ש–ת) was completed after Gesenius' death (1842) by Roediger.

G.-K. . . . Wilhelm Gesenius' *Hebräische Grammatik*, völlig umgearbeitet von E. Kautzsch, ed. 26, 1896.
English translation by G. W. Collins and A. E. Cowley (Oxford, 1898).

GVI. . . . *Geschichte des Volkes Israel*, by Bernhard Stade (Berlin, 1889).

Hengst. . . . E. W. Hengstenberg; see p. 307.

HPN. . . . *Studies in Hebrew Proper Names*, by G. Buchanan Gray (Lond. 1896).

JBLit. . . . *Journal of Biblical Literature* (Mass. U.S.A.).

JPh. . . . *Journal of Philology* (Cambridge and London).

JPTh. . . . *Jahrbücher für Protestantische Theologie.*

JQR. . . . *The Jewish Quarterly Review.*

KAT. . . . See *COT.*

Kays. or Kayser . August Kayser, *Das vorexilische Buch der Urgeschichte Israels und seine Erweiterungen* (Strassburg, 1874).

KB. . . . *Keilinschriftliche Bibliothek*, ed. Eb. Schrader (Berlin, 1889 ff.).
A collection of Assyrian and Babylonian texts transliterated and translated into German by various scholars. Vol. v., containing the Tel el-Amarna correspondence, is edited by H. Winckler; of this there is an English edition with an English instead of the German translation (London, 1896).

Ke. or Keil . . C. F. Keil, *Comm. on Numbers* in Keil and Delitzsch's *Biblical Commentary on the Old Testament.* References are to vol. iii. of the translation (by J. Martin) of the Pentateuch (Edin. 1867).

Kit. or Kittel . R. Kittel, *Geschichte d. Hebräer* (Gotha, 1888).
English translation by J. Taylor, H. W. Hogg, and E. B. Spiers (London, 1895, 1896).

Kön. . . . F. E. König, *Historisch-kritisches Lehrgebäude der hebr. Sprache*, vol. i. 1881; vol. ii. 1895. The concluding part of the work appeared in 1897 with an independent title (*Historisch-comparative Syntax der hebr. Sprache*): this is cited as Kön. iii.

Kue. . . . A. Kuenen, *The Hexateuch* (translation by P. H. Wicksteed: Lond. 1886). References are given either to the section and subsection, or to the pages of the original work (see *Deut.* p. xxii), which are given in the margin of the translation.

Lagarde . . Paul de Lagarde, *Uebersicht über die im Aramäischen, Arabischen u. Hebräischen übliche Bildung der Nomina* (Göttingen, 1889); abbreviated *BN.*

Levy . . . J. Levy, *Neuhebräisches u. Chaldäisches Wörterbuch über die Talmudim u. Midraschim* (Leipzig, 1876–1889).

L.O.T. . . . See under "Driver" (2).

Moore . . . G. F. Moore, "Numbers" in *EBi.*

NHB. . . . See "Levy."

Nöld. . . . Th. Nöldeke, *Untersuchungen zur Kritik des AT* (Kiel, 1869).

The first essay (pp. 1–144) is entitled *Die s.g. Grundschrift des Pentateuchs*, and deals with the extent and characteristics of P.

Now. or Nowack . W. Nowack, *Lehrbuch d. hebr. Archäologie* (Freiburg and Leipzig, 1894).

Onom. or *OS.* . *Onomastica Sacra*, ed. Lagarde (Göttingen, 1887).

This contains several ancient Onomastica, including those of Jerome and Eusebius.

OTJC. . . . *The Old Testament in the Jewish Church*, by W. Robertson Smith, ed. 2, 1892.

PAOS. . . . *Proceedings of the American Oriental Society.*

Paterson . . J. A. Paterson, *The Book of Numbers, critical edition of the Hebrew Text, printed in colours exhibiting the composite structure of the work, with notes* (Leipzig, Baltimore, and London, 1900).

PEF. (*Qu St*) . Palestine Exploration Fund (*Quarterly Statement*).

PRE.[3 (or 2)] . . Herzog's *Real-Encyklopädie für protestantische Theologie u. Kirche*, ed. 2, 1877–1888. Of the third edition by A. Hauck (vol. i. 1896), 12 volumes have at present appeared.

Rashi . . . Rabbenu Shelomoh Yiṣḥaḳi (1040–1105), one of the most learned and typical of the mediæval Jewish commentators. His Commentary on the Pentateuch as edited by A. Berliner (Berlin, 1866) has been used.

Ros. . . . E. F. C. Rosenmüller, *Scholia in Vet. Test.* (pars sec.; Lipsiæ, 1798).

SBE. . . . *The Sacred Books of the East*, translated by various scholars, and edited by F. Max Müller, 1879 ff.

SBOT. . . . *The Sacred Books of the Old Testament*, ed. Paul Haupt.

The volume on Numbers is by J. A. Paterson (see under Paterson).

Schürer . . . E. Schürer, *Geschichte d. jüd. Volkes im Zeitalter Jesu Christi*, ed. 3, 1898–1902).
English translation of ed. 2 (Edin. 1885–1891).

Siphrê . . . *Sifré debé Rab, der älteste halachische u. hagadische Midrasch zu Numeri u. Deuteronomium*, ed. M. Friedmann (Vienna, 1864).

St. or Sta. . . Bernhard Stade, (see *GVI*).

Str. . . . Strack, *Die Bücher Genesis, Exodus, Leviticus, u. Numeri* (in Strack and Zöckler's "Kurzgefasster Kommentar"), 1894.

Th. Ti(jd). . . *Theologisch Tijdschrift* (Leiden).

TSK. . . . *Theologische Studien u. Kritiken.*

We. . . . J. Wellhausen, *Die Composition des Hexateuchs u. der historischen Bücher des AT*, ed. 2, 1889. Cited as *Comp.*
The references to the *Prolegomena* and the *Israelitische u. jüdische Gesch.* are, unless otherwise indicated, to the fourth and second editions respectively.

ZATW. . . . *Zeitschrift für die Alttestamentliche Wissenschaft.*

ZDMG. . . . *Zeitschrift der Deutschen Morgenländischen Gesellschaft.*

ZDPV. . . . *Zeitschrift des Deutschen Palästina-Vereins.*

Biblical passages are cited according to the Hebrew enumeration of chapters and verses: where this differs in the English, the reference to the latter has usually (except in the philological notes) been appended in a parenthesis.

The sign † following a series of references, indicates that all examples of the phrase, word, or form in question, occurring in the OT., have been quoted.

In the translations of the poems (pp. 345, 351, 360, 368) the single inverted commas (*e.g.* 'glory') indicates that the translation is from an emended text.

Cp. = compare.

Ct. = contrast.

INTRODUCTION.

§ 1. *Title.*

NUMBERS, as the title of the fourth book of the Pentateuch, is derived through the Latin from the Greek usage. Ἀριθμοὶ is the title of the book in the earliest codices of 𝔊 (א and B); but it is much older than these: it was certainly known to Melito * (*c.* 175 A.D.), and was in all probability of Alexandrian and pre-Christian origin.† At first, as in the case of the other books of the Pentateuch, the Latins adopted the Greek word as the title; and Tertullian cites the book as *Arithmi.*‡ But whereas the Greek titles, Genesis, Exodus, Leviticus, and Deuteronomy persisted, the Greek title of the fourth book was subsequently translated: hence the title in the Vulgate is *Numeri*, to which the English "Numbers" corresponds.

A similar title used by the Palestinian Jews, and already found in the Mishnah (*c.* 200 A.D.), is חמש הפקודים = "The fifth (part of the Pentateuch treating) of the mustered" (הַפְּקוּדִים).§ Still more similar to the Greek title would be ספר מספרים ("Book of Numbers"), but it appears doubtful whether this title was in actual use among the Jews of the Mishnic

* Eusebius, *HE.* iv. 26.

† Swete, *Introd. to the Old Testament in Greek*, 215. The titles of the other four books of the Pentateuch are cited by Philo (see Di. *Genesis*, p. vii; Ryle, *Philo and Holy Scripture*, p. xx); Ἀριθμοὶ does not happen to be so cited, but may be assumed to belong to the same age as the rest of the Greek titles of the Pentateuch.

‡ "Balaam prophetes in Arithmis arcessitus a rege Balack," etc. (*Adv. Marc.* iv. 28).

§ See, *e.g.*, *Yōmā* vii. 1; *Menaḥoth* iv. 3. In the Bab. Talm. see, *e.g.*, *Soṭa* 36*b* (top), and cp. Origen in Eusebius, *HE.* vi. 25 (Ἀριθμοί Ἀμμεσφεκωδείμ).

period. It is cited by some writers * as "Mishnic," but without any evidence given for the statement.

Other Hebrew titles of Numbers are וידבר, the first word, and במדבר, the fourth word, of the Hebrew text of the book. The second of these is used in modern Hebrew Bibles: from it also was derived the name of the great Haggadic commentary on the book, the *Bemidbar Rabbah*. The title וידבר was already known to Jerome and Epiphanius.†

As indicative of the contents of the book the title Numbers is not aptly chosen; for it is only a small part of the book (c. 1–4. 26) that is concerned with the numbers of the Israelites. Though not chosen for the purpose, the Hebrew title "In the wilderness" would be far more suitable, since the wilderness is the scene of the greater part of the book (§ 2)

§ 2. *Scene and Period.*

The contents of Numbers are very miscellaneous in character (see § 5). The connection between subjects successively treated of frequently consists in nothing more than the fact that they are associated with the same, or successive scenes or periods; and the whole book may be said, in a measure, to be held together by this geographical or chronological skeleton. It will therefore be convenient to indicate at once the scenes and dates that are given.

The scene of 1^{1}–$10^{11. 29-32}$ is the wilderness of Sinai, of 12^{16b}–20^{21} the wilderness of Paran, of 22^{1}–36^{13} the steppes of Moab at the N.E. end of the Dead Sea. The first and second of these sections is connected by an account (10^{12-28} 10^{33}–12^{16a}) of the march northwards from Sinai to Paran

* H. E. Ryle, *Canon of the Old Testament*, 294; Swete, *op. cit.* p. 215. Hottinger (*Thes. Phil.* (1649) p. 463) writes: "ספר המספרים, *Liber Numerorum.* Sic appellatur apud Euseb. *Hist. Eccl.* lib. 6, c. 19, ex Origine." This statement appears to rest on the reading of Stephanus (1544), which has not been admitted by later editors, in Euseb. *HE.* vi. 25 (cited in last note), ἀμμισπαρὶμ ἢ πεκουδίμ; see Heinichen's ed. i. 293, xviii, xix.

† See Jerome, *Pref. in libr. Sam. et Mal*, ed. Migne, xxviii. 552 (Quartus, *vajedabber* quem Numeros vocamus); Epiphanius in Lagarde, *Symmicta*, ii. 178 (οὐἀδαβηρ ἥ ἐστιν Ἀριθμῶν).

(or Ḳadesh), the second and third by an account (20^{22}–$21^{32\,(35)}$) of the march from Ḳadesh on the west, to the steppes of Moab on the east, of the ʿArabah (Jordan-valley). Thus geographically the book falls into three sections: 1^1–10^{11} (also v.$^{29-32}$) Sinai; 10^{12}–21^9 North of Sinai and West of the ʿArabah; 21^{10}–36^{13} East of the ʿArabah (Jordan-valley).

The chronological is in some respects less clear than the geographical articulation of the book; for in a crucial passage (20^1) the number of the year is now missing. But whether or not that missing number was 40 (see 20^1 n.), the main periods of the book are clear: 1^1–10^{11} covers 19 days; 10^{12}–21^9 just under 38 years ($20^{28} = 33^{38}$); and 21^{10}–36^{13} not more than 5 months (cp. $33^{38} = 20^{28}$, 20^{29}, Dt. 1^3: also Ex. 7^7, Dt. 34^7).

Several dates are given either directly or inferentially. Those given inferentially are enclosed in square brackets in the subjoined table. The era is that of the Exodus.

Reference.	Year.	Month.	Day.
1^1 (cp. v.^{18})	ii	2	1
[7^1 (cp. 9^{15} Ex. $40^{2.\,17}$)	ii	1	1]
9^1	ii	1	...
9^5	[ii]	1	14
10^{11}	ii	2	20
20^1	[? xl]	1	...
(20^{22-29}=) 33^{38}	xl	5	1
Dt. 1^3	xl	11	1

In addition to the foregoing references, there is in 33^3 a purely retrospective reference to the 15th day of the 1st month of the year i.

On the value of these chronological statements, see § 15*e*.

§ 3, 4. *Connection with preceding and following books: Scope.*

§ 3. The first section of Numbers (1^1–10^{10}) may be regarded as an appendix to the Books of Exodus and Leviticus. The arrival of the Israelites in the wilderness of Sinai is recorded in Ex. 19^1, their departure therefrom in Nu. $10^{11f.\,(33)}$; and thus the scene of all that lies between these two passages is the same. Not only so: the main subjects of Ex. 19^1–Nu. 10^{11} are closely related, and, indeed, parts of a single conception—the due organisation of the people with a view to securing the sanctifying presence of Yahweh in their midst. The closing chapters of Exodus are primarily connected with the building of the tabernacle for the divine presence; Leviticus, with the institution of the sacrificial system, by means of which the people was to approach Yahweh, and of the priesthood, the members of which were to be the immediate ministers of Yahweh; the opening chapters of Numbers, with the institution of the Levites, who were to be the ministers of the priests, and with the arrangement of the camp in such a manner as to symbolise the holiness and unapproachableness of Yahweh. At present all three sections of Ex. 19^{1}–Nu. 10^{10} contain also miscellaneous laws and regulations not closely related to the main conception (see, chiefly, Ex. 20–23, Lev. 17–26, Nu. 5 f.); but this ought not to obscure the essential unity of the whole. Clearly, then, Exodus, Leviticus, and Numbers might have been much more suitably, though very unequally, divided as follows: (1) Ex. 1–18: The Exodus from Egypt to Sinai; (2) Ex. 19–Nu. 10^{10}: Sinai; (3) Nu. 10^{11}–36^{13}: From Sinai to the Jordan.

As the first section of the book is closely related to Exodus and Leviticus, so the latter part of the last section is, though far less closely, related to Deuteronomy. The laws and instructions recorded in 33^{50}–36^{13}, like those of Deuteronomy (see 4^{1} 6^{1} $7^{1f.}$ 9^{1} 12^{1} and *passim*), are given in prospect of the passage of the Jordan, and with the intention that they shall be carried out only after the settlement in Canaan ($33^{50f.}$ $34^{2.\,17.\,29}$ $35^{2.\,10f.}$). At the same time these chapters cannot be regarded as a detached part of Dt., for (apart from considerations referred to below) they deal to a considerable extent with the same subjects; with 33^{50-56}, cp. Dt. 7^{1-6} $12^{2f.}$; and with 35^{9-34}, cp. Dt. 19^{1-13} (Cities of Refuge).

§ 4. The preceding remarks may suffice to show that the Book of Numbers is a section somewhat mechanically cut out of the whole of which it forms a part; the result is that it possesses no unity of subject.

Unity of subject is only to be found when 1^{1}–10^{10} is disregarded. The subject of the remainder of the book is the fortunes of the Israelites after leaving Sinai, where they had been duly organised as the people of Yahweh, up to the point at which they are ready to enter and conquer the Land of Promise. The Conquest itself forms the subject of the Book of Joshua. The subject of Numbers would have been fitly rounded off by the record of the Death of Moses (Dt. 34), but with the Book of Deuteronomy to follow this was impossible.

In brief, the fortunes of the Israelites, as here described, are as follow:—From Sinai they proceed northwards to the southern confines of the Land of Promise, with a view to entering it from this direction. Spies are despatched to reconnoitre the land; they return with a report that disheartens the people, who refuse to advance. For their unbelief Yahweh condemns the people to exclusion from the Land of Promise for 40 years. Repenting, the people attempt, in disregard of Moses' entreaty, to advance northwards on Canaan, and are defeated. Forty years later they march across to the East of the ʿArabah (Jordan-valley), defeat the Amorites, occupy their country (which at that time extended from the Arnon to the Jabboḳ), and settle, more particularly, on the East of the Jordan in the immediate vicinity of the Dead Sea. Here they yield to the temptation to worship the god of the country and to have intercourse with foreign women, they are numbered a second time, exterminate the Midianites, and receive various laws; the Gadites and Reubenites are given possession of the country E. of Jordan; Moses is warned by Yahweh of his approaching death, and Joshua is appointed his successor. This narrative is enriched by episodes: four of these are connected with the northward march from Sinai, viz. the murmuring at Tabʿerah, the gift of Quails, the imparting of the spirit to seventy elders, and the vindication of Moses' uniqueness against Miriam and Aaron; another, to judge by its present position, was referred to some time during the forty years' exclusion from Canaan; this is the Revolt of Ḳoraḥ, Dathan, and Abiram, another (the Bronze Serpent) to the advance on the East of Canaan. The longest and most famous episode is the story of Moab's machinations against Israel, and of Balaḳ's unsuccessful attempt to use Balaam for his purposes: this is naturally connected with Israel's residence E. of Jordan.

Since at most nothing but the revolt of Ḳoraḥ, Dathan, and Abiram is referred to the Forty Years' Wandering, the main subject of the book is practically limited to the fortunes of the Israelites during their advance towards the south of Canaan before the Forty Years' Wandering, and again during their advance towards the East of Canaan at its close. The story of the "Forty Years" is scarcely more than a blank.

The greater part of the legal matter of the book is very loosely connected with the narrative, and deals with a great variety of matters. It cannot be conveniently classified under general heads; but the subjects of the laws and the points at which they are inserted in the narrative will be most easily gathered from the subjoined table of contents of the whole book.

§ 5. *Contents.*

[Topics derived from JE (§ 7 f.) are italicised.]

I. 1^{1}–$10^{10\,(29-32)}$.

Scene: The Wilderness of Sinai. *Period*: 19 days (1^{1} 10^{11}).

1–4. The census; the arrangement of the camp; the functions of the Levites.

- 1. The numbers of the secular Israelites. Position of the Levites in the camp.
- 2. The arrangement of the camp; the numbers of the secular Israelites.
- 3^{1-10}. Aaron's sons; the relation of Levi to the other tribes.
- 3^{11-39}. The numbers of the male Levites upwards of a month old; the duties of the several Levitical families, and their place in the camp.
- 3^{40-51}. The numbers of firstborn male Israelites.
- 4. The numbers of the male Levites between 30 and 50 years of age; the duties of the several Levitical families.

5, 6. Various laws and regulations.

5^{1-4}. Exclusion of certain unclean classes from the camp.

5^{5-10}. Some priestly dues.

5^{11-31}. The ordeal of jealousy.

6^{1-21}. The law of the Nazirite.

6^{22-27}. The priests' blessing.

7. The offerings of the tribal princes.

8^{1-4}. The golden candlestick.

8^{5-22}. Solemn dedication of the Levites.

8^{23-26}. Age of Levitical service.

9^{1-14}. The supplementary Passover.

9^{15-23}. The cloud over the tabernacle.

10^{1-10}. The two silver trumpets.

II. 10^{11}–21^{9}.

Scene: North of Sinai, West of the ʿArabah.
Period: 38 (or, in round numbers, 40) years.

10^{11-28}. From Sinai to the wilderness of Paran.

10^{29-34}. *Departure from the Mount of Yahweh: Moses invites Ḥobab to act as guide.*

$10^{35f.}$. *Verses addressed to the ark.*

11^{1-3}. *Tabʿerah.*

11^{4-35}. *Ḳibroth-hatta'avah: the seventy elders; Eldad and Medad; the lust for flesh satisfied and punished by the gift of quails. Ḥaṣeroth.*

12. *Moses vindicated; Miriam's leprosy.*

13, 14. Spies, despatched from the wilderness of Paran to spy out Canaan, bring back the report that the land is worthless; the people are disheartened and rebel. *Men despatched from Ḳadesh bring back the report that the land is fruitful, but the inhabitants invincible; the people are disheartened and rebel. Moses' intercession with Yahweh; the present generation condemned to exclusion from Canaan*; the people condemned to forty years' wandering; *futile attempt to invade Canaan from the south; Ḥormah.*

15. Various Laws.

v.$^{1-16}$. The proper quantities of meal-offerings and libations.

v.$^{17-21}$. The cake of firstlings.

v.$^{22-31}$. Propitiation for sins of ignorance.

v.$^{32-36}$. Punishment of the Sabbath-breaker.

v.$^{37-41}$. Tassels.

16–18. The rebellion of Ḳoraḥ, *Dathan, and Abiram*; the blossoming of Aaron's rod, and vindication of the superiority of the tribe of Levi; dues payable to this tribe by the Israelites.

19. Law of defilement by the dead, and of its removal by means of the ashes of a red cow.

20^{1-13}. Arrival at the wilderness of Ṣin. *Death of Miriam at Ḳadesh. Want of water.* The waters of Merîbah; sin of Moses and Aaron.

20^{14-21}. *Permission to pass through Edom sought and refused.*

20^{22-29}. Death of Aaron at Mt. Hor; Eleʿazar succeeds him.

21^{1-3}. *Ḥormah.*

21^{4-9}. Departure from Mt. Hor. *Edom avoided. The bronze serpent.*

III. 21^{10}–36^{13}.

Scene: East of the ʿArabah (Jordan-valley).
Period: Not more than 5 months.

21^{10-20}. Places passed on the march: Obhoth, ʿIyye-ʿAbārim, *wilderness E. of Moab, Zered, Arnon, Be'er, Mattanah, Naḥali'el, Bamoth, Pisgah. Citation from the "Book of Yahweh's Battles." Song of the Well.*

21^{21-32}. *Permission to pass through the land of the Amorites sought and refused. Israel defeats the Amorites, and occupies the country between Arnon and Jabboḳ. Poem on the destruction of Moab.*

21^{33-35}. Defeat of ʿOg, king of Bashan [insertion from Dt.; see § 14*a*].

22^{1}. Arrival at the steppes of Moab.

22^{2}–24^{25}. *Moab and Israel; Balaḳ and Balaam.*
25^{1-5}. *The Israelites seduced by Moabite women; the Baʿal of Peʿor.*
25^{6-18}. The Israelite and the Midianitess; the zeal of Phineḥas; perpetuity of the priesthood in the line of Phineḥas.
26. The second census.
27^{1-11}. The daughters of Ṣelopheḥad; law of succession to landed property.
27^{12-22}. Moses bidden to prepare for death; Joshua appointed to succeed him.
28 f. A scale of public offerings.
30. Conditions of the validity of a vow.
31. The extermination of Midian.
32. The settlement of Gad, Reuben, and (v.$^{33. 39-42}$) Manasseh on the East of Jordan.
33^{50}–36. Various laws relating to the conquest and settlement of Canaan.
- 33^{50-56}. The idolatrous objects of the Canaanites; the distribution of the land by lot.
- 34^{1-15}. The boundaries of Canaan.
- 34^{16-29}. Names of persons appointed to superintend the allotment of Canaan.
- 35^{1-8}. Levitical cities.
- 35^{9-34}. Cities of refuge.
- 36. Marriage of heiresses (Ṣelopheḥad's daughters).

§ 6–13. *Sources.*

§ 6. The question of the origin of Numbers could only be adequately discussed in connection with the wider question of the origin of the Pentateuch; and much of what follows must be read in the light of, or supplemented by reference to, such works as are cited below.

Judged even by itself, Numbers supplies abundant evidence that it is not the work of Moses, or even of a contemporary of the events described. Not only is Moses referred to throughout in the 3rd person, and, in one passage * in particular, in terms that have always occasioned difficulties to those who assumed the Mosaic authorship, but the repetitions, the divergent and contradictory accounts of the same matter, the marked differences of style in different parts, the impossible numbers, and many other features of the book, prove clearly that Numbers is not the work of one who was contemporary with the events described, or familiar with the conditions presupposed.†

In one passage only (33^2; see n. there) does the book lay any claim to the authority of Moses for its statements; that passage is closely related to others (P) which are clearly of far later origin than the age of Moses, and consequently the Mosaic *authorship* even of this particular passage cannot be seriously considered.‡

§ 7. Numbers (and more especially that part of it which is contained in 10^{11}–25) is, like Genesis and Exodus, mainly derived from two earlier works. These works were (1) a compilation (JE) which was made at the end of the 7th century B.C., and consisted for the most part of extracts from a Judæan collection of stories (J) of the 9th century B.C., and a similar

* 12^3 "Now the man Moses was very humble (before God), above all the men which were upon the face of the earth."

† Cp. § 15 on "The Historical Value of Numbers"; and in illustration of the features of the book mentioned above, see pp. 10–15 (on impossible numbers), and, amongst many other discussions, pp. 92 f., 128–134, 186–193 on repetitions, divergences, and differences of style.

‡ The particular evidence for the literary analysis will be found in the discussions prefixed to the several sections of the Commentary. The fundamental arguments, alike for the analysis and especially for the dates and origins of the several sources, cannot be reproduced here, for some of them find only a subsidiary support in Numbers. This is particularly the case in regard to the analysis of JE into its constituent elements, J and E. It would indeed be evident, even if Numbers had to be judged apart from the remainder of the Hexateuch, that JE was itself a composite work; but the actual analysis, so far as it can be carried through, rests largely on criteria established from the clearer evidence of Genesis and Exodus. Some of the matters here presupposed will naturally be dealt with in due course in the Commentaries on Genesis and Exodus; meantime the reader should refer to Driver, *L.O.T.* 116–159; CH. i. 1–179; see also the present writer's article in *EBi.* on "Law Literature" (especially § 10–23).

collection (E) made in the Northern kingdom in the 8th century B.C.; and (2) of a priestly history of sacred institutions (P^g), which was written about 500 B.C. The combined works (JEP^g), or in some cases, perhaps, P^g before it was united with JE, appears to have been gradually but considerably enlarged by accretions (P^x and P^s), chiefly of a legal, but in some cases also of a quasi-historical, character. In the following paragraphs the extent of these various literary elements in Numbers will be briefly considered.

§ 8. *The earliest literary elements in Numbers.*—There is little difficulty in eliminating those parts of Numbers which were derived from JE. To a great extent these extracts stand by themselves, side by side, but not interwoven with, the extracts from P; see 10^{29}–12^{15} 20^{14-21} 21^{12-32} 22^{2}–25^{5}, and note the distribution of italic type in the table of contents given above (§ 5). Even where (as in c. 13 f. 16. 20^{1-13} 21^{1-11}) the accounts of JE and P have been interwoven, they can, for the most part, be separated with ease; the chief difficulties are presented by $14^{1-10.\ 26-38}$ 20^{1-13}; see pp. 132, 258 f.

Far more difficulty attends the attempt to analyse JE into its constituents, J and E. Even where doublets and incongruities are present, which admit of little doubt that the narrative containing them is composite, it is often impossible to carry through an analysis in detail. Thus, for example, in the case of JE's closely interwoven stories of the spies (c. 13 f.), and of Dathan and Abiram (c. 16), no analysis that has been offered can be regarded as anything more than partial and tentative.*

There remains a number of passages that can with some confidence be referred to their ultimate source. The following appear to be derived, at least in the main, from J:—10^{29-32} (the departure from Sinai), $11^{4-15.\ 18b-24a.\ 31-35}$ (quails), 22^{22-35} and other parts of the Balaam narrative. Among the passages which most clearly appear to be derived from E are $11^{16.\ 17a.\ 24b-30}$ (the seventy elders), 12^{1-15} (the vindication of Moses), 20^{14-21} 21^{21-24a}

* See pp. 133 f., 190. Other passages presenting difficulties of which various solutions have been offered are, 20^{1-13} (see p. 258 f.), 21^{1-9} (pp. 272, 274), 21^{11-32} (p. 280 f.), c. 22–24 (p. 312 f.), and 25^{1-5} (p. 380 f.).

(the embassies to Edom and the Amorites), and the larger part of the story of Baalam (c. 22–24). Some, indeed, assign the stories of the seventy elders and of the vindication of Moses to later (7th cent.) amplifications of E, but on grounds which appear to the present writer insufficient and, in part, mistaken (see pp. 99, 116).

The most important passage of JE that is of later origin than the main sources, J and E, is 14^{11-24}; this may have been a 7th century amplification of J or E, or it may be the work of the 7th century editor who combined J and E (see p. 155).

It is not certain that the *order* in which the incidents were related in JE was in all cases the same as at present. There are some reasons for thinking that the stories of the elders and of the vindication of Moses, which now appear as episodes in the narrative of the march from Sinai to Ḳadesh, once formed part of the narrative of the stay at Sinai (see p. 98). Clearly misplaced passages in JE are 21^{1-3} and 32^{39-42}; see also p. 258 f.

§ 9. *The poems.* — Literary elements even more ancient than the stories of J and E are to be found among the poems and poetical fragments ($10^{35f.}$ $21^{14f.\ 17f.\ 27-30}$ $23^{7-10.\ 18-24}$ $24^{3-9.\ 15-17\ (18f.\ 20.\ 21f.\ 23f.)}$). On 6^{24-26}, see pp. xxxvi, xxxviii.

The poems attributed to Balaam (apart from 24^{18-24}) may be of the *same* origin as the prose narratives which now include them. But this is certainly not the case with the rest of the poems. One fragment ($21^{14f.}$) is definitely cited from a literary source, the "Book of Yahweh's Battles," another as a poem that was commonly recited by a professional class of reciters or "ballad-singers"; and it is clear that the "Folk-song" addressed to the well ($21^{17f.}$) and the snatches connected with the setting out and return of the ark ($10^{35f.}$) are older than the writer who has introduced them into the narrative.

It is probable that the verses contained in 24^{18-24} were inserted after the completion of JE (p. 373). But there can be little doubt that the rest of the poems formed an original part of JE. Whether the editor of that work derived them from J or E is less certain: he may have derived some of them from other sources. But, be that as it may, the poems themselves (except 24^{18-24}) are scarcely of later origin than the 8th cent. B.C., and some of them may be considerably earlier. Exact and certain determination of date in any single case is out of the question; to what extent approximate and probable decisions may be reached is discussed in the Commentary.

§ 10. *The later literary elements of Numbers.*—Less than a quarter of Numbers is derived from JE. The remaining and larger parts of the book are sufficiently similar and related to one another to be grouped under the common symbol P. They are all the work of a priestly school employing a large common vocabulary and governed by important and fundamental common ideas. But the activity of this school extended over centuries, and differences as well as similarities appear in what must be regarded as the work of many hands and many generations.

P, the work of this school, consists in part of narrative, in part of legal matter; and different generations contributed both to the narrative and to the legal parts. Thus, to refer to two clear instances, the priestly narrative of Ḳoraḥ has clearly been amplified by later additions intended to give the story a different turn (p. 192 f.); and the law of Levitical service in 8^{23-26} is different from that presupposed in c. 4 (p. 32 f.). The existence of differences is clear; the extent of them is less clear, and the distribution of the material of the book among the different hands, whose work may be detected, is attended with much difficulty and uncertainty. It will be convenient, therefore, to indicate here the general nature and value of the available evidence, and to gather together the more probable results which may be obtained from it. Three symbols have been used to distinguish the different elements of P. P^g denotes the fundamental work, the priestly history of sacred institutions; P^s is used for whatever is clearly later in origin than P^g, and therefore secondary in regard to it; P^x is used for that large amount of matter which can neither be shown to be later in origin than P^g, nor yet to have formed an original part of that work. P^g is the work of a single writer; but P^s and P^x cover the work of an indefinite number of hands; P^s is in part narrative, in part legal; P^x is entirely legal. P^g was written about 500 B.C.; P^s, including some glosses later than 𝔊 (cp. § 14), is the work of various writers and editors between the date of P^g and about 300–250 B.C.; P^x includes laws, some of which may, so far as the substance even of their literary expression is concerned, extend back into the 6th, or even the 7th cent. B.C. The symbol H is retained for that code,* commonly known as the Law of Holiness, which was incorporated by P^s with P^g (or JE D P), but was itself earlier than P^g (early 6th cent.). One or two laws in Numbers appear to be derived from H (15^{37-41} $33^{52f.\ 55f.}$, possibly also $10^{9f.}$).

A complete solution of the literary problem presented by P would show (1) the exact extent of P^g; (2) the matter (if any) contained in P^g which had previously received a fixed written or oral setting; (3) the matter (P^x) which had received a fixed setting at a time prior to P^g, but was only incorporated in P^g (or JE D P) subsequently to the completion of that work; (4) the matter (P^s) later in origin than P^g; (5) the dates at which the various matters defined in (2), (3), and (4) originated, and, in the case of (3) and (4), the dates at which they were incorporated. As a matter of fact the solution is and will remain very far from complete. So far as (5) is concerned, the available evidence is given in the Commentary; but there are certain general considerations which have been frequently alluded to in the Commentary that must be explained here.

§ 11. *Positive criteria for the elimination of P^s.* — Good reasons have been assigned for regarding references to any of the following as distinct signs of P^s: † (1) "the altar of incense" or "the golden altar." This is described in a supplemental section (Ex. 30^{1-10}), and is frequently mentioned from the time of the Chronicler downwards,‡ but appears to have been unknown to the author of Ex. 25–29, which forms an integral part of P^g. After the establishment of a second altar, it became necessary to distinguish the main and original

* Driver, *L.O.T.* 47–49, 145–152; CH. i. c. 13, § 8.

† See We. *Comp.* 139 ff.; Driver, *L.O.T.* 37 f. (with references there); CH. c. xiii. § 10.

‡ *E.g.* 1 Ch. $6^{34\ (49)}$, 1 Mac. 1^{21} 4^{49}; Philo, *De Vita Mosis*, iii. 9; *Yoma* v. 5, 7; *Zebaḥim* v. 2.

altar as "the altar of burnt-offering"; this term also and the reference to "altars" (in the pl.) are, therefore, further indications of P^s. The "altar of incense" may have been a very late addition; it is not clear that it was even known to the Pseudo-Hecatæus (3rd cent. B.C.); see Schürer,[3] ii. 287 (the note is more detailed than in ed. 2, Eng. tr. II. i. 281). (2) The unction of the priests. In P^g unction is a peculiar distinction of the high priest (Ex. 29); subsequently it was extended to the ordinary priests (Ex. 40). (3) The "cords" of the tabernacle, mentioned in Ex. 35^{18} 39^{40} (P^s), appear to have been unknown to Ex. 25–29 (P^g). (4) The sweet incense required in Ex. $30^{7. 34ff.}$, and frequently alluded to in Ex. 35–39, appears to have been unknown to the original text of Ex. 25–29: see CH.'s notes on Ex. 25^6 30^{22}; also 85^P.

Directly these tests of P^s are not widely applicable in Numbers (yet see $3^{3. 26. 31f. 37}$ 4^{11}); indirectly they are more important, for they point to the secondary character of Ex. 35–40, and these chapters afford in turn a standard of style whereby to judge others. Thus the recurrence in a marked degree of the diffuseness and circumstantiality of detail (cp. Holzinger, *Einleitung*, 419 f.) which characterise Ex. 35–40, in c. 1–4. 7. 26. 31, points to the editorial and amplifying activity, if not to the actual authorship, of P^s

The retrospective dates in 7^1 $9^{1. 5. 15}$ are most satisfactorily explained by attributing the sections thus introduced to P^s; they cannot be earlier than P^g, for they presuppose it.

On the ground of vocabulary *only*, it is seldom possible to refer passages with any certainty to P^s. Mere *peculiarity* of expression points at most to *heterogeneity*, not to posteriority; it may render the ascription of a passage to P^g improbable; but it is no criterion between P^s and P^x. And, further, even if it can be shown that the *formula* introducing, or concluding, a law is characteristic of P^s, this only proves the date of the *incorporation* of the law in P^g (or JE D P); it proves nothing with regard to the literary origin of the law itself. These points need to be borne in mind in consulting the collections of the stylistic peculiarities of P^s given by CH. (i. 155) and Holzinger (*Einleitung*, 418).

§ 12. *Difficulty of delimiting P^g.*—Whatever can be defined as P^s formed no part of P^g; but this is not the case with P^x. It is impossible to determine with any confidence how much, if any, of the matter defined as P^x formed an original part of P^g. The provisional answer to the question raised depends on the view taken of the manner in which P^g adhered to his leading motive.

The leading purpose of P^g was briefly to recapitulate the history of the origin and subsequent fortunes of the chosen people, and especially to describe the origin of their institutions. How strictly did he confine himself to that purpose? Did he only suffer his narrative to expand into fulness at points at which the origin of institutions naturally fell to be described, or did he himself at times snap the thread of his history in order to insert laws, or masses of laws, that had no connection with it? The former hypothesis seems to the present writer the more probable. If it be correct, then many sections of Numbers—such as $5^{(1)\,5}$–$6^{21\,(27)}$ 15. 19. 28 f. 30—must be considered to have formed no original part of P^g, simply on the ground that they have no organic connection with the priestly narrative, no such connection as exists, for example, between P^g's story of Ḳoraḥ (c. 16 f.) and the laws regulating dues payable to the priests (c. 18). At the same time, many of these laws, which are unrelated to the narrative, are in themselves by no means clearly later in origin than P^g; it is likely that some of them are earlier, and in that case, even if they were inserted by P^g in his work, they were inserted probably with little modification, and without any attempt to connect them closely with his narrative.

That many of the laws defined as P are in substance earlier than P^g, and may in some cases represent actual pre-exilic practice, has been very generally recognised: see Stade, *GVI.* ii. 66; Driver, *L.O.T.* 142 f.; the introductory notes to Driver and White's "Leviticus" (English) in *SBOT.* pp. 56–59; CH. c. xiii. § 9. Numbers contains one clear instance of older matter not legal in P, viz. the Priests' Blessing (6^{24-26}).

For legal matter which, though it formed no part of P^g, may, in substance, be earlier than that work, CH. adopt the symbol P^t, *i.e.* Priestly Teaching. But the symbol is not altogether suitable; it suggests a unity, though it cannot be shown (as, indeed, is admitted) that the various matters included under P^t ever existed, like H, as a separate code.

Further, a series of symbols like that adopted by CH. (P^h, P^t, P^g, P^s) necessitates, in the case of every passage, a judgment as to relative date which there is frequently no sufficient evidence to justify.

Finally, the question connected with the closing chapters of the book (c. 28–36) must be considered. In 27^{12-23} (P^g) Yahweh bids Moses prepare for death; and in Dt. 34 (P^g) the death of Moses is narrated. In the case of Aaron (20^{22-29} (P^g)), the warning of death and the death itself are related in immediate sequence. Did the writer follow his own model exactly, and was Nu. 27^{12-23} immediately followed by Dt. 34 in P^g? The assumption that this was the case can hardly be made with confidence; for it would not have been unnatural to P^g or, so far as we can judge, inconsistent with his method, to have traced back the regulations regarding the conquest and distribution of Canaan, of which c. 28–36 in part consists, to Moses, and to have represented him as making these after he had been warned of death, and Joshua had been appointed to succeed him. At the same time, little or nothing in these chapters can be conclusively shown to have formed part of P^g, while much in them, partly on grounds indicated above, partly on more specific grounds given in the Commentary, clearly appears to be the work of P^s: such is the case with c. 28–30 (p. 403 ff.), c. 31 (p. 419), c. 32 (apart from the misplaced fragments of JE in it; see p. 426), 33^{1-49} (p. 443 f.), 35^{1-8} (p. 466 f.), c. 36 (p. 477). Three sections (33^{50-56} 34^{1-15} 35^{9-34}) are connected by a similar introductory formula which may point to incorporation by the same hand; the first of these sections is related to P, and may, with the other two, have been embodied in P^g; but even this is far from certain.

§ 13. Starting from the conclusions stated in the preceding sections, the probable contents of P^g (so far as it is preserved in Numbers) may be outlined as follows:—In continuation of the record of the erection of the tabernacle, and the institution of the priests as given in Exodus and Leviticus, the author related the institution of the Levites, the census of the tribes, and the establishment of a camp order (c. 1–4), and possibly, in connection therewith, inserted the laws for securing the cleanness of the camp and for the delivery of the Priests'

Blessing (5^{1-4} 6^{21-27}). In prospect of departure from Sinai two silver trumpets are made (10^{1-8}). The people leave Sinai and encamp in the wilderness of Paran ($10^{11f.}$). From thence the spies, including Caleb and Joshua, are despatched; and the revolt of the people on their return is punished by the condemnation to forty years' wandering in this wilderness (c. 13 f.). At a time and place undefined the whole people, led by Ḳoraḥ, call in question the exclusive rights of the Levites; but the rank of the Levites is vindicated by the destruction of Ḳoraḥ, and by the blossoming of Aaron's rod; and the dues payable to them are fixed by divine revelation (c. 16–18). In the (fortieth) year the people come to Ḳadesh, and murmur at the lack of water; Moses and Aaron sin, and are condemned to die outside Canaan (20^{1-13}). On the way from Ḳadesh to the East of the ʿArabah, Aaron dies on Mt. Hor, and the people mourn for him thirty days; Eleʿazar succeeds him (20^{22-29}). The people reach and encamp in the steppes of Moab (22^{1}). Here Phineḥas, son of Eleʿazar, displays zeal, and is promised the perpetuation of the priesthood in his family, and here (possibly after a second census) Moses is bidden to get up into a mountain of the ʿAbārim and die. At his request for the appointment of a successor, Joshua is solemnly set apart for the purpose, but with the provision that he is to be subordinate to Eleʿazar the priest (27^{12-23}). Possibly before P^{g} recorded the death of Moses (Dt. 34) he inserted certain instructions communicated through Moses relative to the conquest and distribution of Canaan.

H and P^{x}.—The clearest example of matter preserved in P, but in substance earlier than P^{g}, is the Priests' Blessing (6^{21-27}). Probably earlier are passages from H, or a kindred source ($10^{9f.}$ 15^{37-41} $33^{52f.\ 55f.}$); and possibly earlier are many of the laws (including 5^{5}–6^{20}, $15^{17-21.\ 22-31}$ 19) assigned to P^{x}.

P^{s}.—The chief expansions of the *narrative* of P^{g}, and the chief narrative matter added at various times to P^{g} (or J E D P), are c. 7. 8^{5-22} 9^{15-23} 10^{12-28} $16^{8-11.\ 16f.}$ 17^{1-5} (16^{36-40}) 26. (mostly if not entirely) 31 and 36 (if not also 27^{1-11}). Among the laws or *legal sections* that can with most reason be regarded as later than P^{g} are 8^{1-4} 9^{1-14} 28 f. 30. 35^{1-8}.

Besides these additions, the recasting and amplification of c. 1–4 and the insertion of at least most of c. 28–36 are to be attributed to P^s. Minor results of the activity of these later writers, or annotators, may be seen, for example, in the addition of the name of Aaron to that of Moses (1^2 n.); such annotations or modifications of the text continued as late as the 3rd cent. B.C., as is shown by a comparison of 𝔥, S, and 𝔊 (§ 14).

§ 14. *Text.*

Like the remaining books of the Pentateuch, and unlike such books as Samuel and the Minor Prophets, the text of Numbers appears to have suffered comparatively little from simple errors of transcription. The most corrupt passages are to be found in some of the poems, and in these the most serious corruptions are more ancient than 𝔊, and, consequently, only to be emended, if emended at all, by conjecture. Some of the proper names, alike of persons and places, several of which are mentioned only in Numbers, have suffered mutilation, or are otherwise corrupt. But for the assumption of far-reaching corruption of the text and mutilation of (perhaps) the great majority of the names in the book, which has recently led Professor Cheyne to propose a large number of purely conjectural emendations, there is no manifest justification; and, as he still considers the disclosure of his principles of textual criticism "premature" (*Critica Biblica*, p. 5), it is impossible at present to form a final estimate of the probability of any of the several conjectures.*

* The proposed emendations will be found, for the most part, in the *Encyclopædia Biblica*, especially in the articles on the various names occurring in Numbers. Subsequently they are, it appears, to be collected in *Critica Biblica*, of which Part I. (on Isaiah and Jeremiah) has just appeared (Jan. 1903). Only a small proportion of the emendations have been cited in the Commentary, for so many of them, judged by any hitherto recognised principles of textual criticism, are altogether void of probability. The reader who is interested is once for all referred to the relevant articles in *EBi.* In criticism of Prof. Cheyne's methods (so far as they can be inferred from the emendations offered), see G. B. Gray, "The Encyclopædia Biblica (vols. i. and ii.) and the Textual Tradition of Hebrew Proper Names" in *JQR.* xiii. 375–391.

The variations in the codices of 𝔐 are comparatively few and uninteresting. A comparison of 𝔐, S, and 𝔊, the earliest and most important witnesses to the text, brings more variations to light. In large part these are due to amplification, or curtailment, of the original text. It is probable that in the great majority of cases the shorter is the *earlier* reading; whether it is also the *better* reading depends on the view taken as to the date at which the Pentateuch should be regarded as complete. It is difficult to draw a sharp line between the latest editors (P^s; see § 13), whose remarks might be regarded as part of the original work in its final form, and the early scribes who transmitted the text of the completed work. The amplifications due to these two classes are similar, and the variants of S and 𝔊 have been cited freely in the Commentary that the student may the better appreciate to what extent these (for the most part) minor changes were being made as late as the 3rd cent. B.C., in 𝔐 as well, though not so frequently, as in 𝔊 and S.

(*a*) S contains the longest additions. Many of these are of one character: they are derived from parallel, or supplementary, narratives in Dt., and generally with little other modification than was involved in adapting the narrative of Dt., which is in the first, to the narrative of Nu., which is in the third person. These additions * occur as follows:—

Dt.	1^{6-8}	is inserted	after	Nu.	10^{10}.
,,	$1^{20\ 23a}$	,,	,,	,,	12^{16}.
,,	1^{27-33}	,,	,,	,,	13^{33}.
,,	1^{42}	,,	,,	,,	14^{40}.
,,	$1^{44a\beta}$	,,	,,	,,	14^{45a}.
,,	$3^{24-25a\ 26b-28}\ 2^{2\ 6}$		,,	,,	20^{13}.
,,	2^{9}	,,	,,	,,	21^{11}.
,,	2^{17-19}	,,	,,	,,	21^{12}.
,,	$2^{24f.}$	,,	,,	,,	21^{20}.
,,	$2^{28.\ 29a}$	,,	,,	,,	21^{22}.
,,	2^{31}	,,	,,	,,	21^{23a}.
,,	$3^{21f.}$	,,	,,	,,	27^{13}.

* Similar additions occur, though with less frequency, in other books: thus Dt. 1^{9-17} is inserted after Ex. 18^{24}. See Colenso, *Pentateuch*, vi. 531–533.

This series of additions is of special interest, inasmuch as it points to 21^{33-35} (= Dt. $3^{1f.}$; cp. p. 306), which is found alike in 𝕳, S, and 𝕲, being the earliest result of a tendency to interpolate passages from Dt. in Nu. The text of Nu. in both S and 𝕲 is also affected by that of Dt. in $27^{12f.}$, and in 𝕲 only in 32^{11} (see notes there). Another instance of editorial activity that has left a slight trace on 𝕳, but is much more marked in S (and in this case in 𝕲 also), may be detected in c. 32 (see 32^{1} n.).

Among other passages in which S has a longer text than both 𝕳 and 𝕲 are 3^{31} 31^{20} (Moses represented as the source of Ele'azar's communication in v.^{22}).

S is sometimes shorter than 𝕲 (see under (*b*)), very seldom shorter than 𝕳 (but see under (*c*)).

Apart from omissions and additions, S has some readings certainly more primitive than 𝕳 (*e.g.* in c. 22–24; see p. 310 f.), some that are certainly secondary (*e.g.* 25^{4} n.).

(*b*) 𝕲 * frequently has a text longer than 𝕳, and sometimes than both 𝕳 and S. For example, it is longer than both 𝕳 and S in 2^{7} (see phil. n. on 2^{5}) 3^{10} 7^{88} 10^{6} 14^{23} $23^{3.6}$ 24^{23} 32^{30} 33^{36} 36^{1}, and than 𝕳 only in 4^{14} $13^{29\,(30)}$. Frequently 𝕲 assimilates repeated formulæ by adding words omitted in 𝕳 or otherwise; † see the notes on 1^{20-47} (p. 10), 4^{3} $15^{5.6}$ 19^{3} 21^{8} 26. (p. 388 f.), 28 f. (p. 412 f.).

Less frequently 𝕲 has a *shorter* text than 𝕳; see especially, 9^{20-23} 13^{33} 15^{35} 26^{40b} $28^{5f.}$ and under (*c*).

In c. 1. 26 the *arrangement* of the text in 𝕲 is less primitive than in 𝕳 (p. 10); see also 32^{1} n. On the other hand, in placing 10^{34} after $10^{35f.}$ 𝕲 may be more primitive than 𝕳.‡

(*c*) In its greater brevity 𝕳 as a whole represents an earlier stage of the text than either S or 𝕲. But it, too, suffered some amplification at a time later than that of the archetype of 𝕳, S, and 𝕲; a probable instance of such ampli-

* On the characteristics of this version of Nu., see Z. Frankel, *Ueber den Einfluss der palästinischen Exegese auf die alexandrinische Hermeneutik* (Leipzig, 1851), 167–200.

† Cp. Frankel, *Vorstudien zu der Sept.* 78 f.

‡ See Ginsburg, *Introd. to the Hebrew Bible*, 341–343.

fication may be found in the word בתית, which is read by 𝔐 in 28^5, but is absent from both S and 𝔊; another instance may be the gloss (omitted in 𝔊) in 13^{33}, and the true text of 9^{20-23} may lie between the fulness of 𝔐 and the brevity of 𝔊. An amplification of the text earlier than S or 𝔊 is 21^{33-35} (see under (*a*)).

Among the more interesting instances of late modifications of another kind are the substitution in 22^{22} (and possibly elsewhere in c. 22–24) of אלהים for יהוה (p. 310 f.), and the probable replacement of an original מים חיים (cp. 𝔊) in 5^{16} by מים קדשים.

§ 15, 16. *The historical Value of Numbers.*

The Book of Numbers presents itself as a record of the nomadic period in the history of Israel. But the various sources (§§ 6–13) from which the book was compiled were all written centuries later than that period. The historical value of Numbers consists largely in the evidence indirectly given by these sources regarding the periods to which they severally belong. This is considered below (§ 16, 17). We turn first to consider the value of Numbers as a record of the age which it describes.

Much that is here related of the age of Moses can be demonstrated to be unhistorical; much more is of such a nature that it can, with far greater probability, be explained as unhistorical than as historical; there remain, particularly in JE, a certain number of statements and descriptions which are not incompatible with any known historical facts and conditions, and in or underlying some of these it is not difficult to discern what is, historically, entirely possible, not to say probable. Nor is the possibility that reminiscences of actual historical events and conditions are here preserved by any means small. In written form, even the stories of J and E may be no older than the 9th or 8th cent. B.C.; but the *traditions* themselves must be much older. Again, the "Book of Yahweh's Battles," from which a solitary fragment is cited in $21^{14f.}$, may well have contained some old poems recording conflicts of the wandering Israelites with the peoples settled on the border of Canaan; if so, these poems would have formed a stream on which some knowledge of the far-off age may have drifted down. Unfortunately, be this as it may, such facts had only too many opportunities of being distorted, or placed in a wrong light, as the stories were told and retold during the five or six centuries that must have separated JE from Moses. The uncertainty thus created, and the number of alternative interpretations of the frequently conflicting traditions, can only be diminished by the discovery of fresh material.*

But when every allowance has been made for all this uncertainty and ambiguity, the value of this residuum of what cannot, at all events at present, be shown to be unhistorical lies in this: it contains the earliest theory or tradition of the Hebrews as to the nomadic period in their history; through it (and other biblical data) the life and fortunes of the Hebrews under Moses before they settled in Canaan must be read, if any attempt is made to read them at all. For contemporary evidence,† which casts much welcome light on the conditions

* Some sentences from Mr. Haverfield's Essay in *Authority and Archæology* (p. 307) are worth consideration in connection with what is said above. After citing some instances in which Roman archæology has confirmed the traditions preserved in Latin authors, he continues: "There comes into view a new method of testing legends, a new touchstone to try them. The old method of probing the legend itself is useless. It is easy to shew of most legends that they are either impossible, or highly improbable, or self-contradictory, or absurd, or otherwise seriously defective. But that after all is implied when the legend is called a legend. Some external touchstone is wanted which will, in each case, help to sift false from true. We must not, however, exaggerate the significance of such confirmations. If one or two or three stories rest on a basis of fact, it does not follow that all do; and though it is interesting to know that such and such legends are based on fact, we have to learn the fact first before we can say anything about the legend." Unfortunately, at present, archæology does not furnish us with touchstones for the legends in Numbers.

† Most important is the Tel el-Amarna correspondence (ed. Winckler, *KB.* v.; also published with English translation of the text, London, 1896). No mention is made in this correspondence of the Israelites; whether they formed part of the Ḫabiri, who figure in some of the letters, is disputed; but even if they did, only biblical data justify any statement about the Israelite Ḫabiri in particular. An inscription of Menephthah (*c.* 1270 B.C.), discovered at Karnak in 1896, in recording the establishment of peace

of life (especially in Canaan) in this age, says absolutely nothing of the Israelites in the wilderness.

The greater part of Numbers (P) is of no earlier origin than the 6th or 5th cent. B.C.; much of it is still later. A smaller part (JE) contains the earlier traditions. It is possible that some historical facts not found in JE may underlie P, but the general impression given by that work of the Mosaic age is altogether unhistorical, and much of the detail, which consists in large part of statistics and laws, can, with varying degrees of cogency in different cases, be demonstrated to be entirely unreal, or at least untrue of the age in question.

(*a*) The numbers of the Israelites are unreal; cp. pp. 10–15.

(*b*) The *lists* of individuals, though they contain some ancient names, cannot be accepted as genuine records of the Mosaic age; see pp. 6 f., 135 f.

(*c*) The organisation, position, and duties of the Levites, and the fiscal system for the support of priests and Levites, as described and presupposed in various parts of the book, cannot be harmonised with earlier Hebrew evidence; they

says: "Vanquished are the Tehennu (Libyans); the Khita (Hittites) are pacified; Pa-Kan'ana (Canaan) is prisoner in every evil; Askalni (Ashkelon) is carried away; Gezer is taken; Yenoam is annihilated; Ysiraal is desolated, its seed is not; Charu has become as widows for Egypt; all lands together are in peace." The determinative shows that the Ysiraal mentioned in this inscription was the name of a tribe or people, not of a country; and some have seen in the statement an allusion to Israel in the wilderness south of Canaan. If this be so, this inscription forms an exception to the statement in the text. On the other hand, it is at least as probable that the allusion is to "Israel," already settled somewhere in Canaan. Then the chief importance of the inscription would lie in giving a date before which "Israel" was in Canaan. See, further, Driver in *Archæology and Authority*, 62–65 (with the literature there cited). *This allusion of Menephthah's is the only contemporary mention of Israel* in what may be termed widely the age of Moses. This fact, and our consequent dependence on the biblical data for any knowledge of the fortunes of the Israelites in the wilderness, is greatly obscured in works like Sayce's *Early History of the Hebrews*, and Hommel's *Ancient Hebrew Tradition*; see, further, the present writer's criticisms of these works in *Expositor*,[5] vii. (May, 1898) 337–355, vi. (Sept. 1897) 173–190, and (more generally) Driver's article in *Archæology and Authority* (especially pp. 62–76).

correspond to an ecclesiastical organisation that first became established many centuries after Moses; see pp. 21–25, 236–241.

(*d*) Many of the laws are expressly stated to be for the regulation of life in Canaan; few of the rest have any relation to nomadic life. In the abstract this may not be incompatible with the promulgation of them by Moses; but such an origin is highly improbable, and not to be accepted on the evidence of so late a work; many of the particular laws contain much that is definitely inconsistent with Mosaic origin, and point to a relatively late age; for this see the Commentary.

(*e*) The chronological statements of the book cannot be fully judged apart from a consideration of the chronological system of the entire Pentateuch.* They are perhaps not incompatible with what is related in P^g, though nineteen days is short for all that is placed even in that work between 1^1 and 10^{11}. With the account given by the book in its present form the chronological statements cannot be treated as real; this is clearest in the closing section. Between the *departure* from Mt. Hor and the delivery of Moses' final address to the people there elapsed *not more* than five months (cp. 21^4 33^{38} 20^{29}, Dt. 1^3). Into these few months there is now compressed the journey south to the Gulf of ʿAḳabah, thence north to the Arnon, the despatch of messengers to the Amorites, war with the Amorites and occupation of the country between Arnon and Jabboḳ, the attempt of Balaḳ to get Balaam to curse Israel (this alone, if Balaam came from Pethor, extending over at the least three months), the intercourse of the Israelites with the Moabite women, the taking of the second census, the appointment of Joshua, the war with Midian, and the subsequent seven days of purification for the warriors; and in addition to the foregoing, the communication of many laws.

(*f*) It is perfectly possible, not to say probable, that the Israelites, before their settlement in Canaan, were brought into relation with the Midianites, and that at times they were at strife with them; but the account of the war with Midian given in c. 31 is entirely unreal; p. 418 f.

* In criticism of this see, in particular, Nöldeke, *Untersuchungen*, 107 ff.

If we now turn from P to JE, we find less that is so demonstrably unhistorical, especially if we understand the narratives to refer to a relatively small number of people. Even in some cases where there may be reasons for doubting whether the narrative is true of all Israel, it may preserve in a generalised form a reminiscence of the actual fortunes of individual tribes, or sections of Israel. But there is much that is far more probably due to the activity of the popular imagination or religious feeling than to any actual occurrences in the time of Moses; this is the case with the various stories explanatory of the names of places,* with the reference to a gigantic race resident in Hebron ($13^{32f.}$), and with the story of the bronze serpent (21^{4-10}). It is the view of prophecy and of the character of Moses prevalent, not in the age of Moses, but at the time when the story finally became fixed, that gives substance and significance to the stories of the vindication of Moses and of the seventy elders (11 f.).

Underlying the narrative of the spies is the fact of the connection of the Calebites with Ḥebron, and also a possibly correct reminiscence that they came thither from the south; some struggle of the Reubenites for supremacy may lie at the basis of the story of Dathan and Abiram; the traditional names Balaam and Balaḳ, Eldad and Medad, may have attached to historical individuals; but whether these events and persons belonged to the age of Moses we are in no position to affirm. The story of Balaam as told in Numbers is largely poetic rather than historical (314 ff., 340 f.).

The nucleus of history underlying JE is to be sought with most probability in the association of the Israelites during the nomadic period of their history with Ḳadesh, and the temporary settlement, though possibly only of a part of them, East of Jordan immediately before attempting the invasion of Canaan. How much that is related of the actual marches West and East of the ʿArābah (Jordan-valley) and of the relations of the Israelites with the Edomites, Moabites, and Amorites, also corresponds to facts of the Mosaic age it

* Tab'ērah (11^{1-3}), Ḳibroth-hatta'avah (named from the lust for flesh, $11^{4-10.\ 13.\ 18-24a.\ 31-34}$), Eshcol ($13^{23f.}$), Ḥormah ($14^{45}$ 21^{1-3}), Be'er ($21^{16f.}$).

is more difficult to determine; the questions are briefly discussed in the Commentary (see pp. 268, 272, 284, 300 f., 303).

§ 16. The indirect evidence of Numbers as to periods later than the Mosaic bears mainly on beliefs and religious practices. These will be considered in the next section. But Numbers is also comparatively rich in the amount and variety of early Hebrew poetry which it contains; in particular, the value of the obscure fragment cited from the "Book of Yahweh's Battles" and of the "Song of the Well," consists even more in the light shed on the modes and (in the reference of the former to its source) on the extent of poetic expression in early Israel than in the fragments themselves, though the Song of the Well, a perfect specimen of its kind, vividly depicts the customs and feelings of the people. So again the passing reference to the "reciters of *meshālîm*" or "ballad-singers" in 21^{27} is the only extant reference to a class of men who must have formed a conspicuous and, at times, an important element in society and the national life under the early monarchy (p. 299). The historical value of the poem cited in 21^{27-30} would be greater if it were free from ambiguity (p. 300 f.).

§ 17. *Numbers and the Religion of Israel.*

The various parts of Numbers are products of many generations widely separated from one another in time, and in some respects sharply distinguished from one another in the matter of religious belief and practice. The consequence is that Numbers is as lacking in unity of religious expression as in literary unity. It is therefore impossible to summarise the fundamental ideas, or to point out in general terms the religious value of the book; for these are different in the different parts. This being the case, much that might have been said on these matters in an introduction to another book, is in the present work more naturally distributed over various sections of the Commentary. But the value of the contribution made by the book to our knowledge and understanding of the religion of Israel may be better appreciated, if the extent to which the main features of religious life in various periods find expression in it is here briefly indicated.

(1) Many of the early popular beliefs appear in the poems and the narratives of J and E. Israel is Yahweh's son (this thought lies behind 11^{12}), and as such the object of His perpetual care and discipline. This may be said to be the overruling religious motive of the whole story of the Exodus, the journey towards Canaan, and the wanderings as told in the 9th and 8th cent. B.C. Yahweh's care for Israel is conspicuously illustrated by the episode in c. 22–24 (pp. 315–317); and underlies the frequent references to the goodly land which He has promised to His people, and to which He is leading them (10^{29} 11^{12} 13^{27} $14^{7f.}$ $24^{5f.}$). It is also prominent in the story of the provision of flesh (c. 11), though here the disciplinary manifestation of Yahweh's interest in Israel, which was also shown at Tabʿerah (11^{1-3}), is most emphasised. Yahweh marches before His people (10^{33}), fights for them so that their battles are His battles (10^{35} 21^{14}, cp. 14^{9}), and gives them victory (21^{1-3}).

The warmth and intensity of the early popular feeling for Yahweh has its reverse in the limitations of the early conceptions of Him. Yahweh is peculiarly the God of Israel: He is not the only God that exists. The existence and power of Kemosh seemed as real to the men of that age as the existence and power of Yahweh; Israel is "the people of Yahweh," Moab "the people of Kemosh"; and as Yahweh disciplines Israel, Kemosh disciplines Moab. The Baʿal of Peʿor, the gods of the Canaanites, too, are regarded as real gods, though inferior in power to Yahweh, and not to be worshipped in Israel (21^{29} 25^{1-5} 14^{9}). A particularly antique conception, which a later writer (Ps. 132^{8}) found it necessary to modify, as another (Jer. 48^{46}) modified the terms of 21^{29}, appears in 10^{35}, where the ark, as the visible embodiment of Yahweh, moves of its own accord, and is addressed as Yahweh (10^{33-36}). Elsewhere the manifestation of Yahweh in human form under the name of the "angel of Yahweh" (22^{22-35}; cp. 20^{16}) and in or as the theophanic cloud (11^{25} $12^{5.10}$) is referred to, and direct vision of Yahweh is ascribed to Moses (12^{8}). The comparative simplicity of worship in the age to which the stories belong is reflected in E's view of the tent when contrasted with the elaborate ideal of P; it is situated outside the camp, as in some cases the shrines of ancient Israel were above and somewhat away from the city (1 S. 9^{11-27}), and thither men resort to it; it requires the constant presence of but few attendants or guardians.

A vivid light is cast on some of the religious customs of the days of the early monarchy. Many must have been those who made pilgrimage to the bronze serpent (21^{4-9}) down to the time of its destruction by Hezekiah. Like famous relics of other ages and other faiths which have been treasured and credited with similar virtues, the bronze serpent must have raised, and sometimes seemed to satisfy, the hopes of many generations of suffering Israelites. We shall be safe in detecting another feature of early life in the law of 5^{11-31}, though in its present form this law may be no older than the 6th century: women suspected of unchastity, men, as we may reasonably infer, resting under suspicion of various offences, were made to drink specially prepared potions, or undergo, perhaps, various other forms of ordeals; for this purpose in early times they probably made their way to any one of the places specially sacred to Yahweh. The *combination* of customs in the law of the Nazirite (6^{1-21}) is late; but many of the individual customs, such as the practices of making offerings of hair, and submitting to certain forms of abstinence during the period of a vow, are early. What amount of early Israelite custom underlies the law of defilement from the dead (c. 19) is less clear; but the wearing of tassels at the corners of the garments out of religious or superstitious feeling (15^{37-41}) is ancient. See also p. 40.

Not the least important of the features of early Israelite religious life preserved in Numbers is the character of Moses as presented in the stories of J and E. The influence of such an ideal is not to be overlooked or underestimated. Thoroughly human, subject to despondency (11^{10-15}), and at times provoked by the people (JE in 20^{1-13}), Moses is yet pre-eminently distinguished by his submission to Yahweh (12^{3}); by his trust in (10^{29-32}), his intimacy with, and his faithfulness to Him (12^{6-8}); by his affection for his people, which leads him again and again, even when the people provoke him by their rebelliousness, to intercede with Yahweh on their behalf ($11^{2.\ 10-15}$ 21^{7}); by his generosity and public spirit (c. 12. 11^{27-29}).

In $11^{16.\ 17a.\ 24b-30}$ and 12 Moses appears as the ideal and, indeed, the exceptional and unique prophet, or man of Yahweh's counsel. These passages, together with c. 22–24, form a not unimportant contribution to our knowledge of the early Hebrew theory of prophecy. The first is a parallel to the stories in Samuel of the prophetic frenzy that followed the possession of a man by the spirit of Yahweh; but in the second Moses is distinguished as the man who receives the communication of Yahweh's will directly, and not like other prophets in dream or vision. Obviously no member of the prophetic school could distinguish Moses from prophets like Amos or Isaiah in this way: either, therefore, Moses is here the representative of the type of the great prophets of the 8th century B.C., or the passage was written before the time of Amos, and would in this case be proof that the ideal existed, though no living prophets satisfied it. C. 22–24 is important as evidence of the belief that even prophets of other nations might receive communications from Yahweh. Incidentally 16^{28} illustrates the early existence of a mode of distinction between the true and the false prophet which frequently appears later (Jer. $23^{16.\ 21}$, Ezek. 13^{2}): the true prophet comes because he is sent by Yahweh, and says and does what Yahweh directs (cp. also $22^{18.\ 30}$); the false prophet comes unsent, and delivers a message of his own making.

Seventh century.—In the long editorial passage 14^{12-24}, which is referred to this period, the Exodus is regarded particularly as a manifestation of Yahweh's *might*, and the problem presented, especially to Ezekiel, by the certain approach, or the actual endurance, of exile and the consequent destruction of national life, here appears in Moses' argument with Yahweh: how can Yahweh, if He must, in order to satisfy His moral nature, actually destroy Israel, maintain among the nations of the world a reputation for power?

Possibly another product of the religious feeling of this period may be found in the Priests' Blessing (pp. 71–74).

Post-exilic period.—The writings of the priestly school, from which the greater part of Numbers is derived, are in part the expression, in part also the cause, of the religious life of the post-exilic community. The hierocratic organisation of that society is reflected in the description of the arrangement of the camp (c. 1–4. 17 f.), in the story of Ḳoraḥ (c. 16), in the subordination of the secular leader Joshua to the high priest Eleʿazar (27^{18-22}), and in much else that relates to the priests and Levites. For the support of the sacred classes (c. 18, pp. 236–241) novel or heavier claims are made on the people, and much that formerly went in relief of needy classes is wholly reserved for the now highly organised and dominant hierocracy. Somewhat obscurely it is possible to trace modifications of practice and sentiment which must have occurred, though at what exact times it is impossible to say, within the sacred classes during the period extending from the 6th to the 4th centuries B.C. Such changes may be observed in the age of Levitical service (p. 32), and in the esteem in which the lower sacred class, the Levites, were held (pp. 21 ff., 192 f.).

The thought of Yahweh which is most prominent is His holiness or unapproachableness: the place of His presence is ringed off from the secular Hebrews by the sacred cordon of priests and Levites: men approach Him at their peril ($1^{49.50}$ 3^{10} $17^{28f.(12f.)}$ etc.), and only by means of special classes of intermediaries and in a specially defined manner. The spontaneity of religious life which so strongly coloured the earlier time is lost; another illustration which the book affords of this is the precise regulation of quantities which men must bring when they make an offering to Yahweh (c. 28 f. 15^{1-16} (p. 407)). Antique notions of holiness (p. 209–211) are unconsciously retained, probably because they tended to preserve and increase the awe of Yahweh, and in some passages such notions are developed with much elaboration of detail ($4^{5ff.}$). Incidentally * the question of Yahweh's relation to sin emerges

* Directly P concerns himself little with such questions; Driver, *L.O.T.* 129.

as it presented itself to the Jews from the time of Ezekiel onwards (16^{22}).

Ancient customs, which retained too great a hold on the mass of the people to be entirely suppressed, were gradually modified and supplied by the priests with new and more suitable interpretations, and in this way acquired an even prolonged lease of life (see p. 47 f.)

COMMENTARY.

I. 1.–X. 10 (P). *The Wilderness of Sinai.*

THE first section of the book covers the last nineteen days spent by the Israelites in the wilderness of Sinai (1^{1} 10^{11}). Exactly a month before the date given in 1^{1}, the tabernacle had been completed and set up (Ex. $40^{1.\,17}$). The intervening month had been occupied with the consecration of the priests —Aaron and his sons—to the service of the altar (Lev. 8), and with the revelation or communication of various laws, most of which, more or less directly, concerned the priests (Lev. *passim*): to the same interval two retrospective passages in the present section (Nu. 7. 9^{1-14}) refer the offerings of the princes to the tabernacle and the communication of the law of the supplementary Passover.

The tabernacle once erected was to form the centre of the camp, and the priesthood once instituted demanded servants; hence the erection of the tabernacle (Ex. 25–31. 35–40) and the organisation of the priesthood (Lev.) is now followed by the establishment of a fixed camp order and the definition of the functions of the priests' servants, the Levites, with whom, in spite of its title, the Book of Leviticus is, except in $25^{32f.}$ (P^{s}), wholly unconcerned. With these two subjects—the functions of the Levites and the arrangement of the camp— 1–4. 8^{5-26} is concerned. But 5 f. 8^{1-4} consists of various laws which, apart from 5^{1-4}, have no connection whatsoever with either of the subjects just mentioned; while 7 and 9^{1-14} are referred to a date anterior to that of 1^{1}. Then 9^{15}–10^{10}, describing the customary movement of the cloud and the trumpets to be used in connection with the march, forms a suitable transition to the next section of the book, which opens with the departure from Sinai ($10^{11ff.}$).

For the history of the Mosaic age the whole section is valueless: see Introduction.

It is agreed* that the whole section is derived from P. Language, style, subject, and connections with other parts of this work place so much beyond doubt. But the distribution of the material among the various strata of P is attended with difficulty. For details, see the analytical notes prefixed to the several subsections.

I.–IV. *The Census. The Arrangement of the Camp. The Functions of Levi.*

These subjects, as indicated above, are very naturally introduced at the point now reached in P, and, it may be reasonably assumed, were dealt with in P^g. But it is unlikely that these four chapters in their present form are the work of a single hand. They contain much repetition; the order in some places is suspicious; and there are other indications that an original narrative has been recast, amplified, and modified by later writers.

(1) *Repetitions.* $1^{45f.}$ may contain two statements of the total (obscured in RV.). The entire substance of 1^{17-43} (recurring formula and numbers of the tribes) is repeated in $2^{4.\ 6.\ 8.\ 11.\ 13.\ 15.\ 19.\ 21.\ 23.\ 26.\ 28.\ 30}$, and that of 1^{5-15} in $2^{3.\ 5b.\ 7b.\ 10b.\ 12b.\ 14b.\ 18b.\ 20b.\ 22b.\ 25b.\ 27b.\ 29b}$: cp. also 1^{44-47} with $2^{32f.}$. The subscription in 2^{34} disregards the matter common to c. 1 and 2. C. 3 f. is in part briefly anticipated by 1^{48-53}: further, $3^{31.\ 25f.\ 36f.}$ is repeated in $4^{5-15.}$ (greatly amplified) $^{24-26.\ 31f.}$, *i.e.* 4^{1-33} contains nothing new in substance beyond the command to number the Levites between thirty and fifty years of age, and the instruction that the priests are to cover up the objects intrusted to the care of the Ḳohathites before the latter touch them. The mere presence of repetitions might be explained as due to P's diffuseness. But (2) the *order* in which the material is arranged is very curious. Thus the command not to number the Levites (1^{49}) among the other tribes comes oddly *after* the other tribes have been numbered, and details of the census have been given. In c. 3 we have (apparently) a series of statements (v.$^{21f.\ 27f.\ 33f.}$) interrupted by a series of commands (v.$^{23-26.\ 29-32.\ 35-38}$); for v.^{38b} can only be taken as a command, and naturally determines the imperfects in the preceding verses. The difficulty in this case could be overcome, of course, by omitting v.^{38b}. But inversely the same thing happens in c. 2, *e.g.* v.^{3a} command, v.$^{3b.\ 4}$ statement, and so throughout

* Nöld., Kays., Di., We., Kue., Corn., Dr., Str.

the chapter. (3) Definite indications of P^s are to be found in $3^{3. 26. 31. 37}$ $4^{11. 16. 26. 32}$; see Introduction, § 11. In c. 4 CH. draw attention to a number of "small divergences from the phraseology of other parts of P": see also below, the notes on $4^{5-7. 12. 15. 19}$.

Of the substance as apart from the form of this section, it is hardly necessary to assign much to P^s; one of the two Levitical censuses may be his; he may have supplied 4^{34-49} to fill up the lack of statistics as to *adult* Levites; or, if the view that the Levites were substitutes for the firstborn be rightly derived from H (3^{11-13} n.), we may suppose that P^s supplied the census in c. 3 in illustration of the view of H incorporated by R^p. But attempts at a detailed distribution of the chapters among two or more hands are for the most part inconclusive.

If we are right in concluding that P^s recast P^g's matter, he may have been led to the present arrangement, especially of 1^1–3^{39}, by the desire to act in the spirit of 1^{49} 2^{33}, and, so far as possible, to keep the accounts of the Levites and the secular tribes separate. Thus, at present, c. 1 f. deals with the secular tribes, 3^{1-39} with the Levites. But the more natural arrangement in dealing with the camp order would have been to bring together the statements as to the positions of the several tribes, Levites and secular, the Levitical positions being defined first. The order of treatment in P^g may rather have been something as follows:—1. The separation and functions of Levi: this in immediate sequence to the separation and functions of the priesthood (Ex. Lev.). 2. The census: *a.* the appointment of princes; *b.* the numbers of the secular tribes; *c.* the numbers of the Levites. 3. The camp order: *a.* general statement—the central position of the tabernacle; *b.* the positions of the Levites—immediately round the tabernacle; *c.* the positions of the tribes—outside the Levites.

Anticipatory references to the census are found in Ex. 30^{12} 38^{26} (P^s).

I. 1–20. The appointment of twelve eminent men, each representing his tribe, to assist Moses and Aaron in taking the census.—1. *The wilderness of Sinai* (מדבר סיני v.^{19} $3^{4. 14}$ $9^{1. 5}$ 10^{12} 26^{64} $33^{15f.}$, Ex. $19^{1f.}$, Lev. 7^{38}†—all in P) is, according to the last editor of the Pentateuch, the scene of everything recorded between Ex. 19^1 and Nu. 10^{11}; also of 10^{29-32} (cp. ^{33}).—*In the tent of meeting*] the tent of meeting (אהל מועד) is the term most frequently (131 times) used in P to denote the sacred dwelling; it is also used in (J)E (11^{16}, Ex. 33^7, Dt. 31^{14}), and may well have been current for an indefinitely long period before its earliest occurrence in Hebrew literature. It has been conjectured by Zimmern * that its original meaning was the tent

* *Beiträge zur Kenntniss d. bab. Relig.* 88 n. 2; so Haupt in *JBLit.* xix. pp. 58, 70 (Assyr. *adânu=proper time*; and it was one of the functions of the Babylonian diviners to ascertain this).

where the proper time for an undertaking was determined. But the sense attached to the phrase by the biblical writers is clearly different; according to P, it is the place where Yahweh *meets* Moses to communicate to him His will (7^{89}, Ex. 25^{22}); and it meant much the same to E (Ex. 33^{7-11}). "Tent of meeting" or "tent of revelation" is therefore a suitable English equivalent.—Generally speaking, after as well as before the erection of the tent of meeting, a divine command is introduced by a simple formula, such as "And Yahweh spoke unto Moses, saying"—; sometimes a clause defining the geographical situation is added, as here and in Ex. 12^1, Lev. 25^1 (26^{46} 27^{34}), Nu. 3^{14} 9^1 35^1 (3^1); but it is altogether exceptional also to add, as here, "in the tent of meeting," though the fact, in the light of Ex. 25^{22}, must be tacitly understood. The nearest parallel to the present case is Lev. 1^1; but that passage embodies a different conception. According to the present passage, Ex. 25^{22} and Nu. 7^{89}, Moses was *inside* the tent when he received revelations; according to Lev. 1^1, Ex. 29^{42} (cp. Ex. $40^{34f.}$, Ezek. $43^{5f.}$), *outside*. The latter passages may be referred to P^s. Yet another conception occurs in E: see 12^5 n.—**2.** *Take ye*] *i.e.* Moses and Aaron: cp. v.[3] and the plural pronouns in v.[4f.]. $\mathfrak{G}^L$ and $\mathfrak{S}$ read—"Take thou"; cp. the address in v.[1] (to Moses only) and the sing. in v.[19], Ex. $30^{11f.}$. The introduction of Aaron's name and the plural pronouns may be the work of an editor: cp. notes on $3^{5.\ 39}$ 9^6.—*All the congregation of the children of Israel*] here (cp. v.[47ff.]), as in $8^{9.\ 20}$, exclusive of the Levites: generally, of course, the phrase includes them, *e.g.* 14^7 25^6 27^{20}.—*By their families, etc.*] the census is to be taken clan by clan (למשפחת) and family by family (לבית אבתם), but is to have as its ultimate aim the number of all male individuals; similarly, the individual is reached through the family in casting lots (Jos. $7^{16f.}$ (J)). The numbering by families and by "hosts" (v.[3]) is compatible: for the hosts were constituted according to tribes (c. 2).—The precise sense with which the two terms משפחה and בית אב (in the reverse order, 3^{15} n.) are employed varies. In strict usage they are related to one another thus: All Israel consists of a number of tribes (שבט: in P מטה), a tribe of several clans (משפחה), a clan of several "houses" (בית, or בית אב, pl. בית אבות), a "house" of a number of individuals—Jos. 7¹⁴ (JE), 1 S. 10²¹, Jud. 6¹⁵. It is quite exceptional for the widest term "tribe" to be used in a more restricted sense (cp. 4¹⁸ n.); on the other hand, "the (father's) house" is used at times of the tribes (*e.g.* 17¹⁷ ⁽²⁾) or the clan (*e.g.* 1 Ch. 24⁶), and the "clan" of a people or nation (Am. 3¹). In the Mishna בית אב is used specifically of a subdivision of the priests.* The term may be of Canaanite origin; for *bitti a-bi-ia* occurs in the Tel-el-Amarna tablets (127¹⁹), though whether in the sense of family or not seems doubtful (cp. Winckler's translation). Unless the two terms here and in similar cases are employed merely for fulness of expression without any precise distinction being intended, the משפחה will be the larger, the בית אב the smaller unit.— *The names*] *i.e.* the individuals; so in 26⁵³˙ ⁵⁵, 1 Ch. 23²⁴: cp. the use of ὀνόματα in Acts 1¹⁵, Rev. 3⁴ 11¹³. According to a widespread mode of thought (cf. Frazer, *GB.* i. 403 f.), the name is an integral part of the person, and might therefore as suitably denote the individual as, *e.g.*, the soul, which is elsewhere commonly used in P for this purpose.—*By their polls*] *poll*, or rather *skull* (גלגלת), in the sense of person or individual, is confined to P and Ch. (cf. v.¹⁸˙ ²⁰˙ ²² 3⁴⁷, Ex. 16¹⁶ 38²⁶, 1 Ch. 23³˙ ²⁴ †: ct. Jud. 5³⁰).—**3.** *Ye shall number them by their hosts, thou and Aaron*] such is the Heb. order; S 𝔖 have the verb in the sing. and so the original text may have run, "thou and Aaron" being an editorial addition (cp. first note on v.²).—**4.** The tribal representative must in each case be the chief man (ראש) in the families which he represents (cp. v.⁴⁴).

2. שאו את ראש] the same phrase (="calculate the total") also v.⁴⁹ 4²˙ ²² 26² 31²⁶˙ ⁴⁹† (most or all Pˢ); ראש="total," appears to be a late usage : see 5⁷, Lev. 5²⁴, Ps. 119¹⁶⁰ 139¹⁷, Pr. 8²⁶ (?).—כל עדת בני יש'] the regular term for the whole body of the Israelites in P is העדה or כל העדה (some 70 or 80 times) ; it never occurs in JE or D, and only, indeed, where the influence of P may be probably traced—Dr. *L.O.T.* 133 (No. 32). Of the fuller phrases used, the present is the most frequent (21 times): others are עדת בני יש' 1⁵³ 19⁹

---

* Cf. on the whole subject, W. R. Smith, *Rel. Sem.*² 276 ; Nowack, i. 300 ; Benzinger, 292–294 ; Levy's *NHB.* i. 115*a*, iii. 284*b*.

31^{12}, Lev. 16^{5} (and S here); כל קהל עדת יש׳ 14^{5}, Ex. 12^{6}; כל עדת יש׳ Ex. $12^{3.47}$, Lev. 4^{13}, Jos. $22^{18.20}$, 1 K. 8^{5} = 2 Ch. 5^{6}; עדת יש׳ 16^{9} 32^{4}, Ex. 12^{19}; כל עדת י״ Jos. 22^{16}; עדת י״ 27^{17} 31^{16}, Jos. 22^{17}.—**3.** יצא צבא] the antithetical phrase occurs in 31^{14} הבאים מצבא המלחמה; the pl. of the present phrase יצאי צ׳ in 1 Ch. 5^{18} 7^{11}, whence it is clear that צבא is an explicative gen. (Dav. 24*d*; G.-K. 128*x*). Variant forms of the phrase are יצא בצבא 31^{36}, Dt. 24^{5}; י׳ לצ׳ 31^{27}: cp. חלוצי צבא and החלוץ לצ׳ in 1 Ch. $12^{24.25}$.—**4.** מטה occurs 162 times in P; שבט, the regular word in JE D, very seldom (cp. 4^{18} n.), and even then, perhaps, as a result of editorial activity (cp. 18^{2} n.); Dr. *L.O.T.* 134 (No. 45); CH. 165^{P}, 112^{D}.

5–15. The twenty-four persons here named are mentioned also in $2^{3ff.}$ $7^{12ff.}$ $10^{14ff.}$; but, with the probable exception of Naḥshon and ʿAmminadab (cp. Ru. 4^{20}), never again. Several of the names are unquestionably ancient, but the *list* is certainly unhistorical.

Much has been said in defence of the antiquity of this list which is not to the point. It would be insufficient proof even if it could be shown (and it certainly cannot) that *every* individual name in it was ancient; for a late compiler might select only ancient names in composing a fictitious list. This is obvious: but it has been frequently overlooked. The actual facts relative to the list are these. (1) Several (7) of the individual names are known to have been in early use (*i.e.* in or before the time of David), or belong to types which were frequent in early, but had become obsolete by post-exilic, times: these names are עמינדב, עמיהור (on עמישדי see below), אבידן, אחיעור, אחירע, אליאב, אלישמע; further, אליסף is of a formation less frequently used in later times. (2) Five of the names are of types unknown to any OT. author except P, and three are without any well-established analogy among Semitic names. These are the names compounded with שדי (שדיאור, צורישדי, עמישדי) and צור (צורישדי, אליצור, and פדהצור). The only other name of either type in OT. is צוריאל in 3^{35} (P). Among other Semitic peoples we find the Sabæan Ṣûri-ʿaddana in an inscription said to be of the 8th cent. B.C. or somewhat earlier (Hommel, *Ancient Heb. Trad.* p. 320), and ברצור in a Zinjirli inscription of the 8th cent. B.C. (Panammu Inscr. l. 1): possibly we should add the OT. place name ביתצור. Compounds with שדי have not yet been proved to exist apart from the names in this section. Hommel's attempt to find a parallel in the name of a Babylonian king (*c.* 2000 B.C.) rests on an uncertain transliteration, and other hazardous philological hypotheses. The most that can at present be safely said in favour of the antiquity of these names is that one of them is compounded with עמי. (3) נתנאל and נמליאל are unknown to the pre-exilic writings of OT., but the former is frequent in the later OT., and both are frequent in the post-biblical literature. (4) The proportion of compounds with אל to the whole number of names is large (9 out of 24). Nothing like this can be found in early lists or documents; contrast these proportions, 1 out of 28 in Jud. 2^{6}–16; 2 out of 45 in 2 S. 9–20; 9 out of 87 in Jeremiah; compare, on the other hand,

5 out of 17 in Ezr. 10^{18-22}, and (in a list of angels) 13 out of 20 in Enoch 6 (Greek text, ed. Charles, p. 64). (5) The proportion of compounded to uncompounded names (18 out of 24) is also very large: this again can only be paralleled in later times. (6) The number of names in which אל is postfixed (5) is greater than those in which it is prefixed (4). This is very characteristic of post-exilic names, but the reverse is the case with the earliest Hebrew names. Moreover, the tendency to postfix rather than prefix a divine element in compound proper names appears to be a mark of the later periods of other Semitic languages (cp. Hommel, *op. cit.* pp. 74, 83 f., 85 f.). (7) The prefixing of the pf. tense to the divine element in נתנאל, פדהצור (as against one instance of the reverse—אליסף) is noticeable. This also is rare in early, usual in later names. The last five characteristics of the list thus lead to the conclusion that it does not rest directly and *entirely* on an ancient document; with this conclusion neither the first nor the second characteristics in any way conflict. It is quite possible that some of the names are drawn from a lost source, as two of them appear to have been drawn from a source of which, even if it does not actually exist, we yet have other indirect evidence (Ru. 4^{20}). Among such names the compounds with צור and שדי *possibly* ought to be reckoned. But to a very considerable extent the list must have been compiled at a relatively late period by a studied selection from ancient and modern names. For further details see *HPN.* pp. 191–211, and *The Character of the Proper Names in the Priestly Code: a reply to Prof. Hommel* (*Exp.*, Sept. 1897, pp. 173–190). Hommel's *Ancient Hebrew Tradition* (esp. c. iii.) contains much that is of interest on the individual names, but for reasons just indicated breaks down as a defence of the antiquity of this and similar narratives.

5. *Eliṣur*] "God is a rock," or, "My God . . .," and so in similar cases: *HPN.* 84–86, 75 n. 2—*Shede'ur*] "Shaddai is a light"; the meaning and punctuation of "Shaddai" are alike obscure, but it is obviously reasonable to punctuate and interpret it in the same way in all the compounds.—6. *Shelumi'el*] Both the punctuation and interpretation are uncertain. MT punctuates the first element as a passive part., which gives a name of rare and late formation (*HPN.* 200 f.), with some such meaning as "at peace with God"; Hommel (*AHT.* 200), "my friend is God." 𝔊 (also in 34^{20}) suggests the far commoner, but also predominantly late, formation with a pf. prefixed to the divine element; the meaning would then be "God is friendly or conciliated," but cp. the abbreviated Shelomi 34^{27}† (P). The genealogy of Judith (8^1) is carried back to this Shelumiel or Shelamiel.—*Ṣurishaddai*] "a rock is Shaddai."—7. *Naḥshon the son of 'Amminadab*] cp. Ru. 4^{10}. Naḥshon is probably connected with *Naḥash* (also found as a proper name), meaning

"serpent." ʿAmminadab = "the (divine) kinsman is generous."—8. *Nethanʾel*] "God hath given"; the name also of nine different persons mentioned in Ch., Ezr., Neh.; and one in NT., Jn. 1^{45}.—9. *Eliʾab*] "God is Father"; for other persons of the same name, see 16^{1b} (J), 1 S. 16^{6}.—10. *Of the children of Joseph*] by selecting a man from each of the subdivisions of this tribe, Ephraim and Manasseh, the number twelve is maintained in spite of the fact that Levi is not included in this census, and, therefore, furnishes no assessor.—*Elishamaʿ*] "God has heard"; for other Elishamaʿs, see 2 S. 5^{16}, Jer. 36^{12}, 2 Ch. 17^{8}.—*ʿAmmihud*] "the kinsman is glorious"; for others of this name, see 2 S. 13^{37}, Nu. $34^{20.28}$, 1 Ch. 9^{4}. The reading in 2 S. 13^{37} is uncertain (*al.* ʿAmmiḥur); but in view of the general history of compounds with ʿAmmi (*HPN.* pp. 47 ff., 245) the name in any case is probably ancient.—*Gamaliʾel*] "God is a (my) reward"; the name also of many Rabbis of the first and following centuries A.D.; see, *e.g.*, Acts 5^{24}, *Pirḳe ʾAbhoth* 1^{16} 2^{2}.—*Pedahṣur*] "the rock has redeemed"; probably a name of comparatively late origin, to which the formation and the use of the root פדה in names point (*HPN.* 196, 199).—11. *Abidan*] "the (divine) father has judged."—12. *Aḥiʿezer*] "the (divine) brother is a help"; another Aḥiʿezer is mentioned in 1 Ch. 12^{3}; cp. the parallel and early name Eliʿezer.—*ʿAmmi-shaddai*] if this be a genuine early name it will mean "a kinsman is Shaddai"; but if it be a late and artificial creation, it was probably intended to mean "people of the Almighty."—13. *Pagʿiʾel*] the first element of the word is uncertain; possibly the name means the "lot or fate of (*i.e.* given by) God" (cp. פגע in Eccl. 9^{11}), or "the mark (or target) of God" (cp. מפגע in Job 7^{20}).—14. *Eliasaph*] "God has added"; another person of the same name in 3^{24} (P).—*Deuel*] form and meaning of the first element is uncertain.

7. נחשׁון] the philologically younger ending וֹן- occurs here and in v.[9] (MT.), the older form ָן in v.[13. 15]; the latter is common in Arabic, and also occurs in several Hebrew names; cp. Barth, *NB.* § 193–195.—**14.** רעואל] 𝔊 𝔖 here and elsewhere רעואל; so some MS. of 𝔐 in 2^{14}; רעואל is given as an Edomite and Midianite name (Gn. 36^{4}, Ex. 2^{18}); in later Heb. cp. Tob. 3^{7}, Enoch 20^{4}. Reuel, perhaps = "God is a friend," though 𝔊's γ = ע = غ does not favour this. With רעואל cp. אלרעה and دعا = to call.—אחירע] "thy brother is evil"—BDB.: obvious, but most improbable: some detect in רע the Egyptian deity Ra, as Horus in אשחור, חנפר, חור: cp. *EBi.* i. 101, 333, 1966, 2134: others רֵעַ = "friend": cp. רעואל and preceding n.

16. *These are the elect of the congregation, princes of their ancestral tribes, heads of the thousands of Israel*] the twelve assessors are men of already established rank. If the term אֶלֶף, rendered "thousands," be taken literally, the assessors are heads of the largest divisions into which the people were ordinarily divided for judicial (Ex. 18^{21-25} E) or military (2 S. 18^{1}) purposes. But the term also means a "division of a tribe"; if it has that sense here, it corresponds to "fathers' house" in v.[4], just as it corresponds to clan (משפחה) in 1 S. 10^{19-21}. Like other similar terms in Hebrew and Arabic, it is used sometimes of larger, sometimes of smaller divisions of the tribe: cp. n. on v.[2] above; and for Arabic usages, Nöldeke in *ZDMG.* 1886, p. 175 f.—17. *Expressed by name*] נקבו בשמות Ezr. 8^{20}, 1 Ch. 12^{32} 16^{41}, 2 Ch. 28^{15} 31^{19}†.—18. *They declared their pedigrees*] *i.e.* registered themselves. The form of the verb (התילד) occurs only here. Like התיחש, so frequent in Ch., Neh., Ezr., it is a denominative.—19. *As Yahweh commanded Moses*] to be closely connected with the preceding v. and separated from clause b. For the formula, cp. Ex. $39^{1.5.7}$ etc., Lev. 8 (several times), Nu. 2^{33} etc. CH. regard the formula as characteristic of P^s, to whom they assign v.[17–19a], and whose hand they trace in the expressions commented on in the two preceding notes. Paterson refers the peculiarities to glossing and textual accident.—*And he numbered them*] the sentence is introductory to the following details of the census.

16. קריאי העדה] 26^{9} Ḳ'rē; Ḳ'rē here = K'tib in 26^{9} קְרוּאֵי העדה. The form קרא as the more unusual is more probably correct; it is the only form in the similar phrase קראי מועד 16^{2}.—17 f. ויקח . . . הקהילו] Dav. 114*b*; for another possible explanation, cf. 1^{2} first n.—18. ויתילדו] the retention of the secondary י indicates the denominative character of the form; ct. התודע, and cp. Stade, § 31*a*.—19. ויפקדם] For the cstr. as assumed by the verse division, cp. Driver, 127 γ. 𝔊 𝔙 read ויפקדו.

20–47. **The numbers of the twelve tribes.**—The section consists of (1) a recurring formula based on v.[2f.]; (2) the numbers of the several tribes. The numbers are repeated in c. 2. The form and present position of the section may be due to P^s; see above, p. 3, and below on v.$^{47-54}$.

The position of Gad in this list (and in c. 26) is extraordinary, and appears due to the influence of c. 2, where Gad is connected with Reuben and Simeon for sufficient reasons (see introductory note to c. 2). 𝔊, by placing v.$^{24f.}$ after $^{36f.}$, restores Gad to a more normal position.

In the twelve repetitions of the formula there are but three variations. (*a*) לגלגלתם כל זכר v.$^{20. 22}$ is omitted in 𝔐 and S in the remaining ten cases. 𝔊 repeats the phrases every time: 𝔖 retains them only in v.$^{20. 22. 24}$; 𝔖 in all cases and S in v.^{20} reverse the order of the two phrases in agreement with v.^{2}. (*b*) פקדיו v.^{22} (S פקודיהם) is a manifest intrusion in 𝔐; 𝔊 𝔖 and some Heb. MSS. omit it. (*c*) 𝔐 (though not in all MSS.) in v.^{42} omits ל before בני נפ׳: ct. S 𝔊 𝔙.

The style of the formula is redundant and clumsy; תולדתם appears to be in apposition to . . . בני; but in turn gives place to כל זכר, כל יצא, and פקדיהם, the suffix in the last bringing us back to the first term, but being itself explained by the added genitival clause . . . למטה. Cp. König, iii. 284*c*.

44. איש אחד לבית אבותיו] the omission of אחד, or the addition of another איש אחד, would assimilate this cstr. to what we find elsewhere; for the former cp. Gn. 9^5 10^5; for the latter 13^2 34^{18}, Jos. 3^{12}. Read איש אחד איש אחד למטה אבותיו; for מטה cp. 𝔊 S, though the text of the latter as a whole is not preferable to 𝔐. The accents (cf. RV.) connect שנים עשר איש with the first half of the v.; but translate rather, "twelve men were they, each representing his ancestral tribe."—**45 f.** ויהיו in v.^{45} is without complement; it is repeated in v.^{46} with a shortened subject. Lev. 13^3, 1 K. 8^{30} may be cited as somewhat analogous; but it is not improbable that two originally distinct statements of the total have been here combined. See above, p. 2.—**47.** הָתְפָּקְדוּ] if the punctuation be correct, this verb furnishes an isolated instance in Hebrew of a reflexive of the Kal (cf. Arabic Conj. viii., Aram. Ithpe'el, Moabitic הלתחם, Mesha, l. 11). This passive form recurs 2^{33} 26^{62}, 1 K. 20^{27} †; corresponding active forms Jud. $20^{15\ bis.\ 17}$ 21^9 †, cp. Stade, § 162. Others explain the form as Hithpael, with abandonment of the reduplication of the 2nd radical, and compensative lengthening of the preceding vowel (for the first point, cp. Piel forms like בקש)—König, i. p. 198 f.

It will be convenient to gather together here and to consider once for all the numbers yielded by the two censuses recorded in Numbers (c. 1–4. 26). The details given are the numbers (1) of male Israelites over twenty years belonging to each of the twelve secular tribes: (*a*) in the second year of the Exodus, c. 1 f.; (*b*) in the fortieth year,

c. 26; (2) of firstborn male Israelites above a month old, 3^{43}; (3) of males above a month old belonging to the three Levitical families: (*a*) in the second year, c. 3; (*b*) in the fortieth, c. 26; (4) of male Levites between thirty and fifty years of age, c. 4.

1. The tribes in the table below are arranged according to their size at the first census; the order in the text of c. 1 (in c. 26 it is the same, except that Manasseh precedes Ephraim) is indicated by the bracketed number to the left; the sign + or — to the right indicates that the tribe is represented as having increased or diminished in the interval between the two censuses, and the bracketed figure to the right indicates the order of size in c. 26.

	C. 1, year 2.	C. 26, year 40.		
(4) Judah	74,600	76,500	+	(1)
(10) Dan	62,700	64,400	+	(2)
(2) Simeon	59,300	22,200	–	(12)
(6) Zebulun	57,400	60,500	+	(4)
(5) Issachar	54,400	64,300	+	(3)
(12) Naphtali	53,400	45,400	–	(8)
(1) Reuben	46,500	43,730	–	(9)
(3) Gad	45,650	40,500	–	(10)
(11) Asher	41,500	53,400	+	(5)
(7) Ephraim	40,500	32,500	–	(11)
(9) Benjamin	35,400	45,600	+	(7)
(8) Manasseh	32,200	52,700	+	(6)
Totals	603,550	601,730		

2. The firstborn male Israelites above a month old number 22,273.

3. The numbers of male Levites are—

	Above 1 month old.	Between 30 and 50 years.
Ḳohath	8600	2750
Gershom	7500	2630
Merari	6200	3200
Total	22,000 (in text)	8580
	22,300 (actual)	
At the second census (26^{62})	23,000	

These numbers must on every ground be regarded as entirely unhistorical and unreal; for (1) they are impossible; (2) treated as real, and compared with one another, they yield absurd results; and (3) they are inconsistent with numbers given in earlier Hebrew literature.

1. The total represented is impossible. Males over twenty form but very little more than a quarter of a whole population, thus (neglecting the 51,000 odd Levites) the total in c. 1 f. (603,550) represents a total of men, women, and children well exceeding 2,000,000.* And yet this multitude is represented as spending forty years in the wilderness! The impossibility cannot be avoided by the assumption that the two millions wandered far and wide; for (1) this is not the representation of the text, according to which, for example, they camped in a fixed order (c. 2), and marched together at a signal given by two trumpets (c. 10); and (2) the numbers are impossible even if we think of them as dispersed over the whole peninsula of Sinai, the present population of which is estimated at from 4000 to 6000.†

"As we saw the peninsula," writes Robinson (*Bibl. Researches*, i. 106), "a body of two millions of men could not subsist there a week without drawing their supplies of water, as well as of provisions, from a great distance."‡ By a miracle, no doubt, this multitude might have been sustained; but it ought to be observed that the miracles actually *recorded* are not on an adequate scale; for let any one read the story in 20^{1-13}, and ask himself whether this suggests a water supply sufficient for a multitude equal to the combined populations of Glasgow, Liverpool, and Birmingham. It must suffice to bring this number once more to the touchstone of reality. The number at the end of the wilderness period is virtually the same as at the beginning, *i.e.* we are to think of two million people ready to fall on and settle in Canaan, already long inhabited. Now, what data exist point to about one million as the outside population of Israel and Judah when settled in the country; § even this population representing a density of

* For the vital statistics assumed throughout the discussion, see *Ency. Brit.*[9] xix. 514.

† *Ency. Brit.* xxii. 89.

‡ See also Doughty, *Arabia Deserta*, i. 61, ii. 605.

§ Buhl, *Die socialen Verhältnisse der Israeliten*, 51–55; Meyer, *Entstehung des Judenthums*, 108–114.

about 150 to the square mile, *i.e.* a density nearly twice that of Spain, and about the same as that of Denmark or Scotland.

The numbers of the several tribes must stand or fall with the total.

It is the great merit of Colenso to have demonstrated the absolute impossibility of the numbers; and to his discussion (*Pentateuch*, pt. i. c. iv.–xiii.) reference must be made for further detail. Colenso, being concerned with the credibility of the Pentateuch as a whole, very properly tests the compatibility of the numbers with statements in any part of the whole. In what is here said they are compared only with the statements in P.

2. The unreality of the numbers is independently proved by comparing them one with another. Thus: the number of male firstborn is 22,273; allowing the number of female firstborn to be equal, the total number of firstborn is 44,546, and, therefore, the total number of Israelites being between 2,000,000 and 2,500,000, the average number of children to a family is about 50! Again, if, as is probable, the firstborn of the *mother* is intended (cp. 3^{12}), then, since the number of firstborn and of mothers must have been identical, there were 44,546 mothers: but the number of women being approximately the same as of men, the women over twenty numbered something over 600,000, and therefore only about 1 in 14 or 15 women over twenty were mothers! The comparison of the two sets of Levitical figures bring less absurd, but still unreal, results to light. The average European percentage of persons (male and females) between thirty and fifty years of age to the *whole* population is barely 25, and in the U.S.A. the percentage is 22; but the percentage (males only considered) among the Kohathites is 32, the Gershonites 35, the Merarites 52. For the sake of simplicity the numbers are here taken as they stand; some slight difference would be made by allowing for children under a month, or again by adopting the view that firstborn means the firstborn to the father, and then allowing for the influence of polygamy; but no legitimate allowance or device can get rid of the essential impossibility of the figures. For a full discussion and an account of the attempts to surmount the difficulties, see Colenso, *Pentateuch*, pt. i. c. xiv.; pt. vi. p. 500 ff.

3. The 40,000 (? fighting men) of Jud. 5^{8} stands in striking contrast with the 301,000 (first census 273,300) of men above twenty assigned in Nu. 26 to the six tribes (Benjamin, Ephraim, Manasseh, Naphtali, Zebulun, Issachar) celebrated in Deborah's song as participating in the war. Again, the male Danites above twenty, according to the census, just before settling in Canaan numbered 64,000; in Jud. 18 we have a narrative recording a migration of at least a considerable part of the tribe of Dan: yet the migrating party includes only 600 armed men.

But if the numbers are unhistorical, how did they arise, and how much do they mean? The total, 600,000, was derived by P from the earlier work JE (Ex. 12^{37}, Nu. 11^{21}), unless we assume that the original number in these two earlier passages has been removed by a later harmonising scribe in favour of P's 600,000. How the number was obtained we are just as little able to determine as in the parallel cases of high numbers elsewhere (*e.g.* Jud. $20^{2.\,17}$, 2 S. 24^{9}); it must suffice to have shown that they are impossible even under the conditions prevailing after the settlement in Canaan. The exacter totals (603,550 and 601,730) appear to have been given to gain an air of reality; in the same way the numbers of the individual tribes are not precisely $\frac{600,000}{12}$, *i.e.* 50,000 for each tribe; but the numbers are so manipulated that in each census precisely six tribes have over and precisely six under 50,000; somewhat similarly the number of the Levitical cities (48) is represented not as 12×4, but as $13 + 10 + 13 + 12$ (Jos. 21^{4-7}).* Under the circumstances it seems likely that *all* the tribal numbers are purely artificial; though the number assigned to Judah presupposes a population not greatly in excess of a quarter of a million (which may be taken as a rough approximation to the actual population of the Southern Kingdom), and might, if it stood alone, be treated as an anachronism rather than an artifice. The fact that in both censuses Judah shows the largest numbers may be intentional, and due to the writer's desire to illustrate the pre-eminence of Judah (cp. p. 18); but for the most part no significance can be detected in, and

* Nöldeke, *Untersuchungen*, 116–120.

was probably not intended to attach to, either the numbers of the several tribes themselves or the variations between the first and second census.

The numbers of the male firstborn (22,273) and the male Levites (22,000) are intimately connected. Since the impossibility of the proportion noted above forbids us to believe that the number of the male firstborn was inferred from the total number of male adults, we must consider it based on the number of Levites, a slight excess (273) being attributed to the firstborn in order to admit of an illustration of the law of 18[16]. But this consideration leads us further. The number of the Levites was reached independently and without reference to the 600,000. Whence or how we cannot say: it is more moderate than the Chronicler's impossible figure (38,000 over thirty years old = about 94,000 over a month old), but scarcely corresponds to reality at any period.

47–54. The Levites not numbered with the other tribes: their functions and position in the camp.—In v.[47] it is stated as a matter of fact that the Levites were not numbered with the other tribes: in v.[48f.] the command is given that they are not to be so numbered. Further, v.[49], strictly interpreted, implies that neither Levi *nor* the other tribes have yet been numbered. The facts seem best explained by the assumption that v.[17–47] did not originally stand in their present position (We. *Comp.* 178 f.). Kue., however (*Hex.* § 6, n. 35), stands by the present order on the ground that "we cannot be surprised that in a fictitious narrative the succession of details should be open to criticism." It is, of course, altogether illegitimate to surmount the difficulty by rendering with RV. in 48, *for the Lord spake unto Moses*, for the Waw Conv. cannot state a reason (Driver, *Tenses*, 76, Obs.); וידבר must be rendered here as elsewhere, *and Yahweh spake*.—**50–53.** Brief instructions, all of which are elaborately developed in c. 2–4. The Levites are to carry the tabernacle on the march, to set it up on encamping, and to take it down at starting: they are to encamp immediately round it so as to prevent any but themselves coming near it.—**49.** *Thou shalt not number*] note the singular, and cp. notes on v.[2. 3].—**50.** *But appoint thou*] the pronoun is expressed in Heb. and is therefore emphatic (Dav. § 107; Dr. *Tenses*, p. 201). Di. explains the emphatic pronoun as implying "Thou by thyself and not in company with Aaron and the princes" (v.$^{3f.}$). But it is the emphasis of antithesis—Thou shalt not number it . . . *but* appoint.—*The tabernacle of the testimony*] Ex. 38^{21}.—**51.** *The stranger that cometh nigh shall be put to death*] it is a capital offence for any one not a Levite to concern himself with the holy tent and its furniture. The word translated "stranger" (זר) is used of one who does not belong to the circle which the writer has directly in view, whether he explicitly mentions it or not. Thus in Dt. 25^{5} the "stranger" is a person of another family; "strange children" from the standpoint of the husband are the offspring of his wife's adulterous connection (Hos. 5^{7}). The word is frequently used of the "layman" in contrast to the priest (3^{10}, Ex. 29^{33}).—**52, 53.** The whole people are to encamp in an orderly manner (which is fully described in c. 2) around the tabernacle, but kept from immediate proximity to it by the Levites. This inner position of the Levites is to prevent any even accidental contact of the non-Levites with the tabernacle, and, consequently, any such sudden and destructive outburst of Yahweh's anger as we read of in 2 S. $6^{6ff.}$ and in several passages of P (17^{17} (16^{46}) 18^{5} etc.; cp. 8^{19}).—**53.** (*And the Levites*) *shall keep the charge of*] used as here with a gen. of the obj. to be guarded the phrase (שמר משמרת) is characteristic of P and subsequent writings, as also of Ezekiel (cp. *e.g.* Ezek. $40^{45f.}$ $44^{8.\,14f.}$, 1 Ch. 23^{32}); closely connected with this is the limitation in P of the phrase "Yahweh's charge" (Lev. 8^{35}, Nu. 9^{19}) to a particular duty, whereas in earlier writings it was used with a more general reference, *e.g.* Gn. 26^{5} (JE), Dt. 11^{1}.—**54.** A characteristic priestly formula; cp. *e.g.* Gn. 6^{22}, and for a full list see Dr. *L.O.T.* p. 132, n. 11.

II. The position of the tribes in camp and on the march, and their numbers.—The present form and position of this chapter are probably not original: see above, p. 3.

The writer seems to have conceived the Israelite camp in the wilderness as a quadrilateral; round the tent of meeting as a centre was an inner quadrilateral formed by the priests on the E., and the three divisions of Levi on the remaining three sides (v.^{17}, cp. 1^{48-54} $3^{23. 29. 35. 38}$). An outer quadrilateral was formed by the camps of the twelve tribes, three on each side. Of each set of three, one tribe is distinguished above the rest, and gives its name to the entire camp on its side; the meaning of 𝕳 certainly seems to be that this more distinguished tribe occupied the central position on its side; 𝕲 implies that its position was at the end of the side, a view adopted by few modern commentators. The arrangement described in 𝕳 may be shown by diagram thus—

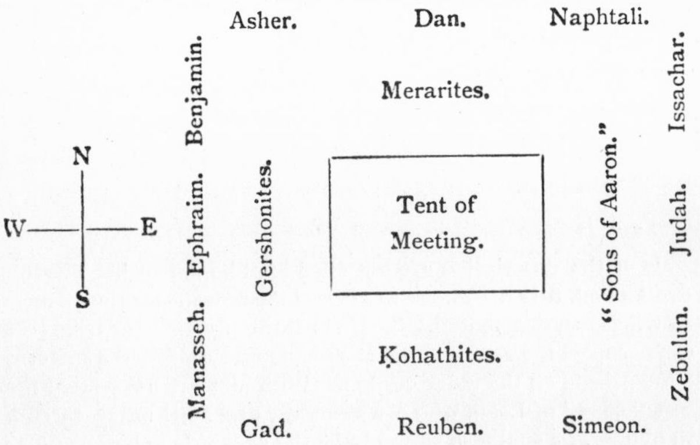

We need not suppose that the writer bases his description on any lingering tradition of what actually occurred in the wilderness, or on knowledge, at first or second hand, of the form of the Bedawin camps in his own time. As a matter of fact the description is at variance with earlier tradition, which placed the sacred tent *outside* the camp (Ex. $33^{7f.}$ E).

What the usual form of the Hebrew military camp actually was we cannot confidently say. From the terms טירה (31^{10} n.), which is not actually used of a *Hebrew* camp, and מעגל many have inferred that it was commonly round (*EBi. s.v.* "Camp," § 1). Modern Bedawî camps are sometimes round, especially when small: Burckhardt, *Bedouin and Wahábys*, i. 33; Doughty, *Ar. Des.* i. 46 ("His people with him were some thirty tents set out in an oval, which is their manner in these parts"—*i.e.* between Ayla and Maon), ii. 309 ("A menzil of B. Aly, sixteen booths pitched ring-wise, which hitherto I had not seen any nomads use in Arabia"—near Hâyil). For Bedawî camps not round (though also not quadrilateral), see Doughty, i. 414, 221, and the picture facing p. 385; also Seetzen, *Reisen*, ii. 298.

The description rather expresses an idea—that of the sanctifying presence of God in Israel's midst (cp. 5^3, Lev. 15^{31}). The sacred presence needs to be guarded against undue approach, hence the sacred caste of Levi separate the tabernacle from the secular tribes. The most sacred caste, the priests, guard the entrance to the tent on the E.

The writer, who thus embodies his ideas in a picture of the past, owes something in all probability to Ezekiel, who, picturing the ideal future, makes Caanan an exact parallelogram enclosing the temple, which is to be immediately surrounded by the priests, the Levites, and the holy city (Ezek. 48). In its turn the present description may have influenced the author of the NT. Apocalypse, who, however, gives yet freer expression to the idea in his depiction of the city which lies four square, and, instead of being sanctified by a fixed centre of the divine presence, is wholly illumined by the glory of God (Rev. 21).

The details of the description are not filled in at haphazard. Though generally overlooked, it is not difficult to detect the reasons for the manner in which the tribes are distributed. Judah, in P the pre-eminent tribe (see above, p. 14), occupies the centre of the most honourable side—the eastern, parallel to the priests on the inner cordon. With him are associated the two youngest "sons" of Leah, who are generally and most naturally connected with him. The southern seems to be the next side in importance; on it the Ḳohathites encamp, who, though descended from Levi's second son, are the Levitical family from which the priests sprang, and who are intrusted with the care of the most sacred objects. Those who encamp on the south, moreover, immediately follow the eastern tribes on the march. The south is occupied by the remaining sons of Leah, Reuben and Simeon, the firstborn naturally occupying the centre. But a tribe is needed to complete the trio; this is naturally found in the eldest "son" of Leah's handmaid—Gad. The next side—third in rank, and occupied within by the Gershonites, the descendants of Levi's eldest son—is filled by the three Rachel tribes, Ephraim (by nature the second-born, but promoted, according to early tradition (Gn. $48^{13ff.}$), to a higher position by Jacob) occupying the centre. Finally, the north is held by the three remaining "sons" of the handmaids, the eldest being in the centre. See, further, Gray, "The Lists of the Twelve Tribes" in *Expositor*, March 1902, pp. 225–240.

1. *To Moses and Aaron*] Moses only is mentioned in v.^{34}; cp. 1^2 n.—**2.** *With his own company*] so in v.$^{3. 10. 18. 25}$ substitute "company" for "standard" of RV.: see phil. n.—*By the ensigns*] The term (אות) is of wide meaning (= "sign," "mark"), and occurs nowhere else with its present signification, except, perhaps, in Ps. 74^{4}. The use of ensigns or standards for the several families forming an encampment is true to modern Bedawî custom, and may have been suggested to the writer by such custom in his day. "The Beduin coming near a stead where they will encamp, Zeyd returned to us; and where he thought good, there struck down the heel of his tall horseman's lance, *shelfa* or *romhh*, stepping it in some sandy desert bush; this is the standard of Zeyd's fellowship,—they that encamp with him and are called his people." * Modern scholars † have generally concluded that the use of two different flags is here implied—the family ensign (אות), and a standard (דגל) for each group of those tribes. But see last n. The meaning of the verse is rather this: the individual Israelites are to keep to their proper quarters; and within these are to encamp by families. The modern Bedawin also encamp "by kindreds" (Doughty, *Arabia Deserta*, i. 414).—**3–10.** If the suggestions made above (p. 2 f.) are sound, in their original form these now overloaded verses ran: *And those who encamp eastwards towards the sun-rising shall be the company of the camp of Judah, and those that encamp beside him shall be the tribe of Issachar and the tribe of Zebulun; these shall start out* (on the march) *first*. So, similarly, in the corresponding sections, v.$^{10-16.\ 18-24.\ 25-31}$.—**3.** *Eastwards towards the sun-rising*] 3^{38} 34^{15}, Ex. 27^{13} 38^{13}, Jos. 19^{13}† (P); cp. Jos. 19^{12} (P), and, for a similar redundancy, see Ex. 26^{18} (P).

17. *And the tent of meeting, the camp of the Levites, shall set forth in the midst of the* (*other*) *camps*] the appositional subject is awkward; the difficulty is concealed in EV., which is simply not a translation of 𝔐. A different view of the order in which the Levites marched is taken in 10^{17-21}: see notes there.—*As they encamp, so shall they start*] The subject is, of course, the Levites, not as Ibn Ezra, in order to avoid the conflict with 10^{17-21}, will have it, the secular tribes. Di. limits the force of the words to a confirmation of clause *a*:

* Doughty, *Arabia Deserta*, i. 221; see also Burckhardt, *Bedouin and Wahábys*, i. 34.

† Di., Now. (*Arch.* p. 362), Buhl, BDB.

as the Levites pitched in the middle of the tribes ($1^{52f.}$), so are they to march in the middle of them. But the following clause, "every one in his place, according to their companies," seems to require a wider meaning, and to imply that the Levites, like the twelve tribes, were divided into (four) companies, each having a set place alike in camp and on the march. These positions in camp are given *subsequently* in the present ($3^{23. 29. 35. 38}$), but may have been given earlier in the original, form of the narrative (above, p. 3). On this view of the words the writer means that the order on the march was: (1) Priests, (2) Ḳohathites, (3) Gershonites, (4) Merarites; cp. the diagram above.—**32.** The subscription to the *statements* in v.$^{4. 6. 8}$ etc.; cp. 1^{44-46}.—**33** corresponds to 1^{49}, but to nothing in the present chapter.—**34.** The proper subscription to the divine *instructions* in v.$^{2f.}$ etc.

2. רגל] some such meaning as company is demanded in v.^{3} and is suitable elsewhere (v.$^{10. 17. 18. 25. 31. 34}$ 1^{52} $10^{14. 18. 22. 25}$). There is, it is true, little etymological support for it, دَجَّالَة "a crowd of men," not counting for much. But there is scarcely more for the usually accepted rendering "standard." Ancient tradition consistently supports such a meaning as that now suggested: 𝔊 *τάγμα*, 𝔖 ܛܟܣܐ, 𝔗 מקם (=*τάξις*); see, further, the discussions by Gray and Cheyne in *JQR.* xi. 92–101, 232–236.—**4.** וצבאו ופקריהם] so 9 times in 𝔐; but in v.$^{6. 8. 11}$ and in S throughout וצבאו ופקריו. Paterson in *SBOT.* argues forcibly in favour of ופקדיהם throughout, and of regarding וצבאו as an interpolation by R^{P} under the influence of $10^{12ff.}$, or of seeing in the two terms traces of two recensions of P here fused together.—**5.** והחנים עליו] the full predicate is מטה יששכר + מטה זבולן v.^{7} (read rather ומטה as in v.$^{14. 22. 29}$), *i.e.* each of the two tribes encamps beside (על) Judah. 𝔊, on the other hand, by inserting at the beginning of v.^{7} *καὶ οἱ παρεμβάλλοντες ἐχόμενοι* (+*αὐτοῦ*, v.^{12}), implies that Issachar only pitched by the side of Judah, and that Zebulun pitched by the side of Issachar; so in the corresponding vv.—**7.** מטה] S 𝔖 and some Heb. MSS. ומטה; cp. last n.—**16.** ושניים] 𝔊 𝔖 𝔙 𝔗 omit the ו: so also (except 𝔗) in v.^{24}; cp. 𝔐 in v.$^{9. 31}$.—**18.** ימה] in v.$^{10. 25}$ the term of position precedes לצבאתם: so here in 𝔊.—**20.** ועליו] read with 𝔖 והחנים עליו.—**31.** לדגליהם] not found in v.$^{9. 16. 24}$. On the other hand, לצבאתם, which we should expect here after מאות, is missing.

III. 1–4. The generations of Aaron.—In substance a mere repetition of Ex. 6^{23}, Lev. $10^{1f.}$. It appears to be inserted here as a preface to v.$^{5ff.}$ with a view to explaining "Aaron and his sons," v.$^{9f.}$ "The anointed priests" in v.^{3} betrays the hand of P^s: cp. Introd. § 11.—1. *Now these are the generations of . . .*] *L.O.T.* 6 ff. The usage is not quite the same as in P's narrative in Genesis, since the subject of what follows ($v.^{5ff.}$) is the descendants of Levi (not Aaron). The insertion of Moses' name *after* Aaron is unusual.—*In mount Sinai*] cp. Ex. 24^{16} 31^{18}, Lev. 7^{38} 25^{1} 26^{46} 27^{34}, Nu. 28^{6}: ct. "in the wilderness of Sinai," 1^{1} 3^{14} 9^{1}.—3. *Who were installed*] lit. "whose hand was filled." The phrase *millē' yād* is ancient (Jud. $17^{5.12}$), and has a parallel in the Assyrian *umalli ḳâti.** It is said, for instance, of Ramman-nirari III. that the god Ashur "filled his hand with an incomparable kingdom" (*KB.* i. p. 190). The precise original sense is uncertain; according to some, it meant "to fill the hand" with money (cp. Jud. $17^{5.12}$ with 18^{4}); according to others, with the office to which one is appointed (cp. the Assyrian usage); and according to others, with the sacrifice (cp. 2 Ch. 13^{9}). Later, the original sense must have been commonly lost sight of, for it is used of the altar (Ezek. 43^{26}; cp. 7^{88} phil. n.); hence in P the phrase may be rendered "installed" or "instituted." †—4. *And they had no children*] not stated in Lev. 10, but repeated in 1 Ch. 24^{2}.

1. ביום דִּבֶּר] cstr. as, *e.g.*, Ps. 138^{3}; Dav. 25. דבר with seghol instead of ṣere (cp. כִּבֶּם, כִּפֶּר) is 3rd pf., not inf. (Str.); G.-K. 52 *l. o.*—2. אביהוא] here as everywhere (except A in Ex. 6^{23} Αβισουρ), in Ch. as well as in the Pent., 𝔊 reads Αβιουδ = אביהוד; with אביהוא cp. אליהוא, יהוא.—4. לפני י״] *bis* as in Lev. $10^{1f.}$; ct. 26^{61}. In 1 Ch. 24^{2} לפני אביהם is substituted for the first. With מות לפני י״, cp. 2 S. 21^{9}.—ויכהן] pl. (1 Ch. 24^{2}) unnecessary; Dav. 113*b*.

5–13. The institution of the Levites as a caste of priests' servants.—$V.^{6-9}$ general description of the functions of the Levites and their subordination to the priests; $v.^{12f.}$ their relation to Israel: they are the representatives of the first-born—a point elaborated in $v.^{40-51}$; $v.^{25.31.36f.}$ the specific duties of the three Levitical families.

In the preceding books of the Pentateuch Levi has been frequently referred to as the eponymous ancestor of the tribe,

* See Fried. Delitzsch, *Assyr. Handwörterbuch*, 439*b*; cp. Winckier in *KB.* v. p. 21*.

† In addition to the Lexicons, see Nowack, *Arch.* ii. 120 f. (with references); Baudissin, *AT Priesterthum*, 183 f.; Weinel in *ZATW.* 1898, pp. 60 f., 42 f.

and as a tribe not possessing the character of a religious caste: Gn. 29^{34} 34. 35^{23} 46^{11} 49^{5}, Ex. 1^{2} 2^{1} 6^{16-25}. Further, there are two passages in JE which may recognise, or contemplate, the sacred character of the tribe: Ex. 4^{14} 32^{26-28}; and two passages belonging to P^{s} which certainly regard Levi as a sacred caste, Ex. 38^{21}, Lev. $25^{32f.}$, the one presupposing Nu. 3, the other Nu. 35^{1-8}. These exhaust the references of all kinds to Levi in Gn. Ex. Lev.

Prior to Nu. 1–3 there is, then, no reference in P^{g} to sacred Levites—a term which may be conveniently used for Levi regarded as a sacred caste, when in the interests of clearness the distinction needs to be made. Yet though the institution of the caste is first described in c. 3, it is quite exceptionally presupposed in 1^{47-53} $2^{17.\,33}$. This may be an additional reason for thinking that the institution of Levi originally preceded the establishment of the camp order (above, p. 3). But be this as it may, the institution of sacred Levites in P^{g} stands entirely apart from and *follows* the institution of the priesthood. A correct appreciation of this is essential to an understanding of the author's view of the hierocratic constitution. Genealogically, priests and sacred Levites are connected: they are sprung from a common ancestor: as religious castes they are from the first and for ever entirely and completely distinct, called into being by two perfectly distinct and independent *fiats* of Yahweh, the priests first (Ex. 28) to a perpetual and exclusive office (Ex. 29^{9}, Nu. 3^{10}), then the Levites. Levitical descent is alike in fact and theory essential to the sacred Levite; what is of the essence of the priesthood is descent from *Aaron*—Levitical descent is, as a matter of fact, implicit in this and necessary, but it is theoretically negligible.

The priests, then, are not exalted Levites; and just as little are the sacred Levites degraded priests. On the other hand, the priests are selected from and stand over against *all Israel*, not merely Levi (Ex. 28^{1}, Lev. $9^{1.\,2}$: so in Psalms dependent on P—$115^{9f.}$ $118^{2f.}$ $135^{19f.}$); and it is all Israel that in P^{g}'s story of Ḳorah claims the priesthood, c. 16.

Priests could and did exist before and without sacred

Levites, but sacred Levites are unthinkable without priests. They are essentially "servants of the priests" (3^6), a subordinate caste "joined" (*nilwah*) on to the previously existing priestly caste (18^2). Thus the order in which the institutions established by Moses at Yahweh's command originated was—the altar or place of sacrifice (Ex. 27); the priests (Ex. 28); the Levites (Nu. 3).

Such is P^g's theory; post-exilic, *i.e.* post-Ezran, practice is governed by it; and the Chronicler reconstructs the past in accordance with it.* But how does it compare with earlier practice and other laws?

In earlier practice, Levites not of the seed of Aaron were priests (Jud. 18^{30}), and the priestly office was at first not even limited to Levites, though they were held to have a superior fitness for it (Jud. $17^{5.\,10-13}$, 1 S. 7^1, 2 S. 8^{18} 20^{26}). All this is entirely at variance with P^g's theory; yet the writers never, except perhaps in Jud. 17^6, take exception to it. That *in practice* there was no distinction between priestly and non-priestly Levites down to the Captivity is clearly implied by Ezekiel, 44^{11-13}.

So with the theory or law: the compiler of the Book of Kings (1 K. 12^{31} cp. 13^{33}) condemns Jeroboam because he had made priests of people who were not Levites; the implication is clear—any Levite might be a priest; the Levites are not yet divided into two classes, one of which consisted of priests, the other of priests' servants.

The same theory underlies Dt. 33^{8-11} and the main body of the Book of Deuteronomy; all Levites have a right to discharge priestly functions ($10^{8f.}$ 18^{1-8}). Here the Levites are, it is true, classified ($18^{6f.}$): but both classes are *priests*; they are priests of the capital or priests of the provincial towns.

Finally, we approximate to P^g's theory in Ezekiel. The prophet writing in exile in the year 572, and sketching the future constitution of Israel, recognises that, *down to the Exile, the Levites had formed* in respect of the priestly function

* The Book of Jubilees throws back the origin of the priesthood to the patriarchal period, when, of necessity, Levi (not Aaron) is the first priest, c. 32.

a single caste, but provides that *in the future they shall be divided into two distinct castes*—a priestly caste, consisting of the sons of Zadok, *i.e.* the priests of Jerusalem, and a caste of priests' servants, consisting of (the descendants of) priests who, before the Exile, had officiated in idolatrous worship, *i.e.* at the high places, and are henceforth, for this offence, to forfeit their priesthood and become subordinates (Ezek. 44^{9-31}, esp. $^{10-16}$).

Thus the division of the Levites into two castes, which elsewhere first appears even as a theory in Ezekiel, and is then consciously and deliberately proposed as a *novelty* for the future, is accepted in P^g as coeval with the institution of worship in Israel.

Since P^g's theory was first placed in relation to parallel theories and practice, the really inevitable inference has gained increasing recognition: P^g is later than Ezekiel: the existence of a Levitical caste, separate and distinct from the priestly, was unknown to the Mosaic age, unknown even to the age of Josiah: it belongs alike in theory and practice to the post-exilic age.

So, *e.g.*, We. *Proleg.* c. iv.; Kue. *Hex.* § 3 n. 16, § 11 n. 13 f., § 15 n. 15, and esp. *Abhandlungen*, 465–500=(*Th. Ti.* 1890, pp. 1–42); König, *Offenbarungsbegriff* (1882), ii. 322 ff; Driver, *L.O.T.* 139 ff.; CH. i. 127 f. So far as the inference as to *practice* is concerned, others (*e.g.* Di., Baudissin) agree; but they argue for a pre-Deuteronomic existence in a then unpublished writing (P) of the *theory* of distinct priestly and Levitical castes. This view as elaborated by Baudissin in his *Gesch. des AT Priesterthums* was criticised by Kue. in the article cited above. Baudissin has lately reiterated his arguments for the pre-Deuteronomic origin of P in an extremely lucid and less encumbered form in his *Einleitung*, pp. 96–102, 139–170, but he has in no way parried Kue.'s criticism. For defences of the traditional view on this matter it must suffice to refer to S. I. Curtiss, *The Levitical Priests* (Edinburgh, 1877), and A. van Hoonacker, *Le Sacerdoce Lévitique dans la Loi et dans l'Histoire des Hébreux* (Louvain, 1899).

Not only does P^g differ from Ezekiel in making the sacred non-priestly Levites an ancient institution, but also in regarding the position of the Levites as the very reverse of a degradation: it is an honour (1^{50-53}): they are chosen freely by God, not, indeed, to the highest position, but to the next highest. They are superior to all except the priests, and hence encamp immediately round the tabernacle between it and the other tribes; cp. also on c. 16. 18.

As in the case of the priesthood, and, indeed, of the nation itself, so of the Levites, no reason is given for the choice; the divine choice is made freely; the distinction is not conferred for any merit. In this respect P^g perhaps differs from earlier writers: cp. Ex. 32^{26-28}, Dt. 10^8 (with Dr.'s note) 33^9.

According to 3^{11-13}, it is true, Levi is chosen as a substitute for the firstborn, to which Yahweh had a claim; but while these verses assign a reason why a tribe had to be set apart, they assign none why that tribe was Levi.

5–10. The Levites in relation to Israel and the priests.—5. *Unto Moses*] Throughout this c. the command is given to Moses alone; see v.$^{11. 14. 40. 44}$, cp. v.$^{16. 42. 51}$, ct. ^{39}; in c. 4 several times to Moses and Aaron (v.$^{1. 17}$, cp. v.$^{37. 41. 45}$); yet also to Moses only (v.^{21}, cp. $^{37. 45. 49}$).—6. *Bring near*] have brought to thee, Ex. 28^1. The technical sense (16^5 n.) is not intended here.—*They shall serve him*] Aaron, *i.e.* the priests. The verb שרת is always, when used of the Levites, limited by an object, which is either, as here and 18^2, the priests, or the assembly (16^9), or the tabernacle (1^{50}); on the other hand, of the priest, the verb is used absolutely, 3^{31}, Ex. 28^{35} etc.; cp. Baudissin, *Priesterthum*, 29.—9. *Aaron and his sons*] *i.e.* the priests: the fuller phrase for "Aaron," v.^{6}. The gift of the Levites to the priests by the Israelites is indirect: they are immediately given to Yahweh, v.$^{40ff.}$, and by Him to the priests: this is elaborately explained in 8^{16-19}.—*To him*] *i.e.* Aaron; cp. v.^{6} n. 𝔊 S read "to me," *i.e.* Yahweh; cp. 8^{16} 18^6.—10. *Aaron and his sons thou shalt appoint*] 𝔊 + *over the tent of meeting.*—*And they shall guard their priesthood*] 𝔊 + *and everything about the altar and within the veil*; cp. 18^7 𝔥. The addition probably goes back to a Hebrew original, since 𝔊 differs in 18^7.—*The stranger*] here = any one not a priest; in the present context the term includes and, indeed, specially refers to Levites; cp. 1^{51} n.

6. והעמדתו לפני] העמיד לפני Gn. 47^7 and 12 other times in the Hexateuch of a formal or ceremonial setting. This particular phrase is in the Hexateuch peculiar to P: but see 11^{24}, Ex. 9^{16} (JE); cp. CH. 141^P.—9. המה לו מאת] S and some Heb. MSS. הם לי מתוך; cp. 8^{16}.—נתונים נתונים] for the repetition, here, perhaps = "wholly given," see G.-K. 123*c*.—מאת] = "on the part of," frequently (though not exclusively) in P: BDB. 86*b*.

11–13. The Levites taken by Yahweh in satisfaction of His claim to the firstborn.—This point of view is hardly identical with that of v.$^{5-10}$; moreover, the substance of the present section would more naturally have been incorporated in the preceding if both sections were from the same hand. Paterson may therefore be right in attributing v.$^{11-13}$, together with the allied passages v.$^{40f. 45}$, to another hand, though whether there is sufficient reason for deriving the verses (at least in their present form; cp. v.^{12} n.) from H is more doubtful; yet note "I am Yahweh," v.$^{13. 41. 45}$; see n. on v.^{13}.

The sanctity of the firstborn and their need for redemption therefrom are recognised alike by the early and the later Hebrew laws, Ex. $22^{28(29)}$ $34^{19f.}$ (JE) 13^{2} (P). It is subsequently provided in P that henceforward every male at a month old is redeemable at 5 shekels, 18^{16}; cp. $3^{40ff.}$ The Levites are substitutes only for those above a month old at the time.

In representing the firstborn as subject to redemption in the wilderness, P differs from J, who dates the claim from the entrance into Canaan, Ex. $13^{11f.}$

According to Rabbinic theory before the time when the tabernacle was erected, *priestly* functions were discharged by the firstborn; *Z'baḥim* 14^{4}, 𝔗^{Jon} on Ex 24^{5} (cp. 𝔗^{O} *ib.*); cp. Rashi on the present passage. Some modern scholars have considered that a similar theory underlies this passage; and some even infer that the theory (cp. Ex. $22^{28(9)}$) corresponds to fact, that the firstborn in early Israel was, as a matter of fact, devoted to priestly duties. So, recently, Baudissin, *Priesterthum*, 55–57; Smend, *ATReligionsgeschichte*,[1] 276, [2]282. But (1) the fact that Samuel, a firstborn, is dedicated to the temple-service by a *special* vow; (2) that Jud. 17^{5} (? cp. 1 S. 7^{1}) appears to regard any son indifferently as available for priestly functions; and (3) the indications that in early times the priesthood vested rather in the father (cp. the ritual of Passover, Ex. 12. $13^{8ff.}$; and father=priest, Jud. 17^{10}) do not favour the *fact* of a priesthood of the firstborn; cp. *EBi.* "Family," § 2; "Firstborn." Further, it seems improbable that P^{g}, who does not recognise the existence of sacrifice among the Hebrews before the erection of the tabernacle, considered that the firstborn had ever been devoted to sacred service. H may conceivably have held the theory.

12b. Cp. Ex. 13^{2} (P). So in v.^{13} the first clause and *I hallowed unto me every firstborn in Israel both of man and beast*, much more closely resemble the phraseology of Ex. 13^{2} than Ex. $13^{12f.}$ (JE). On the other hand, P in Ex.

knows nothing of the assertion here made in clause *a*, that Yahweh's claim to the Hebrew firstborn is based on His sparing of the Hebrew firstborn when He slew the firstborn of Egypt. For this view, see Ex. $13^{14f.}$,—a passage not earlier in origin, perhaps, than the Deuteronomic school.

13. *I hallowed unto Me*] *i.e.* declared them to be my possession; anything belonging to or standing in a special relation to Yahweh is holy, anything claimed by Him thereby becomes holy or "is hallowed"; see Baudissin, *Studien*, ii. 63.—*I am Yahweh*] a formula specially characteristic of H; occasionally also in P, *e.g.* Ex. 6^8 12^{12}; cp. *L.O.T.* 49, CH. 179, 203^P.

12. אני הנה] $18^{6.8}$, Gn. 6^{17} 9^9 17^4, Ex. 14^{17} 31^{16} (all P).—'מבני יש] S and some Heb. MSS. 'בבני יש; so $^{41.45}$ 8^{18}, Ex. 13^2 𝔐.—והיו לי הלוים] S 𝔊 prefix ופרויהם יהיו: cp. v.$^{46.48}$.

14–39. The census of male Levites above a month old commanded and carried out.—V.$^{14f.}$ the command; v.^{16} summary statement of its execution; v.$^{17-20}$ enumeration of the Levitical families.

14. *In the wilderness of Sinai*] 1^1 n.—**15.** *By their fathers' houses, by their families*] 1^2 n.; the phrases occur in this order 4^{22}; more frequently, as here also in 𝔖, in the reverse order, as $1^{2.20}$ and throughout 1. $4^{2.29.34.38.42}$ 4^{46}.—*Every male from a month old and upward*] corresponding to firstborn children liable to redemption; a firstborn child under a month old or of the female sex was not subject to redemption.—**16.** *Moses*] 𝔊 + "and Aaron," cp. v.^{39}, and see 1^2 first n.—**17–20.** = Ex. 6^{16-19}, cp. Gn. 46^{11}. The three main divisions of the Levites are the same in Nu. 26^{57}, but the subdivisions v.^{58} differ.

21–26. The Gershonites number 7500, and encamp W. of the tabernacle. Their prince is Eliasaph the son of La'el, and their charge the tabernacle, the tent, its covering, the curtain before the entrance of the tent, the hangings of the court, the curtain of the entrance to the court, the altar and its cords.—**22.** On the constant change from narrative (*e.g.* v.^{22}) to command (v.^{23}) in v.$^{22-39}$, see above, p. 2 f.—*Even those that were numbered of them*] this second ופקודיהם should be omitted with 𝔖: perhaps it has been accidentally transposed from v.^{28}, from which it is now missing in H.—**23.** *Westwards*] on this and the other positions, see above, p. 18.—24. *Eliasaph son of La'el*] the *list* of six names contained in v.$^{24. 30. 35}$ does not appear to be ancient: for all are compounds, and five are compounded with El; see p. 6 f., and the phil. notes below.—25. *The tabernacle*] since the framework of the tabernacle (the boards, bars, etc.) fall to the charge of the Merarites, v.^{36}, all that can be here intended are the curtains referred to in Ex. 26^{1-6}; this is clearly indicated in 4^{25}.—*The tent*] made of curtains raised over the tabernacle, Ex. $26^{7ff.}$.—*The covering thereof*] the covering of the tent made of rams' skins, Ex. 26^{14}.—*The screen for the door of the tent*] Ex. 26^{36}.—26. *The hanging for the court and the screen for the door of the court*] Ex. 27^{9-16}.—*Which is by the tabernacle, and by the altar round about*] *i.e.* which (viz. the court) encloses the tabernacle and the altar (of burnt-offering).—*And the cords of it*] the pronoun probably refers to the tent. These cords can scarcely be distinguished from those assigned to Merari, v.^{37}, and the double assignment may be due to an oversight of the writer. The cords are the tent ropes fastened to pins and so supporting the goats' hair curtain, or tent-material: cp. Ex. 35^{18} 39^{40}; see Introd. § 11.—*As regards all the service thereof*] the Gershonites are to do whatever these things require to have done to them.

27–32. The Ḳohathites number 8600, and encamp S. of the tabernacle. Their prince is Eliṣaphan b. 'Uzzi'el, and their charge the ark, the table, the lamp-stand, the altars, the sacred utensils, and the veil.

28. Hebrew idiom requires the restoration with 𝔖 at the beginning of the verse of "and those that were numbered of them"; cp. v.$^{22. 34}$, also the n. on v.^{22}.—*Keeping the charge of the sanctuary*] appears to be out of place here, and accidentally repeated from v.^{32}.—*Six hundred*] a textual error (שש for שלש) for *three hundred*: see on v.^{39}.—29. *Along the side of the tabernacle southwards*] cp. v.^{35}, ct. v.$^{23. 38}$. The term "side" is introduced in connection with the longer dimensions of the tabernacle which were N. and S. (Ex. $26^{18ff.}$); so Ex. $40^{22. 24}$.—31. *The altars*] 𝔖 𝔗^{O} the altar. The pl. in 𝔥 includes (1) the altar described in Ex. $27^{1ff.}$, and subsequently called, for sake of distinction, the altar of burnt-offering (*e.g.* Ex. 38^{1}), and (2) the golden altar of burnt incense (Ex. 30^{1-10}); cp. Introd. § 11.—

Wherewith they minister] the subject is "those who minister" (*i.e.* the priests; cp. n. on v.^{6}); cp. Dav. 108. 1.—*The screen*] the curtain which separated the holy place from the holy of holies (Ex. 26^{31-33}), and is elsewhere called either "the veil" (פרכת) simply (Ex. $26^{31.\,33.\,35}$ 27^{21} 30^{6} 36^{35} 38^{27} $40^{3.\,22.\,26}$, Lev. 4^{17} $16^{2.\,12.\,15}$ 21^{23}), or "the veil of the sanctuary" (Lev. 4^{6}), or "the veil of the testimony" (Lev. 24^{3}), or "the veil of the screen" (פרכת המסך Ex. 35^{12} 39^{34} 40^{21}, Nu. 4^{5} 18^{7}), the particular sense of the last phrase being explained by Ex. $40^{3.\,21}$. Probably we should read here with 𝕾 "the veil of the screen" as in 4^{5}. The present ambiguity with the screens mentioned in v.$^{25f.}$ then disappears. The tendency to amplification in these chapters is illustrated here by S, which adds after "the screen" the words "the laver and its base" (cf. Ex. 30^{18}). The same addition is made in 4^{14} by both S and 𝔊.—**32.** The statement that Eleʿazar was chief prince of Levi presumably finds its place here because Eleʿazar belonged to the family of Ḳohath, Ex. 6^{18-25}. Di. considers the verse a later addition; see phil. n. below.

33–37. The **Merarites** number 6200, and encamp to the N. of the tabernacle. Their prince is Ṣuri'el b. Abiḥail, their charge the framework of the tabernacle, viz. its boards, bars, pillars, sockets; and the pillars, sockets, pins, and cords of the court.

In this section, unlike the two preceding, the mention of the prince precedes that of the position in the camp.

34. *Six thousand two hundred*] 𝔊 6050.—**35.** *On the side of*] v.^{29} n.—**36 f.** On the various objects forming the charge of the Merarites, see Ex. $26^{15ff.\,26ff.\,32.\,37}$ $26^{19ff.}$ $27^{10ff.}$ The tenons, rings, and hooks in Ex. $26^{17.\,19.\,32}$ are probably here included in the general term *accessories* (כליו). Cp. 4^{32}.—*Their cords*] v.^{26} n.

38. The **priests** encamp on the E. of the tabernacle, thus guarding its entrance (Ex. 26^{15-30}).—*Before the tabernacle eastwards*] 𝔊 omits; but cp. 2^{3} n.—Aaron and his sons, *i.e.* the priests, are described as *those who paid attention to what required to be attended to in the sanctuary, including everything that had to be attended to for the children of Israel*: the last clause is naturally limited to the sacrificial requirements of the Israelites.—*The stranger*] v.^{10} n.

39. The **sum total** of male Levites above a month old is

22,000. The separate numbers given in v.$^{22. 25. 34}$ give a total of 22,300. That the actual total intended by the writer was 22,000 (not 22,300) is clear from v.$^{40-51}$. The error is in v.^{28} (see note there). The error is an early one: for 𝔊 agrees with 𝔐 in v.^{28}. Many Jewish and some modern commentators (*e.g. Speaker's Comm.*) assume that the three hundred not included in the total were firstborn, and, therefore, not available for redeeming the firstborn of the secular tribes; but the text says nothing of this, and three hundred would be a ridiculously small proportion of firstborn to the whole number. —*And Aaron*] S 𝔖 and some Heb. MSS. omit. The points in MT., already referred to in *Siphrê* on 9^{10}, mark the words as suspicious, and a comparison with v.$^{14-16}$ tells against their originality: cp. 1^2 n.

16. משה 𝔊+ואהרן.—צִוָּה] S צוהו (cp. 20^9 𝔐); 𝔊 (cp. 𝔙) *συνέταξεν αὐτοῖς Κύριος*: cp. 36^2 n.—**20.** הַלֵּוִי] so also in v.^{32} 18^{23} 26^{57}, Dt. 10^8 Jos. $13^{14. 33}$; in all these passages the whole tribe is referred to. The use of the art. with a tribal name is rare (Dr. on Dt. 3^{13}; König, iii. 295*d e*); it is facilitated in the case of Levi by the gentilic form; the word is, indeed, often used with unambiguously gentilic force (*e.g.* Dt. 12^{12}, Jud. 17^7). VV. render by a pl. both here and in v.^{32}: in the latter verse S reads הלוים.—**24.** לגרשני] 𝔊 למשפחת הגרשני, cp. v.$^{30. 35}$ 𝔐.—אליסף] 1^{14} n.—לאל] if rightly read, probably a late name; *HPN.* 206 f.; $𝔊^{ABF}$ Δαηλ, $𝔊^{L}$ Δαουηλ, 𝔖 אליאב.—**26.** לכל עבדתו] this use of ל is specially characteristic of P and Ch.; see BDB. 514*b*; in v.$^{31. 36}$ וכל ע׳.—**27.** ולקהת] the ו is dittographic: cf. v.$^{21. 33}$: also $1^{22. 24}$ etc.—**30.** אליצפן] for the name (="(my) God has sheltered"), cp. 34^{25} (P); it is probably an ancient name, cp. *HPN.* 176 f., 192.—עזיאל]="a (my) strength is God." This and other names containing עזי, עזו, etc., are common in the later OT. writings; see the appendices to *HPN.* under עזיאל, יעזיאל, עזיה, עזויה, יעזיה, and חזיה, also *ib.* pp. 210, 230. For earlier usage the only evidence is the name of king Uzziah who was also, and perhaps originally, known as 'Azariah, in the 8th cent., and עזיו on an ancient Hebrew seal; Levy, *Siegel u. Gemmen*, 39–42.—**31.** עבדתו] S 𝔊 עבדתם: cp. v.^{36} 𝔊.—**32.** נשיא נשיאי] Dav. 34, R. 4.—פקדת] the cstr. would be easiest, if we might assume here the late Heb. use of the form to denote the holder of an office; cp. קהלת and Dr. *L.O.T.* 466; Strack and Siegfried, *Neuhebr. Gramm.* 68*c*. But פקדה nowhere else has this sense. If we retain the text and the sense which the word has elsewhere in these chapters (3^6 4^{16}), we must assume a loose cstr. of the acc.: render "with the charge of." Paterson's conjecture, פָּקָד עַל, is not really supported by 𝔊.—**35.** צוריאל] (="a (my) rock is God"); on the type of name, see above, p. 6.—אביחיל] ancient type of name (cp. *HPN.* 22–34); the actual instance only in P Ch. Esth.—**36.** ופקדת משמרת בני מ׳] variations in v.$^{25. 31}$.

40–51. The number of the firstborn Israelites of the male sex above a month old is 22,273; of these 22,000 are redeemed by the 22,000 Levites, the remainder at 5 shekels apiece. This money is given to the priests. The firstborn cattle of the Israelites is redeemed by the cattle of the Levites.

For the unreality of the relation between the firstborn and the adults, see above, pp. 10–15.

40. *Their names*] 1^2 n.—41. *I am Yahweh*] v.^{13} n.—*The cattle of the Levites instead of all the firstborn among the cattle of the children of Israel*] this is difficult, for the firstborn of cattle that could be offered were not redeemable ($18^{15.\,17}$). It is questionable (with Di.) to limit "cattle" here to unclean cattle (Lev. 27^{27}, Nu. 18^{15}). Baudissin (*Priesterthum*, 42 f.) thinks this passage later than the law requiring the sacrifice of all clean firstborn and of a period when that demand was no longer satisfied in practice. Possibly we should assimilate this sentence to v.^{45} by transposing בהמת (omitting the prep. ב) before כל בכור; then render "the cattle of the Levites instead of the cattle of all the firstborn among the children of Israel"; the firstborn and all their belongings are regarded as properly forfeit to Yahweh; the Levites and their belongings are substituted for them.—45. *Their cattle*] if the text of v.^{41} be correct we should expect here "the firstborn of their cattle," the pronoun referring to the children of Israel. If the suggestion in the last n. be adopted, the pronoun refers to the firstborn Israelites.—47. The fine payable for redeeming a firstborn of men is 5 shekels, *i.e.* about 12 shillings (a shekel = 2s. 5d.: Kennedy in Hastings' *DB.*, *s.v.* "Money," iii. 422 f.).—*By the poll*] 1^2 n. With clause *b* of the v. cp. Ex. 30^{12}.

42. משה] 𝔊^L + ואהרן; אתו 𝔊^L אֹתָם.—46. ואת פדויי וגו'] For this absolute or pendent acc. cp. Kön. iii. 341*o*; and for ולקחת, Dr. *Tenses*, § 123.—פְּדוּיֵי—also v.$^{48f.\,51}$ 18^{16}; both the ground form (*kătûl*) and the plural point to an abstract meaning (Barth, *NB.* 82*e*; Kön. iii. 261; cp. ii. 137 f.); but in this particular instance the word must have acquired a secondary concrete sense (otherwise Kön. iii. 260*d*): it does not mean either the act of ransoming or the state of being ransomed, but the ransom-price (Dietrich, *Abh. z. hebr. Gram.* 41; Ges.-Buhl, "Löse-geld").—העֹדפים] The root, which appears only in Kal (Ex. 16^{23} $26^{12f.}$, Lev. 25^{27}, Nu. $3^{46.\,48f.}$) and Hiph. (Ex. 16^{18}), is in OT. confined to P; it reappears in the Mishnah.—47. חמשת חמשת] For the suspended cstr., see Dav. 28, R. 6; for the repetition, Dav. 29, R. 8 (2).—48. פדויי] resumes and defines הכסף.—49. הַפְּדוּיִם] if the text be right,

a parallel form in ם to פִּדְיֹן (Ex. 21^{30}, Ps. 49^{9}): Lagarde, *Bildung d. Nomina*, 186, 204. But probably the same form was originally read here as in v.$^{46.48}$; so S הפדוים.—פדויי הלוים] פדויי is here the pass. part., which is, however, used with a different meaning from פדויי יהוה Is. 35^{10}.—**51.** הפדים] The K'tib may be pointed הַפְּדֻים, on which see v.^{49} n.; Ḳ'rē and S both read *plene* הפדוים, cp. v.^{46} n.

IV.—V.$^{1-33}$ Levites between thirty and fifty years of age to be numbered; the transport duties of the Levites defined; v.$^{34-49}$ results of the census.

1. *And Aaron*] 3^{5} n.; some Heb. MSS. and 𝔗^{Jer} omit: but see de Rossi's note.

2–20. The Ḳohathites.—In c. 3 the Gershonites, here the Ḳohathites, are first dealt with. With the priority given to the Ḳohathites here, cp. their superior position in the camp; see above, p. 17 f.—**2b.** 3^{15} n.—**3.** The census here required is of Levites qualified for *service* about the tabernacle. It thus corresponds to the census of the rest of Israel (c. 1). The same word (צבא) is used in both chapters, though RV. here renders by "service," there by "war." Originally the word had reference to war (see phil. n.): its use of menial service about the tabernacle or temple is late; for the verb so used, see 4^{23} 8^{21}, Ex. 38^{8}, and the late gloss omitted in 𝔊^{B} in 1 S. 2^{22}; and for the noun, besides the present c., $8^{24f.}$ — Two other and different regulations as to the period of Levitical service are found in OT. (1) Instead of being as here defined from thirty to fifty years of age, it was, according to 8^{23-26}, from twenty-five to fifty, after which latter age a Levite might still render certain auxiliary services. (2) According to the Chronicler (1 Ch. $23^{24.27}$, 2 Ch. 31^{17}, Ezr. 3^{8}), from the time of David onwards the age of entrance on service was twenty, and there was no upward limit of disability.

The simplest way of accounting for the differences would be to assume that they correspond to actual differences in the age of service at the different periods to which the several references belong, *i.e.* that in the time of the Chronicler (*c.* 300 B.C.) the minimum age for Levitical service was twenty, and that at different times between about 500 and 300 B.C. it had been twenty-five and thirty respectively: so, *e.g.*, Kuenen, *Hex.* pp. 93, 299; cp. Str. on 8^{24}. Another view (Baudissin, *Priesterthum*, 167 f.) is that the minimum of twenty years was actual, but that P's fixing of the minimum at thirty is part of his historical fiction, and due to his making allowance for the heavy work of transport (cp. 1 Ch. $23^{24ff.}$); then possibly the twenty-five of 8^{23-26} is simply a mean struck by a later writer between the minimum of actual practice and that required by the law. Of harmonistic explanations it must suffice to mention one: the regulation of the present passage, it is said, is merely intended to be temporary, and has regard to the heavy work of transport; on the other hand, 8^{23-26} contains the permanent law regulating the years of service in and about the tabernacle, but not in the transport of it (so Keil). But this is to disregard the similarity in the definition of service in the two passages, and to limit unwarrantably the meaning of the expressions used in the present chapter—"all who enter into the service *to do work* (לעשות מלאכה) *in the tent of meeting*," v.[3]: "to perform work (לעבד עבדה) in the tent of meeting," v.[23]; "to perform the work of (לעבד את־עבדת) the tent of meeting," v.[30]; "all who worked in the tent of meeting," v.[37]. 𝔊 throughout this chapter substitutes "twenty-five" for "thirty," thus assimilating the present passage to 8^{23-26}. The reason for doing this, rather than correcting 8^{23-26} to agree with the present chapter, would be clear if we could assume that "twenty-five" was the actual age of service at the time of the Greek Version. Is 8^{23-26} later than Chronicles? and was the age which had been lowered from thirty to twenty between the times of Ezra and the Chronicler on account of the scarcity of Levites (cp. Kue. *loc. cit.*), once again raised subsequently to twenty-five when the number of Levites had been increased by the assimilation of the singers and others (cp. We. *Proleg.*[4] p. 145)? The data are insufficient for a decisive answer.

4. *The most holy things*] the phrase קדש הקדשים, which is variously applied (frequently, *e.g.*, to the inner part of the tabernacle, Ex. 26^{33}) refers here, as the following vv. explain, to the furniture and instruments of the tabernacle: cp. Ex. 30^{29}. See, further, Baudissin, *Studien*, ii. 52–54.—5 ff. The most holy things which the Ḳohathites had to carry fall into six groups: all alike, before the camp moved, had to be covered up by the priests that the Ḳohathites might not see them, and were then so carried by the Ḳohathites that they did not actually touch the sacred objects themselves. The six groups of most holy things are as follows:—(1) the ark, v.[5]; (2) the table of the presence, its utensils (Ex. 25^{29}), and the perpetual bread, v.[7]; (3) the candlestick and the utensils connected with it, v.[9]; (4) the golden altar, v.[11]; (5) the utensils of ministration . . . in the sanctuary, v.[12]; (6) the altar (of burnt-offering), and the vessels and instruments attached to it, v.[13f.]. These various things, or groups of things, were all alike packed in a wrapping of "*taḥash*" skin (v.[6. 8. 10. 11f. 14f.]); and, in every case except that of the ark, this wrapping formed the outer covering. On the other hand,

the ark was first covered with the veil (see on 3^{31}), then with the "*taḥash* skin" wrapping, and, finally, with a cloth of blue (v.[6]). Thus, on the march, the blue outer covering at once distinguished the ark from all the other sacred objects. All the rest of the (main) objects except the altar of burnt-offering, whose inner covering was a purple cloth, v.[13], were first wrapped in blue cloth, v.[7. 9. 11. 12]. The table of presence, like the ark, had, in all, three wrappings. It was covered with the blue cloth, then the vessels attached to it were packed on it and the whole wrapped in a scarlet cloth, and, finally, in the "*taḥash* skin" wrapping. The motive for these differences, except in the case of the bright external covering of the ark, is not obvious. The candlestick and the objects connected with it and the vessels of ministration were carried on frames specially provided for them, v.[10. 12]. The remaining objects were carried by means of the staves with which they had been provided at the time of making.—**6.** *Taḥash-skin*] the precise meaning of the Heb. phrase, skin of *taḥash*, is uncertain. The ancient versions incorrectly took *taḥash* to be a colour. From the time of the scholars of the Talmud downwards it has been customary to see in *taḥash* the name of an animal; if this be right, some marine animal of the dolphin kind seems most probable; in Arabic *tuḥas* = "a dolphin." Recently it has been suggested that the word is a loan from the Egyptian *tḥs* = "Egyptian leather." * Since the OT. writers who refer to this skin are Ezekiel and P, it may be an article with the use of which the Jews first became familiar in exile.—*And shall put in the staves thereof*] so RV.; if this means that the staves were removed during packing and then again placed through the rings (Ex. 25^{14}), for which holes could be made in the wrappings, it conflicts with Ex. 25^{15}, which forbids the removal of the staves: such a conflict is perfectly possible, for the two passages are doubtless from different hands. But the vb. שים is of a general significance, and certainly might be

* For various suggestions, see Fried. Delitzsch in Baer's *Ezek.* p. xvi f., and *Proleg.* 77 ff.; Nöld. in *ZDMG.* xl. 732; Lewysohn, *Zoologie des Talm.* 95–98, 152; Toy's note in Ezekiel (*SBOT.* Eng.), 123–126; and for an excellent summary, art. "Badger" in *EBi.*

rendered "adjust", but could any "adjustment" of poles under three wrappings make them convenient for holding?—7. *The table of the presence*] RV. in rendering ". . . *of shewbread*" assumes that the unique phrase שלחן הפנים is an abbreviation of ש' לחם הפנים. This is unnecessary; it may well mean the table of the face or presence of Yahweh. On the table, see Ex. $25^{23ff.}$.—*The dishes and the cups and the cans and the bowls*] see Ex. 25^{29}, where the last two articles are mentioned in reverse order. For the present order, Ex. 37^{16}.—*The continual bread*] *i.e.* the shewbread (Ex. 25^{30}, Lev. 24^{5-9}). The phrase לחם התמיד is used here only, but is readily explained by Ex. 25^{30}. —8. *Its staves*] Ex. 25^{28}.—9. Ex. 25^{31-38}. The full phrase, *the candlestick of the light* (מנרת המאור), is only found here and in Ex. 35^{14} (P^s).—10. *The frame*] see phil. note.—11. *The golden altar*] Ex. 39^{38} $40^{5. 26}$, *i.e.* the altar of burnt incense (Ex. $30^{1ff.}$); see Introd. § 11.—*Its staves*] Ex. $30^{4f.}$.—12. *The utensils of service*] *i.e.* the utensils used by the *priests* in their sacred service, 3^{31} n.—13. *The altar*] of burnt-offering, Ex. $27^{1ff.}$.—*Its staves*] Ex. $27^{6f.}$ At the end of the verse S 𝔊 add—"And they shall take a purple cloth and cover the laver and its base [Ex. 30^{17}], and they shall put them within a covering of *taḥash* skin, and they shall put them on the frame." The addition, with which cp. 3^{31} n., was naturally suggested by such catalogues as Ex. 30^{26-29} 31^{7-9} $35^{11ff.}$ 40^{1-11}, Lev. $8^{10f.}$.—15. *Afterwards the sons of Ḳohath shall come to carry them; without, however, touching the holy things, and so suffering death*] the negative clause is not, as the translations usually make it, adversative, but circumstantial (Dr. *Tenses*, § 159); it defines the manner in which the Levites are to carry the holy things, viz. by the staves or frames, without touching the sacred objects themselves; cp. 18^{3}. For the mortal effect of touching a sacred object, cp. 2 S. $6^{6f.}$.—*The holy things*] הקדש is used collectively of sacred objects, the more precise denotation of the term being suggested by the context (cp. Lev. 5^{16}): so several times in this and following chapters, v.$^{16. 20}$ 7^{9} 8^{19}. —16. Corresponds to the briefer statements of v.$^{28b. 33b}$ that the Gershonites and Merarites were under the general supervision of Ithamar. Ele'azar's duties consist of the general oversight of the tabernacle and all its sacred objects, and the special and immediate care of certain things that are specified, viz.—(1) *the oil for the light* (Ex. 27^{20}); (2) *the incense of sweet perfume* (Ex. 25^{6} $30^{34ff.}$); (3) *the continual meal-offering* (Neh. 10^{34}), which is not mentioned elsewhere in the Pentateuch by this term, but is identical either with the meal-offering that accompanied the burnt-offering which was offered twice daily (Ex. 29^{38-40}), and is often (*e.g.* Nu. 28^{10}, Neh. $10^{33\,(34)}$) called the continual burnt-offering (עלת התמיד), or, more probably, with the meal-offering offered daily by "the anointed priest" on behalf of himself and the other priests (Lev. $6^{13-15\,(20-22)}$); (4) *the anointing oil* (Ex. $30^{22ff.}$).—**17-20.** An amplification in the form of a direct command of what is referred to parenthetically in v.^{15}. The section is possibly an interpolation: it is marked by certain stylistic peculiarities (see phil. notes).—**20.** *They shall not see the sacred things . . . and so die*] for the mortal effect of looking at a sacred object, cp. 1 S. 6^{19}.

2. נָשׂא] Inf. abs. with imperative force (Dav. 88*b*, R. 2); so also v.^{21}; but the imperative is used in 1^{2} 3^{40}.—**3.** כל בא לִצְבָא] in v.$^{30.\,35.\,39.\,43}$ כל הבא לִצְבָא, in v.^{23} (also v.^{30} 𝔖) כל הבא לִצְבֹּא צבא; 𝔊 assimilates the phrase in all six passages—*πᾶς ὁ εἰσπορευόμενος λειτουργεῖν*. The ideas of fighting, army, military service are connected with the root צבא over so wide an area of the Semitic field that they must have become attached to it at an early period. The Assyr. *ṣâbu* means "a warrior," also "an army" (Del.); Arabic ضَبَأَ = "to lie in wait for," and in '*Urwa*, 3^{8} (cited by Nöld. *ZDMG.* xl. 726) = غزا = "to make a raid"; South-Arabian צבא = "to fight" (Hommel, *Süd-Arab. Chrest.* p. 125); Eth. ፀበአ = "to wage war." From this alone we might surmise that in Heb. the sense of "military service" was early, and, since the use of the root for service in general, or liturgical service in particular, is not common in the cognate languages, that the use of the word for the service of the tabernacle was a later extension of the meaning. As a matter of fact, צבא is constantly used in connection with warfare in early Hebrew (cp. *e.g.* 2 S. 2^{8} 10^{7}, Is. 31^{4}); it retained this connotation in the later periods of the language (see, *e.g.*, Zech. 14^{12}, Nu. 1, and Ch. *passim*). But in P it is also frequently used, as in the present chapter, of service about the tabernacle (references above). It is one of several interesting instances in which terms originating in the early and more warlike periods of Hebrew history, and retaining their military reference down to the close of the monarchy, took on after the Exile a fresh meaning, in consequence of the change from a national society under a monarchy to a religious community under a hierarchy. Cp. תרועה in early Hebrew = "the alarum of war"; but after the Exile = "the sound of the temple trumpets": cp. Nowack, *Arch.* ii. 110.—**5.** ובא] Dr. § 119β.—**6.** כסוי] also v.^{14} †, in S also in v.^{8} before בגד; cp. Mand. כסויא (cited by Barth, 124*d*). Synonyms are מִכְסֶה Gn. 8^{13} (J) and 15 times in P (many of the instances in secondary strata); מְכַסֶּה Ezek. 27^{7}, Is. 14^{11} 23^{18}, and, in a special sense (cp. Ex. 29^{13}), Lev. 9^{19} †; and כסות, which appears to have been the form in common use in earlier Heb. (Gn. 20^{16} E; Ex. 21^{10} 22^{26}, Dt. 22^{12}), though it continued in use in and after the Exile (Is. 50^{3}, Job 24^{7} 26^{6} 31^{19} †).—ופרשו] 𝔊 S 𝔗 and one or two Heb. MSS. + עליו; cf. v.^{8} 𝔐.—כְּלִיל תכלת] = "wholly blue" (Dav. 24*d*).—**10.** המוט] v.^{12} (and in the addition to S in v.^{14}), 13^{23} and (in the sense of "yoke") Nah. 1^{13} †. מוטה is more frequent, and is used specifically, in the pl., of the three *bars* (מוטת) *of* which *a yoke* consisted, and, in the sing., with primary reference to the most important part of the yoke, the *cross-bar* (מוטה). Whatever may have been the original meaning of מוט (and on this cp. König, iii. 243*b*), here and in v.^{12} the context requires, and in 13^{23} is best satisfied by, a word meaning something with a considerable flat surface on which a variety of objects could be placed and carried. 𝔊 𝔖 render "staff" or "pole," using the same word by which they render בדים in v.^{6} etc.—**12.** כְּלֵי הַשָּׁרֵת] thus here only; cp. 2 Ch. 24^{14} כלי שרת והעלות. On the art. with the infin., see König, iii. 241*k*.—**15.** ומתו] Dr. *Tenses*, § 115, p. 133.—**16.** פקדת] has two different senses in the same v., (1) things committed to one's oversight; (2) oversight.—**16.** בקדש ובכליו] the ב specifies the parts, viz. the holy things and the vessels thereof (*i.e.* of the tabernacle), of which the whole (וכל אשר or כל המשכן) consists: cp. Gn. 7^{21}, Ex. 12^{19}, Nu. 31^{26}, and BDB. p. 88*b*. The usage is characteristic of P.—**18.** אל תכריתו] though corresponding phrases with the Niph. are frequent in P (*e.g.* Gn. 17^{14}, Ex. 12^{15}) and specially characteristic of H, the Hiph. of כרת does not occur in P proper; and in H, where we find it four times in a similar sense (Lev. 17^{10} $20^{3.5.6}$), the subj. is always Yahweh. The following v. shows that we must understand the word of annihilation, not simply of loss of Levitical status, as the מתוך הלוים might seem to imply; cp. 9^{13} n.—את שבט משפחת הקהתי] appositional genitive, König, iii. 337*c*; cp. G.-K. 128, 2. The use of שבט is remarkable. Regularly the word denotes one of the main tribes of Israel (*e.g.* Gn. 49^{16}, Ex. 24^{4}, 1 S. 10^{20}); cp. n. on 1^{2}. Here it is used for a *subdivision.* The only other passages that imply such an usage are Jud. 20^{12}, 1 S. 9^{21}, which speak of the tribes (שבטי) of Benjamin. But in both passages the pl. is probably due to corruption: cp. Moore on Jud. 20^{12} (p. 430). The only other instances of שבט in P (who regularly uses מטה; cp. 1^{4} n.) are Ex. 28^{21} 39^{14}, Nu. 18^{2} 32^{33} 36^{3}, Jos. 4^{8b}, $13^{29.33}$ and 21^{16}; for Bennett is no doubt right in assigning the six instances of שבט in Jos. 22 to R; and some of the above instances may, probably enough, be traced to the same origin: cp. 18^{2} n.—משפחת הקהתי] also $3^{27.30}$ 4^{37}, Jos. $21^{4.10}$ †: cp. משפחת הק׳ 26^{57}; a variant phrase is משפחת בני קהת 3^{29}, Jos. $21^{20.26}$, 1 Ch. 6^{51} †.—**19.** וחיו] Driver, *Tenses*, § 112.—בגשתם את] 1 S. 9^{18} (but not 1 S. 30^{21} where את = with) also has את for אל. But in both passages the Versions (and here S and many Heb. MSS. also) are probably right in reading אל; cp. Dr. on 1 S. 9^{18}.—על עבדתו] 𝔊 om.—**20.** כְּבַלַּע] lit. "for the likeness of a swallowing" (viz. of one's spittle, cp. Job 7^{19})—a vivid phrase for a moment. For כ as an acc. of time, cp. BDB. 453*a b*. Somewhat differently König, iii. 402*t*.

21–28. The Gershonites.—23. *Thou shalt number them*] the phrase does not occur in the preceding section, v.^{3}, and is in a different position in the next, v.^{29}. On some other variations, cp. the notes in the preceding section; and on some minor details, see phil. notes below.—**25 f.** Cp. 3^{25} n.—**25.** *The covering of taḥash skin*] Ex. 26^{14b}: this is not mentioned in 3^{25}.—**26b.** *All that may have to be done with regard to them* (*i.e.* the objects just mentioned) *they* (the Levites) *shall perform.*—**27b.** *And you shall appoint to them by name the things committed to their charge to carry*] you shall specify in detail the various things they have to carry. So after 𝔊 and v.^{32} 𝔥. The subj. is either "Aaron and his sons" mentioned in clause *a*; or, more probably, Moses and Aaron, this passage, like the rest of the chapter, having been originally addressed to Aaron as well as Moses, who alone is mentioned in v.^{21}; then the v. means that in the first instance Moses and Aaron are to specify the objects committed to the Gershonites, and that subsequently the priests are to give all further directions.

23. לעבר עבדה ב׳] cp. לעשות מלאכה ב׳ v.^{3}; לעבד את עבדת v.^{30}.—**24.** משפחת הגרשני] so מ׳ הקהתי v.$^{18. 37}$ (see note on former v.), but מ׳ בני מררי v.^{33}.—ולמשא] used exactly like the inf. לעבר: cp. מַסַּע 10^{2}, and see G.-K. 45*e*, 115*d*; Ryssel, *De Elohistæ Sermone*, 50, 68; Strack on this passage, and especially König, iii. 233*d*.—**26.** שער] 3^{25} omits.—ועברו] On the general principle of Waw conv. with pf. after various introductory phrases, see Driver, *Tenses*, 123; but instances of the direct obj. thus standing before the Waw are not common; Ex. 4^{21} with repetition of the obj. is rather different.—**28.** בני הגרשני] 1 Ch. 26^{21} †; similarly בני הקהתי only v.^{34} and 2 Ch. 29^{12}. But the same writer sometimes curiously varies the different possible idioms in the same verse, cp. 2 Ch. 29^{12}: see also phil. note on v.^{18}; and cp. below, v.$^{37. 41}$.

29–33.—The Merarites.—29. The section begins more abruptly than the two preceding, v.$^{1. 21}$.—*Thou shalt number*] 𝔊 "ye shall number," and so in v.^{30}: cp. on v.^{27}.—**31 f.** Cp. $3^{36f.}$.—**32b.** Cp. v.^{27} n.—*Including all their accessories*] (לכל כליהם) 3^{36} n.

32. את כלי] S 𝔊 את כל כלי. Note also the expansions of v.$^{31f.}$ in 𝔊.

34–49. The census.—On the numbers, see above, pp. 10–15.

—**34.** *The princes of the congregation*] the same phrase, of a different set of men, in 16^2, Ex. 16^{22}. 𝔊 here has "the princes of Israel": cp. ^{46} 1^{44} 7^2 n. 𝔥. —**41.** At the end of the v. 𝔊 adds—"by the hand of Moses": cp. v.$^{37. 45}$.—**49.** The v. is manifestly more or less corrupt, and cannot be intelligibly rendered: RV. is not a translation, especially in clause *b*. Possibly ביד משה has fallen out of place, ופקדיו is a misplaced fragment, and אשר an error for כאשר (S 𝔊 𝔖); then render—*According to the commandment of Yahweh, by the hand of Moses, they were appointed every one to his proper service and burden, as Yahweh commanded Moses.* For the indef. subj. of פקד see Dav. 108*a*, and for פקד על 27^{16}.

34. ולבית] v.$^{38. 46}$; 𝔊 𝔖 לבית: cp. v.$^{2. 42}$ 𝔥.—**37.** על פי י״ ביד משה] על פי י״ frequent in P, uncommon elsewhere (*L.O.T.* 134, No. 41). Combined with ביד משה, it is entirely peculiar to P—$4^{37.}$ (^{41} 𝔊) ^{45} 9^{23} 10^{13}, Jos. 22^9 †, and, perhaps, originally in v.^{49}; see above. Instead of ביד משה, 3^{16} has כאשר צֻוָּה and 3^{51} כאשר צוה י״ את משה.—**46.** את הלוים] For the noun rather than the pronoun completing אשר, cp. 33^4, Ex. 25^9; König, iii. 414*q*.—**47.** כל הבא] 𝔖 + לצבא: cp. v. ^{8} n.

V. VI. *Miscellaneous Laws and Regulations.*

(1) Seclusion of unclean persons from the camp, 5^{1-4}; (2) some priestly dues, v.$^{5-9}$; (3) the ordeal of jealousy, v.$^{11-31}$; (4) the Nazirite, 6^{1-21}; (5) the priestly blessing, v.$^{22-27}$.

The first of these sections, all of which are introduced by P's characteristic formula (CH. 185*a*), would have formed a suitable conclusion to the description of the camp order, and the last might have rounded off the same subject. It is not impossible, therefore, that both formed the conclusion in P^g of the description of the camp now found in c. 1–4; though some, considering it merely supplemental, have referred the first to P^s.* It is quite improbable that any of the remaining sections, which have as little relation to the preceding and following chapters (7. 8. 9 or 10) as they have to one another, formed part of P^g (Introd. § 12); 5^{5-8} as supplemental to Lev. 5^{20-26} (6^{1-7}) is P^s; the rest, by no means clearly secondary in substance, P^x.

* Kue. *Hex.* 91–93; CH.

1–4. Every one that is leprous, or suffers from a discharge, or is unclean through contact with the dead, is to be secluded from the camp in order to preserve the sanctity conferred on it by Yahweh's presence undefiled (cp. Lev. 15^{31}).—For details as to uncleanness from leprosy, see Lev. 13; from discharges, Lev. 15; from contact with the dead, Nu. 19. All three forms of uncleanness are contagious (Lev. $13^{45f.}$ $15^{4ff.}$, Nu. 19^{22}); but the laws (P^x) just referred to do not require exclusion from *the camp* except in the case of leprosy; and the clauses demanding or implying exclusion even in that case may be editorial additions (so Baentsch). Some (*e.g.* Di.) attempt to account for the greater stringency of the present law by assuming that the laws of uncleanness have general validity, but that this law applies only to the *military* camp. There is, however, no justification in the text for this limitation, nor does the reference to women (v.^{3}) favour it: ct., moreover, the terms of Dt. $23^{10(9)}$, "when thou goest forth (*i.e.* to war) as a camp." But it is true that the Hebrews, like many other peoples,* were subject in war to special taboos, including regulations as to uncleanness (Dt. 20^{1-9} $23^{10-15(9-14)}$, 1 S. $21^{6ff.}$, 2 S. 11^{11-13}). Reminiscences of such actual though special taboos may have furnished the writer with the regulations which he here represents as of general validity in the wilderness in order to heighten his picture of the holiness of the camp. Leprosy in general involved seclusion ($12^{10ff.}$ (E) 2 K. 7^3 15^5); seclusion from the military camp on account of natural discharges is referred to in the references above; and some local or special custom in ancient Israel may well have required the seclusion of women at menstruation, who fall under the second class of unclean persons here enumerated (Lev. 15^{19-24}); for the seclusion of such is widely practised, and in particular "Maimonides tells us that down to his time it was a common custom in the East to keep women at their periods in a separate house," † just as the leprous Uzziah was kept.

* For a large collection of parallels, see Schwally, *Semitische Kriegsalterthümer*, 59–99.

† Frazer, *Golden Bough*, iii. 224; for similar practices, cp. *ib.* 222 ff.; also Halévy in *Revue Sémitique*, vii. 274. The reference to Maimonides is *Moreh Nebuchim*, iii. 47.

2. צו את בני יש' וישלחו] a rare formula: cp. Ex. 27^{20}, Lev. 24^{2}, Jos. 4^{16}. Commoner is דבר אל followed by the persons addressed and Waw with the voluntative—Ex. 6^{11} $14^{2.15}$ 25^{2}, Lev. 16^{2} 22^{2}, Nu. 19^{2} (all P): cp. Ex. 11^{2} (E).—טמא לנפש] cp. טְמֵא נפשׁ Lev. 22^{4} (H), Hag. 2^{13}. In $9^{6f.}$ the present cstr. is repeated, but נפש is defined by אדם. נפש in these phrases means either (1) the soul of the dead person, or, as we should say, the ghost—in particular, perhaps, the soul tarrying in or near the body that has ceased to breathe, but is yet unputrefied (Schwally, *Das Leben nach dem Tode*, 7 f.), or (2) the corpse; this does more justice to the language of 19^{13} (cp. n. on 19^{11}). For נפש of a material representative of the deceased, cp. the widespread use of the word for a monument on a grave, one נפשא being erected for each person buried in the grave: cp. Duval in *Revue Sémitique*, ii. 259–263, and, as illustrations, 1 Mac. $13^{27f.}$ (Syr. and Gr.); *CIS.* ii. 162, 196.—**3.** אל מחוץ למחנה] CH. 120^{P}.—מחניך] *sing.*: G.-K. 93, § 5.—**4b.** For the formula, see CH. 189^{P}.

5–10. Some priestly dues.—5b–8. A law supplemental to Lev. 5^{20-26} (6^{1-7}). It is there provided that any man voluntarily confessing to the wrongful possession of property must return the property + a fifth of its value to the rightful owner, and, in addition to this, offer to Yahweh, as an *'āshām* or guilt-offering, an unblemished ram. Provision is now made that if the rightful owner be dead, and there also be no next-of-kin (*goel*) to whom the property can be restored, it is to become the priest's.—*Any sin that men commit*] lit. "any sins of men." 𝔊 RV. rightly interpret if the gen. be subjective; others, "any of the sins committed against men"; but see phil. n.—*In breaking faith with Yahweh*] Sins against man, shown by the context at least to be intended here, and faithlessness to Yahweh are similiarly connected in Lev. 5^{21}. It is possible to sin against God without sinning against man (Ps. $51^{6(4)}$), but all sins against man are *also* sins against God. Hence, after the offender has made restitution to the wronged man or his representative, he offers God a guilt-offering, v.^{8}, Lev. 5^{25}. Both implications—that God is offended with wrong done to man, and that restitution must be made before the rite of atonement—are of importance in estimating the value and character of the later Jewish law: cp. Mt. $5^{23f.}$.—*And that person incur guilt*] *e.g.* by any of the wrongs referred to in Lev. $5^{21f.}$, such as the denial of the receipt of a deposit, or of the finding of lost goods. For similar uses of the phrase "to incur guilt," cp. Lev. $4^{13.22}$ 5^{4};

for "soul" (נפש) with the meaning of "person, any one,' 9^{13} 15^{30}, Gn. 17^{14}; the usage is frequent in P: CH. 146^{P}, BDB. 660*a*.—**7.** *Then they shall confess*] the other instances in which confession is definitely commanded will be found in Lev. 5^{5} 16^{21}: cp. Jacob, *ZATW.* 1897, pp. 60–62.—*That which he has wrongfully in his possession*] such must be the meaning of the Heb. אשם here and in v.[8], though it is found nowhere else.—*In full*] lit. "with its head." For some parallel idiomatic uses, see phil. n. to 1^{2}. For the principle of repaying $\frac{6}{5}$, cp. Lev. 5^{24} (6^{5}); and for the same fraction in other connections (*e.g.* in certain cases of redemption), see Lev. 22^{14} $27^{13.\,27.\,31}$.—**8.** *But if the man* (be dead and) *have no next-of-kin to whom the property wrongfully held may be restored, the property wrongfully held which is to be restored* (becomes) *Yahweh's, the priest's, over and above the ram of propitiation with which he* (the priest) *makes propitiation for him* (*i.e.* the man who has confessed his error). The property becomes the priest's as Yahweh's proxy, Lev. 23^{20}.—*The ram of propitiation*] the ram which formed the guilt-offering. The phrase (איל הכפורים) occurs here only. The ram becomes the property of the priest according to the general law, Lev. 7^{7}.—**9 f.** Every sacred gift which falls to the priest becomes the property of the particular priest to whom it is offered, not of the whole priestly community: cp. Lev. $7^{7-9.\,14}$, and ct. Lev. $7^{6.\,10}$ 6^{11}; for differences of usage in this matter are found within the Levitical legislation; see Baentsch on the passages just cited, and Baudissin, *Priesterthum*, 40. The present passage appears to be a fragment; its very general terms may have been better defined by the original context, just as 18^{8} is defined by $18^{9ff.}$.—*And every contribution, even all the holy things*] the two terms are best taken as coextensive, as in 18^{8}. The sacred gifts are represented under two aspects—as removed from the mass of a man's property, and as rendered holy by being dedicated to Yahweh. EV. renders *t^erûmah* by the misleading equivalent "heave-offering": see 15^{19} n., and Dr. *Deut.* 142. Some such word as "contribution" or "portion" serves best, whether *t^erûmah* is used in the wide sense of any contribution made for sacred purposes (*e.g.*

15^{19-21}, Ex. $25^{2f.}$), or in the special sense of the portion removed from the whole sacrifice as the priest's due (Lev. $7^{14.32.34}$). Equally comprehensive is the term "holy things" (קדשים): cn. Ex. 28^{38}; and for details, see Baudissin, *Studien*, ii. 44.—10. *And as for every man's holy things, they shall be his* (the priest's): *whatsoever any man gives to the priest, his* (*i.e.* that particular priest's) *shall it be.*

6. דבר אל בני יש׳] add. לאמר (S) or ואמרת (cp. v.[11]) with 𝔊. 𝔐 is unique, for the formula . . . דבר אל is, except in the peculiar case of 17^{17}, always followed either (1) by לאמר (Ex. 16^{12}, Lev. 4^2 6^{18} $7^{23.29}$ 12^2 21^{17} $24^{24.34}$, Nu. 9^{10} 6^{23}, Jos. 20^2†), cp. in commands to Moses and Aaron (*i.e.* after דברו אל), Ex. 12^3, Lev. 11^2†; or (2) by וְאָמַרְתָּ (Lev. 1^2 17^2 18^2 19^2 22^{18} $23^{2.10}$ 25^2 27^2, Nu. 5^{12} 6^2 8^2 $15^{2.18.38}$ 33^{51} 35^{10}†), cp. ואמרתם . . . דברו Lev. 15^2; or (3) by Waw and the voluntative; see note on v.[2].—איש או אשה] is prefixed (cp. Dav. 130, R. 5), as here, to the subordinate sentence, Lev. 13^{29}, Nu. 6^2 (followed by sing. verb or pron.), Lev. 13^{38} 20^{27} (followed, as here, by pl.). The prefixing of the subj. to the conditional particle is critically significant; ct. Ex. 21^7 and other passages in Book of the Covenant; and see 19^{14} n., König, iii. 341 n.—יעשו] The pl. is justified by the instances just cited: 𝔊 translates by a singular (cp. Lev. 13^{38} and ct. 20^{27}), and turns all the remaining plurals in v.[6f.] by singulars. The changes of number in 𝔐 are remarkable, but scarcely unparalleled; cp. Ew. 319*a*.—מכל חטאת] "any one of the sins"; cp. Lev. 5^{24}. See König, iii. 81–83; and cp. the use of مِن (Wright, ii. 48 f., R. b; BDB. 581*a*).—חטאת אדם] the gen. after חטאת is so generally subjective (cp. *e.g.* Gn. 31^{36} 50^{17}, 1 S. 20^1—all instances, as the *context* shows, of sins against men) that it probably is so intended here. If objective (Dav. 23), cp. חמסי (Gn. 16^5) = "the violence done to me."—**9.** וכל תרומה לכל ק׳] the explicative ל = *even, namely, to wit*: cp. Ex. 28^{38}, Lev. 5^3; BDB. 514*b*.—וכל תרומה . . . לו יהיה] one of the numerous instances in which היה ל does not agree with its (apparent) subject: cp. 9^{14} 15^{29}, Ex. 12^{49} 28^7, Dt. 18^2; the grammatical subject is rather the real object of the verbal idea: cp. Ew. 295*d*; G.-K. 145*u*. Otherwise König, iii. 345*d*.—**10.** איש את קדשיו] Dav. 11, R. 1*d*; 72, R. 4.

11–31. The ordeal of jealousy.

Literature.—The Mishnah tractate *Soṭah* (ed. Surenhusius, iii. 178–321, containing Wagenseil's Commentary); Philo, *De specialibus Legibus*, c. 10 (Mangey, 308–310); Josephus, *Ant.* iii. 11^6; Spencer, *De Legibus*, bk. iii. c. ii. § 3 *ad fin.*; Bähr, *Symbolik*, ii. 441–447; Stade, *Die Eiferopferthora* in *ZATW*. xv. (1895) 166–178.

A woman suspected of adultery, which cannot be legally proved, may be subjected to an ordeal. For this purpose her husband, who must bring with him an offering of barley meal, which is termed "a meal-offering of jealousy, a meal-offering of memorial bringing guilt to remembrance," must bring her to the priest. The priest brings her before Yahweh, makes her take an oath of purgation, and then gives her to drink a potion described as "the water of bitterness that causeth the curse," and consisting of "holy water" with which dust from the floor of the tabernacle has been mingled, and into which the written words of the oath have been washed. If the woman be guilty the potion proves harmful; if innocent, harmless; in the latter case, moreover, the woman becomes fruitful.

The custom here regulated has innumerable analogies in practices generally prevalent in antiquity, and still prevalent over large parts of the world. The essential element in the custom is that the accused in test of his innocence subjects himself to a hazard, whether that consists, as here, in drinking a potion, being flung into deep water, walking over hot ploughshares, holding heated metal in the hand, or the like. Such customs figure prominently in the ancient Indian law books, are not infrequently alluded to by the classical writers of Greece and Rome, formed a regular feature in European life down through the Middle Ages, and still have a wide prevalence, especially in Africa.

One or two illustrations are cited below. For others, reference can be made to *The Laws of Manu*, viii. 114–116 (*SBE.* xxv. 274), and the *Institutes of Vishnu*, ix–xiv (*SBE.* vii. 52–61.), for Indian custom; to Frazer's Pausanias, *Description of Greece*, iv. 175 f. (n. on vii. 25. 13) and iv. 253–255 (n. on viii. 17), and Funkhänel's article in *Philologus*, ii. (1847) 385–402 (which also contains some good remarks on the connection between oaths and ordeals), for instances in Greek and Roman authors; to Livingstone, *Missionary Travels in South Africa* (1857), 434, 631, and A. M. Post, *Afrikanische Jurisprudenz*, ii. 110–120, for African custom; and generally to Tylor's article "Ordeal" in *EB.*, and Bastian, *Der Mensch in der Geschichte*, ii. 210 f. A peculiarly interesting parallel is cited by the last named (from Japan): the accused drinks water in which paper inscribed with bird-characters (*Vögelcharakteren*) has been dipped; this causes him pain in his body till he confesses.

The Priestly Code alone among the Hebrew law books, and that only in the present section (P^x), contains a law of the ordeal; and the allusions to the custom in the OT. are at most but few. The presentation of incense by Ḳoraḥ and his company (c. 16) is a story best accounted for by assuming that the ordeal was a familiar custom not confined to cases of suspected unchastity. It is possible that familiarity with the custom also accounts for Ps. 109^{18b}, Pr. 6^{27-29}. More direct and unambiguous allusions are not found.

And yet there are reasons for concluding that the ordeal was more frequent, at least in early Israel, than this unique law would at first lead us to expect, and that the practice of it with the Hebrews, as with other peoples among whom it prevailed, was not limited to cases of unchastity.

For (1) the Hebrews also used other modes of obtaining the direct decision of the deity in cases of doubt, and one in particular which is among other peoples found closely connected with the ordeal, viz. the oath of purgation (Ex. $22^{9f.\,(10f.)}$, 1 K. 8^{31}). In what mode the decision of the deity is given in the case of Ex. $22^{7f.\,(8f.)}$ is not distinctly stated, whether by the oath, as in the next case (Di.), or by the priestly oracle (Baentsch), or by ordeal.

The connection of oath and ordeal is well illustrated by Manu's *Law* (viii. 109–116): "If two (parties) dispute about matters for which no witnesses are available, and the (judge) is unable to really ascertain the truth, he may cause it to be discerned even by an oath. . . . Let the (judge) cause the Brâhmana to swear by his veracity, a Kshatriya by his chariot," and so of the other castes; then, in immediate sequence, "or the (judge) may cause the (party) to carry fire or to dive under water, or severally to touch the heads of his wives and children. He whom the blazing fire burns not, whom the water forces not to come (quickly) up, who meets with no speedy misfortune, must be held innocent on (the strength of) his oath." The *methods* of Yahweh's decision in the early law book is left entirely undetermined or is barely alluded to, just as the detailed *ritual* of sacrifice is omitted even from Dt., though both methods and details of necessity existed in reality. The later law book (P) records the details of sacrificial ritual and of the particular ordeal which perhaps alone maintained its existence after the Exile. Bühler's remarks on the parallel silence or brevity of the earlier and the fulness of the later Indian codes in the matter of ordeals are instructive (*SBE.* xxv. p. ci f.).

(2) The double term for the accompanying offering is noticeable. It is "the offering of jealousy"; it is also "the offering of memorial, bringing guilt to remembrance." Neither term occurs elsewhere; yet the latter looks like the species, the former like the sub-species; this is so in any case, and

especially if Stade's analysis, noticed below, be adopted. But the term for the species seems to indicate that the offerings covered by it were made when a decision was required of the deity in cases of doubt, of which the doubt of jealousy is but one. Stade observes further, "The difference drawn in Lev. 7[10] [see below on v.[15]] would be much more easily explained if the meal-offering without oil and frankincense were used in more than the special cases of Lev. 5[11], Nu. 5[11-31]. But this would be the case if we assume that the מנחת הזכרון was employed in other cases as well as that of suspected adultery."

(3) W. R. Smith (*Rel. Sem.*[2] 181) interprets the names Ên-Mishpaṭ and Mê Merîbah (*i.e.* well of judgment and waters of controversy) with reference to the use of the springs at Ḳadesh in decisions by ordeal. The names outlived the practice, and are possibly not of Hebrew origin (*EBi. s.v.* "Names," § 89–91); yet their significance, taken in connection with the foregoing considerations, is not to be overlooked.

If the force of the preceding argument be admitted, it will not be denied that the custom of ordeal among the Hebrews goes back to the remotest period of their history. It survived, at least in a particular instance, as the incorporation of the present law in P shows, into the post-exilic period. It was an illegitimate conclusion of Ewald's (*Alterthümer*,[3] 275), even on his theory of the pre-exilic origin of P, that the custom fell into early disuse; for the Nazirite's vow, like the ordeal of jealousy, finds a place in P alone of the Codes, and yet we have proof positive that it was practised long after the Exile (below, p. 57 f.). There is no evidence as to when the ordeal of jealousy fell into disuse, except the statement of the Mishnah (*Soṭah* 9[9]), which may be taken for what it is worth, that Joḥanan b. Zaccai, who flourished in the last third of the 1st century A.D., abolished it. Some of the additional details given in *Soṭah*, though not always consistent with the apparent intention of the biblical text, may rest on the actual practice of the 1st century A.D., though much is somewhat clearly mere theoretical discussion. It is doubtful, however, whether the *Protevangelium* (c. 16) in making Joseph as well as Mary drink the waters, rests on actual custom: cp. v.[31] below and note.

The ordeal rests in principle on modes of thought and belief far more ancient than the religion of Israel. Modern anthropological study has abundantly justified the judgment of the great Cambridge divine of the 17th century: "Cum itaque gentes pleræque, mediis hujusmodi prodigiosis, innocentiæ in dubium vocatæ experimentum caperent; probabiliter arbitremur, hunc morem, diu ante Mosis ætatem, inter gentes invaluisse; et Deum aquam zelotypiæ Judæis concecisse, ne privilegium aut miraculum aliquod inter gentes familiare populo suo deesse videretur" (Spencer, *De Legibus*, p. 657, Cambridge edition, 1727).

The origin of the law must constantly be borne in mind in attempting to interpret its religious significance, and to estimate its place in the religion of Israel. A rite incorporated, as in the present case, from ineradicable popular custom into an essentially alien religious system passes, in respect to its meaning, through three stages: in the first stage it possesses a definite meaning; in the second it is deprived of this and, perhaps, of all meaning; in the third it has read into it a variety of new meanings consonant with the religious belief of the times, and, generally, completely at variance with the original significance. So in the present instance: the potion was originally believed to be the actual cause of harm to the guilty woman; when the rite was assimilated to Yahwistic belief, the potion becomes a meaningless survival; for it is Yahweh who causes the harm (v.[21]); finally, various symbolical meanings are read into this as into other parts of the ritual; as, for example, by Philo, who explains that the water used is pure and living (𝔊's equivalent for the holy water of 𝔥 being ὕδωρ καθαρὸν ζῶν), "since a blameless woman is pure as to her life, and deserves to live," and that the dust mingled with it is taken from the temple as being on that account "most excellent, just as a modest woman is." All three stages may very well be represented in different classes of the same age; at the very time that Philo and the Palestinian doctors were finding meanings for the several details of the ritual, to many of the people they either retained some shadow of their original meaning, or had ceased to have any at all; just as the practice of turning to the East, filled by the reflective with a Christian meaning, to the mass of the unreflecting laity means nothing, and among some Christian sects has retained, at least till recent times, something of the significance given to it by the sun-worship from which it sprang.*

Just as myths, not of Hebrew origin, like those of Creation and the Flood, as they gained currency among the Hebrews, gradually exchanged their originally polytheistic for a monotheistic setting, and thus became a fit vehicle for the truths of the Hebrew religion; so rites such as the present, or that of the red cow (c. 19), or of the "scape-goat" (Lev. 16), or of the purification of the leper (Lev. 14^{4-7}), not deriving their origin from the belief in Yahweh, were accommodated to it at the cost of some modifications, and with some incongruous results. The first essential in the present case was that those who used the ordeal should feel that the decision was Yahweh's decision (cp. Dt. $18^{10ff.}$, Is. 8^{19}), the judgment due to Yahweh's activity. This involved obtaining the decision at Yahweh's (one) sanctuary, and this in turn the bringing of an offering. Again, the place whence the dust (and probably also whence the water) was taken is a modification of the original requirements. The present law may embody other modifications of the original, which can no longer be detected with certainty.

In this connection a suggestion made to me by the Rev. H. W. Robinson seems worthy of consideration. In the original rite administered in cases of suspicion aroused by pregnancy the water may have been credited with positive virtue in the case of guilt; being supposed to descend into the womb (מעים v.^{22}, as in Gn. 25^{23}, Ps. 71^{6}, Ru. 1^{11}), it may have been regarded as affecting the offspring of a guilty intercourse, so that, though the woman grows great with child ("the swelling belly"), the birth is abortive (expressed by the euphemistic or modified expression נפל ירך:? compare נֵפֶל = abortion). In the other case the potion may have been regarded as innocuous to the growth of the fœtus, which is duly brought to the birth. The latter point has then been characteristically modified: the innocent woman is promised that she shall *subsequently* conceive, as a reward directly granted by Yahweh (cp. Gn. 17^{15-19} 25^{21}).

* Tylor, *Primitive Culture*,[3] ii. 426.

The interpretation of the section must also take account of certain literary or textual phenomena. In the present text the woman is twice brought before Yahweh, twice made to swear (v.$^{19. 21}$), and twice, if not thrice, to drink the potion (v.$^{23f. 26f.}$). That this duplication occurred in the actual ritual is highly improbable. The text has either been interpolated and otherwise modified, or it rests on a compilation from two parallel but distinct *tôrôth*.

Stade also lays stress on the lack of complete harmony between superscription and subscription; on the assumption that the wife is guilty in v.$^{12f.}$, and, in contrast, on the openness of the question in v.^{14} and on sundry alternative expressions. He argues that the present law has sprung from a literary fusion of two laws of ordeal—(*a*) a מנחת הזכרן consisting of v.$^{11-13}$ (except 3rd clause), ^{15} (except כי מנחת הקנאת הוא), $^{16-19}$ (except the 1st clause and מנחת קנאת הוא and המאררים in ^{18} and טמאה, המאררים in ^{19}), ^{20} (except וכי נטמאת), ^{22a} (except המאררים), $^{23f. 25}$ (last clause), $^{26a. 31}$; and (*b*) a מכחת הקנאת consisting of v.$^{29. 13}$ (3rd clause), $^{30a. 14}$ (והיא לא נטמאה), $^{30b. 18}$ (to יהוה), $^{21. 22b. 25. 27f.}$ (with some slight variations). CH. have attempted another analysis into (*a*) an ordeal; (*b*) a solemn condemnation: for a brief criticism of this, see *EBi. s.v.* "Jealousy," § 5. Any such analysis can in detail only reach a very moderate degree of probability.

11, 12a. "The superscription is the formula well known from the Book of Leviticus [*e.g.* 1$^{1f.}$] by means of which the codifications of older customs are there introduced; it indicates that we have before us here a section of the same character" (Stade). For v.^{11}, cp. phil. n. on v.^{6}.—**13.** *And it be hid from the eyes of her husband, and she be undetected, though she has* as a matter of fact *defiled herself* (Lev. 18^{20})] RV. is wrong: the subj. of the first vb. (masc.) is the fact, of the second (fem.), the woman.—*And there be no witness against her, since she was not taken*] viz. in the act. A woman convicted, on the evidence of two witnesses at least (35^{30} (P), Dt. 17^{6} 19^{15}), of adultery was put to death (Lev. 20^{10} (H), Dt. 22$^{22-27}$). The ordeal is to be resorted to when, as in cases of adultery it must frequently have happened, legal proof was not forthcoming. The husband is not here required in any way to justify his doubt; indeed, the next v. seems to contemplate the possibility of the merest and most baseless suspicion. The Mishnah required the husband first to prohibit the woman, in the presence of witnesses, to hold any further communication with the man suspected; and then only in case of the wife's disobedience could the husband subject her to the ordeal (*Soṭah* i. 1 f.). Philo also says the husband must state the evidence for his suspicions.—14. *And the spirit of jealousy come upon him*] *i.e.* the man becomes jealous or suspicious: cp. "the spirit of whoredom" (Hos. 4^{12}). Spirit in such cases denotes an uncontrollable or unaccountable impulse.—15. *Her offering for her*] The Versions rightly understood that the offering, however described, is the man's; see phil. n. He brings it as one who requires the services of the priest, *i.e.* the help of God, in which case no one must appear empty, without a gift. Though described at length the offering is a mere subsidiary; the *raison d'être* of the law is the ordeal.—*One-tenth of an ephah*] a little under 4 litres or 7 pints; see BDB. *s.v.* בת, p. 144*b*.—*Barley meal*] Everywhere else P requires "fine meal" (סלת) to be used for offerings: cp. Ezek. 46^{14}. But the requirement is scarcely ancient; Gideon and Hannah offer ordinary meal (קמח), which is clearly distinguished in 1 K 5^2 (4^{22}) from סלת, Jud. 6^{13}, 1 S 1^{24}. Barley meal (שעורים) was far less valuable than "fine meal" or "wheat" (2 K. 7^1, Rev. 6^6), but in early Israel it may have been the staple farinaceous food, and throughout it appears to have been not only the food of cattle (1 K. 5^8 (4^{28}), but also the ordinary food of the poorer classes (Ru. 2^{17}, Jud. 7^{13}, Jn. $6^{9.13}$; cp. *EBi.* 483 f.); as such it is only probable that at one time it played a considerable part in sacred offerings, and was generally accepted by the priests of the sanctuaries for services such as the present. As an isolated survival, it subsequently called for explanation; a typical attempt is R. Gamali'el's: "As her acts had been bestial, so her offering consisted of the food of beasts" (*Soṭah* ii. 1); Philo's is similar. Such interpretations fail to do justice even to the law in its present form, much less to the original custom; for the offering is not the woman's, and her action is still subject of doubt.—*He shall pour no oil over it*] Meal-offerings (מנחה), for which see Lev. 2, were divided into two classes: (1) those that were mingled with oil; (2) those that were dry, Lev. 7^{10}. The only other instance mentioned of "dry" meal-offerings is the poor man's sin-offering (Lev. 5^{11}), which, like the present offering, must also be offered without frankincense. Philo, who has been much followed, may very well be correct here in explaining that the absence of the accompaniments is due to the fact that the occasion was no happy one, but one that was very grievous.—*A meal-offering of memorial*] The defining term זכרון is elsewhere used in a good sense; hence the interpretation is added—by the original writer or a glossator—*bringing iniquity to remembrance*. When Yahweh forgets, guilt goes unpunished; when He remembers, He visits the sinner, 1 K. 17^{18}, Ezek. $21^{28f. (23f.)}$ 29^{16}, Hos. 8^{13}, Jer. $44^{21f.}$, Ps. 25^{7} 137^{7}.—**16.** *Before Yahweh*] *i.e.* before the tabernacle, and, in particular, before the altar. In later times, according to *Soṭah* i. 5, the accused were brought to the Nicanor or eastern gate of the temple.—**17.** *Holy water*] "The expression . . . is unique in the language of Hebrew ritual, and must be taken as an isolated survival of an obsolete expression. Unique though the expression be, it is not difficult to assign it its meaning; the analogies already before us indicate that we must think of water from a holy spring" (W. R. Smith, *Rel. Sem.*² 181). The intention of 𝕳 is rather water from the laver (*Soṭah* ii. 2, 𝕿, *Siphrê*). It is, however, highly probable that the phrase מים קדשים is a late substitute in 𝕳 for an original מים חיים (cp. 𝕲) = "running water," which we may assume in any case was used in the original rite; running water is used in the somewhat kindred rites of 19^{17}, Lev. $14^{5f.}$.—*An earthen vessel*] Lev. $14^{5. 50}$. Infected by the holiness of the potion it would after use be destroyed (Lev. $6^{21 (28)}$).—*Dust . . . on the floor of the tabernacle*] also holy in virtue of the place whence it is taken, and calculated, therefore, to increase the intensity of the holiness of the draught. The dust of the original rite may perchance have been taken from graves in virtue of necromantic beliefs; such beliefs must be the *ultimate* cause of the custom of eating dust from the grave of Mohammed as "a cure for every disease" (Lane, *Modern Egyptians*, c. xi., "Minerva" edition, p. 235).—**18.** *And the priest shall set the woman before Yahweh*] Repetition of v.^{16b}, and perhaps originally a gloss explaining that the object in v.^{16b} is the woman and not the meal-offering. If the words were original in their present position, "her hair" would be more natural than "the hair of the woman" in the next clause.—*And he shall unbind the woman's hair*] for the phrase (פרע ראש) cp. Lev. 10^{6} 13^{45} 21^{10}; Nowack, *Arch.* ii. 114. According to *Soṭah* i. 6, the woman was also clothed in black. It would appear from Josephus (*Ant.* xiv. 9^{4}) that any person accused before the Sanhedrin appeared with unbound hair and dressed in black; for the latter point we may then compare Zech. 3^{3}. It has been customary from Philo downwards to explain the unbinding of the hair as pointing to the woman's shame, which must be the meaning of the further action of the priest in laying bare her bosom (*Soṭah* i. 5). W. R. Smith (*Rel. Sem.*^{2} 181) cites an instance of an Arabian woman subjected to shame in connection with an oath of purgation (*Kitāb el 'Agānī*, i. 156. 3).—*He shall place . . . the offering in her hands*] cp. 6^{19}, Ex. 29^{24}, Lev. $8^{27f.}$.—*Waters of bitterness*] *i.e.* waters having an injurious effect, Jer. 2^{19}, 4^{18}; so clearly in v.$^{24.27}$. By itself מי מרים might mean water rendered bitter by ingredients: cp. מי ראש Jer. 8^{14} 23^{15}; and for מר = "bitter to the taste," Ex. 15^{23}, Pr. 27^{7}. This may have been the original meaning of the phrase: for, as Tylor points out (*EB.* xvii. 819), bitter potions are much used in various ordeals.

12. איש איש כי] so 9^{10}, Lev. 15^{2} 24^{15}; see, further, CH. 190^{P}.—תשטה] also $^{19f.29}$, Pr. 4^{15} 7^{25} †; cp. שוט Ps. 40^{5} and? Hos. 5^{2}, Ps. 101^{3}. In Aram. it is frequent; and in 𝔗 often renders Heb. סור (*e.g.* Ex. 32^{8}, Dt. 11^{16}). Treated by Giesebrecht (*ZATW.* i. 196) and Ryssel (*De Elohistæ Pent. Serm.* 70) as an Aramaism; disputed by Dr. (*JPh.* xi. 205).—ומעלה . . . מעל] use of both vb. and noun confined to Ezek. Pr. (16^{10}) P, Ch.-Ezr.-Neh. Dan. Ecclus. (*e.g.* 48^{16}): cp. CH. 164^{P}.—**13.** ושכב . . . אתה] MT. in this phrase makes שכב take a direct acc. אֹתָהּ; but point אִתָּהּ: cp. Lev. 18^{22}, where the indef. obj. precludes את being the sign of the acc., and the parallel phrases שכב עם, שכב אצל; Geiger, *Urschrift*, 407 f.: otherwise König, iii. 329 f.—שכבת זרע] Lev. $15^{16.18}$.—ונעלם] Lev. (4^{13}) 5^{2-4}. The vb. is masc. here as in Gn. 17^{11}; the fem. is commoner, G.-K. 144*b*.—ונסתרה] subj. האשה; but in Stade and CH. ונסתרה is the parallel in another source to the preceding ונעלם.—היא] this and the instance in v.^{14} are two of the eleven instances in which, in the Pent., this fem. pr. is written *plene* in 𝔐; see BDB. 214 f.—עד] emphatically placed before אין; BDB. 34*a b*.—**14.** ועבר] Dav. 113*b*; in v.^{30} fem.—**15.** את קרבנה עליה] 𝔊 𝔙 omit suffix (𝔖 is ambiguous). This is not right; but possibly קרבנה (G.-K. 91*e*) was originally intended, and was glossed by עליה.—עשירית האיפה] For $\frac{1}{10}$ ephah P uses the technical term עשרון 24 times, the present expression only 4 times elsewhere, Ex. 16^{36}, Lev. 5^{11} 6^{13}, Nu. 28^{5}; in the last case it is parallel to עשרון in Ex. 29^{40}.—מנחת קנאות] Dav. 23 and 17, R. 2.—**17.** המשכן] 𝔊 אהל מועד.—מים קדשים] Di. and Str. further argue in favour of 𝔊 (see above) on the ground of the uniqueness of this adjectival use of קדוש: cp. Baudissin, *Studien*, ii. 130 n., and BDB. *s.v.*; G.-K. 128*p*. — **18.** מי המרים] waters resulting in, leading to, bitterness: cp. v.$^{24.\ 27}$, also Dav. 23, 16*b*.

19–22. The oath of purgation is administered to the woman, who accepts it by replying, Amen, amen.—For the connection between oath and ordeal, see above, p. 45. At present the terms of the oath, v.$^{19f.\ 22a}$, are interrupted by a fresh introduction (v.^{21} = v.^{19a}) and a parallel to the concluding part of the oath (v.^{21b} = v.^{22a}). This cannot be right. But if we assume, with Stade and CH., that it has resulted from the deliberate fusion of two laws by the compiler, we must credit him with almost incredible stupidity for not having placed v.^{21} after v.^{22}, where it would have been merely superfluous. It seems preferable to suppose that v.^{21} consists of glosses that worked their way into the text, v.^{21b} being an explanation of v.^{22}, insisting that Yahweh, not the water, is the cause of injury to the woman (above, p. 48). Omitting v.^{21} the oath runs naturally:—If you have not committed adultery, let the water be harmless; if you have, harmful.—**19.** *Be thou free from this water*] be unpunished by it: cp. נקה in Ex. 21^{19}, 1 S. 26^{9}, Pr. 6^{29}.—**21.** *Yahweh make thee a curse*] make thy fate so evil, that people wishing to curse any one will say, Yahweh make so-and-so like this woman: cp. Jer. 29^{22}, also Gn. 48^{20}, Zech. 8^{13}, Is. $65^{13ff.}$ —*When Yahweh maketh thy thigh fall away and thy belly swell*] the phrases are in the reverse order in v.$^{22.\ 27}$. It is doubtful whether any, and, if so, what particular disease is thought of; many, from Josephus downwards, have thought of dropsy. For another suggestion, see above, p. 48. The precise meaning, especially of the first term, is not certain; "thigh" is probably euphemistic: see phil. n. The Jewish interpretation is based on the general principle, "with what measure a man metes, it is measured to him" (במידה שאדם

(מודד בה מדדים לו), and so the Mishnah says, "With the thigh she commenced her transgression, and afterwards with the belly: therefore the thigh shall be first smitten and then the belly" (*Soṭah* i. 7 ff.); for a lengthy illustration of the principle, see the *Pesiḳta* of Rab Kahana (ed. Buber), 128*b*, 129*a*.—**22.** The original continuation of v.[20] (see above): render ובאו וגו *then shall this water . . . enter*, etc.—*Thy bowels*] Hebrew physiology was very primitive: the term מעים covers "the womb" (Gn. 25[23]) as well as other internal organs; see BDB. *s.v.*—*Amen, Amen*] a single "Amen" is the response to a curse in Dt. 27[15ff.]: cp. Neh. 5[13]. The double, uncopulated amen occurs elsewhere only in Neh. 8[6]; copulated in Ps. 41[14] 72[19], 89[53] (𝔐, not 𝔊). See, further, H. W. Hogg in *JQR*. ix. 1–24.

19. תחת אישך] = "being under (the authority of) thy husband": cp. Ezek. 23[5]. The fuller phrase is תחת יד (*e.g.* Jud. 3[30]). —**21.** ירכך] not, literally, "thigh"; the sense can be gathered from the parallel (בטן) and the use of ירך in the phrase (of the male) יצאי ירך.—נפלת] apparently = "waste away"; but the sense is not found elsewhere.—צבה] The roots צבה = صبا = צָבָא and צבה = ظبى = טבא are known in Heb., but give no suitable meaning; nor do the usages of ضبا, which also corresponds. The sense "to swell," used in this section only in OT., thus rests on the use in New Hebrew (see Levy) and on the VV.—**22.** לַנְפִּל . . . לַצְבּוֹת] Hiphils with syncope of ה; but point rather לִנְפֹּל . . . לִצְבּוֹת: cp. v.[27], and see König, ii. 278 f.

23. The words of the curse are now written down and then washed off into the water. Evidently the original purpose was to impart an actual efficacy to the potion. Potions into which written words have been washed off are widely credited with particular virtues. In Tibet "the eating of a paper on which a charm has been written is an ordinary way of curing disease"; in Egypt "the most approved mode of charming away sickness or disease is to write certain passages of the Ḳorān on the inner surface of an earthenware cup or bowl; then to pour in some water, and stir it until the writing is quite washed off: when the water, with the sacred words thus infused in it, is to be drunk by the patient." * The potion thus has

* L. A. Waddell, *The Buddhism of Tibet* (Lond. 1896), 401; Lane, *op. cit.* 233; cp. Köberle, *Natur u. Geist*, 165 f.

two distinct ingredients—the dust, v.[17], and the words of the curse, while the term "water of bitterness" may preserve a reminiscence of a third. It is not improbable that we have here a fusion of originally distinct modes of preparing such potions: cp. below, pp. 60, 62 f.—*A book*] ספר simply means anything fit to receive writing; cp. BDB. *s.v.* 3. The Mishnah (*Soṭah* ii. 4) specifies the character of the material on which and with which the words are written.—**24.** The woman drinks the potion. Since the tenses are consecutive, the present text can only mean that, *after* she has drunk, the priest performs the ritual of the meal-offering, v.[25. 26a], and after that gives the woman a second draught, v.[26b]. Two draughts are unlikely; and, if intended, would probably have been more clearly expressed by the addition of "again" or "a second time" in v.[26b]. The alternatives for meeting the difficulty are much as in v.[19–23], only there is less to be said against the theory of intentional fusion of sources here; if a compiler could kill Ḳorah and his company twice over (16^{31-35}), he would not have hesitated to give the woman two draughts instead of one. Still unintentional disarrangement and glossing may suffice to account for the text. Possibly v.[24a] stood originally after v.[26a]; but, except for a fragment (if original) at the beginning of v.[27], became accidentally disarranged, and was then completed by the addition of v.[24b] from v.[27]; v.[26b] may (as Stade also suggests) originally have been an explicative gloss; that such was necessary is seen from the dispute in *Soṭah* iii. 2 as to the order of drinking and offering.—*Wave . . . before Yahweh*] the rite of waving (6^{20} 8^{10} n.) is, in the case of the meal-offering, exceptional (18^{11} n.).—**26a.** See Lev. 2^{2}.—**27.** *And he shall make her drink the water*] strictly a third draught; 𝔊 𝔖 omit the words. Otherwise, see on v.[24].—**28.** *And she shall conceive seed*] the phrase ונזרעה זרע is the precise legal equivalent of the popular word הרה used in 11^{12}, and 28 times besides in JE, but never by P. Though rendered by RV. in the same way, the present phrase is not quite the same as is used in Lev. 12^{2}, which rather means "to be delivered, bring forth seed" (cp. Gn. $1^{11f.}$).—**29–31.** A subscription summarising the occasion of the law and the manner of putting it into force.—*This is the law of* . . .] cp. Lev. $15^{32f.}$ 12^{7b}, both at the conclusion of laws beginning in a manner closely resembling the present law; with v.$^{11f.}$ cp. Lev. $15^{1f.}$ $12^{1f.}$. The phrase (זאת תורת) is used in all once in Ezek. (43^{12}) and 8 times in P (Lev. 11^{46} 12^{7} 13^{59} $14^{32.57}$ 15^{32}) at the end, and 6 times (6^{21}, Lev. $6^{2.7.18}$ $7^{1.11}$, Nu. 6^{13}) at the beginning of a law; in the form זאת תהיה תורת it occurs at the beginning in Lev. 14^{2}, and in the form זאת התורה ל׳ at the end in Lev. 7^{37} 14^{54}. *Usage*, therefore, does not call for the hypothesis (Stade, CH.) that it is here the introduction to a misplaced superscription.—**30.** *Then shall he set the woman*] subject "the man"; in v.^{16} the priest.—**31.** The man is, in any event, even if the ordeal prove his suspicion unfounded, free of guilt; the woman alone can be proved guilty. The law does not directly state the time within which the potion must work to convict; but from the nature of the case a comparatively speedy result must have been expected: if the accused is to be regarded as pregnant, the term of pregnancy would be an outside limit. In any case, the theory of *Soṭah* iii. 4 (cp. 5), that merit might defer the effect as long as three years, is obviously not original. Josephus, an earlier witness, makes it ten months at longest; for, if innocent, she bears a boy within that period—a view that probably enough already underlies v.^{28}.

23. מי מרים] 𝔊 𝔙 + המאררים (cp. 𝔐 in v.$^{18f.\,24}$); 𝔖 המים המאררים (cp. 𝔐 in v.^{22}).—**26.** וקמץ] S substitutes הרים for the rare verb קמץ (Lev. 2^{2} 5^{12}†).—אזכרתה] Lev. 2^{2}.—**27.** והשקה . . . והיתה] not to be explained with Str. as a hypothetical, as a glance at Dr. *Tenses*, 147 f., will show. The text therefore implies a third draught; but see above. For והיתה read והיה with S; 𝔐 is unique; Dr. *Tenses*, 121, Obs. 2.—**28.** זרע] acc.; Dav. 80.—**30.** איש is the virtual subject of the following sentence; and is placed before the repeated conjunction (אשר) as a new subject, replacing אשה of v.^{29}. Exact parallels hardly occur; but for the general principles involved, see Dr. *Tenses*, 160 Obs., 196 f., and Dav. 146.

VI. 1–21. The Nazirite.

LITERATURE.—Tractate *Nazir* in Mishnah and Talmud; Philo, *De Victimis*, c. xii. (Mangey, 249 f.); J. Spencer, *De Leg. Hebr.*, lib. iii. diss. 1, cap. 6; Bähr, *Symbolik*, ii. pp. 430–440; Vilmar in *TSK.* 1864, pp. 438–484; Grill in *JPTh.* 1880, pp. 645–680; Wurster in *ZATW.* 1884, pp. 129–133; Wellhausen, *Reste des Arab. Heid.*^{1} pp. 117–119; W. R. Smith, *Semites.*^{2}

pp. 323-335 (especially 332 f.: cp. addit. note K); Smend, *ATReligionsgeschichte*,[1] pp. 152–154; Budde, "Judges" (in *Kurzer Hand-Commentar*), p. 94 f.; Frazer, *Golden Bough*,[2] i. 362–389 (on primitive sanctity of head and hair); G. B. Gray, "The Nazirite" in *Journal of Theol. Studies*, i. 201–211.

Here alone in the Pentateuch is any reference made to the Nazirite. The law divides naturally into three sections, dealing with (1) the general conditions to be observed by a Nazirite during the period of his vow—he is to abstain from all intoxicating liquors and all products of the vine, from cutting his hair, and from defiling himself with the dead, v.[2-8]; (2) the case of accidental defilement by the dead, v.[9-12]; (3) the offerings required and the ritual to be followed at the close of the period of the vow, v.[13-21].

The Law has been referred above (p. 39) to P^x. CH. consider it to be in substance earlier than P^g, the first section perhaps earlier still. Indications of P^g, such as "door of the tent of meeting," v.[10. 13. 18], and "the basket of unleavened bread," etc., v.[15] (only in Ex. 29, Lev. 8), must then be "not original." The phraseology they consider closely approximates to H. Incidental indications, in the present form of the law, of a comparatively late date may be found in the demand for a "he-lamb" in v.[14] (see n.), in the sin-offerings, and generally in the precise regulations of quantities (see p. 170 f.).

Nazirites figure in some of the earliest Hebrew stories, the stories about Samson (Jud. 13–16). In the 8th cent. B.C. Nazirites were numerous (Am. 2[11f.]).* In the 2nd cent. B.C. they were also numerous (1 Mac. 3[49f.]), and continued so down to the final destruction of the temple (Jos. *Ant.* xix. 6[1]; *Nazir*, *passim*). But it would be unsafe, and as a matter of fact wrong, to assume that the same conditions were either fulfilled by, or required of, all Nazirites during the thousand years or more covered by these references.

The law of the Nazirite is a law to regulate *an already existing institution*, and that more especially as it is brought into connection with the priesthood through the offerings demanded of a Nazirite on the interruption or completion of

* Indirect evidence of the prominence of Nazirites in pre-exilic Israel is furnished by the metaphorical use of נזיר in Lev. 25[5. 11] of the unclipped vine. There seems no sufficient reason for substituting בציר for נזיר in these passages with Grätz and Che. (*EBi.* 3364).

his vow. The law thus presupposes that persons become *Nazirites for a specified time only*; it makes no provision for the case of a lifelong Nazirite such as Samson. This fact would be explained if lifelong Nazirites were unknown at the time of the law. A more usual, and perhaps a sufficient, explanation accounts for the absence of any reference to the lifelong Nazirites by the fact that these, since they took no terminable vow and offered no special offerings, were never brought into any special relation with the priests.

Nazirites answering to the description contained in the law, in so far at least as their vows are for a definite period, appear somewhat frequently in later Jewish history. Perhaps the best proof of this is *Nazir*; the tract throughout implies that Nazirites who took the vow for a definite period were very numerous; see also 1 Mac. $3^{49f.}$; Jos. *Ant.* xix. 6^1; and cp., further, as probable references to Nazirites, Jos. *BJ.* ii. 15^1; Acts $21^{23f.}$. On the other hand, of the existence of Nazirites of this type before the Exile, we have absolutely no evidence, apart from any inference which the law may seem to justify.

As to lifelong Nazirites, the case is precisely reversed: they certainly existed before the Exile (Samson; cp. Am. $2^{11f.}$ and, perhaps, 1 S. 1^{11}), but whether there were any lifelong Nazirites in later times is quite uncertain. John the Baptist has been regarded as such on quite inadequate grounds. He is never called a Nazirite, nor is it recorded that he left his hair unshorn. His abstinence from intoxicants is but an element in his ascetic character (cp. Mk. 1^6, Mt. 11^{18}); but the Nazirite was not an ascetic. The case of James, "the brother of the Lord," is more to the point: for though he, too, is never called a Nazirite, yet the traditional description of him includes the chief characteristics of the Nazirites (Euseb. *HE.* ii. 23^4).

Whether lifelong devotees and persons who had taken a particular form of temporary vow were in one and the same period alike termed Nazirite, or whether it was only after lifelong Nazirites had died out that the name was passed on to persons under a vow and distinguished by certain features that had marked the lifelong Nazirites, the evidence does not allow us to determine for certain. But in any case there is a marked difference between the two classes.

What, then, are the permanent and universal elements in Naziriteship? The most certain and, as Grill (p. 666) seems to have been the first to suggest, possibly the only one, was the abstinence from cutting the hair. The almost invariable reference to this when Nazirites are mentioned, the part that Samson's hair plays in the stories about him, the transference of the term Nazirite to the unclipped vine, all indicate that this was, in early times, the most marked and, as it proved, the essential and most abiding mark of a Nazirite.

Whether abstinence from intoxicants was also a permanent element in Naziriteship is far more doubtful. Samson, like the young men of his day, gave feasts; but we are not told, and it is precarious to infer from Jud. $13^{4.\,14}$, that, unlike the young men of his day, he abstained either at these or at other times from intoxicants. Perhaps it is most reasonable to infer from Am. $2^{11f.}$ that the custom of Nazirites to abstain from *wine* was as ancient as the 8th cent. B.C., but the passage may be parallel in thought to Is. 28^{7} and simply mean: You stopped the activity of the Nazirites by making them intoxicated, and the messages of the prophets by forbidding them to speak.

Clearly Nazirites like Samson (Jud. 14^{19} 15^{8}) were not bound by the prohibition in the law of coming into contact with the dead. Further, while the Nazirites of the law took a vow, Samson did not, nor, as it would seem, the Nazirites of the time of Amos; they rather are Nazirites, as others were prophets, by divine appointment (cp. Jud. 13^{5}, Jer. 1^{5}).

There is reason for believing that every custom in the law is in itself ancient: the question is, did the particular combination of customs recognised in the law exist in early times? did persons practise this particular combination of customs, or, so doing, did they then go by the name of Nazirites? Hebrews, in early times, certainly took vows; they believed that contact with the dead produced uncleanness, and that this uncleanness must be more rigorously guarded against by some persons than others; there is reason for concluding that some persons at an early time may have abstained not only from all intoxicants, but from all products of the vine. But all this does not prove that Nazirites, such as those indicated in the law, were known in early Israel. They may have been. But if they were, Nazirites of this type had but little public significance; they are quite unlike Samson or the Nazirites who are coupled by Amos with prophets. Into the significance of these lifelong Nazirites we cannot further inquire here.

It appears most probable to the present writer that the combination of observances in the law is not ancient, that in the regulations for the Nazirites of later times we see a fusion of several originally distinct customs which, like many others (see above, p. 47), had lost much and, in some cases, all of their original meaning; and that it would be altogether wrong to attribute to the Nazirites regulated by the law anything of the public or religious significance of the earlier Nazirites or even of the Rechabites.

On the other hand, the living significance of the Nazirite-vow appears to have lain in the expense of the sacrifices involved; perhaps, also, in the inconvenience involved by the conditions of life during the term of the vow. Men undertook to become Nazirites in return for some special manifestation of the divine favour shown, for instance, in restoration to health, or the birth of a child (Jos. *BJ.* ii. 15^1; *Nazir* ii. 7); at times also for purely trivial reasons; indeed, if we may trust *Nazir* (v. 5 ff.), the Nazirite vow degenerated into a bet; *e.g.* of two men walking together and seeing some one at a distance, one says to the other, "I'll be a Nazirite if that man is not so-and-so." The purely private nature of the later Nazirite appears in these illustrations.

The Nazirite vow has considerable resemblances (though not without differences) to the Arabic *Iḥram* thus described by Wellhausen (*Arab. Heid.* 116): "When any one intends to undertake the Ḥagg he submits himself as a matter of course to the condition of those bound by a vow. This condition is termed Ihram. The Ihram is not the actual content or purport of the vow; it is only a restraint laid upon a person making the vow that he may exercise all zeal in his holy duty. This restraint consists especially of certain troublesome abstinences which cease when the vow is discharged. . . . The purpose of the Ihram is the offering. The offering brings the Ihram to an end. It is the accomplishment, consequently also the real purport, of the vow. After the offering has been made, the hair is cut off."

1, 2a. Cp. 5^6 n.—**2.** *When any man or woman*] It was probably not unusual for a woman to take the vow, subject to the conditions of $30^{3ff.}$ (cp. *Nazir* iv. 1 f.). *Nazir* significantly employs the fem. form (נזירה) for women, and mentions in particular Queen Helena's vow (iii. 6). Bernice's vow may also have been that of a Nazirite (Jos. *BJ.* ii. 15^1).—*Shall discharge a vow*] precise meaning uncertain; see phil. n.—*A Nazirite*] etymologically the term means one separated, or who separates himself, or, even more definitely, one devoted; in usage it is, perhaps, an abbreviation of the full phrase נזיר אלהים which occurs in Judges, just as משיח is often used briefly in the sense of משיח יהוה, and means one who separates or devotes himself to God, a religious devotee: cp. the verbal phrase להזיר ל י״י v.[2. 5f. 12]. The vb. followed by מן (and in Zech. 7^3 used absolutely) has, like the Arabic نذر ب, the meaning "to separate oneself, or abstain, from certain things": cp. v.[3. 12]. But this scarcely justifies giving Nazirite the sense of "abstainer."* In Gn. 49^{26} = Dt. 33^{16}, the word may retain a religious sense, or it may have been transferred from the sense of religious separation to that of simple distinction. Such a transference from the religious sense certainly takes place in the case of נֵזֶר, which means (1) the state of consecration or devotion, v.[4. 8], cp. v.[6]; (2) the symbol of such a state, especially the Nazirite's hair, v.[19]; (3) the hair of an unconsecrated person, Jer. 7^{29}.†—**3.** First regulation: the Nazirite is to abstain from all intoxicating liquors and all products of the vine during the term of his vow.—*Strong drink*] שכר is a general term for intoxicating beverages without reference to the material from which they are made. It may therefore include wine, as it appears to do in 28^7, but more commonly the two terms are

* Cp. Hoffmann in *ZATW.* iii. 100.

† See, further, Grill, p. 660; We. *Reste des Arab. Heidentums*,[1] 117 f., 167; BDB. 634, and further references there.

used together as an exhaustive expression for intoxicants (Lev. 10^9, Is. 5^{11} 24^9, Pr. 20^1 31^6).—*Vinegar of wine and vinegar of strong drink*] the Hebrews appear to have prepared their vinegar, or whatever other acid drink may be covered by the term חמץ (Ru. 2^{14}, Ps. 69^{22}), from intoxicants gone sour; a poor form of English vinegar is still largely obtained from sour beer, and much of the continental vinegar from sour wine.—*Dried grapes*] compressed into cakes, constituted an article of ordinary consumption (2 S. 6^{19}, Cant. 2^5), and were also eaten at sacrificial feasts (Hos. 3^1).—4. *All the days of his Naziriteship he shall eat nothing that is borne by the grape-vine, not even unripe grapes* (?) *or tendrils* (?). The general idea is conveyed more briefly and by a different idiom in Jud. 13^{14}—"nothing that comes forth from (יצא) the grape-vine." The verb עשה here used of what a tree bears or produces is, of course, common in that sense (cp. *e.g.* Gn. 1^{11}, Job 14^9). But would it be natural to speak of the vine producing "pips" and "skins" (RV. "kernels" and "husk")? If not, the traditional interpretation of the obscure ἅπαξ λεγόμενα חרצנים and זג falls through. The translations of the two words here given (after Di.) are uncertain, and merely to be regarded as approximating to the exact meaning. See phil. n.

In v.[3, 4] we have two quite distinct rules—(1) abstinence from intoxicants; (2) avoidance of anything connected with the vine. For both we have analogies both among the Hebrews and elsewhere. With (1) cp. the restriction laid on the Jewish priest during service (Lev. 10^9), and on Brahmanas, Kshatriyas, and Vaisyas in the *Laws of Manu* (xi. 91–98): see, further, Frazer, *GB.* i. 359 f.; with (2) cp. the restrictions laid on the Rechabites (Jer. $35^{6f.}$), and on the Roman Flamen Dialis, who was not allowed even to touch the vine (Plut. *Quæst. Rom.* 112; cp. Vilmar, p. 470 ff.; Frazer, *GB.* 241 f.). The Nabatæans were forbidden to sow or plant any fruit-bearing plant, or to build houses, or to use wine (Diod. Sic. xix. 94. 3). The original reason for the latter rule has been sought in the attempt of certain classes to maintain a more primitive mode of life; the cultivation of the vine, though not the use of intoxicants as such, is one of the most marked differences between the nomadic life, which was that of the Hebrews before their settlement in Canaan, and the settled agricultural life (W. R. Smith, *Prophets*,[2] 84 f.). But in later times avoidance of the vine and its products in all forms must have lost much or all of its original meaning; and it is doubtful whether we ought to seek any living meaning for the rule in the law. The prohibition of *all* intoxicants might, if ancient, in the case of the Nazirite, be explained by the belief that intoxication is caused by the entrance of a spirit into man (for illustrations, see Frazer, *GB.* i. 359 f.) combined with the fundamental Hebrew belief that intercourse with other spirits than Yahweh is unlawful; but it is, perhaps, in the case of the Nazirite an extension of the prohibition of wine when the real meaning of that had been lost. The most we can infer about the Nazirites of the time of Amos is that they were forbidden *wine*; for all we know, both they and the Rechabites may have drunk other intoxicants. The general Mohammedan prohibition of wine, which was only gradually made stringent by the prophet, may have found a starting-point in the opposition to the vine among some of the Arabs, such as the Nabatæans referred to above; but abstention on moral grounds from all intoxicants was practised by some Arabs before Mohammed; and the commentators, in accordance with the prevailing theory in Islam, have interpreted the passages in the Ḳoran as a prohibition of all intoxicants—Ḳoran 2^{116} 4^{46} $5^{92f.}$ 16^{69} (with Beiḍawi on the passages); Muir, *Mahomet*, iii. 300 f., ³ 300; Sprenger, *Moḥammad*, i. 387 f.

5. Second regulation: the Nazirite is not to cut his hair.—The treatment of the hair, originally the most prominent feature of the Nazirite, takes the second place in the law (cp. 1 S. 1^{11} 𝔊), possibly because it had ceased to be most prominent when Naziriteship came to be merely a vow for a short period.—*No razor shall pass over his head*] cp. 8^{7}; another phrase with the same meaning in Jud. 13^{5} 16^{17}, 1 S. 1^{11}. For shaving the head bald (גלח), and for trimming or shortening the hair (כסם), Hebrew had different words. The meaning here is that the hair is to be in no way trimmed or shortened; cp. clause *b*; and for the origin of the custom, see p. 68 f. The rule cannot, of course, be a *mere* taboo on the use of iron, such as forbade iron and required bronze razors to be used in shaving the Roman and Sabine priests (Frazer, *GB.* i. 371, 344 ff.; cp. Vilmar, 455 ff.). The present regulation sharply distinguishes the Nazirite from the priests (Lev. 10^{6} 21^{10}, Ezek. 44^{20}), with whom he is associated by the preceding and following.—6 f. Third regulation: the Nazirite is to avoid uncleanness through contact with a dead body, even though it be that of his nearest relative. In this respect the Nazirite is more stringently bound than any one, except the high priest (Lev. 21^{11}); ct. the case of the ordinary priests, Lev. $21^{1ff.}$. This regulation was clearly not observed by Samson (cp. Jud. 14^{19} 15^{8}). In the Mishnah the difficulty is solved by the assumption that there were two types of life-

long Nazirites—(1) The Samson type (נזיר שמש), who was forbidden to trim his hair but allowed to contract uncleanness from the dead without being subject to the necessity of making the offerings required by v.[9-12]. (2) The (ordinary) Nazirite for life (נזיר עולם), who might clip his hair on condition that he made the offerings required in v.[13-20], but was obliged to make the offerings of v.[9-12] every time he was defiled by the dead (*Nazir* i. 2). No doubt the real explanation is that avoidance of uncleanness by the dead formed no part of a Nazirite's duty in early times. When or how it became such we cannot say; but, as in the case of the high priest, it was due to the extreme degree of sanctity attaching to the Nazirite; cp. v.[8].

2. איש או אשה כי] 5^6n.—יַפְלִא] MT. distinguishes the verb here and in Lev. 27^2 as Hiphil from $15^{3.8}$, Lev. 22^{21} Piel. In 𝔐 Piel may have been intended in all cases. The Hiphil elsewhere is used differently. "To make a special vow" (RV.) is unsuitable in the other passages, and is not required here; "to discharge or accomplish a vow" is a sense that satisfies all passages, though how it was acquired is not clear: otherwise Grill, 656 ff. לנדר after יפלא may be dittographic from נדר; cp. the parallels cited above.—**3.** משרת ענבים] probably grape juice or liquor made from grapes; so Di. Paterson, taking משרת from שרה=لَوِس (a derivative from which is here used in 𝔖)=ثرى="to be moist"; Assyr. *mešrû*="moisture" (so Haupt in *SBOT.*).—חרצן] the meaning of this word and of זג was already lost to the earliest extant tradition. Hebrew interpreters explained the words of the grape-stone and the skin of the grape, but differed as to which meant which (*Nazir* vi. 2; see also Levy, i. 517*b*, ii. 116). In 𝔊 חרצן=στέμφυλλον (a mass of pressed grapes) and זג=γίγαρτον (grape-stone); similarly 𝔖. The etymology is indecisive; it has been suggested that grape-stones were called חרצן from their acrid taste (חרץ="to cut"); but the Hebrews thought of the effect of such a taste as blunting (Ezek. 11^2). זג, too, has been explained as the *pellucid* skin (from זגג="to be clear"; cp. זַגָּג in New Hebrew="a glazier"). With חרצן="unripe grapes," cp. حصرم in the same sense. On traditional interpretations, see more fully Ges. *Thes.*—**5.** גדל פרע שער ראש] the antithesis is ופרע לא ישלחו Ezek. 44^{20}. פרע (5^{18}n.) is omitted by 𝔖. On גַּדֵּל (Inf. abs.), see G.-K. 113*h*.

9–12. Accidental defilement and its consequences.—A Nazirite who comes accidentally into contact with the dead is defiled; on the seventh day after the accident he regains his cleanness. He must then be shorn, and on the following day offer a sin-offering and a burnt-offering, each consisting of a turtle dove or young pigeon. He then regains his sanctity, and must thereafter keep the whole original period of his vow. Finally, he offers a young sheep as a guilt-offering.

The conditions under which defilement from the dead is contracted are given in c. 19, and more minutely in their application to the Nazirite in *Nazir* vii. 2f.

9. *And he defile the head*] the act of defilement is attributed to the Nazirite, though his contact with the dead is unintentional. But unintentional sin plays a large part in the priestly law, as indeed elsewhere, Ps. $19^{13\,(12)}$ 90^{8}.—*He shall shave his head*] cp. v.[5] n.—The law does not state what is to be done with the hair in this case (ct. v.[18]); but the Mishnah records what, we need not question, was the ancient practice. This hair was *buried* (*Temûrah* vii. 4)—buried, as analogy suggests, because unclean, and therefore dangerous (W. R. Smith, *Rel. Sem.*[1] 350 ff., [2] 369 ff.).

The following instances, taken from Frazer's *GB.* i. 387–389, will throw light on the probable origin and original significance of the rite: "At Hierapolis no man might enter the great temple of Astarte on the same day on which he had seen a corpse; next day he might enter, provided he had first purified himself. But the kinsmen of the deceased were not allowed to set foot in the sanctuary for thirty days after the death, and before doing so they had to shave their heads" (Lucian, *Dea Syria*, 53). In ancient India mourners at the "end of the period of mourning cut their hair and nails, and use new vessels." "At Agweh (W. Africa) widows and widowers at the end of their period of mourning wash themselves, shave their heads, pare their nails, and put on new cloths; and the old cloths, the shorn hair, and the nail-parings are all burnt." A practice is observed by some Australians "of burning off part of a woman's hair after childbirth, as well as burning every vessel which has been used by her during her seclusion. Here the burning of the woman's hair seems plainly intended to serve the same purpose as the burning of the vessels used by her; and as the vessels are burned because they are believed to be tainted with a dangerous infection, so, we must suppose, is also the hair."

On the day of his (recovered) *cleanness*] no special act of cleansing (cp. RV.) takes place on this day, but the effects of defilement have by this time become exhausted: cp. 19^{12} "On the seventh day he shall be clean." The more active process of propitiation follows on the next day; so also Lev. 15^{13-15}.—10 f. The Nazirite, in spite of his superior sanctity, does not suffer longer than an ordinary Israelite from the effects of defilement; but the rites are more elaborate. The ordinary man simply had to be sprinkled with the "water of uncleanness" (see on 19^{9}), and was not required to present offerings. The offerings exacted of the Nazirite after defilement (two turtle doves or young pigeons) appear also in other connections, Lev. 5^{7} 12^{8} $14^{30f.}$ $15^{14f. 29f.}$. It was the least burdensome form of animal sacrifice (cp. Lev. 5^{7} 12^{8}). The main part of the expense to which a Nazirite was put in the case of an interrupted vow was due to the guilt-offering, which was also required, and consisted of a yearling he-lamb, v.[12].—11. *And he shall hallow his head*] the subject is the Nazirite; he rehallows, after defiling (v.[9]), his head.—12. *And he shall separate unto Yahweh the days of his separation*] he shall, after recovering his cleanness, observe his vow for the full length of time originally devoted, since the days before his defilement are not allowed to count. According to the Mishnah (*Nazir* iii. 6), Queen Helena (fl. 50 A.D.), just at the close of the seven years for which she had taken the vow, was accidentally defiled by a corpse, and consequently had to keep the vow for a further term of seven years.—*A he-lamb . . . for a guilt-offering*] the reason for the guilt-offering (*'āshām*), is not stated, nor is it clear. Possibly, as in the case of the guilt-offering demanded of a cleansed leper (Lev. $14^{12. 21}$), it is for some unknown sin which was certainly, as the argument of Job's friends shows us, according to the thought of the time (cp. even later, Jn. 9^{2}), the cause of such misfortunes as leprosy, and may perhaps have been considered the cause of such misadventures as a Nazirite's defilement by the dead (Di.). Others explain the guilt-offering here as a recompense to Yahweh for the delay in the discharge of the vow (Sta. *GVI.* ii. 257; Now.).

9. בפתע פתאם] lit. "in an instant, instantly," and so "very suddenly," G.-K. 133*i* end. The two words appear to be pure synonyms (cp. Pr. 6^{15}) and in origin identical, פתאם being a softened form of פֶּתַע. Cp. Assyr. *ina pitti* and *ina pittimma*, both = "instantly" (Del. *Assyr. Handwörterbuch*, p. 553*a*).

13–20.—**The rites at the conclusion of the vow.**—At the conclusion of the vow the Nazirite is to offer a burnt-offering, a sin-offering, and a peace-offering, together with the customary meal-offerings and libations, v.$^{13-15}$. After these have been presented by the priest, v.$^{16f.}$, the Nazirite is to shave off his hair at the door of the tent and to burn it on the sacred fire, v.^{18}. After this the priest is to make a wave-offering of a portion of the peace-offering and the cereal-offering; this becomes holy, and, as such, the perquisite of the priest. The Nazirite may now drink wine.

13a. Cp. 5^{29} n.—*He shall be brought*] why the Nazirite should need to be brought instead of coming by himself it is not easy to see. Perhaps, as Di. suggests (see phil. n.), the strangeness of the passage is due to an interpolation, and the law originally ran—"In the day when the days of his Naziriteship are completed, he shall bring to the door of the tent of meeting a yearling he-lamb without blemish for a burnt-offering. . . ."—14. The burnt-offering is here mentioned before the sin-offering (cp. Lev. $12^{6.8}$; ct. v.$^{11.16}$), though the latter was presumably offered first.—*One he-lamb*] according to the Levitical law (at variance in this respect with earlier custom, cp. 1 S. 6^{14}), which required that animals for burnt-offerings should be of the male sex (Lev. $1^{3.10}$ $22^{18f.}$).—*Without blemish*] Lev. 22^{18-25}.—*One ewe-lamb*] the female sheep for a sin-offering, according to Lev. 4^{32} 5^{6}.—*One ram*] the animal for a peace-offering might be either male or female, Lev. $3^{1.6}$.—15a. The phraseology here closely resembles Lev. 7^{12}.—*Cakes*] see 15^{20} n. *Their meal-offering and their drink-offerings*] *i.e.* the meal-offering and libations required as the accompaniment of the burnt- and peace-offerings just mentioned; according to 15^{4-6} these would together consist of $\frac{3}{10}$ of a hin of fine meal (= about $3\frac{1}{2}$ pints), $\frac{7}{12}$ of a hin of wine, and the same quantity of oil. Apparently, therefore, the meaning of the whole verse is that the ordinary accompaniments of the sacrifices in the way of meal, oil, and wine are to be presented, and also a cereal-offering, the character of which is stated in clause *a*, but not the quantities. But the awkward way in which this is expressed, and especially the loose attachment of clause *b*, may well raise a question as to the originality of the final clause of this v. and consequently of v.^{17b}. The pronominal suffixes (in נסכיהם and מנחתם) should refer to all the fore-named offerings, though, as a matter of fact, they cannot refer to the sin-offering, which was never accompanied by these cereal-offerings and libations. For it is too hazardous to argue from Lev. 14[10-20] that the sin-offering under exceptional circumstances was accompanied by a meal-offering; cp. *Siphrê* on the present passage. — 16. *And the priest shall present* (them) *before Yahweh*] הקריב refers to the bringing of the sacrifice to the altar: cp. the alternative idiom 5[25]. — *And shall offer his sin-offering*] the verb here used (עשה) is "meant as a summary description of the process of sacrifice" (Driver in Hastings' *DB*. iii. 538*b*); cp. Ex. 29[38], Lev. 9[7].—17. *With the basket of unleavened bread*] v.[15a].—*Its meal-offering and its drink-offering*] v.[15b]; here the suffix refers to the ram of the peace-offering; in v.[16] the author has not thought it necessary to refer in particular to the offerings accompanying the burnt-offering.—18. *At the door of the tent of meeting*] the Nazirite shaves himself beside the slain peace-offering (cp. Lev. 3[2]), and then throws the hair into *the fire which is under the sacrifice of peace-offerings*, *i.e.* into the fire of the altar which also stood at the door of the tent (Ex. 40[6]). This is more probable than the opinion * that the fire referred to is that on which the flesh for consumption by the priest and the Nazirite is being boiled.—"Deus itaque comam dedicandi et offerendi morem inter Israelitas (populum Gentilismi pervicacem) toleravit: eam autem non nisi ad ostium Tabernaculi vel Templi deponi voluit, ne aliter populus ille crines suos in arbore sacra suspenderet, aut (ad morem seculi) fluviis aut idolis consecraret," Spencer, *De Legibus*, p. 696. The treatment of the hair of a Nazirite who has duly completed his vow is clearly a survival of hair-offerings—a species of offerings widely spread in antiquity, and still existent in more or less primitive forms among many peoples. Samson's hair, which was never cut, cannot have been intended for an offering. Thus, though the growth of the hair is common to the Nazirites of the early stories and of the law, the purpose in the two cases is markedly different.

* 𝔗°, Rashi.

A common belief, that the hair is part of the man's vital being, seems to account for both treatments. If the one main object is to keep the man's power and vitality at the full, the hair is never shorn; if the object is to present the deity with part of the man's life, the hair is a suitable means of achieving this. Hence its frequency in offerings. The same object is obtained in other cases by chopping off and offering a finger. Numerous instances of hair-offering may be found in the works of W. R. Smith, Spencer, and Frazer, as cited above; Tylor, *Prim. Culture*,[3] ii. 401; Goldziher, *Muhammedanische Studien*, i. 247–251. Here it may suffice to refer to one or two: Lucian relates that in Syria the hair of children was cut off and dedicated to the deity (*de Dea Syria*, 60); in an ancient Arabic poem there occurs the oath—"By him in whose honour the hair is shaved off" (Goldziher, 249); it was customary with the ancient Arabs (Goldziher), as it is with the modern Bedāwin (Merrill, *East of the Jordan*, 511) and New Zealanders (Tylor), to deposit the shorn hair at the tomb—a sacrificial act, and different from the mere shaving of the hair in mourning, which is to be otherwise explained (see above, p. 65). The sacrificial nature of the treatment of the hair was still obvious to the later Jews; and though Philo's explanation is highly refined, it so happens that the significance he attributes to the hair is not far removed from the primitive view; the Nazirite's vow, so he argues, is the greatest of all vows, for it is the dedication of the man's self; but since the altar may not be polluted with human blood, the man cannot be offered himself: hence the hair as a portion and representative of the man's self is combined with the sacrifice. The hair-offering even gained a place in Christian history, as the case of Justinian and Heraclius proves (Gibbon, *Decline and Fall*, ed. Bury, v. 169). The practice of offering the hair is therefore in no way peculiar to the Hebrews, nor is the origin to be sought in peculiar Hebrew beliefs. All that is peculiar to the religion of the Hebrews is that the offering must be made to Yahweh and not to others, such as the spirits of dead.

19, 20. After the fat parts and the viscera of the ram of the peace-offering have been burned on the altar (v.^{17}), according to Lev. 3^{6-11} $7^{30f.}$, the priest takes the shoulder, which has meantime been boiled, together with one of the cakes and wafers, v.^{14}, and waves these before the altar. After the rite of waving, these become the property of the priest, together with the breast and the thigh, which fell to him by the general law of the peace-offering (Lev. 7^{28-34}, especially ^{34} 10^{12-15}). The priest thus waves and receives a larger part of the Nazirite's peace-offerings than in ordinary cases. The peace-offering was one in which, even by the priestly law (Lev. 7^{11-21}), the offerer partook; we may therefore conclude that at the close of the specified ritual the discharged Nazirite, together, as we may assume, with his friends, partook of the sacrificial meal. It may have been customary to drink wine at this meal; and to this the final clause of the verse may refer, though, of course, the clause—*And afterwards the Nazirite may drink wine*—may be purely and simply permissive.—**19.** *The shoulder*] in Dt. (18^{3}) this forms one of the regular portions due to the priest.—**20.** *The wave-breast*] so RV. here and Lev. 7^{34} $10^{14f.}$, Nu. 18^{18}, but in Ex. 29^{27} "the breast of the wave-offering." The phrase simply means the breast which was waved (cp. Ex. $29^{26f.}$, Lev. 7^{30}), *i.e.* moved to and fro (very probably, as tradition reports, in the direction of the altar) as a symbol that it was given to Yahweh.—*The thigh of the contribution*] the thigh of the *t'rûmah* (cp. 5^{9} n., 15^{19} n.) was the right (Lev. 7^{32}) thigh, which was removed (*hûram*, Ex. 29^{27}) from the whole offering to be the priest's portion: cp. 18^{11} n.

13. קְלֹּאת] G.-K. 74*h*; Sta. 201*b*, 619*k*.—יביא אתו] lit. "One shall bring him," *i.e.* the Nazirite shall be brought by some person unnamed (Dav. 108*a*). This is on material grounds (see above) unlikely here; other explanations of the text are, however, even more open to objection. Rashi explains it, "he shall bring himself"; but the parallels for the pronominal acc. as a reflexive (unless, as in Jer. 7^{19}, it is emphatic) are unreal; Dt. 34^{6} ויקבר אתו "and he (Moses) buried himself," is an interpretation embodying a ridiculous Rabbinic opinion, and in Lev. 22^{16} the subj. and obj. of השיאו can and should be regarded as referring to different persons. König (iii. 324*d*) treats אתו as resuming the preceding נזרו ("Naziriteship"), but in a different sense—"he shall bring it, viz. his hair." Di. suspects that the words והקריב . . . ליי of v.[14] are an insertion, and that, subsequently, אתו (pointing forward to כבש וגו' of v.[14]) was placed as an obj. to יביא, which, by the former insertion, had been deprived of its original obj. (כבש וגו').—**14.** בן־שנתו] so, in defining the age of a sacrificial victim, 7^{15} 15^{27}, Lev. 12^{6}; with this alternates בן־שנה Ex. 12^{5}, Lev. 9^{3}. König, iii. p. 293 n., discusses the syntax of the present phrase.—כבש . . . תמים אחד] a rare position for the numeral אחד, but cp. 1 S. 6^{7}; in 𝔖 and in the remaining two instances of its use in this verse, it occupies its usual position immediately after the substantive; König, iii. 334*e*.—**19.** הזרע בשלה] either בשלה is acc. of condition = "the shoulder being boiled" (Dav. 32, R. 2), or, as very exceptionally in OT., the indef. adj. qualifies a def. noun (König, iii. 334*m*).

21. The subscription to the law.—*This is the law of the Nazirite who takes a vow*—to wit, *his offering to Yahweh in accordance with his Naziriteship apart from what* (or, anything further which) *his means enable him* (to offer). The construction is awkward; but the view of it underlying this translation is preferable to 𝔊 𝔙—"this is the law of the Nazirite who vows his offering." In either case the subscription confirms the conclusion that the sacrifices formed the main element in Naziriteship as understood by the law and illustrated by later practice.—The point of the subscription appears to be this: the sacrifices provided in the law are a *minimum*; if a man's means admit, he may offer more, but under no conditions less. And if at the commencement of his vow he vows larger offerings than the law demands, then he must discharge them. If, for instance, a Nazirite in taking a vow says, "Lo, I am a Nazirite on condition of offering a hundred burnt-offerings and a hundred peace-offerings when I shave," then he must offer accordingly (*Siphrê*). For the phrase תשיג ידו, cp. Ezek. 46^{7}, Lev. 14^{21}.

21–27. The priestly blessing gives terse and beautiful expression to the thought that Israel owes all to Yahweh, who shields His people from all harm, and grants them all things necessary for their welfare.

Each of the three unequal lines of the blessing consists of a longer, followed by a shorter hemistich.

It would have been more in accordance with P's general method if the blessing had been introduced in connection with the first occasion on which Aaron solemnly blessed the people (Lev. $9^{22f.}$); possibly it once stood there, for we cannot be sure that its present is its original position; see above, p. 39.

The blessing is introduced by a formula characteristic of P (v.$^{21. 22a}$, cp. 5^{6} n.). But while it formed part of P, there neither has been nor can be much doubt felt that it was not composed by P, and that it is, consequently, of earlier origin than the date of its incorporation in P. The linguistic affinities (and, indeed, the general tenor and feeling) of the blessing, while they decisively distinguish it from P, relate it to the Psalms. It appears to have influenced Ps. 67 directly, possibly also Ps. 4^{7}, though this is far more doubtful. It is probable, then, that the blessing is pre-exilic in origin—a citation from an early Psalm, as Addis suggests, or, more probably, a blessing actually used in the temple at Jerusalem before the Exile.

A liturgical poem, such as the blessing is, in which the whole people is addressed in the 2nd pers. sing., would have been a natural product of the period of the Josianic Reformation. The centralisation of worship must have strengthened the sense of the religious unity of the people as well as that of the unity of Yahweh. The blessing may, of course, be considerably earlier; but the positive reasons adduced for holding it to be such are not cogent. Ewald (*History*, Eng. tr. ii. 21) referred it to the Mosaic period on account of its antique simplicity; Del. (*Zeitschr. für kirchliche Wissenschaft u. kirchliches Leben*, 1882, pp. 113–136) to the pre-Davidic period on account of its influence on the Psalms. See also König, *Einleitung*, p. 186.

Of the later use of the blessing (cp. Ecclus. $50^{20ff.}$), the Mishnah gives a good deal of information: it was used in the temple at Jerusalem every morning in connection with the daily sacrifices; the sacred name was pronounced, and not replaced by Adonai. It was also regularly used in the synagogues; in these it was not limited to the morning service, but a substitute for the sacred name was used. For these and a number of other details, see *Tamid* vii. 2 (= *Sotah* vii. 6), Wagenseil in Surenhusius' *Mishnah*, iii. 264; Hamburger, *Realencyclopädie*, ii. Abth. (art. "Priestersegen"); Herzfeld, *Gesch. des Volkes Israel*, ii. 108 f., 162 f.; Schürer, *GJV*³. ii. 457 f. (Eng. tr. II. ii. 82 f.).

23. In limiting the prerogative of blessing to the "sons of Aaron" (*i.e.* the priests), the present law, which governed post-exilic practice, differs from Dt. 10^8 21^5, which made it the prerogative of the whole tribe of Levi. Still earlier we hear of the king blessing the people in the name of Yahweh, 2 S. 6^{18}.—**24–26.** The blessing may be rendered—

Yahweh bless thee	and guard thee:
Yahweh cause His face to shine upon thee,	and show thee favour:
Yahweh lift up His face towards thee,	and appoint thee welfare.

24. *Yahweh bless thee*] by granting fruitful harvests, increase of cattle, and success in all undertakings: cp. Dt. 28^{2-14}.—*And guard thee*] the same wish expressed negatively

Yahweh guard thee from everything, such as drought or hostile invasion, which would prevent the blessing.

Some of the Rabbinic interpretations collected in *Siphrê* are interesting —"Yahweh bless thee with possessions and preserve thee in possessions. R. Nathan said: Yahweh bless thee with possessions and guard thee in body (bodily health). R. Isaac said: Yahweh guard thee from the evil nature (יצר הרע): cp. Pr. 3^{26}. Another interpretation: Yahweh guard thee, so that others may not rule over thee: cp. Ps. $121^{6. 4. 5. 7a. 8a}$."

25. *Yahweh cause His face to shine upon thee*] Ps. $31^{17\,(16)}$, Dan. 9^{17} (על); Ps. $80^{4. 8. 20\,(3. 7. 19)}$ (abs.); 119^{135} (ב); $67^{2\,(1)}$ (אִתָּנוּ); cp. Ps. $4^{7\,(6)}$ $44^{4\,(3)}$ $89^{16\,(15)}$, and, if the text be correct, ct. Ps. 90^{8}. The light or brightness of the face is the sign of inward pleasure, and, when turned towards or upon any one, of a favourable disposition to him; two men reporting to R. Joḥanan that R. Abbahu had found treasure, and asked why they said so, replied, "Because his face shines."* In Pr. 16^{15a} "the light of the king's countenance" is parallel to "his favour," v.^{15b}, and antithetical to "wrath," v.^{14a}. Cp. also Pr. 15^{30}, Job 29^{24} (Duhm, "the light of my countenance comforted the mourners"), Ecclus. 7^{24}, and the use of בלג (= بلج). Perhaps this metaphor for human favour was only used of Yahweh after men had ceased to believe in the possibility, dangerous and generally fatal as it was, of man's seeing the actual face of God (Ex. 33^{20} etc.). With Ex. $34^{29f.}$ (P)—the effect of the fiery glory of Yahweh on Moses' face—the expression has no connection.—*And favour thee*] חנן, frequent in the Psalms, never occurs in P.—26. *Lift up His face towards thee*] the exact phrase does not occur again with a divine subject, and with a human subject it is used in somewhat different senses (2 S. 2^{22}, Job 22^{26}; 2 K. 9^{32}). The nearest parallels are Ps. $4^{7\,(6)}$ 33^{18} $34^{16\,(15)}$: in Assyrian the phrase "to lift up the eye upon" is used of God's favourable regard (Del. *Assyr. Handwörterbuch*, 484*a*). When Yahweh hid His face His creatures were troubled (Ps. $30^{8\,(7)}$ 104^{29} $44^{25\,(24)}$); when He turned it towards them their welfare was secure.—*Welfare*] such rather than peace is the meaning of שלום here: it is freedom from all disaster; cp. Job 21^{9}, Lev. 26^{6}. Some Jewish

* *Pesiḳta* of Rab Kahana, 38*a* (cited by Del.).

interpreters took the clause to be a prayer for the establishment of the Messianic kingdom (Is. $9^{6\,(7)}$), and the light of Yahweh's face (v.[25]) to refer to the Shechinah; so 𝔗° *Siphrê*.—**27**. The solemn thrice-repeated pronunciation of the divine name in the blessing secures the presence and favour of Yahweh; on the sense that lingers here of the power of the duly pronounced name, see Fr. Giesebrecht, *Die alttestamentliche Schätzung des Gottes-namens* (1901).

23. אמור] The infin. abs. has an adverbial (G.-K. 113*k*), or imperative (*ib.* 113*bb*) force. Some emend; Haupt proposes אִמְרוּ, others לאמר; but לאמר followed by ל and a pronominal suffix or noun would be quite unusual.
On the accentuation of the blessing, see Del. (*op. cit.* p. 72), p. 133.

VII. The offerings of the princes.—On the day of the completion of the tabernacle and the anointing of the altar (v.[1. 10. 84. 88]), *i.e.* on the first day of the first month of the second year of the Exodus (Ex. $40^{2.\,17.\,10}$, cp. Lev. $8^{10f.}$), the princes (1^{5-15}), mentioned in the same order as in c. 2, make each a sacred offering (קרבן) of precisely the same amount, and consisting of (1) wagons and oxen, v.[3], which are given to the Gershonites and Merarites for use in connection with the tabernacle, v.[4-9]; and (2) a quantity of sacrificial material in gold or silver vessels, and a number of sacrificial animals. It is directed that the sacrificial gifts shall be formally presented by the several princes on successive days, v.[11]. This is done, v.[12-83], and the total amount offered recorded, v.[84-88].

Thus the date is a month previous to 1^1, but the narrative of 1–4 (*i.e.* of the month following the erection of the temple) is presupposed. This is best explained by referring the chapter to P^s; so We. Kue. It is, of course, not impossible that P^g had some account of an offering made by the princes; only then, as Di. points out, the editor has not only removed the narrative from its proper position after Ex. 40 or Lev. 8–10, but has also recast the original by adapting it to c. 1–4. For the wearisome repetitions in v.[12-83], cp. 1^{20-43}. Linguistically note נשיאי יש׳ v.[2], חנכה v.[10].

The writer desires "to introduce the heads of the tribes . . . as models of liberality towards the sanctuary, which his own contemporaries would do well to copy" (Kue. *Hex.* 94).

1. *The day that Moses completed the setting-up* (להקים) *of* *the tabernacle*] cp. Ex. $40^{17f.}$—"And in the first month in the second year on the first day of the month the tabernacle was set up (הוקם), and Moses set up (ויקם) the tabernacle," etc. The identity of the terms used here and in Ex. is obscured in RV. *Occasionally* יום in the sing. (BDB. *s.v.* 6) is used in the more indefinite sense of "time," as, *e.g.*, in "the day of harvest" (Pr. 25^{13}). But in view of Ex. $40^{1.\,17}$ this meaning cannot satisfactorily be given to it here in spite of v.^{84}.—*And anointed it and sanctified it*] Ex. 30^{26-29} 40^{9-11}, Lev. $8^{10ff.}$. On the anointing of lifeless objects with a view to their consecration as a mark of P^s, cp. We. *Comp.* p. 145.—**2.** *The princes of Israel*] (נשיאי ישראל), "Prince" (נשיא) is P's equivalent for "elder" or "prince" or "captain" (שר) of JE D: cp. CH. 131^P. The particular phrase "princes of Israel," used in a vaguer sense by Ezekiel (21^{17} 22^6 45^9), is in the Pentateuch used only of the twelve persons named in 1^{5-15}. The four passages (1^{44} 4^{46} $7^{2.\,84}$) where it is found all seem to belong to P^s. P^g prefers another phrase, viz. "princes of the congregation" (נשיאי (ה)עדה), Ex. 16^{22} (cp. 34^{31}), Nu. 4^{34} 16^2 31^{13} 32^2, Jos. $9^{15.\,18}$ 22^{30}: cp. Driver, *L.O.T.* 132 f. (Nos. 32, 38).—*The heads of their fathers' houses*] Ex. 6^{14} (P), 1 Ch. 5^{24} 7^9, cp. Nu. $1^{2.\,4}$ n.—**3.** This v. completes the sense of v.^{2}; in v.^{2} the verb (יקריבו) "offered" was left without an object; in v.^{3} the object, cognate to the verb of v.^{2}, is introduced after a new verb—"And they brought their offering (קרבנם)"; the last clause of v.^{3} repeats the verb of v.^{2} and the sense of v.^{3a}.—*Before Yahweh*] cp. 5^{16} n. — *Wagons*] the precise sense of the word rendered in RV. "covered" is uncertain: see phil. note.

4–9. Moses assigns two of the six wagons and four of the twelve oxen, presented by the princes, to the Gershonites, the rest to the Merarites, for use in the transport of the things intrusted to them (4^{21-33}). The Ḳohathites receive none, for they must carry the "holy things" given into their care on their shoulders. C. 4 does not contemplate this distinction; cp. We. *Comp.* 181. Earlier writers saw nothing amiss in the ark being placed on a cart (2 S. 6^3).—**8.** *By the hand of Ithamar*] as the chief overseer of the Gershonites and

Merarites (4^{28-33}).—9. *Holy things*] קדש is wrongly rendered in RV. "sanctuary"; see 3^{31} and cp. 4^{15} 10^{21} n.

2. ראשי] 𝕲 prefixes the numeral 12.—**3.** עגלת צב] but v.$^{3b. 6. 8}$ עגלה and העגלת undefined by צב. If צב be the same word as צבים (Is. 66^{20}), the sing. after pl. עגלת is peculiar. The word is probably a gloss. The meaning is uncertain; neither here nor in Is. does the context require "covered," nor does the etymology support such a meaning, nor the use of *çumbu* in Assyr.: *çumbu* is the draught wagon as distinguished from the *narkabbi* or war chariot (Del. *Assyr. Wörterbuch*, 558). 𝕲 (λαμπηνικάς), Aq. (κατασκεπαστάς), 𝔙 (*tecta*) and 𝕿^{O} (מחפין) give to צב the sense of *covered*; cp. 𝕲, Aq., Theod. in Isaiah. S (ܡܛܝܒܢ) and 𝕿^{Jer} (מזונן) render by *made ready*; 𝕿^{Jon} (מחפן וממקסן) gives both meanings. Symm. (ὑπουργιάς) may have read צבא and understood the phrase to mean *a wagon for* (*military*) *service*. Symm. and 𝔙 in Is. render by *litter*.—**5.** מאתם] BDB. 86*b*.—איש] Dav. 11, R. d.

10 f.—The offering of sacrificial material.—This is presented by all the princes on the same day as the wagons and oxen, v.^{10} (cp. v.^{84}); *after* the presentation, v.^{11}, Yahweh commands that each prince shall offer on a separate day, *i.e.* that the present of each prince shall be offered afresh and formally received on a separate day. This appears to be the meaning of the verses, but it is badly expressed, for the terms of the two verses are the same. Is the view that the offerings were made on separate days (v.$^{11-83}$) an intrusion?

The paragraph division of RV. would be improved if v.^{10} began a new paragraph: the account of the first gift closes at v.^{9}, the account of the second begins with v.^{10}.

The Dedication-gift] חֲנֻכָּה has the same sense in v.$^{84. 88}$ and, perhaps, in v.^{11}, though there it may mean "dedication." Though the root is ancient, the noun in Heb. is confined to late writers, the Chronicler, and an editor of the Psalms (30^{1}). For sacrifices at dedications, cp. 1 K. $8^{62f.}$ (cp. 2 Ch. 7^{9}), Neh. 12^{27-43}, 1 Mac. $4^{53f.}$. The gift consists of materials for each of the main types of sacrificial offerings—the meal-offering, the burnt-offering, the sin-offering, and the peace-offering.—*In the day that it was anointed*] Ex. 40^{10} (cp. v.^{1}); see above on v.^{1}.—13. *Dish*] (קערה) RV. "charger"; see Ex. 25^{29}.—*Bowl*] (מזרק), Ex. 27^{3}.—14. *Saucer*] כף; RV "spoon," Ex. 25^{29}.—*The shekel of the sanctuary*] Ex. 30^{13}.

10. את חנכת המזבח] 𝔊 εἰς τὸν ἐγκαινισμόν,—a paraphrase rather than a variant (=לחנ׳ המ׳): ct. v.$^{84.\ 88}$.—ביום המשח אתו] Dav. 79, 81, R. 3.—**12–83.** The only variations from the otherwise constant formula of the following twelve sections are—(1) In the initial vv. of the first two sections: ct. v.$^{12.\ 18}$ with v.$^{24.\ 30}$ etc. (2) In the second v. of the first two sections we have וקרבנו v.^{13}, הקריב את קרבנו v.^{19}; in all the remaining sections קרבנו v.$^{25.\ 31}$ etc. 𝔖 reads קרבנו simply in v.$^{13.\ 19}$ also. 𝔊 assimilates v.$^{13.\ 19}$. (3) The lack of special forms for the ordinals above ten necessitated a slight change in the reference to the 11th and 12th days, v.$^{72.\ 78}$.—**13.** שלשים ומאה] Dav. 37, R. 4.—**24.** נשיא לבני זבולן] the reason for using ל as a periphrasis of the gen. here and in subsequent and corresponding vv. is not clear: ct. v.^{18}. See König, iii. 280*m*.—**72.** ביום עשתי עשר יום] Dav. 38 (2).—**86.** עשרה . . . הקדש] 𝔊^{BL} omit.—**87.** ומנחתם] 𝔊+וְנִסְכֵּיהֶם: cp. 6^{15}; but here the addition is clearly wrong.—**88.** המזבח] 𝔊+אחרי מלא ידיו (μετὰ τὸ πληρῶσαι τὰς χεῖρας αὐτοῦ): cp Ezek. 43^{26}. The translators must have had the Heb. phrase before them.

89. An isolated fragment of a narrative which recorded the fulfilment of the promise made in Ex. 25^{22}.—*With Him*] presupposes an immediately preceding mention of Yahweh. —*And He spake to him*] The subject is Yahweh. In its original context the words doubtless introduced a divine speech. On the subject-matter of the v., cp. 1^{1} (2nd n.).

מִדַּבֵּר] Hithp. part.; G.-K. 54*c*. The same form occurs in 2 S. 14^{13}, Ezek. 2^{2} 43^{6}: otherwise the Hithp. of דבר is not found. Perhaps we should punctuate מְדַבֵּר, the present punctuation merely representing some false exegesis such as that of Rashi, who explains מדבר אליו as meaning מדבר בינו לבין עצמו, *i.e.* speaking with himself.

The versions make different efforts to get over the difficulty presented by this v. when its fragmentary character is not recognised. 𝔙 goes furthest—Cumque ingrederetur Moyses tabernaculum fœderis, ut consuleret *oraculum*, audiebat vocem loquentis ad se de propitiatorio quod erat super arcam testimonii inter duos Cherubim: *unde et loquebatur* ei. The attempt to make the last clause express the constantly recurring practice, which would, of course, require in the Hebrew the simple imperfect, is perhaps also the cause of the renderings of 𝔊 (καὶ ἐλάλει) and 𝔗 (ומתמלל). 𝔖 inserts ו before מעל and substitutes דבר for וידבר, and so reads, "And from the mercy-seat . . . He spake to him."

VIII. 1–4. The golden candlestick.—The verses contain nothing new in substance. Thus v.$^{1.\ 2a}$ is a formula (cp. 5^{6} n.); ^{2b} = Ex. 25^{37}; v.^{3} the execution of the command of v.^{2b} (not recorded in Ex. 37^{17-24}); ^{4a} = Ex. 25^{31}; ^{4b}, cp. Ex. $25^{9.\ 40}$.

The person to whose care the lamps are intrusted is undefined in Ex. 25^{37} (𝔥), is Moses in Ex. 25^{37} (S 𝔊), but, as here, Aaron in Ex. 27^{21}, Lev. 24^{1-4}.

In view of the character of the section it seems preferable

with Kue. and CH. to refer it entirely, rather than with Di (cp. Paterson, *SBOT.*) only in part (v.[4]), to P^s.

When thou settest up the lamps] so RV. marg. rightly; העלה means *to fix on*, not *to light* (RV.) a lamp.

2. אל מול פני המנורה] the sense is probably the same as that of the parallel expression (על עבר פניה) in Ex. 25^{37}—"on the space in front of the candlestick"; in other words, on the N. side of the outer chamber along which the table of shewbread was placed (Ex. 26^{35}). The phrase אל מול פני occurs elsewhere in [3], Ex. $28^{25.37}$, 39^{18}, Lev. 8^{9} (all P), 2 S. 11^{15}†.—**3.** אל מול פני המנורה]? dittographic from v.[2]; as an interpretation of the text RV. is doubtful.—**4.** פִּרְחָהּ] rather פִּרְחֶיהָ: so 𝔊 S: cp. Ex. 25^{31}.

VIII. 5–22. The purification and presentation of the Levites to Yahweh.—A parallel narrative to 3^{5-13}. All that is new in substance is contained in v.[6b–13], and consists of a command to purify the Levites, and of directions for their purification and solemn presentation to Yahweh. The rest (v.[5. 6a. 14–22]) consists of variants on parts of v.[6b–13], a resetting of 3^{5-13}, and stereotyped formulæ (see notes below for details).

The section contains curious repetitions; *e.g.* the command to purify the Levites is given twice, v.[6. 15], and Aaron is once, v.[11], Moses twice, v.[13. 15], commanded to "wave" the Levites.

It appears probable that an original narrative by P^s of the solemn institution of the Levites, designed as a parallel to the consecration of the priests (Lev. 8), has been subsequently expanded, partly by attempts to emphasise the activity of Aaron and partly by assimilation to 3^{5-13}.

So, substantially, We. (comp. 180 f.), Kue., Baudissin (*Priesterthum*, 44 f.), CH. Others (Di., Str.), though admitting that the passage has been expanded, consider the cleansing and formal presentation of the Levites to belong to P^g. The case is well stated by Kue. "Nu. viii. 5–22 . . . is an insipid repetition and exaggeration of the account of the separation of the Levites for the service of the sanctuary in Nu. iii. and iv. If the author of these last-named chapters had supposed that the Levites, before entering on their duties, had to be purified, and presented to Yahwè by תנופה, like a sacrifice, he would not have passed it over in silence; for he represents them in iii. and iv. as already intrusted with the task which in that case they would only have become qualified to undertake in viii. 5–22. This pericope, then, must be a later addition, as we might have supposed from its setting, viii. 1–4, 23–26. Its author observed that a formal consecration of the Levites, analogous to that of the priests (Lev. viii.), was not recorded, though it seemed to be neither unsuitable nor superfluous. This defect he supplied" (*Hexateuch*, § 6 n. 33).

6a. Cp. $3^{12a. 45}$.—*And cleanse them*] make them ceremonially clean. The priests are sanctified (Ex. 28^{41}, Lev. 8^{10-12}), the Levites merely cleansed.—7. *And thus shalt thou do unto them in cleansing them*] (לטהרם) cp. Ex. 29^1 (of the priests), "And this is the thing which thou shalt do unto them in sanctifying them" (לקדש אתם). Corresponding to this general difference, that the dedication of the Levites involved only the negative process of purification from ceremonial uncleanness, the dedication of the priests, in addition, the positive process of receiving the qualities of holiness, is the absence from the present ceremonial of the sprinkling with blood and the anointing with oil, which play so significant a part in the dedication of the priests, Lev. $8^{12. 23f.}$: cp. Weinel in *ZATW*. 1898, pp. 35 f., 62 f.—*Water of sin*] (מי חטאת) *i.e.* water for the removal of sin; so מי (ה)נדה = "water of impurity," 19^9; for analogous uses of the construct and genitive (Dav. 23). The term is used nowhere else, and there is, therefore, no means of determining with certainty whether it denotes water specially treated, as the analogy of "the water of impurity" or the "waters of bitterness" ($5^{17f.}$) or the water used in the cleansing of lepers (Lev. 14^{4-7}) would suggest, or simply clean water, which might also be used as a means of cleansing from sin (Ezek. 36^{25}, cp. Zech. 13^1). The priests are entirely washed, not merely sprinked, with (simple) water (Lev. 8^6).—*And let them* (the Levites) *cause a razor to pass over their whole flesh*] *i.e.* all the hair, not only of the head but of the whole body, is to be cut. Close shaving, which the English expression suggests, is scarcely intended: cp. 6^5 note. Close shaving (וגלח את כל שערו) entered into the purification of lepers (Lev. $14^{8f.}$), and of Nazirites who had contracted uncleanness from the dead (6^9): cp. also Dt. 21^{12}. Compare the practice of the Egyptians. "The priests shave themselves all over their body every other day, so that no lice or any other foul thing may come to be upon them when they minister to the gods" (Herod. ii. 37); and see, further, on 6^9.—*And let them wash their clothes*] another point of inferiority as compared with the priests, who are clad with entirely new and different clothes (Lev. 8^{13}): cp. with the present, once again the rite of the purification of lepers (Lev.

$14^{8f.}$).—8. The offerings to be made by the Levites are a burnt-offering (cp. v.[12]), consisting of *a young bullock* (Lev. 4^3), with the appropriate meal-offering (15^9), and a sin-offering consisting of a second young bullock.—*They shall take . . . thou shalt take*] the reason for the change of subject, possibly the result of textual accident, is not clear: cp. v.[12b] for the 2nd p.—10. *Before Yahweh*] cp. 5^{16} n.—10b. The people lay their hands on the Levites to indicate that it is they who offer them to Yahweh: for the rite of laying on hands, see Lev. 1^4.—*Children of Israel*] To explain this as meaning the representatives of the people (1^{16}) or the heads of their tribes* is quite gratuitous. Had the writer clearly thought out the ceremony, and intended the one or the other, he would no doubt have expressed it intelligibly. The same remark may hold good with regard to the next rite—the waving of the Levites. Either the practical difficulty that a large body of over 20,000 men could not, like loaves of bread (Lev. 23^{17}) or a sheaf of corn (Lev. 23^{15}) or a piece of a sacrificial animal (Lev. 7^{32-34}, Nu. 6^{20}), be moved or waved to and fro before the altar, never occurred to the writer, and he has introduced the act of waving (תנופה), without thinking how it could have been actually performed, because it suitably symbolises a gift to Yahweh (6^{20} n.); or else the words הניף, תנופה have lost their original meaning and signify nothing more than "to make a sacred gift," "a sacred gift"; cp. Now. ii. 239 f.—11. Probably an interpolation to explain that the "waving" referred to Moses in v.[13. 15] was actually performed by Aaron. Di. further suggests that v.[13b. 14] originally occupied the place of v.[11]. For the introduction of Aaron, cp. 1^2 n.—12. The Levites before entering on their duties must not only cleanse themselves, but also offer atoning sacrifices; the imposition of hands is part of the regular ritual, Lev. 1^4.—14. *And thou shalt separate the Levites*] as Israel is separated from other peoples (Lev. 20^{26}), so the Levites are separated from the rest of Israel. 14b. Cp. 3^{12b}.—15a. After the ritual described in the preceding vv., the Levites are to enter on their duties—this is the natural close to the narrative. Another "cleansing" and another

* Di., Keil.

"waving," v.^{15b}, cannot have been intentionally introduced by the original writer at this point, but is due to expansion of the original narrative.—**16a.** Cp. 3^{9}.—**16b.** Cp. 3^{12b}.—**17.** Cp. 3^{13}.—**18.** Cp. 3^{12}.—**19a.** Cp. $3^{9a.\ 12.\ 8}$.—**19.** *The service of the children of Israel*] the services which, but for the exchange, the firstborn Israelites must have rendered. By discharging these services the Levites *make propitiation for* the people,—secure or cover (כִּפֵּר) them against such a plague (נֶגֶף) as would be the natural result of withholding from Yahweh His due (cp. Ex. 30^{12}), and so provoking His anger. By a kind of afterthought, as it would seem, the writer adds the words *when the children of Israel approach the sanctuary* (cp. 18^{22}), thus indicating that the Levites screen the people not only from the anger which would be evoked if the services of the firstborn or their substitutes were withheld, but also, by forming a ring round the tabernacle, from the wrath which fell on those who, without due qualification, drew near the sacred edifice (1^{53}). The word used for *plague* (נֶגֶף), which is confined to P, commonly implies some calamity inflicted on people who have roused the anger of God (cp. $17^{11f.}$, Ex. 12^{13} 30^{12}, Jos. 22^{17}†); and the verb often has a similar implication (cp. *e.g.* Ex. 7^{27}, 2 S. 12^{15}).—**20–22.** The various directions carried out. The allusion to Aaron, at least in v.^{21a}, is due to modification of the original: cp. v.^{11} n.—**21.** *And the Levites unsinned themselves*] The Hebrews included in the idea of "sin" ceremonial uncleanness, and it is to the removal of sin of this kind that the vb. התחטא refers, alike here and in $19^{12.\ 13.\ 20}$ $31^{19f.\ 23}$. So the Piel חטא is used in Lev. 8^{15} of the removal of the "sin," or ceremonial uncleanness of the altar.

7. וְהִטֶּהָרוּ] G.-K. 27*q*, 54*c*.—**14.** הלוים (2)] 𝔊 om.—**15.** לעבר את אהל מ׳] 𝔊 S לעבר את עבדת אהל מועד, as, *e.g.*, 4^{30} in 𝔓; cp. v.$^{11.\ 19.\ 22}$.—תנופה] 𝔊 𝔖 add לפני יהוה; cp. v.$^{13.\ 21}$ in 𝔓.—**16.** פטרת] occurs nowhere else; even in 3^{12}, on which the present passage is based, we find פטר. S reads here also פטר. The clause seems to have suffered from some corruption; in addition to פטרת, the כל between בכור and בבני is suspicious. The whole clause תחת . . . ישראל is read by S thus: תחת כל בכור פטר רחם בבני ישראל.—**17.** הַכֹּתִי] S הכיתי.—**19.** ואתנה] Dr. *Tenses*, 69*o*; König, iii. 200*a*.

23–26. The age of Levitical service.—Levites between twenty-five and fifty years of age are to undertake the responsibility of the service of the tabernacle. When they have reached the age of fifty, their responsibility ceases, though they may still render voluntary assistance to their fellow-Levites (אחיו v.^{26}).

According to c. 4 the age of service was from thirty to fifty. On the difference, see 4^3 n.

There are also certain stylistic peculiarities which distinguish the present section from c. 4. In c. 4 the age of service is indicated by means of the phrase מבן שלשים שנה ומעלה ועד בן חמשים שנה. Here we have the two direct statements: At twenty-five the Levite enters (יבוא) on service; at fifty he retires (ישוב). The particular combination צבא העבדה v.^{25}, lit. "the warfare of the service" (cp. 4^3 n.), occurs nowhere else.—In 24 זאת אשר ללוים is unique; Paterson supplies התורה after זאת; but even this fails to give any of the usual formulæ; see 5^{29} n. 𝔙 𝔖 are paraphrases rather than variants. The awkwardness of 𝔐 may betray a late hand, or we might supply תעשה after אשר; cp. Ex. 29^1 and below v.^{26b} (cp. Ex. 29^{35}).

IX. 1–14. The supplementary passover. — The passover having been duly observed on the 14th day of the first month of the second year, according to the directions given at the institution of the festival in the previous year, v.$^{1-5}$, certain men complain that they had been prevented, through defilement by the dead, from discharging their passover duties, v.$^{6f.}$. On inquiry Moses receives this instruction from Yahweh, v.$^{8f.}$: all who are prevented, either by defilement from the dead or by absence on a distant journey, from observing the passover on the right day, are to observe it on the 14th day of the next month, v.$^{10-12}$; all who fail to observe the festival, except for these reasons, are to be "cut off from their kinsmen," v.^{13}. The *gêr* or resident foreigner (15^{13} n.), as well as the Israelite by birth, is to keep the passover, v.^{14}.

The supplemental character of the section, the date (v.^{1}, cp. 7^1, ct. 1^1), and the lack of organic connection with the context, are most simply explained as being due to the secondary character of the passage (cf. Introd. § 12). The *insertion* of the passage here is explicable, for through its chief motive it is connected with the middle of the second month, and should therefore stand between 1^1 and 10^{11}. Had it, however, formed part of the original narrative, the main motive would, it is reasonable to suppose, have been stated first, and dated in the second month, and the historical cause, v.$^{1-8}$, would have been introduced by means of a pluperfect paragraph.

Di.'s view is that the original narrative of P contained, at this point, a short account of the supplementary passover (see below on v.[2]), and that this was expanded in the final redaction into the section as now read. The variations in 𝔊 (v.[3-5]) and the faulty text of v.[2] he considers to be at once the result and the indications of such a process. See also We. *Comp.* 177; Kue. *Hex.* § 6 n. 32.

1a. 1^1 n.—The day of the month is omitted, for it is illegitimate to interpret *in the first month* (בחדש הראשון) as meaning "at the first new moon," *i.e.* on the first day of the month. Hebrew writers, when they wish to define the first day, use the numeral אחד; so $1^{1.\,18}$ 29^1 33^{38}, Dt. 1^3, Ezek. 31^1, Hag. 1^1, Ezr. 3^6 7^9 and often. Cp. Di. on Ex. 19^1.—**2.** The rendering of RV., *Moreover, let the children of Israel keep*, is not a translation of וְיַעֲשׂוּ, which presupposes some such phrase as "command the children of Israel (that they keep)"; see phil. n. on 5^2. Either such a phrase has dropped out (𝔊 prefixes εἰπόν), or the tense was originally historical (וַיַּעֲשׂוּ), the present pronunciation being the result of a redaction of the passage (see above). Di. surmises that all that is original in v.[1-5] ran as follows: "And the children of Israel kept the passover at its appointed time, on the 14th day of the first (so 𝔊) month at evening, in the wilderness of Sinai: according to all that Yahweh commanded Moses, so the children of Israel did."—**3.** *Between the two evenings*] the same peculiar phrase is used elsewhere in connection with the passover (first in Ex. 12^6) and in some other connections (Ex. 16^{12} $29^{39.\,41}$ 30^8, Nu. 28^4). It is peculiar to P; with Ex. 12^6 ct. Dt. 16^6. The exact sense of the phrase is obscure; according to the practice of the 1st cent. A.D. it was interpreted to mean the time between about three and five o'clock in the afternoon: cp. Jos. *BJ.* vi. 9^3 with Ex. 12^6, and, further, Jos. *Ant.* xiv. 4^3 and *Pesaḥim* 5^1 with Ex. 29^{39}. See, further, especially for various Jewish interpretations, Gesenius, *Thesaurus*, p. 1065.—**3b.** The passover is to be kept in the manner already established by decree and usage: cp. Ex. 12. But the author of the present section shows no very vivid realisation of a passover in the wilderness. The regulation of Ex. 12^7 could not have been carried out by people dwelling in tents.—**5.** *And they kept the passover*] 𝔊 𝔖 omit.—*At even*] 𝔊 omits.—**6.** Partaking of the sacrificial flesh while in a state of uncleanness is the subject of an express and general prohibition, Lev. $7^{20f.}$; cp. also 1 S. 21^{4-6}, Lev. 22^{1-6}. On uncleanness by the dead, see c. 19; on the phrase here used to express it, 5^2 phil. n.—*And before Aaron*] probably an insertion. Aaron is not mentioned elsewhere in the section; and the pronoun ("to him") in the next verse disregards him: cp. 1^2 n.—7. *Why are we withdrawn from offering*] the Hebrew word (נגרע) is used of withdrawal, especially of a part from the whole: cp. in Kal Ex. 5^8, Dt. 4^2; in Hiph. 36^3 27^4, Lev. 27^{18}. The question seems, therefore, to mean this: Why are we, owing to accidental and temporary defilement, to be excluded from the rest of Israel and, in the matter of the great annual festival, to be in the position of foreigners who would have no part in it? The men did not need to ask why they were *prevented*; they knew that the reason lay in their uncleanness. Their question is virtually a petition for a modification of the law, which, on the present occasion, had prevented them.—8. *Stand still*] cp. the use of עמד in Jos. 3^{16}, Ex. 9^{28}; but the parallels are not exact, and the present phrase is a little abrupt. Possibly כה or פה = "here" has dropped out; cp. 𝔊 𝔖.—9 ff. The law now given provides not only for the case of uncleanness raised by the incident just recorded, but also for the case of those on distant journeys. According to the Mishnah (*Pes.* 9^1), all who were prevented by accident or compulsion from observing the first were bound to observe the second passover. On the second passover, cp. *Pes.* 9 *passim*, and 2 Ch. 30 (Hezekiah's passover celebrated in the second month, 30^{15}).—10. *Of you or of your generations*] *i.e.* belonging to this or future generations.—11. Three of the chief regulations governing the observance of the normal passover are specified as governing also this supplementary passover; with v.^{11b} cp. Ex. 12^8; v.$^{12a\alpha}$, Ex. 12^{10}; and v.$^{12a\beta}$, Ex. 12^{46}. Then in v.^{12b} it is summarily enjoined that the law of the first passover holds in every respect also for the second.—13. *That soul shall be cut off from his kinsmen*] Gn. 17^{14} and often in P (CH. 50). The threat is not made in Ex. 12. On the much debated question whether this is a threat of death or excommunication, Gunkel (*Genesis*, p. 246) seems to hit the mark: "Doubtless men like

P desired the death of such a sinner . . . and when the heathen government permitted it, certainly also inflicted it; in Lev. $17^{9f.}$ $20^{3.\,6}$ we can read between the lines that such capital punishment of the religious transgressor was not permitted by the government, and that it was necessary to rest content with the belief in the destruction of such a sinner *by God*." Note 4^{18} and the context; see also Kuenen, *Rel. of Israel*, ii. 276 f.—*That man shall bear his sin*] (חטאו ישא) *i.e.* shall suffer the consequences of his sin, undergo the punishment of it: cp. 18^{22}, Lev. 20^{20}.—**14.** Ex. $12^{48f.}$; cp. 15^{13} n.

בְּמוֹעֲדוֹ] S, here, and throughout the section, and in 28^{2} במועדיו: cp. 𝔊 κατὰ καιρούς, v.[3]; but otherwise in v.[2. 7. 13].—**6.** ויהי] Dav. 113*b*; S ויהיו; 𝔊 καὶ παρεγένοντο; the latter does not *necessarily* imply a reading ויבאו, cp. 1 K. (S.) 20^{24}.—**10.** איש איש כי] 5^{12} n.—בדרך רחקה] On the epicene character of דרך, see Kön. iii. 249*n*. The point over the ה of רחקה has reference to the Rabbinic exegesis which refers the adjective to the subj. of the sentence instead of to דרך. Cp. 𝔊 here, *Siphrê* on this passage, and Geiger, *Urschrift*, 185–187.—**12.** עד בקר] The art. is omitted in the familiar expression; Dav. 22, R. 3; Kön. iii. 294*e*.—**14.** וכמשפטו] S (cp. 𝔖) וכמשפטיו. The pl. is probably right: cp. v.[3].—יהיה] 5^{9} phil. n.—ולגר ולאורח] Dav. 136; Kön. iii. 376*a*.

15–23. The fiery cloud.—The movements of the Israelites from Sinai onwards were regulated partly by the action of a cloud, partly, as before reaching Sinai, by the express command of Yahweh. This cloud, which at night assumed a fiery appearance, settled on the tabernacle on the day of its erection; subsequently as often and as long as the cloud rested on the tabernacle the Israelites encamped; and as often as the cloud rose from off the tabernacle they broke up the camp and continued their journey.

The section, which is unconnected with either the preceding or the following, is parallel to Ex. $40^{34a.\,36\text{-}38}$ and connected with Ex. $40^{2.\,17}$ by the date in v.[15]. It would have stood most naturally at the conclusion of the narrative of the erection of the tabernacle. In its present form it may best be referred to P^{s}; note the numerous omissions in 𝔊 and certain expressions not found elsewhere in P^{g}, viz. יש אשר v.[20] n., שמרי משמרת י״י (cp. 1^{53} n.), כמראה אש v.[15] (cf. Ezek. 8^{2}). As relating the section to P, note the conception of the cloud (n. on v.[18]), the connection of v.[15] with Ex. 40, also על פי יהוה (CH. 19*a*), המשכן (CH. 54), הערות (CH. 161), ביד משה (CH. 180). See, further, CH.

15a. Cp. 7^{1} n.—*The cloud covered*] the tense is historical, recording the one definite past event that the cloud settled on the tabernacle when it was first set up. On the other hand, all the verbs in v.$^{15b-23a}$ are *frequentatives*, and state what repeatedly happened subsequently (Dr. *Tenses*, 30). — *The tabernacle, even the tent of the testimony*] the tabernacle (המשכן) was contained within the tent (אהל), cp. $3^{25f.}$ n., Ex. 26^{7}; the cloud, therefore, is more accurately described as covering (כסה) the tent, cp. Ex. 40^{34}, Nu. 17^{7} (16^{42}); but it is spoken of indifferently as resting or being on (על) either the tent (Ex. 40^{35}) or the tabernacle (Ex. $40^{36.38}$, Nu. 10^{11}). "Tent of the testimony" (אהל העדות) only occurs again in $17^{22f.}$ 18^{2}, 2 Ch. 24^{6}; "tabernacle of the testimony" (משכן העדות) is found in Ex. 38^{21}, Nu. $1^{50.53\,bis}$ 10^{11}; on "the testimony," see 17^{18} n. No satisfactory reason can be discovered for the addition of the second phrase here, and it may be, as Paterson argues, a gloss.—**15b.** Cp. Ex. 40^{38}. The fiery appearance may have been supposed to result from the presence in the tabernacle of the glory of Yahweh (Ex. $40^{31f.}$), the appearance of which was like devouring fire (Ex. 24^{17}: cp. 34^{29-35} and also Lev. $9^{23f.}$).—**16.** *The cloud used to cover it*] 𝔊 𝔖 𝔙 add "by day." **18.** *At the commandment of Yahweh*] the cloud, according to P, first appeared at Sinai (Ex. 24^{15-18}; Ex. 16^{6-10} is a misplaced narrative), and first became a permanent phenomenon after the erection of the tabernacle. Before reaching Sinai, the Israelites marched according to the commandment of Yahweh, Ex. 17^{1}; such definite direction they still required; for the cloud in P does not, as in J (Ex. 13^{22}), move at the head of the whole host to show the way. In P the cloud is always closely associated with the tabernacle; and the tabernacle formed the *centre* of the host (2^{17}). It is clear, too, from v.^{23b} that v.^{18} is more than another way of stating v.^{17}; the commandment of Yahweh, according to which the Israelites marched, was not merely the action of the cloud, for it was communicated through Moses. For על־פי of directions orally communicated, cp. *e.g.* 13^{3}.—**20.** $𝔊^{L}$ omits this v. and also v.^{22}.—**21 f.** Sometimes the cloud only remained over the tabernacle from the evening of one day to the morning of the next: *i.e.* the Israelites sometimes journeyed day after day, sometimes they remained encamped a whole day (v.[21b]), sometimes a couple of days, or a month, or more indefinite periods, v.[22a]. The last clause of v.[21] is omitted in 𝔊, and is very probably dittographic. Omitting this clause (but not או ימים, which is also omitted by 𝔊[B]), we may translate v.[21. 22a] thus—"Sometimes the cloud would remain from evening to morning, and the cloud would rise up in the morning and (the people) would journey; or (it would remain) a day and a night, or two days, or a month, or for some time." The rendering of ימים by *year* (RV.) is quite unjustifiable, and is not to be defended by a reference to Lev. 25^{29}; it means simply an indefinite period (cp. *e.g.* Gn. 40^{4}, Neh. 1^{4}), which, from the context, may sometimes be inferred to be short (less than ten days, if the text of Gn. 24^{55} be correct) or long—here, for instance, presumably more than a month.—**22b.** 𝔊 om.—**23a.** 𝔊[F] om. This may be according to the original text, but is more probably a further stage in the shortening of the text than that represented by 𝔊[ABL], which omit the first clause only. Manifestly either 𝔐 or 𝔊[F] is right.

15. הקים] subj. המקים; cp. Dav. 108, R. 1. S הוקם (3rd s. pf. Hophal); cp. 𝔊 𝔗[O].—לאהל העדות] Kön. iii. 289*g*. Paterson in *SBOT.* regards the words as a gloss; see his note there.—**20.** יש אשר]="There were (times) when": so only here and in the next v. But cp. יש אשר="there were some who"... Neh. $5^{2. 3. 4}$, and Syriac phrases, such as ܐܝܬ ܕܐܡܪ (*e.g.* 1 Cor. 1^{12} in Pesh.), ܐܝܬ ܕܐܡܪܝܢ: cp. Payne Smith, *Thesaurus Syriacus*, p. 172.—ימים מספר] rather ימי מ׳; 𝔐 has arisen from dittography of ם. מספר in this type of idiom (="few") is always elsewhere in the gen. —**22.** על המשכן] 𝔊 om. Probably the phrase was a gloss on עליו; in 𝔖 it has replaced עליו, in 𝔐 it has gained a place in the text by the side of עליו.

X. 1–10. The silver trumpets.—Their workmanship and purpose, v.[2]; the occasions of their use (*a*) in the wilderness, v.[3–8]; (*b*) in Canaan, v.[9f.].

In v.[9f.], also in v.[5. 6a. 7], the verbs are in the 2nd pers. pl. (ct. 3rd pl. in v.[3f. 6b. 8]); Di. for this reason, and because v.[9f.] deals with a different use of the trumpets, and because of the incompleteness of v.[5. 6a] (see below), regards v.[9f.] as derived by a redactor (or less probably by P) from a different source, viz. S, *i.e.* H, and v.[5. 6a. 7] as redactional expansions. In favour of this conclusion he also notes in v.[9f.] "I am Yahweh your God," בוא מלחמה, צר="enemy" (elsewhere almost confined to the elevated style, yet cp. 25^{18}), and בארצכם (cp. Lev. $19^{9. 33}$ 22^{24} 23^{22} $25^{9. 45}$ 26^{1}). On v.[9f.]

cp. also Kayser, *Das vorexil. Buch d. Urgesch. Isr.* p. 80 (v.[8] contains the customary conclusion); CH.; Baentsch, *Heiligkeitsgesetz*, 8f. (v.[9f.] an earlier source, but whether H doubtful).

The manufacture of these trumpets, which are henceforward to be used for sounding the march, is the last act recorded by P prior to the departure from Sinai, v.[11]. To the trumpet (חצצרה) there is no reference in any preceding part of the narrative of the Exodus; but E mentions the horn (יבל in Ex. 19[13], שופר in Ex. 19[13. 16. 19] 20[18]), and H contains a law (Lev. 25[9]) relative to the use of the horn in Canaan.

1, 2. The trumpets are to be of silver, with chased work, and are to be used to summon the people and to give the signal for breaking up camp.—2. *Trumpets*] (חצצרות) were apparently much less used for secular purposes than the horn (שופר), which is so frequently mentioned in early literature. Of their secular use we read only in Hos. 5[8], 2 K. 11[14]. Of their sacred use there is mention in 2 K. 12[14], P (here and 31[6]), Ps. 98[6], and especially in Ch., Ezr., and Neh. The instrument is described by Josephus (*Ant.* iii. 12[6] *ἀσωσρά*) as rather less than a cubit long, and is no doubt the long straight instrument depicted on the Arch of Titus; see, further, Wellhausen, *Psalms* (*SBOT.*), 220f., where illustrations may be found.—*Of turned work*] מקשה (Ex. 25[18. 31] 37[7] etc.).—3 f. A blast on both trumpets is to be the signal for the whole people, on one alone for the princes (1[16]) to assemble. Kn. Di. compare the practice of summoning the Roman "curia centuriata" by means of a trumpet (Gell. 15. 27. 2; Propert. 4. 1. 13).—5 f. A series of alarms (תרועה) on the trumpets are to give the signal for the several divisions of the camp successively to break up.—5b. Cp. 2[3-9].—6a. Cp. 2[10-16]. After v.[6a] 𝔊 inserts—"And ye shall blow a third alarm, and the camp which encamped westwards shall break up (cp. 2[18-24]); and ye shall blow a fourth alarm, and the camp which encamped northwards shall break up" (cp. 2[25-31]). 𝔙 has a much briefer addition—"Et iuxta hunc modum reliqui facient."—6b. *They shall blow an alarm whenever they* (the Israelites) *are to make a start*] מַסַּע is here used in its strict sense of "the start," and not, as it is used in some cases, of the journey started upon;

so 𝔊 exceptionally, but rightly, ἔξαρσις. The plural (למסעיהם) may have reference either to the several starts of the different divisions on a single occasion, v.[5. 6a], or to the successive future starts of the whole company.—7. *And when bringing together the assembly*] קהל is frequent in P, but much less characteristic of his style than "congregation" (עדה), which is used in v.[2]; on the latter, cp. phil. n. on 1[2].—*Ye shall blow, but not sound an alarm*] The difference intended is uncertain; in Hos. 5[8] the two terms תקע and הריע seem to be synonymous. The noun derived from the latter (תרועה = "alarm," v.[6]) is, especially in early literature, used more particularly of the battle-cry (*e.g.* Am. 1[14], Jer. 4[19]); hence, perhaps, the phrase in 31[6] (חצצרות התרועה). Thus, although in P the word is also used in a very different way (*e.g.* 29[1]), the present command may mean: blow the trumpet, but not with martial notes. Whether the first verb (תקע) means to produce a series of short staccato notes (Di.) or a single long blast (BDB. p. 348*b*), there is no sufficient evidence to decide. —*A statute for ever*] The phrase in the Hexateuch is confined to P, who uses it frequently (CH. 62); it occurs in the pl. in Ezek. 46[14].—*Throughout your generations*] Dr. *L.O.T.* 332, No. 20; CH. 76*b*.—9. When the Israelites are settled in Canaan the trumpets are to be blown in time of battle to keep God in remembrance of Israel, and so to secure Israel's delivery (Ps. 44[1-8]). For if God "forgets," Israel suffers defeat (Ps. 44[22-24]). For this use of the trumpets, cp. 2 Ch. 13[12-16], Mac. 4[40] 5[33] 16[8].—10. On (extraordinary) public festivals, on fixed feasts (Lev. 23) and new moons (28[11]), a blast of trumpets is to accompany the burnt-offerings and peace-offerings to secure God's attention: cp. 2 Ch. 29[27], Ps. 98[6], Sir. 50[16]; also Ps. 47.—*A memorial before your God*] Ex. 28[29]; and see Herzfeld, *Gesch. des Volkes Jisrael*, ii. 164–167.

2. אתם] Dav. 1, R. 3.—ולמסע את] cp. 4[24] n.—3. ותקעו . . . ונועדו] Dr. *Tenses*, 149; so v.[5f.].—ותקעו] 𝔊 καὶ σαλπίσεις; so 𝔙.—6. תימנה] S mistakenly צפונה.—9. תבאו מל׳] the usual phrase is "to go into battle" (יצא למ׳); in 31[21] 32[6] we have בוא למ׳. The present phrase is quite peculiar.—אלהיכם] 𝔊 om.—10. חרשֵׁכם] S and many Heb. MSS. *plene* חרשיכם; G.-K. 91*k*.

X. 11–XXI. 9 (JE P). *The northward march from Sinai; the wanderings and marches west of the 'Arabah.*

The period covered by this second main section of the book is about forty years (14^{33} 10^{11} $20^{23f.}$, cp. 33^{38}); but the bulk of it is concerned with the opening (10^{11}–14^{45}) and closing ($20^{(1)\,1-2}$–21^{9}) months. A single incident,—the revolt of Ḳoraḥ, Dathan, and Abiram and its consequences (c. 16–18),—or at most two, if we include here 20^{1-13}, and some miscellaneous laws (c. 15. 19) are alone referred to the intervening years.

Here as elsewhere the editor adopts P as his main thread. To P's brief account of the removal from Sinai to the scene of the wanderings ($10^{11-12\,(28)}$), he adds the parallel from JE (10^{29-33}) and much other matter from that source (10^{35}–12^{16}). In the story of the spies he opens with a long extract from P (13^{1-17}) and then fuses the stories of P and JE. With P's account of Ḳoraḥ's revolt he combines JE's story of the revolt of Dathan and Abiram; and he again fuses matter from the two main sources in 20^{1-13}; but P's account of the death of Aaron (20^{22-29}) is kept quite distinct from the extracts from JE (20^{14-21} 21^{1-9}), among which it is appropriately placed. To this editor or yet later hands we may attribute the incorporation of the laws in c. 15. 19 (cp. Introd. § 10 ff.) and the matter of 10^{13-28}; also the additions to the story of Ḳoraḥ (see on c. 16), and the suppression of the full details of date in 20^{1}.

X. 11–28. The departure from Sinai (P).—Guided by the cloud, the Israelites on the 20th day of the second month of the second year leave Sinai and (subsequently) encamp in the wilderness of Paran, v.$^{11f.}$ The tribal princes (1^{5-15}) are mentioned, and the order of the march, agreeing in the main with that in c. 2, is described v.$^{13-28}$.

Indications of P are (1) in v.$^{11f.}$ the date, the conception of the cloud (cp. $9^{17ff.}$, Ex. 40^{33-38}), משכן, למסעיהם; (2) in v.$^{13-28}$ the names of the princes, the relation to c. 2, על פי י״י, מטה. But the disagreement of v.$^{17-21}$ with 2^{17} points to another hand—P^{s}; so Di., Bacon, CH. A further expansion of the text here is found in S, where Dt. 1^{6b-8} is cited almost verbatim and prefixed to v.^{10}.

11. The Israelites leave Sinai between ten and twelve months after reaching it (Ex. 19^{1}), possibly in P^{g} exactly twelve months after (cp. Ex. 16^{1}; Nöld. *Untersuchungen*, 73

n. 1).—*The tabernacle of testimony*] 9^{15} n.—12. *By their journeys*] or *stages*. The journey from Sinai to Paran occupied several days. On למסעיהם, see v.[6] n.; and for the phrase in its present sense, 33^{2}, Ex. 17^{1}: cp. Gn. 13^{3} (JE), Ex. $40^{36.\ 38}$. —*The wilderness of Paran*] The precise boundaries of the district are somewhat uncertain. According to P, the W. of Paran is reached by an indefinite number of stages from Sinai in the direction of Canaan; hence the spies are despatched ($12^{16b.}$ 13^{3}) and hither return (13^{26}), and here the forty years of wandering are spent (14^{29-34} in the light of 13^{26}). In the fortieth year the people apparently march out of the W. of Paran to Ḳadesh (see on 20^{1}). From this we may infer that it lay N. of Sinai and S. of Ḳadesh. The other data do not conflict with this, if in 1 S. 25^{1} the Maʿon of 𝔊 be substituted for the Paran of MT. (so We. Dr.). The wilderness of Paran is Ishmael's dwelling-place (Gn. 21^{21} E); Paran itself lay between Midian and Egypt (1 K 11^{18}): cp., further, Gn. 14^{6} (El-paran) and Hab. 3^{3} (Paran ‖ Teman). Mt. Paran is associated with Seir and Sinai in Dt. 33^{2}. Its E. border was, apparently, the ʿArabah. The W. of Paran thus corresponds approximately to the desert of Et-tih (on which see Palmer, *Desert of the Wilderness*, p. 284 ff.). Cheyne (*EBi.* 3583) suggests that the term may have had a wider and a narrower usage, in the former including the W. of Ṣin, and so stretching right up to the Negeb.—13. *And they first departed*] "this was their first departure which followed on the command of God communicated by means of the lifting of the cloud" (Di.)—the least unnatural interpretation of the text. Possibly "first" (בראשנה) has been accidentally repeated from the next v.—14–16. See 2^{3-9}.—14. *The company*] 2^{2} n.—*The children of Judah marched first*] *i.e.* in front: ct. v.[25].—17. *And the tabernacle used to be taken down*] From this v. down to v.[27] all the verbs are frequentatives, indicating the general practice on a series of marches.—*Carrying the tabernacle*] and its appurtenances, $4^{25f.\ 31f.}$.—18–20. See 2^{10-16}. —20. *Deʿuʾel*] *al.* Reʿuʾel: 1^{14} n.—21. *And the Ḳohathites who carried the holy things*] enumerated in 3^{31} $4^{5ff.}$. מקדש cannot here mean "sanctuary" (RV.), though that is its usual meaning; for the building when taken to pieces is carried by the Merarites and Gershonites, v.[17] $3^{25f.\ 36f.}$. The use of מקדש here is quite exceptional and indeed improper; the nearest parallel is 18^{29}; in both cases the text may be at fault (cp. BDB. 574*a*).—*And they* (the Gershonites and Merarites) *used to set up the tabernacle against they* (the Ḳohathites) *came*] Such must be the meaning; but it is clumsily expressed. For the use of עד (= *against*) see Gen. 43^{25}, Ex. 22^{25}. Contrary to the implication of 2^{17}, the Merarites and Gershonites are here made to march off after the first division of the Israelites, apparently in order that the holy things might not be left unsheltered while the tent was being erected in the new camp. If so, the writer did not reflect that this arrangement left them unsheltered before the march.—**22–27.** See 2^{18-31}.

12. פארן] S here and everywhere (except Gn. 21^{21}) פראן. فرّان and فاران are names of Arab tribes; Ges.-Buhl, 616*a*.—**13, 14.** בראשנה] Far the most frequent meaning of the phrase is "formerly," *e.g.* 2 S. 7^{10} 20^{18}, 1 K 13^{6}, Jer. 7^{12}, sometimes specifically "on the previous occasion" (1 K 20^{9}); it also commonly means "first" (adverbially)—*e.g.* Dt. 17^{7}, 1 K. 17^{13}; very rarely also "at the beginning" (Pr. 20^{21}) or "in front" (Is. 60^{9}: cp., perhaps, 1 K 20^{17}). The last sense, which the antithesis of v.[25] requires in v.[14], is expressed by ראשנה in 2^{9}, Gn. 33^{2}.—**17.** וְהוּרד] cp. הוקם Ex. 40^{17}; 𝔊 𝔖 read here וְהוֹרִד, assimilating to 1^{51} 4^{5}.—**18.** ראובן] read בני ראובן with S $𝔊^{L}$ 𝔙 and also some MSS. of 𝔥. In the eleven remaining cases in this section 𝔥 followed by 𝔗 prefixes בני to the tribal name, except in v.[22] where some MSS. of 𝔥 and 𝔊 omit בני; 𝔙 omits בני in v.[16. 20. 24]; 𝔖 in v.[18. 22. 23. 24. 26. 27].—**21.** הקהתים] 𝔖 𝔊 𝔗 בני קהת.—**25.** מְאַסֵּף] Jos. $6^{9.\ 13}$, Is. 52^{12}.—**28.** ויסעו] Dr. *Tenses*, 76. 𝔊 places the word before לצבאתם; but 𝔥 is no doubt original.

29–36. The departure from the Mount of Yahweh (JE).—In contemplation of immediate departure Moses begs his kinsman Ḥobab to accompany the Israelites as guide, and give them the benefit of his great knowledge of the camping places in the wilderness, v.[29–32]. When they actually start, they are led by the ark, v.[33]; in v.[34] a reference is made to the cloud, and in v.[35. 36] poetical addresses to the ark are cited.

The narrative of JE, last cited in Ex. 34^{28}, is here resumed. Proofs of the derivation of v.[29–33] from JE—(1) the vv. are parallel and not consecutive to v.[11-12 (28)]; in v.[12] the Israelites are in Paran, several days' journey from Sinai; in v.[29-32] they are still at Sinai, and only leave it in v.[33]; (2) in v.[21] (cp. 3^{21} P) the ark is carried in the midst of the people, in v.[33] it precedes them; (3) linguistic evidence—נא (CH. 186), עוב (160), כי על כן (35), היטיב (38); see also notes below. As between J and E the evidence favours J (Di., Kue., Corn., Kit., Bacon); note Re'u'el (cp. Ex. 2^{18} J), not Jethro (Ex. 3^1 4^{18} $18^{1ff.}$ E), 29$a\beta$ corresponding more closely to Ex. 33^1 (J) than to Ex. 32^{34} (E) and the phrase אל ארצי ואל מולדתי (cp. Gn. 12^3 24^4 31^3 (J); ct. אל ארץ מולדתך Gn. 31^{13} (E); see CH. 60).—The ultimate source of v.[33], which did not originally form the immediate sequence to v.[32], is less certain. Many detect traces of the hand of E (Kue., Kit., Corn., Di., Moore). In v.[34] we have a conception of the cloud which is that of neither J nor E, but is similar to P's ($9^{17ff.}$): the v. appears to be a note of P^s which has gained its present position in 𝔥, another in 𝔊, where it stands after v.[36]. Whether the ancient poetical snatches in v.[35f.] were derived by the editor from JE or from some other source must remain uncertain, though the idiom ויהי ב in v.[35] is quite favourable to the former alternative (CH. 127^{JE}).

29. *Ḥobab, the son of Re'u'el, the Midianite, the father-in-law of Moses*] Ḥobab has not been previously mentioned. In Jud. 4^{11} he is called the father-in-law (חתן) of Moses, as also perhaps in the original text of Jud. 1^{16} (see Moore, *ad loc.*). Re'u'el is a clan name, and the meaning of the writer both here and in Judges may be that Ḥobab was a member of the clan ("son") of Re'u'el. In that case we may suppose that the name Ḥobab has been suppressed before or in favour of Re'u'el in Ex. 2^{18}, and consequently that in J's narrative he had been mentioned previously to the present section. Even so the present section opens abruptly. Probably in the source whence it was drawn, it was prefaced by an account of Ḥobab coming from his country (cp. v.[30]) to visit the Israelites at Sinai; fragments of this introduction are perhaps preserved in Ex. 18, which consists in the main of a parallel narrative in E of Jethro's visit. Cheyne (*EBi.*) identifies Ḥobab with Jehonadab, the founder of the Rechabites. Though the early Hebrew traditions differ as to the name of Moses' father-in-law—E calls him Jethro—and as to the name of his tribe, which in some cases is said to be Midianite (Ex. 3^1 $4^{18f.}$), in others Ḳenite (Jud. 1^{16} 4^{11}), they agree in connecting him by marriage with an Arab or nomadic tribe, for such were both Midianites and Ḳenites; see also 12^1 n.—

The place of which Yahweh said, I will give it you] Ex. 33^1 (J); see n. on 13^2.—The present story seems earlier in origin than the promise of the accompaniment of the angel (Ex. 33^2). The impress of nomadic life is here fresh and clear. What Moses, as leader of the people from Sinai to Canaan, needed was one who knew the various camping places.—*And let us do thee good*] give thee a share in the prosperity which Yahweh has promised us: cp. v.^{32}, Gn. 12^{16} $32^{10.\ 13\ (9.\ 12)}$, Jos. 24^{30}.—*For it is Yahweh who has promised Israel prosperity*] and having promised will fulfil: the subj. is emphatic. For דבר על virtually = "to promise," see Gn. 18^{19}, Jos. 23^{14}.

30. Ḥobab declines Moses' invitation: he prefers to go home. This implies that the route to Canaan was different from that to Midian. Most justice is done to this if we suppose that Sinai lay somewhere in the neighbourhood of the top of ʿAḳabah; for then the route of the Hebrews to Ḳadesh would lie to the N.W., that of Ḥobab to the E. Apart from the passages connecting Midian with the mount of God, all references imply that the Midianites had their homes on the E. of the ʿArabah and the Gulf of ʿAḳabah (Jud. 6–8, Gn. 25^6 36^{35}, Nu. 22^4 $25^{5ff.}$ 31). There is no reason for locating them in the southern part of the Sinaitic peninsula, except the assumption that Sinai-Ḥoreb lay there; then cp. Ex. 3^1. If, however, in deference to the traditional view of the site of Sinai, we are to conclude that Ḥobab's particular division of Midianites occupied the south of the Sinaitic peninsula (cp. Di. on Ex. 2^{15}), then we must probably think of them as cut off from the Midianites of the E.; otherwise the route of the Hebrews, if, as is usually assumed, it went by the top of the Gulf of ʿAḳabah, would have lain for some distance through Midianite country. Cp., further, Sayce, *Early Hist. of Hebrews*, 186–189, 213, who cites Baker Greene, *Hebrew Migration from Egypt*; and on the survival of the name E. of the Gulf of ʿAḳabah in the *Μοδίανα* of Ptolemy (6^7) and the Madyan of Arabic geographers, see *EBi.* col. 3081.—**31 f.** Moses further presses Ḥobab to accompany him, reiterating, v.^{32}, the promise made before, v.^{29b}. At this point the story breaks off and Ḥobab's final decision is not given. We may infer from Jud. 1[16] that it was favourable.*—31. *Thou knowest our encamping*] *i.e.* where we can and ought to encamp. The inf. (חנתנו) refers to the future; the paraphrastic renderings of 𝔊 and 𝔗 interpret it of the past, and also change the sense of the next clause, so as to avoid the incongruity of Moses seeking a natural guide when (according to the composite narrative, v.[11–13. 33f.] 9[17ff.]) he was so fully assisted by supernatural signs and agents. The rendering of v.[31b] in 𝔗 is as follows: "Thou knowest how we were encamping in the wilderness, and the mighty deeds which were done unto us hast thou seen with thine eyes"; and in 𝔊: "Thou wast with us in the wilderness, and shalt be an elder among us."—31. *But become unto us eyes*] Job 29[15].—33. *The mount of Yahweh*] *i.e.* Ḥoreb-Sinai; so only here: but cp. "the mount of God" (הר האלהים = Ḥoreb), Ex. 3[1] 4[27] 18[5] 24[13] (all E), 1 K. 19[8] †; in a different sense, Ezek. 28[16]. Perhaps "the mount of God" originally stood here, and "Yahweh" is due to an editor. Elsewhere "the mount of Yahweh" is Zion—*e.g.* Is. 2[3] = Mic. 4[2], Is. 30[29], Ps. 24[3], Gn. 22[14] (? originally "God").—*Three days' journey*] Gn. 30[36], Ex. 3[18], Nu. 33[8]: cp. Ex. 15[22]. The repetition of these words in clause *b* may be due to dittography. The only meaning of the whole verse as it stands is that during a three days' march from Sinai the ark was always three days' journey in front of the people—a useless position for a guide: cp. We. *Comp.* 100 f. As here, so in Jos. 3[3f.] (D), the ark precedes the Israelites and acts as their guide along an unknown route; but there it is borne by "the priests, the Levites." Here, if we may judge from so fragmentary a record, it is conceived of as moving by itself: cp. 1 S. 5 f., especially 5[11] 6[9ff.], 2 S. 6[5]. The pillar of cloud is certainly thought to move of itself (*e.g.* Ex. 13[21f.]). Like the cloud, the ark moves because it is the form in which Yahweh accompanies the people. With the conception of Yahweh's going before the people, cp. Ašur-nâṣir-abal's account of the god Nergal—"With the exalted help of Nergal, *who went before*

* Di., Kit. (*Gesch.* 181 n. 5), Sayce (*Early Hist. of the Hebrews*, p. 213 f.).

me (*Nirgal a-lik pa-ni-a*), I fought against them."*—*The ark of the covenant of Yahweh*] (ארון ברית י"י) P's phrase is different (ארון העדות). The present phrase is most characteristic of Deuteronomic writers (*e.g.* Dt. 10^{8} $31^{9.\ 25f.}$, 1 K. 6^{19}), and in passages like this, derived from J or E, the word ברית may be redactorial.†—*To seek out for them a resting-place*] cp. Dt. 1^{33}, Ex. 33^{14}. On תור = "to seek out," see 13^{2}, phil. n. —**34.** The v. coheres very loosely with the preceding. After v.[33] we expect a statement of the place reached after the three days' journey: cp. Ex. $15^{22f.}$. This is not given, though in $11^{1.\ 4}$ previous arrival at a definite place is assumed.—*The cloud of Yahweh*] only here, 14^{14} (R), and Ex. 40^{38}.—*Was upon them*] The idea is not that of J (nor of E), whose cloud precedes the people (Ex. $13^{21f.}$); nor quite the same as that of P^{g}, with whom the cloud rests over the tabernacle (10^{11}).—**35.** *When the ark started, Moses said*] Here, as in v.[33], the ark starts of itself, and the words which follow may be taken as addressed to it. The ark is the visible form in or by which Yahweh manifests His presence, and may therefore, like the angel of Yahweh, be addressed as Yahweh. It would be futile to attempt to date the two sayings; they have the savour of antiquity about them, and may have originated at any time subsequent to the growth of the national consciousness of union through Yahweh, except that the second seems to imply an already existing settled life in Canaan.

> Arise, Yahweh! that Thine enemies may be scattered,
> That they that hate Thee may flee before Thee.

The cry reflects the old Hebrew thought of Yahweh as a God of battles (cp. 21^{14} n.); Yahweh "arose" when He gave His people victory: cp. Is. 28^{21} in its reference to 2 S. $5^{20.\ 25}$. For the ark in battle, cp. 1 S. $4^{3ff.}$; with the second clause, Jud. 5^{31a}. The cry is repeated in Ps. $68^{2\,(1)}$, and is referred to in Ps. 132^{8}, which so modifies the form of the vocative as clearly to distinguish the ark from Yahweh.—**36.** *And when*

* Annal. Inscription, col. ii. l. 27 f.; cp. ll. 26, 50; iii. 52 = *KB.* i. pp. 74, 78, 104; see, further, Del. *Assyr. Handwörterbuch*, 531*a*.

† Cp. Cheyne in *EBi.* 300 f.; Seyring in *ZATW.* 1891, 114–125.

it came to rest] v.[33] n.—*He used to say*] The verb is frequentative.—*Return Yahweh to the ten thousand families of Israel*] an address to the ark returning from victory, and a prayer that Yahweh may dwell again undisturbed with His people. Such words could be suitably addressed to the ark returning from battle to its fixed sanctuary, whether Shiloh, Nob, or some other place, after the people were settled in Canaan. It is less clearly suitable to the circumstances of the march through the wilderness; the people overtake the ark, the ark does not return to them; Yahweh is regarded as being with them on the march as well as in the camp.—*Families*] lit. "thousands" (אלפי); here used of a division of a tribe (cp. n. on 1^{16}) rather than numerically.

Del. (*Zeitschr. f. kirchliche Wissenschaft*, 1882, p. 234) cites the *Return* of Ps. 90^{13} ("the prayer of Moses") as a parallel to the present "Mosaic" verse, and compares also the same cry in the Davidic Psalms, 6^5 7^8, and, further, the *arise* of v.[35] with Ps. 3^8 7^7; but though the words are the same, the conceptions they express in the Psalms are very different.—**29.** חתן] regularly means "father-in-law." In Ar. خَتَن is used not only of the father-in-law, but also of other relatives of the wife. So some here render "brother-in-law" or "relative," making the phrase qualify חבב; so also in Jud. 1^{16} 4^{11}; cp. Moore, *Judges*, p. 33. On the etymology of חתן = "circumciser," see BDB. *s.v.* חתן and the literature there cited.—**31.** כי על כן] Gn. 18^5 19^8 33^{10} 38^{26} (J); also Nu. 14^{43}, Jud. 6^{22}, 2 S. 18^{20} (*K're*), Jer. 29^{28} 38^4; see BDB. p. 475*b*; Kön. iii. 373*e*. —**35.** 𝔊 inserts כל before משנאיך and omits מפניך.—**36.** ובנחה] G.-K. 91*e*.—שובה] is followed by an acc. of direction (G.-K. 118*df*). Others consider שובה trans. (𝔊; Kön. iii. 210 f.). But the use of שוב as a trans. vb. is almost confined to the phrase שוב שבית; and, as Del. (p. 233) points out, "Bring back the ten thousand families of Israel," would give a saying more suited to the march out than to the return home.—For various views of the inverted *nuns* within which v.[35f.] (like Ps. $107^{23-28.\,40}$) are enclosed, see Del. p. 230 f.

XI. XII. *Incidents between Sinai and Ḳadesh* (JE).

The four incidents related in these chapters are referred by the editor who has given them their present position to the march from Sinai ($10^{12.\,33}$) to Paran or Ḳadesh (10^{12} 12^{16} $13^{3.\,26}$). These incidents are (1) the destruction of murmurers at Tab'erah, 11^{1-3}; (2) the lust for flesh, $11^{4-10.\,13.\,18-24a.\,31-34}$; (3) the resting of the spirit of prophecy on seventy elders and also on Eldad and Medad, $11^{16.\,17a.\,24b-30}$; (4) the vindication of Moses' uniqueness against the criticism of Aaron and Miriam, 12^{1-15}. In $11^{11f. 14f. 17b}$ we probably have matter not originally connected with any of the incidents.

Except for a clause or two of his own (11^{17b} 12^{16}), the entire matter of these chapters was drawn by the editor from JE, but with some difference of arrangement and setting.

The entire absence of all traces of P's style (on למשפחתיו in 11^{10} see n. below), together with abundant evidence of the style, motives, and ideas of JE (see margin in CH. and below), and the fact that P's story of manna and quails is preserved elsewhere (Ex. 16), have led to the practically unanimous assignment of these chapters in their entirety to JE. Kittel (*Gesch.* i. 198), exceptionally, finds possible traces of P in $11^{18-22. 24a-35}$. The reference to the wilderness of Paran in 12^{16} is rather an editorial link between 10^{12} and 13^{3} than a direct citation from P.

The present fusion of the second and third incidents may have been effected by the compiler of JE or later, but that they once existed apart will hardly be doubted once they have been read separately (see p. 101 ff.). But if so the original connection of the third incident with Ḳibroth-hatta'avah becomes uncertain. Like the fourth incident, it is not, taken by itself, connected with any place, and we cannot be sure that the present position of either incident in the narrative goes back further than the editor who united P and JE. Bacon refers both incidents to E's account of the stay at Sinai (*Triple Tradition*, 141 ff., 336–338), in which they formed an immediate sequence to Ex. 33^{7-11}. It is probable, too, that v.$^{11f. 14f.}$ also formed part of JE's account of the stay at Sinai (see below). On the other hand, the editor follows tradition in placing the gift of (manna and) quails after leaving Sinai; for though the parallel story in Ex. 16 is placed before the arrival at Sinai, it still in itself clearly presupposes the events at Sinai (see, *e.g.*, CH. on Ex. 16). There being no reason for suspecting the contrary, we may suppose that the incident at Tab'erah is here in its right position.

The analysis of c. 11 f. as between J and E, though much discussed, still remains to some extent uncertain and tentative. The third and fourth of the above mentioned incidents ($11^{16. 17a. 24b-30}$ and 12^{1-15}) are connected with Ex. 33^{7-11} (E) by the view taken of the theophanic cloud and the position of the tent (see below on $11^{25. 26. 30}$ $12^{4f.}$); in c. 12 further indications of E are the conception of revelation (see on 12^{6}) and the prominence of Miriam (cp. Ex. $15^{20f.}$ 2^{1-10} E). In $11^{16.\ 17a.\ 24b-30}$ the part played by Joshua (see on 11^{28}) and the stress laid on prophecy (cp. c. 12) point to E. In the main, therefore, these two incidents may well be before us not only as they lay in JE, but even earlier in E (so Bacon and, so far as c. 12 is concerned, Kit. Dr.). Some (Kue. CH.) refer them to E^s on the ground of the "advanced reflexion on the phases of prophetic activity" contained in them (but see below on 11^{29}); We., too, does not derive them from the main stratum of either J or E. Di. finds traces of J in c. 12, and analyses 11^{11-35} peculiarly. As to the rest of these chapters, such slight evidence as there is favours referring 11^{1-3} to E (Kue. Di. Kit. Bacon, CH.), while in the main at least the story of the manna and quails together with $11^{11f.\ 14f.}$ seems derived from J (Bacon, CH.: earlier critics, *e.g.* Kue. We. Di., less definitely or with modifications). The purely linguistic data are indecisive; much turns on interpretation and relation to other passages, the origin of which is also often doubtful. See We. *Comp.* 101 f., 323–327; Kuen. in *Th. Tijd.* 1880, 281–302 (= *Ges. Abh.*, ed. Budde, 276–294); and *Hex.* 139, 155, 241, 244, 247; Kit. *Gesch.* i. 182, 191; Bacon, *Triple Tradition*, 80–87, 168 f.; Moore in *EBi.* 3440; Di. and CH.

XI. 1–3. Tab'erah.—The story, probably derived from E (see on v.[2]), records a divine judgment. The people murmur on account, no doubt, of some hardship described in the introduction to the story which has not been reproduced here. The fire of Yahweh breaks out among them, and, notwithstanding Moses' supplication, burns (*b'r*) enough of the people to justify naming the place *Tab'ērah* (= "Burning").—1. *The people were as those complaining of misfortune*] רע = "misfortune" is the antithesis of טוב = "good fortune, prosperity"; cp. v.[29] n.; see 1 K. 22^{8}, Job 2^{10}. The complaints of the people were loud, and reached the ears of Yahweh, and roused His anger.—*The fire of Yahweh*] the ultimate physical cause of the conception of the fire that indicated Yahweh's presence or executed His judgments may have been the lightning (cp. Ex. $9^{23f.}$) or other electrical phenomena (cp. "Bush," § 2 in *EBi.*). In Job 1^{16}, 2 K. 1^{10} possibly nothing more than lightning is in the writer's mind; but here and often something much more terrific and destructive is thought of—a fire that, unlike lightning, does not always burst out from the sky: cp. 16^{35}, Lev. 10^{2} (P), Ex. $19^{18ff.}$ (JE).—2. Through Moses' intercession the judgment is arrested now as at other times (21^{7}, Dt. $9^{20.\ 26}$; cp. also below $12^{13f.}$). The effectiveness of prophetic intercession plays a conspicuous part in E's story of Abraham and Abimelech (Gn. 20[7. 17]). The term התפלל is confined in the Hexateuch to the parallels just cited.—3. The name Tabʿerah is probably enough in reality older than the story and its cause. The place is mentioned only once elsewhere (Dt. 9[22]), and then in connection with Massah and Ḳibroth-hatta'avah. The site is unknown, and the story is too loosely connected with the rest of the narrative to afford much clue for identifying it.

1. ויהי . . . כמתאננים] Kön. iii. 338δ; BDB. *226a*, 454*a*. התאנן also Lam. 3[29]†.—באזני] some MSS. בעיני: cp. 𝔊 𝔖 𝔗O Jon.—ויחר אפו] v.[10. 33] 12[9] 22[22] and often; characteristic of JE: CH. 233; ct. היה קצף, קצף (P), *e.g.* 1[53] 18[5] 16[22]; CH. 178.—ותאכל בקצה] the ב is partitive; BDB. *s.v.* ב, i. *2b*.—ותשקע] שקע here only in Hex.

4–6. The lust for flesh.—After eliminating from 11[4-35] the story of the seventy elders (v.[16f. 24b-30]) and also v.[11f. 14f.] we have left a story, almost intact, of the lust of the people for flesh, and its punishment. Sick of the long diet of manna, v.[6b], they recall the succulent fare of Egypt, v.[5], and, led on by the mixed multitude among them, petulently demand flesh, v.[4]. Moses incredulously asks Yahweh how he is to procure the people flesh, v.[13]. Yahweh bids Moses tell the people they shall have flesh for a whole month, till, in fact, they get to loathe it, v.[18-20]. Moses remains incredulous, but, rebuked by Yahweh, communicates the message to the people, v.[21-24a]. Yahweh by means of a wind brings up immense quantities of quails from the sea; the people fall greedily on them, but before the supply is exhausted, they are plagued by Yahweh: the burying of the people who fell in the plague gave the scene of the divine judgment the name of Ḳibroth-hatta'avah = "the graves of lust," v.[31-35].

The reference to the manna in v.[6] is followed by a parenthetic description of the manna and the modes of preparing it, v.[7-9]. Such a parenthesis may be due to the author of the main story, or inserted by an editor. It does not seriously affect the unity of the story itself. The main reason adduced by those who question this is the difference between the actual plague, v.[33], and the warning, v[20].

As compared with Ex. 16, to which, in so far as it refers

to both manna and quails, the present story is parallel, there are these marked differences: in Ex. 16 the manna, here the quails, are most prominent; in Ex. 16 manna and quails are represented as both given at the same time, here quails are first given after the people have been so long familiar with the manna as to have grown weary of it; in Ex. 16 the story issues in no judgment, here the judgment, which gives its name to the scene, may be regarded as the ultimate motive of the story (cp. v.[1-3]).

It is generally admitted that Ex. 16 is most largely derived from P, and the present story entirely from JE. But Kue.'s able discussion (*Manna en Kwakkelen* in *Th. Tijd.* xiv. 281–302 = *Abhandlungen* (Budde), 276–294) fails, in its main thesis, to sustain the criticism of Wellhausen (*Comp.* 323–327), who argued that there must have been a reference to manna in JE before our present passage, and that there are other elements than P in Ex. 16. At the same time there is much in Kue.'s argument that the full description of v.[7-9] belongs to a first reference; we might add—or, as an alternative, to a glossator. Its presence here may therefore be due to an editor who composed it freely on the basis of tradition, or transferred it from the account in JE of the first giving of the manna. Between such alternatives style hardly suffices to decide. So, too, even if the difference between v.[20] and v.[33] seem to indicate the presence of two sources (J and E) in the story, it is impossible to carry the analysis through in detail. In the main the evidence points to J. So Bacon, CH.; Di. Kit. refer v.[7-9. 31-35] to E. See further references cited on p. 99.

The story of the lust for flesh, disentangled from the foreign matter with which it has been encumbered, runs as follows:—

[4] And the mixed multitude that was among them fell a lusting: and the children of Israel also wept again, and said, O that we had flesh to eat! [5] We remember the fish, which we were wont to eat in Egypt for nought; the cucumbers, and the melons, and the leeks, and the onions, and the garlick: [6] but now our soul is dried away: there is nothing at all: we have nought save this manna to look to.* [10] And Moses heard the people weeping throughout their families, every man at the door of his tent: [13] [and he cried unto Yahweh, saying,] Whence should I have flesh to give unto all this people? for they trouble me with their weeping, saying, Give us flesh, that we may eat. [14] And the anger of Yahweh was kindled greatly: [18] and [He said unto Moses], Say thou unto the people, Sanctify yourselves against to-morrow, and ye shall eat flesh: for ye have wept in the ears of Yahweh, saying, O! that we had flesh to eat! for it was well with us in Egypt: therefore Yahweh will give you

* Here v.[7-9] may have been inserted parenthetically by the original writer. See above.

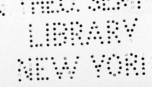

flesh, and ye shall eat. [19] Ye shall not eat one day, nor two days, nor five days, neither ten days, nor twenty days; [20] but a whole month, until it come out at your nostrils, and it be loathsome unto you: because that ye have rejected Yahweh who is among you, and have wept before Him, saying, Why came we forth out of Egypt? [21] And Moses said, The people, among whom I am, are six hundred thousand footmen; and yet Thou hast said, I will give them flesh, that they may eat a whole month. [22] Can flocks and herds be slain for them, to suffice them? or can all the fish of the sea be gathered together for them, to suffice them? [23] And Yahweh said unto Moses, Is Yahweh's hand waxed short? now shalt thou see whether My word fall in with thee or not. [24] And Moses went out, and told the people the words of Yahweh. [31] And there set forth a wind from Yahweh, and brought across quails from the sea, and let them fall by the camp, about a day's journey on this side, and a day's journey on the other side, round about the camp, and about two cubits above the face of the earth. [32] And the people rose up all that day, and all the night, and all the next day, and gathered the quails; he that gathered least gathered ten ḥomers; and they spread them all abroad for themselves round about the camp. [33] While the flesh was yet between their teeth, ere it ran short, the anger of Yahweh grew hot against the people, and Yahweh smote the people with a very great slaughter. [34] And the name of that place was called Ḳibroth-hatta'avah (= "graves of lust"), for there they buried the people that lusted.

4. Neither the departure from Tabʿerah ($v.^{1-3}$), nor the arrival at Ḳibroth-hatta'avah is mentioned. Hence some,* failing to recognise the fragmentary nature of the stories, and the lack of connection between them, have inferred that both names attached to a single place. Cheyne (*EBi.* 2660), on other grounds, comes to much the same conclusion, assuming Ḳibroth-hatta'avah to be a corruption of Ḳibroth-tabʿerah.—*The mixed multitude*] or rabble (והאספסף), who, according to Ex. 12^{38} (J), where they are called by another name (ערב), accompanied the Israelites out of Egypt.—*They fell a lusting*] Ps 106^{14} $78^{29f.}$. The vb. and noun (התאוו תאוה), though mainly used of the appetites, commonly refer to perfectly legitimate excitement of the appetite; see, *e.g.*, Dt. 12^{20} 14^{26}.—*And the children of Israel again wept*] No previous *weeping* (cp. 14^{1}) has been mentioned; but the word need not be pressed. Previous stories of complaints are Ex. 15^{23-25} (J), 17^{2-7} (mainly E). "Again" may refer to one of these, or to $v.^{1-3}$; the word is possibly, but not necessarily, editorial.—*O that we had flesh to eat*] Rashi already perceived

* Keil.

a difficulty here which critical analysis has not yet completely explained. Why should a people rich in flocks (Ex. 12^{38} 17^{3} 19^{13} 34^{3}, Nu 14^{33} 32^{1}) cry out for flesh? Why should Moses, in the midst of a people provided with flocks and herds, feel the difficulty which he expresses in v.^{22}? Clearly the present story goes back to a cycle which did not credit the Israelites with flocks in the wilderness; but whether this point of view was maintained throughout either E or J is doubtful; the above references are not clearly confined to one of these two main sources of JE.—**5.** It is curious that though the people cry out for flesh, their happy memories of Egyptian fare are chiefly of the vegetables.—*The fish which we were wont to eat for nought*] "The quantity of fish in Egypt was a very great boon to the poor classes. . . . The canals, ponds, and pools on the low lands continued to abound in fish even after the inundation ceased." * Another OT. writer shows himself familiar with the conspicuous part played by fish and fishermen in Egyptian life (Is. 19^{8-10}). In later times fish was exported from Egypt to Palestine (Schürer,[3] ii. 57; Eng. tr. II. i. 42 f.). —*The cucumbers*] (קִשֻּׁאִים) the philologically cognate Arabic (قِثَّاء) is the name of the long and slender *Cucumis chate*, L., a variety of the melon which is native to Egypt, and widely cultivated there.—*The melons*] (אבטחים) water-melons (still called بطّيخ), *Cucumis citrullus*, L., are represented on ancient Egyptian monuments, and much cultivated and consumed by the modern Egyptians. They are frequently mentioned in the Mishna (Levy, *s.v.* אבטיח), but here only in OT.—*The leeks*] חציר ("grass") here, but here only in OT., means, as it sometimes does in Aram., "leeks," and specifically, perhaps, *Allium porrum*, L. Pliny (*HN.* 19^{33}) refers to the fame of Egyptian leeks.—*The onions*] Herod. (ii. 125), speaking of the pyramid, says that on it was declared "how much was spent on radishes and onions and leeks for the workmen."

* Wilkinson, *Pop. Account of the Ancient Egyptians*, ii. 193 (see also 181, 186–194). Cp. Seetzen, *Reisen*, iii. 274–276, 497 f.; and among the classical writers, Herod. ii. 92 f.

Hasselquist (p. 562), as cited by Di., says "the Egyptian onions are very mild and agreeable, better than in all other countries: therefore they are much grown in Egypt, and form a favourite dish with all classes, and a common diet especially of the poorer classes."—*The garlic*] (שׁוּמִים) Löw identifies the Aram. שום with *Allium sativum*, L., which is still cultivated in Egypt.

For further details and references, see Ges. *Thes.*, Ges.-Buhl, and BDB. under the several words; the relevant articles in *EBi.* and *NDB.*; also *EBi.* col. 1541 f. Löw, *Aram. Pflanzennamen*, Nos. 278, 169, 336; Seetzen, *Reisen*, iii. pp. 233 (cucumbers), 158, 209, and especially 350 (melons), 158 (onions); and Di. on the present passage.

It will thus be seen that we have here a very vivid and true picture of Egyptian life; and, in particular, of the life of the lower orders.

Speaking of these in his *Modern Egyptians* (c. vii.), Lane describes their food as consisting chiefly of "bread (made of millet or of maize), milk, new cheese, eggs, small salted fish, cucumbers and melons, and gourds of a great variety of kinds, onions and leeks, beans, chick-peas, lupins, the fruit of the black egg-plant, lentils, etc., dates (both fresh and dried), and pickles," and remarks, "It is surprising to observe how simple and poor is the diet of the Egyptian peasantry, and yet how robust and healthy most of them are, and how severe is the labour which they can undergo."

Of the sources of the Hexateuch it is elsewhere E that is particularly characterised by acquaintance with Egyptian life: cp. Dr. *L.O.T.* 118.—6. For lack of the succulent foods of Egypt, the people's *soul* or appetite is *dried up*; nor have they any prospect of other food than the manna, of the very sight of which they have grown sick.—*Our soul is dried up*] cp. "his soul is empty," *i.e.* he is hungry (Is. 29[8]); "to satisfy (lit. to fill) his soul," *i.e.* to stay his hunger (Pr. 6[30]); "a man given to appetite," lit. "a possessor of soul" (Pr. 23[2]).

4. [וְהָאסַפְסֻף] for וְהָאֲסַפְסֻף: G.-K. 35*d*; on the rare noun-form, see Barth, 147 γ.—[בקרבו] singular suffixes or verbs are found also in v.[10. 12. 21]; pl. suffixes or verbs (following the subj.) in v.[7-9. 13. 18-20. 21b. 22. 31. 34]. The sing. here after the כם of v.[3], without an intervening use of the noun, may indicate that v.[4] is not the original sequence of v.[3]. Perhaps v.[4] was originally preceded by a sentence such as this ויסע העם מ . . . ויחן בקברת

התאוה.—**5.** חנם] = "for nothing"; Gn. 29^{15} (E), Ex. $21^{2.\ 11}$, and nowhere else in Hex.—את הקשאים] 𝔊 𝔖 'ואת הק.—**6.** בלתי] as conj. Gn. $43^{3.\ 5}$ (J), Is. 10^{4}† (BDB. 116*b*); "*save that* our eyes are unto this manna."—אל המן עינינו] for the idiom, cp. Ps. 33^{18} 34^{16} 123^{2} and the n. pr. **אליהועיני.**

7–9. A parenthetic account of the manna and the modes of preparing it, inserted between the complaint of the people, v.[6], and the statement that Moses overheard it, v.[10]. Taken by itself the present account does not suggest that the manna was miraculously provided — the prevalent view elsewhere (Ex. 16, Dt. $8^{3.\ 16}$, Neh. $9^{15.\ 20}$, Ps. 78^{23-25} 105^{40}). The writer speaks of it as a natural product of the desert; and it is probable that he had in mind some of the "mannas" described by modern travellers in Sinai and Arabia, such as the sweet-tasting, dirty-yellowish exudation of the *Tamarix gallica*, L., which, exuded by night during the season (June and July), falls to the ground and is melted by the heat of the sun during the day; or the edible lichen (*Lecanora esculenta*, Everson), greyish yellow without, white within, which, in parts of S.W. Asia, is used instead of corn in years of famine.* Certainly no natural mannas are produced in sufficient quantities to support the multitudes contemplated in the narrative. But if the manna in this story is rightly interpreted as a natural, in Ex. 16 as a supernatural, food, we have parallels for the difference in the story of the passage of the Red Sea which, in one account, was rendered possible by the natural action of wind (Ex. 14^{21b} J), in others by the miraculous influence of Moses' rod (Ex. $14^{16a.\ 31}$ E) or hand (Ex. $14^{16b.\ 18.\ 19.\ 22b.\ 23}$ P); and in the staying of the people's thirst by natural wells to which they were led according to one account (Ex. 15^{27} J), by water brought miraculously from a rock according to others (Ex. $17^{1b.\ 2.\ 4-7}$ E; Nu $20^{7f.}$ P).—**7.** *Like coriander seed*] Ex. 16^{31}.—*Bdellium*] it is probable that the Hebrew בדלח (Gn. 2^{12} †) is rightly rendered thus. Bdellium is a resinous substance, transparent, gelatinous, and commonly yellowish in colour. In Ex. 16^{31} manna is said to be white; and Josephus, though he also retains the comparison with bdel-

* The above details are taken from *EBi.* "Manna." See, further, the Commentaries on Ex. 16, especially Di. (176 f.).

lium, exaggerates this, saying the people would have mistaken the manna for snow had not Moses warned them it was food (*Ant.* iii. 1^{6}). Both the biblical descriptions of the colour are justified by one or other of the modern "mannas" referred to above.—8. *And they used to grind it between the mill-stones or pound it in a mortar*] the exuded juice of the tamarisk is never hard enough for such treatment. Seetzen (*Reisen*, iii. 78) suggests that the Hebrew description is drawn partly from this, partly from the very nutritious gum of the *Mimosa nilotica*, L., which is exuded at the same time of year and is found in the same places.—*And boil it*] Ex. 16^{23}.—*And make it into cakes*] the process is differently expressed in Ex. 16^{23} (bake); cakes (עֻגוֹת) are mentioned elsewhere in the Hexateuch only in Gn. 18^{6}, Ex. 12^{39} (J).—*Its taste was like that of a dainty prepared with oil*] the precise meaning of the phrase is not quite certain: see phil. n. Seetzen (*Reisen*, iii. 76) records that at St. Catherine's convent the "manna" was used as "a dainty instead of honey." In Ex 16^{31} the taste is compared to wafers made with honey.—9. The coming of the manna by night is similarly described, though in very different words, in Ex. $16^{13f.}$.—10. Resumes v.$^{4-6}$. The whole v. in its present connection must mean that Yahweh was angry (cp. v.$^{1.\,33}$) with the people, and that His anger displeased Moses, who expresses his displeasure in v.$^{11f.}$. But *Yahweh's* anger, v.^{10b}, is not the natural sequel to *Moses'* overhearing the people's weeping, v.^{10a}; v.$^{11f.}$ appears to have found its way into the present story from a very different context (see below). Possibly the clause, "and Yahweh was angry," has moved to its present position from after v.^{6} (Di.) or v.^{13} (Bacon), and so caused some change in the last clause.

7. וְרַע] G.-K. 93*h*.—עין] = "appearance"; cp. Lev. 13^{55}.—בדלח] the rendering bdellium rested till recently on Josephus and the later Greek VV. (cp. Field's *Hexapla* on Gn. 2^{12} and Nu. 11^{5}), but Peiser has now adduced evidence from Babylonian contract tablets in favour of such an interpretation: a word meaning "spicery" is probably to be transliterated *bid-li-ḥ* = בדלח; *ZATW.*, 1897, p. 347 f.—8. שטו . . . ולקטו] Dr. *Tenses*, 114*a*.—לְשַׁד] cp. לְשַׁדִּי apparently = "my sap or life-juice," Ps 32^{4}. لسد, which appears to be but rarely used, is "to suck." The word, therefore, remains of somewhat uncertain and obscure meaning. VV.

give the whole phrase a meaning similar to that suggested above, *e.g.* 𝔊 ἐνυκρὶς ἐξ ἐλαίου, 𝔙 *panis oleatus*. On Aq. and Symm., see Field, *Hexapla*, i. 237. — **10.** למשפחתיו] the *frequent* use of this phrase (yet not with the sing. suffix) is characteristic of P. Either this is an isolated use in an earlier writer (cp. Dr. *L.O.T.* 132), or redactorial (cp. Kue. *Hex.* 323).

11–15. Moses expostulates with Yahweh.—In v.[13] Moses is asking how he is to satisfy the people's cry for bread, and the answer is given in v.[18ff.]. But the connection of v.[11f. 14f.] with the context is very imperfect. In these vv. Moses complains to Yahweh that he cannot unaided lead the people to Canaan, that he would rather die than make the attempt, and that, since Israel owes its existence to Yahweh, it is on Him and not on His servant that the burden should rest. All this has nothing to do with the story of the quails, nor probably with the temporary effect of the spirit on the seventy elders, though at present these elders are represented in v.[17b] as appointed to share the burden with Moses. On the other hand, the verses in question (v.[11f. 14f.]) fall excellently into place after Ex. 23[1-3] where Yahweh bids Moses lead the people to Canaan, but refuses Himself to go with them. They appear to have been transferred here by the editor who united the stories of the quails and the elders.*

11. Moses expostulates with Yahweh for placing on him the whole trouble and burden of the people (Ex. 33[1-3]).—*Wherefore hast Thou evil entreated?*] why hast Thou injured me, or made my lot so hard? (cp. Gn. 19[9] 43[6]). The verb (הרע) is the antithesis (cp. Jos. 24[20]) of היטיב = "to be a source of good fortune to" (10[29] n.); for another instance with Yahweh as subj., see Ex. 5[22]. — *Thy servant*] this periphrasis for the personal pronoun is specially characteristic of J; see, *e.g.*, Gn. 18[3. 5]; cp. CH. 73.—*Why have I not found favour in Thy sight*] v.[15]; this phrase (מצא חן בעיני) is also characteristic of J (CH. 31); see, *e.g.*, Gn. 6[8] 18[3] and, in what appears to have been the original context of the present passage, Ex. 33[12. 13. 16].—*The*

* So Bacon, to whose discussions (*JBLit.* xii. 38–40, 45 f.; *Triple Tradition*, 139–150, 168) reference must be made for further arguments, and in whose translation (p. 299) the vv. will be found in what is presumably their original context.

burden of all this people] the task of leading the people unaided to Canaan (v.^{12b}) had been imposed by Yahweh on Moses (Ex. 33^{1-3}), but after this expostulation Yahweh promises that His "Face" shall accompany Moses (Ex. 33^{12-16}).—**12.** *Have I conceived*, etc.] the pronoun is emphatic; Yahweh, not Moses, brought Israel into being. Israel is, therefore, Yahweh's people (Ex. 33^{13}). Here, as in Ex. $4^{22f.}$, Dt. 32^{18}, Hos. 11^{1}, and, very probably, in Ps. 2^{7}, the whole nation is regarded as Yahweh's son.—*Carry it in thy bosom*] cp. Is. 40^{11} and, with a different word, 49^{22}. — *A nursing-father*] the nursing- or foster-parent played an important part in the wealthier Hebrew families (2 K. $10^{1.5}$ where RV. renders הָאֹמְנִים by "they that brought up"). They are mentioned in another figurative passage, Is. 49^{23}. If, as some* think, the nurse rather than the foster-father should be mentioned in connection with the "suckling," it is easy to read here הָאֹמֶנֶת (cp. Ru. 4^{16}, 2 S. 4^{4}). — *Unto the land which Thou swearest*, etc.] Moses takes up Yahweh's words in Ex. 33^{1}; the words for "land" in the two passages are, however, different (here אדמה, there ארץ).—**13.** Whence is Moses to obtain flesh to satisfy the people's cry? The verse continues, though not quite immediately, v.^{10}. An introductory clause at least has been suppressed in favour of v.$^{12f.}$; and the immediate continuation of v.^{13} has given place to v.$^{14-17}$. The answer of Yahweh to the question of Moses in v.^{13} stands in v.^{18}; it was, perhaps, originally preceded by a statement of Yahweh's anger at Moses' report about the people which has now been shifted further back to v.^{10b}.—*For they trouble me with their weeping*] בכה על, as Jud. $14^{16f.}$.—*Give us flesh, that we way eat*] תנה לנו בשר ונאכלה; cp. Ex. 17^{2} (E) תנו (𝔊 תנה) לנו מים ונשתה.—**14.** The v. is the immediate sequel, not to v.^{13} which it disregards, but to v.^{12}.—*I cannot by myself carry*] (לא אוכל . . . לשאת) Moses' reply to Yahweh's command (Ex. 33^{1-3}), which has been paraphrased by Moses in the words (v.^{12}), "Carry it (שאהו) in thy bosom." The people are too heavy for Moses. The different renderings in RV. of the same verb (נשא) in v.^{12} and v.^{14} obscure the original connection, though they may do

* Nowack, *Arch.* i. 171 f.; Kön. iii. 299*h*.

justice to the editor's meaning: cp. v.^{17b} n.—**15.** Rather let Yahweh, if He has any regard for Moses, kill him and have done with it (חרגני הרוג, Dav. 67*c*), than insist on his carrying the people alone; for similar requests for death, see Ex 32^{32}, 1 K 19^{4}, Jon. 4^{3}, Job 3.—*Let me not look upon my wretchedness*] let me not continue to experience the unendurable toil and trouble of what in such a case must be my hard lot (רעה: cp. חרע v.^{11} n.). ראה ב, which expresses far more than the simple "see" of RV. (cp. 12^{2} n.), is used somewhat similarly in Gn. 21^{16} 44^{34}.—The terms of Yahweh's reply can be gathered from Ex. 33^{12b}, where Yahweh assures Moses that he has found favour, and shall not carry the people alone; the continuation of the argument is to be found in Ex. 33^{12-16}.

11. מצתי]=מצאתי; G.-K. 74*k*.—משא כל העם] 𝔊 and some MSS. of 𝔍 om. כל; 𝔖 כל משא העם.—**12.** הוה] Peculiar to JE in the Hex. and specially characteristic of J; CH. 21 (J 22 times; E 4 times).—יְלִדְתִּיהוּ] For the punctuation, see G.-K. 69*s*.—**14.** 𝔊 omits כל and paraphrases the last clause wrongly under the influence of Ex. 18^{18}.—**15.** אַתְּ] so Dt $5^{24\ (27)}$, Ezek. 28^{14}. Masc. forms have also survived from the earlier consonantal text elsewhere (*e.g.* 1 S. 24^{19}), but have then been correctly pointed אַתָּה. Cp. BDB. 61*b*; Kön. iii. 8.

16, 17a. Yahweh promises a portion of the Spirit to seventy elders (E).—These vv. are separated from their immediate sequel, v.$^{24b-30}$; in E they may have followed immediately on Ex. 33^{7-11}, and the whole story may have immediately preceded that now found below in c. 12; cp. p. 98, above. In any case, the connection with v.$^{11-15}$ is very loose in spite of v.^{17b}. On the relation of the story to certain kindred narratives in Ex. 18 and 24, and on its general significance and motive, see small print n. following v.^{30}.

16. Moses is to assemble seventy men selected from the whole number of the elders of Israel at the tent of meeting. As in a parallel story (Ex. $24^{1\ (2).\ 9f.\ (11)}$), the manner and ground of selection are not stated.—*The elders of Israel*] the elders are the leading men of the various families (cp. Ex. $12^{21f.}$). They are very frequently referred to in early narratives (*e.g.* 1 S. 4^{3} 8^{4}, 2 S. 17^{15}), including the prophetic narratives of the Hexateuch (CH. 151^{JE}, 42^{D}).

In P they are rarely mentioned (Lev. 4^{15} 9^{1}, Jos. 20^{4}†); in that source the phrase is generally replaced by another—"the princes of the congregation of Israel" (or the like—CH. 131[r]). Benzinger's statement (*PRE.*[3] i. 224), that in the narrative of the march through the wilderness they are mentioned only in E and D, and never in J, is not justified by assured analytical results. On the general subject of the "elders," see Nowack, *Arch.* i. pp. 300 ff., 320 ff.; Benzinger, *Arch.* § 41–43, or *Aelteste* in *PRE.*[3]. For "collecting" (אסף) or "summoning" (קרא ל) the elders, see Ex. 3^{16} 4^{29} 12^{21} 19^{7}, Jos. 24^{1}.

Whom thou knowest to be . . . officers] To judge from the analogy of the sheikhs of the modern Bedāwin, the elders of the nomadic Hebrews were, as occasion required, leaders in war, ready with counsel, or arbitrators in disputes. The division of labour whereby some elders became judges, others military leaders, and others "officers," apparently belongs to the more complex conditions of settled life; and it may be only by an anachronism that it is here referred to the nomadic period of Hebrew history: cp. Nowack or Benzinger as just cited. What precisely is covered by the term "officers" (שטרים) is uncertain; etymologically it seems to mean "arranger" or "organiser" (Dr. *Deut.* p. 17); in Ex. 5 (JE) the persons so called are overseers, persons who have to see that the full task of work is performed; in some later passages they carry orders to the people (Jos. 1^{10} 3^{2}, Dt. $20^{5.\,8f.}$). In several Deuteronomic passages the term is used with several others ("elders," "heads," "judges"), the whole combination being apparently intended to exhaust the idea of leaders of the people. But whatever its precise significance, its presence here implies some already existing organisation of assistants to Moses in the government of the people. The institution of such assistants had been previously mentioned in the same source, if we are right in attributing the present story to E (see Ex. 18).—17a. *And I will come down and speak with thee*] *i.e.* will communicate with you in the manner described as customary in Ex. $33^{9.\,11}$ (E).—*And I will withdraw some of the spirit that is* now *upon thee, and put it upon them*] the spirit (הרוח) is conceived materially* and, as in 2 K. $2^{9f.}$, quantitatively. As in 24^{2}, Jud. 3^{10} 11^{29}, 1 S. 10^{6} 19^{20}, Is. 11^{2} 61^{1}, Ezek. 11^{5}, it is thought of as coming or resting *upon* (על) a

* Cp. Köberle, *Natur u. Geist nach der Auffassung des AT*, 184–186.

person. Moses possesses the spirit in large measure, so that he can spare enough to enable seventy others to prophesy for the nonce, v.[25f.]. One purpose of the narrative, common also to Ex. 33^{7-11} and c. 12 below, appears to be to enhance the superiority of Moses in virtue of his close relation to Yahweh. —17b. *And they shall assist thee in bearing the burden of the people, that thou bear it not alone*] It is difficult to believe that this clause does not presuppose and refer to v.[11–15], and yet the answer is only verbal and superficial. The point of Moses' argument in those vv. is that Yahweh Himself ought to bear at least part of the burden; this comes out most clearly when v.[11f. 14f.] are placed between Ex. 33^{1-3} and [12–16], but is sufficiently clear from v.[12] alone. So when Moses in v.[14] says I cannot bear this people alone, he means he cannot bear it without Yahweh's help. To this v.[17b], with its promise that Moses shall receive human assistance, is no genuine reply. The case is, of course, entirely different in Dt. 1^{9-18} (cp. Ex. 18), where Moses calls on the *people* to give him assistance, since, on account of their increasing numbers, he is *no longer* able to bear the burden of them alone. Further, though v.[24b. 25a] mentions point by point how the commands and promises of v.[16. 17a] were carried out and fulfilled, no further notice is taken of any assistance rendered to Moses; quite the reverse; v.[25b] gives the actual result of the spirit resting on the elders: and this result was that the elders received not the power of assisting Moses, but of prophesying. On both these grounds certainly, possibly also on the ground of the clause "whom . . . thou knowest to be officers" (v.[16] n.), we may judge v.[17b] to be an editorial clause designed to connect the three originally distinct elements brought together in this chapter. To the editor the "burden" in v.[17b] meant the same as in v.[11–15], the task more especially of providing the people with flesh. The connection with Ex. 18^{22} is merely verbal, and if v.[17b] be admitted to be editorial, it accounts for the difficulty which commentators have felt (without surmounting) in attempting to decide the difference between the functions of these elders and those appointed in Ex. 18.

16. אספה] G.-K. 48*i*.—שבעים איש מזקני] so v.^{24} (cp. v.^{25} n.); ct. שבעים מזקני Ex. 24$^{1.9}$.—והתיצבו] התיצב 17 times in Hex.; 13 JE, 4 D; see CH. 214^{JE}.—**17.** ואצלתי] the vb. is rare (v.^{25}, Gn. 27^{36}, Ezek. 42^{6}, Eccl. 2^{10}†), and in each case the context requires a slightly different sense: the nearest parallel to the present meaning is Ezek. 42^{6}; cp. BDB. S reads הצל and in v.^{25} ויצל; 𝔊 perhaps supports S here (ἀφελῶ; cp. ἀφαιρεῖν = הציל Gn. 31$^{9.16}$, Hos. 2^{11}); but the variant is scarcely right; the sense of הציל is too violent.—ונשאו ב] "they shall *bear in, i.e.* take part in bearing": so Ezek. 18^{20}; see BDB. 88*b*; Kön. iii. 84.

18. Cp. v.$^{4b.5}$. The story of the lust for flesh is resumed. In answer to Moses' incredulous question, v.^{13}, Yahweh promises that He will Himself provide the people with flesh. The opening words of this verse may have been modified from some such introductory formula as is found in Ex. 7^{16} 8^{1} 9^{1} and a connecting link between v.^{13} and v.^{18} has probably been suppressed by the editor in favour of v.$^{14-17}$.—*Sanctify yourselves*] make yourselves ceremonially clean by ablutions and abstention from women (Ex. 19$^{10.15}$), that ye may be fit to witness the special manifestation of Yahweh's power in the coming miraculous provision of flesh: cp. especially Jos. 3^{5}; also Ex. 19$^{10f.14ff.22}$, Jos. 7^{13} (all JE). Rashi explains: prepare yourselves for destruction; cp. Jer. 12^{3}.—*Against to-morrow*] a term frequently set (especially in J) for the fulfilment of a divine promise or command—Ex. 8$^{6.19.25\,(10.23.29)}$ 9$^{5.18}$ 10^{4}, Nu. 14^{25}, Jos. 3^{5} 7^{13} (all JE); Jud. 20^{28}, 1 S. 9^{16}; somewhat differently 16$^{7.16}$, Ex. 16^{23} (P). The fulfilment on the morrow (ממחרת) is sometimes recorded—17$^{23\,(8)}$ (P), Ex. 9^{6} (J). Ct. "the third day," Ex. 19^{11} (E).—*It was well with us in Egypt*] (טוב לנו): cp. 14^{3}, Ex. 14^{12}.—**19 f.** But though Yahweh promises to satisfy the people with flesh, He also warns them that as a punishment for their impious discontent they will be kept to the flesh diet till it becomes nauseous to them.—**20.** *Until it come out from your nostril*] this may refer to violent vomiting, or to the rejection of the smell of the flesh as repugnant, or to the repeated taste of food that has disagreed.—**21 f.** Moses doubts even Yahweh's power to provide sufficient food for such a multitude.—**21.** *Six hundred thousand*] Ex. 12^{37}: cp. p. 14, above.—*And yet Thou hast said*] the use and position of the pr. (אתה) gives the sentence an adversative force not brought out in RV.—**23.** Yahweh challenges Moses' incredulity: cp. Gn. 18^{14} (J).—The paragraph division of RV. is wrong; v.$^{23. 24a}$ closely connect with v.^{22}; the new paragraph should begin with v.^{24b} ("and he gathered").—*Is Yahweh's hand short?*] is His power small? cp. Is. 50^{2} 59^{1} and similar phrases with reference to men in 6^{21} (n.), Is. 37^{27}. The opposite idea of might is expressed by the "outstretched arm"; *e.g.* Dt. 4^{34}.—*Now shalt thou see whether My word fall in with thee or not*] a divine word was thought to possess a certain real and independent existence; once uttered, it pursued its own course (Is. 55^{11}): cp. the power attributed to spoken words of men (30^{3} n.).

18. ואל העם תאמר] 𝔖=ויאמר משה אל העם.—**20.** חדש ימים] Gn. 29^{14}† (J): cp. ירח ימים Dt. 21^{13}, and see BDB. *s.v.* יום 6*b*.—זרא] a copyist's error for זרה (S), or a gloss of a scribe familiar with Aramaic (cp. G.-K. 80*h*). The word is found in Sir. 39^{27} mrg., but nowhere else in OT. It seems to come from √זור = ذار = *fastidivit*, though Aq. εἰς ἀλλοτρίωσιν assumes זור = زار. Most of the VV. translate by a word denoting sickness or the like.—**22.** צאן ובקר] acc. with the pass.; see next clause; Dav. 79, 81, R. 3; G.-K. 121*a b*.—ומצא להם] Jud. 21^{14} and (in Niphal) Jos. 17^{16}, Zech. 10^{10}.

24b, 25. Yahweh places the Spirit on the seventy elders, and they prophesy.—V.$^{16. 17a}$ is here continued; the directions and promises there given are carried out and fulfilled.—*And Yahweh came down in the cloud*] to the tent where Moses and the elders were standing, v.^{24b}: cp. 12^{5}, Ex. 33^{9-11} (E). In E the appearance of this theophanic cloud (הענן, so also 12^{10}; עמוד (ה)ענן 12^{5}, Ex. $33^{9f.}$, Dt. 31^{15}) is intermittent; in P continuous after the completion of the tabernacle. In both E and P, as distinguished from J, it is regularly associated with the tabernacle; see *Pillar of Cloud* in *EBi.*—*They prophesied, but they did so no more*] the effect of the spirit resting on the elders was that they fell into prophetic frenzy, just as the messengers of Saul, and ultimately Saul himself, were overpowered by the spirit and made, even against their will, to prophesy, 1 S. 19^{20-24} 10^{10-13}; but the elders are only affected by this form of religious excitement on the present occasion, nor does the narrative (ct. v.^{17b}) relate that their reception of the spirit had any permanent effect on them; it simply relates that they returned with Moses to the camp, v.^{30}.

26–29. **Eldad and Medad.**—The spirit also rests on Eldad and Medad, who had been left in the camp when Moses and the elders went out to the tent, and they fall into the same prophetic frenzy. Nothing further is known of Eldad and Medad (or, as 𝔊 S perhaps rightly have it, Modad), nor does the latter name recur, though it seems identical with Mûdadi, which appears on ancient Babylonian contract tablets.* Eldad, a name of early type (*HPN.* 61, 192 n. 1), reappears under the form Elidad in 34^{21}. The assonance of the names may be paralleled by Jabal and Jubal (Gn. $4^{20f.}$), Gog and Magog (which in Arabic (Ḳoran, 21^{96}) become Yâjûj and Mâjûj), Hârût and Mârût (Ḳoran, 2^{96}). A pseudo-epigraphon, purporting to be a prophecy of Eldad and Medad, is cited in the *Shepherd of Hermas*, Vis. ii.—*Now they were among them that were registered*] this is generally understood to mean that Eldad and Medad were two of the seventy elders. But if the interpretation be correct, the clause seems in several respects at variance with the rest of the passage. Not only is nothing said of any registering of the seventy elders in v.$^{16f. 24f.}$, but v.^{24b} asserts that the seventy actually went out to the tent, and v.^{25} (present text) directly states that seventy there received the spirit. Further, Moses' rebuke of Joshua, v.^{29}, implies that Eldad and Medad did not belong to the number who had been promised the spirit. If the clause be original and not rather the note of a glossator (*EBi.* 1256), it would be better to understand by "the registered" the whole body of elders from whom the seventy were chosen, v.^{16}. The references to the registration or enrolment of persons are chiefly late—Neh. 12^{22}, 1 Ch. 4^{41} 24^{6}; cp. Jer. 22^{30} and, figuratively, Ex. 32^{32} Is. 4^{3}, Mal. 3^{16}, Ps. $69^{29\,(28)}$, Dn. 12^{1}, Enoch 47^{3} (see Charles' note for later allusions); but it would be unreasonable to deny that the practice of registration may have extended back to the 8th or 9th century, and that the original story here may have alluded to it. The mere linguistic evidence therefore does not prove the clause to be a late gloss.—*And they had not gone out to the tent*] Even more clearly than the opening clause of the v., this implies that the tent was outside

* Hommel, *Altisraelitische Ueberlieferung*, 75, 112 (Eng. tr. 76, 113).

the camp; such, too, is the implication of v.^{27} and v.^{30} (cp. $12^{14f.}$). The whole passage is thus connected with Ex. 33^{7-11} (E); ct. the entirely different point of view of P, who, possibly following J (14^{44} n.), makes the tent the centre of the camp (p. 16 ff.).—**27.** A young man brings Moses the news of the sudden outbreak of prophetic frenzy in Eldad and Medad; the bystanders were also astonished when Saul was similarly affected, 1 S. $10^{11f.}$.—**28.** Joshua begs Moses to stop them prophesying. He is jealous (v.^{29}) lest Moses should lose his pre-eminence if not only the seventy but others also manifest the spirit, and that, too, without appearing, like the seventy, to receive only the overplus of the spirit which had rested on Moses, v.^{25}.—*Joshua the servant of Moses*] Ex. 24^{13} 33^{11}, Jos. 1^{1}, cp. Ex. 32^{17}—probably all E. The presence of Joshua at the tent, though he was not one of the elders, needed no explanation if, as is probable (see above, p. 98), in the original source Ex. 33^{11} immediately preceded the present story.—*From his youth up*] or *since he was a young man*; cp. בחור in 1 S. 9^{2}. Others render the phrase "one of his young men," see phil. n.—**29.** Moses replies, Are you so deeply concerned to maintain my rights and honour (קִנֵּא: cp. $25^{11.13}$, 2 S. 21^{2}, 1 K. $19^{10.14}$) that you would have the number of the recipients of Yahweh's spirit limited? Nay, rather would that all Yahweh's people, elders or not, without the camp or within, might receive and manifest it. Moses has more at heart the good of the community as a whole than his own personal honour or continued pre-eminence; whatever obscurity rests on the interpretation of certain details of the story, this fine trait in Moses' character as conceived in early Israel stands out clearly.—The whole episode is an important illustration of the belief that Yahweh did not confine His gifts to particular persons or classes. In itself, it is true, the value set on the prophetic frenzy does not reveal a very advanced religious perception (ct. 1 Cor. 12–14). But the belief in the free range of the spirit, in the possibility of all men, irrespective of class or place, coming under its influence and so into close relation with God, is one of abiding value, and what it was capable of becoming may be seen in Jeremiah's great prophecy ($31^{33f.}$:

cp. Ezek. $11^{19f.}$). At the same time the present passage and Jeremiah's prophecy, so far from showing entirely the same standpoint, and needing on that ground to be regarded as of the same, or nearly the same, age,* are strikingly different. In thought, at least, Jeremiah is far in advance. For there is here no idea of that deep spiritual communion of man with God of which Jeremiah is thinking when he speaks of "the law in the inward parts" and of "the knowledge of God"; nor even of that direct speech of Yahweh which was granted to Moses (Ex. 33^{11}), but simply of that prophetic frenzy described in the narratives of Samuel, and represented there also as descending on men without regard to class or family; cp. especially the proverbial question with regard to persons who fell under the prophetic impulse—"And who is their father" (1 S. 10^{12}).—**30.** Moses and the elders return from the tent into the camp: cp. v.^{26} n.

The relation of the foregoing story of the seventy elders to Ex. 18 and 24^{1-11} has been much discussed. If it be admitted that, as argued above, v.^{17b} is editorial and not an original part of the story, then Ex. 18 and Nu. $11^{16. 17a. 24b-30}$ are not parallel accounts of the same incident; their motives are entirely different, and they may well have been successive incidents in the same source. Thus the fact that Ex. 18 is E is no reason for denying that the present story is from the same source. On the other hand, Nu. $11^{16. 17a. 24b-30}$ and Ex. 24^{1-11} do so far resemble one another that both are stories of seventy elders specially privileged; they may therefore represent variations from a common story whence come the rare vb. אצל of Nu. and the unique אציל (= "nobles") in Ex. 24^{11}. At the same time they are sufficiently unlike to have been included in the same (literary) source from the first, and it is best to consider their literary origin independently. The reference of the story of the elders in Ex. 24 to E would not invalidate, nor the reference of it to J greatly support the conclusion here accepted, that the present story of the elders is from E. For earlier analyses of Ex. 24^{1-11} see Holzinger; for later, Bacon, CH., who assign Ex. $24^{1f. 9-11}$ (the story of the elders) to J, and v.$^{3-8}$ to E; Steuernagel (*TSK.* 1899, p. 322), who exactly reverses this analysis, and Baentsch, who refers Ex. $24^{1 (2). 9-11}$ to a very ancient north-Israelitish tradition.

24. וַיָּאצֶל] cp. v.^{17} n. The form is apparently intended to be Hiphil (= וַיַּאְצֵל)—Kön. i. 390. Otherwise Böttcher (ii. p. 426) and Barth (*ZDMG.* 1889, p. 179: cp. G.-K. 68*f*), who regard the form as Kal, the *â* not

* So Kue. (*Hex.* 241) and many after him.

having been dulled to *ô* as in וַיֹּאמֶר.—**25.** שבעים איש הזקנים] the pl. def. הז׳ after the indef. sing. איש is strange in spite of such partial parallels as Gn. 21^{29} 41^{26} (cp. Dr. *Tenses*, 209 (1)). Possibly שבעים איש is an interpolation.—ולא יָסָפוּ] cp. Dt. 5^{22}. 𝔊 rightly *καὶ οὐκέτι προσέθεντο*: so 𝔖. S ולא יאספו (cp. v.^{30} H). 𝔙 (cp. $\mathfrak{T}^{\text{O and Jon}}$) *nec ultra cessaverunt* as if from סוף. —**27.** הנער] Dav. 21*e*; G.-K. 126, 4.—**28.** מִבְּחֻרָיו] In Eccl. (11^{9} 12^{1}) the fem. pl. is used; but the usage may well have changed in the interval. For the masc. pl. abstractly of an age, cp. זְקֻנִים, נְעֻרִים. S reads מבחיריו = "one of his chosen (servants)": cp. 𝔊 𝔙. But the clause by itself in its present position hardly bears such a sense. It could be well spared altogether; however interpreted, it would be more in place where Joshua is first mentioned; Di. indeed makes its presence here a ground for denying the v. to E.

31–33. Quails.—Continuation of v.$^{18-24a}$. Yahweh fulfils His promise of flesh by bringing to the camp huge flights of quails, which the people kill in immense quantities, and eat. The description is drawn from life, corresponding accurately to modern observations in its various details—the great multitude of the birds, their use of wind in their migration, the lowness of their flight, the ease with which when weary they are netted.

31. *A wind set forth from Yahweh*] The vb. (נסע), which is repeated (in Hiphil) in Ps. 78^{26}, is the same as, *e.g.*, in 10^{33} n.; cp. Jon. 1^{4}, Ps. 135^{7}. Elsewhere also Yahweh is represented as working out His purposes by means of winds—Ex. $10^{13. 19}$ 14^{21} (J), Gn. 8^{1} (P), Ex. 15^{10}, Ps. 104^{4} 148^{8}.—*And brought across quails*] the identification of *salwim* with the common quail (*Coturnix communis* or *C. dactylisonans*) is well secured by the fact that this bird is still called *salwā* in Egypt and Syria,* that its habits justify the description here given, and that it was certainly so understood by Josephus (*Ant.* iii. 1^{5} 13^{1}, *ὄρτυξ*) if not also by 𝔊 (*ὀρτυγομήτρα*).

Quails belong to the partridge family. "In March and April they cross the Mediterranean from the south . . . in large bands," and return southwards from Europe in even more enormous flights towards the end of September. On both migrations they are netted for the market; the flesh of the birds caught in the spring is commonly dry and indifferent, but that of those taken in autumn is excellent. Though they rise rapidly on the wing, they seldom fly far except on their migrations, and then they are

---

* Seetzen, *Reisen*, iii. 80: cp. Robinson, *Biblical Researches*, ii. 620.

often overtaxed and drop exhausted into the sea or on passing ships. (The foregoing details are condensed from *EB.*[9] art. "Quails.")

Speaking of Palestine, Tristram (*Fauna and Flora of Palestine*, 124) says: "A few pairs of quail may be found here and there all through the winter; but in March they return by myriads in a single night, and remain to breed in all the open plains, marshes, and corn-fields, both in the Ghor and the upper country."

It cannot be established that in the original source this story was referred to the spring season, though it is not unnatural to suppose that the editor, if he reflected on the matter at all, had this season in view: cp. 10^{11}.

The sea] presumably the Gulf of ʿAḳabah; a S.E. wind, of which a later poet (Ps. 78^{26}) thinks, would, as a matter of fact, bring up the birds from the Gulf to people on the march from Sinai to Ḳadesh or resident in Palestine.—**32.** The people spend the whole of two days and the intervening night in capturing the birds, so that he who caught least brought home *ten ḥomers, i.e.* about 100 bushels.—*They spread them out*] to cure them by drying: 𝔙, paraphrastically, but rightly, *siccaverunt*; cp. $\mathfrak{G}^{AFL}$. S (cp. $\mathfrak{G}^{B}$), transposing the two last letters of the root, reads *they slaughtered.* With the preferable reading of 𝔐, cp. the ancient Egyptian treatment of fish and quails: "of their fish, some they used to dry in the sun and eat without cooking, others they eat cured in brine. Of birds, they eat quails and ducks and small birds without cooking, after curing them" (Her. ii. 77).—**33.** Before the stock of dried quails was exhausted, Yahweh manifests His anger with the people by destroying many of them.—*Ere it ran short*] For this meaning * of נכרת, see Jos. 3^{16}, 2 S. 3^{29}, 1 K. 2^{4}, Joel $1^{5.16}$; for "ere it was chewed," † there is no parallel. The latter translation would also bring the v. into conflict with the rest of the story; for the remark would be pointless unless it means that before the people had had time to masticate, on their first attempt to eat the quails, the plague broke out; but v.[32a] naturally implies that they had already eaten, and v.[18-24] certainly contemplates the flesh being eaten for a whole month.—*And Yahweh smote the people with a great slaughter*] lit. *smiting* (ויך . . . מכה רבה).

* 𝔊 𝔙 $\mathfrak{T}^{O}$; Di., Reuss, Str., Socin (in Kautzsch, *HS.*), Bacon.
† Arabic V., Ros., Ke., RV. BDB.

מכה is frequently used both of an act of God (Lev. 26^{21}, Dt. 28^{61}, 1 S. 4^{8} 6^{19}) and of an act of man (Dt. 25^{3}, Jos. $10^{10.20}$, 1 S. 14^{14}). The rationalistic explanation, that the mortality among the people was due to the poisonous stuffs on which quails are said sometimes to feed, if intended as an interpretation of the meaning of the story, merely betrays a lack of literary sense on the part of those who offer it. This mortality is not the punishment with which Yahweh threatens the people in v.$^{18-24}$, and it is possible that the whole episode of the lust for flesh as here related is borrowed partly from one, partly from another form in which the story was wont to be told.—**34.** The people who die by the hand of Yahweh as a punishment for their lusting are buried, and their graves give the place its name, "the Graves of the Lusting"; cp. v.^{3} n.

31. רוח] here, exceptionally, masc.: cp. Job 4^{15} 8^{2}, 1 K 19^{11}.—וַיָּגָז] standing between נסע and ויטש should have the same subj., viz. רוח: then שלוים is acc. and ויגז transitive, and therefore rather to be pointed Hiph. than, with MT., Kal. The root occurs only once again (Ps. 90^{10}) in OT., and then with the Syriac sense *to pass away*; but with the present use, cf. Ar. *jāza*, iii. *to cross* (Kor. 7^{134}) and iv. *to make to pass over*, or *through*, and the Targumic גז *to pass over*, or *through* (see Levy).—שלוים] S שלוי, perhaps rightly; for note the following ם, and that the word is elsewhere always sing. in 𝔐 (שלו(י)ו v.^{32}, Ex. 16^{13}, Ps. 105^{40}). On י=â, cp. 12^{3} n.; but the true form is rather שלוי; cp. سلوى, ܣܠܘܝ. The word seems a loan in Heb. and Syr. from Ar.; Lagarde, *BN.* 190. On the renderings of the VV. see Di.'s note on Ex. 16.—**33.** With the vivid construction of the v., cp. Gn. 19^{23} 27^{30} 38^{25} $44^{3f.}$, Jud. 18^{3}, and especially Gn. 29^{9} (all early passages); see Dr. *Tenses*, 169.

35. The people journey from Ḳibroth-hatta'avah to Ḥaṣeroth and remain (ויהיו, cp. Ex. 24^{12}) there. Ḥaṣēroth has been identified by many with ʽAin el Ḥadra, of which Palmer (*Desert of the Exodus*, pp. 260–262, cp. 313 f.) gives a full description. It is two days' journey N.E. from Sinai (*i.e.* in the direction of the top of the Gulf of ʽAḳabah). But this identification rests on altogether inadequate grounds.

The identification seems to have been first suggested by Burckhardt (*Syrien*, p. 808); it is favourably entertained by Robinson (*Bibl. Researches in Palestine*, 1841, 1, p. 223), and defended by Palmer (*op. cit.*: also p. 508); but questioned by Di. (on the present passage), Clay

Trumbull, *Kadesh Barnea*, p. 314 f. The main ground of identification is the similarity of the name, the roots (حضر = חצר) and the general signification of the words being the same. But names derived from this root and of similar form simply mean "an enclosure" (cp. Palmer, pp. 289, 321 f.), and are so frequent that mere similarity of name affords in this case a very insufficient reason for identity of place. In OT. there are several similar place-names of this class. See *EBi. s.v. Place-names*, § 105. The presence of water at 'Ain el-Ḥaḍra is manifestly a still more insufficient ground of identification. How far the *position* supports the identification depends on the validity of particular theories of the route from Sinai to Ḳadesh. See further on c. 33.

XII. 1–15. The uniqueness of Moses.—The motive of this story, which tells how Miriam and Aaron challenge Moses' peculiar right to speak for Yahweh, how Yahweh vindicates Moses, and how Miriam is smitten with leprosy for her sin, and only healed in virtue of Moses' intercession, is the uniqueness of Moses' position and of his intimacy with Yahweh. This appears in (1) the terms of the challenge, v.^{2}, for they imply that, as a matter of fact, Moses' position and authority were supreme; (2) in the direct statement of the divine utterance, v.$^{6-8}$—to other prophets Yahweh spoke by dream and vision; to Moses, mouth to mouth as one man to another; (3) in the vindication of Moses' position by the divine judgment on Miriam, v.$^{9f.}$; (4) in the efficacy of Moses' intercession to remove Miriam's leprosy, v.$^{13f.}$

The same motive is prominent in the stories of the seventy elders ($11^{16f. 24b-30}$), and of the mutiny as related by JE in c. 16.

The scene of the incident, as defined by the editor, is Ḥaṣeroth (11^{35} 12^{16}), but in the source (E) whence the story was drawn it may rather have been Ḥoreb: cp. p. 98.

1. *Miriam and Aaron spoke against Moses*] Miriam is here mentioned before Aaron (cp. 𝔊^{BA} in v.^{4}), and the vb. is in the 3rd sing. *fem.*; subsequently the verbs are pl., and Aaron is mentioned first. The order and cstr. of the present clause (subsequently abandoned) indicate either that Miriam took the lead, or that a story in which Miriam alone offended—she is still alone in being punished—has been modified by introducing Aaron as a second offender. For דבר ב of hostile speech, cp. v.^{8} $21^{5.7}$ (E), Job 19^{18}, Ps. 50^{20} 78^{19}.—*On account*

of the Cushite woman] The Hebrew Cush (כּוּשׁ) is certainly used of two, possibly of three distinct districts or peoples: 1. Ethiopia (so usually); 2. the Cassites (E. of Babylonia); cp. Gn. 10^{8}; * 3. it has been argued by Winckler † that the Kusi mentioned in certain inscriptions of Esarhaddon were a N. Arabian people, and that it is to these that 2 Ch. $14^{9ff.}$ 16^{8} 21^{16} and some other OT. passages refer when they speak of Cush. If this be admitted, then the statement that Moses had married a Cushite, *i.e.* a N. Arabian wife, is best regarded as a variant form of the tradition that Moses' wife was a Midianite (10^{29}, Ex. 2^{15-21} 3^{1}) or a Kenite (Jud. 1^{16} 4^{11}, and see n. on 10^{29}). On the other hand, if Cushite be here taken to mean Ethiopian,‡ the allusion must be to an otherwise unknown wife of Moses, for Ṣipporah could not be called an Ethiopian. In its present position, it is true, the clause itself, apart from any particular interpretation of Cushite, reasonably implies that the marriage was recent, and consequently that the wife mentioned is not Ṣipporah. But without pronouncing the substance of the clause, the invention of a later age,§ or denying that it embodies an ancient tradition,—a decisive choice between these alternatives is scarcely justified,—we may suspect that its insertion here is due to an editor, rather than to the author of the main story; for at most the marriage is the occasion, whereas the real cause of the complaint against Moses is the wounded pride of Miriam and Aaron (v.[2]); and further, the mere assignment

* Schrader, *COT.* 86–88; Delitzsch, *Wo lag. d. Paradies*, 51–57, 72, 127–129.

† *Musri, Meluḫḫa u. Mâin*, ii.; cp. *Musri*, etc. i. 48 on 2 Ch. 14^{14}; also *EBi. s.v.* "Cush"; Hommel in *Exp. Times*, viii. 378, and *Vier neue arab. Landschaften*, 298–303. Augustine on exegetical grounds alone really anticipated this view—"Madianitis . . . qui reperiuntur in Paralipomenon Æthiopes dicti, quando contra eos pugnavit Josaphat. Nam in his locis dicitur eos persecutus populus Israel, ubi Madianitæ habitant (II Paral. xiv. 9–14), qui nunc Saraceni appellantur. Sed nunc eos Æthiopes nemo fere appellat, sicut solent locorum et gentium nomina plerumque vetustati mutari" (*Quæst. in Num.*). The identification is criticised by König (*Fünf neue arab. Landschaften*, 51 ff.).

‡ 𝔊 𝔖 𝔙 Ar. AV.; Jos. (*Ant.* ii. 10); Sayce, *Early Hist. of the Hebrews*, 214 f.

§ Cp. We. *Comp.* 101.

of marriage with a foreigner as a ground of offence savours of an age—the age of Ezra—much later than that to which the main narrative of c. 12 belongs.

Di. considers that the Cushite offended Miriam not because she was a foreigner, but because she was black! A rabbinical interpretation of Cushite is "beautiful" (𝔗° Sam. V., Rashi), the meaning being based on the proverbial beauty of the Ethiopians or on Gematria (כושית being numerically = יפת מראה): for other fancies of this type see *Siphrê*. 𝔗° further recasts the story by basing Miriam's complaint on Moses' *dismissal* of his beautiful wife; and R. Nathan (as cited by Rashi) tells in greater detail how Miriam, happening to be with Ṣipporah when Eldad and Medad prophesied, heard her pity their wives because their husbands would now separate from them as Moses had already separated from her.

2. If the latter part of v.[1] be an editorial insertion, the original text ran, *And Miriam and Aaron spake against Moses, and said, Is it only with Moses*, etc. Then, for the sequence, cp. 21[5].—*Is it only with Moses that Yahweh has spoken? Has he not also spoken with us?*] Miriam and Aaron do not call in question Moses' prophetic position or his right to lead, but only the uniqueness of his prophetic position and his right to sole leadership; nor is there any suggestion in their question that he had done anything to forfeit a position originally held; in other words, the question has no relation to the occasion mentioned in v.[1b]. "To speak with or by" (דִּבֶּר בְּ) is used several times (v.[6. 8], 2 S. 23[2], 1 K. 22[28], Hos. 1[2], Hab. 2[1], cp. הדֹּבֵר בִּי Zech. 1[9. 13] 2[2. 7] 4[1. 4. 5] 5[5. 10] 6[4]) of a divine communication to or through a prophet or other inspired person, though it is much less common than the phrase "to speak to" (דבר אל).

The precise meaning of דבר ב used of a divine communication is not quite certain. We may notice three suggestions that have been offered. (1) Here and in some other passages (*e.g.* 1 K 22[28]) it might be and has been explained (*e.g.* Ges. *Thes.* 314*a*) as meaning "to use as a spokesman"; בְּ certainly has, with some other verbs, a similar force: thus עבר ב means "to use as a slave"; cp. BDB. 89*b*. Further, this meaning would be consistent with the Hebrew view of a prophet's function; see Ex. 4[15ff.]. But the mediation of the prophet in divine communications is otherwise expressed, viz. by דבר ביד (17[5] 27[23], Is. 20[2], Jer. 37[2]); and the proposed meaning of דבר ב is not in harmony with the parallel (במראה אליו אתודע) in v.[6], and it is impossible in the context both in v.[6] and v.[8]. (2) Another suggestion is that the phrase means "to speak in," and refers to the internal voice of revelation; but this is inconsistent with the representation of "the angel who speaks with" (המלאך הדבר ב) Zechariah (Zech. 1^9 and often); for this angel is conceived not to dwell in, but to accompany and sometimes to leave the prophet (Zech. $2^{7\,(3)}$ 4^1 5^5). (3) It is best therefore to explain דבר ב on the analogy of ראה ב, הביט ב, שמע ב, as meaning "to speak to," but as expressing a closer and more intimate conversation than דבר אל. This explanation has the advantage of closely connecting the sense of the phrase as used here and in similar cases with that of the phrase as used in v.^{1}; here the בְּ emphasises the friendly intimacy, there the hostile intent that accompanies the speech; cp. the relation between ראה ב as used in Ps. 54^9 (of the intense gaze of pleasure) and Gn. 21^{16} (of the intense gaze of sorrow and distress); so König, *Offenbarungsbegriff*, ii. 178–180.

And Yahweh heard] 11^1; Di. conjectures that the words may, as in 11^1, have been immediately followed by "and Yahweh was angry" (v.^{9}). Yahweh, unsought by Moses, takes heed of the injustice done to His servant, v.^{3}; for of all mankind Moses is the humblest (ענו), the most submissive before God. The word ענו, here only used in the singular, is generally rendered "meek," and interpreted to mean "patient," "given to bear wrongs without resistance"; but this is a sense which it bears nowhere else in OT.; the meaning "humble before God" is illustrated particularly by Zeph. 2^3, and by the use of ענו with such parallel and synonymous terms as "those that seek Yahweh" (Ps. $22^{27\,(26)}$). Rahlfs (as cited below, phil. n.) has pointed out that the "*'Anāwîm*" or "meek ones" of the Psalms are anything but men who bear patiently wrongs inflicted on them by their fellow-men. See, further, phil. note.—*The man Moses*] (האיש משה) so Ex. 11^3 (E); the phrase in Ex. $32^{1.\,23}$ (J) is different.—The obliqueness of the reference to Moses and the self-commendatory nature of the statement occasioned difficulties to older commentators, who were bound by the theory of the Mosaic origin of the Pentateuch.

1. על אודות] scarcely to be used, with Di., as a decisive mark of E, and consequently as an argument in favour of v.^{1b} forming an integral part of E's narrative. The phrase occurs in Gn. $21^{11.\,25}$, Ex. 18^8, Nu. 13^{24} (all E), and, with a slightly different sense, in Gn. 26^{32} (J), Jos. 14^6 (not JE); but with the same meaning as here it occurs outside the Hexateuch in Jud. 6^7, and על כל אודות is used similarly in Jer. 3^8.—**2.** רק אך] The two synonyms thus combined here only; cp. 6^9 n.—**3.** ענו] The meaning of this word (mainly as used in the Psalms), its relation to עני, and its interpretation in the early Versions, have been fully investigated by Rahlfs in עני *u.* ענו *in den Psalmen* (Göttingen, 1892); see also "Poor" in *DB.* (Driver) and *EBi.* (A. C. Paterson). On the form עניו of the Ḳ're see Rahlfs, pp. 95–100 (י is a *mater lectionis* to indicate that the last syllable is to be pronounced as in דְּבָרָיו).—**3b.** The language, as Di. points out, resembles that of J (Gn. 2^{6} 4^{14} $6^{1.7}$ $7^{4.23}$ $8^{8.13}$, Ex. 32^{12} 33^{16}), but not decisively, as between J and E (cp. CH.).

4–8. Yahweh's vindication of Moses.—4. Suddenly, that is, immediately after the utterance of the complaint, v.^{2}, Yahweh summons Moses, Aaron, and Miriam out of the camp to the tent (cp. 11^{26} n.), and they go out. — **5.** Yahweh descends in the pillar of cloud (cp. 11^{25} n.), and stands at the door of the tent (Ex. $33^{9f.}$ (E), see also Nu. $11^{16f.\ 25}$). He then summons Miriam and Aaron, and they both step forward, viz. from the position which they had taken up together with Moses. Certainly this gives the verb (ויצאו) a sense different from that in which it is used in v.^{4}, and in itself unusual (yet cp. Zech. 5^{5}). Di. explains the verb in both cases of going out from the camp, regarding v.^{4} (J) and v.^{5} (E) as doublets. But (1) it is not in accordance with E's representation elsewhere that the theophanic cloud should appear, and wait for people to come out from the camp; the persons summoned to or seeking God await His appearance, not He theirs; see Ex. 33^{7-11}, Nu $11^{16f.\ 24f.}$. (2) V.^{4} by its reference to the tent, no less than v.^{5} by its reference to the cloud, seems to belong to E.—**6–8.** Yahweh addresses Aaron and Miriam, admitting that He may indeed communicate His will by means of others, but that no other enjoys such direct and intimate intercourse with Him as Moses. The address is poetical in character, rhythmical and parallelistic in form. Adopting one or two necessary emendations, it may be rendered—

6 Hearken now to My words!
If there be a prophet among you,
In visions do I make Myself known to him,
In dreams do I speak with him.
7 Not so with My servant Moses:
In all My house he showeth himself trustworthy.

8 Mouth to mouth do I speak with him,
Plainly and not in riddles,
And the form of Yahweh doth he behold.
Why then did ye not fear,
To speak against My servant Moses?

6. The terms *prophet*, *vision*, *dream* (נביא, מראה, חלום) are singulars with a collective sense; the tenses, imperfects denoting customary and repeated action (Dr. *Tenses*, 32 f.). The v. therefore states Yahweh's customary mode of revelation to ordinary prophets—it is by means of dreams and visions, cp. Joel 3^{1} (2^{28}); it is this mode of revelation to which constant reference is made in E (but not in J)—Gen. 15^{1} 20^{3} $28^{11f.}$ $31^{11.\,24}$ $37^{5ff.}$ $40^{5ff.}$ $41^{1ff.}$ 46^{2}; cp. Nu. $22^{8.\,20}$ ("by night") and, perhaps, Gn. 21^{12} (cp. v.^{14}) and 22^{1} (cp. v.^{3}). Elsewhere revelation by dream is sometimes distinguished from revelation through prophets (1 S. $28^{6.\,15}$, Dt. 13^{1}, Jer. 27^{9}); and with some of the higher prophets, such as Jeremiah, dreams as a source of revelation fell into complete disrepute (Jer. $23^{25ff.}$).—*A prophet among you*] this, though the rendering of EV., is not a translation of the present text of 𝔐, which can only be rendered, *If your prophet be Yahweh*; see phil. n.—*I speak with him*] v.^{2} n.—7. The case is different with Moses, Yahweh's trusted servant.—*My servant*] Dt. 34^{5} (JE), Ex. 14^{31} (R): otherwise this description of Moses is, in the Hexateuch, confined to the Book of Joshua (*e.g.* $1^{1.\,2.\,7}$), and, at least mainly, to its Deuteronomic sections. Abraham is similarly described (Gn. 26^{24} J) and also Caleb (14^{24} J). The term is very naturally introduced here, leading on as it does to the next clause: in all Yahweh's house, *i.e.* in the administration of all that belongs to Yahweh (viz. Israel), Moses has proved himself worthy of Yahweh's confidence (נאמן, cp. 1 S. 2^{35} 3^{20} 22^{14}: cp. the use of the verb אָמְנוּ in Gn. 42^{20}). He worthily sustains the part of a servant intrusted with all his master's affairs, such as Eliʿezer (Gn. 24^{2}) or Joseph (41^{40}; note the usage of ביתי).—8. With His servant, who has thus proved his fidelity in the conduct of all Yahweh's affairs, Yahweh holds more intimate intercourse than with ordinary prophets: with Moses He converses

not through the medium of dream or vision, but as one man with another; and not in dark riddles, but clearly; moreover, unlike other men, Moses sees the form of Yahweh.—*Mouth to mouth*] cp. "face to face," Ex. 33^{11} (E), Dt. 34^{10} (JE).—*Plainly and not in riddles*] The meaning of the first word must be gathered from that of the second phrase in the line; the two phrases are clearly antithetical; the meaning of the second is plain—God does not express Himself to Moses in dark enigmatical sayings (חידות Jud. 14^{12}, 1 K. 10^{1}, Ps. 49^{5}), but clearly and intelligibly; whether 𝔐 or the different reading of S (𝔊 𝔖) can be made to mean this is doubtful; if not, the text must be corrupt; see phil. n.—*And the form of Yahweh he beholds*] the elders as well as Moses "saw God" on Sinai (Ex. 24^{10} JE), but that was a special occasion. No other, like Moses, is allowed in customary and familiar intercourse with God to see His form (תמונה), though others might see it in dream (Job 4^{16}) or ecstatic vision (Ps. 17^{15}). D distinctly states that the people at Ḥoreb heard a voice, but saw no form (Dt. $4^{12. 15}$). The form or *t'mûnah* is something less distinct than the appearance or *mar'eh* (Job 4^{16}); * the present statement does not, therefore, necessarily conflict with Ex. 33^{20} (J). At the same time it would be a mistake to attempt to harmonise all the OT. statements on the visibility of God; they represent different stages of thought and belief on the subject; see *EBi. s.v.* "Theophany."

6. אם יהיה נביאכם יהוה] the only possible translation (see above) is nonsense. The Versions afford no help; 𝔐 seems older than 𝔊. The conjectural emendation אם יהיה נביא בכם is simple, and has been commonly adopted (*e.g.* Di., Str., Kautzsch, Paterson). The superfluous יהוה may be misplaced, having stood originally after ויאמר, or may be a gloss explaining that the prophet must be a true and not a false one. The position makes it impossible to construe it as in apposition to the subject of אתודע.—**8.** פה אל פה] For the acc. and some Arabic as well as Hebrew parallels, see Kön. iii. 402*i*.—ומראה] S and some MSS. of 𝔐 במראה, 𝔊 *ἐν εἴδει*, 𝔖 ܒܚܙܘܐ. 𝔊 quite properly distinguishes this from the במראה (*ἐν ὁράματι*), cp. v.^{6}; 𝔖 and 𝔗^{o} identify them. If the text be sound here, there is a play on similar words differently pronounced (מַרְאָה and מַרְאֶה). But it may be questioned whether this is likely. Paterson (after Ew.)

---

* Dr. *Deut.* n. on 4^{11}.

reads לא במראה ; but this is tautologous after v.[6b. 7]. The rendering "as an appearance" or the like (*e.g. vermittelst Anblicks*, Di.; *sichtbarlich*, Reuss) agrees better with the usual sense of מראה ; on the other hand, it not only destroys the antithesis, but unduly anticipates the next line (ותמונת וגו).—בעברי במשה] Dav. 29*a*.

9 f. **Miriam's punishment.**—Yahweh departs in wrath (see on v.[2]). No sooner has the cloud removed from the tent than Miriam is seen to be smitten with leprosy. Miriam alone is punished (cp. Dt. 24^9), apparently because she took the lead in the complaint (v.[1] n.).—**9.** *And He departed. And the cloud removed*] the tenses are *not* consecutive, as this rendering of RV. might suggest; Yahweh and the cloud departed, as well as arrived, v.[5], simultaneously. Render: *And He departed. And when* (or, *as soon as*) *the cloud had removed . . . behold Miriam was leprous.* With the Heb. cstr. of v.[10a], cp. Gn. 15^{17} 24^{45} and the somewhat similar instances in Dr. *Tenses*, 169.—*From beside the tent*] RV. "from over." This, it is true, is the commoner sense of the prep. (מֵעַל), but it is unsuitable here in view of v.[5]. For מעל = "from beside," see $16^{26. 27}$, Gn. 17^{22} 18^3, 1 K 1^{53}.—*Leprous as* (white as) *snow*] so Ex. 4^6 (J); the story has in view the white or milder form of the disease; cp. Driver and White, *Leviticus* (*SBOT.*), p. 76.

11–15. **Moses' intercession.**—Aaron, perceiving his sister leprous, begs Moses to forgive their folly and sin, and that Miriam may be healed, v.[11f.]. Moses intercedes with Yahweh, v.[13] (cp. 11^2 n.), who insists that Miriam shall be excluded from the camp for seven days. During this time the people do not journey, v.[14f.].—**11.** *O my lord*] בי אדני addressed to men, Gn. 43^{20} 44^{18} (both J), 1 S. 1^{26}, 1 K. $3^{17. 26}$; to God, Ex. $4^{10. 13}$ (J), Jos. 7^8 (JE), Jud. $6^{13. 15}$ 13^8 †. — *Do not lay sin upon us*] *i.e.* do not compel us to bear the consequences of our sin; the phrase (אל תשת על) is the negatively expressed equivalent of the more frequent "take away sin" (נשא חטאת, *e.g.* Ex. 10^{17} 32^{32} (JE)).—**12.** Let not Miriam remain leprous, so that by the ordinary process of the disease she becomes like an untimely birth born with its skin already half consumed.—Like the friends of Job (Job $42^{7f.}$), Aaron and Miriam are compelled to seek the mediation of him whose intimacy with God they had wrongly called in question.—13. *Nay now, heal her, I pray*] MT. runs—*O God, I pray, heal her, I pray*: against this, see phil. n.—14. In answer to Moses' prayer, so Yahweh's words imply, Miriam is immediately healed; but Yahweh insists on her exclusion for seven days from the camp. Had her father put her to shame by spitting in her face, she would keep to herself for seven days to hide her shame; not less must she do so after being put to shame by the divine infliction of leprosy.—For spitting in the face, cp. Dt. 25^{9} (same phrase as here), Job 30^{10}, Is. 50^{6}.—*Let her be shut up*] cp. Lev. $13^{4f.}$—*And afterwards she shall betake herself*] viz. back into the camp; cp. 11^{30}.

10. העגן סר מעל] ct. נעלה הענן מעל 9^{17} 10^{11} (P).—**11.** אשר] as in 1 S. 15^{15} 20^{42}; cp. BDB. *s.v.* אשר 8*c*.—**12.** תהי] 𝕾 נְהִי: for the meaning of this reading and the kindred Tiḳḳun Sopherim, see Geiger, *Urschrift*, p. 384.—ויאכל] Dr. *Tenses*, 127*β*.—**13.** אֵל־נא] MT. is very improbable, for (1) נא elsewhere always follows a particle or a verb; (2) אֵל though common in compound expressions and in poetry (especially Job, Psalms, and Balaam songs), is very rare elsewhere: cp. BDB. p. 42. For אַל־נא, cp. Gn. 19^{18}.—**14.** ואביה ירק ירק] For the omission of the conditional particle, see Dr. *Tenses*, 155; and on the inf. abs. in a conditional clause, Dr.'s notes on 1 S. 1^{11} 20^{6}.

16a. Departure from Ḥaṣeroth (11^{35} n.); **16b.** the people encamp in the wilderness of Paran. V.^{16b} carries us back to the point reached in 10^{12}, and seems to be merely an editorial link: cp. We. *Comp.* p. 104.

XIII. XIV. *The Spies.*

Literature. — Nöldeke, *Untersuchungen*, 75–78; Kayser, *Das vorexilische Buch*, 81–85; Kuenen in *Th. Ti.* xi. 545–566; Wellhausen, *Comp.* 103–105, 336–338; Meyer's article in *ZATW.* i., *Kritik der Berichte über die Eroberung Palaestinas*, especially pp. 139–141; Steinthal in *Zeitschr. für Völkerpsychologie*, xii. 276 ff.; Bacon, *Triple Tradition*, 177–183, and *Hebraica*, xi. 234 ff.; Steuernagel, *Die Einwanderung der israelitischen Stämmen*, 70–83, 106 f.; G. F. Moore in *EBi.* 3441.

From the southern confines of Canaan, spies are despatched to reconnoitre the country. The majority bring back a discouraging report; the people in consequence refuse to go forward; Yahweh is provoked by their unbelief.

Nothing but the baldest analysis of the story as it now lies before us is possible without recognising the numerous incongruities in detail by which it is marked; some of these might be harmonised, others are hopelessly irreconcilable. The point of departure of the spies is now the wilderness of Paran, v.[3. 26a], now Ḳadesh, v.[26b]; the country reconnoitred is now the whole land of Canaan, v.[2. 17a], from the extreme south to the extreme north, v.[21], now only the southern district round Hebron, v.[22–24]; the majority of the spies now report that the land is unfertile, v.[32], now that it is very fertile, but invincible, v.[27–31. 33]; now Caleb alone dissents from the majority, v.[30], and is alone exempted from punishment, 14[24]; now both Joshua and Caleb dissent, 14[6f.], and are exempted, 14[38]. Even when the details of the narrative are not incongruous, they are frequently duplicated, or the style is markedly redundant (*e.g.* 13[17–20], and note the extent to which 14[11–24] and v.[26–35] are parallel in substance).

The reason for these incongruities and redundancies lies in the fact that the editor has fused, without wholly assimilating to one another, various versions of the incident.

The literary origin of the present form of the story appears to have been much as follows:—The story as it ran in the prophetic history of the 7th cent. (JE) was already marked by redundance, but not by striking incongruities, for the stories of J and E, which were then combined, down as far at least as the reception of the reports, resembled one another closely in their leading features. The long argument of Moses with Yahweh (14[11-24]) formed no original part of J or E, but stood in JE; whether it was written by the editor himself, or had been incorporated in J by a somewhat earlier writer, may be left an open question. The story of P was very different; but the editor who combined JE and P has made little attempt to smooth away the differences. This editor has incorporated P almost intact, JE more fragmentarily, and perhaps with some dislocation (*e.g.* 13[30] may be out of place); it is probable also that he has recast some part of Yahweh's speech to Moses (14[29-33]). It is uncertain whether a few unimportant annotations are due to this editor or a later scribe (*e.g.* in 13[26]).

To facilitate the study of the narrative the two main sources (down to the reception of the reports) are here given in parallel columns; the detailed analysis of JE into J and E cannot be carried through with any approach to certainty; for attempts the reader may refer to CH. and Bacon. For brevity's sake the list of names in 13^{4-15} is omitted from P here.

JE

[Arrived at Ḳadesh (13^{26}, cp. 32^{8}, Dt. $1^{19.45}$, Jos. 14^{7}), Moses, at the request of the people (Dt. $1^{22f.}$), despatched Caleb and other men ($13^{30f.\ 27}$), twelve in all (Dt. 1^{23})] [17b] "and he said unto them, Get you up then into the Negeb and get you up into the mountains, [18] and see the land what it is, and the people that dwell therein, whether they be strong or weak, whether they be few or many; [19] and what the land is that they dwell in, whether it be good or evil, and what the cities are wherein they dwell, whether in camps, or in strongholds; [20] and what the land is, whether it be fat or lean, whether there be wood in it or not; and exert yourselves to bring some of the fruit of the land. Now the time was the time of first ripe figs, [21] and they went up, [22] and they went up by the Negeb and came unto Ḥebron; and Aḥiman, Sheshai, and Talmai, the children of ʽAnaḳ, were there. Now Ḥebron was built seven years before Zoan in Egypt. [23] And they came unto the valley of Eshcol, and cut down from thence a branch with one cluster of grapes, and they carried it away on a frame borne by two, and also some of the pomegranates, and of the figs. That place was called the valley of the cluster (Eshcol) on account of the cluster which the children of Israel cut down from thence.

[26] "And they went to Ḳadesh and brought back word unto them, and showed them the fruit of the land. [27] And they told him and said, We came unto the land whither thou sentest us, and surely it floweth with milk and honey, and this

P

[1] "And Yahweh spake unto Moses, saying, [2] Send the men that they may spy out the land of Canaan which I give unto the children of Israel; of every tribe of their fathers shalt thou send a man, every one a prince among them. [3] And Moses sent them from the wilderness of Paran according to the commandment of Yahweh; all of them were men, heads of the children of Israel. [4] And these were their names"—the names, including Hoshea the son of Nun, follow, v.[4-15]. [16] "These are the names of the men whom Moses sent to spy out the land. And Moses called Hoshea' the son of Nun, Joshua. [17] And Moses sent them to spy out the land of Canaan; [21] and they spied out the land from the wilderness of Ṣin unto Reḥob, to the entering in of Ḥamath.

[25] "And they returned from spying out the land at the end of forty days. [26] And they came to Moses, and to Aaron, and to all the congregation of the children of Israel, unto the wilderness of Paran. [32] And they spread abroad among

is the fruit of it. [28] Howbeit the
people that dwell in the land is
strong, and the cities are fortified,
very great; and we also saw the
children of 'Anaḳ there. [29] ('Amaleḳ
was dwelling in the land of the
Negeb, and the Ḥittite, the Jebusite,
and the Amorite were dwelling
in the mountain, and the Canaanite was dwelling beside the sea
and along the side of Jordan.)
[30] And Caleb stilled the people before Moses, and said, We ought to
go up and possess it, for we are
quite able to overcome it. [31] But
the men that went with him said,
We cannot go up against the people,
for it is stronger than we are; [32] and
all the people whom we saw therein are men of stature; and there
we saw the Nephîlîm (the sons of
'Anaḳ are some of the Nephîlîm),
and we were in our own sight as
grasshoppers, and so we were in
their sight.

14[1] ". . . and they gave forth
their voice, and the people wept
that night . . . [3] and wherefore
doth Yahweh bring us unto this
land, to fall by the sword? Our
wives and our little ones shall be a
prey: were it not better for us to
return to Egypt? [4] And they said
one to another, Let us make us
a head and return to Egypt . . .

[8] If Yahweh delight in us, then He
will bring us into this land and
give it unto us; a land which floweth with milk and honey. [9] Only
rebel not against Yahweh. But as
for you, fear ye not the people of the
land; for they are our bread: their
shadow has departed from them,
whereas Yahweh is with us: fear
them not."

the children of Israel an evil report
of the land which they had spied,
saying, The land through which we
passed to spy it out is a land that
eateth up its inhabitants.

14[1] "And all the congregation
lifted up (their voice), [2] and all the
children of Israel murmured against
Moses and against Aaron; and the
whole congregation said unto them,
Would that we had died in the land
of Egypt! or Would that in this
wilderness we had died! [5] Then
Moses and Aaron fell on their faces
before all the assembly of the congregation of the children of Israel.
[6] And Joshua the son of Nun and
Caleb the son of Jephunneh, who
were among them that spied out the
land, rent their garments, [7] and said
unto all the congregation of the
children of Israel, saying, The land
through which we passed to spy it
out is an exceeding good land.
[10] And all the congregation bade
stone them with stones. And the
glory of Yahweh appeared in the
tent of meeting unto all the children
of Israel."

Then follows Moses' argument with Yahweh, His reply, and the exemption of Caleb from the sentence passed on the rest, 14^{11-24}, the command to take the Red Sea route, v.^{25}, and the futile attack on the Canaanites and 'Amaleḳites, v.$^{39-45}$.

Then follows in 14^{26-39} (mainly P) the condemnation to forty years' wandering for all the people, and death to all over twenty years of age except Joshua and Caleb.

Data for the preceding analysis.—(1) P. $13^{3.26a}$ connects with 10^{12}; the glory of Yahweh (14^{10} n.); Aaron (13^{26} $14^{2.5.26}$); the list of names (13^{4-15}), the change of Joshua's name (13^{16}; cp. Gn. $17^{5.15}$ 35^{10} P), the precise determination of age and time ($14^{29.34}$). Linguistically, note v.^{1} (cp. CH. 185*a*), מטה $13^{2.4-15}$ (cp. 1^{4} 4^{18} nn.), נשׂיא 13^{2} (cp. 7^{2} n.), עדה 13^{26} $14^{1.2.5.7.10.27.35f.}$ (1^{2} n.), לון or הלין $14^{2.27.29.36}$, מאד מאד 14^{7} (CH. 63), רגם 14^{10}, נועד 14^{35} (CH. 111); also, as linking parts of this particular narrative, תור $13^{2.16f.21.25.32}$ $14^{6f.36.38}$, and further עבר ב 13^{32} 14^{7}, הוציא דבה 13^{32} $14^{36f.}$.—(2) JE. Note generally the vividness and picturesqueness of this story as compared with P, *e.g.* $13^{20b.23}$ 14^{9} and 13^{17-20} (as contrasted with the simple "spy out" of P). In detail note the absence of P's peculiarities and the presence of certain words or phrases characteristic of JE—רעה . . . טובה v.^{19} (CH. 165), על אדת v.^{24} (12^{1} n.), ספר v.^{27} (CH. 219): see, further, CH. margins.

The extent of P.—In c. 13 only one or two differences as to the literary analysis call for mention. In v.^{21} CH. (followed above) not unreasonably see in ויתרו the immediate continuation of v.^{17a} (P), and regard ויעלו as the doublet in JE to ויעלו v.^{22}: cp. עלו and ועליתם in v.^{17b}. But most assign all of v.^{21} to P. More doubtful is the assignment * of all v.^{32b} to P: it contains no mark of P's style, and the fact that the height of the inhabitants is twice referred to is insufficient proof that one of these references must fall to P; 14^{7} ignores the point. In 14^{1-10} not *less* than is assigned above is derived from P; CH. assign also אך ביהוה אל תמרדו in v.^{9a}, Kue. (p. 562 f.) v.^{3}, Corn. (*Einleitung*, 19) v.^{3} and possibly v.^{4} to P; but there is nothing sufficiently characteristic in the style to justify this, and v.$^{3f.8f.}$ seem to correspond to the nature of the report of the spies in JE. Within 14^{26-38} many detect a fragment of JE, though they differ as to its extent; thus Dr. assigns v.$^{31-33}$ to JE, Bacon to J; Di. v.$^{30-33}$ and ? v.^{28} to J. Bacon urges that the narrative of J in v.$^{11-24}$, incomplete in itself, is completed by v.$^{31-33}$, which latter vv. duplicate P's narrative (cp. v.^{29} with v.^{32}). On the other hand, v.^{31} is not easily divorced from v.^{30}, and v.$^{32f.}$ is connected with v.^{29} by פגריכם. The citation of v.^{31a} in Dt. 1^{39a} proves nothing, for there the clause is a late gloss unknown to 𝔊. The theory that seems to do most justice to the facts is that v.$^{26-38}$ is a passage from P, expanded in v.$^{30-34}$ by an editor using, but recasting, older material derived from or allied to JE; hence the connection of v.^{31a} with v.^{8}; cp. We. Kue. Corn. In 14^{39} clause *a* may well be assigned (with CH.) to P (cp. v.^{28}); but clause *b* to JE; the change of subject from "children of Israel" to "the people" (cp. 14^{1} n.) favours the division.

* Reuss, Gruppe (*ZATW.* ix. 141–143), Str., CH.

In P's story, then, Moses, at the direct command of Yahweh, despatches twelve spies, one taken from each tribe, to traverse Canaan, and report on the country. In forty days the spies pass through from what was subsequently the southernmost to the northernmost point of Canaan (with v.^{21} cp. $34^{3.8}$) and return. The majority report the land unproductive—as indeed the contemporaries of Haggai and Nehemiah in the sixth and fifth centuries found it to be (Hag. 1^6 2^{19}, Neh. 5); but Joshua and Caleb report it good—as it appeared, for example, to the contemporaries of Hosea (c. 2). The people murmur, and Yahweh, in His provocation, condemns the people to forty years' wandering, and all over twenty years of age, except Caleb and Joshua, to death in the wilderness.

The traversing of the whole country, apparently without difficulty or precaution taken, shows the same generalisation of early traditions and the same indifference to historical realities which are found elsewhere in P.

In JE all is different, the men go up from Ḳadesh into the Negeb; they go as far as Ḥebron or Eshcol: they bring home grapes to confirm their report of the great fertility of the country. But they bring back also tales of giants and strong cities; the land, they say, is certainly good, but invincible. Caleb alone dissents from this view and endeavours (or supports Moses' endeavours) to convince the people that, strong in Yahweh's presence, they are more than equal to the people of Canaan. But the people are afraid, and refuse to go forward. Yahweh orders them back into the wilderness. Then the people repent, attack the ʿAmaleḳites and Canaanites, but are forsaken by Yahweh and defeated.

The separate stories of J and E.—Without attempting a complete analysis in detail, for which the data are insufficient, it must suffice to point out here what may have been the main features of the two similar stories that appear to be fused in JE. That two stories are there combined is rendered probable, not only by the numerous repetitions and the differences of names or terms, but also by the fact that Dt. 1^{20-45} follows one set of terms to the exclusion of the other. In one of these stories (E's, followed by Dt.), then, the spies are bidden to go up *into the mountains* (13^{17} last clause), and to bring samples of the fruit of the land (v.^{20a}): they go as far as *Eschol* and bring fruit thence (v.$^{23f.}$). To this story there may further belong v.^{26b} (in part: at least the last clause), ^{27} (last clause), $^{32b.\ 33}$. In the other story (J) the spies are sent into the *Negeb* (13^{17} last clause but one) and go as far as *Ḥebron* (v.^{22}). To this there may further belong $13^{18f.}$ (in the main), v.$^{22.\ 28}$. On 14^{11-24} (neither J nor E) $14^{25.\ 39-45}$ see the separate discussions below.

1–17a. The selection and despatch of the twelve spies (P).—Having reached the wilderness of Paran (10^{12}), Moses is commanded by Yahweh to select twelve men, one from each tribe, and to send them hence, v.^{3}, to spy out the land of Canaan, v.$^{2.\ 17a}$; v.$^{4-15}$ names of the spies; v.^{16} Hoshea' renamed Joshua.

1. *And Yahweh said unto Moses*] According to Dt. $1^{22f.}$ it was the suggestion of the people which led Moses to send men to reconnoitre the land. Nothing is said here of the people's suggestion; nothing there of the divine command. S here combines the two accounts by prefixing to the present chapter the substance of Dt. 1^{20-23a}, changing the persons so as to make the passage read as a narrative in the 3rd person: for similar insertions in S see Introduction.—**2.** *The land of Canaan*] (ארץ כנען) The regular term in P for the land of promise; it certainly has this connotation in 34^{2}, Gn. 17^{8} $48^{3f.}$, Ex. 6^{4}, Lev. 18^{3} 25^{38}, Dt. 32^{49}; probably, also, in many of the remaining passages, about thirty in number, in which P employs the term (CH. 4). In JE, on the other hand, it never appears to possess this connotation; and is much less frequently used than in P, occurring several times in Gn. c. 42. 44. 45. 47, and otherwise only in Gn. 35^{6} 50^{5}, Jos. 24^{3}. For the land of promise JE employs a variety of terms, *e.g.* "the land of the Canaanite" (ארץ הכנעני), Ex. 13^{11}; "the land that I will show thee," Gn. 12^{1}; "this land" (Gn. 12^{7} $15^{7.\ 18}$ 24^{7}—ct. 17^{8} P): cp., further, Gn. 28^{13}, Nu. 10^{29} 14^{40}. These terms are sometimes defined by the context; *e.g.* it is the land in which the Canaanite then dwelt, Gn. 12^{6}; or the land "from the river of Egypt to the Great River," Gn. 15^{18}. In the JE narratives of the sojourn in Egypt, of the Exodus and of the Wanderings, it is "the land flowing with milk and honey" (Ex. 3^{8} and often), the land sworn to Abraham, Isaac, and Jacob, or to the fathers

(Ex. 13^{11} 33^{1}, Nu. 14^{23}, Dt. 31^{23} 34^{4}), "the place which I have prepared" (Ex. 23^{20}): ct. Ex. 6^{4}, Dt. 32^{49} (P). D agrees in this usage with JE against P. Outside the Hexateuch "the land of Canaan" occurs only as follows:—Jud. 21^{12}, Ezek. 16^{29} (17^{4}), Ps. 105^{11} = 1 Ch. 16^{18}.—For the extent of territory covered by the term (as used by P), see v.^{21} and notes there; also $34^{2ff.}$.—*Shall ye send*] the subject is Moses and Aaron and also (?) the whole congregation, cp. v.^{26a}; but in view of v.$^{1.\ 2a.\ 3a}$ it is better to read with 𝔊 𝔖 S '*shalt thou* (the subject being Moses) *send.*—*Every one a prince among them*] Each tribe had more than one "prince" (נשיא); for the spies (v.$^{4-13}$) are not the same people as the representatives of the tribes at the census (1^{5-15}); yet these latter also were "princes of their fathers' tribes" (1^{16}). Note, too, that Ele'azar is archprince (נשיא נשיאי) of the Levites, 3^{32}. See also 4^{34} n. and 16^{2}. The term originally meant "an eminent person" (from נשא = "to lift up"), or, according to a less probable view of the etymology, a "spokesman" (from נשא = נשא קול = "to lift up the voice," cp. Hoffmann, *Phön. Inschr.* 55; and, for the form, Barth, *NB.* 125*e*).—3. *The wilderness of Paran*] 10^{12} n.—*At the commandment of Yahweh*] one of P's favourite and characteristic phrases: Dr. *L.O.T.* 134, no. 41.—*Heads of the children of Israel*] the representatives in 1^{16} are called "heads (ראשי) of the thousands of Israel."—4. *These were their names*] . . . אלה שמות is the common formula for introducing a list of names; it is very frequent in P (*e.g.* Gn. 25^{13}, Ex. 1^{1}, Nu. 1^{5} $34^{17.\ 19}$, Jos. 17^{3}), but is also employed by other writers—2 S. 5^{14} 23^{8}, Ezek. 48^{1}, 1 K. 4^{8}, Ezr. 8^{13}, 1 Ch. 8^{38}, cp. CH. 188^{P}.—None of the twelve spies with the exception of Caleb and Joshua are ever mentioned elsewhere. Although there is no such convergence of evidence as in the case 1^{5-15} that the present is an artificial list composed at a late date, there is little ground for confidence that the list itself, or that *the whole* of the names which compose it, is of ancient origin.

The relevant facts are these: The four names, Caleb, Jephunneh (yet compare *Heb. Prop. Names*, p. 204), Joshua, and Nun belong to the early traditions. Of the remaining twenty, eleven are otherwise quite unknown—these are Raphu, Gaddiel, Sodi, Gaddi (גַּדִּי: yet compare גָּד גַּדִּי Γαδδι(ς), 1 Mac. 2[2]), Susi, Gemalli, Sethur, Naḥbi, Vophsi, Geu'el, Machi. The text and interpretation of several of these is very uncertain. As to the remaining nine names: Ḥori (חורי) is also the name of a Ḥorite clan, Gn. 36[22], 1 Ch. 1[39]: Palṭi of a contemporary of David, 1 S. 25[44] (called elsewhere Palṭi'el); of a late currency of these two names we have no evidence. 'Ammi'el is the name of a contemporary of David (2 S. 9[4]), but occurs also in 1 Ch. 26[5]; on this name cp. *HPN.* 47, 245. We have evidence that the names Shammua', Ig'al (יגאל), and Shaphat were in use both comparatively early (in or before 9th century B.C.) and also late (see, on the one hand, 2 S. 5[14] 23[35], 1 K. 19[16]; on the other, *e.g.* Neh. 11[17], 1 Ch. 3[22] 5[12]); though the evidence for the early use of Shammua' and Ig'al rest on uncertain readings (with 2 S. 5[14] cp. 1 Ch. 3[5], and with 2 S. 23[35], 1 Ch. 11[38]). The same is true of Joseph (but see below on v.[7]). We have no authentic evidence of the early currency of either Zaccur or Mîcha'el among the early Hebrew, though both names are common in post-exilic literature; see *HPN.* 157, 181, 210, 221; 236. The comparatively small number of compounds, and especially of compounds with a divine name, would be well explained by assuming an early origin for the list; the fact that in all four of the compounds with -el the divine name stands at the end, on the other hand, points to a late date, though not very conclusively, for in no instance is the first element a 3rd pf. Cp. on these and other matters the small print note on 1[5]. A noticeable feature of the list is the large number (nine) of forms ending in ־ִי. In favour of the authenticity of the list, see Hommel, *Alttest. Ueberlieferung*, pp. 298–302.

6. *Of the tribe of Judah, Caleb*] cp. 34[19] (P). According to another and earlier tradition, Caleb was a Ḳenizzite, 32[12], Jos. 14[6. 14].—7–11. The vv. do not appear to be in their original order: probably v.[10. 11] once stood before v.[8. 9]; the unusual separation in the present text of Issachar from Zebulon, of Ephraim from Manasseh, and the occurrence of the clause "of the tribe of Joseph" after one half of Joseph has been dismissed, all point to this conclusion: see *Expositor*, 1902 (March), pp. 225–240. Probably, too, the text is not only dislocated, but corrupt: the names Gaddi'el, Sodi, Gaddi, Susi in v.[10f.] are suspiciously alike, and the name of Ig'al's father may have been accidently lost by a repetition of Joseph from the phrase "of the sons of Joseph."—16. *And Moses called Hoshea . . . Joshua*]. This is the first occasion on which Joshua is mentioned in P. Since, according to P, the name of Yahweh was not revealed until after Joshua's birth (Ex. 6[3]), a name containing Yeho = Yahweh could not have been given him at

birth. P therefore attributes the name to Moses. The previous references to Joshua in the Pentateuch occur in JE (Ex. 17$^{9.13}$ 24^{13} 32^{17} 33^{11}, Nu. 11^{28}).

2. ויתרו] תור occurs 11 times in this and the next c. (references above, p. 132); and also (in a different sense) in 15^{39} (P) 10^{33} (JE), Dt. 1^{33}, 1 K. 10^{15}=2 Ch. 9^{14} (text doubtful), Ezek. 20^{6}, Eccl. 1^{13} 2^{3} 7^{25} †. All three instances of the Hiph. (Jud. 1^{23}, Pr. 12^{26}, 2 S. 22^{33}, ct. Ps. 18^{33}) are textually doubtful. Entirely different words are used to express the idea of spying out in Dt. 1$^{22.24}$, which is probably based on the now lost introduction to the JE story, viz. חפר and רגל (the latter also in Jos. 14^{7}). Ct., further, with תור, consistently used by P here, מרגלים in Gn. 42^{9}, Jos. 2^{1} (JE).—ישראל] 𝔊 + לאחוה; cp. Lev. 14^{34}, Dt. 32^{49} in 𝔐; the same addition in 𝔊 in 27^{12} and in 𝔊^{AF} in 20^{24}. For the omission of לאחוה in both 𝔐 and 𝔊, see 15^{2}, Lev. 23^{10} 25^{2}.—למטה אבתיו] 𝔊 *κατὰ φυλὴν κατὰ δήμους πατριῶν αὐτῶν*, *i.e.* למטה למשפחת (בית) אבתם; cp. *e.g.* 1^{20}. For the combination in 𝔐, cp. 1$^{16.47}$.—כל נשיא בהם] כל absolutely and without the article in this sense is rare; BDB. p. 482*b*. The collective subj. (כל) is distributed by the singular predicate—"all (severally) a prince."—**4.** שמוע] so 𝔊^{F} Σαμμου: but 𝔊^{B} Σαμουηλ, ^{AL} Σαμαλιηλ; cp. שלמיאל 1^{6}.—זכור] If an ancient traditional name, the name perhaps means "ventriloquist" (ז=ز, not ذ): Lag. *NB.* 112 n.—**5.** חורי] 𝔊 Σουρει, Σουδρι.—**12** עמיאל] 𝔖 גמליאל.—**14.** ופסי] 𝔊 Ιαβει.—**15.** גאואל] 𝔊 Γουδιηλ (=in v.^{10} גדיאל).—מכי] 𝔖 מכיר.

17b–20 (JE). The men are charged to proceed into the Negeb and the mountains, and to investigate the nature of the country, its inhabitants, cities, and produce.—The redundance in these verses is the result of the fusion of sources (J and E): see above, p. 133 f. The redundance is reduced in 𝔖 by the omission of all of v.^{19} (after "wherein they dwell") and some clauses in v.^{20}. 𝔖 thus proves that the redundance was felt at an early period. But it does not represent the original text, for note the references back to v.^{19b} in v.^{28}, and cp. Dt. 1^{28}, Jos. 14^{12}. Though any detailed analysis can only be very tentative, it appears likely that in both sources the charge directed the men to consider both the natural and the defensive character of the land, but perhaps in J the former, in E the latter point was emphasised; see Bacon's analysis.

17. *Go up then*] RV., wrongly, "this way"; see phil. n.—*Into the Negeb*] AV., most confusingly, "southward"; as a matter of fact, the journey of the spies was *northward*, for Hebron (v.^{22}) lies some 70 or 80 miles N.N.W. of Ḳadesh (v.[26]). RV. renders "into the South," the capital letter being intended to warn the reader that "south" is a technical term. But the Hebrew term did not originally mean "south," but (cp. Aram. נגיב) "dry," "parched." "South" is a secondary sense acquired by the word (*e.g.* 35^5, Jos. 11^2) after settlement in Canaan, to the south of which the Negeb lay; just as "west" is a secondary sense acquired by "the sea" (*i.e.* the Mediterranean), which lay W. of Canaan.* The dry and comparatively verdureless country known as the Negeb stretched some 60 miles northwards from Ḳadesh; the country changes for the better at Dhâheriyah, which lies about half-way between Ḥebron and Beersheba, and may be taken as a point on the northern boundary of the Negeb. The whole district is a "savage high land," the steep ridges mostly running from east to west. Yet it is not lacking in more fertile valleys, where even the grape has been cultivated (see below on v.[23]). In David's time the Negeb belonged to nomads, and supported large flocks (1 S. 27^{7-12}); the ruins discovered there are partly prehistoric, but mainly Byzantine. "South of Beersheba, for 30 miles, the country, though mostly barren, is sprinkled with ruins of old villages gathered round wells. They date mostly from Christian times, and are eloquent in their testimony to the security which the Roman government imposed on even the most lawless deserts."† A list of places in the Negeb is given in Jos. 15^{21-32} (P).—*The mountains*] or "the hill country" (ההר); so [29] $14^{40.44}$. This is best taken as a second reference to the country immediately north of Ḳadesh, called in the preceding clause Negeb, and described in the last n. In Dt. 1^{20} the country round Ḳadesh is called "the hill country of the Amorites" (הר האמרי), and it is said of the spies on leaving Ḳadesh that "they went up into the hill country" (ויעלו ההרה). It is true that N. of the Negeb the hill country of Judah begins, but the absence of any distinctive term, and the use of the same verb in this clause as in the last, render it

* W. R. Smith, *OTJC.* 326.

† On the Negeb, see G. A. Smith, *Hist. Geog.* 278-286; Buhl, *Geog.* 15 f., 87-89; Cheyne, art. "Negeb" in *EBi.*; Palmer, *Desert of the Exodus*, pt. ii. c. v.-vii.; Rowlands in Williams' *Holy City* (1849), ii. 464-468.

unlikely that we have here the work of a writer who wished to express that the spies were to pass through one district and into another.—**19.** *Cities*] The word (הערים) is used here, as in 1 S. 6^{18}, 2 K. 17^{9}, of any inhabited place. The spies are to see whether the inhabitants of the country dwell in camps or fortified places. A camp (מחנה) was sometimes sufficiently permanent to give its name to a place; we know of a Dan's camp (Jud. 13^{15}) and of Maḥanaim (= "the two camps"). The fortified place (מבצר) was, in the first instance, the actual fortress or defensive work with which a walled city was provided; hence the full phrase for a city so provided, "city of fortification or fortress" (עיר מבצר, pl. ערי (ה)מבצר; $32^{17.36}$, Jer. 4^{5}); cp. Nowack, *Arch.* i. 368.—**20.** *And exert yourselves to obtain some of the fruit of the country*] an exhortation to courage implied by RV. is out of place just at this point; for the foregoing translation, cp. the use of התחזק in Gn. 48^{2} (J).—*Now the season was the season of firstripe grapes*] Early grapes are ripe by or soon after the middle of July: Seetzen found them on sale at Acre on July 18th (*Reisen*, ii. 92; cp. Robinson, *BR.* ii. 100).

17. עלו זה] The enclitic use of זה is common only after interrogatives; but cp. with the present the instances of its use after הנה 1 K. 19^{5}, Is. 21^{9}, Cant. $2^{8.9}$.—**18.** הישב עליה] so with על of the land inhabited, Lev. $25^{18f.}$ 26^{35}, Dt. 30^{20} (cp. 1 K. 8^{27}); in v.$^{19.28}$ we have the far commoner cstr. with בְּ.—החזק הוא הרפה] The double ה in an indirect disjunctive interrogation is quite exceptional; the other clauses in these verses show the common cstr. with אם . . . ה; cp. BDB. 210*a*; Kön. iii. 379*bγ*.—**19.** בהנה] so Lev. 5^{22}, Jer. 5^{17}; both here and in Lev. S has the more usual בהן: see BDB. 241*b*; Kön. iii. 20.—הבמחנים] The pl. of מחנה without suffixes is elsewhere always מחנות. On this and some other grounds Paterson judges הבמחנים אם במב' to be a gloss.

21. The spies' journey (P).—The spies spy out the whole land of Canaan (cp. v.^{17a}) from the Wilderness of Ṣin in the S. to Reḥob in the N.—Just as the whole congregation later on (20^{1} P), so now the spies reach the Wilderness of Ṣin *after leaving* the Wilderness of Paran (v.^{3}). The former is not part of the latter; but, according to P, Ḳadesh lay in the Wilderness of Ṣin (see 20^{1a} 27^{14} 33^{36}, Dt. 32^{51}). Thus the district from which, according to JE, the spies started is, according to P, part of the country which they had to reconnoitre. The

Wilderness of Ṣin is referred to elsewhere as the most southern district of Israelitish territory—$34^{3f.}$, Jos. $15^{1.3}$ (P). The Reḥob here referred to is most probably identical with the city which is mentioned by this name in 2 S. 10^{8} (and under the fuller form Beth-Reḥob in 2 S. 10^{6}, Jud. 18^{28}; also in 1 S. 14^{47} ($\mathfrak{G}^{L}$), and which lay in the far north of the country near to Laish-Dan. Another Reḥob is mentioned in Jos. $19^{28.30}$, Jud. 1^{31} in the territory of Asher.—*In the direction of the entrance to Ḥamath*] or, if we may infer that the whole phrase has become virtually a proper name and in the present instance stands in apposition to Reḥob, it may be rendered simply *the entrance to Ḥamath*. The phrase (לבא חמת) occurs frequently in definitions of the N. boundary of Canaan or of the territory of Israel (as distinguished from Judah), 34^{8}, Jos. 13^{5}, Jud. 3^{3}, 1 K. 8^{65}, 2 K. 14^{25}, Ezek. 48^{1} (cf. 47^{20}), Am. 6^{14}, 1 Ch. 13^{5}. The city of Ḥamath itself lay on the Orontes, about 150 miles N. of Dan; but its territory extended at least as far S. as Riblah (2 K. 23^{33} 25^{21}), which is 50 miles distant from the city of Ḥamath; "the entrance to Ḥamath" is understood by some* to be the depression between Lebanon and Ḥermon, which stretches northwards from the neighbourhood of Dan, and is described by Robinson (*Later Bib. Researches*, p. 499) as "a vast and lofty mountain cleft 8 or 9 miles wide"; by others † to be the plain of Ḥöms, about 30 miles south of the city of Ḥamath (modern Ḥamā), but within the ancient Ḥamathite territory. If, as is probable, the Ḥa-mâ-tị of Pap. Anastasi I. (*temp.* Ramses II.) be the city so frequently mentioned in the Bible, we have direct evidence ‡ of its existence before the entrance of Israel into Canaan.

רחב]=בית רחב. For such equivalences, see *HPN.* p. 126 ff.; and for suggested sites of Reḥob, Buhl, *Geog.* 237, 240.—לְבֹא חמת] the use of מן (*e.g.* 1 K. 8^{65}, Am. 6^{14}), or עד (Jos. 13^{5}), or עד נכח (Ezek. 47^{20}), before the whole phrase, shows that the phrase as a whole had become virtually equal to a term for a place or district. Originally לְ may have had a local sense *at*, or *towards*.

---

* *E.g.* G. A. Smith, *Twelve Prophets*, i. 177; Buhl, *Geog.* pp. 66, 110; cp. Driver on Amos 6^{2}, and in Hastings' *DB.* iv. 269 f

† *E.g.* Moore, *Judges*, p. 80.

‡ W. M. Müller, *Asien u. Europa*, 174, 256,

22–24. The spies' journey (JE).—The spies go up into the Negeb and reach Ḥebron, a city built seven years before Ṣoʿan, where they find ʿAnaḳites dwelling [so far, probably J]; they come to the naḥal Eshcol and take away a great bunch (*'eshcol*—hence the name of the place, v.[24]) of grapes and other fruit [probably E].

22. *And they went up into the Negeb*] the sequel to v.[17b]. In contrast to v.[17a. 21] the land represented as traversed is only the south of Canaan; Ḥebron lies about 19 miles S. of Jerusalem.—*Aḥiman, Sheshai, and Talmai, the children of ʿAnaḳ*] These were three clans or individuals, possibly of Aramæan origin, and popularly reputed to be of a gigantic height. The gentilic Sheshai may perhaps represent the Shasu or Bedawin of Southern Canaan so frequently mentioned on the Egyptian monuments (Sayce, *Higher Crit. and the Monuments*, 189). On Talmai, see phil. n.

The children of ʿAnaḳ (ילידי הענק, also v.[28], Jos. 15^{14} JE), called also "the sons of ʿAnaḳ" (בני ענק v.[33], Dt. 9^2; בני הענק Jos. 15^{14a}, Jud. 1^{20}, or, with another form of the pl. of a compound expression (cp. Dav. § 15) בני ענקים Dt. 1^{28} 9^2), or "ʿAnaḳites" (ענקים Dt. $2^{10f. 21}$, Jos. $11^{21. 22}$ $14^{12. 15}$), were a class of very tall men, whose height lingered long in the memory of the Hebrews. ʿAnaḳ—always, except in v.[33], Dt. 9^2 with the art. הענק—is (even in Jos. 15^{13} 21^{11} הענוק) not a proper name; the phrases ילידי הענק, בני הענק בני ענקים are of the same type as בני החיל = "mighty men," בני הנכר = "foreigners," and if ענק has in the phrase the same sense which it bears elsewhere in Hebrew will mean "(long-) necked people." Another term, similar in form to that here used, for the giants of popular tradition was ילידי הרפה 2 S. $21^{16. 18}$, or ילידי הרפא 1 Ch. 20^4; cp. Dt. 2^{11}. The ʿAnaḳites are generally associated with Ḥebron; but in a late passage (Jos. $11^{21f.}$ D[2]) they are represented as scattered over the mountain country of Israel and Judah, whence they were exterminated by Joshua, except for a few who survived in Gaza, Gath, and Ashdod. It is not easy to separate the historical and mythological elements connected with this and other notices in OT. of the giants that lived in the country before the entry of Israel. Certainly some of the terms for giants seem to be of a mythological character; see Schwally, *Ueber einige palästinische Völkernamen* in *ZATW.* xviii. 126–148; and on the origin of tales of giants, Tylor, *Primitive Culture*, i. 385 ff. Stories of other peoples about the gigantic size of the former inhabitants of their countries will be found collected in Lenormant, *Les Origines de l'Histoire*, i. pp. 349–355. There is, of course, nothing intrinsically improbable in the existence in Ḥebron of three individuals famous for their height; but v.[32b. 33] attribute a gigantic size to the inhabitants of the country in general in terms which plainly cannot be accepted in a literal sense as corresponding to fact.

22b. The date of the building of Ṣoʿan—the Tanis of the Greeks and Romans, a city situated in the E. part of the Delta, near to the coast of Lake Menzaleh—is unknown; but it was a city of great antiquity, at least as old as the 12th and perhaps as old as the 6th dynasty, *i.e.* it was in any case built before 2000 B.C. It was rebuilt at the beginning of the 19th dynasty, and some have thought that this rebuilding is alluded to here. Failing knowledge of the origin and value of the present statement and early monumental allusions to Ḥebron, we cannot exactly determine its antiquity; but it certainly seems of pre-Israelitish origin. It is quite unnecessary to derive the name from the Ḥabiri of the Tel el-Amarna tablets, and so make it later in origin or refoundation (Sayce) than the presence of these people in Canaan. On the other hand, the identification of Ḥebron with the Khibur (Sayce) of Ramses III.'s list is hazardous.* Ṣoʿan is frequently mentioned elsewhere in OT. (Is. $19^{11.13}$ 30^4, Ezek. 30^{14}, Ps. $78^{12.43}$). From the fact that it is here coupled with Ḥebron, Flinders Petrie infers that "the building must refer to a settlement by Shemites and not by Egyptians" (*Tanis*, p. 4).—**23.** The Wady Eshcol has not been identified, though various inconclusive hypotheses have been put forward. There is a Wady Bît Iskâhil N.W. of Ḥebron (Buhl, *Geog.* 89). But even the generally accepted conclusion that the Wady Eshcol must be one of the valleys near Ḥebron is uncertain; for in the only other passages where the Wady Eshcol is referred to (32^9, Dt. 1^{24}) it is not associated with Ḥebron; and in the present passage the proximity of the references to the two places may be merely due to a compiler: see above, p. 133 f. The late Midrashic story in Gn. 14^{13} in its association of Mamre (*i.e.* Ḥebron) and Eshcol may very well be dependent on the present compilation (JE). The valleys and hillsides round Ḥebron are, it is true, all rich in excellent vines. "The vineyards belonging to the city are very extensive . . . covering the sides of nearly all the hills. . . . The produce of these vine-

* See Bible Dictionaries, *s.v.* Ḥebron, Zoan; G. A. Smith, *Hist. Geog.* 318 n. 1; Sayce, *Higher Crit. and the Monuments*, 187–192, 333 f., 341: Flinders Petrie, *Tanis* (Memoir of Egypt. Exploration Fund, 1885).

yards is celebrated throughout Palestine" (Robinson, *BR.* ii. pp. 442, 445). "Pomegranates and figs as well as apricots, quinces, and the like still grow there [*i.e.* in the valley near Ḥebron, identified by Robinson with Eshcol] in abundance" (*ib.* i. 316). But grapes might also have been found in wadies among the hill country that lay between Ḳadesh and Ḥebron; for traces of grape culture were found in many places far south of Ḥebron by Palmer; * and ʿAnab, a place some 14 miles S.S.W. of Ḥebron, may have derived its name from grapes grown there.†—*A branch with a single cluster of grapes*] stories of heavy clusters of grapes found in Palestine are told by Reland, *Palästina*, i. p. 351, and Rosenmüller in his *Scholia* on this passage.—*And they carried it away on a frame* (*borne*) *by two*] "frame" rather than "staff" (RV.) is the meaning of מוט; see phil. n. on 4^{10}.—*And some of the pomegranates and some of the figs*] Pomegranates and figs grow round Ḥebron (see above), but this can scarcely be the southern limit of their culture. Palmer (*op. cit.*) sees no difficulty on this ground in identifying Wady Eshcol with the Wady Hanein, not so far N. of Ḳadesh. Some of the places called Rimmon, or by a name containing Rimmon, may recall pomegranate culture in this southern region, though they may, it is true, contain the name of the god Rimmon (*EBi. s.v.* "Names," §§ 103, 95).—**24.** The great cluster, according to the story, gave its name to the valley; perhaps rather the name of the valley gave rise to the story (cp. 11^3 n.).

22. וַיָּבֹא] rather with S 𝔊 𝔖 𝔙, pl. וַיָּבֹאוּ. The exegesis which either occasioned or resulted from MT. is represented by Rashi—"Caleb alone went thither (*i.e.* to Ḥebron) and threw himself down on the graves of the fathers, that he might not be seduced by his companions to be of their counsel." That only Caleb went to Ḥebron was suggested by Dt. 1^{36}, Jud. 1^{20}.—תלמי] the name also appears as that of a king of Geshur, 2 S. 3^3; cp. the Nabatæan n. pr. תלמו *CIS.* ii. 321, 344, 348.—צען מצרים] For the proper name in the cstr., see Dav. 24, R. 6.—**23.** ואשכל ענבים אחד] 𝔊 + עליה; if 𝔐 be the true text the ו in ואשכל is the "waw of association" (BDB. 253*a*).—וישאהו . . . בשנים] "they carried it as two, two at a time": Kön. iii. 332*m*.

* *Desert of the Exodus*, 351–353, 367, 373 f., 411, 512.
† *EBi. s.v.* "Names," § 103.

25, 26. The return of the spies (JE P). — V.^{25} and ^{26a} (except קדשה and, perhaps, וילכו) P—forty days after starting the spies return to the wilderness of Paran; v.^{26b} JE—they bring back a report to Ḳadesh, and display the fruit brought home as a sample of the products of the land.

Nöld. (p. 76) suggests the following restoration: for P ויבאו אל משה ואל אהרן ואל כל עדת בני ישראל אל מדבר פארן; for JE וילכו אל משה קדשה וישיבו אתו דבר ויראוהו את פרי הארץ. The changes of אתו to אתם and ויראוהו to ויראום are thus redactional. The last clause of v.^{26} (cp. v.^{23}) and the phrase וישיבו אתם דבר (cp. Gn. 37^{14}, Nu. 22^{8}, Jos. 14^{7} (E), and, hence, Dt. $1^{22. 25}$, Jos. 22^{32}—so Di.) may be ultimately referred to E. קדשה is secured to JE, even though indirectly, by the references in 32^{8}, Dt. 1^{19}, Jos. $14^{6ff.}$. P places Ḳadesh north of the wilderness of Paran (see on 10^{12} and c. 20). Bacon in *Hebraica*, xi. 234 ff., ultimately refers קדשה to J, thus correcting the analysis in his *Triple Tradition*.

26. *Ḳadesh*] ʿAin Ḳadîs, 50 miles S. of Beersheba. The identification suggested more than half a century ago by John Rowlands * was finally established by Clay Trumbull, whose work, *Kadesh-Barnea* (1884), contains an account and criticism of earlier identifications; see, further, Guthe in *ZDPV.* viii. 182 ff., and the new Bible Dictionaries.

The following extracts are from Clay Trumbull's description of the place (pp. 272–274): "The long-sought wells of Qadees [Ḳadîs] were before our eyes . . .: out from the barren and desolate stretch of the burning desert-waste we had come with magical suddenness into an oasis of verdure and beauty, unlooked for and hardly conceivable in such a region. A carpet of grass covered the ground. Fig trees, laden with fruit nearly ripe enough for eating, were along the shelter of the southern hillside. Shrubs and flowers showed themselves in variety and profusion. Running water gurgled under the waving grass. . . . Standing out from the earth-covered limestone hills at the north-eastern sweep of this picturesque recess was to be seen the 'large single mass, or a small hill, of solid rock,' which Rowlands looked at as the cliff (Selʿa) smitten by Moses. . . . From underneath this ragged spur of the north-easterly mountain range, issued the now abundant stream. A circular well, stoned up from the bottom with time-worn limestone blocks, was the first receptacle of the water. . . . The mouth of this well was only about three feet across it, and the water came to within three or four feet of the top. A little distance westerly from this well, and down the slope, was a second well, stoned-up much like the first, but of greater diameter. . . . A basin or pool of water larger than either of the wells, but not stoned-up like them, was seemingly

* See his letter in Williams' *Holy City* (1849), ii 466–468.

the principal watering-place. It was a short distance south-westerly from the second well, and it looked as if it and the two wells might be supplied from the same subterranean source — the springs under the rock. . . . Another and yet larger pool, lower down the slope, was supplied with water by a stream which rippled and cascaded along its narrow bed from the upper pool. . . . The water itself was remarkably pure and sweet. . . . There was a New England look to this oasis, especially to the flowers and grass and weeds. . . . Bees were humming there, and birds were flitting from tree to tree. Enormous ant-hills made of green grass seed, instead of sand, were numerous. As we came into the wady we had started up a rabbit, and had seen larks and quails." G. L. Robinson (*Bibl. World*, May 1901, 326–338) gives a plan, several photographs, and a description of Ḳadesh as seen in 1900.

And they brought back word unto them] *i.e.* to Moses and Aaron. But in the original source either the pronoun both here and in the next clause was sing., referring to Moses (cp. v.^{27}, Jos. 14^{7}), or the pl. referred to the whole people (cp. Dt. $1^{22.\,25}$).—*And all the congregation*] a gloss, or an editorial addition; on "congregation" (עדה), see phil. n. on 1^{2}.

27–31. The report of the spies (JE).

This report is interrupted, if not by v.^{29} and v.$^{30f.}$ (possibly a note of the narrator's and a misplaced fragment of JE respectively), at least by v.^{32a}—P's account of the report. It is continued in v.$^{32b.\,33}$.

The spies report to Moses that the land is good and fruitful, but invincible owing to the strength of the inhabitants and their cities.

27. *And they told him*] *i.e.* Moses: see v.^{26} n. V.^{27} is hardly the original sequel to v.^{26b} in its present form.—*The land whither thou sentest us*] the Negeb (v.^{17b}), and in particular the neighbourhood of Ḥebron, on the fertility of which see v.$^{22f.}$ nn.—*A land flowing with milk and honey*] 14^{8} 16^{13} (exceptionally of Egypt) ^{14}, Ex. $3^{8.\,17}$ 13^{5} 33^{3} (all, according to CH. 34, passages from J), 7 times in D, once in H (Lev. 20^{24}), and also in Jer. 11^{5} 32^{22}, Ezek. $20^{6.\,15}$ †. Cheyne (in *EBi.* 2104) suggests that the phrase, already conventional in the time of JE, was derived from ancient poetry, and had a mythological origin.*—*Here is the fruit thereof*] cp. v.$^{20.\,23.\,26b}$.—

* Cp. Stade in *ZATW.* xxii. (1902) 321–324. With the Greeks (H. Usener in *Rhein. Museum f. Phil.*. 1902, 177–195) "milk and honey" is a phrase for the food of the gods.

28. *And the cities are fortified, very large*] cp. Dt. 1^{28}, Jos. 14^{12}, and the terms of the charge in v.^{19}.—*The children of ʿAnaḳ*] v.^{22}, Dt. 1^{28}, Jos. 14^{12}.—29. The distribution of the different peoples in the land. The v. coheres somewhat loosely with the context, and, naturally interpreted, refers to a much greater extent of country than is contemplated in the charge of v.^{17b}, or is reported to have been investigated in either v.^{22} (J) or v.$^{23f.}$ (E): cp. v.$^{27f.}$. It may well be an editorial remark. Even if an original part of either of the prophetic sources (J or E), it seems best taken as a remark of the narrator rather than as a part of the report. The meaning of the v. as it stands appears to be—the Negeb was inhabited by ʿAmaleḳites; the mountainous country, that forms the centre of Palestine, by Ḥittites, Jebusites, and Amorites; the coast of the Mediterranean and the Jordan valley lying respectively on either side of the mountains, by Canaanites: cp. Jos. 11^{3}.

Although the extent of "mountain" is not defined, and might, therefore, be limited to the mountains of Judah, so that this detail would harmonise with the view of JE that the journey of the spies was limited to the Negeb and the mountains round about and S. of Ḥebron, yet the distribution of the mountain country among three different peoples, and the threefold division of the whole land into negeb, mountain, and lowland, point to a greater extent of country, and indeed to the whole territory subsequently occupied by the Hebrews. If this be the actual intention of the v. it must be attributed to a late editor influenced by a view of the incident of the spies identical with or approximating to that of P (see on v.^{21}). It has been very generally * recognised that the catalogues of pre-Israelitish inhabitants of Canaan which recur so frequently (in the Hexateuch—Gn. 10^{15-17} 15^{19-21}, Ex. $3^{8.17}$ 13^{5} $23^{23.28}$ 33^{2} 34^{11}, Dt. 7^{1} 20^{17}, Jos. 3^{10} 9^{1} 11^{3} 12^{8} 24^{11}; outside the Hexateuch—Jud. 3^{5}, 1 K. 9^{20}, Ezr. 9^{1}, Neh. 9^{8}) formed no part of the earlier sources, but are the work of D or writers influenced by that school. The multiplication of names in these catalogues was intended to magnify the greatness of Israel's conquest; neither the choice of the particular names nor the order, which varies greatly, in which the names are placed have any geographical or ethnographical reason. Is this v. of similar origin? If so, the probable discrepancy between it and v.$^{17b.22-24}$ and the difficulties which arise when we attempt to harmonise its statements with what is said elsewhere of the various peoples mentioned, are accounted for; so, too, is the conflict of opinion as to the source of this v. Di., Bacon, CH., for example, assign it to E, but on inadequate grounds: for ארץ הנגב is used by J (Gn. 24^{62}, cp. Jos. 15^{19},

---

* See, especially, Budde, *Urgeschichte*, p. 344 ff.; cp. Driver on Dt. 7^{1}.

Jud. 1^{15}) as certainly as by E (Gn. 20^{1}); there is nothing peculiarly characteristic of E in describing some particular *part* of the inhabitants of Canaan as Amorite; and, though it be granted that 14^{43} be J, and 13^{29} not from the same hand, this does not prove the latter to be E. The remaining point cited by CH.—the use of על יד, cp. Ex. 2^{5}—by itself is too slight a proof. Meyer and Budde assign the v., with the exception of its middle clause, which on account of its mixture of ethnographical terms they consider redactorial, to J, on the ground that כנעני is used in J's sense as a collective term for all the inhabitants of Palestine. But this conclusion rests on the highly questionable assumption that the last clause of the v. is a definition of the whole country by its two boundaries—the Mediterranean and Jordan. Had this been intended the text would more naturally have run והכנעני ישב מן־הים ועד הירדן.

'Amaleḳ was dwelling in the land of the Negeb] If treated as part of the report the words must be rendered *'Amaleḳ dwelleth* . . . The 'Amaleḳites were a race of nomads who were particularly associated with the deserts to the S. of Palestine (cp. 1 S. 15. 30). See, further, on 24^{20}. — *The Ḥittites*] a powerful, non-Semitic people called Ḫ-tȧ, who appear to have come from Cappadocia, are frequently mentioned in Egyptian inscriptions of the 18th, 19th, and 20th dynasties. When they are first mentioned (*temp.* Thothmes III., *c.* 1500 B.C.), the southern limit of their empire seems to have lain in the district of Kommagene, *i.e.* well to the N. of Carchemish. Later, they pressed somewhat farther southward, but never apparently beyond the upper Orontes valley in this direction.* The Tel el-Amarna tablets (*c.* 1400) and the Assyrian inscriptions † (from Tiglath Pileser I., *c.* 1100, to Sargon, 721–704 B.C.) agree in confining the Ḥittites (Ḫatti = Egyp. Ḫ-tȧ = Heb. חתי) to N. Syria. This northern home of the Ḥittites is familiar to some, and especially the earlier, OT. writers: see Jud. 1^{26} 3^{3} (read "Ḥittites" for "Ḥivites"), 2 S. 24^{6} (read instead of "to the land of Taḥtim-ḥodshi," "to the land of the Ḥittites, to Ḳadesh," *i.e.* Ḳadesh on the Orontes), 1 K. 10^{29}, 2 K. 7^{6}. On the other hand, later writers, particularly P (Gn. 23^{10} 25^{9} 26^{34} $49^{29f.}$ 50^{13}) and perhaps Ezekiel (16^{3}), locate a Ḥittite population in South Palestine (Ḥebron); early writers speak of *individual* Ḥittites resident in the South

* Max Müller, *Asien u. Europa*, pp. 319–324.

† Cp. Schrader, *COT.*[2] 107 ff.

(1 S. 26^6, 2 S. 11^3); and these individuals have *Semitic* names (Uriah, Aḥimelech). The present passage, like P, ascribes a southern or central Palestinian home to a Ḥittite *population.* The explanations possible are: (1) there was a more or less unimportant Semitic tribe, called in Hebrew Ḥittite, which had no connection with the non-Semitic Ḥittites of the inscriptions, and of which we have at present no information from other than biblical sources; or (2) the Ḥittites located by the biblical writers in S. Palestine are isolated settlements of the great Ḥittite race; or (3) the term Ḥittite was used loosely and inaccurately by later Hebrew writers in reference to the pre-Israelitish inhabitants of Canaan in general. The reference to individual Ḥittites with Semitic names in early Hebrew sources may be thought to favour the first alternative, which, at any rate, seems preferable to the second; the third (cp. Jos. 1^4) is that more generally adopted by modern scholars.* If the third be correct, we should have a parallel to the late Hebrew usage in the Assyrian inscriptions of the 8th cent. B.C., where "land of Ḫatti" is used of Palestine in general (Schrader, *COT.*[2] p. 108). — *The Jebusite*] the Jebusites were a local tribe in possession of Jerusalem at the time of the conquest (Jos. 15^{63}, Jud. 1^{21}), and in the time of David till expelled by that king (2 S. 5^{6-9}). No reference to them on inscriptions has yet been found; but, so far as the scanty data afforded by the biblical sources admit of a conclusion, they appear to have been Semites.† — *The Amorite*] the name (אמרי) is identical with the 'A-ma-ra of the Egyptian inscriptions and the 'Amurru of the Tel el-Amarna tablets. In the 15th and 14th centuries B.C. these Amorites of the inscriptions are a people living in the north of Palestine and still further north, Ḳadesh on the

* Budde, *Urgeschichte*, p. 347; Max Müller, *Asien u. Europa*, p. 319 n. 1; Stade, *Geschichte des Volkes Israel*, i. 143 n. 1 (cp. Schrader, *COT.*[2] 110; Meyer in *ZATW.* i. p. 125). The second of the above-mentioned alternatives is adopted in some measure by Di. (*Genesis*,[5] p. 191), who, however, admits that "Ḥittite" was used by P and Ezekiel for all Canaanite peoples, and Sayce (*Early Hist. of the Hebrews*, pp. 54–56; yet see p. 56, bottom, and art. "Hittite" in *DB.*). Cp. Kittel, *Gesch. der Hebr.* i. 21, and Jastrow's art. in *EBi.* (argues in favour of (1) above).

† Dr. in *DB. s.v.* "Jebusite"; G. A. Smith in *EBi. s.v.* "Jerusalem," § 13.

Orontes being a principal town of theirs in the time of the 19th dynasty. In the Bible the term is used specifically of the kingdoms of ʿOg and Siḥon on the E. of Jordan (Nu. $21^{13.\ 21}$); but also and generally of the pre-Israelitish inhabitants of Canaan W. of Jordan. This latter usage is characteristic of E and D (as against J, who regularly uses "Canaanite" instead): see also Am. $2^{9f.}$, Is. 17^{9} (𝔊). Apparently we have the same usage here, and certainly no data at present known suffice to determine any special district of the highlands of W. Canaan marked off as "Amorite" from other districts occupied by "Ḥittites" and "Jebusites." If, however, "Ḥittites" is also used in this general sense (see above), the combination of terms (cp. Jos. 11^{3}) in the present clause is curious; we have two general terms for all pre-Israelitish inhabitants of the country and one purely local name (Jebusite); and thus to some extent this verse shares the rhetorical character of the catalogues of Canaanite nations referred to above. The Amorites are elsewhere connected with the hill-country, *e.g.* Dt. $1^{19f.\ 44}$; but see Jud. 1^{34}.

On the Amorites in the Egyptian Inscriptions, see Max Müller, *Asien u. Europa*, p. 177 and c. xvii.; in the Tel el-Amarna tablets, *KB.* v. Index, *s.v.* "Amurru"; Jastrow in *EBi. s.v.* "Canaan," § 10; on the biblical usage, Meyer in *ZATW.* i. 122 ff.; Budde, *Urgeschichte*, p. 345 f.; Driver, *Deut.* p. 11 f.; cp. Max Müller, *op. cit.* pp. 229–233; and see the Bible Dictionaries, *s.v.* "Amorites."

And the Canaanite was dwelling beside the sea (*i.e.* the Mediterranean) *and along the Jordan*] Here, in direct contradiction to 14^{45} (cp. notes on $14^{25.\ 45}$) but in agreement with Dt. 1^{7} 11^{30}, Jos. 5^{1} $13^{3f.}$ (all D^{2}), Zeph. 2^{5}, the Canaanites are described as lowlanders, and more especially as inhabitants of the western lowlands. The name has, indeed, very generally been interpreted to mean "lowlander," though for reasons not beyond criticism.* With the present usage we may compare the use of Ki-na-aḫ-ḫi (=כנע) and Ki-na-aḫ-ni (=כנען) in the Tel el-Amarna tablets, if Jastrow is right in limiting these to "the northern 'lowland' or seacoast" (*EBi.* 641). W. M. Müller (*Asien u. Europa*, p. 206) infers that

* Moore in *PAOS.* 1890, pp. lxvii–lxx.

in certain Egyptian inscriptions the geographical term refers especially to the coast-land, whereas ethnographically "Canaanite" was used, as among OT writers by J, of all inhabitants of the country W. of Jordan. But whether the present notice preserves a reminiscence of the ancient seats of the Canaanites, or is based on the actual condition of things when centuries of Hebrew occupation of the country had forced the Canaanites back to the lowlands, must be left an open question.*

30. The counter-report of Caleb (JE).—Caleb stills the people, and encourages them to go up and conquer the land. The v. seems out of place; for the commotion of the people to which it refers is not mentioned till 14^{1}.—*And Caleb silenced* the murmurings of *the people against* (אל) *Moses, and said* to the people (or *to him, i.e.* Moses—so distinctly S (לו), 𝔊) *we ought to go up* (cp. v.^{17b}) *and take it*, viz. the land, *in possession, for we certainly can prove too much for it.*—**31.** *But the men who went up with* Caleb reiterate that the people are *too strong* (חזק, cp. v.^{18}; ct. v.^{28} עז) to be overcome. Both this and the preceding v., as also 14^{24}, are inconsistent with P's story that Joshua was one of the spies, and that he supported Caleb against the others (v.$^{8.\,16}$ $14^{6.\,38}$). Instead of fusing the two accounts of the minority report, $13^{30f.}$ $14^{5f.}$, the editor has preferred to separate them from one another at the cost of a logical sequence in the narrative; the result in the composite narrative is a longer altercation than either of the main sources presented. The position of $13^{30f.}$ in JE may rather have been after 14^{4}.

28. עז העם הישב בארץ] with ישב ב cp. v.^{19}, and ct. ישב על in v.^{18}. With עז ct. חזק in v.^{18}.—**29.** והחתי] S 𝔊 + והחוי—another term that frequently appears in the rhetorical catalogues of the peoples of Canaan.—על יד] cp. Ex. 2^{5} (E); for יד of the side or bank of a stream, see especially Dt. 2^{37}, and, in the pl., Jud. 11^{26} הערים אשר על ידי ארנון.—**30.** ויהס] an apocopated Hiphil form from the prep. הס; cp. the inflection as an imperative in Neh. 8^{11}.

---

* For the data and the theories to which they have given rise, see Meyer, *ZATW*. i. pp. 122–127 (but cp. iii. p. 306–9); Budde, *Urgeschichte*, 346 ff.; W. Max Müller, *Asien u. Europa*, pp. 205–208; the Tel el-Amarna tablets as quoted above; Buhl, *Geographie*, p. 64 f.; G. A. Smith, *Hist. Geog.* p. 4 f.; Moore, *Judges*, pp. 79, 81; Driver, *Deut.* p. 11.

32a. The report of the spies (P).—The spies, with the exception of Joshua and Caleb ($14^{6. 7}$), spread abroad among the people the unfavourable report that the land was barren.—*And they uttered*] הוציא as in Job 8^{10}, Eccl. 5^{1} of the bringing forth of speech: cp. also Dt. 22^{14}.—*An evil report*] the word דבה always has a sinister sense, whether, as here and in the same phrase in $14^{36. 37}$†, it is used of a false report, or, as in Gn. 37^{2} (P) and probably also in Ezek. 36^{3}, Pr. 25^{10}, of the true report of evil doings.—*The land*] *i.e.* the whole land of Canaan: cp. v.^{21}.—*Through which we have passed*] the same Hebrew phrase (עברנו בה) is differently rendered by RV. in 14^{7}.—*A land that eateth up its inhabitants*] *i.e.* does not produce enough to support them; see Ezek. $36^{13f.}$, the point of which passage is—Judæa, devastated by its conquerors, and rendered in consequence infertile during the Exile, ate up its inhabitants; but Yahweh is about to restore the fertility of the land (cp. v.$^{8. 11. 30}$), and then it will no more eat up its inhabitants. The context in Ezek. renders the meaning of the phrase clear; and so, in the present case, does the antithesis in 14^{7}—the land is very good, *i.e.* a very fertile land. The same metaphor is used in Lev. 26^{38}.

32b, 33. The report of the spies (JE), in continuation of v.$^{28\,(29)}$.—All the inhabitants of the land are very tall (cp. Am. $2^{9f.}$), but in particular the Nephîlim, compared with whom the spies had seemed to themselves mere grasshoppers. In v.^{28} the ʿAnaḳites, here the Nephîlim, are singled out for special mention.—*The sons of ʿAnaḳ are some of the Nephîlim*] The clause is certainly parenthetic, and probably a gloss; it is omitted in 𝔊; the "sons of ʿAnaḳ" (בני ענק) is a different phrase from that used in v.$^{22. 28}$ (ילידי הענק), and only occurs again in Dt. 9^{2}. The etymology of נפלים is far too uncertain to add anything to what can be gathered from this and the only other passage (Gn. 6^{2}) in the OT. where the word occurs, as to the Hebrew legends about the class of giants called Nephîlim. Several etymological speculations are cited and criticised by Di. on Gn. 6^{2}; see also Schwally, *Das Leben nach dem Tode*, p. 65; and for a theory based on extensive conjectural emendations, Cheyne in *EBi. s.v.* "Nephîlim."

רבה] is claimed by Giesebrecht (*ZATW*. i. pp. 189, 228) as a possible Aramaism; but see Driver in *JPh*. xi. 208.—**32.** אנשי מדות] the sing. is איש מדה 1 Ch. 20^6 (and hence to be restored in 2 S. 21^{20}); on the double plural see Dav. 15 (3); G.-K. 124*p-s*; in Is. 45^{14} the pl. is אנשי מדה.—**33.** כן] Ch. on Is. 51^6 (crit. note) suggests כנים.

XIV. 1–10. The people murmur at the report of the spies (JE P).—To P belong at least v.$^{2. 5-7. 10}$ and part of v.^{1}, the rest probably to JE; see above, p. 132.

1 f. Disheartened by the report of the spies (13^{27-33}) the people lament and complain, and wish themselves already dead in Egypt or the wilderness. As Di. has pointed out, the subject is stated three times in these two verses; note the three terms for the murmurers—*All the congregation* (1^2 phil. n.), *the people*, *all the children of Israel* (cp. 20^1); the four verbs—*they lifted up their voice* (ותשא . . . ויתנו את קולם), *wept*, *murmured*—might be progressive statements; but they are more probably due in part to the fact that three sources are here combined.—*And uttered their voice*] ויתנו את קולם Gn. 45^2 (JE).—*And the people wept*] $11^{10. 13. 18. 20}$ (J); cp. 25^6 (P), 11^4 (J).—**2.** *That night*] CH. 142^{JE}.—*And . . . murmured*] (וילנו) the same verb (Niphal or Hiphil) in Ex. 15^{24} 17^3 (JE); otherwise, like the noun (תלנות), it is confined to P or R^P (CH. 114^P).—*Would that we had died in Egypt*] cp. Ex. $14^{11f.}$ (J), 16^3 (P), also Nu. 20^4 (P).—*In this wilderness*] v.^{29}.—**3, 4** (JE). The people would rather return to Egypt than perish by the sword in the attempt to conquer Canaan; they therefore propose to replace Moses by another leader, who shall lead them back to Egypt. It is not improbable that it was at this point in the narrative of JE that Caleb came forward, stilled the people, and gave an encouraging account of the land, 13^{30}.—*Why doth Yahweh bring us into this land*] cp. v.$^{8. 16. 24}$.—*To fall by the sword*] v.^{43}. The people fear the military power of the Canaanites ($13^{28. 32b. 33}$); cp. Ex. 13^{17} (E). The complaint against Yahweh is even more explicitly stated in Dt. 1^{27}. With the question cp. Joshua's in Jos. 7^7 (JE).

Between 13^{33} and 14^1 S inserts, with the necessary change of persons, Dt. 1^{27-33}; see also Field's *Hexapla*; cp. the similar insertion before 13^1, and see Introduction.—**1.** ותשא . . . ויתנו] The first verb agrees with the fem. subj.;

the second is pl. owing to the collective character of the subj.; Kön. iii. 346*c*. נשא here stands for נשא קול, as in Is. 3^{7} $42^{2. 11}$.—וילנו] The root is possibly לן (cp. the parallel root رَنّ, רנן). S always has defective forms, never, as 𝔐, *e.g.*, in v.[29], such forms as הלינתם. Note also the subst. תלנה; and see Nöld. in *ZDMG*. xxxvii. 535 n.—**2.** לו מתנו] Dav. 134; Dr. *Tenses*, 140. After מתנו 𝔖 inserts ביד י״י, cp. Ex. 16^{3} 𝔐.—**3.** טוב] the simple adj. with comparative force: Kön. iii. 308*a*.—יהיו לבז] היה לבז in Hex. only here, v.[31], Dt. 1^{39}; בז also Nu. 31^{32}.—**4.** נתנה . . . ונשובה] S נתן . . . ונשוב.

5–7. The counter-report of Joshua and Caleb (P).—The land is not unfertile as the other spies had said (13^{32a}), but very good.—**5.** Alarmed by the blasphemous murmurings of the people (v.[2]), Moses and Aaron fall on their faces before all the congregation,—an act expressive of awe, or entreaty, or contrition before Yahweh; cp. $16^{4. 22}$ 17^{10} (16^{45}) 20^{6}, Gn. $17^{3. 17}$ (see Gunkel), Lev. 9^{24} (all P), Jos. 5^{14} 7^{6} (J; a fuller phrase).—**6, 7.** Joshua and Caleb, separating themselves from their fellow-spies, rend their garments in grief at the conduct of the people, and assert, in contradiction of the report previously circulated (13^{32a}), that the land is good, *i.e.* fertile.

8 f. (JE) The people's fear is groundless; for if only they do not alienate Yahweh's favour by resisting Him, He will bring them into this fruitful country, the inhabitants of which, forsaken by their god(s), will be unable to offer any opposition to Israel advancing accompanied by Yahweh. At present this argument forms part of the speech of Joshua and Caleb, v.[6f.]. In JE, whence it is drawn, it was either addressed by Moses to the people (cp. Dt. $1^{29ff.}$), or, perhaps more probably in view of its position here, formed the conclusion of Caleb's misplaced speech in 13^{30}.—*He will bring us into this land*] v.[3. 16].—**9.** *They are our bread*] we shall conquer them as easily as we eat bread: cp. Ps. 14^{4} ($= 53^{4}$) and the figurative use of "eat" (אכל) in, *e.g.*, 24^{8}, Jer. 10^{25}.—*Their shadow has departed from them*] this might be explained as an idiom springing out of a widespread belief in the intimate relation between a man and his shadow, and the consequent loss of vitality, and extreme peril involved in the loss of this shadow.* But it is preferable to take the genitive as objective (= the shadow hitherto cast protectingly over them). In that case צל is used

* See Frazer, *GB*. i. 285–292.

in a figurative sense (R.V., here, "defence"), similar to that in which it is used in Ps. 91^{1} 121^{5}, Is. $30^{2f.}$ 49^{2}; the origin of the figure may be sought in the more fully expressed metaphors in Is. 25^{4} 32^{2}. That the phrase "their shadow" refers to the god or gods of the Canaanites is favoured by the following considerations: (1) the verbal idiom used here (סור מעל) is the same as in 1 S. 28^{15}, Jud. 16^{20}; (2) in the following and parallel clause *Yahweh* would thus form a pointed and antithetical subject; (3) the thought is parallel, and the metaphor similar to those in Dt. $32^{30f.}$—"How should one chase a thousand . . . except their rock had sold them and Yahweh had delivered them up. For their rock is not as our Rock." Early Hebrew writers recognised the existence and indeed the power of the gods of other peoples, *e.g.* of Moab (2 K. 3^{27}—after the king of Moab's offering to his god (Mesha), Israel experiences the destructive wrath of Moab's god).—**10.** The people are about to stone Joshua and Caleb (v.[6]; also ? Moses and Aaron, v.[5]); but they are stayed by the appearance of the glory of Yahweh (cp. Ex. 16^{10} P). According to P, *the glory of Yahweh* (כבוד י״י) was a fiery appearance (Ex. 24^{16-18}, cp. 34^{29-35}), manifesting the divine presence; it was first seen on Mt. Sinai at the time of the giving of the Law (Ex. 24^{16-18}); subsequently it was a frequent though not constant appearance at the tabernacle (Ex. $16^{7.10}$—for "wilderness" read "tabernacle"—Lev. $9^{6.23}$, Nu. 16^{19} 17^{7} (EV. 16^{42}) 20^{6}). Two passages (Ex. 29^{43} $40^{34f.}$) might seem to imply that the glory was a constant phenomenon; but these must be interpreted in the light of the less ambiguous passages, unless, as is perhaps more probable, this difference is to be attributed to the author of the later strata of P. P's conception of the glory of Yahweh is markedly different from that of other Hexateuchal sources; see below on v.[21]; and, further, art. "Glory" in *DB*.

5. ויפל] Dav. 113 (*b*); G.-K. 145*o*; note 𝔊 *ἔπεσεν*.—קהל עדת] Ex. 12^{6}, and cp. phil. n. on 1^{2}; 𝔊 here recognises only one of the synonyms.—**7.** הארץ . . . הארץ] Driver, *Tenses*, 197, Obs. (2).—מאר מאר] Gn. 7^{19} (P), 30^{43} (J), 1 K. 7^{47}, 2 K. 10^{4}, Ezek. 37^{10}; cp. במאר מאר, which is peculiar to P and Ezek.; see *L.O.T.* 132; CH. 63.—**9.** סר צלם מעליהם] סור מעל with a personal subject denotes the cessation of *protecting accompaniment*; see Driver on 1 S.

28^{15}.—צלם is paraphrased by the Versions: 𝔊 ὁ καιρὸς (influenced, perhaps, by the idea appearing in Gn. 15^{16}); 𝔙 *omne præsidium*; 𝔖 ܬܘܩܦܗܘܢ; Onk. תוקפהון. The last two (= "strength") may well be paraphrases of a word taken to refer to a god; cp. 𝔊's rendering of Ps. 19^{15}. The use of צל metaphorically of the deity is perhaps to be found in the Midianite name צלמנע, Jud. 8^{5} (but see Moore on the passage), and the Hebrew name צלפחד (to be pointed, perhaps, צִלְפַּחַד; see Skipwith, *JQR*. xi. 259). Skipwith (*JQR*. x. 669) suggests צלמם for צלם in the present passage,—an easy emendation, for note the initial מ of the next word. In this case the reference to the deity would be still less ambiguous; see on 33^{52}. Still *their image* is scarcely a natural or probable expression in the present connection.—**10.** רגם] P's term for "to stone" (see Lev. $20^{2.\,27}$ $24^{14.\,16\,bis.\,23}$, Nu. $15^{35f.}$); the regular equivalent in JE is סקל—*L.O.T.* 134. רגם is the regular Aramaic translation (both in 𝔖 and $𝔗^{o}$) of סקל. The Mishnah uses both סקל and רגם.—נראה] 𝔖 + בענן: cp. Ex. 16^{10} 𝔐.

11–24. Moses' intercession.—Yahweh proposes to destroy the rebellious people, and to make of Moses a yet greater nation (v.$^{11f.}$); Moses seeks to deter Yahweh from His purpose by an appeal to (1) His regard for His reputation among the nations (v.$^{13.\,17a}$); (2) His mercy (v.$^{17b-19}$). Yahweh relents (v.^{20}), but insists that none of the present generation, except Caleb, shall enter the promised land (v.$^{21-24}$). With the present intercession cp. Ex. 32^{9-14} 32^{30-35} $34^{9ff.}$, also Gn. 18^{16-33}; and see note on 11^{2}.

It has been very generally felt that in its present form this section is not derived from the early prophetic sources. The close affinity in thought of v.$^{13-17}$ with Ezek. is specially noticeable. Kue. assigns the passage to the 7th century: "Num. xiv. 11–25, in its present form, must likewise date from the seventh century. The pericope [though not necessarily the whole of it: corresponding to Nu. 14^{11-24} there is but $1^{(33).\,34-36}$ in Dt.] is older than Deut. i.–iv., as a comparison of vv. 22–24 with Deut. i. 35, 36 shows beyond dispute: but, on the other hand, vv. 17, 18 proves that it is either dependent upon Ex. xxxiv. 6, 7, or of identical origin with it. Compare, further, vv. 11–16 with Ex. xxxii. vv. 9–14 and 21 with Is. vi. 3, which the writer has followed" (*Hexateuch*, 241). Similarly Wellhausen: "The additions with which here [*i.e.* in c. xiv.] the main narrative (J) is enriched, are mainly composed by the Jehovist himself; so, especially, is the long speech (vv. 11–25) a free composition of his on the basis of an originally quite small kernel; cp. Ex. 32^{12} $34^{6ff.}$, Ezek. 20." (*Comp.* p. 104.) Similarly Meyer, *ZATW*. i. p. 140; Corn. *Einleitung*,[4] p. 73; Socin in Kautzsch's Bible; Bacon, *Triple Tradition*, p. 187, footnote; Di., CH.

11. *How long*] For similar indignant questions put into the mouth of Yahweh, see Ex. 10^{3} (J), 16^{28} (P), Hos. 8^{5}, Jer.

23^{26}.—*In spite of all the signs*] the plagues of Egypt, and the wonders of the Exodus and of the journey through the wilderness; see $v.^{22}$.—*In their midst*] in 𝔐 the suffix referring to the people is sing. here and throughout the next v.; so in reference to the Egyptians in $v.^{13}$; then the suffixes are pl. from $v.^{14}$ onwards; cp. 11^4 phil. n.—**12.** Cp. Ex. 32^{10}, Dt. 9^{14}.—*I will smite them with an epidemic*] the Hebrew word (דבר) is used of diseases in general that cause great mortality; cp. 2 S. $24^{13. 15}$, Jer. 14^{12}, Ex. 9^{15}.—*And disinherit them*] or, with abandonment of the specific meaning of the verb (הוריש), *destroy them*, cp. Ex. 15^9.—*And I will make thee*] 𝔊 S + *and thy father's house*.—Yahweh proposes to make of Moses *a nation greater and mightier* than the present, which by its existence redeemed His earlier and similar promise to Abraham (Gn. 12^2 (J), 18^{18} (J^2); cp. Dt. 26^5, Is. 51^2).—**13–17.** The text of $v.^{13f.}$ is unintelligible, and the Versions furnish no appreciable emendations; see phil. notes. But the point of Moses' appeal is quite clear, for it is contained in $v.^{15-17}$, which is straightforward. If, he says, you destroy the people, the peoples who have heard of your fame will conclude that it is a hollow fame, and that you destroyed your people simply because you were incapable of bringing them into Canaan. The problem, therefore, is: How is Yahweh to inflict that punishment on a rebellious people which His moral nature demands, and yet maintain the reputation of His power among the peoples of the world? The same problem presented itself to Ezekiel, who saw in the Exile the punishment of the nation's sins and the vindication of Yahweh's moral nature, and believed, as a necessary consequence, in a future restoration, which should vindicate Yahweh's power, and prove to the nations that Yahweh was indeed Yahweh: see especially Ezek. 36^{16-36} 39^{21-29} (cp. Driver, *L.O.T.* p. 295), and cp. the prophet's treatment of the problem raised by these rebellions in the wilderness, Ezek. $20^{9ff.}$. The idea occurs also, though with less prominence, in Is. 48^{11} $52^{5f.}$.—**13 f.** Perhaps, since the following verses contain the real point of the speech (see previous note), these verses have been gradually built up of glosses, and their broken construction and unintelligibility is due to such an origin, rather than, as some have suggested, to Moses' emotion. Cp. with them, in general, Ex. $32^{11f.}$.—V.[13] as it stands must be rendered—*And the Egyptians will hear that* (or, far less probably, *because*) *Thou broughtest up by Thy might this people from their midst.* But the Egyptians do not need to hear in the future what they have already experienced in the past. The rendering, *The Egyptians have both heard . . .* v.[14] *and said to the inhabitants,* etc., is in itself most questionable, and, if admitted, hardly yields better sense.—**14.** *This land*] Canaan; cp. v.[8], but here the phrase is inaptly used.—*Eye to eye,* Is. 52^{8}; cp. the similar locutions in 12^{8}, Ex. 33^{11}.—**14b.** A fusion of phrases and ideas to be found in different narratives of the cloud; see Ex. 13^{26} $33^{9f.}$ (עמד), Nu. 10^{34}.—**15.** This conditional sentence would form a very suitable beginning to Moses' appeal, and was, perhaps, originally such: see preceding notes. —*As one man*] completely and without exception, Jud. 6^{16}.— *Who have heard Thy fame*] in itself the Hebrew phrase scarcely means more than "who have heard about Thee"; cp. Gn. 29^{13}.—**16.** Dt. 9^{28}.—**17.** *But now let the power of my Lord be great*] let Yahweh exert His power in some other way than He has proposed, that the nations as well as Israel may realise His might; cp. Jos. $7^{8ff.}$. Or, possibly, as v.[19] would suggest, כח rather means (*moral*) *power,* or *control* by the exercise of which Yahweh pardons; cp. Nah. 1^{3} (also Job 36^{5}). *Adonai* (= "my lord") of and in address to Yahweh is not infrequent in J, especially in J[2]; see, *e.g.*, Gn. $18^{27.30}$, Ex. $4^{10.13}$ 5^{22} 34^{9}: BDB. *s.v.* אדון, 3 (2). 𝔊 𝔖 here read *let Thy power, O Lord.*—*As Thou didst say*] at Sinai.—**18.** The quotation is from Ex. $34^{6f.}$; the clause "keeping mercy for thousands" (Ex. 34^{7}) is here omitted.—**19.** *According to Thy great kindness*] cp. Ps. $51^{3\,(1)}$.— **19b.** Cp. Ex. 32–34.—**20.** Yahweh so far promises to forgive, that He grants Moses' request not to slay the people one and all, v.[15].—**21–23.** Cp. $32^{10f.}$, Dt. 1^{35}. RV. wrongly makes כִּי in v.[22] causal (see phil. n.): v.[21–23] should rather be rendered as follows:—*As surely as I live, and* (*as surely as*) *the whole earth shall be full of the glory of Yahweh, none of the men who have seen My glory and My signs which I wrought in Egypt and the wilderness, and yet have put Me to the proof these ten* *times, and have not hearkened to My voice, shall see the land.*—*As I live*] men swear, though not exclusively (see Gn. $42^{15f.}$, 2 S. 15^{21}, 2 K. 2^{2}), by Yahweh (cp. *e.g.* Jud. 8^{19}, 1 S. 14^{39}), Yahweh by Himself: cp. Gn. 22^{16}. Cp. the oaths of the modern Bedawin: "The nomads will confirm every word with an oath, as commonly *wa hyât*, 'by the life of'; but this is not in the Waháby country, where every oath which is by the life of any creature they hold to be 'idolatry.' They swear *wa hyât*, even of things inanimate; 'by the life of this fire or of this coffee,' *hyâtak*, 'by thy life,' *wa hyât rukbaty*, 'by the life of my neck,' are common affirmations in their talk" (Doughty, *Ar. Deserta*, i. 269).—**21b.** Cp. Is. 6^{3}, Ps. 72^{19}. Here and in the next v. (where note the parallel *my signs*), *the glory of Yahweh* is the revelation of His character and power in history; cp. Ps. 96^{3} (‖ "marvellous works"), and ct. v.[10] (where see note).—**22b.** The verb נסה (cp. Ex. $17^{2.7}$, Dt. 6^{16}) means "to test or prove a person to see whether he will act in a particular way" (Driver, *Deut.* p. 95); the sin of the people consisted in losing their faith in Yahweh, and constantly putting Him to the proof after He had repeatedly manifested His power and goodwill toward them (cp. v.[11]).—*These ten times*] or, as we might say, a dozen times, *i.e.* frequently; cp. Job 19^{3}. The Talmud (ʿArakin 15*a b*) takes "ten" literally, and explains by reference to two temptations at the Red Sea (Ex. 14^{11}, Ps. 106^{7}), two in demanding water (Ex. 15^{23} 17^{2}), two for food (Ex. $16^{20.27}$), two for flesh (Ex. 16^{3}, Nu. 11^{4}), the golden calf, and the spies. CH. also think that the number may belong to a systematised tradition.—**23.** After "to their fathers" 𝔊 here inserts *but as for their children who are here with Me, as many as have not known good and evil, every one that is young and inexperienced, to them will I give the land*; cp. Dt. 1^{39}, and see Bacon, *Triple Tradition*, p. 188 n.—*All them that despised Me*] v.[11].—**24.** But Caleb, in reward for (עקב) the fact that his disposition toward Yahweh had been different, receives the promise from Yahweh that he shall receive, and his seed inherit, the district whither he had gone as spy, *i.e.* Hebron (13^{22}); the sequel is to be found in Jos. 14^{6-15}, especially v.[12-14]. See also Jud. 1^{20} (where, as in Jos.

14^{9}, the promise is referred to Moses), Jos. 15^{13} (to Yahweh through Joshua).—*My servant Caleb*] cp. "My servant Moses," 12^{7}.—*The land whither he went*] more specifically in Dt. 1^{36}, Jos. 14^{9} "the land that he (thy foot) hath trodden upon."

11. עד אנה] in the Hexateuch only here, Ex. 16^{28} (P) and Jos. 18^{3} (D): elsewhere also only from 7th century onwards—Jer. 47^{6}, Hab. 1^{2}, Ps. $13^{2f.}$ 62^{4}, Job 18^{2} 19^{2}†. The synonymous עד מתי (v.^{27}) is found in all periods, *e.g.* Ex. $10^{3.7}$ (J), Hos. 8^{5}, Is. 6^{11}, Zech. 1^{12}, Neh. 2^{6}, Dn. 8^{13}.—בכל] בְּ = "in spite of," as, *e.g.*, Is. 5^{25}; BDB. *s.v.* ב iii. 7.—**14.** ואמרו אל ישב] ? 𝔊 𝔖 𝔙 omit אל: 𝔖 treats ישב וגו as subj. of ואמרו; 𝔊 has ἀλλὰ καὶ πάντες instead of ואמרו (? + אל), and then makes ישב וגו the subj. of שמעו.—אשר . . . נראה יהוה] Read נִרְאָה for the anomalous נִרְאָה: *forasmuch as thou, Yahweh, art seen.*—אתה (2) $𝔊^{B}$ 𝔖 omit.—**15.** והמתה] S והמת.—שמעך] 𝔊 𝔖 שמך.—**16.** יְכֹלֶת] only again Dt. 9^{28}; G.-K. 69*n.*—וישחטם] 𝔊 foolishly וישטחם. On שחט and its Assyrian equivalent, see Paterson and Haupt's n. in *SBOT.*; *to butcher*, suggested by Paterson for the rare cases where the vb. is used of putting men to death (*e.g.* Jud. 12^{6}, 1 K. 18^{40}, 2 K. 10^{7}, Jer. 39^{6} 41^{7} 52^{10}), is over-violent. *To slaughter* would be a sufficiently expressive rendering; cp. the use of שחט with the reference to child sacrifice: Gn. 22^{10}, Is. 57^{5}.—**18.** רב חסד] 𝔊 S $𝔗^{O}$ + ואמת = Ex. 34^{6} 𝔐.—ופשע] 𝔊 S $𝔗^{O}$ + וחטאה = Ex. 34^{6} 𝔐.—על בנים] 𝔖 + ועל בני בנים = Ex. 34^{7} 𝔐.—על שלשים] S ועל שלשים.—**19.** גדל] In Pent. elsewhere only in Deuteronomy.—נשאתה ל־] = נשא עון v^{18}.—לעם הזה] 𝔊 𝔖 להם.—**20.** יהוה] 𝔊 𝔖 + למשה.—**21.** וימלא כבוד י״י את כל הארץ] both acc. are here by a very infrequent cstr. retained with the passive: Dav. 81, R. 2.—**22.** כי] here simply introduces the fact sworn to; so frequently; see, *e.g.*, Gn. 42^{16}, 1 S. 20^{3}; BDB. 472*a*.—**23.** לאבתם] S + לתת להם: for the much longer insertion in 𝔊 see above.—**24.** מלא אחרי] is a pregnant phrase (for מלא ללכת אחרי) = "to follow completely and uninterruptedly"; it is used of Caleb's conduct here and in $32^{11f.}$, Dt. 1^{36}, Jos. $14^{8.9.14}$, Eccl. 46^{6}: otherwise but once—1 K. 11^{6}.—יורשנה] 33^{53} n.

25. *The ʿAmaleḳite and the Canaanite were dwelling in the vale*] the connection of this clause (neglected in Dt. 1^{40} = clause *b* of this v.) with the context is not obvious, nor can we tell to what special "vale" the writer refers. Further a comparison with v.$^{40.43.45}$ 13^{29}, Dt. 1^{44}, raises difficulties that cannot be entirely surmounted. Perhaps the least of these is the apparent direct contradiction (avoided by 𝔖, which reads "mountain" here) between this v. and v.^{45}. Here, the ʿAmaleḳite and Canaanite are said to dwell in the vale; there, in the mountain. But the Hebrew word הר means hill-country as well as an individual peak or mountain; and the word used for valley, *ʿEmeḳ*, "literally *deepening*, is a highlander's word for a valley as he looks *down* into it, and is never applied to any extensive plain away from hills, but always to wide avenues running up into a mountainous country like the vale of Elah, the vale of Ḥebron, and the vale of Ajalon" (G. A. Smith, *Hist. Geog.* p. 384: cp. p. 654 f.; also Driver in *DB. s.v.* "Vale"). Consequently the same people might be described as dwelling in an *ʿEmeḳ* or vale, and in the *hār* or hill-country.* But whether the writer, who speaks consistently of the hill-country in v.$^{40-45}$, would have described the inhabitants of the district in the present abrupt manner as dwelling in a vale which he does not define, is quite another question. Again, although we might harmonise the present v. with 13^{29}, so far as the Canaanites are concerned, on the ground that the Jordan valley, at least a part of it (though certainly not the sea-coast also), was an *ʿEmeḳ* (cp. Jos. 13^{27}); yet why are the Canaanites and ʿAmaleḳites, whose districts are there distinguished, here united as dwellers in the vale? Certainly the Negeb and the Jordan vale are not interchangeable terms; and, moreover, any reference to the Jordan valley would be out of place here. Again, if 13^{29} has any meaning at all, it contrasts the Canaanites as lowlanders with the Amorites and others as highlanders; yet in 14^{45} both Canaanites and ʿAmaleḳites appear as highlanders, and we find no mention of Amorites; while in the parallel account to v.$^{40-45}$ in Dt. 1^{41-44} Amorites take the place of Canaanites and ʿAmaleḳites. See below on v.^{45}: and also above on 13^{29}.

25b = Dt. 1^{40}. *To-morrow*] 11^{18} n.—*Turn*] changing your present northern to a southern course.—*By the way of Yam Suph*] the Gulf of ʿAḳabah (cp. 21^{4}, 1 K. 9^{26}). Clay Trumbull regards the way of Yam Suph (דרך ים סוף) as a specific term, always (Ex. 13^{18}, Nu. 21^{4}, Dt. 1^{40} 2^{1}) denoting the same road, viz. that connecting the top of the Gulf of Suez with Elah at the top of the Gulf of ʿAḳabah (*Kadesh-Barnea*, pp. 7 f., 352–363); but this does not suit the present context; for the people would need to make a long march through the wilderness from Ḳadesh before they struck this road. The meaning

* Cp. also Palmer, *Desert of the Exodus*, p. 427 f.

seems to be, therefore: Turn back into the wilderness in the direction of Yam Suph.

העמלקי] v.$^{43.\ 45}$, Gn. 14^{7}—the only instances in the Hexateuch of the gentilic form. Elsewhere the people are called עמלק, see 13^{29} 24^{20} (Gn. $36^{11.\ 16}$), Ex. 17^{2}, Dt. $25^{17.\ 19}$.—ישב] sing. after two subjects, cp. v.^{45}; so after three subjects in 13^{29}: Dav. 114*a*.—המדבר] S המדברה: cp. Dt. 1^{40} 𝔐.

26–39a. The condemnation to the forty years' wandering (P).—Yahweh swears that as a punishment for their murmuring (v.$^{27f.}$) all the people above twenty years old (v.^{29}), except Caleb and Joshua (v.^{30}), shall die in the wilderness (v.$^{29.\ 35}$), in which they shall lead a nomadic life (v.^{33}) for forty years. At the end of forty years the children of the present generation will be brought into Canaan (v.$^{31-33}$). All the spies except Caleb and Joshua are (? immediately) cut off by a divine visitation (v.$^{36-38}$).

In view of the difficulty of separating with confidence any elements from JE which may be embodied in this passage (above, p. 132), it cannot be safely used as evidence that the term of forty years for the wanderings in the wilderness was found in that source, still less for its presence in either of the two ultimate sources J or E. But it is clear on other grounds that "the forty years" formed part of early Hebrew tradition: see Am. 2^{10} 5^{25}. In the Hexateuch this period of wandering is elsewhere referred to in P (26^{64} 33^{38}), and frequently in D (Dt. 1^{3} 2^{7} $29^{4\,(5)}$). Otherwise in the Hexateuch the references to it (32^{13}, Jos. $14^{7.\ 10}$) are confined to passages which appear to be late eclectic compositions based on P, JE, and D. In both P and D the Forty Years' Wandering is a period of punishment; on the other hand, passages in the early prophets seem to imply that the period was regarded as one of special divine favour (Am. $2^{9f.}$ $5^{25f.}$, Hos. $2^{16\,(14)}$). The two points of view are not necessarily irreconcilable: but, under the circumstances, it cannot be safely concluded that the punitive character of the wanderings was a primitive element in the story. Meyer (p. 140) seeks to show positively that J knew nothing of a forty years' wandering, but regarded the entrance into Canaan as following immediately on the report of the spies; cp. Steuernagel, 70–77.

26. The insertion of the long passage, v.$^{11-25}$, from another source obscures the immediate sequence of the appearance of the divine glory, v.^{10}, and the divine speech, v.$^{26ff.}$, which was expressed in P here as elsewhere (16^{20} 17^{7-9} $20^{6f.}$, Ex. $16^{11f.}$).—**27.** *How long* are the people to *murmur* (cp. v.^{2} note) with impunity? On the construction of the v., see phil. n.—**27b.** Cp. Ex. $16^{9.\ 12}$ (P).—**28 f.** No longer: the murmurers shall be punished by having the wish they had expressed in their discontent (v.^{2}) fulfilled: all above twenty years of age shall die in *this wilderness, i.e.* the wilderness of Paran (13^{3} n.).—**28.** *Say unto them*] the vb. in 𝔐 is sing., the subj. "Moses": ct. "Moses and Aaron" in v.^{26}, and cp. 1^{2} n.—*Saith Yahweh*] the phrase נאם יהוה, so common in the prophets from Amos to Malachi, occurs elsewhere in the Hexateuch only in Gn. 22^{16}, where, as here, it introduces the words of a divine oath. On the different use of נאם in the Songs of Balaam, see on 24^{3}.—*As I live*] v.^{21} n.; though not found elsewhere in P, this formula of the oath in the mouth of Yahweh is common in Ezekiel (see, *e.g.*, 5^{11} $14^{16.18.20}$).—**29.** *Your carcases*] v.$^{32.33}$; the word פגר is used of the dead body whether of men (*e.g.* Am. 8^{3}) or animals (*e.g.* Gn. 15^{11}); as here, it is used contemptuously in Lev. 26^{30}, Ezek. 6^{5}.—*All that were numbered of you . . . from twenty years old and upwards*] for the phraseology, cp. c. 1, *passim.*—**30 f.** You, the men of this generation, with the exception of Joshua and Caleb, shall certainly not enter Canaan; but your little children, fear for whose fate you made the pretext for your complaints, shall be brought thither by Yahweh. It may be assumed that the family of Aaron is tacitly included in the exception. Eleʿazar must be thought of as over twenty years of age at this time (see $3^{3f.32}$ 4^{16}, Ex. 28^{1}, cp. 7^{7}), yet he entered Canaan (Jos. 14^{1} 17^{4} etc. in P, and 24^{33} in E). *You* (אתם), v.^{30}, is in emphatic antithesis to *your little children*, v.^{31}.—*I lifted up My hand*] *i.e.* swore (cp. Ex. 6^{8} (P); Ezek. $20^{5.6.15.23}$ (hence Ps. 106^{26}) $^{28.42}$ 36^{7} 44^{12} 47^{14}†); in all these cases the vb. is נשא; in Gn. 14^{32} the synonymous הרים is used. For the promise here referred to, see Gn. 17^{8}: cp. 28^{4} 35^{12} 48^{4}, Ex. 6^{8}.—*Caleb . . . Joshua*] for this order cp. 26^{65}, 32^{12}: ct. v.^{6}.—**31a.** Cp. v.^{3}; the presence of this clause in Dt. 1^{39} 𝔐 is due to late glossing (ct. 𝔊). The extent to which the parallel narratives were amplified from one another is further illustrated by 𝔖, which here inserts from Dt. 1^{39} *and your children who this day have no knowledge of good or evil, they shall enter the land.*—*And they shall know*] וידעו; or, perhaps, *shall possess* (ויירשו); so 𝔊; cp. Dt. 1^{39} 𝔐.—*The land which ye despised*] owing to the report that it was infertile, 13^{32a}; this last clause shows that we have to do here with a passage from P, or, at least, dependent on P's account of the report of the spies. According to JE the people did not despise, but feared the land.—**32** f. While the present generation gradually dies off, the generation which is ultimately to enter Canaan must lead a nomadic life in the wilderness.—*Your children shall be shepherds*] RV. text *wanderers*, strictly presupposes נעים (cp. 32^{13}), but is really due to Jewish exegesis as represented in 𝔗 Jon and 𝔙 (*vagi*). 𝔗° also paraphrases, *tarrying*.—*And they* (your children) *shall bear* the consequences (cp. 12^{11}), *i.e.* the punishment, of *your whoredom* (probably singular), *i.e.* of your unfaithfulness to Yahweh. Though the children do not bear the full weight of punishment, yet they share it (cp. v.[34]): the forty years in the wilderness are here regarded as a period of punishment for all concerned. The figure of whoredom is used in the prophets and other writers, especially and very appropriately, for unfaithfulness to Yahweh shown in courting foreign alliances (*e.g.* Ezek. 16^{26} $22^{20ff.}$), or practising forbidden cults (*e.g.* Hos. $2^{5\,(7)}$ 9^{1}); here the original force and appropriateness of the figure have been lost, and it is used simply of the reprehensible unbelief of the people.—**33b**. *Until your carcases be complete in the wilderness*] till the last of you shall have died. The verb תמם means "to be complete," cp. Dt. $31^{24.\,30}$; it is often used as here more or less elliptically; cp. *e.g.* Gn. 47^{15}, Nu. 32^{13}, Dt. 2^{15} (but fully expressed in v.[16]).—**34**. *According to the number of the days* (13^{25}) *wherein ye*, *i.e.* the people as a whole by their representatives, the spies, *spied out the land*.—*Shall ye bear* the consequences of *your iniquities*; the subject is again the people as a whole—not the fathers only, for the whole sentence would then imply that these died altogether at the end of the forty years.—*And ye shall know*] shall experience, cp. *e.g.* Hos. 9^{7}.—*My opposition*] the exact meaning of תנואה which 𝔊 paraphrases (τὸν θυμὸν τῆς ὀργῆς μου) is uncertain: the noun occurs elsewhere only in Job 33^{10}, and there the text is doubtful. Cp. the use of the verb in 30^{6} 32^{7}.—**35**. *In this wilderness shall their number be completed, and there shall* *they die*] virtually a hendiadys—one and all shall die there.—**36–38.** The spies, with the exception of Joshua and Caleb, are cut off at once by a visitation of God.—**36.** Cp. 13^{17a}.—**36b.** Cp. $13^{25a.\ 32a.}$ 14^{2a}.—**37.** *The plague*] מגפה is any form of death regarded as inflicted directly by Yahweh for an express purpose, whether for punishment or for some other reason—cp. 17^{13-15} (16^{48-50}), Ex. 9^{14}, Zech. 14^{12}, Ezek. 24^{16}, and see CH. 125^{P}.—**39a.** In accordance with the command (v.^{28a}) Moses reports Yahweh's words (v.$^{28-38}$) to the people.

27. עד כתי לעדה . . . עלי] The explanations generally offered of the construction are (1) there is an ellipsis (or loss) of a verb such as אסלח (v.^{19}) or אשא (Cler., Rosenm., Keil, RV.), hence: *How long shall I forgive this evil congregation*; (2) the sentence אשר . . . עלי is the subj. and לעדה is construed as לכם in Mic. 3^{1}: *How long shall this evil congregation murmur against Me*: so, after some older commentators, Di., Reuss, Kautzsch; cp. 𝔖. There are no very satisfactory parallels for the use of אשר, but see 2 S. 14^{15}, Zech. 8^{20}. Neither explanation is quite satisfactory: the clause אשר . . . עלי might very easily have arisen by dittography from the end of the v.—**30.** לשכן אתכם] שכן with a personal obj. occurs elsewhere only in Jer. $7^{3.\ 7}$.—**31.** והביאתי] Dr. *Tenses*, 123*a*.—אתם] 𝔊+אל הארץ.—**32.** ופגריכם אתם] For the added pronoun emphasising the suffix, see Dav. 1; G.-K. 135*f*.—**33.** זנותיכם] the form is probably not intended to be pl.; see Kön. iii. 258*f*.—**34.** ארבעים יום יום לשנה יום לשנה] Ezek. 4^{6}.—**35.** יִתַּמּוּ] In 𝔐 this was probably intended to be read as a Kal: cp. v.^{33}; the form even as punctuated in MT. can be explained, not as a Niphal, but as a Kal: G.-K. 67*g*; St. 523*d*.—**36.** The whole of v.^{36} qualifies האנשים, which is a *casus pendens* resumed by האנשים in the following v.; the predicate is introduced by waw conv. with the impf. (וימתו) in v.^{37}; cp. Dr. 127*a*.

39b–45 (JE). The presumption of the people, and their defeat at Ḥormah.—At the communication of the divine sentence (v.^{25}) the people are much grieved, and now insist on attempting to enter the land of promise: Moses vainly endeavours to dissuade them, and refuses to go himself or to suffer the ark to go with them. The people make the attempt, are attacked by the ʿAmaleḳites and Canaanites, and driven back to Ḥormah.

V.$^{40-45}$ have been and can be assigned to JE with confidence: the vv. contain no marks of P's style, many of that of JE, such as הננו and השכים v.^{40}, למה זה v.^{41}, בקרב v.^{42} (P uses בתוך), כי על כן and יהוה עמכם v.^{43}; see CH. 104, 200, 89, 58, 35, 130^{JE}. Some have assigned the whole section to E in particular; so Kue., Corn., Kit., Bacon; and Meyer (p. 133) inclines to the same view on the understanding that the "Canaanite and the 'Amaleḳite" is a redactorial substitute for "the Amorite" (cp. Dt. 1^{44}); cp. also We. *Comp.* 104 f. Others (*e.g.* Di., CH.) regard the passage as composite; CH. assign v.^{40} to E, v.$^{41-45}$ to J; Steuernagel, v.$^{40-42.\ 44}$ to E, v.$^{43.\ 45}$ (though not in their present form) to J. Certainly v.^{41} is a bad sequence to v.^{40}, and v.^{40} *as it now runs* was not the original preface to v.^{44} (but see on v.^{40}). In הננו there may possibly be a distinctive mark of E; in למה זה, כי על כן, and perhaps in צלח v.^{41} (cp. CH. 66^{JE}) and בקרב marks of J, and in v.^{44b} a view of the position of the ark that is certainly not E's. Still the data seem insufficient for a detailed analysis. In so far as the passage refers to Ḥormah, its origin cannot be adequately considered without reference to the other notices of Ḥormah. See on 21$^{1-3}$.

In substance this passage is reproduced in Dt. 1$^{41-44}$ with these chief differences: in Dt. nothing corresponds to the going up into the mountain of v.^{40}, the rebuke to the people placed in Moses' mouth in Nu. v.$^{41f.}$ is given as (in the first place) a divine communication to Moses in Dt.; nothing in Dt. corresponds to v.$^{43.\ 44b}$, and for "the 'Amaleḳite and Canaanite" of v.$^{43.\ 45}$ Dt. has "Amorite." In Dt. the incident is immediately *followed* by the record of the stay of the people at Ḳadesh.

39. *And the people mourned*] the vb. התאבל occurs elsewhere in the Hex. only in Gn. 37^{34}, Ex. 33^{4} (JE).—**40.** In Dt. v.^{25b} and v.^{40} are immediately connected; thus v.^{25b} = Dt. 1^{40}; v.^{40} = Dt. 1^{41a}. Instead of obeying Yahweh's commands and starting on the morrow (v.^{25b}) southward from Ḳadesh, they rise up early (on the next day) and go, or propose to go, northward in the direction of Canaan.—*And they went up into the top of the mountain*] this strangely anticipates v.^{40b} (for why should the people ascend to the summit before announcing their intention, and why should Moses suffer himself to be dragged by them so far in the wrong direction) and still more v.^{44}, and appears to be inconsistent with v.^{45}, which represent the 'Amaleḳites and Canaanites *coming down* on the Hebrews. These difficulties are not wholly obviated by assigning, with CH., v.^{40} to E, and v.$^{41-45}$ to J—an analysis, moreover, which is not favoured by the recurrence of the same phrase (עלו אל ראש ההר) in v.^{40} and ^{44}. It would be preferable to regard *and they went up into the top of the mountain* here as an accidental intrusion from v.^{44}. With the phrase, cp. and ct. 13^{17}. *The top of the mountain* generally means the summit of a particular peak (*e.g.* Gn. 8^{5}, Ex. 19^{20}; cp. 17^{9}), but here, apparently, the heights of the hill-country.—*To the place of which Yahweh spoke*] 10[29] (J): cp. also Gn. 22[3. 9] (E).—*For we have sinned*] in refusing to go up; cp. v.[3. 4], Dt. 1[32ff. 41]; for a similar confession of the people, see 21[7] (JE); cp. also Ex. 32[31] (E), Nu. 22[34] (J), 12[11] (E), Jos. 7[20] (JE).—**41.** *Seeing it cannot prosper*] viz. what you purpose.—**42.** Ill-success must attend the attempt of the people; since, in consequence of their disobedience (v.[43], Dt. 1[42]), Yahweh, whose presence secures victory, (cp. v.[9] 10[35]), will not be with them.—*Go not up*] to the land of promise or to the top of the mountain? See n. on v.[43].—**42b.** Cp. Dt. 1[42], Lev. 26[17] (H).—**43.** *The ʿAmaleḳite and the Canaanite*] so in v.[45]; but in Dt. 1[44] "The Amorite": cp. above, p. 145 f.—*There*] this will refer either to the land of promise (v.[40b]), or to the mountain country (v.[40a]), if the clause "and they went up to the top of the mountain" in v.[40a] be original, and v.[40] the original prelude to v.[43]. If the reference be to v.[40b], then the inhabitants of the land of promise are described by the unusual combination "ʿAmaleḳite and Canaanite"; "the Amorite" of Dt. is, on the other hand, E's usual term for the pre-Israelitish inhabitants of Canaan. If the reference be to the mountain of v.[40a], then the Canaanites here, as quite clearly in v.[45], appear as highlanders; ct. 13[29] 14[24], and see the notes there.—**44.** The meaning of the first word of the v. is uncertain (see phil. n.); but in view of the next v. and the parallel in Dt. 1[41f.] it is possible that the statement does not imply that the people actually reached the summit, but that they attempted the ascent heedlessly and lightheartedly.—**44b.** Omitted in Deut.—*The ark of the covenant of Yahweh*] 10[33] n.—The v. seems to imply that the customary place of the ark was *within* the camp. But if this be so, then, since the ark and the tent of revelation can hardly be separated, and it is perfectly clear that, according to E's point of view the tent was *outside* the camp (Ex. 33[7-11]: cp. pp. 98, 114 f. above), this v. must come from another source, presumably J. Then J, in this matter as in several others, is the source from which P draws; for P's elaboration of the idea of the central position of the ark, see above, p. 17 ff. —**45.** *And the ʿAmaleḳite and Canaanite who dwelt in that* *hill-country came down*] to meet the Hebrews as they were attempting the ascent; see on v.^{43} and cp. 13^{17b}. In Dt. 1^{44} the direction is stated more neutrally—"And the Amorite who dwelt in that hill-country *came out* to meet you." Here, as in 13^{17}, the country immediately ahead of the people is described as hill-country.—*Unto Ḥormah*] Ḥormah, originally, according to P, a royal Canaanite city, and subsequently one of the cities allotted to Judah or Simeon, is frequently mentioned as situated in the extreme south of the Hebrew territory, 21^{3}, Jud. 1^{17}, 1 S. 30^{30}, Dt. 1^{44}, Jos. 12^{14} (D), 15^{30} 19^{4} (P), 1 Ch. 4^{30}. The identification of Ḥormah with Sebaiṭa, 25 miles N.N.E. of ʿAin-Ḳadîs (= Ḳadesh), rests on a philologically unsound connection of Sebaiṭa with Ṣephath—the former name of Ḥormah (Jud. 1^{17}). The line of pursuit is more fully described in Dt. 1^{44} as "from (so 𝔊 𝔖 𝔙) Seir to Ḥormah."—𝔊 S add at the end of the v., *And they returned to the camp.*

40. ועלינו] Dr. *Tenses*, 123.—**41.** עבר את פי] here, 22^{18} 24^{13} only in Hex.—הי׳א] Dav. 1, R. 2; G.-K. 135*p*.—**43.** ונפלתם בחרב] v.^{3}; here and there only in Hex.—כי על כן] cp. 10^{31} n.—**44.** ויעפלו לעלות] Dt. 1^{41} ותהינו לעלות; Dt. 1^{43} ותזדו ותעלו. The √עפל in Hebrew is known only by 1. the Pual form עֻפְּלָה Hab. 2^{4}, where the text is probably corrupt; 2. the Hiphil, found only here; 3. the substantive עפל, meaning, *a.* "a hill," *b.* "a boil or tumour." Some such meaning as "to swell" may be the starting-point of the meanings 1 and 3, and also of the Arabic derivatives of عفل: then, metaphorically, ויעפלו may mean "they acted proudly or presumptuously"; cp. זיד in Dt. Or, connecting with غفل (=*neglexit vel omisit rem*), we may perhaps infer that it is parallel to the הין of Dt., and means "they acted carelessly, thoughtlessly." The VV. appear to guess: 𝔊 *διαβιασάμενοι*, 𝔖 ܘܫܪܝܘ (=*and they began*), 𝔙 *contenebrati*, Onk. וארשעו.—משו] the other occurrences in the Hex. of מוש המיש are Ex. 13^{22} (J), 33^{11} (E), Jos. 1^{8} (D).—**45.** ויכתום] Aramaising Hiphil from כתת, G.-K. 67*f*.—החרמה] here only with the art.; the word means "the sacred place"; cp. חרמון, and see *EBi. s.v.* "Names," § 98. The philological resemblance of Sebaiṭa, or Esbāṭā (اسباطا), and Ṣephath (צפת) is remote. On Sebaiṭa, see Seetzen, *Reisen*, iii. 44; Palmer, *Desert of Exodus*, pp. 374–380; and on the general question, Driver on Dt. 1^{44} and Moore on Jud. 1^{17}.—ויכום ויכתם] a doublet (CH. tentatively) or dittographic? Dt. 1^{44} has ויכתו only.

XV. *Miscellaneous Laws.*

(1) The proper quantities of meal, oil, and wine to be offered in connection with animals presented as burnt-offerings or peace-offerings, v.$^{1-16}$; (2) the cake of "the first of *'Arîsoth*," v.$^{17-21}$; (3) offerings to make propitiation for sins of ignorance on the part of the community or an individual, v.$^{22-31}$; (4) the penalty of the man who gathered sticks on the Sabbath day, v.$^{32-36}$; (5) the tassels to be worn at the corners of garments, v.$^{37-41}$.

These laws, like those in c. 5. 6, have little or no connection with one another ((3) quite incidentally presupposes (1): see v.^{24} and n. below), and none with the narrative of the spies (c. 13. 14) which precedes, or with that of the revolt of Ḳoraḥ which follows them. On this ground alone, then, it may be questioned whether this miscellaneous collection of laws stood between the two narratives just referred to in P^g (Introd. § 11), though they clearly belong to P. Note that v.^{22} not merely fails to connect with v.$^{1-21}$, but almost certainly presupposes an original introduction of an entirely different nature: see n. on v.^{22}.

The language clearly points in all sections to P (though in some it also recalls H): with v.$^{1. 2a. 17. 18a. 37. 38a}$ cp. $5^{11. 12a}$ n.; with v.^{30b} cp. 9^{10} n.; and note, *e.g.*, לדרותיכם v.$^{14. 21. 23. 38}$ (Dr. *L.O.T.* p. 132, no. 20; CH. 76), עדה v.$^{24-26. 33-36}$ (cp. 1^2 phil. n.), הַגֵּר הַגָּר v.$^{15f. 26. 29}$ (CH. 145), אזרח v.$^{13. 29}$ (CH. 34), רגם v.$^{35f.}$ (cp. 14^{10} n.), חקת עולם v.^{15} (CH. 62*c*). See, further, marginal references in CH.

The different manner in which the sections are introduced confirms the conclusion suggested by the want of sequence, viz. that the compiler of the chapter has derived his material from different sources. Note that the 1st, 2nd, and 5th sections are introduced by the same formula as that found, *e.g.*, in $5^{11f.}$; the 3rd and 4th sections are distinguished from the others by the absence of this formula; the third also by peculiarities of style at its close. The 4th section (v.$^{32-36}$) so closely resembles in character Lev. $24^{10-13. 23}$ that the two passages should be closely connected. The 5th section more especially resembles H: see below. It has been suggested* that the several sections were connected and incorporated by the same editor who worked H into P; as an additional point in favour of this, cp. v.$^{2b. 18b}$ with Lev. 19^{23} 23^{10} 25^{2}.

On the age of the substance of the several laws as distinct from their literary setting, see below on the several sections.

What reasons induced the editor to refer this particular group of laws, like those of c. 19, to the period of wandering cannot be determined. The only section of the chapter which in itself may presuppose this period is the 4th; cp. v.^{32a}. On the other hand, the 1st and 2nd sections appear like Deuteronomy to contemplate a speedy settlement in Canaan: with v.$^{2b. 18b}$, cp. Dt. $12^{1. 10}$ 19^{1} and constantly.

1–16. The proper quantities of meal, oil, and wine to be offered with animal offerings.—The law requires that meal, oil, and wine, according to a fixed scale, shall be presented with every animal "of the herd or the flock" offered either as a burnt-offering or a peace-offering. The law is *not* "evidently a *novella* to Lev. 2, intended to regulate what was there left to the free will of the sacrificer or to usage" (Kue. *Hex.* 95); for the law of Lev. 2 regulates the presentation of independent meal-offerings, whereas the present law is concerned only with meal-offerings that are demanded as an accompaniment of an animal offering. It is perfectly conceivable that the amount of an independent meal-offering was left optional even long after the amount required as the accompaniment of various forms of animal offering had been fixed. The date of the literary origin and of the custom here regulated must be determined, in so far as it can be, independently of Lev. 2.

A comparison of the present law with Ezek. $46^{5-7. 11. 14}$ points the way to a surer conclusion. There also we find a fixed scale for meal-offerings offered with animal-offerings; but the scale is different. The two scales may be tabulated thus—

* We. *Comp.* 177 f.; cp. Kue. *Hex.* 96; Addis, ii. 405; Bertholet, *Die Stellung der Israeliten zu den Fremden*, 152 f.; Moore in *EBi.* 3448.

The quantities to be offered are, according to

	(1) Ezekiel's Scale. Meal.	Oil.	(2) The Scale of Nu. 15^{2-16}. Meal.	Oil.	Wine.
With every lamb (ordinarily) .	optional	1 hin per ephah	$\frac{1}{10}$ ephah	$\frac{1}{4}$ hin	$\frac{1}{4}$ hin
With every lamb (of the daily burnt-offering)	$\frac{1}{6}$ ephah	$\frac{1}{3}$ hin			
With every ram	1 ephah	1 ,,	$\frac{2}{10}$,,	$\frac{1}{3}$,,	$\frac{1}{3}$,,
,, ,, bullock	1 ,,	1 ,,	$\frac{3}{10}$,,	$\frac{1}{2}$,,	$\frac{1}{2}$,,

Whether Ezek. reproduces the fixed or customary quantities offered in Jerusalem in the years immediately before the Exile, or establishes his scale independently of previous practice, cannot be determined; but, as compared with his, the present scale appears to be the younger; for note (1) Ezekiel's scale is only to govern *public* offerings,—the offerings of the prince or representative of the people,—whereas the present scale applies to *private* as well as public offerings; (2) an optional element remains in Ezekiel; (3) the amount of meal, oil, and wine is systematically adapted to the size of the animal in the present scale.

On this ground, then, the substance of the law may be regarded as at least as late as the middle of the 6th cent. The scale is elsewhere recognised only in P: see c. 28 f., Ex. 29^{38-42}. In Lev. 7^{11-14} we appear to have an older law which leaves the quantities accompanying a private offering entirely undefined; cp. also Lev. 8^{26}.

Any attempt systematically to fix the amount of material to be offered appears to have been first made at a comparatively late period; though Dt. $16^{10. 17}$ is just as little in *direct* conflict with the present law as Lev. 2 (see above). But taken together, 1 S. 1^{24} (𝔖 𝔊) 10^{3} do not favour the conclusion that a fixed relation, such as Ezek. and the present law demand, between the amount of animals and meal and wine offered existed in early Israel. For other illustrations of fixed quantities, see c. 28 f.; also Lev. $6^{13f. (20f.)}$ (P), which fixes $\frac{1}{10}$ ephah of fine meal as the quantity of "Aaron's oblation"; Lev. 23^{17} (H) 24^{5} (P), which fix $\frac{2}{10}$ ephah as the amount for each of the two loaves offered at the Feast of Weeks and for each of the twelve loaves of shewbread respectively. In the offerings mentioned in 5^{15} and Lev. $5^{11ff.}$ (P) $\frac{1}{10}$ ephah of meal without oil is the fixed amount. See also Lev. 23^{17} (P^s)

Considerably more ancient than the exact regulation of the amounts to be offered was the practice of associating meal, wine, and oil with animal offerings. "Among the Hebrews vegetable or cereal oblations were sometimes presented by themselves [$5^{15ff.}$, Lev. 2. $5^{11ff.}$], especially in the form of first-fruits, but the commonest use of them was as an accompaniment to an animal sacrifice. When the Hebrew ate flesh, he ate bread with it and drank wine, and when he offered flesh on the table of his God, it was natural that he should add to it the same concomitants which were necessary to make up a comfortable and generous meal."* Cp. Jud. $9^{9.\,13}$, 1 S. 1^{24} 10^3, Hos. 9^4, Mic. 6^7. The amount of salt, which also, having probably been from an early period a customary, was made an obligatory (Lev. 2^{13}) accompaniment of meal-offerings, is not regulated by this law (cp. Ezr. 7^{22}); nor is the amount of frankincense (Lev. 2^1). In Ezek. wine is not even mentioned; but it would be, in view of the references to early literature just given, a wholly erroneous conclusion to infer that wine was first made an accompaniment of offerings after the time of Ezekiel.

But while it was customary in all periods after the settlement in Canaan to combine meal- and animal-offerings, it is highly probable that the rigid insistence that *every* animal offered as a peace- or burnt-offering *must* be accompanied by a gift of meal, oil, and wine was, like the exact regulation of quantities, and the insistence on the meal being fine meal (5^{15} n.), very far from primitive; that it was, indeed, the result of the divorce of sacrifice from ordinary everyday life, and the increasing priestly organisation which alike resulted from the centralisation of worship effected by the Josianic Reformation. Gradually other customs connected with these offerings passed into fixed regulations, some of which may be found in the Mishnah tractate *Menaḥoth*.

* W. R. Smith, *Religion of the Semites*,[1] 204 f., [2] 222.

The law itself (v.[2]) rightly recognises that offerings of meal, oil, and wine were not coeval among the Hebrews with offerings of animals. Animals, the natural offerings of nomads, were the more ancient form of offering; meal, oil, and wine were later: they are at most occasionally offered by nomads;* on the other hand, they are peculiarly the offerings of an agricultural community such as were the Hebrews in Canaan, the chief products of which country were corn, oil, and wine (*e.g.* Dt. 7[13] 12[17], Hos. 2[10. 24 (8. 22)], Jer. 31[12]).

2. *When ye be come into the land*] this and the next law (v.[18b]) are only to come into force after the settlement in Canaan—a land of corn and wine and oil. Similar introductions to laws, especially such as refer to agricultural conditions, are found frequently elsewhere, 34[2], Lev. 14[34] 19[23] 23[10] 25[2] (the last three H), Dt. 12[1] 18[9] 19[1].—**3.** *A fire-offering*] the term אִשֶּׁה occurs in three Deuteronomic passages (Dt. 18[1], Jos. 13[14], 1 S. 2[28]), otherwise only in P, who uses it 62 times. The original meaning is uncertain. It has commonly been connected with אשׁ = "fire" †; others, deriving it from √אנשׁ = انس, consider it to have been originally a perfectly general term to denote any offering regarded as a means of establishing friendly relations with the deity.‡ Whatever the etymology, in the usage of the period to which the OT. references belong, אִשֶּׁה was probably connected with אֵשׁ; for where the context speaks clearly, the term always seems to be used of offerings consumed on the altar: so even in Lev. 24[7. 9]; on v.[10] see note there. For such a term P had need; for sacred offering, in the most general sense, he had another term at command in קָרְבָּן. But though the term here used only includes offerings consumed in the sacrificial fire, it still needed qualification; hence in v.[3b] the obligation to offer meal, oil, and wine with the animal-offering is limited to burnt-offerings

* Cp. W. R. Smith, *op. cit.* 205 (222); Wellhausen, *Die Reste arabischen Heidentums*,[1] 111.

† Stade, *Heb. Gram.* 189*b*, 301*a*; Di. on Lev. 1[9]; BDB. *s.v.* אשה (by preference).

‡ So, after Wetzstein, Lagarde, *NB.* 68, 190; cp. König, ii. p. 117 f.

and peace-offerings; and, further, to the cases, by far the most frequent, in which the animal offered was of the bovine, sheep, or goat kind.—*A sacrifice*] זבח is here used, as in Lev. $17^{5.\ 7f.}$ 19^6 23^{37} (H), Jos. $22^{26.\ 29}$ (P), for the sacrifices of which the offerer partook, as distinguished from the sacrifices (including the burnt-offering) which were wholly consumed in the fire or made over to the deity. Far more commonly in P a more distinctive term is used for the former, viz. זבח שלמים = "peace-offering" (*e.g.* Lev. 3^1). In early times "burnt-offering and sacrifice" (עולה וזבח), or "burnt-offerings and peace-offerings" (עולת ושלמים) was an exhaustive classification of animal sacrifices (Ex. 20^{24} 32^6 (JE), Jud. 20^{26}, 1 S. 10^8 11^{15}, 2 S. 6^{17} 24^{25}); later, special forms of the burnt-offering became distinguished as the sin-offering (חטאת) and the guilt-offering (אשם): these seem to be deliberately excluded here: cp. the prohibition of the use of oil in a meal-offering substituted for an animal offered as a sin-offering, Lev. 5^{11}.—*To accomplish a vow, or as a free-will offering, or at your appointed seasons*] these clauses illustrate the term *sacrifice* by referring to various circumstances under which peace-offerings were wont to be offered. Different clauses serve the same purpose in v.[8]. It is scarcely intended to limit the scope of "sacrifice" by excluding, for instance, the "thank-offering" (Lev. 7^{12} 22^{29}). Cp. Lev. 22^{31} (especially in 𝔊).—*To accomplish a vow*] 6^2 phil. n. On the vow and the free-will offering, see Lev. $7^{16f.}$. On the *appointed seasons*, see c. 28 f.—*An odour of rest*] or "satisfaction" (ריח ניחח), Ex. 29^{18}, Lev. 1^9 and 35 times besides in P (CH. 158); see also Gn. 8^{21} (J). The phrase is clearly enough ancient. It originated in the antique notion that the gods derived sensuous delight from the fumes of the burning sacrificial flesh: cp. "the gods smelt the savour, the gods smelt the goodly savour, the gods gathered like flies over the sacrifice" (Babylonian Deluge story). Even in P the phrase refers to the smell produced by the burning, especially of the fat, of the sacrifices.—*Of the herd or of the flock*] the two terms are generic and comprehensive: the first (בקר) covers all animals, of whatever age or sex, belonging to the bovine kind; the second (צאן), all small cattle, *i.e.* sheep or goats (see, *e.g.*, Lev.

1[10]). As among the Carthaginians (*CIS.* ii. 165, 167) an animal of one of these kinds was regularly chosen for sacrifice; occasionally, however, a bird was chosen for a burnt-offering, though never for a peace-offering (Lev. 5^7 12^8).—*Fine meal*] 5^{15} n.—*A tenth*] of an ephah; so rightly 𝔊; note the equivalence עשרון Ex. 29^{40} = עשירית האיפה Nu. 28^5. The term here used (עשרון) is confined to P (including H), who uses it 24 times (CH. 160). The amount is a little less than 7 pints: cp. 5^{15} n.—*A quarter of a hin*] adopting the calculation that a hin = 6·06 litres (BDB. *s.v.* הין), this is about $2\frac{3}{5}$ pints.—*Mingled with oil*] "Among the Hebrew offerings drawn from the vegetable kingdom, meal, wine, and oil take the chief place, and these were also the chief vegetable constituents of man's daily food. In the lands of the olive, oil takes the place that butter and other animal fats hold among northern nations, and accordingly among the Hebrews, and seemingly also among the Phœnicians, it was customary to mingle oil with the cereal oblation before it was placed upon the altar, in conformity with the usage at ordinary meals." *—5. *And wine for the libation*] the term נֶסֶךְ, as it happens, is used in only one early passage (Gn. 35^{14}) of a libation offered to Yahweh; but other allusions (Hos. 9^4, 1 S. 1^{24} 10^3) prove that it was a customary form of offering in the early worship of Yahweh as in other cults (Jer. 7^{18}, Ps. 16^4), though hardly as prominent a feature as among the Arabs, with whom the word نسك became a general term for *to sacrifice*. In early times (independent) libations occasionally consisted of water (1 S. 7^6, 2 S. 23^{16}). In P's demand that the libation shall consist of wine we may, perhaps, trace the same tendency as in the demand for fine meal exclusively in meal-offerings (5^{15} n.). It is possible that wine in libations arose in part as a surrogate for blood (cp. Ps. 16^4 50^{13}).†—7. *And wine for the libation . . . shalt thou present as an odour of satisfaction to Yahweh*] the phrase ריח ניחח (v.[3] n.) is generally used of animal sacri-

* W. R. Smith, *Religion of the Semites*, 202 f.; see also *EBi.* and Hastings' *DB. s.v.* "Oil."

† Cp. W. R. Smith, *op. cit.* 213 f., and more fully in ed. 2, 229–231; Nowack, *Arch.* ii. 208.

fices, or at least of sacrifices that were burnt. Some,* therefore, have inferred that the wine in the ancient ritual was, as among the Greeks and Romans, poured over the animal sacrifice, and hence could be spoken of as a "fire-offering" (v.[10] n.). But the inference is hazardous in view of 28^7. Certainly somewhat later (2nd cent. B.C.) the wine was poured out at the foot of the altar (Ecclus. 50^{15}; cp. Jos. *Ant.* iii. 9^4), and yet Ben-Sira still speaks of the libation as ὀσμὴν εὐωδίας (= ריח ניחח here in 𝔊).—8. *A sacrifice* (*which is*) *to accomplish a vow*, or (*to be offered as any other form of*) *peace-offerings*] cp. v.[3] n.—10. *A fire-offering*] v.[3] n.; but the word is perhaps intrusive here; ct. v.[7]. If original, it is best taken as loosely referring to the whole accompanying offerings (v.[9b] 10^a); grammatically, it can scarcely, neglecting v.[10a], refer back to v.[9b] only (so Rashi), though Rashi is probably correct in arguing that the libation is not a "fire-offering" (see v.[8] n.); strictly speaking only the meal and oil could be covered by this term (Lev. 2^{1-3}).—12. *According to the number*, viz. of the animals *that ye offer*, *so*, *i.e.* according to the scale laid down, *shall ye offer for* or with *each* the proportionate amount of meal, oil, and wine.—13–16. The regulations just given are to bind the stranger or sojourner (*gêr*) and the native Jew alike. There is no satisfactory equivalent in English for the Hebrew *gêr*; and even in Hebrew the word underwent serious modifications of meaning. The word goes back to nomadic life; and, like the corresponding *jār* in Arabic, denoted "a man of another tribe or district who, coming to sojourn in a place where he was not strengthened by the presence of his own kin, put himself under the protection of a clan or of a powerful chief" (W. R. Smith, *Rel. Sem.* 75 f.). The two leading characteristics of the *gêr* of P are that he was not of Hebrew descent, but that he was a permanent member of the Hebrew community. The present is one of the many passages in the later laws that assert the identity in respect of civil, moral, and religious rights and duties of the Jews and of the *gêrim*; cp. v.[26. 30] 19^{10-12} 35^{15}, Ex. $12^{19. 48f.}$, Lev. 16^{29-31} $17^{8. 10-12. 13. 15f.}$ 18^{26} $20^{2ff.}$ 22^{18-20} 24^{16}. In the earlier

* *E.g.* Knobel (cited by Di.).

laws, on the other hand, differences in this respect are still recognised; *e.g.* see Dt. 14^{21} (ct. Lev. $17^{15f.}$). For a full discussion of the position of the *gêr* according to the Priestly legislation, see Bertholet, *Die Stellung der Israeliten zu den Fremden*, pp. 152–176; cp. Driver, *Deut.* p. 165.—**14–16.** "The awkward form of v.[14–16] suggests the hand of a late editor or scribe" (Moore).—**14.** *And if a sojourner sojourn* (*yagūr . . . gêr*) *with you, or if any one* (without enjoying the fixed status and recognised protection and rights of the *gêr*) *be in your midst throughout your generations, i.e.* at any future time (ל distributive), *and offer*, etc. Such is Bertholet's (p. 170) explanation of the alternative terms; in view of the general use of *gêr* it seems preferable to that commonly adopted,* *If any sojourner sojourn with you* temporarily, *or whoever abides in your midst as a permanent resident.*—**15.** All members of *the assembly, both yourselves*, viz. the Israelites, *and the sojourner that sojourneth* with you, *shall have one* and the same *statute*, that is to be irrevocable and binding on all future generations. *Both you and the gêr shall be alike before Yahweh.*

2. ארץ מושבתיכם] here only; but ארץ מגורים occurs frequently in P: Driver, *L.O.T.* p. 133. So also does מושבות in other combinations (CH. 55^{P}).—**3.** בנדבה] S נדבה, which is probably intended to be a second direct acc. to פלא: yet cp. Kön. iii. 332*r*.—אשה] 𝕲 renders by ὁλοκαύτωμα, κάρπωμα, or κάρπωσις: the first always possessed, the last two (which, like ὁλοκαύτωμα, elsewhere often render עֹלָה) had acquired, the sense of *something burnt in sacrifice*: see Deissmann, *Bibelstudien*, 134f., and E. L. Hicks in *Journ. of Hellenic Studies*, ix. 323–337, on a sacrificial inscription from Kos, where (l. 33–5) κάρπωμα is so used.—**4.** והקריב] The changes of person throughout this section "may perhaps indicate imperfect assimilation of material" (CH.); the Versions frequently differ from 𝕳, the tendency in 𝕲, and to a less extent in 𝕾, being to use the 2nd pers. pl. (see v.[5. 6. 7. 8. 11]; so in a clause peculiar to 𝕲 in v.[6]; but in an additional clause in v.[5] 𝕲 uses the 2nd sing.).—בלול] here agrees with עשרון (not סלת); cp. Ex. 29^{40}; or the cstr. is loose (cp. v.[9]); in v.[6] בלולה (but S בלול) agrees with סלת. On בלל in Phœnician (*CIS.* 165^{14}) see W. R. Smith, *Rel. Sem.* 203, [2] 220.—**5.** תעשה] so, *e.g.*, Ex. 29^{36}, Lev. 9^{7}: cp. Driver in Hastings' *DB. s.v.* "Offering." 𝕲 adds at end of v. ποιήσεις τοσοῦτο κάρπωμα ὀσμὴν εὐωδίας τῷ κυρίῳ: cp. v.[7. 10] 𝕳.—**6.** לאיל] 𝕲 + ὅταν ποιῆτε αὐτὸν ἢ εἰς ὁλοκαύτωμα ἢ εἰς θυσίαν: cp. v.[8] 𝕳.—**15.** הקהל] 𝕾 𝖁 om.; cp. Geiger, *Urschrift*, p. 358. Bertholet (*op. cit.* p. 170, n. 2) thinks the word a gloss; so also Paterson and Haupt in *SBOT*. For the *casus pendens* cstr., see Driver, *Tenses*, 196 f.

---

* Di., Str., Addis, Kautzsch.

17–21. The first of ʿarîsoth to be offered to Yahweh.—This is a special case of the law of "firsts" or "firstlings"; see on c. 18. Beyond what has been said above as to the connection of the law with P, little can be added as to the date of its literary source and origin: v.[18b] contains a phraseological link with H. The opening of the law (בבאכם; ct. v.[2]) and a clause in v.[19] (באכלכם מלחם הארץ) are phraseologically unique. The custom of regarding "the first of ʿarîsoth" sacred goes back as far as Ezekiel, and almost certainly farther, for it has no appearance of being a novelty introduced by the prophet. The law itself, like the last, recognises that the practice dates from after the settlement in Canaan. The offering is but twice referred to elsewhere: the terms of reference may be compared—

Nu. 15[20f.] ראשית ערסתכם חלה תרימו תרומה . . . מראשית ערסתיכם תתנו ליהוה תרומה.

Ezek. 44[30] וראשית עריסתיכם תתנו לכהן להניח ברכה אל ביתך.

Neh. 10[38] ואת ראשית עריסתיכם . . . נביא לכהנים.

The precise meaning of *ʿarîsoth* is obscure. The reference in Ezek. 44[30] and the use of the term "cake" in v.[20] favour the view that it is some form of cereal food prepared in the house. ראשית need not be taken in the sense of "first-fruits" (see below, p. 227), but may rather mean the first part prepared: then we have to do not with an annual offering of raw produce, but with an offering that might occur often. So 𝔊 (*φύραμα*), We. (*Proleg.*[4] 156, Eng. tr. 158), and Haupt (in *SBOT.*), who suggests that ר׳ ער״ was "originally equivalent to לחם פנים, Assyr. *akal pâni*, *i.e.* 'advance bread,' the first bread baked of some dough." Kennedy * (*EBi.* 1539) would identify *ʿarîsoth* with the Talmudic *ʿarsān*, "a porridge or paste made from the meal of barley or wheat." According to the Talmud (as cited by Levy, *NHWörterbuch*, iii. 702) *ʿarsān* was a barley food good for invalids and babies; in Syriac, too, *ʾarsânâ* is "hulled barley." In the Mishnah the present law is taken to cover preparations of wheat, barley, spelt, and two other kinds of grain (שבלת שועל ושיפון); and the amount to be given is fixed at $\frac{1}{24}$ for private individuals,

* After Lagarde in *Göttingsehe Gelehrte Nachrichten*, 1889, p. 301.

$\frac{1}{48}$ for public bakers (*Ḥallah* i. 1, ii. 7). Cp. Rom. 11^{15} (φύραμα).

17 f. Cp. v.$^{1f.}$—18. *The land whither I am about to bring you*] Lev. 18^{3} 20^{22} (H).—19. *Ye shall contribute* from the whole quantity *a contribution*, cp. 5^{9} n.: the noun and vb. in Heb. are cognate (תרימו תרומה). The vb. denotes the "lifting off" or removal of a portion, which is to become sacred by being offered to Yahweh, from the whole mass which is retained and, after the contribution has been offered, is available for common use; so in 31^{28} it refers to the selection from the whole multitude of captives of one in every 500 for Yahweh; in Lev. $4^{8.10.19}$ to the removal from the whole animal of the fat parts to be burned on the altar. The verb never refers to any rite of elevation such as is suggested by the RV. rendering of the noun by "heave-offering"; of the renderings of the vb. in RV. that in Lev. 4 ("take off") is best. See, further, Driver's art. "Offering" in Hastings' *DB*.—20. *A cake*] חַלָּה: the term, if rightly derived from חלל = "to perforate," describes the bread as "perforated," whether by the rough stones on which it was baked, or intentionally that it might better receive the oil poured over it. In OT. it is mentioned only in sacrificial connections (*e.g.* Ex. 29^{2}, Lev. 2^{4}), and but once outside P (2 S. 6^{19}). In the present passage Moore considers it a gloss on account of its syntactical isolation and its absence from v.^{21} and Ezek.—*The contribution of the threshing-floor*] cp. 18^{27} n., Ex. 22^{29} (𝔊). The exact phrase here used does not occur again.

22–31. Propitiation for sins of ignorance.—(*a*) On the part of the congregation as a whole, v.$^{22-26}$; (*b*) of an individual, v.$^{27f.}$. In the case of (*a*), the offering with which propitiation is to be made is a young bullock for a burnt-offering with the requisite accompaniments, and a he-goat for sin-offering (v.^{24}); of (*b*), a yearling she-goat for a sin-offering (v.^{27}). The law applies equally to *gêr* and native Israelite, v.$^{29f.}$.

In Lev. c. 4 f. we have other laws, not all of the same age and purpose, relative to sins of ignorance. Not only are the laws in Leviticus much more elaborate, but they differ materially from the present. Here two cases are distinguished—sins by the congregation, and sins by an individual: there four—sins by the high priest, sins by the congregation, sins by a prince or chief (נשיא), and sins by an ordinary individual. It is true the first two cases in Leviticus may be regarded as virtually identical, since the high priest is the representative of the whole congregation before God, and the offering required in either case is the same. But the two sets of laws differ materially in the nature of the requisite offerings. Here in the case of sin by the congregation *a young bullock must be offered as a burnt-offering, and a he-goat as a sin-offering* (v.^{24}); in Leviticus *no burnt-offering is demanded, but one young bullock is requirea for the sin-offering* (Lev. 4^{14}: cp. v.^{3} for the case of the high priest). Here in the case of any individual without distinction of rank, what is required is a *yearling she-goat* as a sin-offering; in Leviticus in the case of a prince, *a male-goat* ($4^{23f.}$), of an ordinary individual, *a she-goat* ($4^{28f.}$) *or a female lamb* (4^{32}) as a sin-offering. In Lev. $5^{6.\,11.\,15.\,17}$ goats, lambs, turtle-doves, young pigeons, fine meal, or rams are prescribed under certain circumstances. In the case of two birds being offered, one is offered as a sin-offering, one as a burnt-offering (Lev. 5^{7-10}).

According to many older and some modern scholars, Lev. 4 f. refers to sins of commission, whereas the present section refers to sins of omission. But this distinction is unreal, in spite of the divergent phraseology of Lev. $4^{2.\,13.\,22.\,27}$ 5^{17} and Nu. 15^{22}, which at first sight may seem to justify it; for the phraseology of v.^{24} and ^{29} and the antithesis in v.^{30} show that the writer has in mind positive acts that violate the law, and not merely the omission to do what the law enjoins. Further, the error referred to in Lev. 5^{2} is one of omission, viz. "of the requisite purifications" (cp. Driver and White on the passage; cp. also v.^{1}).

The differences are, therefore, to be explained as due to the fact that the laws date from different periods or circles; and that the practice or theory of the one period was not that of the other. For similar differences, see notes on 4^{3} and at the end of c. 18.

The actual and relative antiquity of the present section and Lev 4 f. cannot be decisively determined. In its present form Nu. 15^{22-31} presupposes 15^{1-16}, for v.^{24b} can hardly but be a reference to v.$^{8-10}$; but v.^{24b} may well be a note of the compiler who combined the laws. The peculiar language of v.^{31} can be and has been differently explained. It is generally agreed that Lev. 4 f. is not homogeneous: that at least 5^{1-6} is of different origin from c. 4: see, *e.g.*, CH., Moore in *EBi.* 2778 f., Driver and White, "Leviticus" (*SBOT.*), 58 f., 67. Of the three sections (1) Lev. c. 4; (2) Lev. $5^{1-6\,(13)}$; (3) Nu. 15^{22-31}, the first only contains unambiguous signs of P^s in its references to the two altars (Introd. § 11). On this ground, as also on the ground of its greater elaboration, especially in the greater graduation of ranks in the offenders (see above), it may be regarded as later than the substance of the other two in spite of the fact that the *total* offerings demanded by it from the unwittingly offending community are smaller than in Nu. 15^{22-31} (the sin-offering alone in Lev. 4^{14} is more important than in Nu. 15^{24}). So Di., CH., Moore against Kue. (*Hex.* 83, 299), who regarded Lev. c. 4 as the fundamental law, Lev. 5^{1-13} an appendix to it, and Nu. 15^{22-31} an expansion and explanation of Lev. $4^{13-21.\,27-31}$. As between the substance of Lev. $5^{1-6\,(13)}$ and Nu. 15^{22-31} it is more difficult to decide; CH. and Moore give the priority to Lev. $5^{1-6\,(13)}$.

22. The section, though unconnected with the last, lacks an introductory formula like those of v.$^{1.\,2a.\,17.\,18a}$, and appears to be torn from a very different context; for the clause, *and when ye err and do not do all these commandments* (*i.e.* leave any one of them unfilled), suggests that this section originally formed the close of an entire series of laws. The two heterogeneous and unrelated laws that now precede it do not do justice to the expression "all these commandments."—**23.** The present law is to hold good with regard to all existing laws of the class contemplated (perhaps, especially, ceremonial) and all laws that may be made in the future.—*By the hand of Moses*] cp. 4^{37} n.—**24.** *A young bullock for a burnt-offering*] in Lev. $4^{3.\,14}$, which requires no burnt-offering, the bullock is offered as a sin-offering, and therefore unaccompanied by the meal-offering and libations which are here enjoined *according to the law* (cp. $29^{18.\,21}$; also Lev. 5^{10} 9^{16}) laid down in v.$^{1-16}$, and specifically in v.$^{8-10}$; cp. p. 170 above. The *sin-offering* is here mentioned after the burnt-offering, as in Lev. 12^{8}. For some conclusions very precariously based on this unusual order of mentioning the two offerings, see Di.'s discussion. For the combination of the burnt-offering and sin-offering in a process of propitiation, see $6^{11.\,16}$, Lev. 5^{7-10}

$9^{3ff.}$ 12^{8} $15^{15.\,30}$; cp. Lev. 16. Each offering by itself also possessed propitiating efficacy; see, *e.g.*, Lev. 1^{4} 4^{20}, and see 17^{11} n.—**25a.** Cp. Lev. 4^{20b}.—*Their oblation*] the general term here refers specifically to the burnt-offering, v.^{24a}.—*Before Yahweh*] *i.e.* to the altar; cp. the alternative expression "before the tent of meeting" in Lev. 4^{14} and the combination of the two phrases in Lev. 4^{4}: see also 5^{16} n.—**26.** The v. adds nothing to what has been said in v.^{25}, and may consist of glosses, clause *a* explaining "that all the congregation" (v.^{25}) includes the *gêrim* (v.^{14} n.). The last clause is a violent ellipsis: *for to all the people* belongs what was committed *in error.*—**27–29.** Any individual, whether Israelite or *gêr* (v.^{29}), who has sinned inadvertently, must present a female goat a year old as a sin-offering. On the divergence from the law of Lev. 4 f., see above.—**29.** Cp. v.^{15} n. — **30 f.** On the other hand, any one wilfully and defiantly violating the law is to be *cut off from the midst of his kinsfolk*; read עַמֶּיהָ with S for עַמָּהּ = *his people* of H; cp. Ex. 31^{14}, and see 9^{13} n.—*With a high hand*] The same phrase is differently used in 33^{3}, Ex. 14^{8} (P).—*He reviles Yahweh*] and therefore from the very nature of the case cannot appease Yahweh. The point is amplified in v.^{31}.

Style of v.$^{30f.}$.—There are several peculiarities in the phraseology of these verses. גדף = to *revile*, does not occur again in the Hexateuch, and בזה only in a passage from E (Gn. 25^{34}); עונה בה recalls דמיו בו, which only occurs in H (six times in Lev. 20) and twice in Ezek. (CH. 195^{P}): הפר מצוה only occurs again in Ezr. 9^{14}, cp. and ct. הפר ברית Gn. 17^{14}; דבר יהוה and הכרת תכרת are strange in P. On the significance of these peculiarities, see above, p. 168 f.

22. תשגו] only here and in Lev. 4^{13} is √שגה = "to err" recognised in the legal literature (Dt. 27^{18} is of course entirely different), and in both cases the recognition may be merely Massoretic. We should point תְּשֹׁגּוּ from שגג, which is unmistakably used in v.^{28}, Lev. 5^{18}, and from which comes the standing term שגגה.—**24.** מעיני העדה] "Away from the eyes of," *i.e.* without the knowledge of: cp. but also ct. Lev. 4^{13} ונעלם מעיני הקהל.—נעשתה] fem. in reference to a subj. not definitely expressed, but suggested by the context; G.-K. 144*b*.—לשגגה] in v.^{26} and elsewhere (as here also in some Heb. MSS.) בשגגה: for the use of the לְ, see BDB. 516*b* (top). בשגגה is characteristic of P (CH. 168); cp. especially the use in $35^{11.\,15}$ corresponding to בבלי דעת Dt. 19^{4}.—אחר] 𝔊 + תמים.—לְחַטָּת] cp. מצתי for מצאתי: 11^{11} n.—**27.** בת־שנתה] 6^{14} n.—**28.** בחטאה] MT. intends the ה to be suffixal, referring to נפש

and the whole to be equal to "when it sins"; the *mappîk* is omitted and ה marked *rāphē'* before the following aspirate, as in עונה בה in v.[31]. BDB. (306*b*) apparently take חטאה as an infinitival form without the suffix, and Kön. (ii. p. 169) treats it as a noun, בחטאה then being parallel to and synonymous with בשגגה.—תורה אחת יהיה] 5^9 n.

32–36. The Sabbath-breaker. — While in the wilderness, some Israelites find a man gathering sticks on the Sabbath day. He is placed under restraint until his fate is determined; and then, in accordance with Yahweh's instructions, stoned without the camp.

This Midrash was probably inserted here in illustration of "sin with a high hand" (v.[30]).

The passage clearly resembles in its isolated character and general style the incident of the man who "blasphemed the name" (Lev. 24^{10-23}). Either they are the work of the same hand or the one is an imitation of the other. The latter alternative is preferable, in view of the presence of differences as well as of similarities.

With Nu. 15^{34a} cp. Lev. 24^{12a} (but ct. אתו, -הו); cp. also the *general tenor* of Nu. 15^{34b} and Lev. 24^{12b}, and the use in each passage of פרש (="to explain")—a vb. common in the Mishnah, but in OT. confined to these passages and Neh. 8^8 and Ezek. 34^{12}. Note also the similarity of the punishment—stoning without the camp. On the other hand, the blasphemer is brought to Moses only, the Sabbath-breaker to *Moses and Aaron and all the congregation*; ct., further, the cstr. of v.[34b] and Lev. 24^{12b}, and the formula of v.[36b] and Lev. 24^{23b}; and note the omission from the present incident of the hand-laying of the witnesses, Lev. 24^{14}.

Both passages are more Midrashic in character than the laws or narratives of P in general, and on this ground may be regarded as comparatively late—later, that is, than P^g or the earlier laws incorporated therewith.

32. *And the children of Israel were in the wilderness*] the remark of a writer who, looking back to the nomadic period of Israel's history as belonging to the past, lacks the systematic and artificial precision of P^g.—*Pieces of wood*] or "sticks," such as might be used to make a fire: cp. 1 K. 17^{12}, and for the vb. קשש (Poel) also Ex. $5^{7.12}$ (JE). For the force of the pl. in עצים, see G.-K. 124*m*. — *For it had not been clearly explained what ought to be done to him*] previously recorded law (Ex. $31^{14f.}$ 35^2) made Sabbath-breaking a capital offence.

What still needed to be explained was how the sentence was to be carried out (Rashi).—**36.** Cp. Lev. 24^{23}. Execution by the whole community is an ancient practice; it was intended, apparently, to involve the whole community in whatever responsibility might be incurred; see W. R. Smith, *Religion of the Semites*,[2] 285.

35. רגם . . . כל העדה] Dav. 89, R. 5; G.-K. 113*bb*. S 𝔊 read (wrongly) רגמו.

37–41. Tassels attached by a blue thread to the four corners of their quadrangular upper garments are to be worn by the Hebrews, and to serve them as a reminder of Yahweh's commandments.

After the formula (v.$^{37. 38a}$) already used in v.$^{1. 2a. 17. 18a}$, the present law opens peculiarly (see phil. n. below). "The peculiar opening 'and they shall make,' followed by the change to the second person, 'and it shall be unto you,' v.^{39}, points to the employment of some older material" (CH.). The law is either derived from H, or deliberately cast in the manner of H: note the characteristic motive—holiness to God (v.^{40b}); also the twice repeated "I am Yahweh your God" in v.^{41}, followed the first time by "who brought you out from the land of Egypt," as in Lev. 19^{36} 22^{33} 26^{13} (cp. 25^{38}), "to go a whoring after" (cp. Lev. 17^{7} 19^{29} $20^{5f.}$). Cp. Dr. *L.O.T.* p. 48 f.; CH. 202, 203^{P}. The only feature at all pointing away from H is the use of מצות rather than חקה or משפטים. Of all the scattered laws outside Lev. c. 17–26 which have been claimed for H, this has best made good its claim; cp. Baentsch, *Heiligkeitsgesetz*, 9 f.; Moore in *EBi.* 2787 f.

The *custom* regulated by this law is certainly older than Deuteronomy (22^{12}), and in all probability quite ancient.

Earlier direct evidence of the wearing of tassels by the Hebrews than Dt. 22^{12} does not exist; but representations on the ruins at Persepolis (Niebuhr, *Reisen*, ii., Table 22) and pictures of Asiatic tributaries on the Egyptian monuments (W. M. Müller, *Asien u. Europa*, 297–299, with pictures reproduced from Lepsius, *Denkmäler*) prove the existence of a similar custom elsewhere. The custom may well have been adopted from the Canaanites by the Hebrews soon after their settlement in Canaan. The tassels in some of the representations referred to are coloured *blue*.

But the *motive* here assigned is not ancient, probably, indeed, more recent than Dt., which gives no motive for this custom, though it gives a similar motive for another custom of like kind (Dt. $6^{6. 8}$). The motive is rather a religious afterthought, an attempt to make a deeply-rooted custom serve a fitting religious purpose (cp. p. 47 f.). It is possible that the tassels once served a very different religious purpose; that the wearing of them was a superstitious custom, just as the *tephillin*, which are worn in fulfilment of the law of Dt. 6^{8} (cp. Driver, *ad loc.*), may be merely substitutes for what was worn for superstitious purposes; cp. W. R. Smith, *Rel. Sem*^{1}. 416 n.

The *practice* of the law among the Jews, to which there are incidental references in NT. (Mt. 9^{20} 14^{36}, Mk. 6^{56}, Lk. 8^{44}, where the singular of κράσπεδα, 𝔊's rendering of ציצת here, is used), continues to the present day, though for long it has been customary to fulfil it by means of a special garment called *ṭallîth* or *'arba' kanphôth* (cp. Dt. 22^{12}), which, like the *tephillin*, must be worn by all males over thirteen years of age. The *ṭallîth* consists of an oblong cloth with a tassel at each corner. The head is passed through a hole in the middle of the cloth, which hangs over the breast and back. See, further, on these points, as also on the precise regulations for the manufacture of the tassels laid down by the later Jews (cp. 𝔗^{Jon} on the present passage), Kennedy's article "Fringes" in Hastings' *DB.*; S. A. Cook's on the same subject in *EBi.*; Driver on Dt. 22^{12}; and Schürer, *GJV.*^{3} ii. 484 (Eng. tr. II. ii. 111 f.). The last gives references to a large amount of literature devoted to the subject. An illustration of a modern *'arba' kanphôth* or small *ṭallîth*, clearly showing the nature of the tassel and its attachment, may be found in the *Jewish Encyclopædia*, ii. p. 76.—38. The law as given here and in Dt. 22^{12} is differently worded, and the command to use a blue cord is peculiar to Nu.

Dt. גדלים תעשה לך על ארבע כנפת כסותך אשר תכסה בה.

Nu. ועשו להם ציצת על כנפי בגדיהם . . . ונתנו על ציצת הכנף פתיל תכלת.

The terms used for *garment* are general, but apparently the ordinary outer garment of the Hebrews is intended. To each of the *corners* or *ends* of this, or, as Dt. more precisely says, to each of the *four* corners a *tassel* is to be attached. For כנף = "corner" or "end" of a garment (not as RV. "border"), see 1 S. 15^{27} 24^{5} (where note the rendering of 𝔊), Hag. 2^{12}; and cp. the use of the same word in speaking of the "four corners of the earth" (Is. 11^{12}).—*Tassels*] The word ציצת, which in S (cp. 𝔊) is read as a pl. (ציציות),

occurs elsewhere in OT. only in Ezek. 8^3, where, like the corresponding Aramaic word (ציציתא, ܨܝܨܝܬܐ), it means a "lock of hair." Since in the parallel passage in Dt. the word used means "twisted cords," and the *ṣiṣîth* actually used by the later Jews consisted of cords twisted and knotted, there is no doubt that what is actually intended here is a "tassel" rather than a continuous "fringe" (RV.).—*And place upon the tassel of the corner a thread of blue*] wherewith to attach the tassel to the garment. Later, possibly on account of the expense of the blue dye, this provision was so far annulled that white threads were permitted (*Menaḥoth* iv. 1; cp. the Gemara thereon in Talm. B. 38*a*).—**39.** *And it shall serve you as a tassel*] possibly there is a play here on two senses of the word ציצת (cp. $12^{7f.}$); the tassel is to serve as an ornament to attract the gaze of the wearer. No longer is it to serve any superstitious purpose, but it is to be a reminder of Yahweh's commandments.—*That you go not about after your heart and after your eyes*] *i.e.* that you do not follow your own inclinations and desires in preference to the requirements of the law. The writer is perhaps specially thinking of the superstitious purposes which the tassels had served. Cp. Dt. 29^{18}, Job $31^{26f.}$, and note the connection in which the similar phrase "to follow the stubbornness of the heart" is frequently used by Jeremiah, 3^{17} (after v.^{16}) $9^{13 (14)}$ 16^{12} (after v.^{11}). With "to go about after the eyes," cp. "my heart followed my eyes," Job 31^7.—The vb. תור has a somewhat different sense from that with which it is used in c. 13 f.; see 13^2 n. With the present, cp. אנשי התרים = "persons who travel about," "merchants" (1 K. 10^{15}).—*After which ye go whoring*] the relative in the present text must refer to the "heart" and "the eyes" of the last clause. But this makes the clause a very pointless addition to the preceding, and gives to the verbal phrase (זנה אחרי) an altogether exceptional use. The object of this phrase regularly refers to some illegitimate cult or superstition of those who practise it; cp. *e.g.* Lev. 17^7 $20^{5f.}$ (H), Ex. $34^{15f.}$ (J), Ezek. 6^9; and see Driver's note on Dt. 31^{16}. Possibly the present text is corrupt, and the original referred to such superstitions here; see last n.

38. ועשו] an unusual instance of the pf. with Waw Conv. unpreceded by a dominant impf.: Dr. *Tenses*, 119; וַיַּעֲשׂוּ would be more in accordance with analogy: cp. 17^2 and see 5^2 n.—39. והיה . . . אתו] the masc. indicates that the reference is not to the ציצת (fem.) simply, but to the whole appendage—tassel and thread together.—לבבכם] H uses the form לבב (*e.g.* Lev. 26^{41}); P, on the other hand, regularly, if not exclusively, לב; see BDB. p. 523*a*.

XVI.-XVIII. *The rebellion of Ḳoraḥ, Dathan, and Abiram. The rank and rights of the Levites.*

LITERATURE.—Kuenen, "Bijdragen tot de critiek van Pentateuch en Jozua, iv. De opstand van Korach, Dathan en Abiram, Num. xvi." (*Th. Ti.* xii. (1878), pp. 139–162). This article has dominated all subsequent discussions, and at once led We. (*Comp.* 339–341) to modify his earlier conclusions (*Jahrb. für deutsche Theologie*, xxi. 572–576 = *Comp.* 105–109). Among others who follow Kue., see Driver, *L.O.T.* 63–65; Baudissin, *Gesch. des ATliche Priesterthums*, 34–36. Di. and Bacon (*Triple Tradition*, 190–195), who, while still dependent on Kue., in some important respects make a new departure, are followed by CH., but adversely criticised by Addis in *EBi.*

Yahweh's choice of the tribe of Levi for superior holiness, for closer access to Himself, and for serving the priests (16^5 $17^{20\,(5)}$ 18^{2-5}), is shown (1) by the miraculous death inflicted on Ḳoraḥ and his followers, who claimed equal holiness for the whole people (c. 16); and (2) by the miracle of the blossoming stick ($17^{16-26\,(1-11)}$). These incidents are followed by a statement of the relation of Levi, on the one hand, to the priests and, on the other, to the rest of the people (18^{1-7}); and then by a series of laws, regulating the dues payable (1) by the people (*a*) to the priests, (*b*) to the Levites; and (2) by the Levites to the priests (18^{8-32}).

Such is the relation of the main subjects of this section to one another. Combined with them are (1) an account of a revolt led by Dathan and Abiram against the civil authority of Moses ($16^{12f.\ 23-30}$), and (2) some passages containing a claim on the part of the Levites to priestly rank and privileges (16^{8-10} 17^5 (16^{40})). It would in the abstract be conceivable that people, discontented with the leadership of Moses, led by Dathan and Abiram, united in a common revolt with others under Ḳoraḥ, who were aggrieved by the claims to a superior holiness on the part of the Levites, to whom Moses and Aaron belonged. But apart from the fact that the leaders are mentioned together in $16^{1.\ 27a}$, the two parties always act separately, and are finally cut off by entirely different acts of God (on 16^{32b} see n. below). Thus Dathan and Abiram are not present when Ḳoraḥ and his company interview Moses and Aaron (16^{3-11}), for at the close of the interview they need to be summoned to Moses (16^{12}). And when, on their refusal to come, Moses seeks them out at their own tents and threatens them, he has nothing to say of Ḳoraḥ (16^{25-30}). Meantime, however, Ḳoraḥ, acting quite apart, has assembled his company before the tabernacle to submit themselves to the ordeal of the censers (16^{19}). Finally, while Dathan and Abiram are swallowed up together with their tents in an earthquake, Ḳoraḥ's followers ("the two hundred and fifty men that offered incense," 16^{35}) perish by the destructive fire that issued from Yahweh's presence in the tabernacle (16^{35}, cp. Lev. 10^{2}).

It is not only in Nu. 16 that Dathan and Abiram stand apart from Ḳoraḥ; for while Dt. 11^{6} refers only to Dathan and Abiram, Nu. 27^{3} refers only to Ḳoraḥ.

It has therefore long been recognised that the story of Dathan and Abiram and the story of Ḳoraḥ were originally quite distinct, and that they have been pieced together in the present narrative very mechanically, and with merely a few very unsuccessful attempts to harmonise them (16^{32b}: see also on $16^{24.\ 27}$).

The story of Dathan and Abiram is older than the allusion to it in Dt. 11^{6}; and, in view of the close similarity of the phraseology, it is probable that the form in which the author of Dt. 11^{6} read the story contained the passage now reproduced in Nu. $16^{(1).\ 32a.\ 33b.\ 34}$. The allusion in Nu. 27^{3} to Ḳoraḥ may be the reference of a writer back to an earlier part of his own narrative, or the reference of a later writer. In either case it is probable, though, in view of some later allusions to Ḳoraḥ only, not certain, that at the time the story of Ḳoraḥ had not yet been united with that of Dathan and Abiram. The allusions in Ps. 106^{16-18}, Nu. $26^{9f.}$ (a parenthesis in a passage of P^s), and Ecclus. 45^{18} show familiarity with the present combination of the stories. On 26^{11}, see note there. Some later writers refer to Ḳoraḥ alone (Jude [11]), some to Dathan and Abiram alone (4 Macc. 2^{17}). If the stories of Dathan and Abiram and of Ḳoraḥ were originally distinct, then since Ḳoraḥ alone is referred to in Nu. 27^{3} which comes from P, and Dathan and Abiram alone in Dt. 11^{6}, the story of Ḳoraḥ is priestly (P), and the story of Dathan and Abiram prophetic (JE). These conclusions are confirmed by the linguistic and other characteristics of the two stories.

In 17^{6} (16^{41})–18^{32}, which hangs together and has been generally recognised as derived from P, it may suffice to notice a few characteristics only, such as the view of the "glory of Yahweh" and the theophanic cloud in 17^{7} (16^{42}) (see notes on 9^{18} 10^{34} 14^{10}), and the formula in $17^{26\,(11)}$; in the vocabulary, note עדה (1^{2} n.) several times, נשיא (7^{2} n.) in $17^{17.\,21}$, אהל העדות in $17^{22.\,23}$ 18^{2}, קצף (CH. 178^{P}) in 17^{11} 18^{5}, קרבן in 18^{9}. On c. 18 see further below; and, as connecting it with P^g, note the *sing.* "altar" in 18^{3}; see Introd. § 11.

In 16^{1}–17^{5} (16^{40}) as between P and JE analysis gives the following result:—

JE $16^{1f.}$ (partly), $^{12\text{-}15.\,25.\,26b.\,27b\text{-}32a.\,33.}$ (except last clause), ^{34}.

P $16^{1f.}$ (partly), $^{3\text{-}11.\,16\text{-}23.\,26a.\,27a}$ (mainly), ^{35} $17^{1\text{-}15}$ ($16^{36\text{-}40}$).

P is not homogeneous, but the analysis of it into its constituent elements does not rest mainly on linguistic differences, though certain peculiarities are noticeable in $16^{8\text{-}11.\,16f.}$ $17^{1\text{-}5}$: see phil. notes below.

In the part just assigned to JE note the following characteristics:— "the elders" (16^{25}), cp. 11^{16} n.; "flowing with milk and honey" ($16^{13f.}$), cp. 13^{27} n.; נם (16^{13}; CH. 126), חרה ל (16^{15}; CH. 233), רשעים, and כל אשר להם ($16^{26.\,30.\,33}$; CH. 231, 124), טף (16^{27}; CH. 52), with a number of minor points noticed in the margins of CH. and in some cases in the commentary below. In the parts assigned to P, note "the glory of Yahweh" (16^{19}), and עדה constantly, בתוך (16^{3}; CH. 22), וידבר . . . לאמר ($16^{5.\,23.\,26a}$ 17^{1}; CH. 185), הבדיל (16^{9}; CH. 53).

Though neither of the main themes combined in c. 16 is preserved quite intact, and the third (see below, p. 192 f.) was never more than a parasitic growth on the combination of the two original stories, each of the first two can be so nearly recovered that it will be well to reproduce them, and consider their leading motives and purpose separately before proceeding to the detailed commentary, though the preliminary discussion and the commentary are mutually supplementary throughout.

1 *The revolt against the civil authority of Moses under the leadership of Dathan and Abiram and ? On.*

Nearly the whole of the story as it was told in JE seems to be preserved here. The precise original form of the opening sentences (v.[1, 2]) cannot be recovered; and something between the opening and what now follows in v.[12] may have been lost.

[1] And Dathan and Abiram, sons of Eliab, and On, the son of Peleth, sons of Reuben . . . [2] And rose up before Moses . . . men of fame. [12] And Moses sent to call Dathan and Abiram, the sons of Eliab: and they said, We will not come up: [13] is it a small thing that thou hast brought us up out of a land flowing with milk and honey, to kill us in the wilderness, but thou must needs make thyself also a prince over us? [14] Moreover thou hast not brought us into a land flowing with milk and honey, nor given us inheritance of fields and vineyards: wilt thou bore out the eyes of these men? We will not come up. [15] And Moses was very wroth, and said unto Yahweh, Turn not Thou to their offering: I have not taken one ass from them, neither have I hurt one of them. [25] And Moses rose up and went unto Dathan and Abiram: and the elders of Israel followed him. [26] And he said, Depart, I pray you, from the tents of these wicked men, and touch nothing of theirs, lest ye be swept away in all their sins. [27] And Dathan and Abiram came out, and stood at the door of their tents, and their wives, and their sons, and their little ones. [28] And Moses said, Hereby ye shall know that Yahweh hath sent me to do all these works; that I have not done them of mine own mind. [29] If these men die the common death of all men, or if they be visited after the visitation of all men; then Yahweh hath not sent me. [30] But if Yahweh make a new thing, and the ground open her mouth, and swallow them up, with all that is theirs, and they go down alive into Sheol; then ye shall understand that these men have despised Yahweh. [31] And it came to pass, as he made an end of speaking all these words, that the ground clave asunder that was under them: [32] and the earth opened her mouth, and swallowed them up, and their households. [33] So they, and all that was theirs, went down alive into Sheol: and the earth closed upon them, and they perished from among the assembly. [34] And all Israel that were round about them fled at the cry of them: for they said, Lest the earth swallow us up also.

The general drift and purpose of the story is clear. Dathan and Abiram are Reubenites, and as such members of the tribe which once possessed, but had lost, the primacy (cp. Gn. 49[3f.]) In some way, not particularly defined in what remains of the story, they had disputed the supremacy of Moses (v.[1f.]). They defy Moses' summons to attend before him; upbraid him with the old taunt that he had not fulfilled his promise to bring them into a fruitful land, but instead had brought them out to die in the wilderness; and charge him with playing the prince over the people on the strength of the promises he cannot fulfil. There is nothing to indicate that the rebellion extends beyond the Reubenites, if indeed beyond the immediate circle of Dathan and Abiram. The taunting message, if intended to gain further support for the rebels, fails of its purpose, for Moses is accompanied by the "elders of Israel," the representatives of the whole people, when he goes to the quarter of Dathan and Abiram to threaten them to their face. The divine judgment, like the judgment on Achan (Jos. $7^{24f.}$ JE), involves the households and belongings of the offenders; but the only households affected are those of Dathan and Abiram: "all Israel" escapes.

Certain features in the story, such as the redundance in v.[32-34] and the presence of distinctive marks of both J and E, make it probable that it is in itself composite; but the analysis of these two sources can only be carried into detail in the most tentative way. Whether J and E differed materially from one another depends on the view taken of On in v.[1] and "the offering" in v.[15].

Di., Bacon, and CH. detect a story, assigned to J, distinguished from the story of Dathan and Abiram (assigned to E largely on the ground that it is quoted in Dt.), partly by its making one of the leaders of the revolt On the son of Peleth, but mainly by its representing the cause of the revolt to have been, in part at least, religious, and to have lain in a claim on the part of the malcontents to exercise sacrificial functions. This is detected in Moses' words, "respect not Thou their offering" (v.[15]). Starting from these points Bacon reconstructs J's story at length, combining with On, Ḳoraḥ the son of Ḳenaz. He argues that this story is the basis of P's, who obtains from it the name Ḳoraḥ and the religious cause of the revolt. Moreover, it was this resemblance of J's story to P's that led the editor to combine the story of JE with that of P, which, so it is argued, he would hardly have done if that story had consisted merely of a civil revolt of Dathan and Abiram. In all important respects Bacon is followed by CH. who analyse thus—

J. V.[1] ("and On the son of Peleth took"), [13. 14] (to "honey"), [15. 26b. 27] (from "and their wives"), [28-31. 33] (to "into Sheol").

E. V.[1f.] ("and Dathan and Abiram, the sons of Eliab, son of Reuben, rose up before Moses"),[12. 14b. 25. 27b] (and Dathan . . . tents), [32a. 33b. 34].

On the other hand, "On the son of Peleth" may be merely the creation of textual corruption; and Moses' reference to the "offering" can be, though perhaps not altogether satisfactorily, explained without the implication given to it by Di. and Bacon. In that case no reason remains for supposing that the story of the revolt was told in any substantially different form in the two sources.

2. *The revolt of representatives of the whole people under Ḳoraḥ against the Levites (represented by Moses and Aaron) in vindication of their equal holiness* (P^g).

This narrative runs as follows:—

2 Now Ḳoraḥ and some men of the children of Israel, two hundred and fifty, princes of the congregation, called to meetings (? men of repute) . . . : 3 and they assembled themselves together against Moses and against Aaron, and said unto them, Enough [ye sons of Levi,] for all the congregation are holy, every one of them, and Yahweh is among them: (? wherefore then lift ye up yourselves above the assembly of Yahweh?) 4 And when Moses heard it, he fell upon his face: 5 and he spake unto Ḳoraḥ and unto all . . . saying, In the morning Yahweh will make known him that is His; and him that is holy will He cause to come near unto Him: even him whom He shall choose will He cause to come near unto Him. 6 This do: take you censers; 7 and put fire therein, and put incense upon them before Yahweh to-morrow: and it shall be that the man whom Yahweh doth choose, he shall be holy. 18 And they took every man his censer, and put fire in them, and laid incense thereon, and stood at the door of the tent of meeting with Moses and Aaron. 19 And Ḳoraḥ assembled all the congregation against them unto the door of the tent of meeting: and the glory of Yahweh appeared unto all the congregation.

20 And Yahweh spake unto Moses and unto Aaron, saying, 21 Separate yourselves from among this congregation, that I may consume them in a moment. 22 And they fell upon their faces, and said, O God, the God of the spirits of all flesh, shall one man sin, and wilt Thou be wroth with all the congregation? 23 And Yahweh spake unto Moses, saying, 24 Speak unto the congregation, saying, Get ye up from about the tabernacle [of Yahweh]. 26 And he spake unto the congregation, saying . . . 27 So they gat them up from the tabernacle [of Yahweh] on every side. 35 And fire came forth from Yahweh, and devoured the two hundred and fifty men that offered the incense.

17[6] (16[41]) But on the morrow all the congregation of the children of Israel murmured against Moses and against Aaron, saying, Ye have killed the people of Yahweh. 7 (42) And it came to pass, when the congregation was assembled against Moses and against Aaron, that they looked toward the tent of meeting: and, behold, the cloud covered it, and the glory of Yahweh appeared. 8 (43) And Moses and Aaron came to the front of the tent of meeting. 9 (44) And Yahweh spake unto Moses, saying, 10 (45) Get you up from among this congregation, that I may consume them in a moment. And they fell upon their faces. 11 (46) And Moses said unto Aaron, Take thy censer, and put fire therein from off the altar, and lay incense thereon, and carry it quickly unto the congregation, and make propitiation for them: for the wrath has gone out from Yahweh; the plague is begun. 12 (47) And Aaron took as Moses spake, and ran into the midst of the assembly; and, behold, the plague was begun among the people: and he put on the incense, and made propitiation for the people. 13 (48) And he stood between the dead and the living; and the plague was stayed. 14 (49) Now they that died by the plague were fourteen thousand and seven hundred, besides them that died about the matter of Ḳoraḥ. 15 (50) And Aaron returned unto Moses unto the door of the tent of meeting, the plague having been stayed.

Then follow in immediate sequence the story of the blossoming of Aaron's stick in vindication of the superiority of Levi ($17^{16-26\ (1-11)}$), and the regulations for the payment of dues to the priests and Levites (c. 18).

The real point of this important story was for long obscured owing to the additions made by a later writer, who turned Ḳoraḥ and "all his company" into Levites. Ḳoraḥ's company in this story are *not* all Levites; probably none of them were Levites; the two parties to the struggle throughout are Moses and Aaron (as representing the Levites) on the one side, and "the whole of the congregation," *i.e.* the whole of the rest of the people (cp. 1^2 n.), on the other. Associated with Ḳoraḥ are 250 princes of the "congregation" (16^2), *i.e.* of all Israel. Ḳoraḥ champions the cause of the whole congregation (16^3), and the people identify themselves with the leaders when they perish by the divine judgment (17^5 (16^{41})). The writer of 27^3 quite clearly assumes that Ḳoraḥ's followers were not exclusively Levites, for he goes out of his way to explain that Ṣelopheḥad, though a Manassite, was not a follower of Ḳoraḥ. When the intrusive passages of P^s have been removed, nothing remains to indicate that either Ḳoraḥ himself or any of his followers ranked in P^g as Levites.

3. *The claim of the Levites to priestly privileges* (P^s).

In c. 16f. there are now inserted in P^g's story of Ḳoraḥ several passages which by their style betray their origin in the priestly school, but which represent an entirely different point of view. These passages, which never formed an independent story, are $16^{8-11.\ 16f.}$ 17^{1-5} (16^{36-40}), in addition to that part of v.[1] which contains the genealogy of Ḳoraḥ. In these verses all Israel except Levi drop entirely into the background, for they have no concern in this dispute: the struggle is confined to the tribe of Levi. The object of these passages is to condemn the non-Aaronic Levites for seeking the *priesthood.* This comes out clearly in 16^{9-11}: Moses recognises in the rebels a class *already* distinguished from "the congregation of Israel," and admitted to a closer access to Yahweh. It is no longer here a struggle for equal rights for the whole congregation, but a struggle for equal rights within a class sharply marked off from the rest. Ḳoraḥ's company are here already in undisputed possession of what in the foregoing story they rise in revolt to claim. The same point of view is represented in 17^{1-5} (16^{36-40}); note, especially, the moral—*that no stranger which is not of the seed of Aaron come near to burn incense before Yahweh* (17^{5} (16^{40})). And to the same hand we may also refer $16^{16f.}$—a parallel to $16^{6f.}$ in P^{g}.

The inserted passages reflect some struggle, of which we have no direct record, between the priests and the Levites. The question has been much discussed, especially by Vogelstein, *Der Kampf zwischen Priestern und Leviten seit den Tagen Ezechiels* (1889), whose work is reviewed in an important article by Kuenen in *Th. Ti.* xxiv. 1–42 (=*Gesammelte Abhandlungen*, ed. Budde, p. 465 ff.), the closing section of which in particular deals with the place of Nu. 16–18 in the history of the priesthood. Vogelstein is inclined to place the struggle of the Levites, reflected in P^{s}'s additions to Nu. 16 f., before the close of the 5th cent. B.C.; Kuenen, with more reason, inclines to a later date. Centuries later, even when the Levites had sunk to the insignificant position which they held in the 1st cent. A.D., they yet succeeded in making good a minor pretension to priestly privileges, obtaining from Agrippa II. the right to wear the priestly linen (Jos. *Ant.* xx. 9^{6}).

1, 2. The leaders of the rebellion.—These are, according to the present narrative, a Levite, Ḳoraḥ, and three Reubenites—Dathan, Abiram, and On; also two hundred and fifty unnamed "princes."—*Ḳoraḥ, the son of Iṣhar, the son of Ḳŏhāth, the son of Levi*] Ex. $6^{16. 18. 21}$, 1 Ch. $6^{22f. (37f.)}$ $5^{27f.}$ 6^{7} ($6^{1f. 22}$). The clause is from P; but the genealogy does not appear to be ancient; it is earlier in origin than Ch. (see preceding references), but later than P^{g}; for Ex. 6^{13-29} is an insertion of P^{s} between the question of Ex. 6^{12} and the answer of 7^{1} in P^{g}'s narrative. A certain Ḳoraḥ, on the other hand, appears in 1 Ch. 2^{43} as descended from Judah (1 Ch. 2^{3}) and as "son" of Ḥebrôn.

Now the Levitical Ḳoraḥ is a "*nephew*" of Ḥebron (Ex. $6^{18.\ 21}$). It is therefore highly probable * that the two Ḳoraḥs are in reality one and the same; that Ḳoraḥ of Judah was, by later genealogists, converted into Ḳoraḥ the Levite, just as the originally Ephraimite Samuel (1 S. $1^{1.\ 19f.}$) is provided in later times with a Levitical descent (1 Ch. $6^{18\ (33)}$). There was good reason for the transformation; for Ḳoraḥ was the eponym of an important guild of singers (cp. the titles to Ps. 42–49) who became incorporated with the Levites, presumably at some time subsequent to Ezra, when the singers were still distinguished from Levites (Ezr. $2^{40f.}$).† Since P^{g}'s story does not require Ḳoraḥ to be a Levite, but rather excludes such an origin for the leader of a revolt of the "whole congregation" against the exclusive claims of Levi, and since it is essential to the point of view of P^{s} that Ḳoraḥ should be a Levite, the insertion of the genealogy of Ḳoraḥ is to be attributed to P^{s}. In P^{g}, then, Ḳoraḥ was probably understood, if not directly stated, to be a Judahite; the leader of the revolt is thus a member of the leading secular tribe (p. 14, 18). It is possible, as Bacon suggests, that P obtained the name from J; in any case it is probable that some ancient tradition lies at the base of P's story, and that the name of Ḳoraḥ belonged to that tradition. —*Dathan and Abiram*] These names come from JE. Whether the names appeared in both sources of JE is uncertain; probably they appeared at least in E, since they are referred to in Dt. 11^{6}. Abiram, meaning "the (my) father is exalted," is an ancient personal name (*HPN.* 22–34); both origin and meaning of Dathan are obscure. *On the son of Peleth* plays no further part in the story, nor is he ever referred to in any of the allusions to this narrative. Harmonists (*e.g.* Keil) explained this on the ground that "he probably withdrew from the conspiracy." Two plausible explanations have been offered of this isolated reference: (1) Many ‡ have considered

* The appreciation of the extent of this probability rests on familiarity with the methods of ancient and, especially, Hebrew genealogists. The reader may consult on this point with much profit Mr. S. A. Cook's article "Genealogies" in *EBi.*

† Cp. W. R. Smith, *Old Test. in the Jewish Church*,[2] 203.

‡ Graf, Köhler, Kue., Di., Nöld., Str., Paterson.

the present clause to be textually corrupt, ואון being a corrupt repetition of the last letters of the preceding word יאב (אל) and בן־פלת a corruption of בן־פלוא. On this assumption On disappears, and v.[1] (from "Dathan" to the end) originally ran—*And Dathan and Abiram, sons of Eli'ab, son of Pallu, son* (𝔊 S here: Dt. 11^6 𝔥) *of Reuben.* This genealogy is certainly known to P (26^{6-9}, Gn. 46^9, Ex. 6^{14}), but how much earlier it may be cannot be determined, for Dt. 11^6 does not mention Pallu. (2) Others * see in *On the son of Peleth* the name of one of the ringleaders in J's parallel to E's story of Dathan and Abiram. This explains the *isolated* reference to On less well than (1). The name On is closely allied to the Edomite and Jeraḥmeelite clan-name Onam (Gn. 36^{23}, 1 Ch. 2^{26}), the Judahite clan-name Onan (26^{19}), and the name of an ancient southern town, Ono (Neh. 6^2; list of Thothmes III., cp. W. M. Müller, *Asien u. Europa*, 159), and Ben-oni, according to story, the name given by his mother to Benjamin (Gn. 35^{18}). This affinity of On with a series of names belonging to Southern Palestine might be explained either, if On is correctly described as Reubenite, by assuming an earlier settlement of Reuben W. of Jordan,† or by assuming that On in the source was described as Judahite; the latter is probable enough, if On be derived from J. Note also that *Peleth* is elsewhere a Jerameelite name, 1 Ch. 2^{33}. For Bacon's identification of Peleth with Philistine there seems little ground.—*Now Ḳoraḥ . . . took*] the verb ויקח is left without an object. That there is an intentional ellipsis of the object "men" (RV.) is highly improbable. Either ויקח is a corruption, possibly of ויקם = *now Ḳoraḥ arose*; ‡ or it is a fragment of a sentence, the object of the verb having been omitted by accident or design in the process of compilation from the several sources. Adopting the latter view, Bacon and CH. suggest that the original object was "the offering" referred to in v.[15].—**2.** The construction of the v. is loose in consequence, perhaps, of the insertion in P, whence its main substance is drawn, of some clauses from

* Bacon, CH.; see above, p. 190.

† Cp. Steuernagel, *Einwanderung*, 15 ff.; Cheyne in *EBi. s.v.* "On."

‡ Kue., Di., Str., Paterson.

JE.—*And they rose up before Moses*] JE; P's parallel, *and they assembled together against Moses and Aaron* (cp. 17^7 (16^{41})), follows in v.^{3}. The difference is characteristic. Dathan and Abiram rebel against Moses (v.$^{12. 15. 25. 28}$), Ḳoraḥ against Moses and Aaron (v.$^{3. 18. 20}$ $17^{6. 7. 8}$ ($16^{41. 42. 43}$)).—*And men of the children of Israel, two hundred and fifty*] The number is certainly from P; see v.^{35}. Bacon may be right in assigning the first clause to E, but it scarcely formed the immediate sequence in the source to the clause that precedes it.—*Princes of the congregation*] 4^{34} n. 31^{13} 32^2, Ex. 16^{22} (all P). The phrase must come from P, for both terms are highly characteristic of that writer; for נשיא, see 7^2 n., and for עדה, 1^2 phil. n. In JE such people would be called "elders," as indeed they are in v.^{25}, or "captains" (שרים). The assignment of this clause to P is important in determining the point of the story; the leaders who act with Ḳoraḥ are representatives of the non-Levitical tribes: cp. 27^3, and see p. 192, above.—*Called to meetings*] the phrase (קראי מועד) is not the same as that found in 1^{16}; but see phil. n. there. It occurs nowhere else, and the precise meaning is uncertain; the undefined מועד may have a collective force, and the whole phrase may define these persons as those who were summoned to meetings for consultation; cp. 𝔊 σύνκλητοι βουλῆς.—*Men of name*] with אנשי שם here, cp. אשני השם in Gn. 6^4 (J), and אנשי שמות in 1 Ch. 5^{24} 12^{30}. In its present position the phrase scarcely means more than "men of repute, of recognised social position": cp. Job 30^8 where social outcasts are termed "nameless" (בני בלי שם), and the use of "name" in Pr. 22^1, Ecclus. 41^{12}. If the phrase come from JE it may in its original position, like the similar phrases in Gn. and Ch., have had the slightly fuller sense of "famous men"; for "name" often means "fame" (*e.g.* 2 S. 7^9).

3–7. Ḳoraḥ maintains the equal holiness of all Israel.—Ḳoraḥ and his company assemble before Moses and Aaron, assert the equal holiness of the whole people, and condemn Moses and Aaron for their assumption of superior holiness. Moses invites the rebels to subject themselves and their claim to the test of a divine decision by a kind of ordeal (cp. p. 44 f.), and for this purpose to attend before Yahweh the next day with censers filled with fire and incense.—3. *And they came together to Moses and Aaron*] In itself the phrase expresses no hostile intent: cp. Ex. 32^1. According to the present composite narrative, the subject must include all the persons mentioned in v.$^{1f.}$; but this is inconsistent with the implication of v.$^{12. 25}$ that Dathan and Abiram remained in their tents till Moses came to them. In P the subject of the verb is Ḳoraḥ and the two hundred and fifty princes. See, further, on this clause the n. on *and they rose up before Moses* in v.^{2}.—*Enough!*] of your pretensions. The meaning of רב לכם may be gathered from passages like Dt. 1^6 2^3, in which the subject is expressed. The phrase is often used, as here, elliptically: see Dt. 3^{26}, Ezek. 45^9; but the instances do not favour the view of the ellipsis represented in RV, "Ye take too much upon you." The phrase recurs in v.^{7}, with the addition of "ye sons of Levi," and there forms the conclusion of Moses' words to Ḳoraḥ and his company. But the final clause of v.^{7} is really out of place, for the persons addressed are not (all) Levites, nor is *enough* a suitable sequence to the words that precede. On the other hand, Ḳoraḥ may well have addressed Moses and Aaron as "sons of Levi." It is probable, therefore, that in P^g, Ḳoraḥ's speech began with *Enough, ye sons of Levi*, or, possibly, as CH. suggest, that these words originally stood at the end of v.^{3}. The speech, in that case, began and ended with the same abrupt reproof. The words owe their place in v.^{7} to P^s, who turns Ḳoraḥ and his followers into Levites.—*The whole congregation*, yea, *all of them are holy*] not merely as a whole is Israel holy in virtue of Yahweh's presence in their midst (cp. 5^3), but the individual Israelites are, one and all, irrespective of the tribe to which they belong, holy: such is the principle for which Ḳoraḥ contends.—*And Yahweh is among them*] The clause is from P; J, to whom Di. and Bacon assign it, would have written not בתוכם (cp. 5^3, Ex. 25^8 (P)), but בקרבם (11^{20} (J)): see CH. 22^P 58^{JE}.—*Why do ye lift yourselves up above the assembly of Yahweh*] this sentence might, with better reason than the last, be referred to JE on the ground of its style; but if so, an originally sing. vb. addressed to Moses has been turned into a pl. addressed to Moses and

Aaron. The vb. (התנשא) occurs, not quite with its present signification, in two poetical passages (23^{24} 24^{7}): otherwise it is not found again in the Hexateuch; but see 1 K. 1^{5}, Ezek. 29^{15}; cp. also 1 Ch. 29^{11} where, with Yahweh as subject, the signification is necessarily different. The interrogative (מדוע) is found but once besides in P (Lev. 10^{17} (P^{s})); it occurs 9 times in JE (*e.g.* 12^{8}; CH. 230^{JE}).—*Yahweh's assembly*] 20^{4} (P), Dt. $23^{3.4.}$ (cp. Lam. 1^{10}, Neh. 13^{1}) $^{9. (1. 3. 8)}$, Mic. 2^{5}, 1 Ch. 28^{8} †. On קהל, see 10^{7} n.; and, on the usage of the whole phrase, Corn. in *ZATW*. xi. 23–25.—4. *And Moses . . . fell on his face*] 14^{5} n. The same action is twice referred to both Moses and Aaron later in the narrative (16^{22} 17^{10} (16^{45})). The restriction of it to Moses here may be the result of fusion of sources at this point, v.^{3b} possibly coming from JE.—5. *All his company*] עדה is so regularly used by P^{g} of the whole of Israel (1^{2} phil. n.) that the present very restricted use is decidedly strange: further, in the present story Ḳoraḥ speaks for and represents "all the congregation" (v.$^{19. 21. 24}$ $17^{6. 7. 10. 11}$ ($16^{41. 42. 45. 46}$)). Either "all the congregation," or, rather, "the two hundred and fifty princes of the congregation" (who, as a matter of fact, accept Moses' challenge, v.^{35}), was originally read here in P^{g}; the present phrase has been substituted by P^{s} (cp. v.$^{11. 16}$ 17^{5} (16^{40})) in order to maintain his different point of view, that not all Israel, as in P^{g}, but only a section, viz. the Levites, are calling in question the position of the leaders. —*In the morning*] Ex. 16^{7} (P).—*Yahweh will make known him that is His; and him that is holy will He suffer to come near Him, even him whom He chooses will He suffer to come near Him*] the balance of the clauses favours the foregoing rather than the rendering of RV., "Yahweh will show who are His, and who is holy, and will cause him to come near," etc. In using the sing. here and in v.^{7} the writer has in mind a whole class (the Levites who are represented by Moses and Aaron) rather than an individual; cp. the representative character of the individual in $17^{20 (5)}$, the representative use of *thou* in v.^{17} (= Ḳoraḥ and his followers), and see n. on 20^{14}. According to the degree in which Yahweh appropriates anyone, in other words, according to the degree of His holiness (see n. after 17^{5}), can he approach

Yahweh with safety; such is the general principle embodied in the arrangement of the camp (see p. 18). But the term "bring near" (to Yahweh) may here include a somewhat more specific sense, strictly applicable only to the priests who were included among the Levites. In P the regular term for a sacrificial offering is the thing "brought near" (קרבן). Not unnaturally, then, the same writer uses the vb. "to come near" (קרב) with the special technical sense of approaching Yahweh at the altar. Hence it was used predominantly of the priests, 17^{5}, Lev. 16^{1} 21^{17} 10^{3}; so also by Ezek. (40^{46}). But the use of this phrase with reference to the Levites, *as distinguished from the priests*, in v.$^{9f.}$ is probably confined to P^{s}. In 3^{6}, probably also in 18^{2}, the Levites are said to "be brought near" to the priests, which is a different matter; cp. Baudissin, *Priesterthum*, 29 f., 116. In Ps. 65$^{5\,(4)}$ P's technical sense of the vb. may be in the writer's mind, but he himself uses the vb. metaphorically.—**6.** *Censers*] or, as RV. renders the same word in Ex. 27^{3}, *fire-pans*. מחתה means something with which hot coals could be snatched up (חתה Is. 30^{14}) and taken from one place to another. Except in the present narrative the מחתה is mentioned as a receptacle for incense only in Lev. 10^{1} 16^{12}. A more distinctive term for censer is מקטרת (Ezek. 8^{11}, 2 Ch. 26^{19}).—*Ḳoraḥ and all his company*] scarcely a true vocative clause in spite of the principle explained in Dr. *Tenses*, 198, Obs. 2. It is rather a note by P^{s}; see 1st note on v.^{5}.—**7.** *Put fire in them and set incense on them*] Lev. 10^{1}.—*Before Yahweh*] *i.e.* as defined in v.^{18} (cp. v.^{35}), at the "tent of meeting": cp. 5^{16} n.—*Enough! ye sons of Levi*] the clause is out of place: see n. on v.^{3}. The persons addressed in v.$^{5-7}$ are not Levites.

1. ויקח] The versions contain paraphrases rather than variants. The present text already existed and its difficulty was felt when they were made: 𝔊 *καὶ ἐλάλησεν*, 𝔖 (and similarly 𝔗^{O}) ܘܐܬܦܠܓ : 𝔙 *ecce autem*.—**3.** כל העדה כלם] כלם strengthens the preceding phrase with כל as in Is. 14^{18}, Ezek. 11^{15} (Kön. iii. 340*k*); the pl. קדשים distributes the collective subj.—**5.** בקר וְיֹדַע] The cstr., which is comparatively rare (Dr. *Tenses*, 125), is found also in Ex. 12^{3} (P).—5^{b} is, in 𝔊^{AFL}, less verbally tautologous with 5^{a} than in 𝔐—*καὶ οὓς οὐκ ἐξελέξατο ἑαυτῷ οὐ προσηγάγετο πρὸς ἑαυτόν*.

8–11 (P^s). The Levites claim an equal right to the priesthood with the priests.—Moses, addressing Ḳoraḥ in particular, and the whole body of Levites generally, upbraids them with discontent at the position assigned to them by God in virtue of which, as distinguished from the other tribes, they "come near" to Yahweh, or, in other words, attend to the service of the tabernacle. In claiming, as they now do, the priesthood, it is not Aaron's, *i.e.* the priests', self-assumed authority that they are calling in question; they are rebels against Yahweh Himself, since the distinction between priests and Levites is by divine ordinance.

These verses by themselves are clear enough: it is the *priesthood* that is in question; Ḳoraḥ, representing the Levites, claims it for the whole tribe; Moses insists that it is the right of Aaron and his seed alone. The contrast is between the Levites and the family of Aaron; Moses is the arbiter: cp. v.[16f.] 17^{1-5}. This is irreconcilable with the preceding verses and the passages connected with them, in spite of the attempts of the editor in v.[6.7] (see notes) to make them consistent. Note in particular that the distinction to the existence of, or to the attempt to establish, which Ḳoraḥ objects, on behalf of the whole congregation in v.[3], is here a distinction which Ḳoraḥ himself already enjoys, but considers insufficient. In v.[3–7] Ḳoraḥ claims the right, which is withheld from him, to "draw near" to God; in v.[9] he is distinguished by the possession of this right.—**8.** Moses addresses the Levites. Ḳoraḥ is here a Levite; see v.[1] (the genealogy). He is addressed, as the leader of the tribe, by name; but the speech is to the whole tribe—*ye sons of Levi.*—**9.** *Is it too little for you that the God of Israel hath separated you* (8^{14} P^s) *from* the rest of *the congregation of Israel to bring you near to Him* (v.[5] n.), *to serve the service of the tabernacle of Yahweh* (3^7), *and to stand before the congregation to serve them* (3^6 n.)? To "stand before" and "to serve" are synonymous expressions; cp. Dt. 1^{38} with Nu. 11^{28}.—**11.** *Therefore thou and all thy company* (v.[5] n.) *are those who have gathered together against Yahweh* (14^{35})] in seeking the priesthood Ḳoraḥ and the priests are rebels against Yahweh; why should they murmur against Aaron, since the priesthood is not of his but Yahweh's making. A similar condensed argument occurs in Ex. 16^{8b} (P).

8. שמערנא] נא also occurs in P^s in Jos. 22^{26}; but though used over a hundred times in JE, it never occurs in P^g (CH. 186). Its occasional use in P^s is one indication that P^s was more influenced than P^g by the earlier styles.—9 f. המעט . . . כי . . . ובקשתם] virtually the same construction is found in Jos. $22^{17f.}$ (P^s) (the last clause introduced by the waw; but, on account of the intervening subj., the verb is impf.). For other instances of sentences after המעט, see BDB. p. 590; and for the interrogative sentence without an interrog. particle, G.-K. 150*a*; Dr. *Tenses*, § 119.

12–15 (JE). Dathan and Abiram summoned. Moses defied, and his leadership questioned on the ground of incompetence.—12. *We will not come up*] The message ends with the same flat refusal to attend the summons (v.^{14}). The vb. (עלה) is sometimes used of going to a superior, or a judge (Gn. 46^{31}, Dt. 25^7, Jud. 4^5).—13. *A land flowing with milk and honey*] 13^{27} n. The phrase occurs 8 times in J, never in E, according to CH. (34^{JE}). Quite exceptionally it is here used of Egypt—effectively from the standpoint of the rebels.—*To kill us in the wilderness*] 20^4, Ex. 17^3.—13b. Cp. Ex. 2^{14}.—14. Is Moses bent on throwing dust in the eyes of the Israelites by the promise, which he cannot or will not fulfil, to lead the people into *a land flowing with milk and honey*? cp. Ex. 4^{30} in the light of Ex. $3^{7f.}$. The figure in the Hebrew phrase *wilt thou bore out the eyes*? (used literally in Jud. 16^{21}) is stronger than, but seems equivalent to, the English "throw dust in the eyes of."—*Fields and vineyards*] the terms are collective singulars: cp. 20^{17} 21^{22} (E), Ex. 22^4, and also, in the pl., 1 S. 22^7.—*These men*] scarcely with Rashi to be treated as a periphrasis for "us"; but it refers to the Israelites who followed Dathan and Abiram, mentioned in part of the story not reproduced here, or referred to in the clause "men of the children of Israel" in v.^{2}.—15. *Turn not to*] pay no heed to. Cp. the parallel in Ps. $102^{18\,(17)}$ (לא בזה = פנה אל): see also Dt. 9^{27}, Lev. 26^9, Ezek. 36^9. The phrase is not the same that is used in Gn. $4^{5f.}$.—*Their offering*] the term (מנחה) could not have been used by P in reference to the incense of v.^{7}; his general term for offering is different (קרבן), and he uses the present term only in the specific sense of meal-offering: cp. Driver in

Hastings' *DB.*, *s.v.* "Offering," iii. 587; also CH. 118^{P}. On this ground alone, then, the clause must be referred to JE. But no further reference to an offering is made in what remains of JE's narrative. Unless there is here an allusion to some part of the narrative of JE not retained in the compilation (see above, p. 190), the whole clause, "pay no heed to their offering," is simply a prayer that Yahweh may withhold His favour, and, therefore, in effect a curse such as "while all Israelites were allowed to sacrifice, might be naturally invoked against any enemy" (Addis, *EBi.* 1018).—**15b.** Cp. 1 S. 12^{3}. The connection between $v.^{15a}$ and $v.^{15b}$ is not very close, and the two clauses may be from different sources.

12. וישלח . . . לקרא ל] 22^{5}; קרא with ל, אל, or acc., 51 times in JE, 9 in P (always, except Ex. 7^{11}, with אל): so CH. 139^{JE}.—**13.** Throughout this v. 𝔖 has 2nd pl.—המעט . . . כי . . . כי] unlike $v.^{9f.}$ above (where see note). The מעט in the present case (as, *e.g.*, in Gn. 30^{15}) gains comparative force simply from the context: Kön. iii. 308*a*.—תשתרר] The Hithp. of this vb. only here. On the force of the Hithp. ("to play the prince"), see G.-K. 54*e*.—**14.** ותתן] The force of the negative in the previous clause continues; cp. 23^{19}; Dav. 128, R. 6; G.-K. 152*z*.—**15.** ויחר ל . . . מאד] cp. Gn. 4^{5} 34^{7} (J), 1 S. 18^{8}, 2 S. 3^{8} 13^{21}, Neh. 4^{1} 5^{6}; see, further, CH. 233^{JE}.—חמור] 𝔊 ἐπιθύμημα = חמוד; see Geiger, *Urschrift*, 439 ff.—את אַחַד מהם] the acc. אחד being defined by מהם is rightly preceded by את; Kön. iii. 288*f*.

16 f. (P^{s}). These verses are a sequel to $v.^{8-11}$, but a parallel to $v.^{6f.}$. Ḳoraḥ and his company of Levites are to assemble at the tabernacle with Aaron, each man bringing his censer.

17. מחתתו (1)] 𝔖 + ותנו בהן אש; see $v.^{7. 18}$ 𝔥.—עליהם] Dav. 1, R. 3; S עליהן.

18–24 (P^{g}). **The scene before the tabernacle.**—The sequel to $v.^{3-7}$.

18. Accepting the test proposed by Moses ($v.^{6f.}$), Ḳoraḥ and the two hundred and fifty princes prepare their censers and take up their position at the door of the tent of meeting together with Moses and Aaron. Some intervening narrative explaining that Ḳoraḥ accepted the test proposed by Moses, and that he and his companions went away to prepare for it, may well have been included in P^{g}'s original story; but if so it has been rejected by the editor (P^{s}) to make room for his own words (v.$^{8-11.\ 16f.}$).—19. Ḳoraḥ assembles all Israel, whose rights he was championing (v.^{3}), to watch the trial. The *glory of Yahweh* appears ominously as in 14^{10} (see note there).—20–22. Yahweh bids Moses and Aaron separate themselves from the rest of the people, and so save themselves from the destruction He intends to send on them. Moses and Aaron beg that the whole people may not perish for one man's sin.—21. The people as a whole must be supposed to have favoured Ḳoraḥ (cp. v.^{19}); hence the divine intention to destroy them.—*That I may consume them immediately*] 17^{10} (16^{45}). Similar motives are expressed somewhat differently in Ex. $32^{9f.}$ 33^{5} (JE).—22. *And they fell upon their faces*] v.^{4} n.—*And said, O God, God of the spirits of all flesh*] On the usage of אֵל ("God"), see 12^{13} phil. n.; in 27^{16} Yahweh is used instead; for אֵל, before a defining appositional phrase, cp. Gn. 33^{20} (JE). The phrase *God of the spirits of all flesh*, which recurs only in 27^{16} and is therefore peculiar to P, betrays the advanced theological standpoint of P. Yahweh is to him far more than the God of Israel; He is the one and only author of all human life, and, as its author, capable of destroying it (cp. Gn. $6^{12ff.}$ P; but so also Gn. 6^{7} $7^{22f.}$ J^{s}): cp. Job $34^{14f.}$, also Ps. $104^{29f.}$. The term "all flesh" (כל בשר), characteristic of the later literature, occurs 18 times in P; see *Expos.*, Sept. 1893 (On Joel), p. 215.—*Should one man sin and Thou* in consequence *be indignant against*, and, therefore, destroy not him only, but *the whole congregation* (Lev. 10^{6}, Jos. 22^{18}—P), *i.e.* the people of Israel; cp 18^{5}. The one man must be the single ringleader, viz. Ḳoraḥ; the question, inconsistent with the point of view in v.$^{1f.}$ which gives several leaders, is a valuable clue to the original form of P's narrative. Is one man to sin in leading others astray, and are all to perish though their only sin consists in having been led astray? Again the theological standpoint is advanced; it is far removed from the dominance of the early doctrine of solidarity, and is most easily explained if referred to a period influenced by Ezekiel's strong individualism (see, *e.g.*, Ezek. 18. 33). The writer is indeed in some respects beyond Ezekiel's standpoint; he shows an awakening to the difference between the leaders and the led in wrong-doing, and inclines to judge the latter very lightly. On the other hand, the present writer is less dogmatic than Ezekiel: he raises a question; he does not make an assertion. For the divine indignation which is apt to break loose in destructive activity, cp. Lev. 10^6, Nu. 1^{53} 18^5, Dt. 9^{19}.—**23 f.** Yahweh, acceding to the intercession of Moses and Aaron (v.[22]), directs the people through Moses to retire from the tabernacle in order to avoid being involved in the destruction (v.[35]) of those who present the incense. The people obey, v.[27a].—*The tabernacle* (משכן) *of Ḳoraḥ, Dathan, and Abiram*] the phrase in the present text, both here and in v.[27], is due to an editor. For, note (1) the word משכן is constantly used in the Hexateuch of the dwelling of Yahweh, but never, in the sing., of the dwelling-place of men. The pl. is used in a *poetical* passage (24^5) of human habitations. (2) The sing. noun (ct. v.[26]) followed by the three names is strange: Ḳoraḥ, Dathan, and Abiram did not share one dwelling between them. The difficulty is not satisfactorily surmounted by arguing that משכן here means "district," and is therefore suitably followed by the names of the three men, since all—the Ḳohathite Ḳoraḥ, and the Reubenites Dathan and Abiram—had their position on the S. of the tabernacle (2^{10} 3^{29}). (3) The phrase is pointless in the context. For, since the people are assembled before the tabernacle (v.[19]), the command in its present form directs the people to depart from a place in which they are not. There can be no reasonable doubt that the command in P^g ran, *Depart from about the tabernacle of Yahweh* (cp. $17^{28\,(13)}$). When the story of Ḳoraḥ was united by the editor with that of Dathan and Abiram, the fact that Ḳoraḥ and his comrades were destroyed in the immediate proximity of the tabernacle was obscured (though it is still clear enough from v.[35]); the editor wished to suggest that all alike were destroyed in their tents. $\mathfrak{G}^B$, taking exception perhaps to the sing. משכן with the three names, omits "Dathan and Abiram" both here and in v.[27].

18. עליהם] The pl. suffix refers to the plural implicit in the distributive phrase איש מחתתו: Kön. iii. 346*p*.—ומשה] 𝔊 𝔖 omit the ו—perhaps rightly, for we should then have this natural sequence: Ḳoraḥ and the princes prepare for the trial (v.[18a]); Moses and Aaron take up their stand at the tent (v.[18b]); Ḳoraḥ assembles the people there (v.[19]).—**22.** האיש אחד] There are several possible explanations of the cstr. The simplest, and by far the most probable, is that the ה is interrogative and should be pointed הַאִישׁ (G.-K. 100*m*); then for the subordination of the two sentences to the interrog., see G.-K. 150*m*. Or it might be a case of the omission of the art. with the numeral (cp. 28[4]): so Kön. iii. 334*s*; then the sentence is interrogative without an interrogative particle, as in v.[10]. Or the אחד may be an acc. of the state (Dav. 70)—"The man being one and only one"; cp. Is. 51[2].

25–34. The scene before the tents of Dathan and Abiram (JE).

These verses, with the exception of v.[26a. 27a] (P^g and P^s) and v.[32b] (P^s), form the sequel to v.[12–15].

25. Dathan and Abiram having refused to come to Moses (v.[12]), Moses, accompanied by *the elders of Israel* (cp. 11[30] E, and n. on 11[16]), goes to them.—**26.** Moses bids the people remove from the neighbourhood ot the tents of Dathan and Abiram. The introductory clause and the speech itself are from different sources. The word *congregation* (1[2] n.) prevents the former being referred to J (E), to which several words in the speech conclusively point. *And he spake unto the congregation saying* is best with CH. referred to P^g, though it may be, as Di. regards it, the work of the editor. In the former case Moses' announcement of the divine warning (v.[24]) has been suppressed in favour of JE's speech.—*Depart now from*] (סורו נא מעל); P in v.[24. 27] expresses the same idea differently (ויעלו מעל . . . מסביב, העלו מסביב ל). With the present vb., cp. 12[10] (E); the enclitic נא is highly characteristic of JE; v.[8] phil. n.—*These wicked men*] Dathan and Abiram. רשע occurs 8 times in JE, once only in P (35[31]); CH. 231.—*Anything that is theirs*] the same phrase (כל אשר להם), though of necessity differently rendered in English, occurs in v.[30. 33]. The idiom is used 26 times in JE, twice only in P; CH. 124[JE].—*Lest ye be swept away in all their sins*] For the sentiment and the vb. (ספה), cp. Gn. 18[23f.], also Gn. 19[15. 17] (all J).—**27a** (P^g). Sequel to v.[24 (26a)].—**27b** (JE). Moses and Aaron having arrived at the tents of Dathan and Abiram, the latter with their wives and children come out and stand at their tent doors. The Hebrew may also mean that they had come out before Moses had arrived. V.^{27b} might well follow v.^{25} immediately, and very probably did so in E, since the intervening passage of JE (v.^{26b}) appears to come from J. In the last clause of the v. the editor of JE perhaps falls back on J, with whom טף = *little ones* is characteristic (CH. 52).

28–31 (J). Moses, addressing the assembled people, proposes a test of his own divine appointment and the blasphemy of the rebels. If the rebels die a natural death, Moses is an impostor; but if they are swallowed up alive in the earth, Yahweh has sent him, and the rebels in calling in question his divine appointment have contemned Yahweh.

The phraseology here appears to be predominantly that of J; and Bacon points out that it is characteristic of that source solemnly to propose tests of this kind; so Ex. $7^{16f.}$; cp., somewhat similarly, Gn. 24^{14} 42^{33}.—*Hereby ye shall know*] cp. Gn. 42^{33}, Ex. 7^{17}, also Gn. 24^{14} (all J). The people are addressed: Dathan and Abiram are referred to in the 3rd person, v.$^{29f.}$.—*Yahweh hath sent me*] cp. Ex. 3^{10-15} (E) 4^{28}, Jos. 24^{5} (E), Ex. 5^{22} 7^{16} (J).—*That* I have *not* done them *of my own mind*] the same contrast between what is done of personal will and desire, and what is done under divine constraint is drawn in 24^{13} (J). Similar is the contrast between the true prophet called and sent of Yahweh and the false prophet in Jer. $23^{16. 21}$.—29. *If these men die as all mankind die*] *i.e.* a natural death, *and be visited with the visitation of all mankind*, *i.e.* suffer no extraordinary and significant fate, such as descending alive into Sheol or dying "in the midst of their days," which was the special fate of sinners; cp. *e.g.* Ps. $55^{24. 16 (23. 15)}$ (the latter v. alludes to this narrative).—*It is not Yahweh that hath sent me*] The position of the negative before Yahweh rather than before the vb. emphasises the former; cp. Gn. 32^{29} 38^{9}.—30. *But if Yahweh creates a creation*] causes something new and marvellous to come to pass; cp. Ex. 34^{10} (JE), Jer. 31^{22}.—*And the ground open its mouth*] exactly as Gn. 4^{11} (J); both noun and vb. are different in v.^{32} where ארץ (also v.$^{33b. 34}$) and פתח occur instead of אדמה (also v.^{31}) and פצה (also Dt. 11^{6}).—*And they go down . . . to Sheol*] Sheol, the place of departed spirits, was conceived of as below or within the earth; people go *down* to it (cp. *e.g.* Gn. 37^{35}), and the spirits at times come *up* from it (1 S. $28^{11ff.}$). See the Lexicons (*s.v.* שאול).—*They have despised Yahweh*] נאץ as in $14^{11.23}$ (JE).—31, 32. As soon as Moses had finished speaking, the ground under Dathan and Abiram is cleft asunder, and they and their households are swallowed up.—V.$^{31.33a}$ records, with a repetition of the same phraseology (note especially v.^{33a}), the fulfilment of Moses' prediction in v.^{30}. V.^{32a} contains a statement of the same or a similar event, but in different phraseology. Probably v.^{32a} (cp. Dt. 11^{6}) is derived from E, and with it goes the clause *and the earth covered them up* (v.^{33}).—32. *Their households*] the wives and children (v.^{27}) and other persons belonging to Dathan and Abiram. The same word (בתיהם) is used in the reference to this story in Dt. 11^{6}, also with the same signification in Gn. $42^{19.33}$ 45^{18} (all E). It appears to be E's equivalent for J's phrase *all that was theirs* (cp. v.^{26} n.) in v.^{33a}.—32b. *And all the men who belonged to Ḳoraḥ and all their goods*] an unskilful attempt of the editor to unite in death the two sets of rebels who, even in his form of the story, had in life been constantly divided. The effect of the insertion is that after all the men that belonged to Ḳoraḥ have been swallowed up by the earthquake about the tents of Dathan and Abiram, they are done to death again by fire at the tabernacle (v.^{35}). The hand of the editor is also apparent in the phraseology; the last word of the v. (רכוש) is characteristic of P and the editor; CH. 155^{P}.—33. Cp. v.^{30b}.—33b. *And they perished from the midst of the assembly*] either another editorial addition, or, perhaps, E (cp. 22^{4}).—34. Alarmed by the sound of the cries of the perishing people, the Israelites who had been present (cp. v.^{23}) flee away to avoid a like fate. This v. scarcely seems to presuppose v.^{26}.

35 (P^{g}). **The destruction of the two hundred and fifty princes.**—The sequel to v.^{27a}.

As at the destruction of Nadab and Abihu (Lev. 10^{2}), so now fire comes out from Yahweh, *i.e.* from the tabernacle; it consumes the two hundred and fifty (v.^{2}) who offered the incense (v.$^{18f.}$). The name of the leader, Ḳoraḥ, has been suppressed on grounds which will be found stated on 26^{10}.

27. נצבים] a secondary predicate determining the subject; Driver, *Tenses*, 161 (2).—פתח] acc. of place: Dav. 69.—ונשיהם . . . וטפם] is grammatically somewhat loosely connected with the subj. דתן . . . ואבירם (which is prefixed to the vb. either because it is the new and contrasted subject as compared with v.[25], or in order to give יצאו a plupf. sense); for this loose connection see Kön. iii. 375*b*. It might easily result from fusion of sources: Bacon assigns this last clause to J. Or, since בניהם between נשיהם . . . וטפם is unusual and really superfluous, we may in the phrase itself have fusion of sources; so CH.—**30.** בריאה] here only.—אתם] 𝔊 + *καὶ τοὺς οἴκους αὐτῶν καὶ τὰς σκηνὰς αὐτῶν*, probably under the influence of Dt. 11[6].

XVII. 1–5 (16^{36-40}) (P^s). The censers converted into a memorial.—At the command of Yahweh, communicated through Moses, Eleʿazar collects the censers which had been rendered holy (*i.e.* unfit for future profane use) by having been presented to Yahweh, and converts them into a covering for the altar, which is to serve as a reminder that no one, who was not descended from Aaron, might draw near to offer incense to Yahweh.

This last insertion of P^s is a kind of Midrash, to explain the bronze covering or overlaying of the altar. According to Ex. 27^2 (P^g), the altar was overlaid with bronze at the time that it was made. 𝔊 attempts (at the expense of an anachronism) to harmonise the two versions of the origin of this bronze covering by explaining, in the account of the completion of the tabernacle and its belongings, that "he [Beṣal'el] made the bronze altar out of the bronze censers which belonged to the men who revolted with the congregation of Ḳoraḥ" (Ex. 38^{22} 𝔊 = 38^2 𝔥). The present divergence from the representation of P^g is merely another indication of the secondary character of the section, which also appears very clearly in v.[5]. Eleʿazar, too, though known to P^g, is prominent in P^s (see, *e.g.* c. 19, 31, Jos. 22: also Ex. $6^{23.\,25}$, Lev. $10^{6.\,16}$).

2 (37). Eleʿazar is selected for the task of collecting the censers rather than Aaron; for the latter as high priest had to avoid contact with the dead even more scrupulously than the ordinary priests, Lev. $21^{10-15.\,1-4}$.—*From the midst of that which is burnt*] here as in $19^{(6)\,17}$ שרפה appears to have the concrete sense *that which is burnt*; either the word is so taken here by 𝔊 𝔖 𝔙 $𝔗^o$ or these versions read השׂרפים (cp. v.[4])

= *those who are burnt.* If, with RV., the usual signification of שׂרפה *burning* (Lev. 10^6, Am. 4^{11}, cp. Zech. 3^2) be adopted, the meaning would be that the censers are to be collected from among the still burning corpses of those burnt by the fire of Yahweh.—*Scatter the fire yonder*] the fire is the burning coals which had been placed in the censers ($16^{7.18}$); these are to be scattered lest, though holy, they should still be profanely used.—*For the censers . . . have become holy*] so, rightly, 𝔖 𝔙; see phil. n. The censers had contracted holiness in virtue of having been presented before Yahweh, and all that they contained, including the fire, would have been rendered holy at the same time (v.[3]); holiness in such cases is, like uncleanness (cp. *e.g.* Lev. 15), the result of physical contact with or propinquity to holy things: see small print n. at the end of this section.—3 (38). *These sinners at the cost of their lives*] If the text of 𝔐 be retained, the clause must be rendered thus, not as in RV. (text) "these sinners against their own lives"; for (1) "to sin against" is חטא ל and not חטא ב; (2) the men in question could not be said to have sinned against themselves: they had sinned against God. For the ב of price with נפש, cp. 1 K. 2^{23}, 2 S. 23^{17}. With the reading adopted in the last note, *at the cost of their lives* is connected, as in the passages just used, with the vb., and the whole passage becomes more pointed, *The censers of these men became holy at the cost of their lives.* The censers became holy *because they presented them before Yahweh,* but at the cost of their lives to those who, not being priests, had no right to present them, and did not possess the degree of holiness requisite to render such propinquity to the Deity safe.—5 (40). *A memorial*] an object serving to bring something to remembrance; cp. Jos. 4^7 (of the stones in Jordan).—*That no stranger*] 3^{10} n.—*As Yahweh spoke to him* (Ele'azar) *through Moses*] the clause refers to the action of Ele'azar.

Holiness.—A complete understanding of the standpoint and argument of the preceding section depends on an appreciation of certain ideas relative to holiness. Whatever the etymological sense of the root קדש, and however deep and spiritual the meaning imparted to its derivatives by the prophets, in many connections it retained throughout the period of OT. literature, and even later, a signification that can best be represented by the term "taboo." In these cases it was not a term of moral import. Holiness and uncleanness (the two ideas are in origin closely connected) are contagious qualities, and, under certain circumstances and to certain people, dangerous, and even fatal. (1) Holiness is contagious: thus the altar is "most holy," and whatever touches it becomes holy (Ex. 29^{37} 30^{29}). So, again, the flesh of the sin-offering is "most holy," and whatever touches it becomes holy; the vessel in which it is boiled, becomes holy, and, if of bronze, must have the holiness scoured out of it, or, if of earthenware, must be destroyed, since, so we must suppose it was felt, the holiness, having percolated into its pores, has rendered it incurably holy (Lev. $6^{20f. (27f.)}$). Ezekiel provides special boiling-houses for the sacrificial flesh, lest being brought into the outer court it should infect the people with its holiness (Ezek. 46^{20}). Aaron washes himself after putting off his holy garments before donning his ordinary garments again, the object, in the light of the foregoing, clearly being to wash off the holiness acquired from the holy garments, lest it should infect the ordinary garments and render them useless for ordinary purposes (Lev. $16^{23f.}$). When the Scriptures came to be regarded as holy, touching them "defiled" the hands, *i.e.* required a hand-washing to remove the acquired holiness before the hands were used for profane purposes (*Yadaim* $3^{2.5}$: cp. Budde in *EBi.*, "Canon," §§ 3 f.). (2) Holiness is dangerous if acquired suddenly, without due precaution, or by unfit persons: in Ex. $19^{11b-13. 20-24}$ the unconsecrated people are warned against suddenly touching the sacred mount, *i.e.* against suddenly acquiring holiness, and perishing in consequence. The priests on the same occasion are warned that they may only approach Yahweh with safety, if they have been previously made holy in proper form: cp. Nu. 1^{49-53}. So in the present incident the "seed of Aaron," being duly possessed of holiness, offer the incense with safety; the Levitical followers of Ḳoraḥ, not being thus equipped, become holy by the process of offering, but die in consequence. (3) What is holy must be kept from profane use: *e.g.* the firstborn of cattle is holy, and, therefore, may not be used for ordinary purposes (see below, p. 229 f.); holy food, such as tithe, may not be used for the ordinary domestic meal (Dt. 26^{13}); a vessel rendered holy must be destroyed, or purged of its holiness before being again used for ordinary purposes (Lev. $6^{28 (21)}$). So here the censers or firepans were not originally holy (see n. on v.[6]), but were rendered so by the rite of offering; they must, therefore, in future be kept from profane use. The end in the present case is obtained by permanently keeping them, in the form of a covering for the altar, within the sacred precincts. The fire in the censers being also holy, is cast away and thus removed from ordinary use. See, further, on the present subject, W. R. Smith, *Religion of the Semites*, App. C; also for parallels, from many fields, to the contagion of holiness or uncleanness and the necessity for removing things and persons affected by it from ordinary use, Frazer, *Golden Bough*,[2] i. 318–343. From the last a few instances may be cited: "The Mikado's food was cooked every day in new pots and served up in new dishes; both pots and dishes were of common clay, in order that they might be broken and laid aside after they had been once used. They were generally broken, for it was believed that if anyone else ate his food out of these sacred dishes, his mouth and throat would become swollen and inflamed. The same ill effect was thought to be experienced by anyone who should wear the Mikado's clothes without his leave" (p. 318). "In Tonga . . . it was believed that if anyone fed himself with his own hands after touching the sacred person of a superior chief, or anything that belonged to him, he would swell up and die; the sanctity of the chief, like a virulent poison, infected the hands of his inferior, and, being communicated through them to the food, proved fatal to the eater . . . until the ceremony of expiation or disinfection had been performed, if he wished to eat, he had either to get some one to feed him, or else to go down on his knees and pick up the food from the ground with his mouth like a beast" (p. 319 f.). "In New Zealand the dread of the sanctity of chiefs was at least as great as in Tonga. Their ghostly power, derived from an ancestral spirit or *atua*, diffused itself by contagion over everything they touched, and could strike dead all who rashly or unwittingly meddled with it" (p. 321). "The garments of a high New Zealand chief will kill anyone else who wears them" (p. 322). "In general, we may say that the prohibition to use the vessels, garments, and so on of certain persons, and the effects supposed to follow an infraction of the rule, are exactly the same whether the person to whom the things belong are sacred or what we might call unclean and polluted" (p. 325). On some parallel customs in case of uncleanness, see on c. 19.

1. משה] In 𝔊 Moses is not bidden to pass on the command to Ele'azar; he and Ele'azar are both commanded to take up the censers.—**2.** וירם] For the cstr., cp. 5^2 n.—ואת האש זרה] 𝔊 *καὶ τὸ πῦρ τὸ ἀλλότριον τοῦτο σπεῖρον*; cp. Lev. 10^1 𝔥 and 𝔊.—**3.** את . . . אתם] Driver, *Tenses*, 197 (6). But it is far more probable (see notes above) that the את here is intrusive, and that מחתת (v.^{3}) is the subj. of קרשו (v.^{2}); so 𝔖 (cp. 𝔙). G^{BL} (*ἡγίασαν*) apparently retain את and read קִדְּשׁוּ; but MSS. 29, 54, 75 of 𝔊 read *ἡγιάσθησαν* in agreement with 𝔖.—הקריבם . . . ויקרשו] the masc. suffix (similarly אתם above) refers to the fem. מחתת; similarly the 3rd masc. pl. in יקרשו; Dav. 1, R. 3; 113. 𝔊 *προσηνέχθησαν* (*i.e.* הָקְרבו) . . . *καὶ ἡγιάσθησαν*.—רקעי this word occurs only here (but cp. Ex. 39^3), פחים (not the same as פח *a bird trap*) only here and Ex. 39^3 (P^s), and צפוי only here and Ex. $38^{17. 19}$ (P^s), and Is. 30^{22}.—**4.** אלעזר] 𝔊 S + בן אהרן (cp. v.^{1}).—וירקעום] רקע elsewhere in Hex. only in Ex. 39^3.

6–15 ($16^{41–50}$) (P^g). **The people plagued for murmuring at the fate of Koraḥ.**—The sequel to 16^{35}. On the day following the destruction of the two hundred and fifty princes, the whole body of the Israelites complain that by the death of Koraḥ, their representative, they have themselves been attacked (v.^{6}). The cloud and glory of Yahweh appear ominously (v.^{7}). Moses and Aaron, drawing near at this sign to the tent, are warned to stand away from the people, that

Yahweh may destroy the latter (v.[10]). They intercede with Yahweh, and then Aaron, under Moses' direction, places fire from the altar on his censer, and with it passes among the people, thus staying the destructive activity of Yahweh's anger, though not until after it had caused the death of 14,700 of the people (v.[11-15]). It is noticeable that Aaron here (P^g) risks that contact with the dead, to avoid which Eleʿazar was substituted for him in the previous section (P^s).

6 (41). *Ye have slain*] The pronoun is emphatic. Moses and Aaron are thus charged with having invoked the destructive intervention of God; cp. $16^{4f.}$.—*The people of Yahweh*] cp. 11^{29} (E), Jud. 5^{11}, 1 S. 2^{24}, 2 S. 1^{12} 6^{21}, 2 K. 9^{6}, Ezek. 36^{20}, and also Zeph. 2^{10}. The expression is of ancient origin; cp. the parallel "people of Kemosh," 21^{29}, Jer. 48^{46}. In causing the death of their representatives, "the princes of the congregation" (16^{2}), Moses and Aaron might be said to have slain the people.—7 (42) a. Cp. 16^{3a}.—*They turned towards the tent of meeting*] cp. Ex. 16^{10} (P^g), where read "tabernacle" (המשכן) or "tent of meeting" (as here) for "wilderness" (המדבר).—*And, behold, the cloud covered it, and the glory of Yahweh appeared*] another way of expressing what is said in Ex. 16^{10} "the glory of Yahweh appeared in the cloud." It is the glory of Yahweh which is the really significant and ominous sign; cp. 16^{19} n. The cloud was a permanent phænomenon (9^{16}, Ex. 40^{38}); the appearance of the glory was intermittent. Whether, with Di. and others, we ought to draw a further distinction between an intermittent "covering" or complete envelopment of the tent by the cloud (9^{15}, Ex. $40^{34f.}$) and a constant hovering of the cloud above it ($9^{18ff.}$ 10^{12}, Ex. 40^{38}), is uncertain. Note that the term "to cover" is used in 9^{16} of the regularly recurring appearance by day when the tabernacle was at rest.—9 (44). *And Yahweh spoke unto Moses*] 𝔊 + *Aaron*. Moses and Aaron in any case constitute the subject of the following plural imperative in 10 (45). *Get you up*] a different vb. from that used in 16^{21}; otherwise this verse is verbally identical with $16^{21.\,22}$ (first clause).—11 (46). From the last clause of the previous v. we may infer

that Moses and Aaron again (cp. 16^{22}) intercede for the people, and that Moses received from Yahweh the instruction which he here gives to Aaron. For the idioms in clause *a*, cp. $16^{6f.}$.—*Put fire therein from off the altar*] *i.e.* some live coals from the fire which was always burning on the altar (Lev. $6^{6\,(13)}$; cp. Is. 6^{6}); in virtue of the place whence they were taken, these would be holy; see n. after v.[5] and also 5^{17} n.—*Lay incense thereon*] the last word is not expressed in 𝕳, but should be restored from 𝕲 𝕾 𝖁.—*And make propitiation for them*] cp. 8^{19}. By far the most usual means of making propitiation is blood (Lev. 17^{11} (H); cp. $6^{23\,(30)}$ $16^{15f.}$), or offerings like the sin-offering and the burnt-offering (Lev. 1^{4}), which involved the effusion and ceremonial use of blood. But propitiation could also be made by other means, such as the half-shekel paid at the census (Ex. 30^{15}): cp. Driver in Hastings' *DB*. iv. 130 f. The method here adopted may show the influence of a principle analogous to that noticed in 5^{21} n., and illustrated in the passage from Pesiḳta there cited. As the people had sinned by means of censers and incense, so propitiation was made for them in the same way. Cp. also the story of the Bronze Serpent, 21^{6-9}. —*For the wrath*, whose coming outbreak is indicated in Yahweh's words in v.[10], *has gone forth from Yahweh*. The divine wrath is here very independently conceived; cp. 2 Ch. 19^{2} and such Targumic idioms as "against me also there was anger from before Yahweh" (Dt. 1^{37} 𝕿°). A similar independence is given to the "truth" of God in Ps. 43^{3}. In the references back to this passage in 18^{5} the weaker phrase found also in 1^{53}, Jos. 9^{20} 22^{20} is used.—*The plague*] 8^{19} n.—12 (47). Relates the carrying out of the instructions given in v.[11], but rather ineptly; note the order, *and Aaron took*, etc., *and ran* . . . and *put*; ct. v.[11].—13 (48). *The plague*] the same word as in v.[14] 14^{37}: though derived from the same root it is not the same as that used in v.[11f.].—*Those that died in the matter of Ḳoraḥ*] the two hundred and fifty princes who presented the censers (16^{35}).—15 (50). After the plague had been stayed (v.[13]), Aaron returns to Moses, who is still (cp. v.[8f.]) at the tent. RV. obscures the point by its rendering of the last clause, which should rather run, *the plague having been stayed*: cp. Driver, *Tenses*, 16.

8. אל פני] The equivalent, after vbs. expressing motion, to לפני after vbs. of rest: cp. 20^{10}, Ex. 23^{17}, Lev. 6^{7} 9^{5} 16^{2}: so Di. on Lev. 6^{7}.—**10.** הרמו] Niphal also in Ezek. $10^{15. 17. 19}$†. On the form, see G.-K. 72*dd*.—**11.** הולך] Imperative Hiph.; 𝔊 𝔖 𝔗ᴼ translate by transitives, 𝔙 *pergens*, which may also be the intention of S הלך, *i.e.* הֲלֹךְ, the rarer form of Imper. Kal. Cp. the intransitive vb. (וירץ) in the next v.

16–26 (1–11). The superiority of the tribe of Levi vindicated by the blossoming of Aaron's stick.—V.$^{17-20\ (2-5)}$, Moses is to take a stick from each of the twelve secular tribes, and to inscribe on each stick the name of the tribal prince; he is also to take a stick from the tribe of Levi, inscribing on it the name of Aaron. He is then to leave them all before the ark. By a miraculous sign Yahweh will still the complaints of the people against the exclusive rights of the Levites to approach Yahweh; for the stick of the representative of the tribe whom Yahweh chooses to approach Him will bloom; v.$^{21-24}$, the directions given in v.$^{17-20}$ carried out with the promised effect; v.$^{24b-26}$, Aaron's stick blossoms and bears ripe almonds. Subsequently the princes receive their sticks back again, but Aaron's is put back and kept before the ark as a warning token. The meaning is not too clearly expressed in the original; but the foregoing seems to be the correct interpretation, especially in regard to two points. (1) The number of sticks is in all thirteen. In c. 1–3 the secular tribes regularly appear as twelve in number, and Levi stands apart as a thirteenth. Similarly, in c. 7 there are twelve secular princes (נשיאים). This interpretation does most justice to v.^{21}, the last part of which is rendered by 𝔙 periphrastically, but not unreasonably, *fueruntque virgæ duodecem absque virga Aaron.* So Di. and Str. Others (*e.g.* Keil, Reuss) consider that only twelve sticks in all are intended, and that the two tribes of Ephraim and Manasseh here count as one, as in Dt. 27^{12}. (2) The point of the story is to illustrate the distinction between the secular tribes on the one hand, and the sacred tribe of Levi as a whole on the other. Aaron is the *tribal* representative (cp. v.^{23}), corresponding to the representatives of the other *tribes*; he is not here the representative of the priestly section of that tribe as distinguished from the merely Levitical families. The motive of the story is thus in accord with P^{g}'s story of Ḳoraḥ in c. 16. See p. 191 f.

17 (2). *And take from them one stick for each family, from all their princes of their families twelve sticks*] *A stick* (מַטֶּה) seems to have been as regularly carried by the Hebrews (see Gn. $38^{18. 25}$, 1 S. 14^{43}) as by the Babylonians (Herod. i. 195); it was with this stick of ordinary life that Aaron wrought his miracles in Egypt (see Ex. 7^{9} $8^{1. 12 (5. 16)}$ (P)), and it is dried sticks of this kind that are here intended. It is only quite exceptionally (as, perhaps, in Ezek. 7^{10} $19^{11. 12. 14}$), if at all, that the word is used of a fresh rod. By metonymy the word מטה is used (in P and Ch.) for "tribe"; it is probably because the writer here uses the word מטה in its original sense that he selects the expression *father's house* or *family* (בית אב) for "tribe." The "family" is generally a subdivision of a tribe (see on 1^{2}); but the specification of the number both in this v. and in v.$^{21 (6)}$ quite clearly shows that it here denotes one of the twelve tribes. The princes may be identical with those mentioned by name in c. 1. 2. 7. 10 and called in 1^{16} "princes of the tribes of their fathers."—*The name of each shalt thou write upon his stick*] The name of the prince is written on behalf of his tribe: cp. v.$^{20 (5)}$.—18 (3). The Levites also are to present one stick, but one only, inscribed with the name of Aaron. The v. would be superfluous if Levi's was one of the twelve sticks referred to in v.$^{17 (2)}$; for there could be no question that Aaron was the prince or representative of this tribe.—*For there is one stick for the head of their families*] the Hebrew does not admit of the distributive rendering of RV. *Their* must refer to the collect. sing. *Levi* (cp. 18^{23} phil. n.), and the *families* must here be the main divisions of the tribe of Levi. The whole tribe is to have a single representative; its several divisions are not to be separately represented in the ordeal. This appears to be the meaning (cp. Rashi), but it is obscurely expressed.—19. *Before the testimony*] v.$^{25 (10)}$; cp. v.$^{22 (7)}$ *before Yahweh in the tent of the testimony*. "The testimony" or "law" (Ex. $25^{16. 21}$ 40^{20}), written on two tablets (Ex. 31^{18} 34^{29}), was kept in the ark,

which was therefore commonly called "the ark of the testimony" (4^5 7^{89}; CH. 161^P); of this phrase "the testimony" may in some cases, such as Lev. 16^{13}, if not also in Ex. 16^{34} and the present passage, be regarded as an abbreviation. In any case the position intended is before the ark. Since Yahweh there meets with Israel through its representative, this may be described as "before Yahweh" (cp. v.$^{22(7)}$ and 20^9).—*Where I am wont to meet you*] *You* refers to the children of Israel, whom Yahweh met in the person of their representative Moses: cp. Ex. $29^{42f.}$ (𝔐; ct. 𝔊 S 𝔙). S 𝔊 𝔙 and some Heb. MSS. read *thee*, *i.e.* Moses; cp. Ex. 25^{22} $30^{6.36}$.—20 (5). *The man whom* as representative of his tribe *I choose* that he and his fellow tribesmen may approach me; cp. 16^5 n.—*I will cause the murmurings to cease . . . from* troubling or annoying *me*] the double preposition מעל is expressive; cp. 21^7 25^8, Am. 5^{23}, and see BDB. 758*b* (bottom).—22 (7). *Before Yahweh*] here and in v.^{24} = "before the ark": cp. v.^{19} n., also Ex. $16^{33f.}$; but the phrase generally means "before the tent"; see 5^{16} n. —*The tent of the testimony*] see 9^{15} n.—23 (8). The next day Moses returns to the tent and finds that Aaron's stick has borne ripe almonds.—*And, behold, the stick of Aaron of the house of Levi had sprouted, and brought forth buds, and fully flowered, and ripened almonds*] the terms of growth are probably multiplied in order to emphasise the fact that in a single night the complete process of growth, up to the production of the mature fruit, had been accomplished in the previously dry and dead stick. Whether the second and third terms are to be so sharply distinguished as above, or whether they are more completely synonymous, and simply used together here for rhetorical purposes, is somewhat uncertain. The verb of the first clause (פרח), which is primarily used of the budding of the flower (*e.g.* Is. 35^1, Cant. 6^{11} 7^{13}—note the parallels), is here perhaps used of shooting forth in general; such is its meaning in Job 14^9, where it is used of the growth from the root of a felled tree, and its use of the shooting forth of leaves is implied in Pr. 11^{28}. The noun (פרח) of the second is cognate with the verb of the first clause. It, too, sometimes denotes budding shoots or foliage (Nah. 1^4); if it had this meaning here the second clause would be synonymous with the first. But it primarily denotes the bud or blossom (Is. 18^5), and is probably used with this meaning here. The noun (ציץ) in the third clause which forms a cognate object to the verb (ויצץ) occurs elsewhere of flowers growing from the ground ("the flowers of the field," Is. 40^{6-8}, Ps. 103^{15}, cp. Job 14^2), but not of the blossoms of a tree. Derenbourg (*ZATW.* v. p. 301 f.) is inclined to interpret the word of the fruit in its immature state as the blossom falls away; cp. Is. 18^5. The fruit produced by the stick is the almond (שקד), which derives its name, meaning "wakeful," from the fact that the tree is the first to awake from its winter sleep and produce blossoms.

There are many somewhat similar stories of the miraculous vegetation of dried sticks. An Englishman readily recalls the legend of Joseph of Arimathea's stick, which, placed in the ground of Weary-all hill, became the miraculous thorn of Glastonbury. The stories of Hercules' club and Romulus' spear are further parallels. Of the former, Pausanias relates the story: "They say that Hercules leaned his club against this image [a Hermes], and the club, which was of wild olive wood, struck root in the ground, if you please, and sprouted afresh; and the tree is still growing" (*Description of Greece*, ii. 31^{13}, ed. Frazer). For the story of Romulus, see Plutarch, *Romulus*, 20, and Ovid, *Met.* xv. 560 ff.—

Utque Palatinis hærentem collibus olim,
Quum subito vidit frondescere Romulus hastam
Quæ radice nova, non ferro stabat adacto,
Et iam non telum, sed lenti viminis arbor
Non expectatas dabat admirantibus umbras.

Reland (*Pal.* p. 712) recalls the stories of the sacred terebinth at Hebron which sprang from the stick of the angel who appeared to Abraham; the terebinth at Smyrna which sprang from Polycarp's stick; and the ash which grew out of St. Ethelred's stick. The connection with the omen of rods flourishing or withering claimed by W. R. Smith (*Rel. Sem.* 179 n. 5, [2] 196) seems less close. There is no suggestion in the story that anything happened to the remaining eleven sticks.

25 (10). *To be kept*] (למשמרת) Ex. 16^{32-34}.—*For a sign*] cp. v.[3].—*The sons of rebellion*] the precise phrase (בני מרי) occurs nowhere else; but cp. "rebellious people" (עם מרי), Is. 30^9, and Ezekiel's frequently recurring term for Israel, "house of rebellion" (בית (ה)מרי—Ezek. $2^{5.6.8}$ $3^{9.26.27}$ $12^{2.3.9.25}$ 17^{12} 24^3). Both in the present phrase and in Ezekiel's, "rebellion" is a rhetorical substitute for the national terms in the idioms "sons of Israel" (בני ישראל) and "house of Israel" (בית ישראל) respectively.

17. איש את שמו] For different views of the cstr., see König, iii. 76; G.-K. 139*c*.—**18.** At the end of the v. 𝔊 adds *δώσουσιν*; and for לראש it has *κατὰ φυλήν*. Possibly this difficult clause (see above) is corrupt.—**19.** והנחתם] v.[22], Ex. 16[33] (P).—שמה] 𝔊 S (unnecessarily) שם.—**20.** השכתי] lit. "to cause to sink"; the verb is used here only in Hiph.; the Kal is used in Gn. 8[1] (P) of the sinking of the waters; Est. 2[1] 7[10] of the cessation of wrath; Jer. 5[26]† of the stooping of fowlers.—**23.** משה] 𝔊 + *καὶ* 'Ααρών: cp. v.[26].—אהרן לבית לוי] the ל after the proper name is a periphrasis for the gen.: König, iii. 280*k*.—**25.** וּתְכַל] syntax, according to Driver, *Tenses*, 60 ff. MT. points as 2nd pers. Piel (subject Moses), and implies the meaning "to cause to cease," found elsewhere (according to BDB. p. 478*b*) only in Ps. 78[33]. 𝔊 translates *καὶ παυσάσθω*=וְתֵכֶל, 3rd fem. Kal—"that the murmurings may cease"; similarly 𝔖; for the meaning of the Kal, cp. Is. 10[25]; for the fem. sing. subj., Dav. 116.—תלונתם] S תלנותם; cp. v.[20] 𝔥 and phil. n. on 14[1].—**26.** משה] 𝔊 + *καὶ* 'Ααρών; at end of v. *ἐποίησαν*=עשו.

27, 28 (12, 13). These verses, containing the alarmed confession of the people that access to Yahweh, which they had claimed through Ḳoraḥ (16[3-5]), was fatal, and that they are all on the point of perishing for their sins, form really the introduction to the next c., which regulates the functions and privileges of the Levites, who do the service of the tabernacle and, by guarding access to it, secure the safety of the rest of the people.

27. *Behold we expire! we perish, we all perish!*] The tenses in the Hebrew are perfects of certainty: cp. Is. 6[5], Jer. 4[13]; Driver, *Tenses*, 13. The first vb. (גוע) is very characteristic of P: cp. 20[3], Gn. 6[17]; CH. 51.—**28a.** Cp. 18[7]; also 1[53] 3[10. 38].

On the connection and origin of these verses, see Wellh. *Comp.* 182; Kuenen in *Th. Tijd.* xii. 147; Di.

28. האם] a strengthened interrog. (Kön. iii. 353*h*; BDB. 50*b*): "Shall we ever finish dying?"; it is used just thus only here; Job 6[13] is different.—תַּמְנוּ] G.-K. 67*e*.

XVIII. The various parts of this chapter have been to a large extent anticipated; with v.[1-7] cp. 1[50-53] 3[5-10. 38], and with v.[8ff.] cp. *e.g.* Lev. 2[3. 10] 6[9-11. 19. 22 (16-18. 26. 29)]. In spite of this it seems clear that the present chapter, with the possible exception of v.[25-32], formed part of the main priestly work (P^g).

Positive indications of this are (1) the close connection with P^g's account of Ḳoraḥ's rebellion: as in the story, so here the main antithesis is Levi and the rest of Israel; whereas in 17[27f. (12f.)] Israel exclaims that they must all perish, Yahweh in 18[1f. 5. 21-23] regulates the functions of Levi, so that Israel in future may suffer no further destruction such as they have just experienced (with 18^5 cp. 17^{11} (16^{46})). Levi as a whole is to be occupied with the tabernacle, that the rest of Israel need not come into perilous proximity to it ($18^{21f.}$). Altogether subordinate to this main distinction is the distinction between the priests (v.$^{8-20}$) and the Levites (v.$^{21-24}$) in respect of the dues payable to them: for this is merely made because the writer wishes not simply to catalogue the dues payable by the Israelites, but also to describe the different destinations and different treatments (v.$^{10. 11. 13}$) of the several dues. As contrasted with all Israel, priests and Levites are alike distinguished by the fact that they have no landed possession (v.$^{20. 24}$). (2) The reference to "the altar" in the sing. (v.$^{5. 17}$); cp. Introd. § 11. (3) The inconsistency between v.^{20} and 35^{1-8} (P^s).

At the same time the c. is marked by certain peculiarities. "The laws in v.$^{1. 8. 20}$ are addressed to Aaron (so only Lev. 10^8; elsewhere instructions for Aaron are imparted through Moses, *e.g.* Lev. 8^2 16^2 21^1, Nu. 6^{23} 8^2); and the customary formula 'spake . . . saying' is not employed, v.$^{1. 8. 20}$, ct. ^{25}" (CH.). On the general priestly character of the language, see above, p. 188.

1–7. The duties of Levi.—The priests are to have the immediate care of the sanctuary and the altar (v.^{5}); the rest of the tribe are to assist them, but in such a way that they do not come into direct contact with the sacred objects or the altar (v.^{3}). The object of the whole arrangement is to prevent the rest of Israel approaching the sanctuary, and so perishing (v.^{5}: cp. $17^{27f. (12f.)}$).

1. *Thou and thy sons*] *i.e.* the priests.—*The house of thy father*] Genealogically this includes the previous phrase; but from an ecclesiastical standpoint it is quite naturally used to define the whole of the tribe of Levi, exclusive of the family of Aaron; see p. 22.—*Shall bear the guilt of the sanctuary*] shall bear the consequences of any guilt incurred in connection with the sanctuary, such as that of coming too near it (1^{50}). For the phrase, cp. Ex. 28^{38} (CH. 28^P); and for "guilt" (עון) in the sense of "the consequences, the punishment of guilt," see 14^{34}. Since the danger of attending to the sanctuary is thus confined to Levi, the fear expressed by the people ($17^{27f.}$) is groundless.—**2.** *The tribe of Levi, the tribe of thy father*] the term מטה in the first clause is regularly used by P (see n. on 1^4), that in the second (שבט)

very rarely (4^{18} n.); the second clause is probably editorial, and suggested by "the house of thy father" in v.[1].—*Bring near with thee*] scarcely in the technical sense (16^5 n.) "bring near to God in company with thyself"; but rather, in view of the clauses that immediately follow, "Have brought unto thee (cp. 3^6), to be with and assist thee" (אִתָּךְ). But 𝔊, perhaps rightly, assimilates the clause to Ex. 28^1 and reads הקרב אליך = "have brought unto thee."—*That they* (Levi) *may join themselves* (*w^e yillavu*)] a similar paranomasia may be found in Gn. 29^{34}.—*And serve thee whilst thou and thy sons with thee are before the tent of testimony* (9^{15} n.)] the Levites are to assist the priests when the latter are engaged in ritual duties. The last clause is circumstantial (Di., *Tenses*, 156–159), not, as in RV., antithetical.—**3a.** Cp. 3^7.—**3b.** Cp. 4^{15}.—**4.** The Levites, but the Levites only, may thus assist the priests, for *no layman* (זר), *i.e.*, no one not of the tribe of Levi (cp. n. on 1^{51}), *shall draw near to you* (אליכם) the priests, or, with 𝔊 (πρὸς σέ), *to thee, i.e.* Aaron; note the singular pronoun at the beginning of the v.—**5.** *Ye shall keep the charge of the sanctuary*] *Sanctuary* (הקדש) is used with a variety of implications; it may refer to the whole sacred enclosure (cp. *e.g.* Lev. 10^{18}), or to the tent (Lev. 10^4), or to the "holy place" (as distinct from the "holy of holies"), *i.e.* the outer of the two chambers into which the tabernacle was divided by the veil (Ex. 26^{33}), or to the inner chamber—"the holy of holies" (Lev. $16^{2.3.16.17}$ etc.). If the present v. be intended to distinguish between the objects of priestly and Levitical care, the term is best regarded either as an abbreviation for "objects of the sanctuary" (v.[3]), or as referring to "the holy of holies" (v.[7]). But since the subject of the vb. is not separately expressed (ct. v.[7]), and is therefore not emphasised, it is doubtful whether the writer at this point makes the transition from the Levites, who have constituted the main subject of the previous vv., to the priests exclusively. The subject *ye* may rather *include* priests and Levites—all alike must keep their charge if the Israelites are to be prohibited from outbreaks of the divine wrath. Then in this case "sanctuary" may be used with its widest signification and refer to the sacred enclosure.—5b. Cp. 17^{11}.—6. Cp. 3^{9} $8^{16.\,19}$.—7. *But thou and thy sons*] The priests, as distinguished from the Levites, have peculiar priestly duties to discharge (cp. 1^{b}), especially in connection with *the altar and* with service *within the curtain* (Ex. 26^{33}, Lev. $16^{12f.}$).—*And ye shall serve; as a service of gift I give your priesthood*] The priesthood is a favour conferred by Yahweh on the priests. But the phraseology is strange, and the rest of the first clause abrupt; very possibly there is some corruption: cp. 𝔊.—*And the stranger*] here, any one not a priest.—*Who draws near*] to perform priestly duties: 16^{5} n.

2. וילוו . . . לוי] such puns have no etymological value. For suggested etymologies of לוי, see the literature cited in BDB. p. 532*a*.—3. כל האהל] 𝔊 om. כל.

8–20. **The priests' dues.**—A summary statement (v.[8]) that all the "holy things" of the children of Israel are to become the property of the priests is followed by a series of specific directions, as follows:—Except those parts which are burnt on the altar, the whole of all meal-offerings, sin-offerings, and guilt-offerings falls to the priests, and may be eaten by any *male* member of a priestly family in a holy place (v.[9f.]). All the contributed portions of peace-offerings, all the "fat" of oil, wine and corn, and all first-ripe fruits, become the property of the priests, and may be eaten by any member of the priestly households, *male or female*, who is ceremonially clean (v.[11–18]). Further, the priests are to appropriate all "devoted things" (*ḥerem*), all firstborn of clean cattle and the redemption price of all firstborn of men and unclean cattle (v.[14–17]). All these are in the first instance the property of Yahweh, and are given by Him to the priests because they have no landed possessions in Canaan (v.[19. 20]). On the value and significance of these dues, see below, p. 236 ff.

8. *I have given unto thee that which is kept of the contributions made to Me*] *i.e.* that part of the offerings which is not burnt on the altar, but kept over. The translation assumes a very rare concrete sense of the Hebrew word משמרת; but see 1 S. 22^{23}, and cp. the corresponding abstract use in 17^{25} 19^{9}, Ex. 12^{6} $16^{23.\,32}$. To translate (with RV.), "I have given

thee the charge of" the offerings is pointless; dues, not duties, form the subject of the v.—*The contributions—even all the holy things*] 5^9 n.—*To thee I have given them as a share*] Lev. 7^{35}. RV. text is wrong; see phil. n.—*A perpetual due*] the word חק is commonly used for any prescribed or established quantity, especially of food, as, *e.g.*, of the food regularly granted to the Egyptian priests by Pharaoh (Gn. 47^{22}); the present phrase recurs frequently in P (Ex. 29^{28}, Lev. 6^{11} 7^{34} 10^{15} etc.).—**9.** *This shall be thine of the most holy things* in so far as they are not burnt, and are, therefore, reserved *from the* altar-*fire*. This is substantially the meaning, though the very terse phrase (מן האש) of the original might be differently paraphrased. Cp. Lev. 2^3, "And that which remains [after a handful has been withdrawn to be burnt on the altar (v.^{2})] of the meal-offering shall be Aaron's"; see also Lev. 2^{10} 6^9. The term "most holy" may be used of the offerings mentioned in this and the next verse, because they "obtained a higher consecration" as compared with those mentioned in v.$^{11ff.}$ (see Driver and White, *Leviticus*, p. 63 f.; or, more fully, Baudissin, *Studien*, ii. 52 ff.); but the terms "holy" and "most holy" are used rather indifferently, as is shown by a comparison of the last clauses of v.^{9} and ^{10}. The portions of these offerings which were burnt on the altar, and, therefore, did not fall to the priests were in the case of every meal offering a handful (Lev. 2^2 5^{12} $6^{8\,(15)}$), or an undefined amount (Lev. $2^{9.\,16}$); and in the case of animal sin-offerings or guilt-offerings, "the fat pieces" as defined in Lev. 4^{26} (3^{3-5}) 7^{3-5}. In the case of all animal offerings, moreover, the blood was withheld from human, even priestly, consumption. The burnt-offering is not mentioned in the present passage, for no part of it was eaten; yet although the whole of the flesh was burnt on the altar (Lev. $1^{9.\,13}$), the skin was previously removed, and became the property of the priest, Lev. 7^8. The peace-offerings are treated in v.^{11} (cp. v.^{18}).—*Their guilt-offering with which they make restitution to Me*] the relative clause is best thus rendered, and so limited to the last term; cp. $5^{7ff.}$. The *'āshām* was originally a compensation for wrong done; see

1 S. 6.—10. *In a most holy place shalt thou eat it*] in Lev. $6^{9.\ 19\ (16.\ 26)}$ 7^{6} it is laid down that the meal-offering, the sin-offering, and the guilt-offering shall be eaten "in a holy place." In the two former passages "the holy place" is defined by a following clause (which may well be a gloss, yet, if so, an early and correct one) to be "the court of the tent of meeting." The same place must be intended here (*Siphrê*: Rashi, Di.), though it is uniquely described by the phrase which commonly defines the inner part of the tent (Ex. 26^{33}). Ezekiel (42^{13} 46^{20}) also requires the holy things to be eaten in a holy place, viz. in the chambers of the inner court. — *Every male*] Lev. $6^{11.\ 22\ (18.\ 29)}$ 7^{6}. — 11. *The contribution from their gift, including all the wave-offerings*] The peace-offerings are here referred to; parts of these were contributed to the priest, and a part was waved (Lev. 7^{28-34}). For some unknown reason, instead of using the technical term שלמים, the writer here refers to these offerings by the vague word *gift* (מתן), which is used but once again in the Hexateuch, and then not of a sacrificial offering (Gn. 34^{12}). The word, it is true, is not an unsuitable description of the peace-offerings even from the standpoint of P, who classes them as *ḳorbān*, "gifts made at the altar" (Lev. 3). Nevertheless, though presented at the altar, the greater part of a peace-offering was not in any further sense a gift to Yahweh: it was consumed at a sacrificial meal, in which any one ceremonially clean might partake (Lev. 7^{19-21}). Ordinarily the portions *contributed* from the whole offering to the priest were the breast and the right thigh (Lev. 7^{31-34}); in exceptional cases, such as that of the Nazirite's peace-offering ($6^{19f.}$), additional portions were contributed: together these parts constituted the *t^erûmah* (5^{9} n.), or *contribution* from the peace-offering. Of these pieces one (in exceptional cases others, $6^{19f.}$), viz. the breast, was ceremonially waved (6^{20} n.); this part of the *t^erûmah* was called specifically *t^enûphah* or *wave-offering*. All the parts, then, of the peace-offering given to the priest are referred to in the first of the two clauses in the text; the part waved is particularly specified in the second. This is the most probable interpre-

tation; for in spite of the universal phrase (*all the wave-offerings*), everything called *t'nûphah*, or subject to the rite of waving, cannot be intended here. For, described as *t'nûphah*, or as subject to the rite of waving, are the following:—(1) the gold and bronze given for the tabernacle (Ex. 35^{22} $38^{24.\,29}$); the Levites ($8^{11.\,13.\,21}$); (2) portions of the "ram of consecration" and its accompaniments subsequently burnt in the altar-fire (Ex. 29^{22-25}, Lev. 8^{25-28}); (3) certain guilt-offerings (Lev. $14^{12.\,21.\,24}$); (4) the sheaf of first-fruits and the bread of first-fruits with certain accompanying sacrifices (Lev. 23^{10-20}); (5) the meal-offering presented in connection with the ordeal of jealousy (5^{25}); (6) quite exceptionally the thigh as well as the breast of the peace-offering is required to be waved, Lev. 9^{21} 10^{15}. The *t'nûphoth* contemplated in the present law, since they are to be eaten, cannot include the first and second groups; nor, presumably, do they include the third and fifth groups, since these already fall under the law of v.$^{9f.}$; nor the fourth group, which falls under the law of v.$^{12f.}$. As to (6), if the theory of Lev. 9^{21} 10^{15} govern the present law, which is improbable, the two terms in the text must be treated as coextensive, and rendered *the contribution from their gift, even all the wave-offerings*, the last clause being limited by the context to the parts of the peace-offering which were waved.—*Every one that is clean*] Lev. 22^{3-7}.—*Every one . . . in thy house*] Lev. 22^{10-13}. The necessity for being ceremonially "clean" when partaking of sacred food was an ancient regulation (1 S. $21^{4ff.}$).—12. *All the fat*] fig. for "best": cp. Dt. 32^{14}, Ps. $81^{17\,(16)}$ 147^{14}.—*Oil . . . must . . . corn*] the terms (יצהר, תירש, דגן) denote the new produce as contrasted with שמן, יין, and שבר. On תירש (= *must*, or *new wine*), see Dr., *Joel*, 79 f.—*The first of them*] This repeats by means of the more technical word (ראשית), used in the parallel law of Dt. 18^{4} (cp. Ex. 23^{19}), the sense of "*the best of* . . ." How the part to be given to the priests was computed is not stated. On later practice, see below.—13. *The first-ripe fruits of all that is in thy land*] Some (*e.g.* Di.) have taken this to be a generalising repetition of v.^{12}, intended to correct the inference that the offerings in question were to be confined to corn, wine, oil. But this is hardly probable. A distinction is drawn in Neh. $10^{36.\,38\,(35.\,37)}$ between "the first-ripe fruits (בכורי) of our ground and the first-ripe fruits of all fruit of all trees" which were brought "yearly to the house of Yahweh" on the one hand, and a "contribution" (distinct from tithe) of agricultural produce made to the priests on the other. This distinction reappears in the Mishnah; and the two offerings, there clearly distinguished as *bikkûrîm* and *trûmah*, are discussed at length in the tracts bearing those names. Probably the בכורים of this v., like the בכורים of Neh. $10^{36\,(35)}$ and the Mishnah, were comparatively small *offerings* of raw produce, which became indeed, like other offerings or portions thereof, the property of the priests, but only after being *presented with religious ceremony at the temple*, whereas the ראשית of v.[12], like the offerings mentioned in Neh. $10^{37a\,(36a)}$ and the *trûmah* of the Mishnah, was *a contribution* of meal, fruit, wine, oil, etc., *given as a tribute* simply and immediately, without religious ceremony, *to the priests*. See, further, the small print n. that follows.—*Which they bring to Yahweh*] cp. Neh. $10^{36\,(35)}$ "to bring the first-ripe fruits . . . to the house of Yahweh." The first-ripe fruits were offered with a solemn ceremonial at the temple, as they must have been earlier at the local sanctuaries: cp. Ex. 23^{19} 34^{26}, Dt. 26^{2-11}, *Bikkûrîm*, c. 3 (cited below). Philo, *De testo cophini* (Tischendorf, *Philonea*, 69–71; Young's translation, iii. 291–293).

The dedication to the deity of a portion of the new produce of the year is a widely prevalent custom. "Primitive peoples often partake of the new corn sacramentally, because they suppose it to be instinct with a divine spirit or life. At a later age, when the fruits of the earth are conceived as created rather than as animated by divinity, the new fruits are no longer partaken of sacramentally as the body and blood of a god; but a portion of them is presented as a thank-offering to the divine beings who are believed to have produced them. . . . Till the first-fruits have been offered to the deity . . . people are not at liberty to eat of the new crops" (Frazer, *GB*. ii. 458). The following are cited from a large number of examples collected by Frazer (*ib*. 318–340, 459–471): "Among the Basutos when the corn has been threshed and winnowed, it is left in a heap on the threshing-floor. Before it can be touched a religious ceremony must be performed. The persons to whom the corn belongs bring a new vessel to the spot, in which they boil some of the grain. When it is boiled they throw a few handfuls of it on the heap of corn, saying, 'Thank you, gods, give us bread to-morrow also!' When this is done the rest is eaten, and the provision for the year is considered pure and fit to eat" (459). "At the close of the rice harvest in the East Indian island of Buro, each clan meets at a common sacramental meal, to which every member of the clan is bound to contribute a little of the new rice. This meal is called 'eating the soul of the rice.' . . . Some of the rice is also set apart and offered to the spirits" (321). "The Chams of Binh-Thuan, in Indo-China, may not reap the rice harvest until they have offered the first-fruits to Po-Nagar, the goddess of agriculture, and have consumed them sacramentally" (323). In Fiji the new yams may not be eaten before the first-fruits have been dedicated; but the custom as to disposing of the first-fruits differs: in some parts they are presented in the sacred enclosure, and there left to rot; in others they "are presented at the principal temple of the district, become the property of the priests, and form their revenue" (p. 464). "In the Punjaub . . . when the sugar-cane is cut the first-fruits are offered on an altar, which is built close to the press, and is sacred to the sugar-cane god. Afterwards the first-fruits are given to the Brahmans" (461 f.).

Dedication of a part of the new produce was unquestionably an ancient custom with the Hebrews also. The early lawbook forbids delay in making the offering, and requires it to be made at the house of Yahweh, *i.e.* at the local sanctuary (Ex. $22^{28 (29)}$ 23^{19} 34^{26}). In H it is required that a particular kind of first-fruit offering must be made before the new crops may be eaten (Lev. 23^{10-14}). But unfortunately the early references give no information as to the disposal of the offering; it is consequently impossible to decide whether the first-fruits among the Hebrews were in early times consumed sacramentally, as the tithes at one time unquestionably were (see on v.^{31}), and as the first-fruits themselves, according to the customs of some countries just described; or whether from the first among the Hebrews they formed a gift outright to Yahweh or His representative the priest. The former view is adopted by We. (*Proleg.* 155 f.) and Nowack (*Arch.* ii. 255–257), the latter by W. R. Smith (*Religion of the Semites*, 222 f., ² 240 f.). In the former case the later assignment of the contribution to the priests, which had taken place by the time of Dt. 18^{4} (cp. Ezek. 44^{30}), was merely due to the same tendency which, at a later date than Dt., changed the disposal of the firstborn and of the tithe (see below, on v.$^{15-18. 21-24}$).

All the new produce that came to the priests (even in the 7th cent.) was scarcely subjected to such elaborate ceremonial as is described in Lev. $23^{10-14. 15-20}$ or Dt. 26^{2-11}. Consequently the distinction which is certainly drawn in Neh. $10^{35. 37}$, and probably in the present passage, may rest on earlier differences—differences in the mode of presentation, if not in the ultimate mode of disposal of the produce offered.

But such a difference, if indicated here, is not indicated by the mere use of the two different terms ראשית and בכורים. For in themselves they are, though not indeed in all cases, interchangeable, yet certainly not mutually exclusive. They are two among several terms that are used to denote (some of) the new produce of the year, or, specifically, that part of it which was dedicated to the deity; other terms are מלאה ודמעה (Ex. 22^{28}, cp. v.^{27} below); תבואה with the addition of such a genitive as יקב, גרן (v.^{30}), כרם or שדה; תרומה (v.^{27}) or תרומת ידכם (Dt. 12^{6}), or, specifically, תרומת גרן (15^{20}). Of these, תרומה only is necessarily confined, when used in reference to the new produce of the year, to that part of it which was withdrawn from the whole for sacred purposes. Both בכורים and ראשית are primarily wider terms than תרומה, though less wide than תבואה; and it is, strictly speaking, only *part* of what is so termed that is offered to the deity; hence the partitive מן in Dt. 26^{2}, Prov. 3^{9}, and the defining clauses added here, "the ראשית which they give unto Yahweh," "the בכורים which they bring to Yahweh." So in Lev. 23^{10} the sheaf that is offered is "the sheaf *of* the first (ראשית) of thy harvest" (in Ex. 23^{19} 34^{26}, on the other hand, ראשית and בכורים are coextensive rather than part and whole; the case may be different in Ezek. 44^{30}).

But commonly the partitive construction is dropped, and then *rē'shîth* and *bikkûrîm* are tacitly understood to mean that part of the produce so termed that is to be offered or given; so Dt. 26^{10} (ct. v.^{2}), Neh. 10^{36} 13^{31}, 2 Ch. 31^{5}, and Ex. 22^{28} 23^{16} 34^{26} are best understood in the same way. But observe that "bread of first-fruits" (לחם בכורים) is eaten by ordinary people on an occasion which nothing suggests was in any way sacred, 2 K. 4^{42}.

The two terms *rē'shîth* and *bikkûrîm* are rendered indifferently in EV. by "first-fruits," though the latter is here and in Nah. 3^{12} exceptionally rendered "first ripe (fruits)"; cp. the same rendering of בכורה in Hos. 9^{10}, Mic. 7^{1}. 𝔊 in the Hexateuch distinguishes the words, rendering ראשית by *ἀπαρχαί* (which also renders מעשר, חלב, תנופה, and תרומה) and בכורים by *πρωτογεννήματα* (in Ezek. 44^{30} 48^{14}=ראשית); in this way 𝔊 also brings out the close etymological connection between the first-fruits and the firstborn (בכור=*πρωτότοκος*). But ראשית though in itself of far more general meaning (="the first part"), and, therefore, almost always defined by a genitive such as קציר, פרי (in Lev. 2^{12} it is exceptionally undefined), is, when applied to agricultural produce, virtually synonymous with בכורים, and thus, for example, עמר ראשית קצירך (Lev. 23^{10}) might equally well have been termed עמר הבכורים, and similarly the מנחה חרשה (Lev. 23^{16}) or לחם הבכורים (v.^{20}, cp. v.^{17}) might have been called לחם ראשית. As a matter of fact, Dt. does not employ the term בכורים, and uses the word ראשית alike of the offering made with religious ceremony in Dt. 26^{2-10} and of the contribution simply required for the priest in 18^{4}. So again, though in the present passage בכורים (v.^{13}) probably is an offering of raw produce, this distinction is not made clear by the mere use of the term; for while ראשית certainly is used of raw produce in Dt. 26^{2-10} and Lev. 23^{10}, בכורים is not limited to offerings made in that form; for see Lev. 23^{17-20} (H) 2^{14} (P). The two *terms*, then, are sufficiently coextensive to *admit* of Di.'s interpretation of v.^{13} mentioned above.

But the facts that the two different terms are used in two consecutive verses, that the second is strictly the narrower, and still more the difference in the two defining clauses render the alternative view more probable; "the ראשית . . . which they give unto Yahweh" (v.^{12}) is a contribution or tribute paid outright, with little or no religious ceremony, to the priests (cp. Dt. 18^4, Neh. 10^{38}, 2 Ch. 31^5); "the בכורים . . . which they bring to Yahweh" (v.[13]) are offerings of the raw produce which were brought to the sanctuary and offered with ceremony, offerings such as are described in Lev. 23^{10-14}, Dt. 26^{2-10}, and in *Bikkûrîm*, c. 3.

The distinction just drawn was familiar to the Jewish scholars of the Mishnah. Though some of the details there given are manifestly far more recent than the present law, others may be much earlier than the 1st or 2nd cent. A.D., and illustrate at least the outcome of the laws given in the text.

According to the Mishnah, the products of the soil were subject to four exactions named as follows, and exacted in the following order (*Terûmoth* iii. 6): (1) *bikkûrîm*, (2) *terûmah*, (3) tithe (*ma'asēr*), (4) second tithe (*ma'asēr shēnī*). Of these the fourth resulted from an attempt to reconcile the two different but not originally coexisting laws of tithe stated in Dt. 14^{22-29} and Nu. 18^{21-28} respectively, at some time subsequent to the union of Dt. and P in the Hexateuch, and earlier than Tob. 1^7, Jos. *Ant.* iv. 8^2 (cp. Driver, *Dt.* 169–173). The first tithe of the Mishnah corresponds to the tithe of this c., discussed below. The Mishnah recognises that both the *bikkûrîm* and the *terûmah* were included under the OT. term ראשית (*Terûmoth* iii. 7). Nevertheless the *bikkûrîm* and *terûmah* of the Mishnah differ widely from one another. The *bikkûrîm* are clearly offerings of the same nature as the offerings of *rēshîth* described in Dt. 26^{2-10} and Lev. 23^{10}, and apparently identical with the *bikkûrîm* "brought to Yahweh" (Nu. 18^{13}) or "to the house of Yahweh yearly" (Neh. 10^{36}). According to the Mishnah (*Bikkûrîm*), the *bikkûrîm* were only offered of the "seven kinds," *i.e.* of wheat, barley, vines, fig-trees, pomegranates, oil, and honey (i. 10; cp. ii. 3, iii. 9); they had to be brought to Jerusalem (ii. 2), fresh by those living near, dry by those living at a distance (iii. 3), and ceased to be offered with the fall of Jerusalem (ii. 3). The *bikkûrîm* were selected as follows: "If any man went down into his field and saw a fig, grape-cluster, or pomegranate grown ripe he tied it with bast (גמי) and said, 'Lo these are *bikkûrîm*'" (iii. 1). When they were to be taken to Jerusalem all the inhabitants of a district assembled at the chief town. They achieved their journey to the music of pipes, with the ox, to be offered as a peace-offering, preceding them, his ears tipped with gold and crowned with olive leaves. On approaching Jerusalem they were welcomed by the inhabitants, and the music was kept up till they reached the temple-mount. Arrived there, every man shouldered his basket containing the fruits, and proceeded to the fore-court, where they were met by Levites reciting Ps. 30. The animal offerings were offered; the offerers began to recite Dt. $26^{3ff.}$, and, in the middle of the recitation, the basket was removed and placed by the priest on the altar (c. iii.). Thus to the very last this offering of first-fruits retained much of its primitive character; the fruit indeed fell to the priest, but was of comparatively small value; the religious ceremony was still the predominant feature in the custom.

Very different was the *terûmah* of later times. It did not need to be brought to Jerusalem, and could consequently be contributed after the fall of the city (*Bik.* ii. 2 f.). It was exacted on all vegetable produce (כל הפירות :

Bik. ii. 3; cp., perhaps, πάντων τῶν ἐκ τῆς γῆς φυομένων καρπῶν, Jos. *Ant.* iv. 4^4, and Philo, *De præm. sac.* 1 (Mangey, ii. 233)); and in *T^e^rûmoth* reference is incidentally made not only to the more important products like grain, wine, and oil, but also to cucumbers, melons, onions, and the like, as subject to the exaction (*T^e^rûmoth* ii. 5, 6, iii. 1, ix. 6). The amount of *t^e^rûmah* was not fixed, but was expected to be not less than $\frac{1}{60}$ and might be anything up to $\frac{1}{40}$ or, according to Shammai, $\frac{1}{30}$ (iv. 3). When the amount of the new produce to be given to the priest became even so much fixed as this cannot be determined; the present law, like Dt. 18^4, says nothing on the subject.

14. Cp. Ezek. 44^{29}.—*Every devoted thing*] *ḥerem* here, as in Lev. $27^{28.\ 29}$, appears to mean anything so dedicated to Yahweh that it could not be redeemed. Obviously the present law cannot contemplate the objects of such acts of banning or devotion as are described in, *e.g.*, $21^{2f.}$ (n.), Dt. $7^{1f.}$, Jos. $6^{17.\ 21}$, 1 S. 15; for in these cases the objects of the ban are primarily human beings, and the effect of the ban is that they are put to death. The germ of the present use of the term may be found in the custom of placing the silver and gold of a "devoted" place in the sacred treasury (Jos. 6^{19}). But the phraseology here—*everything devoted in Israel*—as well as the passage cited from Lev. favours the view that *ḥerem* in this law is used of objects directly dedicated by individual Israelites, rather than objects belonging to an individual or people placed under ban by the whole of Israel; see Now. *Arch.* ii. 268.—**15–18.** The rights of the priests in the firstborn consist of the redemption price of the firstborn of men, which is fixed at five shekels, equivalent to about twelve shillings, a head (3^{47} n.), the redemption price of unclean animals, and the whole of the flesh of the firstborn of clean cattle. The claim of Yahweh to the firstborn was unquestionably ancient; the early laws are familiar with it (Ex. 13^{13} $32^{28f.\ (29f.)}$ 34^{20}). But the assignment of the firstborn or of the fine paid for their redemption to the priests is probably more recent than Ezekiel, who does not include the firstborn among the dues payable to the priests (Ezek. 44^{28-31}), and almost certainly more recent than Deuteronomy, which gives different directions for the disposal of the firstborn.

In Dt. only the case of the firstborn of clean cattle is considered (15^{19-23} $12^{17f.}$ 14^{23}). On the incompatibility of the law of Dt. and Nu. 18^{15-18}, and also on the probably superior antiquity of the former, see below, p. 236 f., and Dr. *Deut.* p. 187. Here it may suffice to record the known differences in the disposal of the three classes of firstborn (men, clean animals, unclean animals) as described in this law and elsewhere. (1) *Unclean cattle.* These, according to the present law, must be redeemed, and the price of redemption paid to the priest; according to Ex. 13^{13}, in the (typical) case of the ass, redemption was *optional*; if adopted, it is not stated that the price of redemption goes to the priest; nor is it likely, for it was redeemed in kind by a lamb, and this, in all probability, was treated like a firstborn of clean animals. In any case, if the option of killing the ass was adopted, there being no redemption price, the priest received nothing. (2) *Clean cattle.* These, according to Dt., were eaten, not as the present law requires, by the priests alone, but, at a sacred meal, by the man and his household to whom the firstborn belonged. The Levite is simply commended to the hospitality of the Israelites on such occasions (Dt. $12^{18f.}$ 14^{27}). (3) *Men.* Various views have been held as to the original effect of Yahweh's claim to the firstborn of men: one has been noticed above (p. 26); according to another the firstborn were sacrified; see Frazer, *GB.* ii. 43–52; and, briefly, Nöld. in *ZDMG.* xlii. (1888) 483: *e contra* We. *Proleg.*[4] 87 f.; W. R. Smith, *Rel. of the Semites,*[1] 445; Kamphausen, *Die Verhältnis des Menschenopfer zur israelitischen Religion,* 63 ff. However this may be, from the time of the earliest codes the custom in Israel was to redeem the firstborn. So far the present law agrees with at least comparatively ancient custom in Israel. But the early law is at least silent as to any assignment of the redemption to the priest, nor does it fix the redemption at any definite price. Possibly in earlier times the price was variable. W. R. Smith argues at length in *The Religion of the Semites* (note K) against the theory that the firstborn originally constituted a source of tribute to the deity (or priest).

15. *Everything that openeth the womb* (3^{12}), *of all flesh*] In contrast to the precision of the earlier laws (Ex. $13^{12f. 15}$ $34^{19f.}$, Dt. 15^{19}), this general term is not subsequently limited by any direct statement to males either here or in Ex. 13^{2} (P). Some,* therefore, have inferred that P required all firstborn, whether male or female, to be redeemed. If this be correct, the divergence from earlier usage would be another instance of the increasing demands of the priests: but the inference is open to some doubt; for in 3^{40-51} (P) the male firstborn only are considered, and the redemption price here fixed (v.^{15}) is the value of a male between a month and five years of age, but in excess of the value of a woman of the same age (Lev. 27^{6}).—*Only for the firstborn of man thou shalt receive a redemption price*] the subj., as throughout

* Kue. *Hex.* 30; Nowack, *Arch.* ii. 255.

the section, is Aaron, the representative of the priests; but since the priests *receive* the price, the vb. פדה, if correctly pointed, is here used exceptionally of *receiving* the price of redemption; so in v.[16f.].—**15b.** Ct. Ex. 13^{13} (JE), and see small print n. above.—**16.** Cp. 3^{47} n.—*And its redemption price*] On the meaning of the term פדוים, see 3^{46} phil. n. The sing. pronominal suffix here refers to the sing. collective term (בכור "firstborn") in v.[15]. Grammatically, it should at least include a reference to the last clause of v.[15], whence it would follow that every firstborn of unclean animals as well as of men, was to be redeemed at five shekels. The redemption price for male children is fixed elsewhere also at five shekels (3^{47}, Lev. 27^{6}); but that of unclean animals appears to have been, as we should naturally suppose it was, variable (Lev. $27^{11f. 27}$). It is unlikely, therefore, that the present law was actually intended to fix the same price for firstborn of men and firstborn of unclean cattle. Possibly v.[15b] has been transferred by accident to its present position from the end of v.[16], or unreflectingly placed where it now stands by an editor, or, with Di., we may suppose v.[16] a later insertion.—*From a month old*] *i.e.* immediately after attaining the age of a month, and so, virtually, *at a month old.* Any age from a month upwards is differently expressed; see 3^{40}. For illustrations of the present use of the מן, see BDB. *s.v.* מן 4*b*. The age at which children were redeemed is not stated in the earlier codes. The firstborn of oxen and small cattle were, by early custom, given to Yahweh on the eighth day (Ex. 22^{29}) from birth, the same day on which children were circumcised; at a later period (Dt. 15^{20}), within a year from birth (Dt. 15^{20}). —**17.** The firstborn of cattle, of sheep, or goats is treated, so far as the blood and the fat is concerned, in the same way as when one of these animals is presented as a peace-offering (Lev. 3^{2-5}), *i.e.* the fat is burnt on the altar and the blood poured or tossed in full volume against the altar. RV., as usual, erroneously renders זרק by "sprinkle," and so confuses the term with the entirely different הזה. But the *flesh* of the firstborn is treated differently from that of the peace-offering; for, whereas the greater part of the peace-offering could be eaten by any one ceremonially clean (Lev. 7^{19-21}), the *whole* of the flesh of the firstborn, like the right thigh and the breast of a peace-offering, is to be given over to the priests for consumption.—*Thine* (Aaron's) *shall their flesh be as the wave-breast, etc.*] cp. Lev. 7^{29-34} and v.[11] with n. above.—**19.** A summary of the preceding vv.; cp. v.[1].—*A covenant of salt*] cp. "Yahweh . . . gave the kingdom . . . to David . . . for ever . . . by a covenant of salt" (2 Ch. 13^{5}). The phrase means an inviolable covenant. Its origin is probably to be sought in old nomadic custom, whereby a bond was established between those who had shared the same food. The principle is, "If I have eaten the smallest morsel of food with a man, I have nothing further to fear from him; 'there is salt between us,' and he is bound not only to do me no harm, but to help and defend me as if I were his brother."* The root *malaḥa* in Arabic means "to salt," a derivative *milḥat*, "a treaty"; and the sacred character of salt is recognised in a line cited from El-Aʿsha (Kitāb el-'Agānî, xx. 139, 28), "I swear by the salt and the ashes and Ozza and Lât." Salt was mingled with all Hebrew sacrifices (Lev. 2^{13}, Mk. 9^{49}: cp. in reference to particular species, Lev. 24^{7} 𝔊; Ezek. 43^{24}; Jos. *Ant.* iii. 9^{1}; *Zᵉbaḥim* vi. 5) and with the holy incense (Ex. 30^{35}), and continued perhaps to symbolise the inviolability of Yahweh's covenant with Israel.—**20.** *Thou shalt not inherit in their land*] Aaron is addressed as representative of the *priests*; Aaron can, it is true, be *chosen* to represent the whole tribe of Levi ($17^{18ff. (3ff.)}$); but here at the close of the section dealing with dues to the priests (v.[8-20]), and before the section dealing with the Levites (v.[21-24]), Aaron must be interpreted in the narrower sense, for which "Aaron and his sons" is often, but not exclusively (cp. v.[28] $3^{6.9}$ n.), used. In v.[23f.] exclusion from inheritance in the land of Canaan is extended to the Levites, to whom the tithes are assigned in compensation as the sacred offerings are here assigned to the priests. Unlike the rest of Israel, then, priests and Levites receive no landed inheritance in Canaan, but certain sacred dues instead; a corresponding

* W. R. Smith, *Rel. of the Semites*[1], 252, [2]270; cp. We. *Reste des Arab. Heid.* 124.

theory is found in Deuteronomy (Dt. 10^{9} 12^{12} $14^{27.\,29}$ 18^{2}, Jos. $13^{14.\,33}$ 18^{7}) and Ezekiel (44^{28}). But, strictly speaking, the present theory is inconsistent with the alleged assignment of forty-eight cities to the priests and Levites in other, presumably later, passages of P (Jos. 21, Nu. 35^{1-8}). Passages in P agreeing with the present are 26^{62}, Jos. 14^{3}.—*I am thy portion and thy inheritance in the midst of the children of Israel*] *i.e.* the priests are to live by means of the sacred gifts of the Israelites, which are handed over by Yahweh to the priests (v.^{8}). Cp. "Yahweh is his inheritance" (Dt. 10^{9}); but observe that there and in other passages of D (Dt. 18^{2}, Jos. $13^{14.\,33}$) this statement extends to the whole of the Levites, and is not limited, as here, to the priests; see Driver's n. on Dt. 10^{9}.

8. מָשְׁחָה] = "portion": cp. מִשְׁחָה Lev. 7^{35} and the Targumic כְּשַׁח and כְּשָׁחָא = "a measure"; Syr. ܡܫܚ = "to measure"; ܡܫܘܚܬܐ (note the justification for the *o* in מָשְׁחָה) = "a measure"; Ar. *massāḥ* = "a geometrician"; Assyr. *mišiḫtu* = "measure." It is very questionable whether משח = "to measure" has any connection with משח = "to anoint," or the meaning "consecrated portion," given to משחה in BDB., any justification; cp. Fried. Delitzsch, *Proleg*. p. 178 n. 1; Weinel in *ZATW*. 1898, p. 13.—נתתים] The suffix refers to תרמתי (Dav. 1, R. 3; G.-K. 135*o*) or קדשי; these, as distinct from the משמרת of them, are only given under conditions which are subsequently more closely defined.—ולבניך] 𝔊 𝔖 + אתך (cp. v.^{11} 𝔓).—**9.** מקדש] S מקדשי; cp. 𝔊.—**10.** אתו] 𝔊 + σὺ καὶ οἱ υἱοί σου.—**15.** תִּפְדֶּה] v.$^{16.\,17}$; we must either assume a sense for the Kal here which it nowhere else possesses, or point תִּפָּדֶה; cp. Ex. 21^{8}. The use of the inf. abs. Kal in v.^{15} is not conclusive against the latter; see G.-K. 113*w*.—**17.** ורק and הזה are already correctly distinguished in *Speaker's Comm.* ii. 499*b*.

21–24. The Levites' dues.—In return for their service about the tent, and in lieu of any tribal possession of land, the Levites are to receive the tithes offered by the Israelites to Yahweh.

21. *But to the children of Levi*] exclusive of the priests: cp. the similar usage of "tribe of Levi" in v.^{2}. As contrasted with the different subject (Aaron and the priests) of the last v., the clause is placed first for emphasis. — *Every tithe*] According to Lev. 27^{30-33} tithe was taken on both cattle and crops; but Dt. (14^{22-29} 26^{12-15}) refers only to a tithe on crops; and in the present chapter the tithe seems to be similarly limited (cp. v.$^{27.\,30}$). A *royal* tithe on cattle is alluded to in 1 S. 8^{17}, but of a tithe on cattle to be paid to the Levites we find no trace in OT. except in 2 Ch. 31^{6}, Lev. 27^{30-33}; cp. Jubilees 32^{15}. On the other hand, in the full list of dues given in Neh. $10^{36-38\,(35-37)}$, the tithe paid to the Levites is defined as "the tithe of our ground" (מעשר אדמתנו), *i.e.* a tithe on the crops; cp. Neh. $13^{5.\,12}$. Probably, then, the claim to a tithe on cattle was first put forward between the time of the P^{g} and that of P^{s} or Ch., at some time between the 5th and 3rd centuries B.C. Even then the claim appears to have met with but very partial response (Driver, *Deut.* p. 169 f.). In respect, then, of the substances on which tithe was levied the present passage agrees with D and disagrees with P^{s}; it is a tithe on agricultural produce. On the other hand, as to the disposal of the tithe, P is here at the same serious disagreement with Dt. (14^{22-29} 26^{12-15}, cp. 12^{17-19}) as in the matter of the disposal of the firstborn of clean cattle (above, p. 230). In Dt., in two years out of three, the Levite was simply called to share with the offerer and his household in the sacred meal for which the tithe was used; in the third year the tithe was withdrawn from the enjoyment of the landowner and given to the Levites *in common with other needy classes*, the *gêrîm* (15^{13} n.), the widows and the fatherless. According to this law the tithe became the sole property of the Levites, from which they were compelled to contribute a tenth to the priests (v.^{26}). The completely different character of the tithe of Dt. and P was early perceived, and led to the institution of the "second tithe" (above, p. 228). But the institution of two tithes—one payable *in toto* to the Levites, the other intended to form a sacred meal for laymen and Levites—is not recognised by this law, which demands *every tithe* for the Levites; for proof that two tithes were also not required by (nor indeed known to) D, and for a fuller discussion of the subject of tithe generally, see Driver, *Deut.* 168–173.—**22.** The service of the Levites, in return for which they are to receive the tithes, is required in order to prevent the Israelites from again incurring such fatal results of the divine anger at their approach to the tent of meeting as they had recently experienced, $17^{11ff.\,28}$ ($16^{46ff.}$ 17^{13}): cp. 1^{53} 8^{19}.—**23.** *They shall bear their iniquity*] be responsible for and suffer the consequences of any guilt they may incur in the discharge of their duties; cp. v.[2] n. By Ezekiel (44[10]) the same phrase is used in the very different sense of paying the penalty for guilt actually incurred. The difference in the meaning of the phrase illustrates a fundamental difference of attitude towards the Levites on the part of Ezekiel and P respectively: in Ezekiel the Levites are a class degraded from the priesthood in consequence of their guilt (Ezek. 44[10–16]); in P[g] they are a class chosen of Yahweh to a position of honour and distinction, though of less honour, and, therefore, of less responsibility, than that of the priests; see above, p. 22; and, further, Kuenen in *Th. Tijd.* xii. 150 f.; We. *Comp.* 340 f.—**24.** *The tithe . . .* which *they contribute as a contribution*] 5[9] n.

21. חֵלֶף] here and v.[31] only in OT.; cp. חִלַּף and ܚܘܠܦ, which are the regular equivalents in 𝕿 and 𝕾 respectively for תחת in 𝕳.—**23.** הוא] the addition of the pr. gives emphasis to הלוי in antithesis to בני ישראל (v.[23]): cp. 35[33]; Kön. iii. 340*d*.—הם] the pl. pr. referring to the collect. gentilic noun הלוי, Kön. iii. 346*l*.—The variations בני לוי (v.[21]), הלוי (v.[23]), לוים (v.[24]) in this short section are worthy of observation; cp. 4[18. 24] n.

25–32. A tithe of the tithe is payable by the Levites to the priests.—The section is supplemental to v.[8–20], but necessarily follows v.[21–24]. The tithe of the tithes is referred to in Neh. 10[39 (38)].—*And Yahweh spake to Moses, saying*] ct. v.[1. 8. 20]. This change, together with "the curious opening [v.[26]] 'and to the Levites thou shalt speak and say,' etc., implying some previous utterance," has suggested to CH. that we have here an incorporation of fresh material.—**27 f.** The Levites, as well as the rest of Israel (note גם אתם v.[28]), are to make a "contribution" to Yahweh. As the Israelites set aside a part of the new produce of the year, of the corn sifted on their threshing-floors and the wine that fills their vats, so the Levites are to set aside for Yahweh a tithe of what they receive in tithe from the rest of the Israelites; and (v.[30f.]) as the latter, once having paid their sacred dues, enjoy the rest of the produce of their fields where and as they please, so the Levites may consume the remaining nine-tenths of the tithe with like freedom.—**27.** *The fulness*] an old term for the new produce of the year; see Ex. 22[28 (29)] and above, p. 226 f.—**29.** *Of all your gifts* (*i.e.* the tithes) *ye shall contribute the whole of the contribution due to Yahweh*, (to wit) *the hallowed part thereof*, (selecting it) *from the best part thereof*. The tithe of the tithe is to be given in full, and to consist of the best part (חלבו; cp. v.[12] n.) of the tithe.—**30 f.** See on v.[27f.].—**31.** The tithe, not consisting, like the dues payable to the priests, of holy things, may be eaten anywhere; ct. v.[10].—**32.** If the Levites duly pay the tithe of the tithe they *will bear no sin on account of it*; cp. Lev. 19[17] 22[9]. The meaning of the last half of the v. is not too clear; the tithe apparently was not one of the *holy things of the children of Israel* within the meaning of the chapter; moreover, the position of the phrase in Hebrew suggests that it refers to something other than what has been mentioned in the previous sentence. Probably, therefore, it is a warning that the Levites are to be content with their tithes and not profane, by consuming, what might only be eaten by the priests.

26. בנחלתכם] BDB. *s.v.* בְּ i. 7[b].—**29.** כל תרומת] Some Heb. MSS. and 𝔊 om. כל (cp. v.[28] 𝔐).—ממנו . . . מקדשו . . . חלבו] the suffixes refer to כל at the beginning of the v.; Kön. iii. 306*a*.—מִקְדְּשׁוֹ] see 10[21] n. The abnormal punctuation may be intended as a warning that the word has not its usual meaning of "sanctuary": cp. Kön. ii. 97. BDB. (874*a*) propose קָדְשׁוֹ here. But it is possible that the whole clause is corrupt; as an apposition to the clause next but one before it, it is strangely placed.—**30.** ללוים] 𝔙 *vobis*, which Paterson thinks original.

The 18th chapter of Numbers, when compared with other passages dealing with the priestly or Levitical dues, forms a valuable contribution to the history of the Jewish priesthood.

The salient fact is this: the dues here assigned to the tribe of Levi are immensely more valuable than those which are assigned, by direct statement or implication, to the Levites in Dt. or any pre-exilic literature; and considerably more valuable than those required, for the priests, by Ezekiel. They are less valuable than those required in the Mishnah, and, in one respect, than those required in Lev. 27[30-33] (P^s).

It is possible in the abstract to suppose that this chapter contains the most ancient priestly claim, that that claim could not be made good, and that, therefore, the Deuteronomic legislators demanded only the smaller dues which it had become the custom to pay, and that, half a century later, Ezekiel reasserted, to a great extent, the more ancient claim. On this assumption, Nu. 18 might be regarded as earlier in date than Dt. or Ezek., and as containing a programme of claims which the priests would like to have made good if they could. But this is an improbable hypothesis: and it is certain that *the practice of the pre-exilic period*, so far as it may be gathered from notices scattered through the early literature, though it corresponds somewhat closely with the laws in Dt., *differs widely from the regulations of Nu.* 18, *with which*, on the other hand, *the practice of the post-exilic age is in fundamental agreement.* The most natural conclusion from this fact is that Nu. 18 is a regulation later in date than Dt. This conclusion is greatly strengthened by the fact that there is a similar agreement in a number of other matters between the regulations of P and the practice of the post-exilic age (Kue. *Hex.* § 11).

At all periods sacrifices consisted of two great classes: those of the one class (עלה, כליל) were withheld from human consumption and, being made over wholly to the deity, were consumed by the altar fire or ultimately given to the priest; those of the other class formed the substance of a sacrificial meal in which the offerer, his family, and those who might be associated with him, participated.* It was sacrifices of the latter class that formed the prominent feature in early Hebrew life: sacrifices were festal occasions which the people were very ready to multiply (cp. *e.g.* Ex. $32^{5f.}$, 1 S. $1^{4ff.}$ $9^{11ff.}$ 16^{1-13}, Am. 4^{4}, Hos. 8^{13}); this continued to be the case at least as late as Josiah's reformation, for in Dt. the phrases "to sacrifice," "to eat before Yahweh," and "to rejoice," are virtually synonymous (Dt. 12. 16 *passim*). In these sacrificial feasts the Levites, or priests of the time, used to be invited to take a share (above, pp. 230, 234).

But mere participation in sacrificial meals was an inadequate means of support for a class of men. And, apart from any income that may have accrued to them as arbitrators,

* Cp. Jos. *Ant.* iii. 9^{1}.

some, at least, of the priests appear at a quite early period to have laid claim, and to some extent to have substantiated their claim, to more fixed sources of income.

At the famous shrine of Shiloh, as we learn from a narrative (1 S. 2^{12-16}) probably as old as the 8th cent. B.C., the priests sent their servants to remove portions from the pot in which the sacrificial flesh was boiling. This is regarded in the story as a comparative innovation; yet it was tolerated; what roused opposition and ill-feeling was the claim of the priests to parts of the raw flesh.

But long before the close of the 7th cent. this claim must have been decided in favour of the priests. Dt. (18^3) lays down that certain fixed parts of every head of oxen or small cattle offered as a sacrifice (of peace-offerings) must be given to the priests.

The "holy bread," referred to in 1 S. $21^{3ff.}$, though not invariably, was probably, as a general rule, consumed by the priests. A passage in 2 K 23^9 referring to the consumption of unleavened bread by the priests of the high places after the suppression of these latter is obscure.

Apart from these sacrificial portions, the priests at Jerusalem must have derived some income from the "money for guilt" and "the money for sin" (כסף אשם and כסף חטאת) which are referred to in 2 K. $12^{17 (16)}$, but unfortunately in so brief a manner as to leave us in doubt as to its exact nature or extent (cp. Nowack, *Arch.* ii. 226).

In Dt. 18^4 the "first" (ראשית) of corn, wine, oil, and fleece is a due to the priests.

These pre-exilic references do not suffice to give us a complete account of what the priests received. Dues to which we find no reference may have been paid them. On the other hand, we should not be justified in putting all the few references that do exist together, and inferring that the sources of income so mentioned formed part of a contribution regularly made to all priests from the time of David to Josiah. Manifestly, the priests at Jerusalem may have obtained payments that priests at less important sanctuaries failed to secure; and the particular portions of sacrifices which gradually became fixed dues may have differed at different sanctuaries.

And, again, in attempting to form a conception of the income of the priests before the Exile, two facts must be borne in mind. (1) That the form of sacrifice prominent alike in pre-exilic narratives and codes, and presumably, therefore, in the life of the people, was that in which the bulk of the sacrificial flesh was eaten by the offerer and his friends. (2) That the early literature, though it is acquainted with the rarer practice whereby certain victims were altogether removed from use as food and made over entire to the deity, says nothing of victims removed from use as food by the offerer, but handed over for consumption by the priest.

Turning now to sources of priestly income alluded to in Nu. 18 and actually paid after the Exile, we find that some are simply not mentioned before the Exile; it is possible, therefore, that even then the priests received them. Others are there mentioned, but they are assigned for entirely different purposes; these, therefore, had not always contributed to the support of the priests. The dues in P include—

(1) All meal-offerings; all sin-offerings; all guilt-offerings (cp. Ecclus. 7^{31}). The assignment of these to the priests is required by Ezekiel (44^{29}), but is previously unknown. The germ of the law may, however, be seen in (*a*) 1 S. 21^{3-6}; the bread was not necessarily eaten by the priests only; but they might more readily preserve that ceremonial cleanness which was required when eating it; (*b*) 2 K. $12^{17(16)}$: the fines—as they appear to have been—may have been paid for errors committed at the sanctuary; with the increasing sense of the necessity of offerings for sin, offerings took the place, as also the names, of these fines. The sin-offering and the guilt-offering are first referred to by Ezekiel, though they must, it would appear from his mode of reference to them, have arisen before he wrote—possibly between the time of Josiah's reformation and the Exile (cp. Nowack, ii. 225 ff.). Owing to the extreme frequency of these offerings in the later ritual, they constituted in themselves a very large revenue in kind; apart from the sacrifices required at frequently-recurring

public solemnities (see, *e.g.*, c. 28 f.), sin- or guilt-offerings from private persons must have been offered daily, since they were required from women after childbirth (Lev. 12^{6-8}), for touching an unclean thing, and for other frequent occurrences (Lev. 5). Lev. 4, which withdraws certain sin-offerings from priestly consumption, appears to belong to P^s. But even so, the amount of flesh falling to the priests must have been more than they could well consume (cp. Nowack, *Arch.* ii. 234). Even if the question of the disposition of these offerings before the Exile were left an open question, the far greater frequency of them after the Exile would account for a very considerable increase in the income of the priests.

(2) *Ḥerem.* The demand that all "devoted things" should be given to the priests is not *mentioned* before Ezekiel. The value of this due is uncertain; see on $v.^{14}$.

(3) First-fruits and tithes (on vegetable produce). These dues were among the most valuable paid to the priests after the Exile. First-fruits and tithes were withdrawn from ordinary private use before the Exile, but the part of the priest in them was small; for details, see above on $v.^{12f.\ 21}$.

(4) Firstborn. This included a payment to the priests of five shekels (about 12s.) on every (male) firstborn child, a payment for all firstborn of unclean animals, and the assignment to them of all firstborn of clean cattle. Before the Exile the priests received little or nothing of this valuable due; see above on $v.^{15}$.

(5) Fixed portions of the peace-offerings. This, the least valuable due in the list, probably constituted the main perquisite of the earlier priests. Even here P (Lev. 7^{32-34}) requires more than D (18^3).

(6) A number of dues mentioned in P are not mentioned in this c.: some, such as the skin of the burnt-offering, probably because they are of a different nature from those which are here included, but others more probably because they are later in origin than P^g; such are the tithe on cattle (see on $v.^{21}$) and the Levitical cities (c. 35).

These sources of priestly income, which are not distinctly specified in the present c., though some may be covered by its general terms, are the skin of the burnt-offering (Lev. 7^{3}), the shewbread (Lev. 24^{5-9}), amounts paid in compensation for fraud in cases in which no representative of the defrauded person exists (Nu. 5^{8}), certain similar payments (Lev. 5^{16} 22^{14}), unredeemed fields (Lev. 27^{21}), and certain specially large dues for regular offerings in specific cases (*e.g.* Nu. $6^{19f.}$).

Scribal ingenuity in the attempt to reconcile the irreconcilable still further increased the priestly exactions; see above, p. 234.

Literature on the subject of the Priestly dues and their history.—We. *Proleg.* 149–166 (Eng. tr. 152–167); Kue. *Hex.* 31–33, 198–201; Baudissin, *Priesterthum*, 39-43, 86–88, 122–127; Schürer,[3] ii. 243–262 (Eng. tr. II. i. 230–254); Nowack, *Arch.* ii. 125–129; Di. (on this c. and also) *Exodus u. Leviticus*, 634 ff.; Driver, *Deut.* 168–173, 186 f., 213–221, 290; van Hoonacker, *Le Sacerdoce Lévitique*, 383-435 (mainly harmonistic in its treatment).

XIX. *Purification from Uncleanness by the Dead.*

LITERATURE.—Spencer, *De Legibus Hebræorum Ritualibus*, bk. ii. c. 26; Mishnah, tractates *Ohaloth* and *Parah*: *Midrash Rabba* (ed. Berlin), vol. iv. folio עה *a*; Bähr, *Symbolik*, ii. 493–511; Winer, *Biblisches Real-Wörterbuch*, ii. 504–506; Nowack, *Arch.* ii. 287–290; Kennedy's art. "Red Heifer" in Hastings' *DB.*; and Simcox in *EBi.* 846 f.

The present chapter, like c. 15, though it clearly belongs to P, has no intimate connection either with what precedes (c. 16–18—the revolt of Ḳoraḥ) or with what follows (c. 20—the arrival at Ḳadesh). Unlike c. 15, it is devoted to a single subject—pollution through contact with the dead, and its removal by the use of a liquid in which the main ingredient consists of the ashes of a red cow; v.$^{1-13}$ deals mainly with the method of purifying those polluted; v.$^{14-22}$ with the circumstances under which the pollution is contracted.

The actual want of organic connection between this chapter and those that follow is proved rather than disproved by the attempts to establish one; the law, it is said, is placed here on account of the wholesale slaughter that followed the rebellion of Ḳoraḥ.

Not only is the present section entirely unrelated to the preceding and following, it is also separated by much intervening matter from that part of the Hexateuch with which it is in subject most closely connected—viz. from the laws dealing with various forms of ceremonial uncleanness (Lev. 11–15); and that although uncleanness from the dead has been frequently referred to, or discussed, in previous parts of the Hexateuch, Lev. 5^{2} $11^{8. 24-28}$ $21^{1-4. 10f.}$ 22^{4-7}, Nu. 5^{2} 6^{6-12} $9^{6f. 10f.}$.

The present law is presupposed in 31^{19-24}. On the other hand, the method of purification here described is not recognised in the case of the polluted Nazirite: in his case an entirely different method is followed; he purifies himself by shaving his hair and making certain offerings, 6^{9-11}. Lev. 5^{1-6} requires a guilt-offering from one who has *unwittingly* suffered by pollution from the dead.

The reason why neither of these laws refers to the "water of uncleanness" may be that they presuppose it, and refer simply to the special requirements of the special circumstances with which they respectively deal. But the absence of allusion to it in Lev. 22^{4-7} (H) 11^{24-28} is more difficult of explanation if the present law at the time enjoyed a general sanction: so far as the priests are concerned, Lev. 22^{4-7} appears to place uncleanness from the corpses of men on the same footing as other forms of uncleanness, and to require for it, as for them, simply bathing in plain water; and Lev. 11^{24-28} requires nothing more than this simpler cleansing in the case of any man defiled by the carcase of an unclean beast.

Though, therefore, the law has been edited in the priestly school, it does not appear to have formed part of P^{g}, nor to be of the same origin as the laws of uncleanness in Lev. 11–15, nor, perhaps, of the same origin as Nu. 6 or Lev. 5^{1-6}. That it is *younger* than any or all of these there is little or no positive ground for saying; the law is P^{x} rather than P^{s}. Least of all can the absence from the present c. of any demand for offerings on restoration to cleanness be cited in favour of a late origin of the law.

As connecting the c. with P, note, amongst other things, the introductory formula, v.[1] (CH. 185), דבר אל בני ישראל ויקחו v.[2] (cp. 5^{2} n.), עדה v.[9] (cp. 1^{2} n.), and the numerous ritual terms. On the other hand, phraseological peculiarities are, in addition to מי נדה (only again in 31^{23}), חקת התורה v.[2] (also 31^{21} †), התחטא = *to unsin one self*, v.[12. 13. 20] (also 8^{21} n., $31^{19f. 23}$, and in a different sense Job 41^{17} †), מת לכל נפש אדם v.[11] (ct. 6^{6}); see also the notes below on "Ele'azar the priest" (v.[4]), צמיד פתיל (v.[15]), חמאת (v.[9]). We. and Kue., who refer the whole c. to P^s (cp. Di.), consider v.[14-22] an explanatory addition to the main law. CH., on the other hand, refer v.[1-13] to P^s, but v.[14-22] to P^t, judging the latter "less like an addition than an independent ordinance on a similar basis." It has been argued that v.[12] implies that the polluted man sprinkles himself, v.[19] that he is sprinkled by another. But with v.[12] cp. v.[20a], and note that v.[13] (like v.[20b]) implies that the man has the water thrown over him by another: see note there.

But whatever the exact age of the literary origin of the law, the belief on which it is based and the custom which it regulates are ancient and primitive. Purification from pollution through the dead by the use of the ashes of the red cow is but one of many primitive or popular practices which were assimilated and regulated by the later priestly religion and described by its writers; such were the bells on the high priest's cloke (Ex. 28^{33-35}), the water of bitterness (Nu. 5^{11-31}), the goat for Azazel (Lev. 16): see what is said above, pp. 46–48. The belief or doctrine underlying the law and the *specific* regulations here enforced are not, however, necessarily of the same origin and age. The doctrine is this—a dead body is a source or cause of pollution; and this doctrine is both ancient and widespread. There is nothing peculiarly Hebrew, or even peculiarly Semitic, about it.

Thus to refer to some parallel practices that indicate the prevalence of the same doctrine: "Among the Navajos [of North America], the man who has been deputed to carry a dead body to burial, holds himself unclean until he has thoroughly washed himself in water prepared for the purpose by certain ceremonies." "Among the Basutos of South Africa, warriors returning from battle must rid themselves of the blood they have shed. . . . Therefore they go in procession . . . to the nearest stream to wash. . . . It is usual in this ceremony for a sorcerer, higher up the stream, to put in some magical ingredient, such as he also uses in the preparation of the holy water which is sprinkled over the people with a beast's tail at the frequent public purifications." "The Zulus . . . purify themselves by an ablution after a funeral." "Tibetan . . . mourners returning from the funeral stand before the fire, wash their hands with warm water over the hot coals, and fumigate themselves thrice with proper formulas" (Tylor, *Primitive Culture*,[3] ii. pp. 433 f., 437; cp. Frazer, *GB*. i. 322–325). The Madangs of Borneo, after depositing the coffin, pass through a cleft stick, the ends of which, when all have passed through, are tied close together again. Then all who have taken part in the ceremony bathe before returning home, and rub themselves with rough pebbles (Hose in *Geographical Journal*, xvi. 45 f.). The foregoing are customs that have come under modern observation; but they prove the wide prevalence—in America, Africa, and Asia—of the doctrine. The classical authors, the Zendavesta, the laws of Manu, and other ancient Oriental lawbooks show its prevalence among the ancient Romans, Greeks, Persians, and Indians. For Roman practices, cp. Virg. *Æn.* vi. 228–231—

> Ossaque lecta cado texit Corynæus aeno.
> Idem ter socios pura circumtulit unda,
> Spargens rore levi et ramo felicis olivæ,
> Lustravitque viros, dixitque novissima verba;

and ii. 717–720. In Greece a bowl of water was placed before the door of the house where a death had taken place that persons entering the house might purify themselves with it; after the funeral the house was purified; dead bodies were excluded from sacred enclosures, and contact with a dead body rendered a person polluted (μυσαρός) and unfit to approach an altar (Eur. *Alc.* 98–100; *Iph. in Taur.* 380–383; *Helen*, 1430 f.; Paus. ii. 27, together with Frazer's note in *Pausanias Descr. of Greece*, iii. p. 239). In India a death renders the relatives of the dead man unclean, whether they come into contact with him or not: for this and other matters connected with the Indian doctrine of pollution by the dead, see *Gautama*, c. 14 f. = *SBE.* ii. p. 246 ff.; *Manu*, v. 57–104 = *SBE.* xxv. p. 177 ff.; cp. Oldenberg, *Die Relig. des Veda*, pp. 577–591. The doctrine of pollution from the dead is peculiarly influential in Zoroastrianism, and is seen to be closely connected with demonology; see *Vendîdâd* (*SBE.* iv.), esp. Fargards v–xii; cp. *Shâyast lâ shâyast*, c. ii. (*SBE.* v. pp. 245–276), and Darmesteter's introduction to the *Vendîdâd* (*SBE.* iv. pp. lxxxv–xcv), from which this summary of the doctrine may be cited—"Impurity or uncleanness may be described as the state of a person or thing that is possessed of the demon: and the object of purification is to expel the demon.

The principal means by which uncleanness enters man is death, as death is the triumph of the demon.

When a man dies, as soon as the soul has parted from the body, the Drug Nasu or Corpse-Drug falls upon the dead from the regions of hell, and whoever thenceforth touches the corpse becomes unclean, and makes unclean whomsoever he touches" (p. lxxxvi).

For other illustrations of the connection between uncleanness from the dead and the belief in the danger to the living from the spirits of the departed, see Frazer, *GB.* iii. 397–401.

The susceptibility of the dead body to the attacks of demons was also held by the Babylonians, and, with them, led to the custom of purifying the corpse itself (Jastrow, *Religion of Babylonia and Assyria*, p. 602 f.); with which custom we may compare that of the Aztecs mentioned by Tylor (*Prim. Culture*, ii. p. 436).

Clearly, then, there is nothing in any way peculiar to the Hebrews in the belief that a dead body is a cause of pollution; and consequently the *origin* of the belief and the original significance of the customs must be sought not in what is peculiar to the Hebrew religion, but in that system—if the term may be used—of primitive thought out of which the higher religions and the Hebrew among them sprang. Consequently, too, there is no reason for thinking that the belief was borrowed by the Hebrews; and, indeed, although the present law and other references in the Hexateuch (Lev. $11^{31ff. 39f.}$ $21^{1ff.}$ H, Nu. 5^{2} 6^{9} 9^{10} $31^{19ff.}$ P, Dt. 26^{14}) to the subject do not carry us further back than the 7th cent. (Dt. 26^{14}), the belief is unmistakably referred to in Hos. 9^{4}; other references outside the Hexateuch are Hag. 2^{13}, Ezek. 44^{25}; cp. 2 K. 23^{14}. In none of these passages is there any suggestion that the demonological beliefs, with which the doctrine seems to have been originally connected, were still consciously held by the Hebrews. This also is true of subsequent allusions: see Tob. 2^{9}, Ecclus. 31^{30} (34^{25}), Bar. 3^{11}.

When we turn from the doctrine to the *specific* regulations of this law, it is less easy to establish the antiquity of the usage in Israel, or to find exact parallels to it elsewhere. Purification in some form is naturally as ancient and general as the doctrine. But with the particular means of purification here decreed it is different. Generally speaking, ceremonial impurity in Israel, as among many other peoples, was removed at the end of a certain period after the impurity was incurred (sometimes on condition of the discharge of certain other regulations also, such as the presentation of offerings), by the use of simple water, which is often, however, expressly required to be "living," *i.e.* running, and not stagnant (cp. Lev. 13. 15). And this mode of purification appears to be regarded in some of the laws cited above as sufficient even in the case of pollution from the dead. The peculiarity of the present law is that it requires this purification to be made by means of water which has been mixed with the ashes of a red cow.

Three questions naturally arise, though they can be but very partially answered. (1) What is the history of the use of this particular mixture? (2) What analogy has it in Hebrew ritual? (3) What analogy has it outside Israel?

(1) As to the history. The use of this mixture cannot be actually traced further back than this law; unless, perchance, we should find some indirect evidence of it in the story of the people being given water mixed with the ashes of the golden calf to drink (Ex. 32^{20} JE).* Subsequent allusions to or discussions of the use are found in Heb. 9^{13} and the Mishnah. The influence of the story rather than of the actual practice accounts for the allusion to the red cow in the *Ḳoran* (ii. 63–68), on which see Geiger, *Was hat Muhammad aus dem Judenthum genommen*, p. 172.

(2) Water specially treated—with, amongst other things, "cedar wood, scarlet, and hyssop," as in the present law (v.[6]) is employed in the rite of cleansing lepers or a leprous house, Lev. $14^{4f. 49-52}$. The "bitter" or "holy waters" employed in the ordeal of jealousy ($5^{11ff.}$) afford another parallel to the imparting of special virtues to water by adding to it ingredients. Once, again, the *origin* of such preparations is not to be sought in anything peculiar to Hebrew religion. These medicated waters are mere survivals from primitive practice, or the result of borrowing on the part of the Hebrews at a late period. For

(3) Analogies, more or less close, are to be found outside Israel. Passing over remoter parallels, some of which will be found in the customs cited above, it must suffice to call attention here to the use of the cow in lustration.

So far as the present writer is aware, this is, apart from the Hebrew rite under discussion, confined to the Arians.† It is peculiarly common in the Zendavesta, where the use of *gomez*, *i.e.* oxen's urine, is frequently enjoined in connection with pollution from the dead; see, *e.g.*, *Vendîdâd*, v. 51 (a woman who has born a still-born child drinks "*gomez* mixed with ashes" to purify her womb); vii. 73–75 (cleansing of polluted vessels by *gomez*, earth and water); viii. 11–13

* Cp. Simcox in *EBi.* 547: "Is the putting away of the heifer with something of a royal funeral an almost unconscious reminiscence of a well-nigh forgotten cultus of sacred animals? Is the red heifer the last trace of a cow goddess?"

† We. (*Comp.* 178) speaks of the use of the ashes of the red cow as "recalling Arian methods of purification.'

(corpse-bearers wash their hair and bodies with the urine of sheep or oxen). Cows' urine also ranked as a peculiarly valuable means of purification in India (cp. Oldenberg, *Veda*, p. 490). Have we, then, in this use of the cow a trace of Persian influence on the Jews? So far as the known literary history of the chapter is concerned, this is not impossible. On the other hand, this would not account for the slaughter of the cow. To this we may find a closer parallel in the Roman use of the ashes of calves in lustration: cp. Ovid, *Fast.* iv. 639, 725, 733. Cp., further, W. R. Smith, *Rel. Sem.*[1] 362, [2] 382. For Egyptian and Roman instances of red victims, see below on v.[2].

In origin many of the elements in the present ritual are not peculiarly Hebraic or Jewish. But what did they signify to the Jews? Philo naturally allegorises. The mixture of water and ashes is to remind men of what they consist, for knowledge of oneself is the most wholesome form of purification (*De victimas Offerentibus*, c. ii.; Mangey, ii.252). Needless to say, the rite had no such meaning for the ordinary Jew. But is Bähr much nearer the mark? According to him, the purpose of the whole rite is to symbolise the antithesis between life and death. The pollution has been caused by death; everything in the rite of purification must point to life: hence the redness of the cow and the scarlet, for red is the colour of life: the female sex of the animal, for the female is the source of life: the cedar, for cedar wood is incorruptible; and so forth. For another suggestion, see *EBi. s.v.* "Clean," § 16 *ad fin.*

To Christian interpreters the c. gave from the first (cp. Heb. 9[13]) a wide scope for allegorising—to them, indeed, the meaning of the rites here recorded was evident, to the Jews obscure (*Ep. of Barnabas* 7[9]). In *Barnabas* (c. 7) the allegory is already elaborate, but later it was much more fully developed. Many of the requirements of the law, such as the spotlessness of the victim and its being burnt outside the camp, had an obvious meaning for the allegorist. Augustine in his lengthy discussion (*Quæst. in Num.*, No. 33 in Migne, *Patrologia Latina*, xxxiv. 732–737) interprets amongst other things the victim itself as symbolising Christ in the flesh; the female sex, the weakness of the flesh; the red colour, the bloody passion; the cedar, hope; the hyssop, faith (quæ cum sit herba humilis, radicibus hæret in petra); the scarlet thread, charity. In the burning he sees a sign of the resurrection: since fire naturally ascends, and what is burnt becomes fire. That the victim is burnt before Ele'azar, portends that Christ's resurrection was witnessed by those who were to become a royal priesthood. The dead which make men unclean are dead works—and so forth.

1–13. The preparation, effect, and use of the waters for the removal of uncleanness.—A red cow which is without blemish, and has never borne the yoke, is to be slain outside the camp, v.$^{2f.}$; Ele'azar is to sprinkle some of its blood seven times towards the tent of meeting, v.^{4}; then the cow—skin, flesh, blood, and fecal matter—is to be burnt, v.^{5}; with the ashes, cedar wood, "hyssop," and scarlet thread are to be mingled, v.^{6}; the whole constitute the ingredients of the "water of impurity," v.^{9}. Every one concerned in the preparation of this water is rendered unclean, v.$^{7f. 10}$. Every one defiled by contact with the dead is to get himself sprinkled with this water on the third and seventh day from defilement, under pain of being "cut off"; and thus on the seventh day to recover his cleanness, v.$^{11-13}$.

1. *Unto Moses and Aaron*] 2^{1} n.; Moses only is recognised in v.^{2}.—2. *This is the statute of the law*] or "teaching" (חקת התורה); also 31^{21} †; cp. the similar double phrase חקת משפט 27^{11} 35^{29} †.—*Speak*] the Hebrew is sing. (דַּבֵּר); Moses is the subject: cp. 1^{2} n. — *That they take unto thee*] the verb here used (לקח) is not the same as, but virtually synonymous with, that commonly rendered "bring" (הביא); the two interchange in Lev. $12^{6.8}$.—*A red cow*] no unnatural colour is intended: for though the word אדם at times denotes a brilliant red colour (as of blood), it is also used where we should rather speak of a brown or reddish brown (Zech. 1^{8}, Gn. 25^{30}—of lentils); cp. *EBi.* 873. Hebrew terms for colour were not precise: see G. W. Thatcher's art. "Colour" in Hastings' *DB*. Why the cow had to be red is uncertain. Possibly because red is the colour of blood; so the colour was commonly understood by the allegorists. But the equivalence of red and blood is also primitive (cp. Clay Trumbull, *Blood Covenant*, 236 f.). On the other hand, in the offerings by the Romans of reddish-golden puppies (*Rutilæ canes*) to make the crops grow ripe and ruddy, and of red-haired men, whose ashes were

scattered with winnowing fans, and of red oxen by the Egyptians, Frazer (*GB.* ii. 311, 142, 254 f.) detects a symbolism of the ruddy golden corn.—The animal is a female, in this resembling an animal brought as a sin-offering, 6^{14}, Lev. 4^{27} 5^{6} 14^{10}, and the animal used in the rite described in Dt. 21$^{1-9}$. But the term used (פרה) does not define the age or condition of the animal; it means simply a female of the bovine kind. "Heifer" (RV.) is wrong; for פרה is used in 1 S. 6^{7} of cows that had borne calves; cp. also Job 21^{10} and the metaphorical use in Am. 4^{1}. Nor does the specification that the animal is never to have been yoked necessarily imply that a heifer is intended; for the kine of 1 S. 6^{7} are also such as have never before been yoked.—*Faultless, wherein there is no defect*] for a similar redundance of expression, cp. Lev. 22^{21} (H). The cow, like a sacrificial animal (*e.g.* Dt. 17^{1}, Lev. 22$^{20ff.}$), is to be free from such defects as lameness or blindness.—*Upon which a yoke hath never come*] (אשר לא עלה עליה על) 1 S. 6^{7} †; cp. Dt. 21^{3} (אשר לא משכה בעל): cp. the ἄζυγες and *injuges* of the Greeks and Latins. The animal is to be one that has never been used for profane purposes. This provision is not made for cows offered as sacrifices. The cows of 1 S. 6^{7} are indeed ultimately sacrificed (v.^{14}); but they were not selected for this purpose. Neither the heifer of Dt. 21, nor the red cow (see below) is offered as a sacrifice; but in each case the animal is selected for a special sacred purpose, and for this reason must be one that has not previously been used for ordinary domestic purposes: cp. the case of the firstborn, Dt. 15^{19}.—The Jewish doctors disputed about the degree of redness and the age of the cow; most agreed that it must be at least two years old (for a פרה would be older than a עגלה), and some admitted that it might be as old as five years. As to the colour, some maintained that the presence of two black or white hairs rendered an animal unsuitable (*Parah*, c. 1. 2); this may be mere extravagance, arising from erroneously connecting תמימה with אדמה in the sense "wholly red" (so *Siphrê*); but a similar scrupulosity is attributed by Plutarch (*De Iside*, 31) to the Egyptians in the choice of their red victims.—**3.** *And ye shall give it*] the pl. subject in accordance with v.^{1}; 𝔊 καὶ δώσεις, following up the "speak" and "for thee" of v.[2].—*To Ele'azar*] the preparation of the "water of impurity" entails pollution; hence Ele'azar is intrusted with it, rather than the high priest Aaron himself; cp. the strict injunction of Lev. 21^{11} (H), and also 17^{2} n.—*And it shall be taken outside the camp and slain before him*] on these passive renderings, see phil. n. RV. is only right with regard to the second verb. The fact that the sacred victim is slain outside the camp is quite exceptional, and is inconsistent with the view that it is a sacrifice, an offering to Yahweh; that the flesh of certain sin-offerings, *after* presentation and undergoing sacrificial rites at the altar, was burnt outside the camp (Lev. $4^{11f. 21}$ 8^{17} 9^{11} 16^{27}: cp. Ex. 29^{14}), is only a partial parallel, and to be differently explained (cp. p. 65, 209 f.). Nor is it a complete explanation to cite 5^{1-4} and to say that the victim, having reference to death, is therefore removed from the camp. W. R. Smith (*Rel. of Semites*,[1] 354 ff., [2]374 ff.) cites a number of instances from other religions in which human sacrifices were burnt outside the city.—4. Ele'azar is to sprinkle (הזה; ct. זרק 18^{17} n.) some of the blood of the cow seven times (cp. Lev. $4^{6. 17}$ $16^{14. 19}$) towards the front of the tent of meeting; this, apparently, is to indicate that the cow is sacred to Yahweh.—5. The cow is to be burnt entire in the sight of Ele'azar. With clause *b*, cp. the somewhat differently expressed directions of Ex. 29^{14}, Lev. 4^{11} 8^{17} 16^{27}: the present is the only instance in which the blood is dealt with in the same way as the skin, flesh, and fecal matter (פרש); and this for the reason that the blood of all sacrifices was drained off either to be tossed against the altar or used for sprinkling. Only quite exceptionally, too, was the skin of a sacrifice burnt (Lev. $4^{11. 20}$). — 6. *Cedar, hyssop, and scarlet thread*] these are cast into the yet burning carcase of the cow and reduced with it to ashes, so that with the ashes of the cow they form the ingredients of the cleansing mixture. The use of the same three objects in Lev. $14^{4. 6. 49. 51f.}$ in the rite of purification from leprosy is different; for there it appears that the cedar and hyssop, bound together by the scarlet, are used as a sprinkler with which the liquid is sprinkled on the person to be cleansed: cp. the use of the bunch of hyssop below in v.[18] and in Ex. 12^{22}. "Hyssop," after the ὕσσωπος of 𝔊, is the conventional rendering of the Heb. אזוב; but appears to be wrong, since *Hyssopus officinalis*, L., is not native to Palestine. That some climbing plant is intended, is clear from 1 K $5^{13}(4^{33})$. Beyond this all is very uncertain. The favourite identification is with the caper (*Capparis spinosa*), a vivid green creeper which grows, amongst many other places, on the walls of Jerusalem, and was held in high esteem for its cleansing and medicinal properties. Jewish tradition rather favours *Origanum marjorana*, L. (a kind of marjoram).* Whatever the plant, it was doubtless used in this and the parallel rite of purification from leprosy on account of its cleansing properties (Ps. $51^{9\,(7)}$). The scarlet thread was presumably selected for its colour, for the same obscure reason that required the cow to be red; the cedar, perhaps on account of its soundness and endurance, and its supposed property of imparting these qualities—a virtue also attributed to the juniper, which many † argue must be intended by the Heb. ארז here. Pliny remarks (*HN*. bk. xvi. § 76): "Cedri oleo peruncta materies nec tineam nec cariem sentit; Junipero eadem virtus quæ cedro." Numerous medicinal qualities with which cedar and hyssop were credited in the ancient world are mentioned by Pliny; see the Index to *HN*. in Silleg's edition (Gotha, 1857), *s.v.* "Cedrus" and "Hysopus."—7 f. The priest and the man who actually burnt the cow are alike rendered unclean by their duties; they must wash their persons (cp. Lev. 15 *passim*) and their clothes (cp. Lev. $11^{25.\,28.\,40}$ 15^{5} and *passim*); at the close of day they recover their cleanness: cp. v.[10]. Similarly, some of those who were concerned in the rites of the Day of Atonement, the effect of which was to cleanse the people, are themselves rendered unclean: see Lev. $16^{26.\,28}$; cp. the notes below on v.[20f.].—*Until the evening*] (עד הערב) so, as defining the close of (the shortest) period of uncleanness, Lev. $11^{24f.\,27f.\,31f.\,39f.}$ 14^{46} $15^{5-8.\,10f.\,16f.\,19.\,21-23.\,27}$ 17^{15}, Nu. $19^{7f.\,21f.}$ (all P); Lev.

* Tristram, *Natural History of the Bible*, 456 f.; Löw, *Aram. Pflanzennamen*, 93; and the Bible dictionaries under "Hyssop"; also *EBi. s.v.* "Caper-berry."

† See, especially, Post in Hastings' *DB. s.v.* "Cedar."

22^6 (H) †. The same term of time is differently defined in Dt. 23^{12} (לפנות ערב . . . וכבא השמש).—9 f. A man ceremonially clean is to collect the ashes and deposit them in a clean place outside the camp, where they are to be kept for mixing, as occasion may arise, with running water to produce "water of impurity," v.[17]. The man who collects the ashes is rendered unclean by the duty (cp. v.[7f. 21f.]).—*Water of impurity*] (מי נדה, also v.[13. 20] 31^{23}: מי הנדה v.[21] †) *i.e.* water for the removal of impurity: see n. on "water of sin" (מי חטאת) 8^7. Cp. Zech. 13^1 "a fountain . . . for [*i.e.* for the removal of] sin and impurity." The term נדה, which is also used of menstruation, refers to ceremonial uncleanness under its aspect of something that is abhorrent, to be shunned or avoided; cp. the figurative use of the word in Ezek. $7^{19f.}$. The root in Heb. and Arab. means "to flee from"; in Aram. "to abominate" or "shrink from" (see BDB.).—*It*, viz. the cow thus reduced to ashes, *is a means of removing sin*] cp. 𝔊 (ἅγνισμα); the Heb. חטאת (= "sin") received a number of secondary meanings, such as "punishment for sin," "offering for sin": there is no necessity for adopting the latter sense here; it would be pointless. Moreover, unlike actual sacrificial offerings, this cow is not slain at the sanctuary.—10a. Cp. v.[7f.].—10b. Cp. 15^{13-16} n. — 11–13. Touching a dead person entails uncleanness for at least seven days: but by making use of the "water of impurity" on the third and seventh days from defilement, the uncleanness is removed at the end of that period; failure thus to remove the uncleanness is punished by being "cut off."—11. *He that toucheth the dead, even any human corpse*] נפש is clearly used in v.[13] of that with which it is possible to come into physical contact, *i.e.* of the corpse; and so it is best rendered here: the לְ in לכל נפש is then not genetival (RV.), but summarising (cp. BDB. p. 514*b*). See also 5^2 phil. n.—*Shall be unclean seven days*] this longer term of uncleanness (ct. v.[7]), the observance of which is referred to in 12^{14} (E), is due to the more serious nature of the defilement as compared with that which entailed only one day's defilement (v.[7] n.); other causes of defilement that last seven days are menstruation and other issues (Lev. c. 15), or the birth of a male child (Lev. 12^2).—12. In v.[19] two sprinklings, one on the third day and one on the seventh, are quite clearly required. The same requirement is presupposed here in clause *b*, and might, with difficulty, be read into clause *a* even as it now stands in 𝔐. But for יטהר in clause *a* read, with S 𝔊, וטהר, and render—*He must unsin himself* (or, *get himself unsinned*, $8^{21.\,26}$) *therewith on the third day and on the seventh, and so become clean; but if he do not unsin himself on the third day and on the seventh, he will not become clean.* — 13. *Every one who toucheth a dead person*, i.e. *the corpse of any man that may have died*] cp. v.[11].—*Hath defiled the dwelling of Yahweh*] Lev. 15^{31}.—*That soul shall be cut off*] 9^{13} n.—*From Israel*] after the preceding phrase only occurs again in Ex. 12^{15} †.—*Because the water of impurity was not thrown over him*] so also v.[20]; the verb (זרק) means "to throw in quantities," *e.g.* in handfuls or bowlfuls; it is quite distinct from the verb הזה = "to sprinkle," v.[4]. See BDB. *s.v.* זרק. In v.[19] a rite of sprinkling is described; in v.[20], again, the water is described as thrown in a quantity. The distinctly passive vb. here indicates that the water is thrown over the person to be cleansed by another.

2. ויקחו . . . דבר] cp. 5^2 n.—**3.** ושחט . . . והוציא] Dav. 108*a*; G.-K. 144*d*. 𝔊 renders both verbs in the pl.—למחנה] 𝔊 + *εἰς τόπον καθαρόν*: cp. v.[9] 𝔐.—**4.** באצבעו] 𝔊 omits.—**5.** ושרף] 𝔊 *κατακαύσουσιν* (cp. n. on v.[3]), and for ישרף at end of v. *κατακαυθήσεται*.—**5.** פרשה] פרש does not mean *excrement* (RV.), but, like فرث and Assyr. *piršu*, the *contents of the intestines*: see Haupt's n. in *SBOT.*, "Judges," p. 30.—**6.** והשליך] 𝔊 *καὶ ἐμβαλοῦσιν*; but wrongly: this verb, like the preceding and following, refers to Ele'azar.—**8.** במים (1)] 𝔊 𝔖 𝔙 and one or two Heb. MSS. om.; cp. v.[7. 10. 19] 𝔐. במים, common after רחץ, is never used after כבם in Piel, and but once after Pual (Lev. 15^{17}): so Paterson in *SBOT.*—**9.** אפר here and in v.[10], but עפר v.[17]; neither is the word used of the ashes of burnt sacrifices, which is דֶּשֶׁן.—מֵי נִדָּה] EV. "water of separation"—a Jewish, but incorrect, interpretation: cp. Ibn Ezra מי נדה פירושו רחוק כמו מנדיכם (Is. 66^5). Another traditional and incorrect interpretation is "water of sprinkling"; so 𝔊 (*ὕδωρ ῥαντισμοῦ*) 𝔖 (ܡܝܐ ܕܢܨܘܦܐ) 𝔗° 𝔙 Rashi. This sprang from giving to נדה the sense of the Aram. נדה = Heb. נזה. Rashi defends it by a reference to ידה = "to cast" in Lam. 3^{53}, Zech. 2^4. But the noun נִדָּה in Hebrew always means "impurity"; cp. *e.g.* Ezr. 9^{11}.—**10.** והיתה] G.-K. 144*b*.—**11.** וטמא] Dr. *Tenses*, 123*a*. S reads יטמא; cp. 𝔊.—**13.** מי נדה לא זרק] acc. with pass.: Dav. 79 f.; G.-K. 121*ab*; otherwise Kön. iii. 349*g*.

14–22. This section repeats in greater detail and in somewhat different phraseology the substance of v.$^{11-13}$ — the occasion, effect, and means of removal of defilement by the dead.

Among the differences of phraseology note the different ways of expressing "any dead body" (with v.$^{11a. 13a}$, ct. v.$^{16a. 18b}$) and the "ashes" of the cow (אפר v.$^{9f.}$; עפר v.^{17}); note also that נפש is used in different senses in v.^{11} (cp. v.^{13}) and v.^{18} (cp. v.^{22}); and, further, ct. v.^{12} and ^{19}, and מתוך ישראל (v.^{20}) with מישראל (v.^{13}), and את מקדש יהוה טמא and טמא הוא (v.^{20}) with את משכן יהוה טמא and טמא יהיה (v.^{13}).

It is not unlikely, therefore, that v.$^{14-22}$ and v.$^{1-13}$ were originally distinct laws, which have been combined by the compiler for the sake of completeness. For different views as to their relative antiquity, see above, p. 242 f.

14 f. A death in a tent defiles all persons who are in the tent at the time, or who enter it at the time, and all uncovered vessels. The defilement in the case of persons lasts seven days. This is more comprehensive than v.$^{11-13}$, which only speaks of defilement being occasioned by physical contact with a corpse. In Indian law a death defiles all relatives of the deceased, whether near or far away at the time (Manu, v. 74 ff.); so also in the Zend-avesta (Fargard xii.): cp. further, above, p. 244.—*When any man dies in a tent*] the term "tent" is chosen out of regard to the supposed situation in the wilderness. It must mean any dwelling: 𝔊 rightly expresses the sense by οἰκία.—**15.** *Which hath no covering* and *no cord upon it*] the meaning perhaps is, which has no covering tied over it; but the exact meaning of the words here used is uncertain: see phil. n.—**16.** Contact in the open with the corpse of any one who has died through violence or naturally, or with any human bone, or with any grave, also entails seven days' defilement; cp. 31^{19}.—**17 ff.** The mode of purification.—**17.** Cp. v.^{9}. Some of the ashes of the cow, here referred to as the *ḥaṭṭāth* (see on v.^{9}), are mixed in a vessel with spring water (מים חיים: cp. Gn. 26^{19}, Zech. 14^{8}, Cant. 4^{15}): cp. Lev. 14$^{5f. 50-52}$.—**18.** Some man, ceremonially clean, takes a bunch of *hyssop* (v.^{6} n.), and by means of this sprinkles the mixture over the persons defiled (v.$^{14. 16}$), over the tent where a death has occurred, and over all the vessels defined in v.[15]. This use of "hyssop" as a lustral sprinkler may be compared with that of the laurel by the Greeks and Romans, which is discussed by Bötticher (*Baumkultus der Hellenen u. Römer*, 369 f.).—**19.** Not inconsistent with v.[13]; see n. there. But in addition to what is stated in v.[12], it is here laid down that after the ceremonial sprinkling with the mixture on the seventh day, the defiled person is to wash his person and his clothes; cp. 31^{24}.—**20.** Cp. v.[13].—*From the midst of the assembly*] ct. v.[13] "from Israel": the phrase here used is in two respects singular: see phil. n.—*He is unclean*] a different mode of expressing "his uncleanness is still in him," v.[13].—**21a.** The foregoing regulations are of perpetual validity; cp. v.[10b]. — **21b.** While the water of impurity cleanses the unclean, it defiles clean persons who touch it; hence the clean person (v.[18]) who sprinkles the unclean is himself rendered unclean: uncleanness in this case is of the lighter kind (cp. v.[7. 9]), lasts only till the close of day, and is removed by simple washing of the clothes. With the defiling effect of the water which is sacred (see on v.[4]), Nowack (*Arch.* ii. 288 n. 1) aptly compares the later Jewish doctrine that the Holy Scriptures "defiled the hands" (cp. *Yadaim*, c. 3 f.; especially 4^{6}).—**22.** Every thing that the person defiled by the dead touches, becomes unclean, and any one touching it is rendered unclean for the rest of the day; cp. the similar cases of persons, male or female, rendered unclean by a natural discharge—Lev. $15^{4-6.\ 9f.\ 20-23.\ 26f.}$. The clause כל אשר . . . בו is no doubt, as the parallels in Lev. suggest, to be taken neutrally, but as including persons, *i.e.* any one who touches a person during the period of his defilement is defiled. Cp. *Gautama*, xiv. 30 (=*SBE.* ii. p. 250)—"On touching an outcast, a *Kandala*, a woman impure on account of her confinement, a woman in her courses, or a corpse, and on touching persons who have touched them, he shall purify himself by bathing dressed in his clothes."

14. וזאת התורה אדם כי ימות באהל] The accents (note the athnaḥ under באהל) mean: *This is the law when a man dieth in a tent*; so RV.; rather, *This is the law. When a man dies*, etc. In either case the Hebrew is very unusual. The phrase וזאת התורה nowhere else stands thus by itself. Elsewhere we have זאת התורה לעלה or the like; see 5^{29} n.; more frequently . . . זאת תורת followed by a word defining the subject of the law, *e.g.* 5^{29} 6^{13}, Lev. $6^{2.7.18}$.—אדם כי ימות] a characteristic construction at the beginning of a law in P; cp. *e.g.* $5^{6.12}$, Lev. 1^{2}. So also in the Mishnah (*Ber.* 2^{8} 3^{6}); but not in Ex. 21–23 (see, *e.g.*, $21^{7.14}$), nor Dt. (see, *e.g.*, 19^{11} 22^{13}). See 5^{6} n.—**15.** אשר אין צמיד פתיל עליו] 𝔊^{B} ὅσα οὐχὶ δεσμὸν καταδέδεται ἐν αὐτῷ; 𝔖 ܘܠܐ ܗܘܐ ܡܫܠ; 𝔗^{O} דלית מגופת שיע מקף עלוהי. These renderings scarcely carry us beyond the general sense, and contain no precise tradition as to the meaning of צמיד, which elsewhere means a "bracelet." Nor can a suitable meaning be safely established by etymology; صماد, cited, *e.g.*, by Ges. (*Thes.*) in the sense of "stopper" or "cover" (the meaning of the מגופה of 𝔗^{O}), is uncertain and rare. Perhaps צמיד was already obsolete when the law was edited and was explained, whether quite rightly we cannot say, by the addition of פתיל = "a cord" (15^{38}). S reads צמיד ופתיל.—**17.** ונתן] S 𝔊 נתנו; cp. לקחו at the beginning of the v. Either both vbs. were sing. (cp. והוציא . . . ושחט in v.[3]) or both were pl. Haupt in *SBOT.* favours the sing., noting ולקח in v.[18] and regarding its present subj. איש טהור as a gloss.—**19.** ורחץ] 𝔊^{L} + בשרו; cp. v.[7f.] 𝔐.—**20.** מתוך הקהל] cp. 16^{33}; never elsewhere after the phrase ונכרתה הנפש ההיא, which is regularly completed by מקרב עמ(י)ה Ex. 31^{14}, Nu. 15^{30}; cp. Lev. $17^{4.10}$ 18^{29} $20^{3.5f.18}$: for other completions of the phrase, see v.[13], Ex. 12^{15} (מישראל) and Ex. 12^{19} (מעדת ישראל).—**21.** להם] S 𝔊 𝔖 לכם.

XX. 1–21. *Events at Kadesh.*

The events here recorded—the death of Miriam, the miraculous production of water from a rock, the sin and doom of Aaron and Moses, the embassy to the king of Edom—carry the narrative down to the close of the period of wandering. The final march, concluding with the conquest of Canaan from the E., is already contemplated. The present section mainly serves the purpose of an introduction to the account of the march itself, which begins in 20^{22} and is continued in the following chapters; for it explains (1) why Moses and Aaron were cut off by death before the completion of their undertaking to lead the people into the land of promise, v.[2–13]; and (2) how, in the first instance, the Israelites sought to get at Canaan by a peaceful passage through Edom, v.[14–21].

Thus, according to the chronological scheme of P^{g}, to which the composite narrative of the Hexateuch is accommodated, these events are nearly forty years later than those recorded in c. 13 f. (the spies and the condemnation to forty years' wandering). But the fusion of divergent accounts, the attempt of the editor to make the divergences less apparent, and the insertion of miscellaneous laws and stories connected with no definite time or place in c. 15. 19, have obscured this lapse of time, and also the original representations of the various sources. To a considerable extent this obscurity can be cleared up by analysis, though in detail much remains doubtful or ambiguous.

According to P^g, the spies had been despatched from, and the people were condemned to wander in, the wilderness of Paran (13^3 14^{32}): the wilderness of Ṣin lay between Paran and the land of promise (13^{21}). Now that the period of wandering is over, the whole company advances to the district first reconnoitred by the spies a generation before. This is the wilderness of Ṣin, or Ḳadesh. Here the people lack water, and murmur. Moses and Aaron, bidden by Yahweh to produce water for the people in a miraculous manner, so as to impress upon the people Yahweh's holiness, show themselves unbelieving, and are punished; like the rest of their generation, they had been guilty of the sin of unbelief, like them they must now be punished by exclusion from the holy land.

This incident is apparently all that P^g related of Ḳadesh. But the editor thought it a suitable occasion to introduce into his narrative from his other sources some further matters connected with the same place. Since, however, according to these sources (JE), Ḳadesh had been reached by the people before the period of wanderings (see 13^{26}), the editor has omitted from v.[1] the number of the year, which must have been given in P^g, and has inserted (from JE) the clause "and the people abode in Ḳadesh," and the notice of Miriam's death, leaving the reader free to place the arrival at Ḳadesh at an indefinitely earlier point in the period of the wanderings; and the transition to the fortieth year at some point of the narrative between v.[1] and v.[23] (cp. 33^{38}). Still the date originally given in P^g was in all probability the fortieth year; see on v.[1].

But this is not the whole of the editor's work. Other

stories of the murmurings for water were current, and also other stories of the particular murmurings which gave rise to or were told in order to explain such names as Massah ("temptation") and Merîbah ("strife"). The editor appears to have fused some of these different stories both here and in Ex. 17^{1-7}. Here he draws in the main on P; in Ex. mainly on E; but in both cases he has also incorporated matter from J. By fusion and some modifications of his own he has here succeeded in representing the sin of Moses and Aaron in a milder form than it assumed in his sources, though at the expense of leaving the reader without any clear idea of the character of the sin. The close connection between the present section and Ex. 17^{1-7} is apparent not only in the general similarity of the story and the identity of one of the names explained (Merîbah), but also in the common clause, "And the people strove (וירב) with Moses," which plays on the name to be explained (Ex. 17^2, Nu. 20^3).

Certain linguistic peculiarities also point to considerable editorial treatment of the present section.

In detail Cornill (*ZATW*. xi. 20–34) has discussed the analysis of the present section in the most thorough manner. His conclusions cannot rank as certain, but they are as probable as any that can be drawn from the data at command. The following brief summary of his argument will, in connection with the commentary that follows, open up to the student the chief questions at issue and the nature of the evidence available for a decision.

E clearly associated the miracle of the smitten rock with Ḥoreb (Ex. 17^6), and, consequently, with the early period of the wanderings. Parts of the story in Ex. (17^{2-7}) are derived from J. In Nu. 20^{1-13} the analysis is as follows—

E. V.^{1b} (the reference to Miriam).
J. V.^{1} (וישב העם בקדש), ^{5} (|| to v.^{4} P).
P. V.^{1} (to "month"), $^{2.3}$ (from לו), ^{4} (except אנחנו ובעירנו), $^{6f. 8-11}$ (but much recast by R), $^{12f.}$.
R has modified v.^{3}, inserted אנחנו ובעירנו in v.^{4}, and radically recast v.$^{8-11}$, and is wholly answerable for יען לא האמנתם בי and בעירם.

In this analysis Corn. agrees in the main with earlier critics like Colenso, Nöld., Schrader, and Kayser; he differs from Di. and others, and that chiefly in deriving a far larger part from P and reducing the amount derived from E to a minimum. In particular Di. finds it necessary, chiefly on account of the reference to *Moses'* rod, to refer v.$^{8-11}$ to E. Other clear indications of this source are lacking, for בעיר is not such; whereas עדה (1^2 n.) certainly points to P, and Corn. argues that the rod in question is *Aaron's* rod—"the rod before Yahweh" of v.[9] being the rod of $17^{25\,(10)}$. Di. eliminates these words in v.[9] as editorial. Recently Bacon and CH. have attributed the difference between speaking to and smiting the rock to difference of source, and have consequently assigned v.[8b] (*and speak . . . its waters*) to J; whereas Corn. refers both to the original story of P, in which Moses and Aaron are first commanded by Yahweh to produce the water by merely speaking to the rock, and only in consequence of their unbelief are bidden to smite it (see on v.[8-11]).

Corn.'s theory of the relation between Ex. 17 and Nu. 20 and their respective sources is as follows:—Before the editor there lay JE and P; JE contained *two* stories of the miraculous production of water—one (E) was connected with Rephidim, the other (J) was connected with the *arrival* at Ḳadesh, and explained the two names Massah and Merîbah. P contained a similar story, explaining the names Merîbah and Ḳadesh. The editor, as usual, follows P most closely, and, accordingly, throws forward the story to the *close* of the period of the wanderings, whereas in J it stood at the beginning; to reduce the divergence of the two accounts, he omits the number of the year (Nu. 20^1). Similarly, the editor frames his story so as to explain both Merîbah and Ḳadesh, but omits J's Massah. For this he finds a place in the earlier story (E) now found in Ex. 17, and provides that story with what it originally lacked—an etymological motive. Since there he retains both J's etymologies (Massah and Merîbah), he necessarily retains there also the clause וירב העם עם משה. Hence the identity of Nu. 20^{3a} and Ex. 17^3.

For other discussions of the relation between Ex. 17^{1-7} and Nu. 20^{1-13} and the analysis, see Kuenen, *Hexateuch*, § 6 n. 42 (where references to earlier discussions may be found); Bacon, *Triple Tradition*, 86 f., 196 f.; Holzinger, *Exodus*, p. 55; S. A. Cooke in *EBi.* "Massah and Meribah."

1. Arrival (P) and residence (J) at Ḳadesh, and death of Miriam (E).

1a (P). *The children of Israel, the whole congregation*] the same unusual combination of phrases, each by itself frequent in P (CH. 11, 45), occurs again only in v.[22] (P).—*Came*] from the wilderness of Paran, which lay further south (10^{12} 13^{21} n.), and in which the years of wandering had been spent (14^{29}).—*To the wilderness of Ṣin*] in which Ḳadesh was situated; cp. 27^{14} 33^{36}, Dt. 32^{51} (P), and the paranomasia in v.[13] below; see also on 13^{21}.—*In the first month*] the number of the year has been omitted deliberately (see above). In all probability it was the fortieth; for (1) the event to be related is given as the reason why Moses and Aaron, who had led the people all through their wanderings, are cut off just before the entrance into Canaan (v.[22-29] 27^{12-14}, Dt. 32^{48-52} (P), and Dt. 34 (so far as it is derived from P)); (2) in c. 33, which, though not derived from, is dominated by P^g, the wilderness of Ṣin is the station next before Mount Hor, where Aaron died in the fifth month of the fortieth year. Thus, according to P^g, Ḳadesh was merely visited by the people for a short period at the *end* of the wanderings. In JE Ḳadesh is the scene of a prolonged stay. The people go thither straight from Sinai (cp. 13^{21}), and are still there at the end of the period of wanderings (v.^{14}). To this source, therefore, and perhaps in particular to J, we may refer *and the people abode in Ḳadesh*; cp. Jud. 11^{17} and also for the vb. (וישב) Nu. $21^{25.\,31}$ (JE). The change of subject (*the people* for *the children of Israel*, etc., in clause *a*) corresponds to the change of source: cp. $14^{1f.}$ n. In Dt. c. 1 f. we find a third view of the place of Ḳadesh in the wanderings, viz. that Israel "abode" (וישב) there for an indefinite time (not exceeding a few months) at the *beginning* of the period. On the inadequacy of harmonising efforts, see Driver, *Deut.* pp. 31–33.—*And Miriam died there, and was buried there*] with the phraseology, cp. Dt. 10^6 (E). It is E who elsewhere is interested in Miriam; see p. 98 f. The traditional date of Miriam's death must remain unknown; since the date in clause *a* and the statement of death are derived from different sources, and had no original connection with one another.

2–13. Lack of water miraculously supplied. The sin of Moses and Aaron.

2–4. Distressed by want of water, the people reproach Moses and Aaron for having brought them into the wilderness. The lack of water would naturally be felt soon after arrival at Ḳadesh: on this, as well as on other grounds, v.^{1b} may be recognised as interrupting the immediate sequence of v.^{1a} and v.^{2}.—**2a** (P). V.^{5} (last clause) and Ex. 17^{1b} (JE) are differently worded: Nu. 33^{14} (P^s) mixes the phraseology of both sources.—**2b** (P). Cp. 16^{3a} (P); as in 16^3, the words spoken (v.^{3b}) originally followed immediately on the statement of the assembling of the people (v.^{2b}).—**3a** = Ex. 17^2 (JE). In v.^{3a} (in contrast with v.$^{2b.\,4.\,6}$ etc.) it is with Moses alone, and not with Moses and Aaron, that the people quarrel: cp. 16^{2a} n.; the subject as in 1^a (J) is *the people*.—**3b** (P). *Would God we had died*] 14^2, Ex. 16^3 (P).—*When our brethren died before*

Yahweh] at the time of the revolt of Ḳoraḥ; see :. 16f., especially $17^{27\,(12)}$.—*Yahweh's assembly*] 16^3 n.—*We and our cattle*] Cp. Ex. 17^3 (JE), but note that a different word (מקנה not בעיר) is there used for cattle; see also 11^4 n. P^g does not mention cattle in the corresponding complaint of Ex. 16^3; but his account of the establishment of the sacrificial system *presupposes* that the Hebrews were accompanied by cattle. Still the clause is scarcely from P^g; see phil. n.—**5** (JE). Why has Moses brought the people up from Egypt to this infertile and waterless region? The parallel from JE to the preceding v.: cp. Ex. 17^3, Nu. 16^{13} 21^5 (all JE). The vb. in 𝔐, as in the first two passages just cited, is singular, and addressed to Moses (cp. $v.^3$). The pl. punctuation of MT is an accommodation to the composite narrative.—**6 f.** (P: in continuation of $v.^4$). Moses and Aaron withdraw from the complaining people to the tent of meeting, where the glory of Yahweh, ominous of the divine anger, appears; cp. 14^{10} 16^{19} (P).—**8–11.** These vv. should describe the sin of Moses and Aaron, for evidently up to this point (cp. $v.^{13}$) it is the people and not their leaders whose conduct has provoked the divine anger. The sin which excluded Moses and Aaron from Canaan is described in $v.^{12}$ as unbelief, in $v.^{24}$ 27^{14} as rebellion. But in $v.^{8-11}$, as they now stand, neither unbelief nor rebellion on the part of Moses and Aaron is recorded; either the one or the other has often been read into the verses, but neither is there. Yahweh bids Moses take the rod ($v.^{8a}$), and he obeys ($v.^9$); Yahweh bids Moses and Aaron speak to the rock and so bring water from it ($v.^{8b}$); it is not recorded either that they obeyed or disobeyed the command to speak to the rock, but they carried out the divine intention of procuring the people water. In its present form the narrative does not record what directions Yahweh gave as to the use of the rod, so that it is impossible to say whether in striking the rock at all or in striking it twice, Moses was guilty of disobedience or unbelief. It is possible that Moses struck the rock and refused to speak to it through lack of faith in Yahweh's power; it is possible that he struck it twice, because he thought a single stroke would be insufficient. But if it is difficult to discover Moses' sin, it is more difficult still to discover Aaron's; for he did not strike the rock either once or twice, and, indeed, all that the story says of him is that he assisted Moses to assemble the people at the rock.

The truth is, the story is mutilated; and as any attempt to reconstruct it must be tentative, the exact nature of the sin of the leaders must remain doubtful. But the subsequent allusions favour the view that it was an act of open rebellion, rather than of simple unbelief. In v.[12] the editor has softened down the terms of the original story. According to Cornill's reconstruction, Pg's original story ran as follows:—Yahweh first bade Moses and Aaron publicly address the rock, and so bring forth water. Moses and Aaron refuse, sceptically asking Yahweh (in words now addressed to the people), *Can we bring forth water for them out of this rock?* Yahweh replies (with words now addressed by Moses to the people), *Hearken to Me, ye rebels,* and bids them strike the rock: this they do. Afterwards Yahweh pronounces doom on the leaders, *Because ye were rebellious against My command, that ye should sanctify Me,* and so forth, as in v.[12b].

In Dt. the cause given for the exclusion of Moses from Canaan is entirely different: it is Yahweh's anger with him on account of the disobedience *of the people* when the spies returned to Ḳadesh (Dt. 1^{37} 3^{26} 4^{21}).

8. *Take the stick*] this is defined in v.[9] as the "stick before Yahweh"; but that cannot well refer to anything but Aaron's stick, which was put back, after it had budded, to be kept "before the testimony" ($17^{25\,(10)}$), *i.e.* before Yahweh (cp. $17^{19\,(4)}$ with $17^{22\,(7)}$). Probably it is merely by a textual error (מטהו for מטה) of more recent date than 𝕲 that the stick is described in v.[11] as "his (*i.e.* Moses') stick." The stick with which wonders is wrought is, generally, in P's narrative, used by Aaron (Ex. $7^{9.\,19}$ $8^{1.\,12\,(5.\,16)}$); another instance of its use by Moses is possibly to be found in Ex. 14^{16-18}, which is mainly derived from P, though most refer the single clause about the rod to E; cp. also the part played by Moses in the miracle of the stick blossoming in c. 17.—*The rock*] a description of the conspicuous rock at 'Ain-el-Ḳadîs, around which the present story gathered, is cited in the n. on 13^{26}.—9. Moses obeys, and takes the rod as directed. Whether the use he makes of it (v.[10]) was also in accordance with Yahweh's command cannot be determined, for the divine instructions as to the use of the rod are now missing from the story: see above.—10. *Hearken now*] If 𝕳 be original, the נא of שמעו־נא

is due to the editor: see 16[8] n. But 𝔊 reads *Hearken unto me* (שמעוני); cp. Gn. 23 (P) where שמָעֵני, שמָעֵנו, and שמעוני, which are found nowhere else in the Pentateuch, occur in all five times: Corn. (*ZATW.* 1891, p. 26).—*Ye rebels*] המרים is not quite suitably used by Moses in addressing the people: for they had murmured, but not rebelled. On the other hand, Moses and Aaron are elsewhere spoken of as having on this occasion rebelled against Yahweh's command (מרו את פי); hence it has been suggested * that in the original form of the story these words were addressed by Yahweh to Moses and Aaron.—*From this rock must we produce water for you?*] these are the "rash" words which, according to Ps. 106[32f.], called down on Moses the divine sentence. In their present context they are best understood as an expression of ill-temper. The impf. נוציא might equally well be rendered, *can we produce?* But inasmuch as the words are immediately followed by Moses' production of the water, such an interpretation of the clause *in its present position* would be unnatural. See, however, above, p. 262.—**11.** *With the stick*] so 𝔊: 𝔥 "his stick," see n. on v.[8].—**12 f.** Moses and Aaron condemned, on account of their unbelief, not to enter Canaan. On the incongruity between these verses and v.[8–11], see on the latter.—*To sanctify Me*] cp. 27[14], Dt. 32[51]. With these words (*l*ᵉ*hakdishēnî*) the writer plays on the name of the place of the incident (Ḳadesh); so again in v.[13]. By their sin Moses and Aaron prevented the full might and power of Yahweh becoming manifest to the people, and so robbed Him of some of the fear due to Him: for the sense of "sanctity," cp. Is. 8[13] 29[23], Ps. 99[3] 111[9].—**13.** The waters of Ḳadesh were called Merîbah ("strife"), because the people strove (*rābû*; cp. *bim*ᵉ*rîbath hā*ᶜ*edah*, 27[14]) with Yahweh there; and the place Ḳadesh, because in spite of Moses and Aaron's sin, Yahweh vindicated His holiness (*wayyiḳḳādēsh*: cp. Lev. 10[3]) there. The two names Merîbah-Ḳadesh are combined in 27[14], Dt. 32[51], Ezek. 47[19] 48[28], if not also in Dt. 33[2] (cp. 𝔊: and see Di., Dr.). Whether Merîbah was also really called Massah (Ex. 17[7]) is more doubtful.

* Nöld., Corn.

3. ויאמרו לאמר] אמר followed by לאמר without any intervening word is unusual; but see Ex. 15^{1} (overlooked by Corn.) and also 2 S. 5^{1} 20^{18}, Jer. 29^{24}, Ezek. (12^{27}) 33^{10}, Zech. 2^{4}: cp. Corn. *ZATW.* xi. p. 22.—ולו] The Waw is used forcibly with nothing previously *expressed* for it to connect with; cp. 11^{29b} (ומי יתן) and (as here at the beginning of a speech) 2 S. 24^{3} (ויוסף), 2 K. 1^{10} (ואם: v.[12] אם alone), 7^{19}: see, further, Dr. *Tenses,*[3] p. 141 n. —גוענו] a favourite word with P: Driver, *L.O.T.* p. 131, No. 9; CH. 51. —אל המדבר הזה] Ex. 16^{3} (P).—ובעירנו] a much less usual word for cattle than מקנה (Ex. 17^{3}). The latter is common alike in P and J, and used, though less frequently, by E and D (CH. 18^{J}). בעיר, except in the present c., occurs only in Gn. 45^{17} (E), Ex. 22^{4}, Ps. 78^{48}; see, further, Corn. *ZATW.* xi. 24 f.—**5.** העלתנו] העלה of Yahweh bringing Israel out of Egypt is characteristic of JE; CH. 136.—**8.** והוצאת . . . והשקית] 𝔊 has three verbs in the 2nd pl. (under the influence of the preceding ודברתם): but v.[9] shows that the singulars of 𝔐 are original. For דברתם read דברתָ with 𝔖; even if the clause containing it be from JE the 2nd sing. is required: cp. 3*a*. 5.—**10.** ויקהלו] 𝔊 𝔖 ויקהל; note ויאמר and, according to 𝔊, שמעוני following; and in v.[11] וירם; but, on the other hand, נציא in v.[10] and the pl. subj. of והקהל in v.[8].—יען לא האמנתם] neither יען nor האמין is used by P; Corn. *ZATW.* xi. 29.

14–21 (JE). The Israelites send messengers from Ḳadesh to the king of Edom asking to be allowed a peaceful passage through his country. They are refused.—The original sequel to this passage is in $21^{4b. 12. 13}$. Refused a passage across Edom, the Israelites march south to the head of the Gulf of ʿAḳabah, pass round the *southern* end of Edom, and then, keeping to the E. of Edom and Moab, march northwards to Arnon: cp. Jud. $11^{17f.}$.

It is probable that P related neither the petition to Edom, nor its rejection; and that, on the other hand, in entire disagreement from the foregoing story, he represented the Israelites as actually crossing the *northern* end of Edom in their passage from Ḳadesh on the W. to the E. of the ʿArabah.

The present passage, which is intimately connected in style and motive with 21^{21-23}, Jud. 11^{16-18}, is clearly derived from JE. Note the general vividness of the narrative and such details as נא in v.[17] (16^{8} n.), צעק in v.[16] (CH. 141. 23), and the "angel" in v.[16]. JE appears, in the main at least, to have derived the incident from E; so Kue. (*Hex.* 151), Meyer (*ZATW.* i. 121), Di., Str., Dr., Corn., Bacon. The conception of the "angel" in v.[16] is E's: then with כל־התלאה אשר מצאתנו in v.[14], cp. כל־התלאה אשר מצאתם in Ex. 18^{8} (E), and note that נתן = *to suffer, permit* (v.[21]), occurs also in 21^{23}, Gn. 20^{6} 31^{7} (all clearly E) and 22^{13} (probably the same source), twice in D (Dt. 18^{14}, Jos. 10^{19}) and only twice besides in the Hex., in Ex. 3^{19} 12^{23}—passages which are perhaps to be attributed to JE rather than J. CH. assign v.[14-18. 21a] to E and v.[19f. 21b] to J; but their argument is inconclusive, and rests in part on the hazardous assumption that v.[22a] (ויסעו מקדש) is from E rather than P (or R). We. (*Comp.* 110), exceptionally, refers the passage in the main to J, but on the wholly inadequate ground of the use of the singular pron. of the nations.

14. *And Moses sent messengers*] the sending of messengers is directly attributed to the whole people in 21^{21}, Jud. $11^{17.\,19}$.—*The king of Edom*] Hebrew tradition assigned to the monarchy a more ancient origin in Edom, and, indeed, among many of the neighbouring peoples, than among themselves; Gn. 36^{31}, Nu. 22^{4}, 1 S. 8^{5}.—*Thy brother Israel*] Edom is Israel's "brother"; consequently also an individual Israelite may be described as "brother" of an Edomite; see Dt. 2^{4} $23^{8\,(7)}$, Ob. $^{10.\,12}$, Am. 1^{11}. The mode of speech shows how closely the Hebrews felt themselves to be connected with the Edomites. Another expression of the same feeling is found in the patriarchal stories where Edom = Esau is the brother of Jacob = Israel.—*Thou knowest*] the subj. refers to the whole people of Edom, who on account of their kinship are expected to be moved by this recital of Israel's sufferings and deliverance, rather than to the king mentioned in clause *a*. See last n. So *thy border*, *thy land*, in v.$^{16f.}$, is the border, the land of Edom. The case is different in the communications with Siḥon, king of the Amorites, in 21^{21-23}.

The personification of a whole class or people so that it is spoken of or represented as speaking in the singular is frequent in Hebrew. In these cases the pronouns referring to the class or person are naturally in the singular, though rapid transitions to and from plural pronouns are frequently made, as in the present passage (v.^{19}). The result in some cases is so strange that the singular pronouns can scarcely be retained in an English translation; in RV. the pl. is frequently substituted for the sing. The following passages, in all cases literally rendered, may serve as illustrations of the usage: "And Egypt said, Let me flee" (Ex. 14^{25}); "And the man of Israel said unto the Hivite, Perhaps thou art dwelling in my midst" (Jos. 9^{7}); "The children of Joseph spake unto Joshua, saying, Why hast thou given me but one inheritance . . . seeing that I am a numerous people?" (Jos. 17^{14}: cp. v.$^{15-18}$); "The 'Eḳronites cried out, saying, They have brought about the ark to me . . . to slay me and my people" (1 S. 5^{10}). See also $21^{1-3.\,22}$, Jud. 1^{3}, 2 S. $19^{44\,(43)}$. All the foregoing are from early prose narrative. The same usage is found in Deut., where all Israel is constantly addressed as "thou" (see, *e.g.*, c. 8. 9), and not unnaturally in poetry: see, *e.g.*, Lam. 1^{15-22}. To what extent the "I" of the Psalter stands for Israel is disputed: it obviously does so in Ps.

12_9^{1-3}. See Smend, "Ueber das Ich der Psalmen" in *ZATW.* 1888, pp. 49–147; G. Beer, *Individual- u. Gemeinde- Psalmen*; Driver, *L.O.T.* 389–391. The usage is closely connected with the fact that the characteristic and original names of nations are singulars—Moab, Edom, Israel, Midian, Jeraḥme'el; ct., in Greek, Ἴωνες, Αἰολεῖς, Δωριεῖς. The derivative eponyms—Ion, Aeolus, Dorus—of the Greeks are entirely different in character from Moab, Edom, etc. See We. *Reste d. arab. Heidentums*,[1] 176f.; Nöld. in *ZDMG.* xl. 170f.; Smend, *Alttestamentliche Religionsgeschichte*,[1] 27. In the light of the usage it is easy to see that it was not difficult for Hebrew tribal traditions, though generally cast in the form of narratives of tribes (*e.g.* Israel and Edom as here), to assume also the form of narratives of individuals (as, *e.g.*, of Jacob and Esau).

All the hardship] תלאה; Ex. 18^{8} (E), Lam. 3^{5}, Neh. 9^{32} †. The vb. לאה in Hebrew means "to be weary"; the noun in Lam. is used as a synonym with "gall."—**16.** *And Yahweh sent an angel*] Ex. 14^{19a} 23^{20} 32^{34} (E). The angel in E plays the same part in preventing the Egyptians from overtaking the Israelites as the pillar of cloud in J: with Ex. 14^{19a} (E), ct. v.^{19b} (J). The angel, as usual in earlier writers, is theophanic in character; Yahweh Himself is present in the angel: see *EBi. s.v.* "Theophany."—*Ḳadesh, a city on the edge of thy territory*] Ḳadesh (13^{26} n.) lay on the southern border and within the territory of Judah (34^{4}) and on the W. border of Edom. The earlier attempt to gain an entrance into Canaan from the S. (c. 13. 14) left Edom unaffected; but in order to get into position to invade Canaan from the E. the Israelites had either to traverse Edom, or to make a long and circuitous march. The territory of Edom, as the present statement most clearly shows, and as Buhl has argued at length (*Edomiter*, 22–26), extended W. of the ʿArabah; the north-western border was probably formed by the Wady Fiḳreh which runs south-westwards from the southern end of the Dead Sea.—**17.** Israel promises, if suffered to traverse Edom, to keep to the regular road without molesting the cultivated land; to pass through the country, not like an enemy, but peaceably like traders, paying the king's toll, and for all they need in the way of food and water (cp. v.^{19}). The terms of the v., which are, however, repeated in reference to the Amorite country N. of Arnon in 21^{22}, refer to two striking features—the fertility and the roads—of Edom, or rather of the territory of Edom E. of the ʿArabah. Speaking of this Palmer * says: "The country is extremely fertile . . . goodly streams flow through the valleys, which are filled with trees and flowers; while on the uplands to the east rich pasture lands and corn fields may everywhere be seen." A story in the Talmud describes the astonishment of two Rabbis visiting Gebal (the N. part of Edom) at the size of the grapes produced there.† At a later period Edom was certainly traversed by trade routes over which the frankincense from S. Arabia and other commerce to and from the port of Elath on the Gulf of ʿAḳabah were carried, and it can scarcely be doubted that the trade which created them was very ancient. Some ancient through route (or routes) of this kind is intended by the term *the king's way*.‡ In modern Palestine such a through route is known by the name of the *darb es-sulṭân* or "Sultan's way." But neither the term here used nor מסלה in v.[19] implies that the route was a thoroughly made and well-kept road.§ Such roads hardly existed before Roman times. The earlier roads were scarcely better than the modern "Sultan's roads," one of which is described by Seetzen (ii. 336) as an almost invisible path, rocky and stony.—**18.** Edom refuses Israel's request, and threatens to meet any attempt to traverse the country with armed resistance.—**19.** The Israelites repeat their peaceable intentions. The repetition may possibly be the result of the fusion of J and E: see above. The speech begins in the plural *we will go up*, but passes over to the singular *I* (*i.e.* Israel) *and my cattle*: see on v.[14].—*Only—it is no matter* of offence or annoyance (cp. 1 S. 20^{21})—*on my feet would I pass through*, *i.e.* as ordinary, peaceful foot-passengers: cp. Ps. 66^{6}, Jud. 4^{17}. Cp. Dt. 2^{28}. According to 𝔊 the request of v.[19] is a modification of that in v.[17]. At first the Israelites ask permission to pass *through* Edom (παρελευσόμεθα διὰ

* *Desert of the Exodus*, 430 f.: cp. Buhl, *Gesch. der Edomiter*, p. 15, with the literature there cited.

† *Ketuboth* 112*a*, cited by Neubauer, *Géographie du Talmud*, 67.

‡ On ancient routes through Edom, see Buhl, *Gesch. der Edomiter*, 44, 18; G. A. Smith in *EBi.* art. "Trade and Commerce," § 32 f.

§ Cp. Nowack, *Arch.* i. 151 f.; otherwise, Buhl, *Geog.* 126.

τῆς γῆς σου . . . ἕως ἂν παρέλθωμεν τὰ ὅρια σου); on being refused this, they ask permission to pass along the borders of Edom (παρὰ τὸ ὅρος παρελευσόμεθα).—**20, 21.** Again refused, Israel turns away from Edom in order, as the continuation of JE in 21^4 explains, to turn the southern extremity of Edom. V.^{20} and v.^{21a} are in substance identical, and may be from different sources (v.^{20} J: v.^{21a} E).

The traditions as to the early relations between Israel and Edom are to a large extent cast in the form of patriarchal stories; cp. the small print n. on p. 265 f. Among these stories of Esau (=Edom) and Jacob (=Israel), the account of the meeting of Esau and Jacob in Gn. 32 forms in some respects a striking parallel to the foregoing narrative. In Gn., it is true, the story concludes by bringing the two brothers into friendly relations with one another; but such a conclusion is as little anticipated by the reader as by Jacob himself, when on first learning of Esau's advance with four hundred men (Gn. $32^{7b\,(6b)}$, cp. v.^{20b} here) he prepares for the worst (Gn. $32^{8-12\,(7-11)}$). There, as here, on approaching the land of Edom, Jacob (=Israel) sends messengers to find favour for him with his brother Esau (=Edom); the messengers are repulsed (Gn. $32^{7\,(6)}$), and return to Jacob with the news of Esau's hostile intent. Cp. Steuernagel, *Die Einwanderung d. israelitischen Stämmen*, 105.

D does not refer to the present incident, but in Dt. 2^{1-8} relates that subsequently, on the northward march E. of the 'Arabah, Israel did actually cross a part of Edom in the same peaceable way which they here seek in vain to pursue. The two stories are not necessarily incompatible, but it is impossible to determine what amount of historic fact lies at the basis of the stories, or how far they merely reflect later relations between the two peoples.

In all these traditions there are two common and fundamental assumptions: 1. that the Edomites were more ancient than the Israelites; 2. that they already occupied the country in and about the 'Arabah, subsequently called by their name, at the time of the immigration of Israel into Canaan. Certain passages in early Egyptian sources have a bearing on these assumptions. It was for long supposed that Edom was mentioned in the romance of Sinuhit (Dyn. xii.: before B.C. 2000); but the name formerly transliterated Eduma (Sayce, *Higher Crit. and the Monuments*, 203) should be read *ḳdm*=קדם (E. Meyer, *Gesch. Aeg.* 182; W. Max Müller, *Asien u. Europa*, 46). On the other hand, the identification of 'A-du-ma̦ in Pap. Anastasi vi. 4^{14} (*c.* 1300 B.C.) with Edom, though questioned by Winckler (*Gesch. Isr.* 189 f.) and Cheyne (*EBi.* 1182), is generally admitted. In this document the request is made by an Egyptian official that "the Bedawin tribes (tribes of Ša-su) (belonging to the land) of 'A-du-mḁ" be allowed to pasture on the N.E. frontier of Egypt (Max Müller, *op. cit.* 135). Rameses III. (about B.C. 1200) relates: "I inflicted a defeat on the Sa-'a-ïra belonging to the Bedawin tribes." The equivalence of Sa-'a-ïra with שעירים (the inhabitants of Mt. Seir) is not questioned.

Max Müller (*op. cit.* 136 f.) argues that this excludes the possibility that the *Edomites* had up to that time occupied Mt. Seir. If his argument were admitted, the placing of *Edomites* in and about the ʿArabah in the Biblical stories would be an anachronism. But against the validity of his argument, see Nöld. in *EBi. s.v.* "Edom," § 3. 6; Buhl, *Gesch. d. Edomiter*, 53. Further evidence may yet come to light: what exists at present, unless the identification of ʾA-du-må̦=Edom, be denied, proves the existence of the name Edom at or prior to the time of the Hebrew immigration: it neither proves nor at all clearly or necessarily disproves that Edomites already occupied the country later known by their name.

14. וישלח . . . מלאכים . . . כה אמר] cp. Gn. $32^{4f.}$ (JE): כה+some part of אמר with a human or (as so frequently in the prophets) a divine subject is very characteristic of JE as contrasted with P: see CH. 87 and 222.—אתה ידעת] the expression of the pronominal subject with ידע is characteristic of JE: CH. 174.—**16.** קצה גבולך] cp. 22^{36}; גבול in these vv. is clearly used not of the *boundary* or *border*, but, as often (BDB. *sv.* גבול 2), of the *territory* enclosed with borders. Hence we have the alternative expressions נעברה נא בארצך, נעבר גבלך (v.^{17}), תעבר בי (v.^{18}), עבר בגבלו (v.^{21}). קצה is here used of the *border* or *boundary*: cp. קצה המדבר Ex. 13^{20}, קצה ארץ Ex. 16^{35}.—**17.** בשרה ובכרם] cp. 16^{14} 21^{22}.—**21.** נְתֹן] G.-K. 66*i*; the same form occurs in Gn. 38^{9} (J); E elsewhere uses peculiar infinitive forms; see phil. notes on $22^{13f.}$.—עבר] is one of the two accusatives (Dav. 90*c*) governed by נתן; cp. Job 9^{18}; but as both here and in 21^{23} עבר is preceded by a word ending in ל, we should perhaps restore לעבר: so Paterson in *SBOT.*

22–29. Arrival at Mt. Hor; death of Aaron, and investiture of Eleʿazar (P).

Apart from v.^{22a} the whole section is clearly derived from P^g; with v.^{24} cp. v.$^{12f.}$ (P), and generally Dt. 32^{50} (P); see also Nu. 33^{38-40} (P^s); and note, *e.g.*, העדה (1^2 n.) v.$^{22. 29}$; יאסף אל עמיו v.^{24}; גוע v.^{29}; see *L.O.T.* pp. 131, 133 (Nos. 25*b* and 9). Mt. Hor (v.$^{22f. 25. 27}$ 21^{4} $33^{37-39. 46}$, Dt. 32^{50}) is referred to only by P. It has been questioned whether v.^{22a} is from P, on the ground that he would have written ממריבת קדש (cp. 27^{14}), or ממדבר צן (v.^{1}) rather than מקדש; hence some (*e.g.* Di.) refer the clause to R; others, in view of ויסעו (ct. $21^{12f.}$) more questionably, to E (CH.). In any case v.^{24} suffices to show that, according to P^g, Mt. Hor was reached after leaving Ḳadesh.

The continuation of P's narrative is to be found in $21^{4a. 10f.}$ 22^{1}. In one respect certainly, and probably in two, it conflicts with other Hebrew traditions. It makes Mt. Hor the scene of Aaron's death, whereas according to E that event took place at Moserah (Dt. 10^{6}), and it appears to imply that the Israelites marched straight across Edom to the E. of Jordan instead of making a circuit of Edom, as according to another tradition they did (see above on v.$^{14-21}$).

22. *The children of Israel, all the congregation*] v.[1] n.—*To Hor the mountain*] the site is unknown; but since it is situated, like Ḳadesh, on the border of the land of Edom (v.[23] 33[37]), the traditional site, near Petra, which is in the midst of the country of Edom, is certainly wrong. Some recent scholars have identified Jebel Madurah with Mt. Hor; this is described as "a round isolated hill," and lies a short day's journey S. of the southern end of the Dead Sea, on the eastern bank of the Wady el-Fiḳreh, which may have formed the N.W. boundary of Edom (v.[16] n.). The site satisfies the conditions of the text; it was on the border of Edom, and, like the site of Moses' death, near the land of promise; but the data are insufficient to render the identification certain. Jebel Madurah lies N.E. of *'Ain el-Ḳadîs* (Ḳadesh), and therefore on the route which would naturally be followed in marching direct from Ḳadesh across Edom.

Clay Trumbull (*Kadesh-Barnea*, 127–139) has argued at length for the identification of Jebel Madurah and Mt. Hor; but, from a critical standpoint, much of his argument is vitiated by his indiscriminate use of the various sources. Further, his attempt to identify the names Madurah (مدرة) and Moserah (מֹסֵרָה) in Dt. 10[6] is philologically most hazardous. For other descriptions of Jebel Madurah, see Seetzen, *Reisen*, iii. 14 ff.; Robinson, *BR*. ii. 589; Palmer, *Desert of the Exodus*, 415 f.—The traditional site was determined by the erroneous traditional identification of Petra and Ḳadesh. Josephus (*Ant*. iv. 4[7]) already places Aaron's death near Petra. Jerome's note in the *Onomasticon* runs: "Or mons in quo mortuus est Aaron juxta civitatem Petram, ubi usque ad præsentem diem ostenditur rupes qua percussa Moyses aquas populo dedit." Similarly Eusebius; Lagarde, *Onom.*[2] pp. 175, 291. The tradition is perpetuated in the modern Arabic name of a mountain near Petra, the Jebel Nebi Hārūn (described by Palmer, *op. cit.* 433 f., 520; Robinson, *BR*. ii. 651–653).

23. *Mt. Hor on the border of the land of Edom*] (על גבול ארץ אדם); cp. "on the edge (בקצה) of the land of Edom," 33[37]. Since in both places Mt. Hor is mentioned immediately after Ḳadesh, which lay on the W. of Edom, it is on the western border of Edom, whose territory stretched westwards of the 'Arabah, and therefore far beyond Petra, that we must seek Mt. Hor.—**24.** *Shall be gathered to his kinsmen*] The word, rendered in AV. "people," is plural (עמיו), and denotes "one of the same kin," in Arabic (عَمّ) "one of the father's kin"; in this and similar phrases (*e.g.* "to lie with one's fathers") used of death, earlier writers use the synonymous term "fathers"; see, *e.g.*, Jud. 2^{10}, 1 K. 1^{21} 14^{31}; and for further references, BDB. *s.v.* אב 4.—*Because ye rebelled against My commandment*] (פי, cp. 10^{13}): an allusion to the story preserved, though probably only in a distorted form, in v.[7-13]; see above, p. 261 f. In what Aaron's sin consisted is certainly obscure; it is described by the same term as here in 27^{14}, by a milder one in v.[12], and by the specifically priestly term מעל *be faithless* (5^{6}) in Dt. 32^{51} (also P).—**26.** *Strip Aaron of his garments*] his official garments, as described in Lev. 8^{7-9}, are evidently intended; clothed in these Eleʿazar descends from the mountain as Aaron's successor in the high priesthood (v.[27f.]).

28. It is not explicitly stated where Aaron was buried (cp. Dt. 34^{6}), but obviously popular tradition regarded the top of Mt. Hor as the site. The modern Bedawin have a great liking for being buried on mountain tops, and sometimes the body of a distinguished person is brought three or four days out of the steppe that it may be so buried. According to a statement made to Wetzstein, they believe that thus buried they retain their union with their tribe, if from the mountain top they can look out over the tribal camp.*—**29.** The people mourn for Aaron 30 days: cp. Dt. 34^{8} (P).

22. הֹר הָהָר] this peculiar order and cstr. is always found with this phrase (even when the northern Mt. Hor is intended, see $34^{7f.}$); ct. הר סיני, הר עיבל, etc.; see Kön. ii. 333*u. v.*—**24.** עמיו] S עמו; the versions also have the sing.—**25.** 𝔊 adds ἔναντι πάσης τῆς συναγωγῆς: cp. v.[27] 𝔐.—**26.** והפשט] S והפשטת.—**27.** ויעלו] S (𝔊) ויעלהו; 𝔊ᴸ = ויעלם: cp. v.[25] 𝔐.

XXI. 1–3. Ḥormah.—The Canaanites of the Negeb (under the king of ʿArad, a place some 50 or 60 miles almost due N. of Ḳadesh), hearing of Israel's advance in the direction of their territory take the offensive, fight against Israel, and take some of them captive. Israel vow to Yahweh, if granted revenge, to place the Canaanite cities under the ban (*ḥerem*).

* Wetzstein, *Reisebericht über Hauran und die Trachonen*, 26; see also Baudissin in *PRE.*[3] viii. 183; We. *Reste des arab. Heidentums*,[2] 15 f.

Success is granted them, the ban is put into force, and the region or city (? ʿArad) is consequently called Ḥormah (Ban).

It has long been recognised that the section is, in part at least, out of place, and does not refer, as from the position which the compiler has given it it should do, to the period spent at Mt. Hor (20^{22} 21^{4}), nor, indeed, to any time immediately before the Israelites took their departure to the E. of Jordan. For why, as Reland (*Palestina*, *s.v.* "Chorma") pertinently asked, should they abandon the country in the S. of Canaan W. of the ʿArabah, in which they had just proved themselves victorious? It has been frequently considered a sufficient solution to regard v.^{3} as a parenthetic anticipation of Jud. $1^{16.\,17}$. Yet the last thing that ought to be said of v.^{3} is that it is "evidently" parenthetical.* On the other hand, there is no indication whatever that the writer regarded Israel's success as far removed in time from the defeat. It is more satisfactory to assume that the whole section, though already found in its present position by the compiler of 33 (see v.^{40}), is badly placed.

It is difficult to reach any certain conclusion as to the original position of the section. The style, from which all marks of P are absent, but which is marked by some characteristics of JE, such as נלחם ב, שמע בקול, proves that it is not derived from P, and, consequently, that the assignment of the incident to the stay at Mt. Hor is no older than the editor who united P and JE. Further, the story did not, even in JE, stand after 20^{21} and before 21^{4}; for that passage speaks of the Hebrews taking a *southern* course from Ḳadesh; the present incident implies that they were moving towards the Negeb, which lies N. of Ḳadesh. As between the two sources J and E, הכנעני (v.^{3}) favours referring the passage to the former.

As to the relation between the present passage, 14^{45} and Jud. $1^{16f.}$, Moore (*Judg.* 36) considers that the present passage has no connection with Jud. $1^{16f.}$, but is a parallel and different explanation of the name Ḥormah. Steuernagel (*Einwanderung*, 76 f.), on the other hand, considers all three passages scattered fragments of one and the same narrative, which immediately followed the narrative of the spies and, in its original form, described how *Judah* (cp. Judges), which took no part in the conquest of Canaan from the E., gained its footing in Western Canaan from the S. The present passage, on this theory, generalises a tradition which originally related to only a section of Israel, and makes it apply to the whole people.

---

* Palmer, *Desert of the Exodus*, 522.

1. *The Canaanite, the king of ʿArād, who dwelt in the Negeb*] *the king of ʿArād* may be an interpolation, for (1) the personal title is strange after the collective national term, which alone is subsequently referred to (*this people*, v.[2]; *them and their cities*, v.[3]); and (2) after the mention of ʿArād, which is situated in the Negeb, the clause *who dwelt in the Negeb* would be redundant. See also on v.[3]. With *the Canaanite who dwelt in the Negeb*, cp. "the Canaanite dwelt in the valley" (14^{25}); see also 14^{45}.—*The king of ʿArād*] also mentioned (immediately after the king of Ḥormah) in Jos. 12^{14}. ʿArād, according to Jerome (*Onom.* 88^2), lay 20 Roman miles S. of *Ḥebron*. The name survives in Tell ʿArād, which lies 17 English miles almost due S. of Ḥebron,* about 30 miles due N. of Jebel Madurah, and about 50 miles N.N.E. of ʿAin Ḳadîs (Ḳadesh).—*The way of (the) Atharim*] Atharim (האתרים) seems to be a proper name. Di.'s view, that the whole phrase means the "caravan route," is not very probable, and "the way of the spies" (AV. after 𝕿, etc.) must be abandoned; see phil. n.—**2.** *Them I will devote*] or *place under the ban*, and so destroy; cp. 18^{14} n. The name *Ḥormah* is here explained as a place that had been laid under the ban and destroyed, though, like the similar names Ḥermon and Ḥŏrēm, it may actually have acquired the sacred or inviolable character which is implied by the name in some other way.—*And the name of the district was called Ḥormah*] In Jud. 1^{17} it is distinctly stated that Ḥormah was the name given to a *city*, and that the former name of the city was Ṣephath. It is commonly supposed that the present passage also asserts that the name Ḥormah was given to a city; then the city should be ʿArād (v.[1]); yet in Jos. 12^{14} Ḥormah and ʿArād are distinct cities. But the term מקום, though it may be used of a city, may also refer to a wider area including many cities: *e.g.* it is used of the whole land of Canaan (Ex. 23^{20}, 1 S. 12^8; cp. CH. 65^{JE}). In the present instance, after the preceding clause, *and they devoted them* (the Canaanites) *and their cities*, it is most natural to take מקום in the wider sense. In Jos. 12^{14} 15^{30} 19^4,

* Robinson, *Biblical Researches*, ii. 473; Smith, *Hist. Geog.* 278 f.; *EBi. s.v.* "Arad."

1 S. 30^{30}, 1 Ch. 4^{30}, Ḥormah (without the art. as here and in Jud. 1^{17}) is mentioned among a number of cities; but in *from Seʿir to Ḥormah* (Dt. 1^{44} 𝔊) it may well be, like Seʿir, the name of a district; cp. *the Ḥormah* in 14^{45}.

1. דרך האתרים] 𝔊 (ʼΑθαρειν(μ)) certainly and, in all probability, the other versions also presuppose the present text of 𝔐. The rendering *the way of the spies* (𝔖 𝔗 𝔙, Sam. V., Aq., Symm.) is due to the resemblance of אתרים and תרים; but there is no philological connection between the two words. Di.'s suggestion noted above rests on a comparison with the Arabic أَثَر = *a trace, sign.* Cheyne in *EBi.* (2651 n. 5) proposes דרך הר אמרי.—**2.** והחרמתי את עריהם] 𝔊 *ἀναθεματιῶ αὐτὸν καὶ τὰς πόλεις αὐτοῦ*; cp. v.[3] 𝔐.—**3.** הכנעני] Add with S 𝔊 (cp. 𝔖) בידו; cp. v.[2] 𝔐.—אתהם] see BDB. 84*b*.

4–9. The bronze serpent (JE).—The people complain of the unsatisfying manna and of the lack of water. Yahweh plagues them with serpents. At the people's request, Moses intercedes with Yahweh, who instructs him to make an artificial serpent, and set it on a pole. Moses makes the serpent of bronze and sets it on a pole; and every one suffering from a serpent-bite who looks at it is healed.

V.[4a] (*and they journeyed from Mt. Hor*) is taken directly from, or composed by the editor in the manner of, P. The rest of the passage is from JE, and, probably, in particular from E. V.[4b] continues 20^{21} (E), and explains how, on the Edomites' refusal to give Israel passage through their country, they gained their purpose of getting E. of Jordan. With דרך ים סוף cp. 14^{25}, Ex. 13^{18} (E), Dt. 1^{40} 2^{1}. Whether the story of the bronze serpent stood in its present position in JE, or was placed there by the editor, cannot be determined. Characteristic of JE are העלה (of the Exodus) in v.[5] (cp. 14^{13} 16^{13}; CH. 136); הביט v.[9] (cp. 12^{8} 23^{21}; CH. 179); התפלל v.[7 *bis*] (cp. 11^{2} n.) The last word, as also אלהים in v.[5] and perhaps דבר ב in v.[5] (cp. 12^{1} (E)), point to E, to which source the passage is referred by Di., Kue., Bacon, Kit., CH.

From a notice in the Book of Kings (2 K. 18^{4}), it appears that in the 8th century B.C. the "bronze serpent" was an object of popular worship in Judah: the people burnt sacrifices (מקטרים) to it. It was therefore destroyed by Hezekiah, who acted, as we may suppose, under the influence of Isaiah's iconoclastic teaching (Is. 2^{8} 17^{8} 30^{22} 31^{7}). The notice in the Book of Kings agrees with the present in attributing to Moses the manufacture of the serpent.

The relation between these two notices may be regarded in two ways. Either (*a*) the present passage records the actual origin of the bronze serpent, and the symbol, originally erected by Moses without idolatrous intent, came to be an object of idolatrous worship; or (*b*) Nu. 21^{4-9} is an etiological story told to explain a symbol that actually owed its origin to other than Yahwistic belief. The acceptance or rejection of explanation (*a*), which is adopted, for example, by Strack, will be largely determined by the general conclusion as to the date and historical value of the Pentateuchal sources: it need only be pointed out here that the story contains no adequate explanation of the choice of this particular form of miracle, nor of how the Israelite nomads on the march were in a position to manufacture, with the speed which the circumstances demanded, so important a work in metal. Explanation (*b*), which is now very generally adopted, accords with a general tendency in religion to endeavour to impart new and more appropriate significance to incongruous rites and practices which happen to possess a great hold on the people: cp. p. 48.

Beliefs in the connection between the serpent and healing, which, if the present story is rightly regarded as etiological in character, must have been recognised by the Hebrews, are widespread. A conspicuous instance is the Greek god of healing, Asklepios, who is said to have appeared in the form of a serpent, and is constantly represented accompanied by serpents.* Possibly another trace of such a belief among the Hebrews may be found in "the Dragon's spring" (עין תנין Neh. 2^{13}), for the "Arabs still regard medicinal waters as inhabited by the *jinn*, which are usually of serpent form." †

Whatever its origin, the mass of the Hebrew people came to attribute healing power to the bronze serpent itself. Not so those who had come under the higher prophetic teaching among whom, at some time prior to Hezekiah, this story must have been framed to controvert the popular belief, and

* Pausanias, *Description of Greece*, ii. 10. 3; and see Frazer's n. on ii. 10. 3 (vol. iii. 65–67), where parallels from Greek and Roman writers and wider fields may be found.

† W. R. Smith, *Rel. of the Semites*,[2] 168.

to trace back the power of healing to Yahweh Himself, who, as the prophets taught, both bruised and healed (see, *e.g.*, Hos. 6^1 11^3, and compare such stories as that of the healing of Naaman (2 K. 5)). The point of the story is clearly seized by the author of Wisdom; the bronze serpent is a σύμβολον σωτηρίας, and "he that turned toward it was not saved because of that which was beheld, but because of thee, the Saviour of all" (Wisd. $16^{6f.}$).

In later times the story readily lent itself to allegorizing. To Philo the serpent erected by Moses is καρτερία, *patient endurance* (the metal symbolising strength); this is equal to overcoming *pleasure*, which is the real meaning of the serpent who tempted Eve (*De Alleg.* ii. 20 (Mangey, 80); *De Agricul.* 22 (Mangey, 315)). Less elaborate is the explanation in *Rosh hash-Shanah* iii. 8. The allusion in Jn. 3^{14} has given rise to a large typological literature, for which see references in Winer, *Bibl. Realwörterbuch*, *s.v.* "Schlange, Eherne."

The place of the serpent in Semitic and especially Hebrew religion has been fully discussed by Baudissin in *Studien zur semit. Religionsgeschichte*, i. 257–292. The data are insufficient to justify any certain inference as to the actual origin of the cult of the bronze serpent. In view of the slight influence of Egyptian religion on the Hebrews it is unlikely that the cult of the serpent is of Egyptian origin. Of various other views that have been held, two or three may be mentioned. (1) W. R. Smith (*Journal of Philology*, ix. 99 f.) argued that the serpent was originally a totem symbol, and that other traces of the serpent as a totem were to be found in certain proper names (on which see also *HPN.* p. 88 ff., Nos. 24, 44, 45, and p. 108 ff., Nos. 3 and 9). (2) Cheyne in *EBi. s.v.* "Nehushtan," has skilfully argued that the "bronze serpent" in the temple, like the "bronze oxen" and "the sea," was a symbol connected with the Babylonian dragon myth which certainly has left its mark on Hebrew mythology (Gunkel, *Schöpfung u. Chaos*, esp. pp. 29–114); see also Zimmern, *Die Keilinschriften u. das AT*,[3] 505. (3) Frazer (*GB.* ii. 426 f.) cites the present story in connection with the custom of getting rid of vermin by making images of them. Thus the Philistines, when their land was infested by mice (1 S. 5^6 𝔊), made golden images of the creatures, and sent them out of the country. "Apollonius of Tyana is said to have freed Antioch from scorpions by making a bronze image of a scorpion, and burying it under a small pillar in the middle of the city. Gregory of Tours tells us that the city of Paris used to be free of dormice and serpents, but that in his lifetime, while they were cleaning a sewer, they found a bronze serpent and a bronze dormouse, and removed them," whereafter they abounded. See also Jacob, *Altarab. Parallelen zum AT*, p. 11, who cites instances from Ḳazwīnī (ii. 369, 373), and amongst others the case of a well near Toledo which became infested with leeches: a bronze leech was cast into the well and the real things disappeared.

4. *And they set out from Mt. Hor*] the clause connects the narrative of P (20^{22-29} $21^{10f.}$), now interrupted by the insertion of two passages from JE ($21^{1-3.\ 4b-9}$). With ויסעו מן, cp. v.[10f.] (ct. v.[12ff.]) 10^{12}, Ex. 13^{20} 16^{1} 17^{1} (P).—**4a** *β*. The continuation of 20^{21} (JE): the original source ran—*And Israel turned away from him* (*i.e.* Edom: 20^{21}) *by the way of Yam Suph to compass the land of Edom.* They went southwards from Ḳadesh, which was on the boundary of Edom (20^{16}), to pass round the southern extremity of Edom to the E.; cp. Jud. $11^{17.\ 18}$. On *the way of Yam Suph*, see 14^{25} n.—**4b, 5.** The people, unable to restrain their impatience at being led about in so barren a country, *spoke* angrily *against* (12^{1} n.) *God and Moses*, and complained that there was no food to be had, but the unsatisfying manna which they loathed.—*The soul of the people was short*] *shortness of soul* (נפש) or *spirit* (רוח) is impatience or incapability of restraining one's anger. For example, under Delilah's persistent teasing, Samson's soul grew *short* till he revealed his secret (Jud. 16^{16}). *Short-spirited* is the antithesis in Prov. 14^{29} to *long-suffering* (ארך אפים); see, further, Ex. 6^{9}, Jud. 10^{16}, Mic. 2^{7}, Zech. 11^{8}, Job 21^{4}. The prep. בְּ gives either the ground of complaint, as in Jud. 10^{16}, Zech. 11^{8}—*because of the way*; or the place—*in the way*.—*Wherefore have ye brought us up*] According to MT. the subject is God and Moses: see last clause. But the verb should be pointed as a sing. (העליתָנו: so 𝔊^BFL 𝔖 𝔙), the subject being Moses only, as in 16^{13}, Ex. 17^{3}.—*Why hast thou brought us up?*] For the complaint, cp. 20^{5}.—*This worthless bread*] *ḳᵉlōḳēl* occurs only here, but the root in Heb. means literally *to be light*, and so *contemptible* (*e.g.* 2 S $19^{44\,(43)}$, Is. 8^{23} (9^{1})). On account of a *special* development of the root-meaning in Assyr. (*ḳalḳaltu* = *hunger*), some interpret *ḳᵉlōḳēl* here *unsatisfying*.—**6.** *The burning serpents*] If the adj. *sārāph* is connected with vb. שרף *to burn*, it refers to the burning sensation of the inflammation produced by the bite, rather than to the fiery appearance of the serpent or, in particular, of its eye, for the vb. does not mean *give light*. Formally the word here used as an adj. is identical with the noun in Is. 6^{2}, *sᵉraphim*. The *sᵉraphim* of Is. 6^{2} are mythological in character: that is scarcely the case with

the serpents that in this story attack the Israelites. As a matter of fact, serpents of various kinds abound both in the Sinaitic peninsula and in the deserts south of Palestine; either this actual fact is reflected in the story, or the plague of serpents in the story is entirely due to the need for explaining the existence in later times of the bronze serpent: see above, p. 275 f.—*We have sinned*] Aaron and Miriam make a similar confession (12^{11} (E)). After the confession, Moses, as on other occasions, intercedes with effect (11^{2} n.).—*Make thee a serpent*] 𝔊ᴸ 𝔖 add *of bronze*, as in v.[9].—The words נחש = *serpent*, and נחשת = *bronze*, are very similar, and the one word might very easily be omitted by accident after the other. The conventional rendering of נחשת is *brass*; but this is almost certainly incorrect. The word denotes in the first instance an ore, or natural metal (Dt. 8^{9}; cp. נחושה Job 28^{2}). It is used for all sorts of utensils (17^{4}, 2 K. 25^{14}), is less valuable than gold (Is. 60^{17}) or silver (Dan. 2^{32}), and was a bright metal (1 K. 7^{45}, Ezr. 8^{27}). All this points to copper, a metal in early use among various peoples of antiquity. Copper articles have been found, for example, in the tomb of Menes, the "first king of Egypt," copper and bronze at Tell el Ḥesy and Troy. From the fact that some of the OT. allusions (*e.g.* 1 S. $17^{5f.}$, 1 K. 4^{13}, Is. 48^{4}, Job 40^{18}) seem to imply a stronger and harder metal than unalloyed copper, it is inferred that נחשת may also mean bronze. Bronze (an alloy of copper and tin) was much employed by, whereas brass (an alloy of copper and zinc) was hardly known to, the ancients.*—*On a pole*] The word נס is generally used of a conspicuous object round which people, especially troops, mustered; see, *e.g.*, Is. 5^{26} 11^{12} 18^{3} 62^{10}, Jer. 50^{2}: here it seems to mean nothing more than a pole sufficiently high to be conspicuous.

6. מישראל] 𝔊 = מבני ישראל.—**8.** והיה] 𝔊 + ἐὰν δάκῃ ὄφις ἄνθρωπον: cp. v.[9] 𝔐.—**9.** את איש] On the את with the formally indefinite but quasi-pronominal איש (=*any one*), see Dav. 72, R. 4; Kön. iii. 288*g*; G.-K. 117*c*.

---

* *EBi.* *s.v.* "Copper," "Brass"; Nowack, *Arch.* i. 243 f. In AV, *brass*=*copper*; see Wright's *Bible Word Book*.

XXI. 10–XXXVI. (JE P). *Marches and Events East of the 'Arabah and the Jordan.*

After a march northwards from the gulf of 'Aḳabah along the E. of Edom and Moab ($21^{10\,(12)}$–22^{1}) the Israelites come to rest, before attacking Canaan W. of the Jordan, in the country immediately to the N.E. of the Dead Sea. With the story of the Israelites in this district are connected the episode of Balaam (22^{2}–24^{18}), the seduction of the Israelites by the (Moabites or) Midianite women (25^{1-9}), whose conduct is visited on the whole people of Midian (c. 31), the taking of the second census (c. 26), the selection of Moses' successor Joshua (27^{15-23}), the communication of numerous laws and instructions (27^{1-14} 28–30. 33^{50}–36). The greater part of c. 32 also finds a suitable place in this section; and the itinerary of c. 33 is as well placed here as anywhere else.

The greater part of the section is derived from P, much of it from P^{s}. But it is the view of JE with regard to the march that most clearly appears in the compilation. If it was P's view that the Hebrews marched across the N. of Edom (see 21^{11} n.), the editor has succeeded in obscuring it.

XXI. 10.–XXII. 1. *Marches and Conquests East of the Dead Sea and Jordan Valley.*

LITERATURE.—Nöldeke, *Untersuchungen*, 85 f.; Wellhausen, *Comp.* 110 f., 343–346; Meyer, *ZATW.* i. 117–146; Stade, *Geschichte des Volkes Israel*, 116–118, 130 n. 1; Kuenen, *Hexateuch*, 151 f., 230, and *Th. Tijd.* xviii. (1884), 516–532; G. A. Smith, *Hist. Geog.* c. xxvi. and Appendix iii.; Bacon, *Triple Tradition*, 209–212; Kittel, *Geschichte der Hebräer*, 81–83, 192–194, 206–209; Sayce, *Early History of the Hebrews*, 222–228; Steuernagel, *Die Einwanderung der israelitischen Stämmen*, §§ 11 and 13 (especially).

The passage contains the work of many writers. The poetical passages (v.$^{14f.\ 17f.\ 27-30}$), in view of the manner in which they are introduced, are obviously older than the narrative with which they have been incorporated. V.$^{33-35}$ are derived from Dt. 1^{1-3}. The repeated formula of marching and encamping in v.$^{10.\ 11a}$ 22^{1} is in Hebrew different from that in v.$^{12f.}$. That in v.$^{10.\ 11a}$ 22^{1} is the same as is found elsewhere in P (v.^{4} n.); v.$^{12f.}$ has the same formula as Dt. 10$^{6f.}$ (E).

Even the narrative that remains, after removing the poetical passages, the extract from P, and the citation from Dt., is not homogeneous or self-consistent. For in v.^{20} the people have reached Pisgah in the very heart of the country between Arnon and Jabboḳ: in v.$^{21f.}$ they are still outside of this country, and only enter it after conquering the Amorites who then possessed it. Minor incongruities are the difference in the formulæ of the march in v.$^{12f.}$ and $^{18b-20}$, the description of the country occupied by the Hebrews as "land" in v.$^{24a-31}$ but as cities in v.$^{25.\ 32}$, the fact that v.^{25b} and v.^{31} are doublets, and that "these cities" in v.^{25} refers to nothing in the present context. Taken together these differences point to connecting (*a*) v.$^{11b-13.\ 21-24a.\ 31}$; (*b*) v.$^{16.\ 18b-20.\ 24b.\ 25\ (26).\ 32}$. (*a*) can be read consecutively—After passing several stations Israel reaches the border of the Amorite country which stretched from Arnon to Jabboḳ; they ask to be allowed to make a peaceful passage through this country; the Amorites refuse: the Israelites conquer the Amorites, and occupy the country. This story can be assigned with some confidence to E: for (1) v.$^{21-24a}$ closely resembles 20$^{14-18}$ (E); (2) it agrees with Jud. 11$^{12ff.}$ and Dt. 2$^{24ff.}$ in locating the Amorites between Arnon and Jabboḳ; (3) the formula of the march in v.$^{12f.}$ agrees with Dt. 10$^{6f.}$ (E). The narrative (*b*) is not consecutive; for v.^{25} presupposes something not expressed. Nor can it on any strong positive grounds be assigned to its ultimate source; as belonging to JE yet inconsistent with E, it may provisionally be referred to J.

The analysis here adopted is virtually that of Bacon and CH. We., on the insufficient ground noted above (p. 265), assigned the whole of v.$^{21-31}$ to J. Otherwise the general tendency was to refer a much larger part of v.$^{17-30}$ to E; Kit. and Kue. referred the whole section, Meyer all except v.$^{18b-20}$ to that source. Kuenen, slightly modifying the older harmonistic exegesis, thus attempts to get over the difficulty of the inconsistency of v.$^{16-20}$ and v.$^{21-24}$; E "prefaced his own narrative by a passage from an older *itinerarium* . . . and illustrated certain points by poetical citations

. . . just as he did with the main feature of his own narrative also" (*Hex.* 152). Steuernagel has recently denied the presence of J in the section; arguing that v.$^{21-30}$ are out of place, that v.$^{18b-20}$ not less than v.$^{11b-18}$ belong to E, and that v.$^{11b-20}$ immediately preceded the episode of Balaam, which he refers entirely to E and E^2.

When the poetical fragments were introduced into the narrative is uncertain. The introduction of the first and third may be due to the same hand (note על כן v.$^{14. 27}$; ct. v.^{17}); but whether this was E or R^{JE} or even (though this is less likely) a later editor, must remain uncertain. The second poem (v.^{17}) is introduced in the same manner as the song at the Red Sea (Ex. 15^1), and possibly, therefore, by the same hand (J).

10, 11a (P). *And the children of Israel set out*] The point of departure is omitted: ct. v.^{4a}, Ex. 13^{20} 16^1 etc. In 33$^{42f.}$ between Mt. Hor (v.^{4a}) and Oboth, two other places, Ṣalmonah and Punon, are mentioned.—*Oboth*] site unknown.—*'Iyye-'Abārim*] The first part of the name is the cstr. of 'Iyyim (33^{45}) and plural of 'Ai or 'Î, which, defined by the art., also appears as the name of a place. It appears to mean "heaps" or "ruins." 'Ai and another 'Iyyim in Judah were on the W. of the Jordan valley. The addition of the words "of the 'Abārim" here and in 33^{44}, defines this 'Iyyim as being on the E. of the Jordan valley; for "the 'Abārim," meaning literally "places on the other side," is a name given to the country E. of the Jordan valley, specifically to that on the other side from Judah (cp. 27^{12}, Dt. 32^9; and see G. A. Smith's art. "Abarim" in *EBi.*). Little that is more precise can be said of the site of 'Iyye-'Abarim with certainty; for the next clause and the following verses appear to be from a different source. If, however, the compiler has here been careful so to combine his sources as correctly to represent geographical facts, 'Iyye-'Abarim lay E. of Moab (clause *b*) and S. of Arnon; for between 'Iyye-'Abarim and Arnon (v.^{13}) the present compilation places the Wady Zered. In 33$^{44. 45}$ the next station beyond 'Iyyim on the northward march is Dibon-Gad, which was only two or three miles N. of Arnon. In 33^{44} 'Iyyim is said to be *in the territory* or *on the border of Moab*; if the latter translation of the ambiguous phrase be adopted, 'Iyyim should be located at the S.E. corner of Moab, and, therefore, most probably at some part on the upper course of the Wady el-Aḥsā which flows into the southern end of the Dead Sea from the S.E. But however this may be, the main point is certain: ʿIyye-ʿAbarim lay E. of the Jordan valley (including the ʿArabah); and thus the narrative of P^g, in so far as it is extant, mentions between Mt. Hor (20^{22} 21^{4a}) on the W., and ʿIyye-ʿAbarim on the E., of the ʿArabah only one place, Oboth (the site of which is unknown), and gives no indication whatever that the passage from W. to E. was made by a long detour southwards from Ḳadesh by the head of the Red Sea. The fuller itinerary of c. 33, which, though the work of P^s, is in the main governed by P^g's point of view, mentions, indeed, a larger number of intervening stations; but it also gives no indication of a detour south. It is therefore highly probable that P^g represented the people marching, unmolested and with ease, straight across the northern end of Edom. Just as forty years before the spies passed through the whole length of Canaan at will, so now the Israelites approach Canaan by the direct and chosen route with entire disregard of the people then in possession of the country.

11. עִיֵּי הָעֲבָרִים] the existence of a עיים in Judah is a little uncertain: of the versions 𝔙 (*Iim*) alone supports 𝔐 in Jos. 15^{29}, the only passage where the place is mentioned; $𝔊^B$ reads Βακωκ; 𝔖 ܟܠܟܒ; $𝔊^{AL}$ Αυειμ, pointing to עוים (cp. Jos. 18^{23} $𝔊^{AL}$). Even of the present name it is doubtful whether the original form was not rather the sing. עִי העברים (distinguished from הָעַי near Bethel in western Canaan). 𝔙 (*Ijeabarim, Jeabarim*) clearly supports the pl., and, possibly, $𝔊^L$ (Γεει) does the same; 𝔖 always reads ܟܐܦܐ ܕܥܒܪܝܐ, which is ambiguous; but, with the exception just mentioned, all the readings of 𝔊 are either curious or point to the sing.; for Γαι, the regular equivalent of (ה)עַי (see Hatch and Redpath, *Supplement*, *s.v.* Γαι, Αγγαι), is read in $𝔊^{ABF}$ in $33^{44f.}$, and here $𝔊^{AF\,(vid)}$ have Αχελγαι, ^{B}χαλγλει, ^{L}Αχιλειμ χαιειμ. So in *Onom.* Αιή, ἡ καὶ 'Αχελγαί (211^8), *Aie quæ et Achalgai* (86^1). The origin of 𝔊's Αχελ (cp. in NT. 'Αχελδαμαχ, here = Aram. חֲקַל) is not obvious; it might (after ν) be a corruption of Ναχελ = נחל; but if so, whence came נחל? It is worthy of notice that the hard pronunciation of ע which still influences 𝔊 is neglected in the forms of the *Onom.* (Αιη, *Aie*). On this point and on the possible presence of עַי in עיבל, see *Academy*, June 21, 1896.

11b–15. A fragment of E's itinerary, describing how the Israelites advance, keeping outside Moabite territory and the border of the Amorites (v.$^{11b.\,13}$). This is followed by a fragment of an ancient poem (v.[14f.]). Previous fragments of E's itinerary are to be found in 20^{21} 21^{4b}, Dt. 10^{6-8}. Evidently, from the position which they occupy in c. 33, the places mentioned in Dt. 10^{6-8} belong to the march southwards from Ḳadesh: those mentioned here, to the march northward from ʿEṣion-Geber on the Gulf of ʿAḳabah. In view of the different definition of ʿIyye-ʿAbarim in 33^{44} and the similarity to Jud. 11^{18}, CH. seem justified in referring v.[11b] (*in the wilderness which is over against Moab on the east*) to E rather than P. Whether in E v.[11b] defines ʿIyye-ʿAbarim or some other place cannot be determined, but the fact that ʿIyye-ʿAbarim in $33^{45f.}$ immediately precedes Dibon-Gad favours the latter alternative.—*The Wady Zered*] Dt. $2^{13f.}$ Taken by itself the context in Dt. favours the identification * with the Wady el-Aḥsā, formerly the southern border of Moab, and still "the recognised boundary between the districts of Petra and Kerak"; for the command not to vex Moab would be more suitably given as the Israelites were approaching the southern border, than after they had been for some time skirting the eastern border of Moab. But if the compiler of the present narrative was accurately acquainted with and accurately represents the topography of the district, ʿIyye-ʿAbarim must lie on or N. of the Wady el-Aḥsā, and consequently the Wady Zered must be some wady further north, such as el-Franji (the upper course of the Wady el-Kerak) or the Seil Lejjûn (cp. p. 286).†—**13.** *Beyond Arnon*] if the writer speaks from the standpoint of the march, this must mean *north* of the Arnon: this is the most natural interpretation both here and in Jud. 11^{18} (see Moore, *ad loc.*). If the phrase is used from the fixed standpoint of an Israelite, *beyond Arnon* would mean on the side of Arnon out of Israelite territory, and hence *south* of Arnon; so it is commonly taken here.‡—*Which is in the wilderness*] the clause apparently defines Arnon (rather than עבר). Such a definition is not unnecessary, for the name Arnon in the OT. covers a number of branches of the great wady whose

* Robinson, *Biblical Researches*, ii. 555 f.; Tristram, *Land of Moab*, 50.
† Di.; Driver on Dt. 2^{13}.
‡ Di., Str., Meyer, *ZATW.* v. 45 n. 1.

modern name is Wady Mojib (cp. v.[14] n.). G. A. Smith (in *EBi.* 3170 n. 1) suggests that the particular stream here intended is one of the branches of the W. Wāleh, which comes from the N. into the main wady 4½ m. from its mouth.—*The wilderness which stretches away from the territory of the Amorite*] viz. to the east. The whole description points to some locality on the upper Arnon, in agreement with 21[4. 11b] and Jud. 11[18], which represent the march as outside of and therefore necessarily east of Edom and Moab. The upper Arnon could be easily crossed by a large body of men: not so the lower Arnon, which runs through a chasm two or three miles across and 1700 feet deep.*—*For Arnon is the Moabite border between Moab and the Amorite*] What this statement is intended to substantiate is not clear, possibly owing to an incomplete citation of the source. For the view that at the time in question the country N. of Arnon was occupied by the Amorites, see v.[24–26], Jud. 11[22], Jos. 12[2]. The Moabite N. boundary shifted in later times, as the contemporary evidence of the Moabite Stone suffices to show. Under ʿOmri and Aḥab Arnon formed the border between Israel and Moab; Meshaʿ reconquered many of the towns N. of Arnon (*e.g.* ʿAroʿer, Mehēdeba, ʿAtaroth, Nebo), and reoccupied the country. Meshaʿ's inscription, in fact, refers to three changes: (1) in the time before ʿOmri, Moab occupied country N. of Arnon; (2) in the time of ʿOmri, and Aḥab, Moab was confined to the S. of Arnon; (3) in the period of Meshaʿ (and subsequently, cp. Is. 15 f.), Moab again extended N. of Arnon. There is thus nothing historically improbable in the representation of this chapter that at a much earlier period Moab had to fight, and not always successfully, to maintain its claim to the country N. of the Arnon.—14 f. A snatch from *the book of Yahweh's Battles* is cited to show that Arnon was the border of Moab.—*Wherefore it is said*] or *that is the meaning of the saying* (על כן יאמר): cp. Gn. 10[9], and the similar phrase על כן יאמרו in v.[27]. *The book of the Battles of Yahweh*] To judge from the specimen here preserved, and from its title, this book, like *the book of the Yashar* (Jos. 10[13], 2 S. 1[18]) or the *Ḥamāsa* and similar

* G. A. Smith, *Hist. Geog.* 558; Tristram, *Land of Moab*, 125 ff.

collections of the Arabs,* appears to have been a collection of ancient popular songs that had been handed down orally till the fuller establishment of a national life brought with it a period of literary activity. The date of the collection cannot be determined with any certainty.† The *book of the Yashar* cannot be earlier than David (2 S 1^{18}); and *the book of Yahweh's Battles* may well have arisen in the same period. The subject of the collection, as indicated in the title, was the struggles of the nation or its heroes against its foes; for these were what the Hebrews meant by "battles of Yahweh" (1 S. 18^{17} 25^{28}); and the battles were so called because they were waged by the help of Yahweh (*e.g.* 1 S. $14^{6.\ 23}$) and by the presence in the heroes of Yahweh's spirit (Jud. $6^{34ff.}$ 1 S. $11^{6ff.}$) and against Yahweh's enemies (Jud. 5^{31}). War with the Hebrews, as with other peoples of antiquity, was a sacred undertaking,‡ and as such demanded consecration (Jos. 3^5, Is. 13^3, Jer. 6^4 51^{27}, Joel 3^9, Micah 3^5).—The snatch itself is an obscure fragment beginning in the middle of one sentence and breaking off in the middle of the next—

. . . 14b Waheb in Suphah, and the valleys, Arnon.
15 The cliff of the valleys which extends to the site of ʿAr,
And leans on the border of Moab . . .

The verb on which *Waheb* is dependent may have been עבר, or לקח, or the like, and so—*We* (*i.e.* the Israelites, Yahweh's warriors) *passed through* or *took Waheb*. Waheb (𝔊 Ζωόβ) is quite unknown; Suphah, the district in which it is situated, may possibly be identical with the obscure Suph of Dt. 1^1 (see Driver, *ad loc.*), but scarcely, as suggested by Tristram (*Moab*, 50 f.) with the Ghôr eṣ-Ṣâfiyyeh, a small oasis just S.E. of the Dead Sea (see Dr. in *DB. s.v.* "Zoar"). The

* On which see Brockelmann, *Arab. Litteratur*, 17–21, and Fried. Rückert's German metrical translation with notes of the *Ḥamāsa* of Abu Temmâm (2 vols.; Stuttgart, 1846).

† Reuss, *Gesch. d. Heiligenschrift ATS.*,[2] 215 (temp. David–Sol.); Meyer, *ZATW.* i. 131 f. (*c.* 850–800 B.C.; cf. Sta. *GVI.* 50).

‡ Schwally, *Semitische Kriegsaltertümer* (*Der heilige Krieg im alten Israel*), 1901.

sibilants do not correspond, and Ṣâfiyyeh is a specifically Arabic term (Wetzstein in Del. *Gen.*[4] 586 n. 2), which does not seem to be a likely explanation of Suphah.—*The valleys, Arnon*] the valleys which constitute Arnon, *i.e.* the present Wady Mojib, which is formed by the junction just above ʿArâʿir, some thirteen miles from the Dead Sea, of three deep wadies: two of these (the Lejjûn and the Baluʿa) coming from the S. first unite and then join the Seil Saʿîdeh from the E. (F. Bliss, *PEF Qu. St.*, 1895, 204 (map), 215). "The whole plateau up to the desert is thus not only cut across, but up and down, by deep ravines, and a very difficult frontier is formed. . . . but all the branches probably carried the name Arnon from the main valley right up to the desert. It is not *the valley* but *the valleys* of Arnon which are named in the ancient fragment of song celebrating Israel's passage" (G. A. Smith, *Hist. Geog.* 558 f.). The second and third lines of the fragment seem to introduce a notice (in the citation left incomplete) of one particular Arnon valley—that, viz., which *turns towards* or *extends to ʿAr*, and forms the Moabite border; and this is probably the main valley, with its lofty and precipitous cliffs. "Cliff" seems the most probable meaning of אשד, which is only here used in the singular, but occurs in the pl. of "the slopes of Pisgah" (Dt. 3^{17} 4^{49}, Jos. 12^{3} 13^{30}†), and, with a general reference, in Jos. 10^{40}, where it forms one of four divisions (*the hill-country*, *the negeb*, *the shephelah*, and *the slopes*) into which the whole land was divided according to physical aspect.—*The site of Ar*] (שבת ער), a poetical expression; ct. מושב העיר, 2 K. 2^{19}.—*ʿAr* is also mentioned in Dt. $2^{9.\,18.\,29}$, and in the fuller form ʿAr Moab in v.[28], Is. 15^{1}. *ʿAr* means *city*, and may have been the regular Moabitic equivalent of the Heb. *ʿir* (pl. *ʿarîm*). ʿAr, therefore, is presumably the same as ʿIr Moab (22^{36}; RV. "the city of Moab"). In that case (and even Dt. 2^{18} with the context almost suffices to prove it) ʿAr was situated on the upper (eastern) course of the Arnon. In Is. 15^{1} 𝔊 renders ער מואב by Μωαβεῖτις, and it has been suggested that ʿAr was a district rather than a town. The identifications with individual sites, such as Muḥâtet el-ḥajj, just south of the Wady

Mojib, lack proof, or are definitely unsuitable.* The cliff of the valley which forms the border of Moab is poetically said to lean upon that border. It is for this last statement that the fragment is quoted.

11. At the end of the v., S and the margin of codices 85 and 130 of 𝕲 and the Syr. Hex. (see Field's *Hexapla*) add (with the change of אלי to אל משה and the omission of מלחמה) Dt. 2^9 which forbids Israel to fight with or take possession of Moab. After v.[12], S adds Dt. $2^{18f.}$.—**13.** מעבר] S בעבר (cp. 𝕲): so Jud. 11^{18} 𝕳.—**14.** את והב בסופה] 𝕲 τὴν Ζωὸβ ἐφλόγισεν. The obscurity of the fragment offered much scope to the Haggadic faculty. סופה suggested ים סוף, והב (in some MSS. אתוהב is read as one word, which gives an Aramaic verbal form) was taken to refer to a gift of, or a miracle wrought by God. Hence 𝖁, depending on Jewish exegesis as represented in 𝕿 Jer, *Sicut fecit in mari rubro sic faciet in torrentibus Arnon*: similarly AV. 𝕿 Jon connects סופה both with סופה *a storm*, and סוף *end, extremity*. In the next verse אשר, taken in the sense of *pouring out*, suggested a story of how the Edomites and the Moabites, hiding in the valleys with a view to surprising the Hebrews, were crushed by the mountains coming together at the command of Yahweh, and of how the valleys "poured" with their blood.—That את והב is rightly divided, and והב (possibly a corrupt form) a place-name, is clear from the following clause.—הנחלים ארנן] on the appositional cstr., see Dr. *Tenses*, 190.—**15.** ואשר] Either a third acc. to the two in the preceding v. (Di.), or, in view of the absence of את, more probably a nom. (*casus pendens*) of a sentence left incomplete in the citation. The precise meaning of אשר is uncertain. The root in Heb. appears only in this one word (pl. אשדת). In Aram. אשד ܐܫܕ means *to pour out*, and is especially used of "shedding blood." Hence the Targum renderings. On أسد, see Nöld. in *ZDMG.* xl. 160; and on Sabæan אסד, D. H. Müller, *ib.* xxxvii. 8. Fried. Del. (*Heb. in Light of Assyr. Research*, p. 30 f.) compares *išdu=base*; cp. 𝖁 *radices* in Dt. 3^{17}. The sense *sloping side, cliff*, which is suggested by תחת אשדת הפסגה, may have been developed from one or other of these root meanings. 𝕲 and 𝕾 translate by verbs; S reads אשר.

16–20. The itinerary continued: Be'er (Mattanah), Naḥali'el, Bamoth, Pisgah.—This section of the itinerary seems to be derived from a source different from the foregoing; and, strictly regarded, it is certainly out of place before v.[21–24]. See p. 280. Of the places mentioned here, the Pisgah at least lay N. of Arnon, and the entire description in v.[20] points to a spot above the N.E. shores of the Dead Sea. If read as a continuation of the preceding section, the remaining places

* For suggested identifications and criticisms of them, see Buhl, *Geog.* 269; G. A. Smith's art. "Ar" in *EBi.*

lie between the upper Arnon (v.[13] n.) and the N.E. of the Dead Sea, and thus the line of march is north-westerly.

16. *Be'er*] Like the synonymous term ʿÊn (ʿAin), Be'er, which means ***a well***, frequently appears by itself or defined by a following genitive, as a place name. The OT. mentions Be'er (Jud. 9^{21}), Be'eroth (2 S. 4^{2}), Be'er-shebaʿ, Be'eroth-bene-yaʿaḳan (Dt. 10^{6}), Be'er-elim (Is. 15^{8}). The present *may* be an abbreviated form of the last. Such abbreviations are common (*EBi. s.v.* "Names," § 92). If so, to judge from Is. 15^{8}, it lay in northern Moab. But the site is quite uncertain. —16b reads like a note inserted by another hand; in v.[16a] Be'er = *Well* is a proper name; otherwise, as in v.[16b], it would have the article: moreover, had the writer of the itinerary wished to define the well meant, he would more naturally have written, "And from there to the well whereof Yahweh spake," etc. The note appears to refer to a story no longer extant; ct. the terms in which a similar incident is described in 20^{8}; for the rabbinic interpretation, see phil. n.—*Then sang Israel this song*] Ex. 15^{1} (J). The clause with the song introduced by it would follow v.[16a] suitably enough; it is less suitable after v.[16b], which speaks only of Yahweh's promise of water, not of the fulfilment of such a promise. Moreover, the terms of the promise in v.[16b] lead the reader to expect that Yahweh will provide the water miraculously: if this be really intended, then the song itself does not answer to the situation, for it speaks of a well naturally made of service by the leaders of the people.

On the song, see W. R. Smith, *British Quarterly Review*, lxv. (Jan. 1877), 45 f.; *Religion of the Semites*, 127, 167; [2] 139, 169 n. 3, 183 (and in criticism of this Köberle, *Natur u. Geist*, 114); Budde in *New World* (1895, March), 136-144=*Preussische Jahrbücher*, 1895, pp. 491-580; Cheyne, art. "Beer" in *EBi.* The original character of the song is obscured by the historical setting which is given to it. It is scarcely a historical poem, but belongs rather to a particular class of popular poetry, of which, unfortunately, very few Hebrew examples survive. Such poetry consisted especially of short snatches sung in honour of the vine at time of vintage, or of wells and springs, and even, as Ewald (*History* (Eng. tr.), ii. 203 n. 3) put it, "of popular songs accompanying the alternate strokes of hard labour." No complete vintage song survives, though a line of one is probably quoted in Is. 65^{8} (cp. Ps. 57 title), and imitations of the class may be found in Is. $5^{1f.}$ 27^{2-5}. The present lines are a complete, or all but complete, popular song, addressed to a well, in which, perhaps, as W. R. Smith suggested, "the Hebrew women as they stand round the fountain waiting their turn to draw, coax forth the water, which wells up all too slowly for their impatience." Budde and Cheyne trace the origin of the song to the Negeb, where wells were highly prized (cp. Gn. $21^{22ff.}$ $26^{15ff.}$), and without which it is impossible to live (Jud. 1^{15}, Jos. 15^{19}). Budde may be right in detecting in the song an allusion to a custom by which when a well had been discovered it was lightly covered over, and then, on a subsequent occasion, solemnly opened with a symbolic action of the sceptre-like staves of the Sheikhs of the clan, and formally declared clan property. Two interesting parallels are cited: Ḳazwīnī (i. 189) relates, "When the water [of the wells of Ilabistān] failed, a feast was held at the source, with music and dancing, to induce it to flow again . . ." And Nilus (Migne, *Patrologia Græca*, tom. lxxix. col. 648), as Goldziher (*Abhandlungen*, i. 58) has pointed out, reports of the nomadic Arabs, that when they found a well they danced by it and sang songs to it (Καθελόντες οὖν τῶν καμήλων τὰ φορτία, ἐκείνας μὲν ἐκμένεσθαι διαφιᾶσιν ἐλευθέρῳ ποδί· αὐτοὶ δὲ περιτρέχουσι τῷ ὕδατι πίνοντες, περικλυζόμενοι, λουόμενοι, οὐκ ἔχοντες ἁπλῶς, ὅπως χρήσωνται τῇ φιλοτιμίᾳ τοῦ ὕδατος. τουτῷ δὲ προσχορεύοντες καὶ τὴν πηγὴν ἀνυμνοῦντες ὁρῶσιν κατὰ τὴν ὑπώρειαν ἴχνος δωματίου μικροῦ). Modern travellers speak of the songs used by the Bedawin as they draw water for their flocks; Seetzen, *Reisen*, ii. 223.

Whether W. R. Smith is justified in seeing in the song the influence of well-worship is less certain; the well, it is true, is addressed as a living thing; but so also, to cite merely the closest parallel, is the vineyard in Is. 27^{2}; see, further, Köberle, *loc. cit.*

To attempt any more precise determination of the date when this ancient popular song was composed than is suggested by the foregoing remarks, would obviously be fruitless.

Spring up, O well! Sing ye to it!
To the well which the princes dug,
Which the nobles of the people delved,
With the leader's wand, with their staffs.

The song is addressed to a well that is already known and celebrated, rather than to one just discovered. The perfect tenses in the second and third lines are historical. The drawers, as they stand round the well, pray it to supply them again as in the past, exhort one another to sing to the well, and recall the fact that the well was found and secured to them by the Sheikhs of their clan. A similar popular tradition attached to Jacob's well near Shechem (John 4^{12}).

Sing ye to it] cp. Is. 27^{2}.—*With the wand*] not, as in AV., "by the direction of the lawgiver," for מחקק signified the *commander's* or *leader's wand* as well as *the commander* himself See Gn. 49^{10}, Dt. 33^{21}, with Di.'s and Driver's notes thereon. The second word (משענת) is regularly used of the staff employed in ordinary life (Ex. 21^{19}, Zech. 8^{4}). A story told of Mohammed illustrates the use of the staff referred to in the poem: some wells at Hodeibia being choked with sand, Mohammed made one of his followers descend one of them, and with an arrow—the only implement at hand—scrape away the sand; afterward the water flowed freely.* Di., however, on the ground that the well must have been too considerable for its waters to have been thus brought to the surface, explains *with the wand* as meaning *at the instruction and under the superintendence of the leaders.* But this assumes an unparalleled and improbable use of ב. Preferable to this is the explanation that the action with the wand is symbolical (see above).—*And from Wilderness to Mattanah*] If the text be right, Wilderness (מדבר), being without the article, must be a proper name. But this is improbable. Moreover, the place last reached, and from which, therefore, the departure is actually made, is Be'er (v.[16a]); hence many, with 𝔊, read, *and from Be'er to Mattanah.* But Budde questions whether this was the original text of 𝔊 (see phil. n.), and, omitting the ו (= *and*), regards the last two words of v.[18] as the last line of the song, and renders, *From the wilderness a gift.* For *mattanah = a gift*, see, *e.g.*, Gn. 25^{6}. The omission of the article before *wilderness* would be in accordance with common poetical usage (Kön. iii. 292).—19. *And from Mattanah*] the words are omitted in $𝔊^{L}$; and rightly, if Budde's view of the text (see last note) be correct. In any case the site of Mattanah is unknown; in *OS.* (137^{30}, 277^{82}) *Mathane, Μαθθανέμ,* is identified with Maschana, said to be situated on the Arnon, 12 miles E. of Medeba; but the two definitions of the site of Maschana are incompatible, since Medeba was considerably N. of Arnon. According to Budde the original text of the itinerary (v.[16–19]) ran, *And from there to Be'er, and from Be'er to Naḥalī'el, and from Naḥalī'el to Bamoth.*—*Naḥalī'el*] the name means *the wady of God,*

* Muir, *Mahomet*,[3] 343 f.

"which is not an unfit name for the Wady Zerḳā Maʿīn with its healing springs."* The Wady Zerḳā Maʿīn bisects that part of the eastern shore of the Dead Sea which extends northwards from the mouth of the Arnon. A station on its course would therefore be about half-way between the Arnon and the Wady ʿAyûn Mûsa (v.[20] n.). Still the identification of Naḥali'el with the Wady Zerḳā Maʿīn must either govern or be governed by that of *Bamoth*, itself uncertain. *Bamoth*, or *high places*, were as characteristic of the land of Moab (*Meshaʿ*, l. 3; Is. 15^2 16^{12}, Jer. 48^{35}) as they were, down to the time of Isaiah's reformation, of the land of Israel; and, consequently, the generic term *Bamoth*, like others, such as Be'er (v.[16] n.), may in more than one instance have become the proper name of a place. This being so, the identification of the Bamoth of this passage with the Bamoth-Baʿal of 22^{41}, Jos. 13^{17}, and the Beth-Bamoth of *Meshaʿ*, l. 27, is, though probable, not certain. The alternative forms of the name of the same place would be in accordance with well-established custom.† This identification of Bamoth, Bamoth-Baʿal, and Beth-Bamoth being assumed, the place lay in the territory north of Arnon which passed to and fro between Israel and Moab, was loftily situated, and commanded a view over "the plains of Moab" (22^{41}, Jos. 13^{17}). Some high place not far south of the valley of v.[20] (? the Wady ʿAyûn Mûsa) seems best to meet the requirements. Some ‡ place it near the Wady Jideid, "in the dolmens immediately north of El-Maslûbîyeh," the view from which is described by Tristram (*Moab*, 322 f.). In considering the claims of this identification, too much ought not to be made of the presence of dolmens, for they are particularly prevalent in Moab.§ Others,‖ attaching importance to the order of mention in Jos. 13^{17}, seek Bamoth between Dibon and Baʿal Maʿon (see notes on v.[30] and 32^{38}), and in particular on Mt. ʿAṭṭârûs, which rises south of the Wady

* G. A. Smith, *Hist. Geog.* 562.

† See the present writer's discussion in *EBi.*, "Names," § 92 f.; *HPN.* 125–136, 324.

‡ G. A. Smith, *Hist. Geog.* 562; Conder, *Heth and Moab*, 145 f.

§ Conder, *Palestine*, 156.

‖ Hengst., Di., Str.

Zerḳā Maʿîn. In this case Naḥali'el, being mentioned before Bamoth in a northward march, must be one of the less important wadies between Arnon and the Wady Zerḳā Māʿîn.—20. From Bamoth the route is followed to a valley (גיא) near the N.E. of the Dead Sea. So much seems tolerably clear; but in detail the v. is difficult of interpretation. Nothing *excludes* the identification * of the "valley" with the Wady ʿAyûn Mûsā, and on certain views of the text and meaning of the passage there is much that favours it; but it is not fully established.—*The region of Moab*] שדה מואב is an alternative term for *the land* (ארץ) *of Moab*. It is found in Gn. 36^{35} and several times in Ruth. Cp. *the land* (ארץ) *of Seʿîr, the region* (שדה) *of Edom*. This wide definition of the district where the "valley" lay required limitation; this follows in the words *the head* (or *top*) *of the Pisgah*, which may be intended as an appositional clause limiting *the region of Moab*, or as in apposition to and explanatory of *the valley*. In either case the effect is sufficiently awkward to justify a suspicion that the text is corrupt, or that the words *the head of the Pisgah* have been inserted by an editor without regard to style. *The Pisgah* (הפסגה) appears to be used of the western edge of the Moabite plateau which falls steeply to the Dead Sea, and, perhaps, more particularly of that part of it which lies to the N.E. of the Dead Sea: † the term is elsewhere used in 23^{14}, Dt. $3^{17.27}$ 4^{49} 34^{1}, Jos. 12^{3} 13^{20} †. The root פסג in Aramaic (Dr. *Deut.* p. 58) and Mishnic Hebrew (Levy, *Neu-hebr. Wörterbuch*) means *to cleave*; the name may therefore have been given on account of the aspect of the range as seen from below. *The head of the Pisgah* (ראש הפסגה), mentioned also in 23^{14}, Dt. 3^{27} 34^{1}†, appears by itself to be a collective term for the promontories or headlands which run out from the Moabite plateau, generally at a slightly lower level than the plateau itself. The several individual headlands, which, regarded from below, are peaks 4000 feet high, had separate names: two of these are mentioned elsewhere, viz. the Field of the Watchers (23^{14}) and Mt. Nebo (Dt. 34^{1}).—*And it looks out*

* Di., G. A. Smith, *Hist. Geog.* 564.

† Buhl, *Geog.* § 76; G. A. Smith, *Hist. Geog.* 562.

upon the Jeshîmon] The word ישימן, from the root ישם = *to be waste, desolate*, is used in poetry, without the art., of the wilderness of wandering; see, *e.g.*, Dt. 32^{10}. With the art. it is used in certain prose passages virtually as a geographical proper name. Such is the use of the word here. Used thus it appears in 1 S. $23^{19.\,24}$ $26^{1.\,3}$ to be the name of the desolate country of Judah above the northern part of the *western* shore of the Dead Sea.* It is commonly supposed,† in view of the present passage and 23^{28}, that the same name also attached to the waste country in the Jordan valley just N. of the Dead Sea and *east* of the river, a district in which was situated Beth-Jeshimoth (33^{49} n.).—The verb *and it looks out* (ונשקפה) is in 𝔐 fem.; the subst. should therefore be *the Pisgah*, the only unambiguously fem. noun in the context. But the reading of the verbal form is open to suspicion (see phil. n.). If corrected to a masc. it would still be preferable to refer it to *head* (cp. 23^{28}) rather than, with Di., to *the valley*. But in any case if the Jeshimon intended lay to the N.E. of the Dead Sea, the whole description points somewhat clearly to identifying the "valley" with the Wady ʿAyûn Mûsa,‡ which descends from Mt. Nebā through the district which, on the hypothesis, was called the Jeshimon, into the northern end of the Dead Sea.

The following passages from G. A. Smith, *Hist. Geog.* 562–565, will substantiate some of the statements in the preceding notes, and further elucidate the passage:—"During their journey over the Tableland, Israel had no outlook westward across the Dead Sea. For westward the Plateau rises a little and shuts out all view, but on the other side of the rise it breaks up into promontories slightly lower than itself, which run out over the ʿArabah and Dead Sea valley, and afford a view of all Western Palestine. Seen from below, or from across Jordan, these headlands, rising three or four thousand feet by slope and precipice from the valley, stand out like separate mountains. But eastward they do not rise from the Moab Plateau—they are simply projections or capes of the latter, and you ride from it on to them without experiencing any differences of level, except, it may be, a decline of a few feet."

"One thing is certain: this journey [Nu. 21^{16-20}], though it is described

---

* G. A. Smith, *Hist. Geog.* 312, 513; Buhl, *Geog.* 96.

† *E.g.* Di., Ges.-Buhl (*s.v.* ישימן), Str., G. A. Smith, *Hist. Geog.* 564 n. 1.

‡ Di., G. A. Smith, *Hist. Geog.* 564.

in the book of Numbers before the war with Sihon [Nu. $21^{21ff.}$], must have come after the latter. No host, so large and cumbered as this, could have ventured down any of the glens from the Plateau to the Jordan before their own warriors had occupied Heshbon [v.^{25}], for Heshbon, standing above them, commands these glens."

16. ומשם בארה] 𝔊 καὶ ἐκεῖθεν τὸ φρέαρ: so also 𝔖 𝔙 (*ex eo loco apparuit puteus*): 𝔗^{O} (ומתמן אתיהיבת להון בירא). These renderings probably embody the Haggadah that the water produced from the rock at Ḳadesh ($20^{8ff.}$) followed the Israelites in their subsequent wanderings (cp. 1 Cor. 10^{4}). 𝔗$^{\text{Jer and Jon}}$ take the following verses as a description of the places through which the water followed the people. See Driver in *Expos.*, 1889 (Jan.), 15–18.—הבאר אשר אמר] cp. 10^{29}.—**17.** עלי באר] 𝔊 (wrongly) *ἐπὶ τοῦ φρέατος*. S עלה, which should be pointed either עֲלֶה, באר being treated as masc., or עֲלִי *the well is springing up*.—**20.** ונשקפה] Frequentative, *and it used to look*, if the text be correct: Driver, *Tenses*,[3] p. 162 n. 1. But we should probably read הנשקפה (cp. 23^{28} and the *τὸ βλέπον* of 𝔊 here), or with S הנשקף. גיא is regularly masc.; the single instance of גיא as a fem. (Zech. 14^{4}) is decidedly suspicious in view of the fact that it is treated in the following verses as masc.

21–33. The conquest and occupation of the country between Arnon and Jabboḳ, then held by the Amorites under king Siḥon.

The story of the defeat of Siḥon is told elsewhere, rhetorically expanded in Dt. 2^{24-37}, and in a shorter form in Jud. 11^{19-22}. There are many allusions to it (see v.^{21} n.).

The present story is probably compiled from two sources at least, and possibly from three; for the song (v.$^{27-30}$) may have been derived direct from an ancient collection by the compiler. Jud. 11^{19-21} appears related to one only of these (E), but Dt. 2^{24-36} may depend either on the present composite story or on both of those that lie behind it; for it refers to the occupation of "cities" (Dt. 2^{34-36}) as well as of the country as a whole (2^{31}). S has in turn expanded the story in Numbers by interpolations from Dt., viz. of Dt. $2^{24f.}$ before v.^{21}, of the words דברי שלום after האמרי (v.^{21}) from Dt. 2^{26}, of the fuller message of Dt. 2^{27-29a} (mainly in place of v.^{22}), of Dt. 2^{31} (with the necessary change of אלי to אל משה) after בגבלו in v.^{23}; cp. Introduction, § 14.

21–24a (E). The Israelites send messengers to the Amorite king Siḥon, asking, as they had previously asked the Edomites ($20^{14ff.}$), to be permitted to pass peaceably through his country. Siḥon refuses, marches against Israel, engages in battle with them at Jahaṣ, and is defeated. The Israelites occupy his country.

21. *And Israel*] so Jud. 11^{19}, but 𝔊^{ABL} *Moses*; cp. 𝔐 in 20^{14} and Dt. 2^{26}.—*Siḥon, king of the Amorites*] Siḥon is similarly titled (מלך האמרי) in v.^{26} 32^{33}, 1 K. 4^{19}, Ps. 135^{11} 136^{19} (cp. Dt. 31^{4}, Jos. 2^{10} 9^{10}): cp. מלך אמרי v.^{29}. Frequently he is entitled after his chief city, *king of Ḥeshbôn*; so Dt. 2$^{26.30}$ 3^{6} 29^{6}, Jos. 12^{5} 13^{27}, cp. Neh. 9^{22}. Frequently also the two descriptions are combined: e.g. *Siḥon, king of Ḥeshbôn, the Amorite* (Dt. 2^{24}): *Siḥon the king of the Amorites, who dwelt in Ḥeshbôn* (Dt. 1^{4}): see also Dt. 3^{2} 4^{46}, Jos. 12^{2} 13$^{10.21}$, Jud. 11^{19}. In the parallels to the present passage, Dt. 2^{26} gives the alternative description only (*king of Ḥeshbôn*), Jud. 11^{19} gives both. How closely associated were the names of Siḥon and Ḥeshbôn appears in v.$^{26-28}$, Jer. 48^{45}.—The territory of Siḥon at this time extended, according to the present narrative, from Arnon to Jabboḳ (v.^{24}), and from the wilderness to Jordan (Jud. 11^{22}). The embassy, as in the similar negotiations with Edom (20^{16}), would naturally be sent when Israel had reached or were stationed on, but before they had crossed, the *borders* of the country through which they requested permission to pass, and therefore while they were still in the wilderness E. of the Amorite territory. That the embassy was, as a matter of fact, sent from the wilderness appears indirectly from v.^{23}, and the direct statement to this effect is preserved in Dt. 2^{26}, which defines the point as "the wilderness of Ḳedēmoth." In v.^{21}, then, the people are still where they were in v.^{13}.—**22.** The message closely resembles, but is slightly shorter than, that sent to the Edomites (20^{17}). It appears in a much shorter form in Jud. 11^{19} and much expanded in S and Dt. 2$^{27-29}$.—*Let me now pass through*] see n. on 20^{14}. The remaining vbs. of the v. are 1st pl. in 𝔐: but the singular is retained almost throughout in the parallel matter in S and Dt. 2$^{27-29}$.—**23.** *To the wilderness*] N. of Arnon and E. of Moab; cp. v.^{13}, Dt. 2^{26}, and n. on v.^{21} above.—*To Jahaṣ*] the site* remains uncertain. It lay somewhere on the Moabite plateau (Jer. 48^{21}), and in 1 Ch. 6$^{63\,(78)}$

* Tristram, *Moab*, 124 f.; G. A. Smith, *Hist. Geog.* 559 n. 8. In addition to the references to Jahaṣ given in the text, the OT. references are Dt. 2^{32}, Jos. 13^{18} 21^{36}, Jud. 11^{20}, Is. 15^{4}, Jer. 48^{34}.

is mentioned along with "Beṣer in the wilderness" and Ḳedemoth, which must also be sought in or near the wilderness, since it gives its name to a part of it (Dt. 2[26]). Mesha''s allusion to Jahaṣ ("I took it to add it to Daibon"; l. 20) may imply that it lay not far from Dibon. These data for what they are worth point to a place not far north of Arnon * and close to the wilderness; and this would quite satisfy the requirements of the present story. It is unnecessary to locate Jahaṣ actually in the wilderness. Israel, hearing of the approach of Siḥon, would march to meet him as he was on his way towards the wilderness.—**24.** *From Arnon to Jabboḳ*] On the Arnon, see v.[13] n.—The Jabboḳ is by common consent † identified with the Nahr ez-Zerḳā (distinct from the Wady Zerḳā Ma'īn mentioned in the n. on v.[20]), the head waters of which "rise on the edge of Moab, only some 18 miles from the Jordan, yet to the east of the water-parting. So the river flows at first desertwards, under the name of Ammân, past Rabbath-'Ammon to the great Hajj road. There it turns north, fetches a wider compass north-west, cuts in two the range of Gilead, and by a very winding bed flows west-south-west to the Jordan [which it joins at a point about 25 miles in a direct line from the Dead Sea]. The whole course, not counting the windings, is over 60 miles" (G. A. Smith, *Hist. Geog.* p. 584). Like the Arnon, it has always formed one of the frontiers of E. Palestine (*ib.*: cp. also p. 539). In Jud. 11[22] (cp. v.[13]) Jabboḳ is quite clearly given as the *northern* boundary of the Amorites, the eastern and western borders being also given as the wilderness and the Jordan respectively. It is probable, therefore, that here also the Jabboḳ is the northern boundary, and consequently that *unto the children of 'Ammon* (cp. Jos. 13[10]) is not in apposition to Jabboḳ, but states tersely a third, viz. the *eastern*, boundary (cp. Jud. 11[13]). The whole means, then, that Israel occupied the land between Arnon on the S. and Jabboḳ on the N., as far

* North of Dibon, if we may suppose Jerome well informed, and Debus an error for Dibon in his statement "et usque hodie ostenditur inter Medaban et Debus," *Onom.* 131[17].

† See, *e.g.*, Buhl, *Geog.* 122; G. A. Smith, *Hist. Geog.* 583 f.

east as the ʿAmmonite country; this last lay round about the upper courses of the Nahr ez-Zerḳā on which Rabbath-ʿAmmon was situated; cp. Jos. 13^{10}, Dt. 2^{37} 3^{16}. Still this mode of defining the eastern border may be due merely to the compiler (see next note); and the original definition may rather be found in Jud. 11^{22}.—*For Jaʿzer was the border of the children of ʿAmmon*] This is the reading of 𝔊, and probably of the original text. The meaning is that Jaʿzer was on the boundary between the Amorites and the ʿAmmonites (cp. v.^{32}). In Jud. 11^{19-22} (‖ v.$^{21-24a}$ here) no reference is made to ʿAmmon. Since the reference to cities indicates that the compiler in v.^{25} draws on a source different from that used in v.^{24a} (see p. 280), the transition to this source may well be placed at the words *unto the sons of ʿAmmon* in v.^{24b}, which attach awkwardly to the preceding. If this be admitted it is unnecessary to regard the last clause of the verse as a gloss.* The text of 𝔐, *for the border of the children of ʿAmmon was strong* (in which עז, *strong*, is probably a corruption of יעזר, *Jaʿzer*), has been explained (1) as giving the reason why *Siḥon* had not extended his conquests further: † such a clause might have followed v.^{26}; it is out of place here; (2) as accounting for the fact that the Israelites did not capture the ʿAmmonite as well as the Amorite country; in that case the passage would represent a different point of view from Dt. 2^{19}, according to which Yahweh commanded the Israelites to leave the ʿAmmonites unmolested in the possession of their ancestor Lot. Linguistically the rendering of עז by *strong* in the sense of "*well fortified*," whether naturally or artificially, is unparalleled and questionable. Jaʿzer is mentioned frequently in OT.; see more particularly Jos. 13^{25}, which supports the suggestion of v.^{32} that it was not at this time, as in the Maccabæan period it had become (1 Mac. 5^{8}), ʿAmmonitish. During parts of the interval it belonged to Moab (Is. $16^{8f.}$, Jer. 48^{32}). The site is uncertain; according to Eusebius (*Onom.* $264^{98ff.}$) it lay 15 (Roman) miles from Ḥeshbôn and 10 W., according to Jerome about 8 W. (*Onom.* $86^{23f.}$; cp.

* Meyer, *ZATW.* i. 120 n. 1; Stade, *GVI.* 120 n. 1.
† Knobel, Keil.

Eusebius, *Onom.* 262^{29}) of Philadelphia (= Rabbath-ʿAmmon). These data are tolerably satisfied by the *site* of Sar (two hours S.W. of Rabbath-ʿAmmon), or the neighbouring place Ṣîr; * but the sibilants in these names are not the same as in Jaʿzer. Cheyne † identifies Jaʿzer with Yājūz, a little W. of El-Jubeihāt (= Jogbehah, 32^{35}), N.W. of Rabbath-ʿAmmon; others with Beit-zeraʿ, a long way S.W. of Rabbath-ʿAmmon.‡ —**25.** Israel captures and enters on the occupation of all the Amorite cities. This is parallel to v.[24a]; but it is differently expressed, and represents a rather different point of view. Here the cities, there the country as a whole, is occupied. —*All these cities*] There is nothing in what now precedes for these words to refer to. The verse is probably a closing summary of the capture of several individual Amorite cities (cp. v.[32] and 32^{3}), and the source from whence it is derived may have represented the conquest of the Amorite country E. of Jordan in the same manner as the conquest of Western Canaan is represented in Jud. 1, *i.e.* as a gradual conquest city by city rather than as a sudden and complete occupation of the whole country (v.[24]).—*And Israel dwelt in all the cities of the Amorites*] the parallel statement in E, "and Israel dwelt in the *land* of the Amorites," is postponed to v.[31]. Possibly as an editorial link with the following verses, the most famous of these Amorite cities is now specially mentioned, *Ḥeshbôn and all its daughters*, the last phrase meaning all the dependent towns. According to $32^{1ff.}$ Ḥeshbôn, though conquered, was still unoccupied by the Hebrews at a later time than this. The site of Ḥeshbôn is certain, the name surviving in Ḥesbân, which is finely situated on hills higher than Mt. Nebā, which is 5 miles away to the S.W.§—**26.** Ḥeshbôn was at the time in question one of the Amorite cities; for though it had previously belonged to Moab, it had been wrested, with all the country N. of Arnon, by Siḥon from the former king of Moab.—*For Ḥeshbôn was the city of Siḥon the king of the Amorites*] cp. v.[21] n.—*All his land*

* Seetzen, *Reisen*, i. 397 f., 406, ii. 318, iv. 216; Buhl, *Geog.* 263 f.

† In *EBi.*, following Oliphant, *Land of Gilead*, 231 ff..

‡ *Survey of Eastern Palestine*, i. 91.

§ *Ib.* i. 104–108.

out of his hand unto Arnon] perhaps this originally ran, *All his land from Jabboḳ to Arnon*: cp. v.[24], Jud. 11[22], and see phil. note, below. In any case, as in v.[13], Arnon is the southern limit of Siḥon's conquest.

23. יהצה] The original name of the town was יהץ (Is. 15[4]. Jer. 48[34], *Mesha'* ll. 19 f.); but in OT. it is more frequently found with the locative ending (note the penultimate accentuation), whether (as here and in Dt. 2[32]) with or, as elsewhere, without any locative force; cp. תמנה and תמנתה (*e.g.* Jud. 14[2]); Kön. iii. 269*a b*.—**24.** לפי חרב] an old phrase; not used by P, but common to JE D (CH. 150[JE]).—**26.** מידו] the position of the clause between ארצו and the clause that defines it עד ארנן is suspicious. 𝕲 *from 'Aro'er* is in itself quite improbable, for the well-known 'Aro'er lay close to the Arnon, and it is unlikely that the boundary would have been defined by the 'Aro'er of Jos. 13[25]; but ידו (𝕳) and ערער (𝕲) may be different corruptions of יבק: see above and Meyer, *ZATW*. i. 129 n. 3.

27–30. At this point the editor introduces an old poem in illustration of his narrative. The point which he probably intends it to illustrate is the conquest of Moab by the Amorites (v.[26b]).—*Wherefore the reciters of meshālīm say*] the *similarity* of the introductory formulæ here and in v.[14] may point to the same editor; but if so the *difference* between them indicates that he has taken the two songs from different sources, the one from a book, the other directly from men's lips. The frequently repeated suggestion that this poem, like that in v.[14f.], was derived from the *Book of Yahweh's Battles* is therefore improbable. The persons who were accustomed to recite this poem are called הַמֹּשְׁלִים; the pl., the art., the frequentative tense of the following vb. (יאמרו) all indicate that a *class* of people is intended. The vb. משל is a denominative; it might mean *to make a māshāl*: in usage it actually means *to utter or repeat a māshāl*, and that not always, at all events, of one's own making (*e.g.* Ezek. 18[2f.]). So the class here described consisted of men who were primarily *reciters* of poems. It is easy to imagine how these reciters went about in Israel and, especially in time of war, by reciting poems like the present (cp. Is. 14[4ff.]; also Hab. 2[6]), and thus recalling former victories, stimulated and encouraged the people (cp. Jud. 5[31]). But possibly the *repertoire* of these "ballad-singers" (Perowne in Smith, *DB*. ii. 584*a*) was not confined to odes of war and victory; and there is certainly no justification for limiting the sense of the participle of the denominative verb here used to *satirists*, for *māshāl* (23^7 n.; see also *Addenda*) is a term of various applications, and *satire* is neither the original nor even the most frequent meaning of the word. Consequently the interpretation of the following poem must be determined purely by internal evidence, and without any prejudice that it must be a satire.

The view that the poem is the work of an Amorite poet celebrating the victory of his people over Moab* may be dismissed as inherently improbable. Sufficient ambiguities and possibilities of interpretation remain, however, when the poem is regarded as being, what it doubtless was, the work of a Hebrew poet. The one thing that is clear is that the poem celebrates a victory over Moab. Every thing else is more or less uncertain. The ambiguous details are dealt with in the notes. It is necessary here to discuss briefly the general motive and purpose of the poem.

1. Since Ewald,† the view most commonly held has been that the poem is a satiric ode.‡ In the words of W. R. Smith, "the children of Israel invite the Amorites to return and fortify the demolished fastness of their king, Siḥon, exalting that monarch's prowess against Moab, in order to bring into stronger light the valour of Israel, beneath which the invincible Amorite and his stronghold had for ever fallen." § On this view, v.[27f.] is addressed mockingly by the victorious Israelites to the now conquered Amorites; in v.[29] the Israelites address the Moabites, who had been conquered not by themselves, but by the Amorites: in v.[30] the Israelites exultantly record their own conquest of the Amorites. In brief, the thought is—the Amorites destroyed Moab, but *we*, the Israelites, have destroyed *them*, viz. the Amorites. It will thus be seen that v.[30] should contain a strong antithesis,

* Knobel. † *History* (Eng. tr.), ii. 205–207.

‡ Ewald's view is substantially adopted by W. R. Smith (*Brit. Quarterly Review*, lxv. (Jan. 1877) 67), Keil, Str., G. A. Smith (*Hist. Geog.* 560); cp. Sayce, *Early Hist. of the Hebrews*, 227.

§ *British Quarterly Review*, lxv. (Jan. 1877) 67.

both subject and object requiring emphasis. Unfortunately the text of v.[30] is very questionable; but one thing is certain: it does not contain an emphatic antithesis. The first word of the v. (ונירם) may be a verbal form with a pronominal suffix; but even if so, neither subject nor object is emphasised; the construction with the impf. and waw conversive should smoothly carry on what precedes. There is not the slightest indication that the conquerors of v.[30] are different from those who are represented as conquerors in v.[27f.], and consequently the poem itself contains no indication that v.[27f.] are tauntingly spoken. On this ground the view in question appears to the present writer in the highest degree improbable.

2. Breaking loose from the suggestion of the Hebrew editor and the last line of v.[29] (which they regard as a gloss) that the poem has anything to do with the Amorites, Meyer and Stade have argued that it is a triumphal ode celebrating throughout a victory of Israel over Moab. They regard the first word of v.[30] as a noun. But even if it should be taken as a verb, it is no longer open to the same criticism as in the case of the first view of the poem. No emphatic antithesis is required at this point by the present theory; for the same people (the Israelites) who in v.[27] exhort one another to occupy the cities captured from Moab, continue, though no longer in the second person of mutual exhortation, but directly in the first person, to describe their destruction of Moab. This theory is not without difficulties, though the necessity for regarding v.[29e] as a gloss is scarcely one of these. The chief difficulty lies in the fact that the natural, though perhaps not the inevitable, inference is that Siḥon was actually a king of *Moab*, and only became turned into a king of the Amorites in later traditions.

The determination of the date or the poem must obviously depend on the interpretation. Stade not unreasonably refers it to about B.C. 900, the period of the conquest of Moab by 'Omri which is referred to in Mesha''s inscription; cp. Wellhausen, *Comp.* 343. On the first view of the interpretation the poem might be much older.

[27] Come ye to Ḥeshbôn! Let it be rebuilt!
Let the city of Siḥon be established!

28 For fire went out from Ḥeshbôn,
Flame from the town of Siḥon;
It devoured ʿAr of Moab,
The lords of the high places of Arnon.
29 Woe to thee, Moab!
Undone art thou, people of Kemosh:
Who has made his sons fugitives,
And his daughters captives,
[To an Amorite king Siḥon.]
30 So their posterity has perished from Ḥeshbôn to Dibon
. . . . . to Medeba.

Come ye to Ḥeshbôn] the speakers are the Israelites: either they exhort themselves to occupy and rebuild the cities destroyed in their conquest of the Amorites, or they mockingly address the conquered Amorites, according to which of the views discussed above be adopted.—*The city of Siḥon*] an epithet of Ḥeshbôn, just as "the city of David" (2 S. 5^7, 1 K. 2^{10}, and often) is of a part of Jerusalem. That Ḥeshbôn ranked as the chief city of Siḥon is evident from the fact that *king of Ḥeshbôn* and *king of the Amorites* are alternative titles given to him (v.[21] n.). Certainly such a description of *Ḥeshbôn* in an Israelitish triumphal ode over Moab would be most easily accounted for if Siḥon were a king of Moab. Yet it is possible that among the Israelites this name clung to Ḥeshbôn long after the Amorite power had passed away.——*Be rebuilt*] בנה frequently has this sense; see Jos. 6^{26}, Am. 9^{14}.—**28.** *For fire went forth from Ḥeshbôn*] this appears to give the reason for the summons of v.[27]:—Come and rebuild Ḥeshbôn, for now, together with the country as far S. as Arnon, it lies overthrown and wasted by war. Those who adopt Ewald's view of the poem give no satisfactory explanation of the *for* (כי): Di., for example, says vaguely that the ground or explanation of the mocking summons of v.[27] is not contained in v.[28] alone, but in v.[28-30]. It has, indeed, been subtly argued that the phrase *fire went forth from Ḥeshbôn* cannot refer to the desolation of Ḥeshbôn itself by a foreign foe, but must mean that Ḥeshbôn caused the desolation of Moab.*

* Kuen. *Th. Tijd.* xviii. 525; Di.

But two of the passages (Lev. 10^2, Nu. 16^{35}) cited by Kue. to prove this ought at once to be dismissed from consideration, since the phrases used are significantly different, viz. not *from*, but *from with* (מאת) and *from before* (מלפני). It is true that in the others (Jud. $9^{15.20}$, Ezek. 19^{14}) the phrase is used of the *starting-point* of the conflagration, but surely not of *the cause*; the bramble of Jotham's parable, from which fire goes forth, is itself consumed, and not apparently, in the intention of the writer, by self-combustion: the case is similar in Ezek. 19^{14}. The actual meaning of the phrase is rendered still clearer by the use of the Hiphil (followed by מתוך), which admits of the statement of the cause as well as of the starting-point of the conflagration (Ezek. 28^{18}). To judge, then, by the use of the phrase, the meaning of the poem is that Ḥeshbôn and the country southwards to Arnon suffered the same fate, the cause of which is not directly stated, but is most naturally understood to be the speakers in the poem. Obviously, if this be the meaning, it does not apply to a war victoriously made on Moab by the king of Ḥeshbôn. Further, since the line of devastation and conquest proceeds *southwards* from Ḥeshbôn, it cannot refer to Israel's conquest of the Amorites, which proceeded northwards from Arnon towards Ḥeshbôn. On the other hand, it describes the natural line of conquest in a war waged victoriously by Israel, during the period of the monarchy, on Moab. It is, of course, legitimate, and, if the first view of the poem were adopted, it would be best to render *for fire had gone forth*. But this rendering is not necessary: the emphatic word naturally stands first after the causal כי, even when no pluperfect sense is required or even possible (cp. Gn. $2^{3.23}$ 3^{20}): here the subj. (*fire*) is put first because it is the emphatic word, since it and not the verb contains the idea of destruction.—*'Ar of Moab*] v.[15] n.—*The lords of the heights of Arnon*] For the first word (בעלי), 𝔊 has a verb (κατέπιεν) parallel to the verb in the previous clause. 𝔊 apparently read the word ותבלע = *and swallowed down*, which is hardly suitable. But some verb implying destruction may well have stood in the original text. If 𝔥 be right, the *lords* are the *proprietors*, *freeholders* of the district (Jos. 24^{11}, Jud. 9^{2}, 1 S. 23^{11}). The word במות appears to be used here without a religious reference simply of the heights along the Arnon (cp. Ezek. 36^{2}, Dt. 32^{13}): but 𝔗 interprets the phrase *lords of the heights* as *heathen priests*.—**29.** The poet addresses Moab, the conquest of whose northern territory has been just described. *Kemosh* was the name of the national deity of Moab: 1 K. 11^{7} and Mesha''s inscription, *passim*. The Israelites, who called themselves *the people of Yahweh* (Jud. 5^{11}, Ex. 15^{16}), quite naturally called the Moabites *the people of Kemosh*: for in early times the Israelites questioned the real existence of the god of a neighbouring people just as little as the real existence of Yahweh; see, especially, Jud. $11^{24ff.}$. The disasters that had befallen the Moabites proved to the author of the poem the anger of the Moabite god with his people; for it is to Kemosh that he ascribes the flight and capture of the Moabite men and women. The same view was taken of similar disasters by the Moabite king Meshaʿ himself, who writes: "ʿOmri . . . afflicted Moab for many days, because Kemosh was angry with his land" (Mesha''s Inscr. ll. 4 f.). The Moabite men and women are described as *sons* and *daughters* of Kemosh in accordance with an ancient mode of thought which has left its mark on a type of personal names common to many of the Semitic peoples: instances are Abi'el, Abibaʿal, Abiyahu, meaning respectively God, Baʿal, Yahweh is Father.* In the citation from this poem in Jer. 48^{46} these traces of early thought are obliterated; the people are described as sons and daughters of *Moab*, and their capture is not attributed to the anger of their god, but is expressed by a passive vb. —*To the king of the Amorites, Siḥon*] the style is somewhat strange; see phil. n. The line is questionable, since it forms the single exception to the two-lined parallelism which otherwise extends uniformly through the poem. It is not improbably a gloss.—**30.** The text is corrupt, and nothing certain can be made of the verse. If, as in the above translation, we adopt the reading of 𝔊 (καὶ τὸ σπέρμα αὐτῶν = וְנִינָם), it continues the description of the calamity that had befallen

* G. B. Gray, *Hebrew Proper Names*, 21–86.

Moab; and if we may further restore *from*, with 𝔙 and 𝔗 (cp. 𝔊[L] ἐν = ב which is very frequently confused with מ), before *Ḥeshbôn*, the extent of the calamity and the direction from which it came correspond to what is differently described in v.[28]; see note there. *Dîbôn* is the modern Dhîbân, about 4 miles N. of Arnon.* Others find in the v. two verbs in the 1st pers. pl., and suppose that there is a sudden return (cp. v.[27]) to the Israelites' victory over the Amorites; then *we* = *Israel*: *them* = *the Amorites.* On various conjectures of varying degrees of uncertainty, see phil. note. The name of Medeba mentioned at the end of the v. (and also Is. 15^2, Jos. $13^{9.16}$, 1 Ch. $19^{7f.}$) survives in the modern Mâdeba, which lies between Ḥesbān and Maʿīn. According to MT. another place, *Nophaḥ*, is also mentioned; it is quite unknown.—**31.** Israel settles down in the Amorite country. This is the sequel to v.[24a], and a parallel statement to v.[25b] It is the conclusion of one of the narratives of the conquest of the Amorites.—**32.** Here the editor has added a detail from another account, viz. the capture of Jaʿzer and the dependent cities, and the expulsion of the Amorites resident therein.

27. ותכונן] see for the form, G.-K. 54*c*; for the (comparatively) rare passive sense of the Hithpael, Kön. iii. 101.—**28.** להבה] 𝔊[L] 𝔖 + ו, cp. Jer. 48^{45} (𝔐).—מקרית] Jer. מבין, which is probably an error for מבית.—אכלה] Jer. ותאכל (cp. 𝔖 here).—ער] 𝔊 𝔖 S erroneously עד: in Jer. פאת is from Nu. $24^{17e f}$, which is there substituted for the present close of the v.—**29.** אבדת] Jer. אבד.—שבית] S שבי; שבית elsewhere occurs only in the phrase שוב שבית: for the present sense, we find elsewhere שבי or שביה.—אמרי] if adjectival, cp. Gn. 14^{13}, Dt. 2^{24}. The people are elsewhere referred to collectively by the sing. *with the art.* in poetry (*e.g.* Ps. 136^{19}) as well as in prose. The omission of the art. (which S supplies) may be due to the fact that the word is here intended to be taken adjectively (*to an Amorite king*), which gives a strange expression, or to poetic licence (Kue.), or to a glossator's brevity of style (Meyer). The quotation in Jer. breaks off with the preceding line.—**30.** ונירם . . . ונשים] none of the ancient versions recognise verbs in these words. The modern attempts to translate the words as verbs make the lines extraordinarily harsh and obscure: Di. *e.g.* renders the former line, *we shot at* (ירה) *them* (and in consequence of our shooting, *i.e.* of our fighting) *Ḥeshbon was undone unto Dibon* (*i.e.* the whole district unto Dibon was undone as well as Ḥeshbon). For other views, see Di. The

* Tristram, *Land of Moab*, 131 ff.; Buhl, *Geog.* 268.

second line is still more irrecoverable. For אשר S 𝕲 read אש, a reading which is probably indicated in MT. by the dot over the ר: otherwise the Versions show variations through misunderstanding rather than variants. 𝕲, for example, renders *καὶ αἱ γυναῖκες αὐτῶν ἔτι προσεξέκαυσαν πῦρ ἐπὶ* Μωάβ, which Meyer (*ZATW.* i. 130) takes seriously and adopts, with the substitution of מידבא from 𝕳 for the Μωάβ of 𝕲. An extraordinary suggestion of Delitzsch's should be mentioned, since it has gained the approval of Di., Str., and, hesitatingly, of BDB. (under נפח): according to this, the line read ונשים עַד נֻפַּח אֵשׁ עד מידבא = *and we laid waste until fire was blown as far as Medeba.* Paterson and Haupt (*SBOT.*) make the whole v. satisfactory to themselves by the simple process of omitting אבד השבן and אשר עד מידבא as glosses. The punctuators probably took ונשים as 1st pl. Hiphil of שמם (G.-K. 67*y*). For the punctuation of the suffix in ונירם, if a verb, see G.-K. 60*d*.—**31.** בארץ] S בערי, 𝕲 בכל ערי by assimilation to v.^{25} 𝕿

33–35. The conquest of ʿOg and occupation of Bashan.—V.$^{33f.}$ is verbally identical with Dt. $3^{1f.}$, except that the 1st persons of Moses' speech in Dt. here become the 3rd persons of narrative, as in similar interpolations in S from Dt. V.^{35} is abbreviated from Dt. 3^{3}. The clause *and his sons*, which appears here in 𝕳 though not in S, is not found in Dt. 3^{3}: but cp. Dt. 2^{33}. The last clause of the v., *and we possessed his land*, may be regarded as a summary of the subsequent narrative in Dt. (especially 3^{12a}). In view of these facts there can be little doubt that the story of ʿOg has been incorporated in Nu. from Dt.; and this accounts for the lack of reference to it in 22^{2} (cf. also Jud. 11^{22}). The tendency to interpolate the text of Nu. from Dt., which is so marked in S (Introd. § 14*a*), has here also influenced 𝕳. For notes on the passage, see on Dt. 3^{1-3}.

XXII. 1 (P). Israel encamp in the steppes of Moab, opposite Jericho.—The v. forms no natural sequel to the account either of the occupation of Bashan (21^{33-35}), or even of the occupation of the country between Arnon and Jabboḳ (21^{21-32}). It belongs to the itinerary which was broken off at 21^{11} by the introduction of matter from another source.

And the children of Israel journeyed] the same phrase as in $21^{10f.}$. The point of departure has been omitted; probably it was given in the source as "the mountains of the Abarim" (33^{48}).—*The steppes of Moab*] is a term peculiar to P ($26^{3.\,63}$ 31^{12} 33^{48-50} 35^{1} 36^{13}, Dt. $34^{1.\,8}$, Jos. 13^{32} †). It denotes the low country E. of Jordan and immediately N. of the Dead Sea. The corresponding flat country on the W. of Jordan went by the name of the steppes of Jericho (Jos. 4^{13} 5^{10} (P); 2 K 25^5 = Jer. 39^5 = 52^8†). The *steppes of Moab* extended at least from Beth-Jeshimoth to Abel-Shiṭṭim (33^{49} n.), and the term no doubt covers the whole of the open plain from 5 to 7 miles broad, into which the Jordan valley expands on the E., some 9 miles from the mouth of the river. This plain is covered with trees, and well watered; see Driver's note on Dt. 34^1.

ירדן ירחו] ירדן is cstr. (G.-K. 125*h*), since in prose it always takes the art. when absolute. The phrase thus means *the Jordan of Jericho*, *i.e.* that part of the Jordan which flows in the neighbourhood of Jericho.

XXII. 2–XXIV. 25 (JE). *Moab and Israel.*

LITERATURE. — Verschuir, *Dissertatio de oraculis Bileami* (1773); Hengstenberg, *Die Geschichte Bileams u. seine Weissagungen* (1842); Reinke, *Beiträge zur Erklärung des AT.* (1855) iv. 179–287; Ewald, *Jahrbücher der bibl. Wissenschaft* (1856), viii. 1–41; Oort, *Disputatio de Pericope Num. xxii. 2–xxiv.* (1860); Kalisch, *Bible Studies*, part i. (1877); Kuenen, "Bileam" in *Th. Tijd.* (1884) xviii. 497–540; Wellhausen, *Comp.* 111–113, 346–351; Van Hoonacker, "Quelques Observations Critiques sur les Récits concernant Bileam" in *Le Muséon* (1888), vii. 61–76; Franz Delitzsch, "Zur neuesten Literatur über den Abschnitt Bileam" in *Zeitschr. f. kirch. Wiss.* (1888) pp. 117–126; Cheyne, "Some critical Difficulties in the Chapters on Balaam" in *Expository Times* (1899), x. 399–402; Wobersin, *Die Echtheit der Bil'amsprüche* (1900); von Gall, *Zusammensetzung u. Herkunft der Bileam-Perikope* (1900). For other earlier literature, see Reinke, *op. cit.* 205–207.

The Israelites, fresh from their conquest of the Amorites (22^2), are now settled on the border of Moab, and fill Balaḳ, king of Moab, and his people with fear (v.$^{3f.}$). The Moabites prepare for battle (v.$^{6.\ 11}$); but in order that his undertaking may be successful, Balaḳ sends messengers, carrying a suitable fee for the service required (v.^{7}), to a foreigner whose name is Balaam, and who is distinguished for the effect of his cursings and blessings, that he may come and formally curse Israel before the war begins (v.$^{6.\ 11}$). Balaam at first refuses on the ground that Yahweh withholds His permission (v.$^{8-14}$); Balaḳ sends a more impressive embassy (v.$^{15-17}$); Balaam receives

Yahweh's permission to go, but only to do as He tells him, and goes (v.$^{19-21}$). On the way Yahweh manifests Himself to Balaam and his ass (which miraculously addresses its master), and makes known His anger with him for going; Yahweh gives him permission to go, but only to speak what He tells him (v.$^{22-35}$). Balaḳ meets Balaam at the frontier of Moab (v.^{36}) and leads him successively to Ḳiriath-huṣoth (v.^{39}), "the field of Ṣophim on the top of Pisgah" (23^{14}), and the top of Peʿor (23^{28}). At each place he shows Balaam the Israelites encamped below, and endeavours to get him to curse them. But on each occasion Balaam pronounces a blessing, which in every case consists of a poem celebrating the prosperity, present or future, of Israel ($23^{7-10.\ 18b-24}$ 24^{3b-9}). After the second blessing, Balaḳ bids Balaam say nothing further (23^{25}); and after the third, bids him go home (24^{11}). Balaam, however, before going home (24^{25}) recites unsolicited a fourth poem (24^{15b-19}), predicting the ultimate destruction of Moab by Israel, and a similar fate for Edom. Without any demur from Balaḳ, Balaam further recites three much shorter poems, predicting the fate of ʿAmaleḳ (v.^{20}), the Ḳenites (v.$^{21f.}$), Asshur and ʿEber (v.^{24}).

Such is a brief analysis of these chapters in their present form; it necessarily leaves certain things, such as Balaam's country and the reason of Yahweh's anger with him for setting out on his journey, obscure or ambiguous; for in these respects the present narrative is itself obscure. This obscurity is not lessened but enhanced by attempting, as was formerly the custom, to interpret this narrative by the allusions to Balaam in $31^{8.\ 16}$. To these obscurities earlier interpreters devoted the utmost ingenuity. But in vain. The obscurities have been occasioned by the existence in the OT. of widely different stories about Balaam. Two of these have been combined in the present narrative. With the recognition of this, some of the difficulties of older interpreters disappear. But not all. It is impossible to recover in detail and with any certainty the original forms of the stories here combined. Consequently, the interpretation of these chapters still remains an incompletely solved problem.

The narrative, as distinguished from the poems which it contains, is certainly a compilation from at least two sources. This appears most clearly in c. 22. Here the most conspicuous evidence of compilation is as follows:—(1) the doublet in 22^{3a} and ^{3b}; (2) the irrelevance of v.^{4b} after v.^{2}; (3) the inconsistency of the two definitions of Balaam's home in v.^{5}, one clause placing it on the Euphrates, the other in "the land of the children of Ammon" (so read with 𝔊); and (4) the parallelism and inconsistency of v.$^{22-35}$ with much of what precedes. A number of smaller points, such as the different terms used for Balak's messengers, taken together, also support the conclusion that the narrative is composite, though taken separately some of them might be otherwise explained without serious difficulty. Any detailed analysis must of necessity largely rest on this less conclusive evidence.

Quite the most important of the points mentioned in the last paragraph is the inconsistency of 22^{22-35} and the preceding section. This consists mainly in the fact that *in v.*$^{20f.}$ *Balaam, having received God's permission to go, is on his way accompanied by the princes of Balak*, whereas *in v.*^{22} *Balaam is on his way accompanied by two servants, and without having received Yahweh's permission:* for that is the obvious meaning of Yahweh's anger.

There is no such conclusive evidence that c. 23 f. is derived from two sources. But 23^{25} looks like the original conclusion of a narrative; the statement in 24^{1}, that Balaam "went not, as at other times, to seek for enchantments," attaches to nothing that precedes; $24^{1f.}$ might well imply that Balaam now, for the first time, sees Israel, and for the first time realises Yahweh's purpose to bless Israel, in which case it could not have been the original sequel to c. 23. The repetition of $23^{22.\,24}$ in $24^{8.\,9}$, and the postponement of Balaam's solemn introduction of himself ($24^{3f.\,15f.}$) to the third and fourth poems, also favour the conclusion that c. 23 and c. 24 are not the work of a single writer.

Most writers,* therefore, are now agreed that the present narrative is a compilation from the two sources J and E.

* We., Di., Kit., Driver, Corn., Bacon, CH., Addis, Moore (*EBi.* 3442).

Kalisch, Kuenen, Steuernagel, and von Gall take more or less considerable exception to this conclusion. Kalisch argued that Nu. 22^{2}–24^{25}, apart from two interpolated passages (22^{22-35} and 24^{18-24}), formed an independent book, dating from the age of David, and had no connection with either J or E. Kuenen comes nearer to the general position, but holds that the section as a whole is derived from E, who himself derived 22^{22-35} from J, and incorporated it with his narrative. Von Gall maintains that 22^{2-41} $23^{1-6.\ 11-13}$ is compiled in the usual manner from J and E, but that 23^{13}–24^{25} is the work of five successive editors all later than JE, and that all the poems, including 23^{7-10}, are post-exilic. Both the sources (J and E), he further argues, related one blessing only, and the original compiler (JE) retained this feature of the story. Now, that there is some editorial work in 23^{13}–24^{25} is highly probable (see below on 24^{20-24}; see, further, CH.), but some of the features referred to in the last paragraph but one are not well accounted for by the theory that the whole of this section was written by editors before whom 22^{2}–23^{6} and $23^{11f.}$ already lay in its present form: in particular, the terms of $24^{1f.}$ and Balaam's self-introduction in the third and fourth poems present as much difficulty to this theory as to the theory that the chapters are a unity. Steuernagel's theory is that the whole section consists of the work of E^1 and additions by E^2 which are distinguished by the use of the divine name Yahweh, and consist of $22^{8.\ 13.\ 18f.\ 22-35}$ $23^{3.\ 4a\beta-6.\ 12-13a\alpha.\ 15-17.\ 26.\ 27a\alpha}$ $24^{1.\ 11a\beta b.\ 12b.\ 13}$ (*TSK.* (1899) 340 f.: *Einwanderung*, 72, 103–105). This is also open to some of the foregoing objections, and entirely fails to meet the difficulty presented by 22^{22-35}, and bases more than is safe on the use of the divine names (see below).

It is true, however, that the characteristics of E are more apparent than those of J. But before attempting to indicate the positive indications of either of these sources, it is necessary to consider, in the first place, from a purely textual point of view, the use of the divine names. The divine names used in 𝔐 are: *Yahweh*, 29 times; *God* ((ה)אלהים), 9 times, and also twice with a suffix; *God* (אל), 8 times; *Shaddai*, twice; and *Elyon*, once. The last three may be dismissed from consideration; for although both 𝔊 and 𝔖 give *God* for *Shaddai*, there is every probability that wherever these three occur, 𝔐 represents the original text (*Shaddai* = ὁ θεὸς ὁ ἐμός in Gn. 49^{25}; *El Shaddai* regularly becomes ὁ θεός μου, σου in the Hexateuch). In the use of *Yahweh* and *Elohim*, on the other hand, 𝔐 does not always preserve so early a text as S or 𝔊.

The variations of S trom 𝔐 are as follows:—

S has אלהים instead of the יהוה of 𝔐 in 23^{3}.
" " האלהים " " " 23^{26}.

S has מלאך יהוה instead of the יהוה of 𝔐 in $23^{5.\ 16}$.
,, ,, יהוה ,, אלהים ,, 22^{22a}.
,, ,, מלאך אלהים ,, ,, ,, 22^{20}.

𝔖 has throughout ܡܪܝܐ for יהוה and ܐܠܗܐ for (ה)אלהים. The variations of 𝔊 are as follows:—

(1) (ὁ) θεός = יהוה 15 times without variants (besides 23^{8}).
(2) ,, ,, 3 ,, with ,,
(3) ὁ Κύριος = האלהים 2 ,, ,, ,,

The instances of (1) are $22^{23-28.\ 31f.\ 35}$ $23^{3.\ 5.\ 12.\ 16.\ 26}$ 24^{13b}. In 23^{8} ὁ θεός = יהוה, but in the parallel line $\overline{Κς}$ = אל. The MSS. supporting $\overline{Κς}$ in the six cases of (2) and (3) are as follows (cursives not cited when the reading is embodied in Lagarde):—(2) in 22^{13}, L; in 22^{22b}, 44. 74. 84. 106. 134; in 22^{31}, BL; (3) in 22^{9}, 16. 73; 22^{22a}, FN 53. 71.

The fact that in the great majority of the cases S agrees with 𝔐 against 𝔊's (ὁ) $\overline{θς}$ would by itself cast grave suspicion on 𝔊's readings; but there is further evidence of 𝔊's tendency here to use ὁ $\overline{θς}$; thus it is ὁ $\overline{θς}$ that appears in the interpretation of שפי in 23^{3}, and, naturally indeed, in the addition at the end of 23^{6} (cp. 24^{2} 𝔐 and 𝔊).

It follows (1) that an unsupported reading ὁ $\overline{θς}$ in 𝔊 is valueless as evidence of the original reading; (2) that such a reading adds little or nothing to other evidence favouring an original reading (ה)אלהים; but (3) that wherever (ὁ) $\overline{Κς}$ appears in 𝔊, it deserves attention as a possible indication of the original text.

Thus on purely textual grounds (1) it is highly probable that in 22^{22a} *Yahweh* (S and important MSS. of 𝔊) is an earlier reading than *God* (𝔐); (2) in $23^{3.\ 26}$ *God* (S) is at least as probably original as *Yahweh* (𝔐); (3) in 22^{9} *Yahweh* read by certain MSS. of 𝔊 may possibly be earlier than *God* (𝔐). In all other cases 𝔐 probably presents a text earlier than 𝔊, though it is still, of course, perfectly possible that in certain cases 𝔊 *accidentally* reverts to the text of the ancient source. But that is not a question of textual criticism.

It will be convenient to tabulate here the usage of *Yahweh* and *God*.

Yahweh is used (reading thus in 22^{22a})—

(*a*) in narrative, 16 times—22^{22-35} (13 times) $23^{5.\ 16}$ 24^{1};

(*b*) in speeches of Balaam, 12 times (two doubtful)—$22^{8.\ 13.\ 18.\ 19}$ 23^{3} (S *God*) $^{8.\ 12.\ 21.\ 26}$ (S *God*) $24^{6.\ 13\ bis}$;

(*c*) in speeches of Balaḳ—24^{11}.

God ((ה)אלהים) is used—

(*a*) in narrative, 6 times—$22^{9.\ 10.\ 12.\ 20}$ 23^{4} 24^{2}. In 22^{9} some MSS. of 𝔊 read *Yahweh*;

(*b*) in speeches of Balaam, twice (22^{38} 23^{27}), and twice besides in S ($23^{3.\ 26}$).

No conclusive and complete explanation of this usage can be given.

It is partly due to fusion of sources; it is perhaps partly due to an editorial principle incompletely carried through. It is to be observed that in 22^{2-21} *God* is consistently used in the narrative, *Yahweh* in the speeches of Balaam. It is possible that *God* stood originally in (some of) the speecnes, and has been deliberately altered by an editor in order to make it clear that Balaam owes what he has to say to the God of Israel (Di.). The principle is not carried through, for in 22^{38} 23^{27} the reading *God* is, on textual grounds, beyond suspicion; for a similar incompleteness, see 𝕲, particularly in 22^{22b-35}, where $\overline{\theta s}$ takes the place of יהוה 11 times, but $\overline{K s}$ is allowed to stand in 22^{34}.

The consistent use of *Yahweh* (13 times) to the entire exclusion of *God* in 22^{22-35}, and the consistent use of *God* in the narrative parts of 22^{2-21}, favour referring 22^{22-35} to J, and the parts of 22^{2-21} containing *God* and inconsistent with 22^{22-35} (see above) to E. The only OT. parallel to the speaking ass in 22^{22-35} is the speaking serpent, and this also appears in J (Gn. 3); revelation by night (v.^{2a}: cp. v.$^{19.\ 21.\ 8-10.\ 12f.}$) is characteristic of E (12^{6} n.). Some slight indications of J's style (as distinct from E's) will be mentioned in the notes on v.$^{29.\ 31}$, and of E's (as distinct from J's) on v.^{13}.

Further analysis must proceed from this starting-point; and the more remote it becomes, the more uncertain also. The following suggestions are offered merely from this point of view. In 22^{5} *the land of the children of 'Ammon* is from J, *Pethor, which is by the river* (*Euphrates*) from E; for from 'Ammon Balaam might well be represented as coming on an ass with a couple of servants, but the long journey from the Euphrates would call for a larger retinue, such as that of the *princes of Balaḳ*, who are closely connected with passages referring to Balaam's receipt of revelation by night. In J, then, Balaam is an *'Ammonite*, in E an *Aramæan*; hence 23^{7} (*from Aram Balaḳ brought me*) is E. Thus in this episode E appears to term the messengers *princes* (or, when God is speaking, *men*—$22^{9.\ 20.\ (35)}$); and hence there falls to E $22^{14f.\ 40}$ $23^{6.\ 17}$. Different terms (*messengers, elders, servants of Balaḳ*—$22^{5.\ 18}$ 24^{12}) may point to the other source—J.

In the main at least c. 23 and c. 24 cohere respectively. But if this be so, c. 23 is mainly from E on account of *Aram* in 23^{7} and *princes* in $23^{6.\ 17}$: note, further, *God* in 23^{4} and in S also in $23^{3.\ 26}$, yet in the present text *Yahweh* is more frequent. Cp., further, 23^{20} with 22^{12} (E). In c. 24 *God* (אלהים) is used but once (24^{2}), *Yahweh* several times; 24^{12} in virtue of *messengers* connects with 24^{5} (J). Attention should, however, again be drawn to the comparatively slight positive evidence of J. In particular, note that 24^{25} more closely resembles Gn. $32^{1f.}$ (E) than 18^{33b} (J).

Further analysis proceeds from the conclusion that c. 23 is E and c. 24 J, or turns on minuter points of evidence. $22^{17f.\ 37b}$ is J if $24^{11.\ 13}$ is; $22^{5b.\ 11}$ contains a curious phrase (כסה את עין הארץ) found again only in Ex. $10^{5.\ 15}$

generally assigned to J. In $22^{6.\ 11}$ עצום and אולי are more characteristic of J than E (CH. 59, 64). There is no obvious reason for separating (with CH.) 22^{37a} from clause *b*; note rather a point of connection with 22^{5} (לקרא לך and לקרא לו). 22^{37} as a whole may then be J and, consequently, 22^{36} is E, if Wellhausen's suggestion (see on 22^{37}), that in 22^{37} Balaḳ has come to Balaam's home, be accepted, for certainly in E Balaam goes to Balaḳ; in the original form of the ass episode he *may* have returned home.

The tentative analysis thus reached may be tabulated thus—

J 22^{5} (except *to Pethor, which is by the river*) $^{6.\ 7.\ 11.\ 17f.\ 22\text{-}35a.\ 37}$ 24 (in the main except v.^{25}).

E 22^{5} ("*to Pethor, which is by the river*") $^{8\text{-}10.\ 12\text{-}15.\ 19\text{-}21.\ 36.\ 40}$ 23 (in the main), 24^{25}.

The result agrees for the most part with the analysis of CH. who, however, carry the analysis further.

If c. 23 and c. 24 are from different sources, then *these three times* in 24^{10}, part at least of the transition from the one source to the other (*e.g.* $23^{27.\ 29}$), and perhaps *Pe'or* in 23^{28}, may be regarded as editorial; possibly, also, the peculiar formula (cp. Job 27^{1} 29^{1}), common to both chapters, which introduces the first four poems. On the subsequent interpolation of $24^{(18f.)\ 20\text{-}24}$ see the introductory note to these verses.

The date of the narratives is the date of the sources (J and E) to which they have been traced, *i.e.* the 9th? or 8th? century B.C. The date of the poems is not necessarily the same. Like those in c. 21 they may be older than the narrative; or the two in c. 23 may be the work of E, the two in c. 24 of J; or they may be either ancient or more recent poems subsequently inserted in the completed narrative by an editor in place of Balaam's original words. Under these circumstances the poems must be briefly considered by themselves.

In the first place, the poems were obviously written to fit into *a* story of Balaam: see $23^{7f.\ 18.\ 20}$ $24^{3.\ 15}$; though it is only in the first two that a close structural connection with a story of Balaam is found. It is quite possible that $24^{3b\ (4).\ 15b\ (16)}$ are merely introductions attached to poems that originally had no connection with such a story.

The strongest point in favour of the antiquity of the poems, and, in the opinion of the present writer, it is very strong, is the feeling of national confidence, success, prosperity, and contentment which pervades them, and in virtue of which they are most closely connected with the ancient poems known as "the blessing of Jacob" (Gn. 49) and "the blessing of Moses" (Dt. 33). If the allusion to Agag in 24^7 could be relied on, the third poem would belong to the age of Saul; but it cannot. If it were certain, which it is not, that $24^{18f.}$ were an original part of the fourth poem, the only actual king satisfying the reference would be David, who alone conquered both Edom and Moab. If the poems be post-exilic the only mode of accounting for the tone would be to regard them as depicting the Messianic age; and this is the view of those who argue for a post-exilic origin. But, especially in the case of the third poem, it seems to the present writer singularly improbable. If pre-exilic, the poems which contemplate in Israel and Jacob something more than Judah must have been composed before the fall of the northern kingdom in B.C. 722, if not also before the disruption of the kingdoms. On the other hand, $24^{7.17}$ (though probably not 23^{21}, see note there) presuppose the monarchy: a date earlier than Saul is therefore out of the question, a date earlier than David improbable. The poems in their present state contain some interpolation (see on 23^{23}), and the second and third common matter. The reappearance of 24^{17ef} in Jer. 48^{45} is inconclusive; for there is the difficulty, common in the case of parallel passages, of determining which is the original.

Until recently the antiquity of the first four poems was not questioned. Diehl (*Erklärung von Ps. 47* (1894), 8–10) drew attention to certain linguistic and other features common to the poems and later literature. CH. (n. on 23^{7a}) just raise the question whether the poems may "belong . . . to the reproductive style of after times"; and recently von Gall has argued at length in favour of a Messianic interpretation throughout and of a post-exilic date of all the poems. Some of his arguments are criticised, or in some cases, when they turn on interpretation, tacitly met in the commentary; but see, in particular, notes on $23^{7.19}$. Many of the instances cited by him as late usages have slight weight, or rest on insufficiently established results as to the late date of many of the passages in which the words or phrases in question occur elsewhere. Some in themselves are of some weight, such as מלכות (instead of ממלכה) and עליון; and it becomes a question then whether they suffice to outweigh the evidence indicated above for an early origin of at least the main part of the poems.

Bela', son of Be'or, is the name of the first of the kings of Edom of whom a list is given in Gn. 36^{31-43}. His city was

Dinhabah, and he reigned some considerable time before the establishment of the monarchy in Israel. There is no reason to question the historical accuracy of these statements.

Virtually, if not exactly, identical with the name of this Edomite king is that of Balaam the son of Beʿor, who, though not an Israelite, received communications from Yahweh, and was specially and widely distinguished for his power of cursing and blessing. Balaam played this part in Hebrew traditions at least as early as the 9th century B.C. (J). The connection between the historical king of Edom of say the 12th or 11th century and this traditional figure of the 9th century can be only a matter of speculation. The tradition already had a history (which cannot, indeed, be traced) as early as the 8th? century: for Balaam has by then already become in one form of the tradition an Aramæan (E) whose home was in the region of the Euphrates, in another (if the view taken of 22^{5}, pp. 312, 326, be correct) an ʿAmmonite (J), possibly in a third a Midianite, for this last description may be much earlier than the first direct literary reference to it (Nu. $31^{8.16}$ P^{s}).

This traditional figure is one of the chief elements in the episode of Nu. 22–24. An even more important element, the fear and hostility felt by Moab for Israel, not improbably has some foundation in history. But in the main the episode is a creation of the Hebrew national spirit in the days of national prosperity, and self-confidence sprung from reliance on the national God, Yahweh. It may, indeed, contain other historical features; such as the name of Balaḳ, who may have been an actual king of Moab; but no means at present exist for distinguishing any further between the historical or legendary elements and those which are supplied by the creative faculty and the religious feeling of the writers.

The motive of the story and its religious presuppositions are in this case the points which it is most important to determine. The motive is perfectly clear, though it has generally been obscured, or at least cast into the shade, by undue prominence given to what is not a matter of leading interest with the writer, viz. the character of Balaam. Balaḳ, except in so far as he represents Moab, and Balaam are in reality subordinate figures in the story; the protagonists are Israel and Moab; the overruling thought is Yahweh's power to defend His people and His purposes of good concerning them; and the fatal madness of those who, through them, oppose Him. As at the outset, when Yahweh determined to bring His people to the land of promise, Pharaoh, and through him Egypt, opposed Israel to their own undoing, so at the close, as Israel is on the point of entering on its inheritance from Yahweh, Moab attempts, with like hardness of heart, a similar opposition, and suffers a similar fate. This motive was clearly felt by a prophet of the 7th century; the outstanding proofs to him of Yahweh's care for His people are summed up in Yahweh's appeal to Israel, "I brought thee up out of the land of Egypt; and from the house of slaves I redeemed thee, and sent before thee Moses, Aaron, and Miriam. O my people! remember now what Balaḳ, king of Moab, devised, and wherewith Balaam, the son of Beʿor, answered him . . . that thou mayest recognise the proofs of Yahweh's faithfulness (צדקות יהוה)" (Mic. $6^{4f.}$).

The same motive governs the two different stories which have been brought together by the editor (JE); and it was carefully preserved in the story as it left his hands. Drawing on both sources (J and E), the editor is indifferent to incongruities, produced by his method, which strike the modern reader; but he is careful so to combine his material as to give fuller effect to the leading motive. Not once nor twice only, but thrice in this final form of the story does Balaḳ persist in his attempt to get Israel cursed; and at each attempt his own doom approaches nearer: for, as the editor has arranged them, the poems rise to a climax. In the first Balaam speaks of Israel's freedom from Yahweh's curse, of its security from its foes, and of its countless numbers; in the second of Yahweh's irrevocable promise and unalterable determination positively to bless Israel, of Yahweh's presence in Israel's midst, and briefly of Israel's conquests; in the third of the fertility of Israel's land, of the celebrity of their king, of the national prowess, and of the utter destruction of all who oppose them. In the fourth unsolicited poem the climax is reached; Moab itself is singled out by name as about to perish before Israel; and on this note the episode in JE closed: all that followed it was the simple statement that Balaam and Balaḳ went their respective ways. One point in the earlier part the editor may have suppressed, viz. the personal visit of Balaḳ to Balaam, if this once formed part of J's story (22^{37} n.). But he retains with all clearness the corresponding development of the main motive in E; in the earlier as in the latter part of the story Balaḳ, like Pharaoh in the story of the plagues, blinded and rendered fatuous by his enmity to Israel, increasingly provokes, to the frustration of his plans and his people's undoing, the anger of Yahweh. Had he rested content with Balaam's first refusal, he would merely have lost the assistance he hoped to derive from a powerful curse; he sends again, and Balaam comes to bless, and so to range against him the very forces with which he wished to be allied.

Of the religious presuppositions of the story the most striking is the recognition of Yahweh's revelation of His purposes concerning Israel to one who was not an Israelite; and of the familiar intercourse of this foreign seer with the God of Israel. In one place (22^{18}) Balaam indeed speaks of "Yahweh, my God," just as an Israelite did (*e.g.* Jos. 14^{8}, 1 K. 3^{7}). It is indeed possible, as was pointed out above (p. 312), that one of the stories in its original form used throughout the term *God*. Even so, the Hebrew writer can only be thinking of the God who was God of Israel. In either case, to the writer's mind, the God of Israel reveals Himself outside the limits of the chosen people; we have here, therefore, an approximation to the idea of God which is found in Amos and other prophets of the 8th century. Whence this idea came cannot be determined; it is not clear that it is due to a knowledge on the writer's part of the fact, for which there is some evidence, that the divine name Yahweh was known outside of Israel, or had, in the first instance, been obtained by the Hebrews from without. There are some partial parallels for the writer's point of view; J makes all men at the beginning call on the name of Yahweh (Gn. 4^{26}); in E (Gn. 20) God reveals Himself by night to Abimelech, king of Gerar, a place where a Hebrew would naturally have expected that the worship of God would be unknown (Gn. 20^{11}); in the same source God reveals Himself in a similar manner to Laban the Aramæan (Gn. 31^{24}).

There are perhaps in the two stories two different points of view as to the manner in which Balaam received or obtained communications from God. In E, certainly, Balaam resembles the conspicuously true Hebrew prophet Michaiah the son of Imlah (1 K 22); each alike waits for God to speak, and each alike repeats what Yahweh says, whether it be pleasant or unpleasant to the person affected. In J Balaam's *custom* was to obtain oracles (24^{1}: cp. 22^{7}), by observation of omens or casting of lots if we are to press the probable implication of the terms employed; but he delivers his messages to Balaḳ overmastered, like a Hebrew chosen of Yahweh for any special task, by the Spirit of God. In J, too, Balaam proves incorruptible by Balaḳ's proffered gifts.

The motive of the story is clear; but the subsidiary religious beliefs of the writer beyond a certain point become obscure. Yet more is obscure when we pass on to ask what was the writer's estimate of the character of Balaam. The truth is, this question can easily be, and has generally been, pressed too far. The writer himself is, comparatively speaking, indifferent to it. It is hardly overstating the case to say that Balaam is an accident, and is not of the essence of the story. He is the instrument by which the proud opponent of Israel and Yahweh is led on to his destruction. But if the question of Balaam's character be raised, the outstanding fact to be kept in view is that nothing suffices to seduce him from carrying out the will of Yahweh. Balaḳ may think, it may be the intention of the writer to express this in passing, that Balaam is open to a sufficient appeal to his avarice. But if so, the event proves him wrong. It may be said that Balaam does all that he does under divine compulsion; this, however, is only in another way to neutralise the character of the prophet. But if it be further said that he does everything *unwillingly*, that he would if he could have satisfied his avarice, this is simply to import into the story what is not there.

The position taken up in the last paragraph is entirely at variance with the interpretation that till comparatively recent times entirely held the field. It was criticised in great detail by Kalisch, who, through a not unnatural reaction, laboured to prove Balaam as admirable as to previous writers he had been a detestable character. The older interpretation of necessity depended on ingenious and forced explanations of details which were fully exposed by Kalisch; it was justified on one assumption and one assumption alone, viz., that all the details mentioned in all the references are actual and true descriptions of one and the same real life; if Balaam's last act was to counsel Balaḳ to seduce the Hebrews to the worship of his god by means of the sensuous attractions of the Moabite women (31^{16}), then he was indeed a hypocrite, and the most natural explanation of his conduct is avarice. Bishop Butler's sermon, which represents the high-water mark of this mode of interpretation, is then not only a characteristic and masterly study in an unquestionably real type of human character, but a faithful delineation of Balaam's character in particular. But the assumption is no longer justified. The story of c. 22–24 is complete in itself; the allusion in 31^{16} first appears centuries later, and (see p. 320) is of doubtful historicity. Hence it is illegitimate to allow it to dominate the interpretation of c. 22–24.

Though in the main they have broken free from the older interpretation to a juster estimate of Balaam's character, Di. (138: cp. 140) and Bacon (p. 221) are still so far under its influence that they attribute to the Balaam of J a certain greed or avarice which they make no attempt to prove. That the final editor of the Hexateuch thought out a consistent character for Balaam before he admitted both representations to a place in the same work * (though by no means to stand side by side) is incapable of proof: as to its probability, each reader can judge for himself.

With Balaam's departure for his home (24^{25}) the story, whose motive is as described above, is complete. The sub-

* Cp. "Balaam," by W. Lock, in *Journal of Theol. Studies*, ii. 163.

sequent fortunes of the seer were irrelevant to it. But the curiosity out of which the Haggadic Midrash on the Old Testament sprang wanted to know more both of his fate and of his character and personality: and after its wont it created what it wanted, till in the course of time it gave Philo material for his lengthy and spirited description. In particular, the exclusive spirit of a later age could not tolerate the appearance of a true prophet of God among the heathen: it consequently took care to represent him in an unfavourable light. Such is the general tendency, though even later there are rare exceptions to it. The later references in the OT. prove that this depreciatory Haggadah developed early; and much of which there is only later evidence may be considerably earlier in origin.

Apart from a reference in a subsequent passage of E (Jos. $24^{9f.}$), on which see below, the earliest OT. reference (Mic. $6^{4f.}$) to Balaam is that already cited (p. 316); this, most naturally interpreted, regards Balaam favourably; as God frustrated the evil purposes of Egypt by means of Moses, Aaron, and Miriam, so He frustrated those of Moab by means of Balaam. But in the next reference, though it belongs only to the end of the same (the 7th) century, Balaam already appears in a more sinister light; by the end of the 7th century it had become impossible for a prophet who received pay to retain the same esteem which a Samuel or Ahijah, though they took fees, enjoyed; the Deuteronomist (Dt. $23^{5f. (4f.)}$) is, therefore, depreciating Balaam when he expressly states what the story of Nu. 22–24 merely implies (for in the age of that story it was a prevalent custom) that Balaam received fees; he also attributes to him a desire to curse which Yahweh would not gratify. Neh. 13^{2} is merely an echo of this, and a similar echo is probably to be found in Jos. 24^{10}, where what seems to be the original reading preserved in 𝔊 (*but Yahweh would not destroy thee*) has been replaced in 𝔐 by *but I would not hearken unto Balaam*. The latest OT. references are found in P, but belong to P^s rather than P^g; in these Balaam is the "oracle-monger" (קסם)—in so late a writer there is no question that the term is one of the utmost reproach; it is he who counsels the employment of the Moabite women to seduce the Hebrews (cp. 2 Pet. 2^{13-15}, Rev. 2^{14}), and he who fills up what was felt to be lacking in the earlier story by recording that Balaam died in battle in the war of Israel against Midian ($31^{8.16}$, Jos. 13^{22}).

The earliest writers in which the charge of avarice is explicitly made appear to be Philo (*De Vit. Mos.* i. 48 (Mangey, 123)) and 2 Pet. $2^{15f.}$ (cp. Jude [11]). It is less vigorously charged against Balaam by Josephus (*Ant.* iv. 6), though in other respects he presents him in nearly as unfavourable light as Philo.

The favourable judgments on Balaam in later writers are few; but some of them are emphatic. Thus commenting on Dt. 34^{10} (*There hath not arisen in Israel a prophet*), *Siphrê* (ed. Friedmann, 150*a*) adds, "but among the heathen there has, viz. Balaam," and then points out various points in which Balaam was even superior to Moses as, *e.g.*, in receiving his revelations lying down, whereas Moses received them standing up; see, further, Kalisch, p. 27 f.

Of the details of the Haggadic elaboration the following are among the more interesting or important: Balaam was lame or blind of one eye (deduced from the sing. עין in 24^{15}); he died as a bloody and deceitful man at the age of thirty-three or thirty-four, *i.e.* before he was half seventy (cp. Ps. 55^{24}: so Sanh. 106*b*); and, like Doeg, Ahithophel, and Gehazi, he had no part in the world to come, while the lot of his disciples also, who are the exact opposites of the disciples of Abraham, is Gehenna (Sanh. 10^2, Abhoth $5^{19(29)}$). The two who accompanied Balaam on his journey (22^{22}) were Jannes and Jambres, who had counselled Pharaoh to destroy the Hebrew male children and rivalled Aaron before the Egyptian king ($\mathfrak{T}^{Jon}$ on Nu. 22^{22}, Ex. 1^{15} 7^{11}).

Balaam is, moreover, identified with various persons who had opposed Israel, such as Laban ($\mathfrak{T}^{Jon}$ on Nu. 22^5, Sanh. 105*b*), an identification which has, in a sense, been revived by Steuernagel (*Einwanderung*, 104 f.). There is far more spirit about Philo's (*De Vit. Mos.* i. 48–55; Mangey, 122–128) description, but it is too long to quote or summarise: Josephus (*Ant.* iv. 6) is less interesting. See, further, Kalisch, 22–32; and *Jewish Encyclopædia*, ii. 467–469: for references to patristic and later Christian estimates of Balaam's character, which are always more or less unfavourable, and differ mainly on the point whether he was a mere heathen magician or actually received revelation from God, see Reinke, 221 ff.; and, for some modern English estimates, Locke in *Journ. Theol. Studies*, ii. 161–163. On account of the supposed similarity in the meaning of the names, Balaam has been connected with the Nikolaitans (Rev. $2^{6. 15}$) and the Arabic fabulist Loḳman: for literature on both points, see Kalisch, 23 and 53 ff.; Mohammedan scholars, though not unanimously, explain Ḳor. $7^{174f.}$ as a reference to Balaam (see, *e.g.*, Beiḍâwî thereon).

XXII. 2–4. Moab's fear of Israel.—Moab's fear is occasioned by the success of the Israelites over the Amorites (see, however, also v.[4] n.), and their occupation of the Amorite country (21^{21-24} E, or 21^{25} J). This feature in the story may reflect actual historical circumstances. It is in no way improbable. Even though Moab may, in the first instance, have actually called in Israel to attack their troublesome neighbours, or, at least, have maintained a friendly neutrality during that attack, their feelings may well have changed now that they found the Hebrew tribes settled on their borders, fresh from war and hungry for land.—*Bālāḳ the son of Ṣippôr*] king of Moab (v.[4. 10]). The first name is from a root which in Hebrew means *to lay waste*, and may therefore signify *the devastator*. The second is identical with the Hebrew and Phœnician (*CIS*. $165^{11f. 15}$) term which denotes *a small bird* of the sparrow type, but is scarcely confined in usage to a single species. Ṣippôrah, the fem. form of Ṣippôr, is the name of Moses' Midianite wife, and occurs in the form צפרא in Palmyrene inscriptions (de Vogüé, 11 = Lidzbarski, *Nordsem. Inschriften*, p. 458, No. 3^2). The attempts to give these and the names in v.[5] an allegorical significance are unsuccessful; these names are no doubt traditional. See, further, phil. n. Nothing is recorded of Balaḳ independently of what is told of him in the present connection; but he is once mentioned without Balaam (Jud. 11^{25}).—*To the Amorites*] the Hebrew collective term refers to Siḥon and his people ($21^{21. 25f. 31f.}$), but does not include ʿOg and his people, mentioned, but not termed Amorites, in 21^{33-35} (= Dt. 3^{1-3}). All the passages in the Hexateuch which speak of ʿOg as king of the Amorites appear to be later than the main Deuteronomic history; see

Dt. 3^{8} 4^{47} 31^{4}, Jos. 2^{10} 9^{10} 24^{12}. — **3.** Moab's fear of Israel is stated in two materially identical clauses; a similar tautology, probably due to the same cause, viz. fusion of sources, occurs in Gn. 21^{1}. The repetition of the subject *Moab*, and the expression of the object in the second clause by a fresh term *children of Israel* instead of by a simple pronoun referring to the people (14^{1} n. 20^{1} n.), also, point to the fact that the verse combines the similar statements of two sources. The verb in clause *a* (גור) occurs elsewhere in the Hexateuch in Dt. 1^{17} 18^{22} 32^{27}; cp. also, *e.g.*, 1 S. 18^{15}; the verb (קוץ) in clause *b* is stronger, the fundamental meaning being *to feel loathing for*: the nearest parallels to its present use are Ex. 1^{12}, Is. 7^{16} (and the Hiphil, if the text be right, in Is. 7^{6}); the original sense is clearer in Gn. 27^{46}, Lev. 20^{23}, Nu. 21^{5}, 1 K. 11^{25}, Pr. 3^{11} †.—**4.** Moab, very largely a pastoral people (2 K. 3^{4}), fears that the Israelite hordes will devour all the pasturage around them. The occasion for the following episode, and the cause of Moab's fear here assigned, are perhaps not the same as in v.^{2} It is the mere approach, rather than (as in v.^{2}) the conquests, of the Israelites.—*The elders of Midian*] these are again mentioned in v.^{7}, there in combination with the *elders of Moab*. But the narrative takes no further account of them; Balaam's dealings are with the Moabites only; the Midianites are not mentioned, even where they might be expected, and where Josephus, indeed, found it necessary to insert them; see, *e.g.*, in E $23^{6.17}$ (*princes of Moab* only) and in J $24^{10.14}$ (ct. Jos. *Ant.* iv. $6^{5f.}$); of the fate of Midian, Balaam has nothing to say. Some,* therefore, attribute these references to the Midianites to a redactor who thus attempted to connect the present story with extraneous notices which connect Balaam with Midian ($31^{8.16}$, Jos. $13^{21f.}$). Others † think that they are derived from J, whose story, fragmentarily preserved, was introduced by an explanation that Moab and Midian were neighbours, and made common cause against Israel. The latter view still leaves the omission of any reference to Midian in c. 24 unexplained. The association of Midianites and Moabites need in itself occasion no difficulty;

* Kue., We. † Di., Bacon.

for see Gn. 36^{35}, and cp. n. on 10^{30}.—*And Balaḳ b. Ṣippor was king of Moab at that time*] This remark comes in somewhat late after Balaḳ has been already referred to in v.[2] without explanation. Harmonists * argue that in v.[2] Moses had only his contemporaries in mind who needed no explanation, but that by the time he reached v.[4] remembering that he was writing for posterity also, he added this note † for their benefit.

4. ילחכו] pl. before coll. קהל, as, *e.g.*, Lev. 4^{14}; G.-K. 145*bc*; S (cp. 𝔊) ילחך, sing. with coll. קהל, as, *e.g.*, Gn. 35^{11}; G.-K. 145*f*.—הקהל] S 𝔊 𝔖 𝔙 + הזה, which is necessary in the mouth of a non-Israelite speaking of Israel, and therefore evidently original. It was passed over by an inattentive copyist, familiar with P's common custom of using הקהל absolutely of Israel: see, *e.g.*, 10^{7} 16^{32}. — כלחך] The vb. לחך occurs 6 times in OT.; but in no case does the consonantal text happen to distinguish the conjugation. MT. here points as Kal; in the remaining five cases as Piel. In Aram. and Arabic the simple conjugation is used, with the sense *to lick up*.—מלך למואב] cp. Jos. 12^{18b}, 2 K. 19^{13}; Kön. iii. 280*m*.

5–14. The fortune of the first embassy sent by Balaḳ to Balaam.—V.[5f.] (mainly J) Balaḳ sends messengers to the country of the ʿAmmonites—or to Pethor on the Euphrates (E)—to summon Balaam b. Beʿor to curse the people which, having come out of Egypt, is now settled opposite Moab. With the help of Balaam's curse Balaḳ hopes to bring the war against the Israelites, which he contemplates, to a successful issue.

And he (*i.e.* Balaḳ) *sent messengers*] cp. 24^{12} (J); ct. *princes*, v.[8. 13. 21] etc. (E); see above, p. 312.—*Balaam b. Beʿor*] the resemblance to Belaʿ (בלע) b. Beʿor, king of Edom (Gn. 36^{32}), is remarkable, and scarcely accidental. In 𝔥 Balaam (בלעם) differs from Belaʿ merely by the presence in the former of the afformative *-am*. Belaʿ occurs as the name of two other persons (26^{38}, 1 Ch. 5^{8}); but the name Beʿor is otherwise unknown. If the textual tradition in Genesis be correct, or if Balaam be there read with Ball (*SBOT.*) for Belaʿ, the ultimate identity of Belaʿ king of Edom and Balaam is highly probable.‡ The

* *E.g.* Hengst.

† Kalisch (p. 88 f.) criticises this and similar explanations at length.

‡ So, *e.g.*, Nöld. *Untersuchungen*, 87 n. 1; Hommel, *Altisraelitische Ueberlieferung*, 154, 222.

meaning of *Balaam* is ambiguous; for it would be possible to treat it as a compound of בל = *Bēl* and עם = *kinsman* (or *ʿAmmu*: see $1^{7.10}$ n., and cp. *HPN.* 43, 63, 123). The meaning of the root בלע is *to swallow down*: hence the identification of Balaam and Loḳman (لقم = *deglutivit*). The interpretation, *swallower* or *destroyer of the people* (בלע עם), already appears in 𝔗^Jon^. It is entirely unphilological, but has possibly caused, if it be not in part due to, the late pronunciation Bilʿām (MT.); 𝔊 (EV.) keeps what was probably the original pronunciation Balʿām. On this and other interpretations of the kind both of Balaam and Beʿor, see Kalisch, 90–96. —*Pethôr, which is by the river*] *i.e.* the river Euphrates: cp. Ex. 23^{31}, Jos. $24^{2.3.14f.}$ (all E). The identification of Pethôr with Pitru, which is mentioned by Shalmaneser II. (860–825 B.C.), and with *pe-d-rüi̥*, which appears in the lists of Thothmes III. (*c.* 1500 B.C.), has been generally accepted.* Some scholars, however, have recently questioned the identification on the philological ground that in view of the long *ô* in Pethôr (פתורה, 𝔊 *Φαθουρα*) the Assyrian form should be Pitâra. Then explaining away the statement of Dt. 23^5 that Pethôr was in Aram-naharaim, they have sought for the place somewhere on the "river of Egypt" (34^5 n.), which, they allege, is in Gn 36^{37} called "the river" simply.† Pitru was situated a little S. of Carchemish, not indeed actually on the Euphrates, but on the Sājūr, a few miles from its junction with the Euphrates. The Sājūr is a tributary from the W.; it is a considerable stream, and in its lower course flows between two ranges of low chalk hills.‡ Shalmaneser II. thus refers to Pitru: "At that time I restored to their former condition Ana-ašur-utîr-aṣbat, which the Hittites (Ḫatti) call Pitru, which is situated on the Sagura, on the far side of the

* Sayce, *Academy*, x. (1876, Sept.) 291, and *Early History of the Hebrews* (1897), 40, 228; Schrader, *COT.*² 155 f.; Fried. Delitzsch, *Wo lag das Paradies?* 269; Max Müller, *Asien u. Europa*, 98 n. 1, 267; *Records of the Past* (2nd series), v. 38 (No. 280); Driver in Hastings' *DB.* iii.

† Marquart, *Fundamente israelitischer u. jüdischer Geschichte* (1896), 73 f.; Cheyne in *EBi.* 3685 f.

‡ Chesney, *Survey of Euphrates*, i. 419; cp. Sachau, *Reise in Syrien*, 156.

Euphrates, and Mutkînu . . ., which Tiglath-Pileser [I.: *c.* 1100 B.C.] . . . had filled with settlers, and which in the time of Ašur-kirbi, king of Aššur, the king of Arumu [the Aramæans] had captured by force: I settled Assyrians therein." * The description of Pethor as situated in Aram-naharaim (Dt. $23^{5\,(4)}$) quite agrees with the Assyrian definition of the site of Pitru: for Aram-naharaim is not merely the country between the Euphrates and the Tigris; it is the Naharin (*River-country*) of the Egyptian inscriptions, called Nahrima or Narima in the Tel el-Amarna tablets—a district which appears to have extended from the valley of the Orontes eastwards across the Euphrates.† The journey from Pitru to Moab would be something like 400 miles, and would occupy over twenty days,‡ and from any other place on the Euphrates the time-distance would not be appreciably less. The four journeys of the story would therefore have required about three months. A journey to Aram-naharaim, related elsewhere, was undertaken with camels (Gn. 24^{10}); the ass of v.$^{22-34}$ belongs to a story which locates Balaam's home much nearer Moab.§

To the land of the children of Ammon] (ארץ בני עמון) this is the reading of S 𝔖 𝔙, and appears to have been the original.‖ In MT. it has been accidentally, or rather, perhaps, deliberately, changed, by the simple omission of the final ן, into בני עמו *sons of his people* (cp. Gn. 23^{11}, Lev. 20^{17}). The residence of Balaam among the Ammonites, who were neighbours of the Moabites, would agree with the features of v.$^{22-34}$, which are unsuitable in a story that locates Balaam a great distance off by the Euphrates, viz. the journey on an ass, without a numerous escort, and between fields and vineyards. Those who prefer MT.¶ see in the clause an explanation that Balaam

* Monolith Inscription III. Rawl. 7–8, col. ii. ll. 36–38, translated *KB.* i. 163, 165 (on which the above translation is based); also, though differently, in *Records of the Past* (1st series), 92 f.; cp. *Records of the Past* (2nd series), iv. 40; *KB.* i. 133.

† Max Müller, *Asien u. Europa*, 249-267: *EBi. s.v.* "Aram-Naharaim."

‡ Merrill, *East of the Jordan*, p. 268 (twenty-five days or a month).

§ Cp. We. *Comp.* 351; Merrill, *op. cit.* (last n.).

‖ So Geddes, Houb. (see Oort, p. 6), We., Bacon.

¶ *E.g.* Hengst., Oort, Kue. (p. 504).

was not a mere sojourner in Aram, but that it was his native land; the point of such a remark here is not obvious. It becomes more pointed if the suffix be referred to Balaḳ,* who would then appear as a foreign conqueror of Moab. But the phrase elsewhere used in Heb. for native land is different, viz. ארץ מולדת (Gn. 11[28] 24[7] 31[13]). Others,† also retaining MT., render *the land of the children of ʿAmm*, ʿAmm being regarded as the proper name of a deity, which is detected by some scholars in the proper names compounded with ʿAm, ʿAmmi.—*To call him*] cp. v.[20. 37]. *Behold it has covered the face* (lit. *eye*; עין) *of the earth* like locusts (Ex. 10[5. 15] J), *and it is* now *dwelling* or settled *over against me.*

5. פתורה] פתור (Dt. 23[5]) + ה ָ, the acc. ending. 𝔙 (*ariolum*), 𝔖 (ܦܫܘܩܐ *the interpreter*), make the word an appellative in app. to בלעם. Many (*e.g.* Hengst.) while treating it as a place-name, misled by the Heb. פתרון, base much on the supposition that it means "Interpreters' Town," overlooking the fact that the Aramaic *to interpret* has ש for the Heb. ת. The meaning is really quite uncertain.—ארץ] not, of course, genitive (𝔊 AV.): for see G.-K. 125*a*: scarcely locative (Driver, *Tenses*, 191, Obs. 2), but rather acc. of direction (Kön. iii. 330*b*): cp. 32[32], Gn. 45[25], Jud. 1[26] 21[21], 1 S. 13[7]. The awkward position of the word, as also of לקרא לו לאמר, is probably due to the fusion of sources at this point.—הנה כסה] S 𝔊 (also v.[11] in 𝔊[B]) and some MSS. of 𝔐 והנה כ׳: in v.[11] 𝔐 has ויכם (cp. 𝔖 both here and there).

6. *And now come curse me this people*] Balaḳ contemplates fighting the Israelites, and wishes them effectually cursed beforehand, so as to ensure his success. Balaam's curses have the reputation for hitting the mark. Obviously the Hebrew writer shares the belief, which he attributes to Balaḳ, in the objective power of the curse.

The objective power and independent existence attributed by the Hebrews, as by other peoples of antiquity, to a blessing (6[22-27]) or curse (5[23f.]) is but a special case of the belief in the power and independent existence of the spoken word (30[2] n.). Such blessings or cursings had peculiar power when uttered by men in close communication with the deity—by a priest or magician. Among the solemn blessings or cursings recorded in the OT. the more noticeable are those of Noah (Gn. 9[25-27]), Isaac (27[27ff.]), Jacob (c. 49), Joshua (Jos. 6[26], cf. 1 K. 16[34]), and Elisha

---

* Midrash Rabbah, Rashi; cp. Marquart, *Fundamente*, 74.

† Sayce, *Records of the Past* (2nd series), iii. p. xi. In criticism of this view see Gray, *Heb. Proper Names*, 52 f.; also *EBi. s.v.* "Ammi."

(2 K. 2^{24}); Isaac's blessing, though pronounced by mistake over Jacob instead of over Esau, once uttered is beyond even his own control; the reality is inseparably associated with the form of blessing (Gn. 27^{33}); in blessing Jacob, Isaac gives him the service of his brethren (Esau), and though against his will all he can do subsequently is to decree Esau to be Jacob's servant. See, further, Köberle, *Natur u. Geist*, 165–169.

Where such beliefs prevail, it is a very natural development to attach importance to having an enemy duly cursed. Goliath, when David came to engage with him in single combat, cursed him by his gods (1 S. 17^{43}). When it was a case of warfare between tribes or nations, it would seem to have been customary to obtain the services of some man possessing, owing to his exceptional power with the deity, peculiar skill and efficacy in cursing. In an account of a much later period a closer parallel to the story of Balaam occurs. In the civil war between Hyrcanus II. and Aristobulus II. (69–63 B.C.) the troops of Hyrcanus, largely consisting of Arabs under Aretas, insisted on calling in the help of Onias, *δίκαιος ἀνὴρ καὶ θεοφιλής*, who once in a time of drought had by his prayers obtained rain. Brought unwillingly into the camp, Onias was required to place curses on Aristobulus and his party (*ἵν' οὕτως ἀρὰς θῇ κατὰ Ἀριστοβούλου καὶ τῶν συστασιαστῶν αὐτοῦ*). Instead of complying, he prayed God not to listen to one party against the other. For this he was murdered by the baser Jews (*Ant.* xiv. 2^{1}). Goldziher, in his Essay on the origin of the *hijâ'* poetry (*Abhandlungen zur arabischen Philologie*, i. 1–121), has brought together much evidence that serves to illustrate the power attributed to Balaam, and the part which he was asked by Balaḳ to play. The poet, Goldziher argues, was supposed by the pre-Muhammedan Arabs to be inspired by the *jinn*. The *hijâ'*, *i.e.* the utterances of these poets, spoken at the beginning and during the course of the tribal wars, was as important as, perhaps indeed more important than, the use of arms. Consequently the *hijâ'*, no less than warfare itself, was forbidden during the sacred month. One of the Ḳureish on the way to the battle of Bedr, addressing a poet, said, *You are a poet, help us with your tongue.* The value of the *hijâ'* rested on the fact that it was originally a magical formula. The independent existence of such a solemnly uttered speech or curse was very materially conceived: it is an arrow shot from the bow, and "it was said that if, when a man was cursed, he was thrown down, it avoided him" (Ibn Hishâm, 641, 15—cited by Goldziher, 29 n. 1); in other words, the curse-arrow passes over him, leaving him untouched and uninjured. The poets employed to assist in war were not always of the same tribe as that which was fighting (p. 26ff.).

This view of the power of a curse is practically discarded in one of the later OT. writers: see Prov. 26^{2}; and for later Judaism, cp. the principle stated in *Tᵉrumoth* 3^{8}, cited below on 30^{2}.

For it (Israel) *is stronger than I am*] cp. Ex. 1^{9}. Balaḳ speaks as representing his people; 𝔊 read, or paraphrased, *than we are* (ממנו for ממני). On the singular pronoun referring to Israel, see 20^{14} n.; and on the change of persons in 𝔥, see below.—7. The elders of Midian (see on v.[4]) and of Moab deliver Balaḳ's message (v.[5b], also v.[11]) to Balaam.—It was customary to pay seers or priests or others having special relations to the deity for their services, and the fee, whether in money or kind, was offered beforehand; *e.g.* Saul's servant proposes to pay Samuel ¼ shekel for telling Saul and himself what will happen to them (1 S. 9[8]); and people, when sick, sent presents to the seer of whom they inquired whether they should recover (1 K. 14[3], 2 K. 8[8f.]). See also 1 K. 13[7], 2 K. 5[5f.], Am. 7[12], Mic. 3[5]. So Balaḳ's messengers bring (though only as an earnest of what he might receive, v.[17f.]) fees for Balaam; these fees are here called קסמים, literally, *enchantments*, that is, *the fee for enchantments*; so בשרה *glad tidings*, in 2 S. 4[10], means *the fee given to one for bringing such tidings*; see also phil. n. on 3[46]. The Hebrew writer cannot intend it to be an evil trait in Balaam that he is offered, or even that he received fees: for though prophets like Micah and Amos denounce or indirectly condemn the priests or prophets who prophesy for a reward (Mic. 3[5. 11], Am. 7[12–15], Ezek. 13[19]), in earlier times men held in high esteem, like Samuel and Ahijah, received fees, as the references cited above suffice to show. It is, however, possible that the particular term employed may contain some reflection on Balaam's methods; for קָסַם, קֶסֶם (see 23[23] n.) are always used in the OT. in connection with illegitimate means of obtaining knowledge. But for the avarice attributed to Balaam by many commentators, there is no support in the text either here or in v.[15]; ct., rather, v.[18] 24[13]. It is true that the rewards offered to Balaam were far greater than those offered to Samuel; but so were the services required of him; they were of national importance to Moab; Samuel was offered ¼ shekel to tell an individual about some lost asses.—8–14. Balaam promises the messengers an answer in the morning; in the night (cp. v.[13a]) God forbids Balaam to go (v.[12]). The messengers report their ill-success to Balaḳ.—*As Yahweh shall tell me*] On Balaam's use of the name *Yahweh*, see above, p. 311 f.—9. That the divine manifestation took place by night is clear from a comparison of v.[8a] and v.[13a]; it is stated directly in the case of the second visitation (v.[20]). The trait is characteristic of E; see 12^{6} n. For a question of the kind here attributed to God, cp. *e.g.* Gn. 3^{9} 16^{8}.—**11.** Balaam repeats to God in a slightly abbreviated form and with some verbal variations (see phil. n.) the message of Balaḳ as given in v.$^{5b. 6a}$ (J).

6. אָרָה] the form which is repeated in 23^{7} is abnormal for אֹרָה. So in v.$^{11. 17}$ is קָבָה for קָבָּה: G.-K. 67*o*.—ואגרשנו . . . אוכל נַכֶּה] the נכה of MT. is an impf. subordinated to a preceding vb.; the cstr., common in Syr. and Arabic, is rarer in Heb.; yet see (after יכל as here) Lam. 4^{14} and, for further instances, Driver, *Tenses*, 163 Obs. The text, however is suspicious. The change of persons (1st sing., then 1st pl., then again 1st sing.) must be explained on the principle discussed in 20^{14}; cp. also König, iii. 206. But apart from נכה, the 1st sing. is preserved throughout in this v. and in v.^{11}; moreover, in v.^{11} אוכל is quite clearly followed by an inf. with לְ. Probably נכה has arisen by corruption from an infinitival form, the לְ of the inf. having been first accidentally dropped after (אוכ)ל. But it is unnecessary to invent an unknown inf. Piel נַכֵּה (Kön. iii. 399*d*). 𝔊 𝔖 render אוכל by a 1st pl.—a paraphrase, rather than a real variant. 𝔗^{o} assimilates v.^{6} to v.^{11}.—נכה בו] For בְּ after הכה, see 1 S. 14^{31} 18^{7} 23^{2}. Paterson in *SBOT.*, following Grätz, reads הַכּוֹתוֹ, restoring the more usual cstr. with the acc. and also getting rid of נכה (see last n.).—**8.** והשיבתי אתכם דבר] $13^{25f.}$ n.—**11.** The versions assimilate the reported message to the original (v.$^{5f.}$): thus, for—

העם היצא of MT. S 𝔊 𝔖 read עם יצא.
ויכם „ 𝔊^{B} 𝔖 read as in v.^{5} (see note there).
after הארץ „ 𝔊 inserts והוא ישב ממלי.
עתה „ S 𝔊 reads ועתה.
after וגרשתיו „ 𝔊 inserts מן הארץ.

Further, 𝔊 𝔖 𝔙 $𝔗_{o}$ fail to represent differently the different words for *to curse* (קבה and ארה). The word קבב (not נקב, for see 23^{27}) occurs only in Nu. 22–24 (in both sources J and E) and Job 3^{8} 5^{3}, Prov. 11^{26} 24^{24}.—**13.** ארצכם] 𝔊 ארנכם.—להלך] This peculiar inf. cstr. (G.-K. 69*x*) occurs twice besides in E, v.^{16} (cp. also v.^{14}), Ex. 3^{19}; otherwise only in Eccl. $6^{8f.}$. The use of such peculiar infinitives (for another see 20^{21} n.) is somewhat characteristic of E; G.-K. 69*m*; CH. 119^{JE}.—**13.** לתתי] For נתן=*to suffer, allow*, as characteristic of E, see p. 264.—**14.** הלך] This might be, so far as the consonants go, inf. abs. used as the direct obj. (G.-K. 113*d*); but MT. is justified in printing as cstr. (on the form see preceding note), since כאן clearly takes the cstr. without ל in Jer. 5^{3a}.

15–21. The fortunes of the second embassy (E, except v.$^{17f.}$).—Balaḳ sends more numerous and more eminent princes to Balaam. They also spend the night with Balaam, who, having obtained permission from God, departs with them in the morning.

Assuming the avariciousness and insincerity of Balaam, commentators have contrived to read into these verses much that is not there; thus the reason that the second embassy is more eminent in *personnel* (v.[15]) and carry richer presents (v.[17]) is that Balaḳ saw in Balaam's refusal an indication that he had not been offered a sufficiently high reward. This is probably enough the writer's view of *Balaḳ's* attitude; it proves nothing with regard to Balaam's. Then it is quite gratuitously assumed that v.[18b] is hypocritically spoken; and it is argued that Balaam was wrong to inquire of God the second time (v.[19]), instead of dismissing the princes at once. As a matter of fact the text says nothing of Balaam making a second request. Balaam bids the messengers wait in case God of His own accord should visit Balaam by night and give him directions. In v.[20] as in v.[9] God, not Balaam, opens the conversation.

16. *Hold not thyself back from coming*] the verb here used is the reflexive (Niphal) of that used (with Yahweh as subject) in 24[11]. Possibly the words are chosen to indicate that Balaḳ regarded Balaam's previous refusal as an excuse.—17a. Cp. v.[37] 24[11].—17b. The request is as before (v.[6]); the verb for *to curse* (קבה) as in v.[11].—18. Cp. 24[13]. Balaam warns the messengers, here called *the servants of Balaḳ* (cf. 2 S. 10[2-4], Gn. 40[20] 41[37. 38]), that he can do nothing either *great or small*, *i.e.* nothing at all (cp. 1 S. 20[2] 22[15] 25[36]; Kön. iii. 92), without the permission of his God, Yahweh, however great the inducement Balaḳ may offer, even though it were *his houseful of silver and gold*; but (19) he suggests that they should stay the night, that he may have an opportunity of a nightly visitation of Yahweh, and of learning thereby any change in the wishes of Yahweh.—20. This course is justified by the event; Yahweh now commands him to go, but to speak only according to His direction. On the former occasion (v.[10]), Balaam tacitly asked two things—permission to go to Balaḳ and permission to curse Israel; both were refused (v.[12]). Now the first is granted; the second is neither definitely granted nor definitely refused; but Balaam appears rightly to have gathered that what Yahweh would put in his mouth would not be the curse that Balaḳ desired; and immediately on meeting Balaḳ he warns him to this effect (v.[38]; cp. 23[12. 26]). Balaḳ, blinded like

Pharaoh, calls down on himself more and more of the anger and punishment of Yahweh (see above, p. 316).—**20b.** *That shalt thou do*] cp. 23[26]; otherwise in the similar locutions the verb *speak* is used—22[35. 38] 23[12] 24[13].—**21a** *a*. Cp. v.[13a].—*He saddled his ass*] the *ass* (אתון) is a *she-ass*; other references to she-asses used for riding are Jud. 5[10], 2 K. 4[22]; otherwise the he-ass (חמור) is more frequently referred to in this connection (Ex. 4[20], Jos. 15[18], 1 S. 25[20], 2 S. 16[2] 17[23] 19[27], 1 K. 2[40] 13[13], Zech. 9[9]). The ass was used by persons of all ranks, as the references already cited show, and was in early Israel the animal regularly employed for riding, except for long journeys such as that to the Euphrates country, when camels were used (v.[5] n.). Even after the introduction of other riding animals (the mule and, later, the horse), the ass remained in great demand (Nowack, *Arch.* i. 75 f. 224).

18. עברי] 𝔊 שרי.—מלא ביתו כסף וזהב] Driver, *Tenses*, § 194.—**19.** שבו נא בזה] a variation on לינו פה of v.[8]: but cp. וישבו v.[8b]; בזה 23[1. 29] and שבו לנו בזה Ex. 24[14] (E). בזה is characteristic of JE (9 times) as against P who never uses it, but it is not distinctive of either J or E individually (CH. 168).—יֹסִף] Kön. iii. 191*c*.

22–35 (**a** *a*). **Balaam and his ass** (J).

22. *And the anger of Yahweh* (so S: 𝔥 *God*; see p. 311) *was kindled because he was going*] This is clearly not the original sequel to v.[20f.] in which God expressly directs Balaam to go. It is only the incidents recorded in the following verses that show Balaam that his journey displeases Yahweh; when he discovers it, he offers to go back (v.[34]). It was the belief of the early Hebrews that Yahweh frequently first manifested His anger towards any one who, however unwittingly, had offended Him, by subjecting them to inconvenience or disaster, *e.g.* Uzzah's well-meaning act draws down on him the fatal anger of Yahweh (2 S. 6[6]); cp. also 1 S. 6[19], 2 S. 21[1ff.]. Balaam, in J's narrative, we must suppose, after warning Balak's messengers that he cannot curse or bless except as Yahweh permits (v.[18]), sets out without consulting Yahweh on the mere question of going or not.

The harmonistic explanation really explains away the statement and replaces it by another; Yahweh was not angry with Balaam for going, but for the avarice which induced him to go. See, *e.g.*, Hengst. (pp. 43–45), and somewhat similarly Keil; Rashi's explanation, like the text itself, really ignores v.[20f.], ראה שהדבר רע בעיני המקום ונתאוה לילך.

The angel of Yahweh] *i.e.* a temporary appearance of Yahweh in human form; note *in his hand*, v.[23]; see 20[16] n.—*Placed himself in the way as one who would oppose him*] or *would place a hindrance in his way*. The word (שטן) here used purely attributively becomes later the name (Saṭan) of the arch-opponent of God and men: see already 1 Ch. 21[1] (ct. 2 S. 24[1]). The sense of the word, which is confined to this passage and v.[32] in the Hexateuch, is sufficiently illustrated by 1 S. 29[4], 2 S. 19[23] (EV. v.[22]), 1 K. 5[18 (4)] 11[14. 23. 25].—The angel of Yahweh thus meets Balaam as the latter *was riding upon his ass* (v.[21] n.), *his two servants being with him*; the princes of v.[21b] have disappeared, and Balaam is here accompanied by two servants, the same number that Abraham took with him for a three days' journey in Canaan (Gn. 22[3]); sometimes for a short journey a single servant only was taken (Jud. 19[3], 1 S. 9[3]). This mode of travelling suggests that Balaam's home was much nearer to Moab than the Euphrates; as a matter of fact in J's narrative Balaam appears to have come from ʿAmmon (v.[5] n.), which would be but two or three days' journey away; Rabbath-ʿAmmon is about 40 miles from the Arnon.—**23.** Balaam and his party are proceeding along a road or track (דרך) through cultivated but open country (שדה; cp. 20[17] and, *e.g.*, Ex. 23[16], Mic. 3[12]), when, unperceived by Balaam (and apparently by his servants) but seen by the ass, the angel of Yahweh, *with his sword drawn in his hand* (cp. v.[31], Jos. 5[13], 1 Ch. 21[16]), blocks the way; the ass turns off the track on to the cultivated land, and is beaten by Balaam to bring her back into the way. In cases of this kind it is not unusual to represent one or more of the party as perceiving what the others do not perceive, either at first or at all; cp. 2 K. 6[16f.], Ac. 9[3. 7] (ct. 22[9]). Apologetic interpreters, such as Hengstenberg and Keil, sought to establish the credibility of this particular instance by an appeal to the fact that irrational animals have "a much keener presentiment of many natural phœnomena, such as earthquakes, storms," etc., than men, and possess a power of clairvoyance.—The scenery of this and the following verses is not that of the Syrian desert (v.[5] n.); if the Euphrates were really Balaam's starting-point in this story, we should be compelled to conclude that the present incident occurred on the last day or two of the long journey.*—**24 f.** The angel of Yahweh retreats some distance before the advance of Balaam (cp. v.[26a]) till the track across the open cultivated country becomes a way between vineyards which are enclosed by walls of stone (Pr. 24[31]), or rather perhaps of thorns (Is. 5[5]); here he again blocks the way, and is again seen by the ass alone; the ass having now no open country to turn into, tries to pass the angel, and in so doing *she crushed herself against the wall, and she crushed Balaam's foot against the wall.*—**26 f.** The angel again retreats, and now takes up his stand in a place so narrow that he completely blocks the way; the ass seeing him crouches down, and is angrily beaten by Balaam.—**28.** Then a marvel happens; Yahweh enables the ass to speak and upbraid Balaam. A piece of folklore is here utilised for the purposes of the story. Many similar marvels are related by ancient authors,† who record instances of speaking horses, cows, rams, lambs, and dogs. For example, in the Egyptian *Tale of the two Brothers*,‡ the cow says to its keeper, "Verily, thy elder brother is standing before thee with his dagger to slay thee"; Livy more than once relates that in a certain year an ox was said to have spoken with human voice. The speaking serpent in Gn. 3 is the only OT. parallel, and that speaks of itself without any direct assistance of Yahweh. The marvel has occasioned considerable trouble to some commentators, who have regarded the narrative as historical, but have been unwilling to admit that the ass actually spoke. They have consequently endeavoured to explain the difficulty away on the ground that the whole incident is the record of a vision that Balaam

* Hengst.

† See the collection of Bochart in *Hierozoicon*, Pt. I. lib. ii. c. xiv. (ed. Rosenmüller, 1793, p. 168 ff.); see also Kalisch, 129, 132–134.

‡ *Records of the Past* (1st series), ii. 142.

saw.* Unfortunately for this view the text says absolutely nothing of a vision. But the majority of writers and commentators who regard the narrative as historical have correctly interpreted it as referring to a miraculous occurrence; † and some have been at pains to defend and account for the marvel, discussing such questions, for example, as whether the vocal organs of the ass were changed in order to adapt them to human speech.—*And Yahweh opened the mouth of*] The same phrase is used of Yahweh's enabling a prophet to deliver his message, Ezek. 3^{27} 33^{22} (cp. Ps. 51^{17}).—**29.** Balaam, unsurprised at the speech of the ass as was Eve at that of the serpent, replies to her question why he had thrice beaten her, *because thou hast made sport of me*; the verb (התעלל) means *to treat some one* (maliciously) *for one's own pleasure.* 𝔊 ἐμπαίζειν; cp. Ex. 10^{2}, Jud. 19^{25}, 1 S. 6^{6} 31^{4} (= 1 Ch. 10^{4}), Jer. 38^{19}. Had he only a sword with him, Balaam would slay the ass outright.—**30.** The ass hints that there was "reason in her madness"; all his life Balaam had used her for riding, and never before had he found room for complaint.—**31.** *And Yahweh uncovered Balaam's eyes*] so that he saw what the ass had previously seen (cp. v.^{23}) and fell down before the angel.—*To uncover the eyes* (גלה עינים) occurs also in Ps. 119^{18}: cp. below, $24^{4.16}$. Similar is the phrase *to open the eyes* (פקח); 2 K. $6^{17.20}$.—**32 f.** The angel addresses Balaam; the angel, not the ass, is the real hinderer of Balaam's journey. The ass, so far from injuring, had preserved the life of her master. *It is I* (the pronoun is emphatic) *who have come forth* (Dan. 9^{22}) *as a hinderer* (v.^{22}).—The meaning of the last clause of v.^{32} is obvious enough from the context: cp. especially v.$^{22a. 34b}$. The angel, here identified with Yahweh (cp. *before me*, and see *EBi.* "Theophany"), explains that the reason of his opposition is that he disapproves of Balaam's journey. But the precise

* *E.g.* Maimonides, *Moreh Nebukim*, ii. 42; Hengst. pp. 48–65; Strack; see also the literature cited by Di.

† 2 P. 2^{16}; Jos. *Ant.* iv. 6^{3}; *Pirkê Abôth* v. 9 (6); Aug. *Quæst. in Num.* l.; Rashi (n. on ואתה החייתי in v.^{33}), Calvin, Kurtz (*History of the Old Covenant* (Eng. tr.), iii. 406–423), Wobersin, p. 12.

meaning of the verb (ירט) in 𝔐 is uncertain, and the text of the clause suspicious; see phil. n.—**33.** *Unless she had turned aside*] EV. here adopts an emendation without acknowledgment: 𝔐 reads (senselessly) *perhaps she turned aside*. Read לולי = *unless* for אולי = *perhaps*.—**34.** Balaam admits that he has made a mistake (חטאתי, cp. Ex. 9^{27}) in pursuing his way against hindrances, the meaning of which he had at first failed to recognise, and offers to go home.—**35.** The original reply of the angel in J has been suppressed in favour of a repetition by the editor from E (cp. v.^{20}), *Go with the men* (so only v.$^{9. 20}$ E): *but thou must speak only what I* (the angel) *speak unto thee*.—**35b.** = v.^{21b} (cp. for *Balaḳ*, v.^{13}). It is possible only to speculate as to the conclusion of the incident in J: perhaps the angel bade Balaam return home.* Most naturally interpreted v.^{37} seems to imply that Balaam was at home, and Balaḳ had come to him. Then instead of the two embassies in E, the story in J told of one embassy, consisting of Balaḳ's servants or courtiers, and of one personal visit of Balaḳ. Both narratives would, however, agree in making Balaḳ's insistence the occasion of his complete discomfiture.

22. הולך] the participle is *followed* by the subj. after כי (Driver, 135 (4); S הלך (cp. 𝔊 𝔖) is probably intended to be pf.—לשטן] for the לְ cp. Ex. 21^{2}, 1 S. 3^{20} 22^{13}; Kön. 332*m*.—**24.** משעול] ἅπ. λεγ. Apparently from the same root as שעל (= 1. *hollow of the hand*, Is. 40^{12}; 2. *handful*, 1 K. 20^{10}: cp. ܦܣܠܐ). Hence, perhaps משעול means *the confined place between walls*. 𝔊 (ἐν) ταῖς αὔλαξιν (τῶν ἀμπέλων), S משעאל.—**26.** לנטות ימין ושמאול] cp. 20^{17}.—**28.** זה] Cp. 14^{22}: BDB. p. 261*b*.—שלש רגלים] Cp. v.$^{32f.}$, Ex. 23^{14}. Otherwise פעמים; cp. Ex. 23^{17}, Nu. 14^{22} 24^{10} (S רגלים).—**29.** לו . . . כי עתה] Cp. BDB. *s.v.* לו, 2 end. Cp. כי עתה after לולי in v.^{33} (reading לולי for אולי), Gn. 31^{42} 43^{10} (JE). Either the כי is simply asseverative (as in כי אז 2 S. 2^{27} 19^{7}), or (less probably) the sentences are, strictly speaking, aposiopeses: König, iii. 415*m*; Driver, 141.—יש] occurs 20 times in J, only 3 (and rather doubtfully) in E: so CH. 84.—**30.** מעודך עד היום הזה] Cp. Gn. 48^{15}; and with מעודי = *ever since I was, all my life long*, cp. בעודי (Ps. 104^{33} = 146^{2}) = *so long as I shall continue to be*. Literally the statement is, of course, in the present passage an exaggeration. 𝔊 𝔖 (as also in Gn. 48^{15}) *from my youth, i.e.* מנעוריך (cp. 1 S. 12^{2}, Jer. 3^{25})—a prosaic paraphrase rather than a variant.—הסכנתי] 𝔗^{O} *I have been accustomed*, and so many modern versions and scholars, *e.g.* RV., Reuss, Socin (in Kautzsch, *Heilige Schrift*), Oort, Str. But the sense of סכן (used but twice besides in Hiphil, Ps. 139^{3}, Job 22^{21}, and there with different senses),

* Wellhausen.

though possibly correct and certainly suitable here, is not well established. Di. thinks 𝔊 may have read הסכלתי (cp. Gn. 31^{28}), *Have I dealt foolishly in acting thus?*—**31.** ויקד וישתחו] in the Hexateuch the use of these two verbs together is confined to J, who uses it 7 times: CH. 12*b*.—**32.** לשטן] S 𝔊 𝔖 𝔙 לשטנך.—ירט הדרך]. The √ירט occurs at most once besides —in Job 16^{11}; there, if the text be correct, the Kal is trans. (יִרְטֵנִי, Baer, but doubtless ◌ְ should have metheg). ירט is explained by most modern scholars, who admit the reading, by reference to ورط=*to throw, cast headlong*; hence, *the way is* (or, reading Pual, *has been made*) *precipitate before me*; or, reading יָרַטְתָּ, *thou hast made the way precipitate*, i.e. *hast rushed headlong against me* (Di., Haupt in *SBOT.*). הדרך looks wrong: we should expect דרכך (so S 𝔊 𝔙); ירטה may be the corrupt remainder of some word or words expressing the wrongness of the way. The versions paraphrase or guess. Rashi, who refers to the view that ירט was a notarikon for (ראה)י (ראתה)ר (נטתה)נ, himself connects it with רטט *fear*, Jer. 49^{24}, which is, of course, impossible.—**33.** לפני] S (cp. 𝔊 𝔖 𝔙) מלפני.—**35.** אפס]=אך (v.[20]). אפס used thus only occurs again in 23^{13} (which is probably like the present passage redactorial).—תדבר] S 𝔊 תשמר לדבר: cp. 23^{12} 𝔓.

36–40. Balaḳ's reception of Balaam.—36 (E). The original continuation of v.[21].—Hearing of Balaam's approach, Balaḳ goes to meet him at the frontier town of *'Ir* (*city of*) *Moab* (21^{15} n.; p. 286), *which is on the boundary of* (*i.e.* formed by) *the Arnon, which is at the extremity of the boundary* (cp. 20^{16} E): both relative clauses define 'Ir Moab: the first explains that it lay on the northern boundary of Moab (for cp. 21^{14}), the second that it lay at the end of that boundary, *i.e.* the eastern end, since Balaam is coming from the east (cp. 23^{7}). Meyer (*ZATW.* i. 120 f.) insists that the words must mean *which is in the territory about the Arnon on the border of the* (Moabite) *territory*. This journey of Balaḳ's to *meet* Balaam may be the modified form of an earlier story of his going to *fetch* him from his home, the modification being perhaps a necessary result of locating Balaam's home so far away as the Euphrates. The place at which Balaḳ meets Balaam fits in with a form of the story that brings Balaam from the N.E.: in itself it is not decisive between the competing claims of 'Ammon and the Euphrates region to be the home of Balaam, but it is inconsistent with the suggestion that Balaam came from the river of Egypt (see p. 325). It is further to be observed that this description of the northern border of Moab agrees with the view of c. 21 that the country N. of Arnon was not at the time held by Moab.—37 (J). Balaḳ inquires why Balaam did not come to him? Did he doubt his power to reward him? Taken by itself the verse seems to imply that Balaḳ has himself come to Balaam in consequence of his messengers having failed in their mission. If so, the lost portions of J's narrative must have recorded how Balaam sent Balaḳ's messengers back with the evasive answer of v.[18] (cp. 24^{12}); how he started himself, but went home after meeting the angel of Yahweh (v.[34]); and how he received permission from Yahweh, when Balaḳ himself came, to return with him.—*Did I not send unto thee to call thee?*] Cp. *And he sent messengers unto Balaam . . . to call him*, 22^{5} (J).—*Why didst thou not come to me?*] Those who assume that these words were spoken *after* Balaam had come to Balaḳ, explain, Why didst thou not come when I *first* sent to thee? This finds but very insecure support in the *now* of v.[38].—*Am I really unable to honour thee?*] cp. v.[17] 24^{11} (J).—38. Balaam warns Balaḳ that though he has come, he can only speak as Yahweh directs him. Is this the original answer to v.[37]? If so, render, *Lo, I am come unto thee now*,* though I refused at first. But the position of the word עתה favours rather the rendering, *Lo, I am come unto thee; have I now any power?* † etc. For עתה thus before questions, cp. Is. $36^{5.\,10}$ (as here before הֲ).—38b. Cp. 1 K. 22^{14}. Balaam is as little ready to gratify Balaḳ, as was Michaiah to gratify Aḥab, by speaking except as Yahweh directed.—*The word which God puts in my mouth*] (ישים . . . בפי) cp. $23^{5.\,12.\,16}$ (E), Ex. 4^{15} (JE).—39. Balaam accompanies Balaḳ to Ḳiriath-ḥuṣoth. This v. may well belong to the same source (J) as v.[37], and refer to Balaam's journey from the land of ʿAmmon with Balaḳ to Moab. It is unnecessary and, perhaps, out of place between v.[38] and [40] (see on v.[40]). In the present composite narrative it refers to the journey from ʿIr Moab (v.[36]). Ḳiriath-ḥuṣoth (= *City of Streets*) is mentioned only here and, since it is by no means necessarily identical ‡ with Kiriathaim

* *E.g.* Hengst., Kue.

† AV., RV. (cp. 𝔙), Keil, Str.

‡ As suggested by Dietrich (cited by Di.) and Tristram, *Moab*, p. 305.

(? mod. Ḳureiyat N.W. of Dibon; cp. 32^{37} n.), the site is unknown, but it probably lay north of Arnon: see below, p. 340.— 40 (E). In honour of Balaam's arrival Balaḳ sacrifices cattle, large and small (בקר וצאן, cp. 2 S. 12^{4}), and gives portions of the sacrificial flesh to Balaam and the princes who had brought him (v.^{21b}). Such seems to be the meaning of the v., though the interpretation is not free from difficulty, the phrase *and* Balaḳ *sent to Balaam* being obscure: it cannot mean that Balaḳ sent to fetch Balaam from a distance, since they have already met and are together (v.$^{38f.}$); it seems best, therefore, on the analogy of Neh. 8^{12} to take the verb transitively, the unexpressed object being supplied in thought from the preceding clause.* In illustration of the custom of giving special portions to visitors, cp. 1 S. $9^{23f.}$. Von Gall (p. 10) thinks that the last clause of the verse is a gloss replacing perhaps the original object of the vb., which mentioned the entrails of the sacrificial animals from which Balaam was to discover God's willingness to curse Israel. If the sacrificial feast be in honour of Balaam's arrival, v.^{39} is in all probability intrusive, since the feast would naturally be made at the place where Balaam and Balaḳ met, viz. at ʿIr Moab (v.^{36}). Others † explain the sacrifice as the commencement of the supplicatory offerings of the following day: this is less satisfactory, for would not Balaḳ have left this till he reached the scene of operations at Bamoth Baʿal (v.^{40})?

37. הלא שלח שלחתי] The inf. abs. is here as often (*e.g.* v.$^{30.38}$, Gn. 24^{5} $37^{8.10}$) used to emphasise the question: Kön. 329*r β*. There is therefore no necessary reference in the question to the sending of two embassies, and We.'s criticism (*Comp.*[2] 348) of Kuenen is on this point unquestionably sound.—האמנם] cp. Gn. 18^{13}.—38. ארבר] S 𝔊^{AL} אשמר לרבר; cp. v.^{35} n.—39. ויבאו] S 𝔖 ויבאהו.

XXII. 41–XXIII. 6 (E). Balaḳ makes arrangements for Balaam to curse Israel in due form.

—22^{2-40} contains the account of Balaḳ's attempt, at first unsuccessful, to get Balaam to come; 22^{41}–24^{25} the account of Balaḳ's increasing ill-success in bringing Balaam's visit to the desired issue. It is im-

* Hengst., Oort, Di. † Hengst., Di., Str.

portant to determine as clearly as possible the duration and scene of the actual visit.

According to 22^{41}, on the morning after Balaam's arrival, Balaḳ takes him to Bamoth Baʿal. There is no other note of time, and apparently the whole of the following events—the sacrifices at the several places, the several utterances of Balaam, and Balaam's departure—are thought of as occurring in a single day.

The scene of these events is in view of part or the whole of the Hebrew hosts (22^{41} 23^{13} 24^{2}, cp. 23^{9}), and the places specifically mentioned as visited by Balaam are Bamoth Baʿal (22^{41}), "the field of Ṣophim" on "the top of Pisgah" (23^{14}), "the top of Peor that looketh down upon the Jeshimon" (23^{28}). Unfortunately for none of these places has any precise and certain identification been made. Nevertheless it seems probable that all the traditions alike placed the scene *North of the Arnon.*

This is certainly the implication of the present composite story: for the Israelites are encamped N. of the Dead Sea and E. of the Jordan (22^{1} 25^{1}), and sites overlooking them there must be at least N., and, indeed, considerably N. of the Arnon. The same holds good of the combined source JE, to which 25^{1} (mostly assigned to E) belongs, if we may take that as determining Israel's position during the events here recorded; not *necessarily*, however, if Israel's position is to be defined more widely, according to $21^{25.31}$, as being in the "Amorite country," for that included all land N. of the Arnon (21^{13}). A similarly indefinite description of Israel's position occurs in the narrative itself—24^{1} (J). If this excludes the position at the N.E. end of the Dead Sea, the present episode in J must have stood before the fragment in 21^{16-20}.

Of the places mentioned, we know that "the Pisgah" lay at least in part very considerably N. of Arnon (see on 21^{20}); there is no evidence that it extended S. of Arnon; moreover, no site overlooked from one of the headlands of the Moabite plateau S. of Arnon would be suitable for the Israelitish encampment. Peʿor (23^{28}), if not a mere editorial substitute for the Pisgah, must, in view of the identical definition of the site, have lain in the same neighbourhood. Bamoth Baʿal must at least have lain N. of Arnon (cp. Jos. 13^{17}). E, then, certainly places the entire events N. of the Arnon (22^{41} 23^{14}; cp. 25^{1}); J also, if we assign to him 23^{28}, or identify Ḳiryath-ḥuṣoth (22^{39}) with Ḳiriathaim; or assume that the compiler has not violated the order of events as given in J in placing 21^{16-20} before this story.

Thus for the following events, according to the composite

narrative, the source E and possibly also the source J, we reach the conclusion—

Duration: one day. *Scene*: various sites N. of Arnon. Now the mere events would have crowded a single day unduly; but when it is considered that the solemn sacrifices were offered on three different sites (not immediately contiguous, and, according to some identifications, separated from one another by more than a day's journey), it will be seen that we are here moving (as, *e.g.*, in Job 1^{13-22}) in the realm of poetry, not of fact. "We should very surely do the author wrong if we should take him literally, and begin to reckon out how all this can possibly have taken place within the limits of time. He is a poet, and will be understood as a poet."* Once this is appreciated we may also dismiss the question how the king of Moab and his princes ventured unprotected into the territory N. of the Arnon, though it had been just captured by the Israelites from the Amorites.

The unreality or, in other words, the poetical character of the narrative extends apparently to the source E. It is less obvious that the reasons stated apply to the source J.

41. In the morning of the day following the sacrificial feast of v.[40] Balaḳ, accompanied by the princes of Moab (23^{6}), takes Balaam from ʿIr Moab (v.[36] E, rather than, as the composite narrative implies, from Ḳiriath-ḥuṣoth, v.[39] J) to Bamoth Baʿal, which lay near Dîbon, not far north of the Arnon, or, according to others, much further north, near the modern el-Maṣlûbîyeh (see 21^{19} n.). The site was chosen mainly in order that Balaam might deliver his curse in sight of the objects of it (23^{13} 24^{2}), but also because it was, as its name, *the high places of Baʿal*, indicates, an ancient shrine. "The places at which Balaam took his stand and looked for omens were all probably sanctuaries. The range is covered with the names of deity—Baʿal, Nebo, Peʿor. Nor could there be more suitable platforms for altars, nor more open posts for observing the stars, or the passage of the clouds, or the flight of birds across the great hollow of the ʿArabah. *The field of Gazers* was rightly named. To-day the hills have many

* Kuenen, *Th. Ti.* 530; cp. Oort, 68 f.

ancient altars and circles of stones upon them."* *The extremity of the people* (קצה העם), *i.e.* the nearest part of the Israelites, or the part unobscured by the intervening hills: not the whole, including the most distant part (cp. מקצה אחיו and the use of מקצה Gn. 19^4); for cp. 23^{13}.

XXIII. 1f. At Balaam's direction Balaḳ builds seven altars, doubtless of material on the spot, such as earth or undressed stones (cp. Ex. $20^{24f.}$), and offers on each a bullock and a ram. The same solemn rites are gone through at the Field of Ṣophim (v.[14]) and on the top of Peʿor (v.[29]). Their object is favourably to dispose God, that He may grant Balaḳ's desire, and suffer Israel to be cursed. For other instances of the use of seven sacrificial victims, or the repetition of a ritual act seven times, see, *e.g.*, Gn. $21^{28ff.}$, Lev. 4^6, Job 42^8; see also the introduction to c. 28.

Discussions of the sacred significance of the number "seven" among various peoples may be found in Hengstenberg, *Gesch. Bileams*, 70–73; Hastings' *DB.* iii. 565 (König); *EBi.* 3436 (Barton). The seven walls of the underworld of Babylonian mythology, the seven evil spirits (Jastrow, *Religion of Babylonia and Assyria*, 570, 264 f.), the constantly recurring seven-fold obeisance ("At the foot of my lord the king seven times and seven times I fall") of the Palestinian correspondence of *c.* 1400 B.C. (Tel el-Amarna), may serve as illustrations. A single close parallel from a Latin writer may be added: "Nunc grege de intacto septem mactare iuvencos Præstiterit, totidem lectas de more bidentis" (Vergil, *Æn.* vi. 38 f.).

And Balaḳ did as Balaam had said, and offered a bullock and a ram on each altar] So 𝔊 correctly reads. In 𝔥 the words *Balaḳ and Balaam* are inserted as the subject of *offered*, but the addition is obviously a gloss. The subject of the two verbs (ויעש . . . ויעל) is the same: it is Balaḳ alone who offers the sacrifices. Note "thy (his) burnt-offering," v.[3. 6. 15. 17]. The gloss appears to be due to v.[4b], a misplaced and consequently misunderstood clause.—**3.** Balaam goes some way off alone, in the hope that *Yahweh* (S *God*) *may cross* his *path*; the verb נקרה is also used of the meeting of God and man in v.[4. 15f.], Ex. 3^{18} and (נקרא) 5^3 (all JE). It is generally supposed

* G. A. Smith, *Hist. Geog.* 566.

that Balaam goes away to make observations of natural phenomena, with a view to discovering in them, as a magician, the will of God.* But this view is not established by a reference to 24^1, and gains no support from it if that passage be from a different source. The view is rather to be rejected on the ground of the parallels in Ex. 3^{18} 5^3 (cp. also Am. 4^{12}),† and also because Balaam had reason to believe that God would speak to him as directly as He had previously done (22^{20}). Moreover, in the following narrative no allusion is made to discernment by magical means, but to direct revelation of God (v.$^{5. 16}$).—On this, as on other grounds, the emendation must be rejected which has been suggested for the corrupt word (שפי) at the end of the v., making the last clause run, *And he went to seek enchantments* (לכשפים).‡ *And he went to a bare height* (RV.) can be just defended. But it is suspicious. Why a bare height? Scarcely because it was sacred, for Bamoth Baʿal itself was sacred; nor (on grounds stated above) in order that, like the Roman augurs, who chose open and lofty places for their observations, Balaam might perform magic rites. See phil. note.—4 f. God meets Balaam and gives him "a word," and bids him return and deliver it to Balaḳ. V.^{5a} should immediately follow ^{4a}; cp. v.^{16}. The intervening clause (v.^{4b}) is a misplaced speech of Balaḳ's (which originally stood between v.^{2} and ^{3}), informing Balaam that he had done according to his request. It was Balaḳ, not Balaam, who prepared and offered the sacrifices (v.^{1} and note on ^{2b}). 5a. This, no doubt, originally ran: *and he* (viz. God, v.^{4a}) *put a word in his* (Balaam's) *mouth* (cp. 22^{38} n.), as in v.^{16}; an editor inserted *Yahweh* and *of Balaam* for clearness' sake after the accidental misplacement of v.^{4b} (see last note). Originally, then, v.$^{2-5}$ ran: ^{2} *And Balaḳ did as Balaam had said unto him, and offered a bullock and a ram on each altar.* ^{3} *And he said to him, I have arranged the seven altars, and offered a bullock and a ram on each altar. And Balaam said to Balaḳ, Stand here by thy burnt-offerings and let me go; perhaps God will fall in with me, and whatsoever he shows me*

* *E.g.* Hengst., Di., Kue., Keil. † Oort.
‡ Kuenen, Robertson Smith.

I will tell thee. And he went away. . . . [4] *And God fell in with Balaam,* [5] *and put a word in his mouth.*—6. Balaam returns to Balaḳ and the princes of Moab.

41. במות בעל] 𝔊 τὴν στήλην τοῦ Βαάλ ; 𝔗° רמת דחלת׳ה = *high place of his god.*—**XXIII. 1.** בזה] see 22^{19} n.—בנה] S עשה.—**3.** ודבר מה יראני והגדתי לך] Either, *if He show me aught, I will tell thee*—a hypothetical sentence similar to the type discussed in Driver, § 149 (BDB. p. 553*b*) ; or rather, *whatsoever He shows me, I will tell thee* ; מה, as 2 S. 21^{4} (BDB. p. 553*a* (*e*)). The latter view is favoured by the fact that Balaam expects a "word" from Yahweh. In either case the whole idiom is unusual. Kuenen's suggestion, to read וְדָבָר and connect with the preceding, is not acceptable.—שפי] apparently the sing., used only here, of שפיים *bare heights* (Jer. $3^{2.21}$ 4^{11} 7^{29} 12^{12} 14^{6}, Is. 41^{18} 49^{9}†). The sing. שפי perhaps occurs with the meaning of *baldness* in Job 33^{21} (Kt.). The simple acc. of direction is possible, though the present is an improbable instance (cp. Kön. iii. 330*c*). None of the ancient versions recognise the meaning *bare height*, nor is it favoured by the verb here used ; if such were the meaning, ויעל would be more natural. It is possible that וילך שפי is but a corrupt fragment of an originally longer text. 𝔊 has *καὶ παρέστη* Βαλὰκ *ἐπὶ τῆς θυσίας αὐτοῦ. καὶ* Βαλαὰμ *ἐπορεύθη ἐπερωτῆσαι τὸν θεόν· καὶ ἐπορεύθη εὐθεῖαν* ; yet the last two clauses of 𝔊 are clearly doublets ; 𝔙 has *cumque abiissit velociter.* It is not clear that the Versions had anything but the present Heb. text before them.—**6.** מואב] 𝔊 + *μετ' αὐτοῦ* ; cp. v.[17] 𝔐.

7–10 (E). Balaam's first utterance.—In a poem of 14 lines (7 distichs), consisting for the most part of three or four words each, Balaam explains the cause and purpose of his visit (v.[7]), and that it is doomed to failure (v.[8]) ; he dwells on the independence (v.[9]) and the vast numbers of Israel (v.[10a]), and closes with the wish that their fortune may be his.

7. *And he took up his discourse*] so v.[18] $24^{3.15.20.21.23}$. For נשא *to take up* (on the lips) = *to utter*, cp., in addition to נשא קול, נשא . . . אלה = *to utter a curse* (1 K. 8^{31}), נ׳ קינה = *to utter a dirge* (Jer. 7^{29}), and the noun משא = *an utterance.* There is no satisfactory equivalent in English for the term *māshāl* which is applied to all Balaam's poems. *Discourse*, though preferable to *parable* (RV.), which is here wholly unsuitable and even misleading, is itself inadequate, and must be understood as implying something poetical and conceived in an elevated strain. Any suggestive saying that implied more than it actually said might apparently be called a *māshāl*, as being a *likeness*, a *representation*, *i.e.* a statement standing for or representing other facts (see Fleischer in Delitzsch's *Proverbs* on 1^{1}). Haupt (*SBOT. Prov.* p. 32 f.) has recently argued that the original meaning was simply *a verse of poetry* or *a verse* as something that consisted of two halves; cp. Assyr. *mišlu* = *half.* But wide as the actual usage of *māshāl* is, this seems too general, and does not explain certain *early* applications of the term (1 S. 10^{12} 24^{14}); the same criticism applies to another suggestion (offered, *e.g.*, by BDB.) that *māshāl* means speech cast in parallelism. The early *māshāls* cited in 1 S. 10^{12} 24^{14} are short current sayings which are neither cast in parallelism nor are verses. Other instances of *māshāl* used of popular proverbs may be found in Ezek. 12^{22} 18^{3}. *Māshāl* is also used of lamentations (exultant or otherwise) over some one's fall (Is. 14^{4}, Mic. 2^{4}, Hab. 2^{6}: cp. n. on 21^{27}), whence probably arose the transferred meaning common in Deuteronomy, and later, *a byword, an object of taunting* (*e.g.* Dt. 28^{37}); or of parabolic or allegorical utterances (Ezek. 17^{2} 24^{3}). In later Hebrew it came to be used specifically of didactic and artistically constructed sentences, such as constitute and give its name to the Book of Proverbs or *M'shālîm* (Prov. 1^{1} 10^{1} 25^{1} $26^{7.9}$, Job 13^{12}, Eccles. 12^{9}). The present use (cp. Job 27^{1} 29^{1}) seems to be an extension of the last; these poems of Balaam have in them something of a declaratory, sententious, or didactic character. The term is never used of the ordinary discourse of the Hebrew prophets, or of ordinary Hebrew poetry.

7 Balaḳ bringeth me from Aram,
The king of Moab from the mountains of East:
"Come, curse me Jacob,
And come denounce Israel."
8 How can I curse whom God hath not cursed?
Or how denounce whom Yahweh hath not denounced?
9 For from the top of the rocks I see him,
And from the hills behold him—
Lo! a people dwelling alone,
And not accounting itself as one of the nations.
10 Who hath numbered the dust of Jacob?
Or 'who hath counted the myriads' of Israel?

May my soul die the death of the upright,
And may my closing days be like his!

7. Cp. $22^{5f.}$. Aram, according to Dt. 23^5 and the prevalent view of Nu. 22^5 (see note there), here refers in particular to the region of the Euphrates. Generally Aram standing by itself refers to the Aramæan region round Damascus, whence the country about the Euphrates is commonly defined either as Aram-naharaim or (in P) as Paddan-aram. But Hos. $12^{13 (12)}$ refers to the same district as "the region of Aram" (שדה ארם), of which the present use may be regarded as a not unnatural poetical abbreviation. In any case, however peculiar, there is nothing to show that the present is a very late usage;* it might quite as well be very early.—*The mountains of the East*] הררי קדם occurs also in Dt. 33^{15}, but there means *ancient mountains*, which von Gall (p. 19) adopts here. The land of the children of the East (ארץ בני קדם) lay between Canaan and the home of Laban the Aramæan (Gn. 29^1 E). The "children of the East" were nomad tribes (Gn. 25^{1-6}), wandering E. of the cultivated lands of ʿAmmon, Moab, and Edom (Ezek. $25^{4. 10}$, Jer. 49^{28}, Jud. 6–8). *The mountains of the East* may therefore be the high ranges of the Syrian desert, visible on the far southern and western horizons from above the lower courses of the Sajur on which Pethor lay,† hardly the low ranges (22^5 n.) of the Sajur valley itself.—*Jacob . . . Israel*] the use of these terms in parallelism is common to all four poems (v.$^{10. 21. 23}$ $24^{5. 17 (18f.)}$). The frequent use of the parallelism is characteristic of two other writers only, viz. Isaiah 40–55 (17 times) and Micah 1–3 (4 times).‡—8. The poetical equivalent of 22^{38}.—9, 10a. The sight of Israel is proof to Balaam that God will bless and not curse the people. If the poem is to be interpreted by the prose introduction, Balaam sees only part of the people (22^{41}); possibly, however, it should be inferred from this verse, which does not suggest a partial and impeded view, that an existing poem was incorporated by the prose writer in his narrative, and not specially written by himself for it.—*Dwelling alone*] securely and unmolested; cp. Dt. 33^{28}, Mic. 7^{14}, Jer. 49^{31}, and

* Von Gall, *Bileam-Perikope*, 17 f. † Sachau, *Reise*, 159.
‡ Gray in *Crit. Review* (1898), viii. 281 f.; von Gall, 19–22.

perhaps Ps. 4^9.—*Not accounting itself one of the nations*] but peculiar, unique in its prosperity and good fortune; the Israelites thought of themselves as so conspicuously fortunate, that all other peoples must wish to be equally fortunate (Gn. $12^{2f.}$ $28^{14f.}$). Others * take the phrase to mean constituting of itself a state, and not merely the province of a great empire; others,† a people distinguished by its peculiar religion. For Israel's sense of its peculiar relation to Yahweh, and consequent unique position in the world, see Ex. 19^5 (JE) and the kindred passages, which are, however, presumably later than the present.—10. *The dust of Jacob*] *i.e.* the number of the descendants of Jacob, which is like the dust; Gn. 13^{16} 28^{14}.—*Who hath reckoned the myriads of Israel?*] This translation is based on 𝔊, and is probably correct; ‡ with *the myriads of Israel*, cp. 10^{36}. It is in the highest degree improbable that the present text of 𝔥 (whence RV., *or by number the fourth part of Israel*) is the original. On it is based the very prosaic conclusion that Balaam only saw one of the four camps into which Israel was divided (c. 2 (P)).§ RV. margin is not a rendering of 𝔥. See, further, phil. n. In the closing couplet Balaam illustrates the saying that by Israel all nations should bless themselves, *i.e.* in invoking blessing on themselves should use Israel as the type of blessing, and say, May God make me, or may I be, like Israel (cp. Gn. 48^{20}). For *the upright* (*yᵉshārîm*) are the typical or ideal individuals among Israel (Yisrāēl); in v.^{10c} Balaam expresses the desire to die the death of individual true Israelites, in v.^{10d} to enjoy a future like that of the people—prosperous and secure as it has just been described. A similar tacit reference to Israel is probably to be found in the title of a collection of early Hebrew (national) poems, *The Book of the Upright* (*Sepher hay-yāshār*); cp., further, the poetical title for Israel, *Yᵉshurûn*. At the same time *the death of the upright* expresses its own proper meaning, a death not premature or violent (cp. Job 4^7), but peaceful and in a good old age, such a death as the heroes of national story died (Gn. 15^{15}). On the locution *may my soul die*, see phil. n.

* Oort. † Di., Keil, von Gall (p. 25).
‡ Cp. *e.g.* Di., Ges.-Buhl (*s.v.* רבע), Kautzsch. § 𝔗, Keil.

on 5[2]. By *my end* or *future* (אחריתי), which Balaam wishes to be prosperous like Israel's (now referred to in the collective singular—כמהו), is intended the closing days or years, the latter part yet to come contrasted with the first part (ראשית, cp. Job 8[7] 42[12]), now over, of this present life. The old unhistorical view which saw in these words an allusion to a Hebrew belief in a future life of blessedness beyond the grave, and, consequently, a wish on the part of Balaam for such a blessed after-life, was criticised at length by Hengstenberg (pp. 94–101), and has been generally abandoned. Some regard v.[10cd] as a subsequent addition to the poem.*

7. 𝔊 (under the influence of 24[2]) inserts at the beginning of this v. καὶ ἐγενήθη πνεῦμα θεοῦ ἐπ' αὐτῷ.—ינחני] Dr. *Tenses*, 27; Dav. 45 n. 2.—ועמה] The usual sense of √זעם in Heb. is *to be indignant*, and it is always used of Yahweh except in Dan. 11[30] and (the noun) in Hos. 7[16], Jer. 15[17]. In the present passage and in Pr. 24[24], Mic. 6[10], this meaning is hardly suitable. Our best clue to the meaning is the parallel (here and in Pr.) which suggests a synonym for *to curse*; so 𝔊 (ἐπικατάρασαι, καταρᾶται), 𝔙 (*detestor*), Ges. (*Thes.*), BDB., Ges.-Buhl. The rare Aram. ܙܥܡ means *to find fault with, to blame.* The Arabic زعم is used of speaking simply; تزغّم (with غ), a rare verb, is used of angry speech (*Lisān el-'Arab*).—10. מי מנה] On the pf. in such questions as this (cp. 17[28]), see Dr. *Tenses*, 19[2]. —ומספר] Those who retain the text explain this as an acc. of closer definition; so Ew. (*Syntax*, 283*a*), *according to number*, i.e. *exactly*, as though the thought were, the people are too numerous to number quite accurately! The closer definition is here manifestly not only superfluous (in spite of Hengst.'s curious contention to the contrary, strangely accepted by Oort), but objectionable. Read מִי סָפַר; so 𝔊 (cf. 𝔙), Geddes, Di., Kautzsch, König (iii. 330*qβ*). For מנה and ספר together, cp. 1 K. 3[8]; and for ספר used, as here, with reference to an innumerable host, Gn. 15[5]. רבבת=*myriads* for רבע=*fourth part*, is conjectural but probable. 𝔊 (δήμους) does not appear to have read רבע.—כמהו tersely for כאחריתו: cp. משוה רגלי כאילות, Ps. 18[34].

11–17. Introduction to Balaam's second utterance.—11 f. Balaam, in reply to Balaḳ's angry reproach for the blessing just pronounced, reminds the king that he had fairly warned him (22[38]) that he would not be answerable for the character of his utterances, which would be determined by Yahweh and not by himself.—11. *To curse my enemies I took thee*] (לקחתיך;

* *SBOT.*; von Gall, 25 f.

cp. 22^{41} $23^{14. 27f.}$); 𝔊 𝔖, *I called thee* (קראתיך; cp. $22^{5. 20. 37}$).—*And lo! thou hast done nothing but bless*] such is the force of the infin. abs. ברכת ברך; Dav. 86*c*.—12. Cp. $22^{35\,(20)}$ 23^{5}.—13. Balaḳ proposes to take Balaam to another place in the hope of getting a curse pronounced from thence. It was a matter of constant experiment to find out the place in and the circumstances under which a god would favourably regard special requests; some places were more adapted for one kind of manifestation; others for another. Even the Hebrews had one special mountain of cursing (ʿEbal) and another for blessing (Gerizzim). Balaḳ's first attempt to obtain a curse from Balaam, like his first attempt to get Balaam to come, had been unsuccessful; but he hoped that as Balaam's God had changed His mind before, so He might again. Balaḳ's persistence is entirely explicable on the analogy of the widely prevalent custom of persisting, when oracular replies or omens were unfavourable, till they became favourable.* This view of the inconstancy of God's purpose is not shared by the Hebrew writer, nor attributed by him to Balaam (v.[19]). Balaḳ, on the other hand, is led on by it to his own destruction: see above, p. 316.—*Another place whence thou mayest see him*] *i.e.* Israel (תראנו coll. sing. suffix, see 20^{14} n.). From the site on which the first utterance had been delivered Balaam had seen only part of the people (22^{41}), now he is to see Israel without restriction; such is what is obviously to be expected, and what the present sentence implies. But there now follows a qualification (inserted probably by a redactor), stating (but with more emphasis) that Balaam is now to see exactly what he saw before, viz. a part only of the people—*only his* (*i.e.* Israel's) *extremity shalt thou see, but thou shalt not see the whole of him.* The difficulty presented by the clause may be best appreciated in the light of the desperate exegesis which it has occasioned. Thus (1) Keil interprets: "only his extremity *dost* thou see" now and here on Bamoth Baʿal (22^{41}), whereas from the next place thou *shalt* see the whole people; but this is to import into the text all that is most crucial. The verbs throughout are im-

* See, *e.g.*, Gardner and Jevons, *Manual of Greek Antiquities*, 255 f., 260.

perfects, and there is neither adversative conjunction nor adverb of time or place to indicate that the second clause of Balaḳ's speech refers to something other than the first. (2) Equally foreign to the statement of the text is Hengstenberg's explanation: Balaam is to see a part, but a larger part than before. The difficulty is most probably due to redactorial activity. Hengstenberg (p. 105) very wisely remarks: "If Balaam already saw the whole people from here [the field of Ṣophim], no reason can be discovered why Balaḳ subsequently took him up to Peʿor." The editor felt this, and inserted the qualification, betraying his hand linguistically also in the peculiar use of אפס (see phil. n. on 22^{35}).* The sight of all Israel dwelling according to its tribes (24^{2}) is thus reserved for Balaḳ's third and last attempt.—**14.** Balaḳ accordingly takes Balaam to the field of Ṣophim on the top of the Pisgah, and, as before (v.$^{1f.}$), makes altars and offers sacrifices. The site of the field of Ṣophim is uncertain, for the top of the Pisgah was not the name of any particular peak (21^{20} n.), and it cannot therefore be inferred that the outlook from the field of Ṣophim was that described in 21^{20}. It is likely enough, however, that it lay far away from Bamoth Baʿal (see above, p. 340 f.), and the name indicates that it commanded an extensive view: it is the field frequented by *the watchmen* (צפים; cp. *e.g.* 1 S. 14^{16}, 2 S. $18^{25.\,27}$, 2 K. 9^{17}, Is. 52^{8}).—**15.** *And let me fall in with* (Yahweh) *yonder*] the suppression of the object is curious. In the light of v.^{4} what is intended is clear.—**16.** Cp. v.$^{4f.}$.—**17.** Cp. v.^{6}.

13. לָךְ] more generally written לכה (G.-K. 48*i*): but see Jud. 19^{13}, 2 Ch. 25^{17} †.—קָבְנוֹ abnormal for קָבֶנּוּ. Various views as to the significance of the punctuation are fully discussed by König, i. 357 f.—**15.** כה . . . כה] *here . . . there*, or *here . . . yonder*; so somewhat similarly 11^{31}, Ex. 2^{12}, S omits the first כה.—**16.** יהוה] 𝔊 ὁ θεός; so also some MSS. of 𝔐.

18–24 (JE). Balaam's second utterance.—This is considerably longer than the first, consisting of 22 lines (11 distichs); the greater length is probably in part, though not wholly, due to interpolation (see on v.^{23}).

Addressing Balaḳ (v.^{18}), Balaam admonishes him that God

* Di., Bacon, CH.

does not change His purpose (v.^{19}), and consequently he (Balaam) cannot recall his former blessing (v.^{20}). He then depicts Israel's freedom from trouble (v.^{21a}), its happiness in the possession of Yahweh (v.$^{21b. 22}$), and its irresistible attack on its foes (v.^{24}). The reason for this, or the proof of Yahweh's presence, is, if the verse be original, traced to Israel's abstention from magic (v.^{23}).

18 Arouse thee Balaḳ and listen,
Give ear unto me, son of Ṣippôr!
19 God is not man that He should break His word,
Nor of human kind that He should repent:
Is *He* to have promised without accomplishing,
To have spoken without fulfilling it?
20 Behold to bless I received (instruction),
That I should bless and not recall it.
21 I behold no misfortune in Jacob,
I see no trouble in Israel;
Yahweh his God is with him,
And shouts in honour of his king in his midst.
22 God who brought him forth out of Egypt
Is for him like the 'glory' of a wild ox.
24 Behold a people, like a lioness, standing up,
And, like a lion, lifting itself up;
It lieth not down till it devour the prey,
And drink the blood of the slain.

18. *Arouse thee*] "Rise up" (RV.) is unsuitable, since Balaḳ is already standing (v.^{17}). קום is really pleonastic; cp. Is. 32^{9}, Gn. 13^{17}; on this and other pleonasms, see Dalman, *The Words of Jesus*, 20 ff.—19. Balaḳ hoped to change Yahweh's disposition (v.^{13} n.); Balaam now warns him that God, unlike men, cannot be induced to break his word of promise; he does not change his purpose; cp. 1 S. 15^{29} (cf. v.$^{11. 35}$), Judith 8^{16}. He has decreed that Israel is to be blessed (v.^{20} 22^{12} 23^{8}); and blessed Israel will therefore be. The promise, the word of God is no matter of question: it is a fact. The sentences are not double interrogatives (RV.); but the interrogative governs the whole sentence (cp. Is. 5^{4b}). Render as above or, *shall he, having promised, not accomplish?*—*Son of man*] This is

the only instance earlier than Ezekiel (who uses it some 90 times) of בן אדם in the singular. There is no evidence that Ezekiel adopted the phrase from the Aramaic; * on the other hand, many of the instances of the corresponding phrase in Aramaic literature are somewhat clearly Hebraisms.† The phrase may very well have been created, if necessary, by a poet of the 8th or 9th cent. B.C. who wished to express the thought of this verse.—**20.** *I have received instruction*] *i.e.* it has been revealed to me; this is tersely expressed by לקחתי, perhaps with a thought of v.[11] לקב איבי לקחתיך: Balaḳ took Balaam to curse; but in vain, for God took him to bless. The connection is still more suggested by 𝔖 𝔙 (*ad benedicendum adductus sum*), but it is scarcely possible to point לֻקַּחְתִּי.—**20b.** 𝔐 is best rendered, *And if He* (*i.e.* God) *bless, I cannot recall it*; cp. Am. 1[3ff.]; and see Driver, *Tenses*, § 149. RV. implies questionable Hebrew. But v.[19] has stated the unchangeableness of God's purpose, v.[20a] that that purpose is to bless Israel; a hypothetical statement is therefore out of place in v.[20b]. This clause, on the other hand, states that *Balaam* is not going to change his note: he blessed before, he will bless again; and for the same reason—because Yahweh thus instructs him. Read, therefore, with S 𝔊 אברך for וברך and render, *I will bless, and will not recall it*: or with We. ואברך and render as above. 𝔖 𝔙 𝔗[O] probably paraphrase from the present text of 𝔐, but they make *Balaam* the subject throughout.—**21.** As in the first utterance after explaining that he is about to bless (v.[8]), Balaam proceeds to describe how Israel appears to him. For with 𝔖 we must read, as in the parallel v.[9] and in continuation of the 1st persons of v.[20], the verbs in the 1st and not with 𝔐 in the 3rd person (אביט . . . אראה (also S) for הביט . . . ראה; לאאראה first became לאראה, and then אביט was changed to agree with it).‡ In any case Yahweh is not the subject of the verbs.§ If 𝔐 be retained, the subject must be the cognate

* Von Gall, *Bileam Perikope*, 27.

† Dalman, *The Words of Jesus*, 234–241.

‡ Kuenen, *Th. Tijd.* xviii. 507 n. 1; We. *Comp.* 350; cp. 𝔗[O].

§ Hengst., Keil, Paterson. Hab. 1[3] is at least as much in favour of the 1st as of the 3rd person here.

participle understood, *i.e.* from the English point of view the indefinite pronoun, *One does not see . . . one does not behold** (Dav. § 108).—What Balaam sees in Israel is an absence of און and עמל; the same two words are explained in Hab. 1^3 by the parallel שד וחמס *destruction and violence*; cp. also Ps. 90^{10} (RV. *labour and sorrow*), Job 5^6; very clear instances of this physical or material sense of און are to be found in Pr. 12^{21} 22^8, Jer. 4^{15} (RV. *mischief, calamity, evil*); עמל is regularly used in such a sense. Most recent commentators,† therefore, (with 𝕲) rightly interpret both clauses of the absence of disasters from Israel; for it is the external glory and security of Israel that is uppermost in the poet's mind, if not indeed in complete possession of it (if v.[23] be an interpolation). But און has also, and not infrequently, a moral significance (cp. such phrases as מתי און), and some ‡ have so interpreted it here (*iniquity*); some have given a similar meaning (*perverseness*) even to עמל,§ though no clear instance of such a use can be found elsewhere. Others ‖ make the words refer specifically to idolatry: note the use of און in Is. 66^3, 1 S. 15^{23}.—Having in v.[21a] described Israel's happy state negatively, in v.[21b] the poet proceeds to its positive aspect: Yahweh is with His people (cp. 14^{43}, Is. 8^{10}; CH. 130^{JE}), and the shout of triumph and welcome with which the people were wont to greet their divine King (cp. 1 S. 4^5, 2 S. 6^{15}) is heard in Israel. The parallel and the continuation of the reference to God in v.[22] are in favour of thus understanding *the king* to be Yahweh; ¶ the view taken by others,** that the human king of Israel is here, as in 24^7, referred to, is less probable. For Yahweh as the King of Israel, cp. Dt. 33^5 (though some there also take מלך of the earthly king) and such passages as Jud. 8^{23}, 1 S. 8^7, Is. 33^{22}, and the use of מלך (*king*) as a divine title in proper

* Oort, Di., Str., Kautzsch, Kön. (324*d*); cp. 𝕲 𝖁. In *Het Oude Test. . . . overgezet* (ed. Oort) the reading with the vbs. in the 1st pers. sing. is adopted.

† Di., Oort, Kue.

‡ Hengst., Keil, Kalisch.

§ 𝕾, Rashi, Ibn Ezra, RV.

‖ 𝖁; cp. Ew.

¶ 𝕿° (ושכינת מלכהון ביניהון), Hengst., Keil, Kue., Di., Che., Str.

** Ew., Oort, We. (*Proleg.*[4] 256), Stade (*Gesch. des Volkes Israel*, i. 177).

names (*HPN.* pp. 115–120, 138–148).—22 (= 24^8). God is Israel's strength (or glory), whereby He bears down all opposition; directly or indirectly stated, this is the meaning of the v. It can be rendered as two co-ordinate sentences*—*God* (*El*) *is bringing them* (*i.e.* the Israelites, or reading "him," *i.e.* Israel; see below) *out of Egypt; he* (Israel) *hath as it were the toʿaphoth of the wild ox.* This represents the Exodus as still in progress, as lasting up to the entrance into Canaan: for the participle in an independent sentence indicates continuous action (Driver, *Tenses*, 135). In consequence of God's presence, of what He does for them, therefore, Israel is as irresistible as the wild ox. This is directly stated when the verse is translated as a single sentence; then clause *a* is subject, *b* predicate, and the participial clause, referring to the Exodus as past, is an attributive to *God*; so rightly 𝔊 θεὸς ὁ ἐξαγαγὼν αὐτοὺς ἐξ Αἰγύπτου.†—"Thou said'st, Lo a people has come out of Egypt [22^5]. It came not out of itself, but God brought it out" (Rashi).—*The wild ox* (ראם) is the *rîmu* of the Assyrian inscriptions. It is represented on the Assyrian sculptures as a huge species (now extinct) of the bovine kind, and was hunted among other large game by the Assyrian kings; Tiglath-pileser I. (*c.* 1100 B.C.), who claims to have slain ten male elephants and nearly 100 lions, also writes, "In the service of Adar who loves me I slew four male *rîmu* . . . in the desert in the land of Mitâni and in Araziḳi which was before the land of the Ḥattî, with my mighty bow, my iron arrow (?) and pointed lance." ‡ With the Hebrews it was regarded as untameable (Job $39^{9f.}$) and dangerous (Ps. 22^{22}), and is suitably, therefore, used both here and in Dt. 33^{17} of a warlike people capable of bearing down all before it. Cp. "In my manly power I trampled down his land like a *rîmu*." § The belief in the existence of unicorns was widespread in antiquity, and Haupt is inclined to revert to the ancient interpretation of ראם by *unicorn* (𝔊 μονοκέρως). But the Hebrew credited the ראם with more than one horn, Ps.

* Hengst., Oort. † Cp. 𝔖, 𝔗ᴼ, Di., Cheyne.

‡ *KB.* i. 39.

§ Shalmaneser's Monolith Inscr. col. ii. line 52; *KB.* i. 167.

$22^{22\,(21)}$.* The meaning of the word *tóaphoth* is obscure, but probably it refers directly or indirectly to the horns (cp. Dt. 33^{17}) of the wild ox, its most conspicuous and formidable characteristic.—**23.**—

a For there is no observation of omens in Jacob,
b Nor divining by lots in Israel:
c Now can it be said to Jacob and to Israel,
d What hath God done!

This verse presents many difficulties both in itself and in the connection in which it stands; and the ambiguity has been unnecessarily increased by the suggestion of impossible meanings. For example, a formerly popular interpretation of *a* and *b* was, *no divination prevails against Israel.*† But the words used (נחש and קסם) signify means of discovering future or secret things, not magical means of injuring others; the interpretation, moreover, implies an improbable use of the preposition ב. This interpretation was fully criticised by Hengstenberg, and has seldom been suggested since. The meaning of these lines in themselves is clear. In Israel men do not resort to oracles (קסם obtained, *e.g.*, by drawing lots with arrows,‡ Ezek. $21^{26f.\,(21f.)}$) or to omens (obtained, *e.g.*, by watching the play of light in water, Gn. $44^{5.\,15}$).§ The two terms no doubt stand typically for all similar means (such as are indicated at length in Dt. $18^{10f.}$) of obtaining knowledge of secret things; cp. the use of the cognate verbs in 2 K. 17^{17}. Such practices were at an early period discountenanced among the Hebrews (Ex. $22^{17\,(18)}$; cp. 1 S. 28^{7-9}, a source of the 10th or 9th cen-

* See, further, on the *re'em* the art. "Unicorn" in Hastings' *DB.* and *EBi.*; also Driver, *Deut.* 407; Haupt in *SBOT.* (*Psalms*, Eng. ed. 172 f.; *Numbers* (Heb. Text), 58).

† Calv., Ew. *et al.* (cited by Hengst. and Oort), RV. mrg.

‡ Commenting on Mohammed's prohibition of استقسام (from the same root as קסם), Beiḍâwî (on Ḳoran 5^4) says that it had been customary to use three arrows, one inscribed with "my lord commands me," another with "my lord forbids me," and another blank. If the blank was drawn, the process of drawing was repeated (viz. till a clear answer was obtained).

§ See, further, on both words, Driver, *Deut.* 223–225; W. R. Smith, *J.Ph.* xiii. 273 ff., xiv. 113 ff.

turies B.C.); but they continued to be practised, as the laws of H (Lev. 19^{31} $20^{6.27}$) and D (Dt. $18^{10f.}$) and other references suffice to show (Is. 2^6 3^2 8^{19}, Hos. 4^{12}, Mic. $3^{6f.11}$, Jer. 27^9 29^8, Ezek. $13^{6ff.}$, Is. 44^{25}, Zech. 10^2). Balaam, according to a parallel narrative (24^1 J), himself employed such means. The connection between lines *a*, *b* and *c*, *d* has been differently regarded; certainly the best and, if possible, a quite satisfactory view, is that which is thus expressed by Kuenen,* who refers to Am. 3^7, "the poet reckons it among the advantages of Israel that, whenever it is fitting, God causes to be announced what He intends to do. . . . Other peoples may have recourse to augurs and soothsayers, Israel is told what the future shall bring them forth." But for this sense the verb in the last clause should certainly be impf.; and the absence of any adversative particle, the unemphatic position of "to Israel," the necessity of making יאמר virtually = *shall be said by God*, *i.e.* revealed through prophets or others, and of giving כעת an unparalleled sense, all render the proposed interpretation improbable. In the absence of any satisfactory connection, the most probable conclusion is that the lines (which are of a clumsy character) are an exclamation that has found its way from the margin into the text. כעת (line *c*) in the light of the parallels, Jud. 13^{23} 21^{22}, if we must not in both these cases rather read כי עתה, and in any case on the analogy of כיום, must mean *now*; יאמר means either *can be said* (Driver, *Tenses*, § 37), or *is wont to be said* (cp. 21^{27}; Dr. § 33); לישראל, either *to* or *of*, *concerning Israel* (cp. *e.g.* Jud. 9^{54}); מה either *that which* or, as an exclamation, it may be almost equivalent to *quanta*; פעל, instead of being pointed as a pf. could be pointed as a part. פֹּעֵל or as a noun פֹּעַל (Wobersin, 35 n. 1); but neither would justify Kuenen's interpretation given above. The choice between these various ambiguous renderings must depend on the view taken of the context and the connection. But if a connection within the v. is difficult, if not impossible, to establish, the connection of the v. with the surrounding context is even more so. Not to lay stress on the fact that we should expect the assertion of God's presence in Israel (v.$^{21f.}$) to be followed

* Cp. Hengst., Keil

by the effect (v.^{24}) and not prosaically by its proof (כי * v.^{23}), v.^{23} (even admitting the interpretation of the whole verse discussed above) cannot naturally be made the proof of v.$^{21f.}$. Some intrusion in the text has therefore been very generally recognised. Some † suppose v.^{22} interpolated here from 24^{8}. But the connection of v.^{23} with v.^{21} is not essentially better than with v.^{22}. On the other hand the sequence, v.$^{21f.}$ (God's presence in, and the strength thus given to, Israel), v.^{24} (Israel's consequent irresistibility), is excellent. V.^{23} is therefore best regarded as an interpolation.‡ Then v.$^{23a\ b}$ may be a prose commentator's erroneous explanation of v.^{21a} (We.), or, less probably, inserted in anticipation of 24^{1} (Di.).—**24.** In consequence of Yahweh's presence (v.$^{21f.}$), Israel is like a lion proudly taking its prey. The metaphor reappears in a slightly different form in $24^{8b.\ 9}$. For similar metaphors elsewhere, see Gn. $49^{9.\ 27}$, Dt. 33^{20}.

18. בנו צפר] the old nom. ending as in בנו בער $24^{3.\ 15}$; חיתו־ארץ Gn. 1^{24} (P) and elsewhere; מעינו מים Ps. 114^{8}; G.-K. 90 n.; Kön. iii. *268b*. The instances must be regarded as archaisms; almost all occur in the later literature.—**19.** איש . . . בן־אדם] for the parallelism cp. 2 S. 7^{14}, Jer. $49^{18.\ 33}$ 50^{40} 51^{43}, Ps. 80^{18}, Job 35^{8}.—ודבר) Dr. *Tenses*, § 132.—**20.** בָּרֵךְ] S, but unnecessarily, לברך.—**21.** תרועת מלך] Che. proposes תפארת מ׳ = *the glory of the king* (cp. 𝔊 τὰ ἔνδοξα ἀρχόντων), *i.e.* "the visible presence of Yahweh, symbolised and represented by the ark" (cp. Ps. 78^{61}).—**22.** תועפת] also 24^{8}, Ps. 95^{4}, Job $22^{25f.}$: the meaning of this word was early lost (cp. the Versions), and it can hardly be claimed to have been rediscovered. Something like *heights* seems required in Ps. 95^{4}; and the word is so rendered there by 𝔊 𝔖 𝔙. This meaning might be poetically given here, *the heights*, i.e. *the lofty horns, of the wild ox*; but it quite fails to explain the כסף תועפת of Job, which gave the Versions much trouble (𝔊 πεπυρωμένον; 𝔙 *coacervabitur*; 𝔖 [illegible]). Here and in 24^{8} the Versions differ; 𝔊 gives δόξα; 𝔖 𝔙 𝔗^{o} *strength.* The meaning *height* has been precariously supported in modern times by a reference to the Arabic يفع = *to ascend.* Cheyne rejects תועפת from the Hebrew vocabulary and proposes תפארת (cp. 𝔊): it is unlikely that תפארת stood both here and in the preceding v. (see last n.).—**23.** פעל] of the great deeds of Yahweh: cp. Dt. 32^{27}, Hab. 1^{5}, Job 33^{29} and often.—**24.** יתנשא] 16^{3} n.

---

* It is hazardous with RV. and Bacon to avoid (so far) the difficulty by translating כי *surely*; see BDB. *s.v.* כי 1*e.*

† Oort, Kue.

‡ We., Di., von Gall (p. 30 f.); Bacon and CH. consider both v.^{22} and v.^{23} as interpolated.

25 (E). Balaḳ brings his engagement with Balaam to an end.—If Balaam will not curse, at any rate he shall have no further opportunity of blessing; this alone can be the meaning of Balaḳ's words, *Thou shalt neither curse him nor bless him*; in other words, Balaḳ has done with Balaam. The difficulty would not be appreciably diminished by translating with Hengst., *thou shalt indeed not curse him, but thou also shalt not bless him*; but as a matter of fact גם . . . גם (after a negative) means *neither . . . nor* (BDB. p. 169*a*), and not *indeed . . . but also*. The original close of the story is reached, and all that needs to be added is a statement that Balaam departed; this may be found in 24^{25} transferred to its present position of necessity by the compiler of the composite story. But inasmuch as the editor wished to incorporate Balaam's utterances in J, he composed an introduction to what forms, in the composite story, the third utterance, partly from J's own narrative ($24^{1f.}$ and perhaps 23^{24}), and partly by repeating appropriate details from the foregoing narrative of E ($23^{26f.\ 29f.}$).

26–XXIV. 2 (JE). Introduction to Balaam's third utterance—**26.** Cp. v.[12] 22^{20}.—**27.** Cp. v.[13].—**27b** *a*. Cp. 24^1; and for אולי 22^6.—**28.** Cp. v.[14].—*To the top of the Peʿor which looketh out* (הנשקף) *over the Jeshimon*] cp. 21^{20} (J), *the top of the Pisgah which looketh out over the Jeshimon.* The similarity is suspicious, and some* consider that *the Pisgah* originally stood here, and was replaced, when J and E were combined, by *the Peʿor* to obtain a variation from v.[13]. In this case both J and E make the Pisgah the scene of one of the utterances of Balaam, E adding the precise spot. A mountain of the name of Peʿor is not mentioned elsewhere in OT.; but there are places of the names Beth-peʿor and Baal Peʿor in the neighbourhood in which the Israelites are represented as encamped at this time; and in the time of Eusebius an ὄρος Φογώρ existed near Shiṭṭim, and on the ascent from Livias to Heshbon.† The name does not exist now, and the mountain referred to by Eusebius cannot be identified. See, further, Driver in *EBi.* 563 f.—**29 f.** = v.[1f.]

XXIV. 1 f. (J). Balaam, seeing that Yahweh was determined

* We., Bacon, C and B.

† Lagarde, *Onom.* $213^{47f.}$: cp. also 232^{39} 292^2 300^3

to bless Israel, does not trouble to observe omens, but, turning to the wilderness, and seeing all Israel encamped below him, falls under the influence of Yahweh's spirit and (v.^{3a}) utters his verses.—*He went not to meet omens* (נחשים, cp. 23^{23} n.) *as time upon time* he had done. The phrase כפעם בפעם is used of several immediately preceding successive occurrences (*e.g.* 1 S. 3^{10}), or of successive occurrences constituting a general custom or habit (*e.g.* 1 S. 20^{25}). If it is used in the former way here, it refers to previous observation of omens by Balaam during his visit to Balaḳ; if in the latter, to his general custom in his profession of curser and blesser (22^{6}). In either case the phrase indicates a change of source from c. 23; for, in his former utterances, Balaam does not seek omens (see on 23^{3}); and had the writer wished to remark that Balaam did not follow his usual custom, he would have stated this before the first, not merely before the third, utterance. If the phrase be taken in the former sense, previous utterances in J must have been suppressed by the editor; but if in the latter, we may here have the immediate sequel of $22^{37\,(39)}$ (23^{28}). The phrase might have been suppressed, but is less likely to have been added (Bacon) by an editor; and its presence vindicates the whole v. for J against Di.'s reference of it to R. Cp. the use of הפעם *now, this time*, which, in the Hexateuch, is confined to J (CH. 62).—*Towards the wilderness*] usage, especially in the Hexateuch, suggests as the most obvious meaning for this the wilderness lying E. of Moab, "the wilderness" (המדבר) being used especially of the wilderness of wanderings (*e.g.* c. 14, *passim*), including the wilderness on the E. of Moab and Ammon (*e.g.* $21^{13.\,23}$, Jud. 11^{22}). If this be the meaning here, as Dillmann supposes, the scene in J is not the same as in E. But if the traditions should be harmonised, *the wilderness* is that part W. of the Dead Sea called in 22^{1} (P) ʿArboth-Moab.—**2.** *And the spirit of God came* (ותהי) *upon him*] cp. 1 S. $19^{20.\,23}$ and (with צלח instead of היה), *e.g.*, Jud. $14^{6.\,19}$, 1 S. $10^{6.\,10}$. On his journey the divine communication was preceded by omens (the behaviour and speech of the ass); now without any such preparation (v.^{1}) Balaam receives, or rather becomes the vehicle of, the divine communication by falling into an ecstatic state; contrast the way in which the communications are recorded in E's narrative, $23^{5.\ 16}$; 24^{13} (J) is rather different. For the resting of the spirit on men, cp. $11^{24ff.}$ (n.); that the Hebrews did not themselves regard such an experience as limited to themselves is also implied in Gn. 41^{38}.

3–9 (J). **Balaam's third utterance.**—The text of this poem is much more corrupt than is that of the two that precede. And this is probably why this poem does not now, like the others, consist entirely of distichs. It contains at present 9 distichs and 2 tristichs (4 and 8 *c d e*). The Versions afford comparatively little help for the restoration of the true text, but conjecturally some of the difficulties can be overcome. The following translation depends on some conjectural emendations.

3 The oracle of Balaam the son of Be'or,
The oracle of the man . . .
4 The oracle of him that heareth the words of God (El),
Who seeth the vision of the Almighty (Shaddai),
Fallen down (?), and having the eyes uncovered.
5 How beautiful are thy tents, O Jacob,
Thy dwellings, O Israel,
6 Like far-stretching valleys,
Like gardens by the river side,
Like 'cedars' which Yahweh hath planted,
Like 'poplars' beside the waters.
7 'Let peoples tremble at his might,
And his arm be on many nations';
And let his king be higher than . . .
And his kingdom be exalted.
8 God who brought him forth out of Egypt,
Is to him like the 'glory' of the wild ox:
Let him devour nations his adversaries,
[And break their bones,]
And shatter his oppressors.
9 He has crouched, he has lain down like a lion,
And like a lioness, who dares stir him up?
Every one that blesseth thee is blessed,
And every one that curseth thee, accursed.

3 f. Balaam introduces himself: combined with the fact that the poems in c. 23 contain no such introduction, this is another indication that we have passed to another source (see above, p. 309).—3. Cp. 2 S. 23^1; one of the passages must be dependent on the other. This and the next poem, 2 S. 23^1 and Ps. 36^2 (possibly corrupt) are the only passages in which נְאֻם (*the oracle*) is used before any other than a divine name; the usage thus constitutes a remarkable dissimilarity between Balaam's poems and the discourses of the Hebrew prophets who very frequently employ the phrase *the oracle of Yahweh* or the like. The description of Balaam (שְׁתֻם העין) in v.[3b], left untranslated above, has been variously rendered: (1) *who sees truly** (𝔊 ὁ ἀληθινῶς ὁρῶν); (2) or *whose eye is closed*,† generally interpreted to mean *whose bodily eye is closed* (in distinction from *hath the eyes uncovered* in v.[4], which refers to spiritual vision); (3) *whose eye is open*,‡ which leaves v.[4] tautologous. Of these the first, if the two words be divided differently (שֶׁתַּמָּה עין; We. *Comp.* 350), is intelligible, but unnatural (lit. *whose eye is perfect*); both (2) and (3) rest on a very insecure philological basis (see phil. n.); (2) is also over-subtle. The Hebrew language was quite capable, when there was need, of distinguishing between ordinary human and superhuman vision (Job 10^4). It is hazardous to base on a phrase so uncertain as the present any speculations as to the manner in which a seer received his communications from God; for such, see Hengst. p. 137 ff.; König, *Offenbarungsbegriff des AT*, ii. 95 ff.—4. This v. at present constitutes a tristich, whereas, with but one other possible exception (in v.[8]), the whole poem is in distichs. It may originally have consisted of two distichs (cp. v.[16]). S reduces it to a single distich by omitting l. 1.—*Who seeth the vision of the Almighty*] *i.e.* who is accustomed to see (יחזה, Dr. *Tenses*, 32 f.); Balaam describes himself as one who is in the habit of receiving communications from God. The divine name *Shaddai* is not used in the poems of the preceding chapter;

* In addition to 𝔊, cp. 𝔗[O] (דְשַׁפִּיר חָזֵי), We.

† 𝔙, Hengst., Keil, Oort, Di., Str., various Jewish authorities cited by Rashi, RV. text.

‡ 𝔖, Ew., König, Kalisch (p. 231 f.), RV. marg. Cp. 𝔗[Jon Jer].

𝔊 𝔖 do not distinguish it here. The antiquity of the name is proved by the occurrence in Gn. 49^{25}. The use of *Shaddai* by itself is almost confined to poetry; here it seems to be used simply as a synonym for *God* (*El*) in the preceding line.—The last line of the v. begins in MT with נֹפֵל, which may be rendered *falling down*, or (cp. Jud. 3^{25}, 1 S. $5^{3f.}$) *fallen down*. It has been differently interpreted: (1) *fallen down*, *i.e.* on his bed, or in sleep; * then the clause refers to the fact that Balaam saw his visions and received his communications by night; cp. 22^{19} (E). The idea is natural enough, but by no means naturally expressed. In Ex. 21^{18} למשכב defines the meaning of נפל. (2) *Fallen down* in awe; † cp., though the verb is there used with a defining phrase, Ezek. 1^{26} and often, Jud. 13^{20}; (3) *fallen down* under the overpowering (cp. Is. 8^{11}, Ezek. 3^{14}) influence of the spirit; ‡ but 1 S. 19^{24}, which is cited in favour of this interpretation, is a bad parallel; for the reference there is to the physical exhaustion *following on* the completion of the prophetic frenzy, whereas here the phrase, standing where it does, must refer to the state *during* the communication of the divine will. None of these interpretations are acceptable, and it is reasonable to suspect the text, § though no satisfactory attempt to recover the original has been made. **5 f.** The fair sight of Israel's tents pitched below him lead Balaam to apostrophise the people, and to compare them to large and fertile tracts of country, and to strong and flourishing trees; in doing this the poet is not unmindful of the fertility of the land in which Israel is to settle.—*Thy dwellings*] is merely a synonym for *thy tents* in the parallel line: cp. Cant. 1^{8}.—**6a.** Literally, *like valleys that stretch themselves out*; cp. the use of נָטָה of long shadows in Jer. 6^{4}. MT. rightly points כִּנְחלים not כַּנ׳, for the translation,‖ *as valleys are they* (*i.e.* the tents) *spread forth*, would destroy the symmetry of the four lines of the verse, each of which consists of an object

* 𝔊 (ἐν ὕπνῳ), $𝔗^{O}$, Ibn Ezra.

† König (*Offenbarungsbegriff*, ii. 99); cp. 𝔗 Jon and Jer.

‡ Hengst., Keil, Oort, Di., Str.

§ We. *Comp.* 350 (where the suggestion made on p. 112, that נפל is Niph. part. of פלל, is withdrawn).

‖ Hengst., Keil, RV.

of comparison and a defining clause. For similar reasons it is better to reject a translation recently proposed,* *Like spreading palm trees are they stretched out* (נחלים = Ar. نَخْلٌ = *palm trees*). — *Like gardens*, etc.] Israel, enjoying Yahweh's favour, is like a well-watered garden (Is. 58[11]); when that favour is withdrawn the people are like a waterless garden (Is. 1[30]).—The comparisons with tracts of countries (v.[6ab]) are followed in the next distich by comparisons with trees. The last two lines of the v. in MT. read—

Like *ahālim* which Yahweh hath planted,
Like cedars beside the waters.

Cedars do not grow beside water; † but they are referred to elsewhere as planted by Yahweh (Ps. 104[16])—a poetical indication of their majestic size and strength. It is probable, therefore, that the terms of comparison in the two lines have been accidentally transposed.‡ *The ahālim* are generally said to be *aloes* (EV. *lign-aloes*); but elsewhere aloes (אהלים or אהלות, Pr. 7[17], Ps. 45[9], Cant. 4[14]) are mentioned along with other fragrant substances (myrrh, cinnamon, cassia), and what is alluded to is clearly the fragrant wood, not the tree itself. The aloe *tree*, indeed, was not a familiar object with the Hebrews: it was a native of S.E. Asia, whence the wood was exported.§ But would a Hebrew (or even a Mesopotamian) writer have referred, in a connection like the present, to a tree with which neither he nor his readers were familiar? Cant. 4[14] (even if the tree and not the wood be there intended) is different. Either, then, some other tree was originally intended by this word or it is corrupt; Di. suggests אילים = *palms*, but the meaning is questionable. Cheyne proposes ערבים = *poplars*; cp. Is. 44[4], Ps. 137[2].—**7.** Abandoning the apostrophe (to return to it in v.[9b]), Balaam now speaks of Israel in the third person. The last two lines of the v. celebrate the glory of the Hebrew monarchy: in MT. these are preceded by two obscure lines

* Perles in *JQR.* xi. 688; adopted in BDB. p. 636*b*.
† See Post's art. "Cedars" in Hastings' *DB.*
‡ Cheyne in *Exp. Times*, x. 401.
§ See the Bible Dictionaries, esp. *EBi. s.v.* "Aloe."

which are most generally interpreted either directly of the fertility of Israel's land, or as a figure of Israel's prosperity suggested by scenes in agricultural or settled life; by others they are explained as referring to Israel's posterity. The first line can be rendered,

Water flows (or *shall flow*) *down from his pair of buckets.*

In MT. דָּלְיָו is a dual, and therefore means either *his pair of buckets* or (G.-K. 88*e*) *his buckets in pairs.* The word can also be read דָּלְיוֹ *his bucket.* The line may be explained as depicting Israel's prosperity under the figure of a man returning from his abundant springs with water dripping over from two full buckets carried over his shoulders.* Still figuratively, but less picturesquely, the general sense of prosperity would be expressed by the singular—water flows down from his bucket, *i.e.* he is rich in the chief blessings of life. Less probably the line has been taken literally: Israel's land is rich enough in springs for him to be able therefrom to fill his drinking-troughs and to provide his house † (Gn. $24^{11ff.}$)—a very roundabout way of making a literal statement: ct. (even in poetry) Gn. $27^{27f.}$ 49^{25}, Dt. 33^{13}; also Dt. 8^{7} 11^{11}. In Arabic as in Hebrew (cp. *e.g.* Toy, *Prov.* 112 ff.) the store set by water has given rise to many metaphors. Hariri thus describes the action of the audience after being moved by Abu Zayd's sermon: "Each of them put his hand into his bosom, and filled for him a bucket from his stream, and said, 'Use this for thy spending, or divide it among your friends'" (Chenery's translation of the *Maḳāmāt*, p. 111). So Chenery writes in his note (p. 283): "In poetical language water and moisture are almost synonymous with benefit: to seek bounty is to go to the spring, to confer it is to fill the bucket or skin-bag of the suppliant. It is in accordance with this sentiment that 'cloud' has in Arabic poetry a favourable signification. . . . The prosperous are a well-watered meadow, and their life is a moistened one." A fourth, but certainly incorrect, mode of interpreting the line is to take it as a metaphor for a large posterity ‡ (cp. Is. 48^{1}), or, perhaps (? Messianically), of a

* Hengst., Keil, Di.; cp. Kalisch. † Kn., Oort.
‡ Ges. (*Thesaurus*).

single descendant; so, *e.g.*, 𝔊* *ἐξελεύσεται ἄνθρωπος ἐκ τοῦ σπέρματος αὐτοῦ*, where *ἄνθρωπος* is probably a paraphrase for *water* and *σπέρμα* for *bucket*.—The second line is much more difficult, and, indeed, really defies explanation. As pointed it must be rendered,

And his seed is in many waters.

His seed, taken metaphorically, would mean *the seed produced by Israel*, *i.e.* Israel's posterity, and then, as line *a* states the prosperity of Israel in the present, line *b* should state its continuance to Israel's seed; but to say of future generations of Israel that they will be *in* (ב, not על = *by*, as in Ezek. 17^{5}) *many waters*, is not a natural mode of expressing their possession of many waters, or blessings. Nor can the line mean that the seed sown by Israel will be always so well watered that it is *in water*.† Had the writer wanted to express the thought, which often enough occurs, that Israel's land was well watered with rain, he would not have done so in such a ridiculous manner; Ps. $65^{10f.}$ does not support, but refutes the interpretation. MT. must be corrupt. 𝔊 is unfortunately paraphrastic in this v. (see on line 1), and its evidence in consequence less certain with regard to the original. Still for what it is worth, it supports עמים (so 𝔗) *peoples* in place of מים *waters* (the repetition of מים in the two parallels is certainly suspicious); זַרְעוֹ *his seed*, can just as well be punctuated זְרֹעוֹ *his arm*, of which 𝔊's *κυριεύσει* (cp. 𝔗° ישלוט) may be a paraphrase. Then we obtain the line,

His arm shall be upon many peoples,

i.e. Israel's power shall be felt among many nations; cp. (in reference to God) Is. 30^{30} 48^{14} (text?). This sentiment accords excellently with the general tenor of the poem, but, if admitted, demands a parallel entirely different in character from line 1 in MT. Something is required such as is furnished by Cheyne's emendation adopted in the above translation (ירגזו לאמים מחילו for יזל מים מדליו); לאמים and עמים frequently stand in parallelism, *e.g.* Gn. 27^{29}, Is. 17^{12}; the corruption may have been facilitated by למים having been written (in the undivided

* Also 𝔖 𝔗 (מלכא=מים).

† Oort, Di.; cp. Rashi, בזרע הזורע על כני המים, and then cp. Eccl. 11^{1}.

text) for לְאֻמִּים; cp. מוּם for מְאוּם: G.-K. 19*k*. The emended text forms a good introduction to lines *c*, *d*; first (*a*, *b*) the poet dwells on the fear inspired in other peoples by Israel's might, then on the renown of the Hebrew monarchy. In line *c*, 𝔐 runs, *His king shall be higher than Agag*; for this 𝔊 S read *than Gog*, Cheyne *than 'Og*. Agag would be just possible if the poem were written during the reign of Agag, before the destruction of the 'Amaleḳite power by Saul (1 S. 15); but 'Amaleḳ in the days of Agag was scarcely so formidable a kingdom as to justify such an allusion. Probably, therefore, the anachronism which the mention of Agag introduces into the text is due to a textual accident. The reading Gog (on which see Geiger, *Urschrift*, 366) cannot be seriously considered, unless, indeed, the poem be regarded as a late Messianic composition, in which case the allusion to Gog would be suitable enough (von Gall, p. 35).—**8a b.** Identical (but for the variant מוציאו, מוציאם) with 23^{22}.—**8c d e.** A tristich, and as such in this poem suspicious; see on v.[4]. If one of the lines is intrusive, it is most probably *d*, with which Mic. 3^{3} may be compared. It is barely possible to translate the last line, *And with his arrows smite* (*them*) *through*; the text is probably corrupt. Emend with Di. as in the translation above (ולחציו for וחציו), which gives a perfect parallel to *c*; or, preferably if *d* be retained, read חלציו for חציו * and translate, *and shatters their loins* (cp. Dt. 33^{11}), a good parallel to *d*.—**9.** In v.[8] Israel has been tacitly compared to a beast of prey (אכל) to whom its enemies fall victims; he is now compared, with a view to the rest that follows a conquest, to a lion resting in its lair whom no man ventures to arouse. The figure to some extent resembles that of 23^{24} and is identical with that of Gn. 49^{9b}.—**9b.** Perhaps a current saying in Israel: cp. Gn. 27^{29} (also 12^{3}). But even if so, it is effectively introduced here as the climax of the blessing. So far from cursing, Balaam will, as he values his own welfare, bless Israel.

3. נְאֻם] a noun of the form זְבוּל, רְכוּשׁ; Barth, *NB.* 82*e*.—שתם העין] For שתם = *to open*, Mishnic and Talmudic usage is cited; the word is very rare, and means *to open a vessel*: cp. 'Abodah Zarah 5^{4}; Levy, *NH Wörter-*

* 𝔖, Oort, We. For other suggestions see Di.

buch, also cites קולא שתימא = *an open vessel*, from *Ab. Zarah Jerus.* v. 44*d*, and שתם, שתימה, שתומא = *the act of opening*. For שׂתם = *to close*, reference is made to the similar but not identical roots סתם (*e.g.* 2 K. 3^{19}, Dan. 8^{26}, and written שׂתם Lam. 3^{8}), ܣܛܡ, سطم. The article with the noun of the part affected in such combinations as שְׁתֻם הָעָיִן (Dav. 24*d*), is not usual; We.'s emendation שתמה עין gets rid of this, but introduces the relative שׁ, which is not elsewhere found in these poems. If adopted, read rather עינו.—**6.** Doubtless these four comparisons in a strictly accurate and grammatically regular sentence should refer to the אהלים and משכנת of v.[5], which are, from a grammatical point of view, the main subjects. But the thought dominant in the poet's mind is Israel, and it is Israel who is referred to in each of the comparisons.—**7.** וְתִנַּשֵּׂא] G.-K. 54*c*. The present form, unlike that of 23^{24}, could be pointed as a Niphal.—**8.** חציו] RV. assumes an acc. of the instrument which can scarcely be justified. The acc. of manner or specification (Dav. 70*f*) is different: see, however, Ew. 283*a*; Kön. iii. 332*u*. The vb. מחץ, judged by its usage in Heb. (= *to shatter, smash*), would not be suitably predicated of arrows: cp. Paterson and Haupt's notes in *SBOT*.—**9.** There are slight verbal variations from Gn. 49^{9b}, viz. שכב for רבץ, and ארי for אריה. For ארי, both here and in 23^{24} (the only occurrences in the Pent.), S reads אריה: but see König, iii. p. 157 n. 1.

10–14. Balaḳ's displeasure and Balaam's apology.—10. Substantially equal to 23^{11}, but here the fact of Balaḳ's anger is directly expressed, and not merely indicated by his speech.—*He smote his hands*] as a sign of contempt (Job 27^{23}, Lam. 2^{15}) for a magician who had so little control over his god as to be unable to secure a reward (v.[11]).—10b verbally = 23^{11b}, except that קראתיך replaces לקחתיך and the phrase *these three times* is added (by the editor).—**11.** *And now flee* (ברח לך, cp. Am. 7^{12}) *to thy place*, cp. v.[25].—**11b.** Cp. $22^{17.37}$.—*And, lo! Yahweh hath held thee back* (מְנָעֲךָ) *from honour*] cp. 22^{16} n. (תִּמָּנַע).—**12.** Cp. 22^{18a}.—**13.** = 22^{18b} with slight variations.—*What Yahweh speaketh*, etc.] slightly different from 22^{35} (R), and possibly dependent on the idea that Yahweh took possession of Balaam and spoke through him; cp. v.[2].—**14.** Balaam is quite willing to go, but before doing so advises Balaḳ unasked what the Israelites will do to Moab. Balaam now specialises the general theme of his former speech (or speeches), that Balaḳ may be under no mistake that Moab also will go down before Israel: *I will counsel thee* (איעצך), almost = *I will announce to thee, tell thee beforehand*: cp. Is. 41^{28} 44^{26}. Jewish interpreters (*e.g.* Rashi) by a characteristic piece of exegesis find in this word the point of contact with the story in 31^{16} (P), and recently van Hoonacker has argued at length for this view.—*In the end of the days*] a phrase "denoting the final period of the future so far as it falls within the range of the speaker's perspective" (Driver, *Deut.* p. 74, which see).

10. פעמים] S רגלים.—**13.** ידבר] $𝔊^{AF}$ 𝔖 S + אלי, perhaps under the influence of 22^{35}, though this kind of addition is common in the Versions; cp. *e.g.* 22^{9} 𝔊 𝔖, ^{17} 𝔊, ^{30} 𝔖, 23^{2} 𝔊 𝔖, $^{5.\ 16\ bis}$ 𝔖, ^{30} 𝔊.—**14.** לעמי] 𝔊 𝔖 למקומי; cp. v.$^{11.\ 25}$ 𝔐.

15–19. Balaam's fourth utterance.—The theme promised in v.^{14} is given in v.^{17}; it is followed by a halting and prosaic statement of the contrasted futures of Israel and Edom (v.^{18}), and by a general prophecy of Israelitish dominion and success (v.^{19}). Style and subject alike suggest that v.$^{18f.}$ is not an original part of the poem.

15 The oracle of Balaam the son of Beʿor,
The oracle of the man . . .
16 The oracle of the man who heareth the words of God (El),
And knoweth the knowledge of the Most High (ʿElyon);
Who seeth the vision of the Almighty (Shaddai),
Fallen down (?), and having the eyes uncovered.
17 I see him, but not now;
I behold him, but not near:
A star hath 'arisen' out of Jacob,
And a sceptre is established in Israel;
And he smites through the temples of Moab,
And the 'skull' of all the sons of 'pride' (?).

15. See v.^{3}.—16a c d; see v.^{4}; line *b* does not occur in the present text of the preceding poem.—*The knowledge of the Most High*] must here mean, in contrast, *e.g.*, to Hos. 4^{1}, *what God knows;* in some measure (at least according to later thinkers) God imparts what He knows to men generally (Ps. 94^{10}, Pr. 2^{6}). In the present context the whole clause means that Balaam, as another writer might have put it, has hearkened in the council of God, and consequently knows what other less privileged men do not know (Job 15^{8}), *i.e.* he has

gained his knowledge, as Ibn Ezra tersely and correctly comments, by prophetic, not by magical art (בדרך נבואה לא בקסם); cp. the theory of the Hebrew prophets, Am. 3^{7}, Jer. $23^{18.\ 22}$.—The divine name ʿElyon, which was a favourite one with some of the later writers, occurs elsewhere in the Pentateuch only in another song (Dt. 32^{8}) and in Gn. 14 (Cheyne, *Origin of the Psalter*, 83 f.).—**17.** The prophet's vision is wholly of the future; he sees Israel not as it now lies before him, simply menacing Moab, but under a mighty and illustrious king, actually destroying Moab, *i.e.* depriving it of independence. Previous visions have reached forward to the time of the Hebrew monarchy (cp. certainly v.[7]), but have also contemplated the Israel of the present. In view of the subject as announced in v.[14], and of the fact that Israel is the subject of the other poems (cp. 23^{9} in particular), the pronouns in *a*, *b* are to be referred to Israel * rather than to be treated as neuters (*illud*),† or referred by anticipation to the *star* or king ‡ whose emergence in history is metaphorically described in *c*, *d*. The phrases *not now* and *not near* (the latter, as well as the former, being temporal; cp. Jer. 48^{16}, Ezek. 7^{7}, Joel 1^{15}) are rather pointless unless used to contrast the Israel of the future with the Israel of the present.—*A star hath arisen*] The prophetic pf. is carried on in *d*, *e* by the pf. with waw consec.; see Driver, *Tenses*, 14*a*. The verb (דרך) of 𝔐 is highly questionable, since it regularly means *to tread* or *to trample on*; the nearest parallel to the present usage is in Jud. 5^{21}, where דרך is commonly rendered *to march*; but there also the text is corrupt. Read זרח.§ The *sceptre* (שבט) was one of the insignia of the king (Ps. 45^{7}, Am. $1^{5.\ 8}$, cp. Gn. 49^{10}); with the present metaphorical use of *star*, cp. Is. 14^{12}, where the Babylonian king is termed "the morning star," and Ezek. 32^{7}, where the king of Egypt is implicitly compared to a luminary; in Rev. 22^{16} Jesus, the offspring of David, is termed "the bright,

* Verschuir, Oort.

† Rosenmüller; cp. Rashi (רואה אני שבחו של יעקב וגדולתו).

‡ Hengst., Ibn Ezra, Keil, Str., Di., von Gall, Kalisch.

§ So We., Haupt, von Gall; cp. 𝔊 𝔖 𝔙.

the morning star"; and in Arabic, where the cognate word (كوكب) is used in several metaphorical expressions for that which is pre-eminent, the prince (سيد القوم) is termed "the star" (*Lisân-el-ʿArab, s.v.* كوكب). The subject of lines *e*, *f* is again best taken as Israel; they describe what in the future time Israel does to Moab (v.^{14}). Israel is, as often (20^{14} n.), referred to in the sing., and all the more appropriately here, since Moab is personified (much as Israel is in Is. $1^{5b.\,6}$) as a man smitten by his antagonist through *his two temples* (פַּאֲתֵי dual). For other interpretations of *e*, as also of the Hebrew text of *f*, see phil. note: the above translation of *f* rests on an emendation based on Jer. 48^{45}, where these lines are cited. The final phrase of *f* must contain a synonym for Moab; cp. *Jacob*, *Israel* in *c*, *d*; also *Edom*, *Seir* in v.^{18}. The suggestion in the translation seems the least hazardous that has been offered; with it cp. the references to Moab's pride in Is. 16^{6} 25^{11}, Zeph. 2^{10}. See, further, phil. note. The specific reference, if any, in the v. cannot be determined with certainty; line *d* might easily be interpreted of the monarchy as a permanent institution (cp. Gn. 49^{10}, and above, v.^{7}), but *the star* of line *c* rather suggests a specific individual.* Most † who have adopted an individualising (yet non-Messianic) interpretation have seen in the v. a reference to David's conquest of Moab (2 S. 8^{2}); but in view of the testimony of the conquered themselves (Meshaʿ's *Inscr.*) a Hebrew poet might equally well have written thus of ʿOmri's exploits. If, however, v.^{18} were original, then David, as the conqueror of *both* Moab and Edom (2 S. $8^{13f.}$, 1 K. $11^{15f.}$), would alone seem to satisfy the reference.

A Messianic interpretation, though obviously uncalled for, was early attached to the words, as we may infer from R. Akiba's giving to the pseudo-Messiah in the time of Hadrian the title Bar-Kokba, *son of the star*. Such an interpretation is found in $\mathfrak{T}^{O}$ (כד יקום מלכא מיעקב ויתרבא משיחא מישראל) and $\mathfrak{T}^{Jon}$, but not in the Samaritan Targ. (Cowley, *Exp.* 1895 (1), 173). From Justin Martyr (*Dialogus cum Tryphone*, 106), Irenæus (*Contra*

---

* Among those who interpret both *c* and *d* of the monarchy in general are Hengst.

† *E.g.* Rashi, Ibn Ezra, Di.

Hæreses, iii. 9^{2}), and Cyprian (*Testimonia*, ii. 10) onwards, the Messianic interpretation became general among Christian interpreters down to 1771, when it was challenged by Verschuir. Subsequently some writers have maintained that the entire outlook (including v.$^{18f.}$) is only satisfied by the *inclusion* of the Messiah. This view is defended at length by Hengst. (172–181), though he admits that it is doubtful whether Balaam so understood it himself. In the Christian Messianic interpretation "the star" becomes a prophecy of "the star" seen by the Oriental Magi (Mt. $2^{2.\ 9f.}$); this, probably enough, does justice to the meaning of the evangelist, however alien from the intention of the author of the poem. On the history of the interpretation, see Reinke, 186–204. Recently von Gall (37 f.) has argued in favour of a purely Messianic interpretation.

17. שבט] 𝔊 ἄνθρωπος; cp. v.^{6} 𝔊.—ומחץ פַּאֲתֵי] Jer. 48^{45} ותאכל פְּאַת. מחץ demands as its object, if not persons, at least parts of the person (*e.g.* heads, loins). Hence the *dual* פַּאֲתֵי must be the two *sides* of the head, *i.e. the temples*, the full phrase in prose being פאת ראש (Lev. 19^{27}) or פאת פנים (Lev. 13^{41}); but the word is used by itself, as here, in the phrase קצוצי פאה. It is therefore unnecessary with the Versions (𝔊 𝔖 𝔙 𝔗^{o}) to give פאתי a unique metaphorical sense (*leaders*), and unsuitable (with, *e.g.*, Hengst. and ? RV.) to give it (after מחץ) the sense commonly borne by it of *side* or *district of a country*.—וקרקר] S rightly וקדקד (cp. Jer. 48^{45} and the parallel פאתי). 𝔊 𝔖 𝔙 𝔗^{o} Symm. render by various verbs of different significations. A verb is no doubt intended by MT., and that the same that is implied in the textually doubtful passage Is. 22^{5}. The root (قرقر, ܩܪܩܪ, and New Hebrew קרקר) is used of sounds made by men and animals (*e.g. to cry, roar*); in certain post-biblical passages (Levy, iv. 391*b*) קרקר is also used, apparently as a denominative from קיר, with the meaning *to break down*,—a sense which, though wholly unsuitable to the object, has been commonly adopted here by those who retain 𝔐; so Hengst., Ges. (*Thes.*; cp. also *Gesch. d. Hebr. Sprache*, § 12, p. 37), Kön. (i. 456 f.).—כל בני שת] שת being taken as the name of Adam's son (𝔊 𝔖 𝔙 AV.) (Gn. 4^{25}), the phrase was interpreted *all men* or *all nations* (𝔗^{o} Rashi). Sayce (*Exp. Times*, xiii. 69) understands it to mean the Bedawin, who were known to both Egyptians and Babylonians as "Sutu." But most have regarded שת as an appellative, and explained it as = שְׁאֵת, which occurs in Lam. 3^{47}†, and is supposed to have the same meaning as שאון Jer. 48^{45} (Verschuir, Hengst., Oort, Di., Reuss, RV.). The sense thus yielded (*sons of tumult*) is not inappropriate (cp. Am. 2^{2}); but it is by no means clear from the context in Lam. 3^{47} that שאת actually meant *tumult*. It is preferable, therefore (unless Jer. 48^{45} be adopted as the better reading), to treat שת as = שְׂאֵת = *pride*; cp. We. *Comp.* 351.

18 And Edom shall become a possession,
And Se'ir, his enemies, shall become a possession,
While Israel is gaining success.

This inartistic tristich, the more noticeable after the previous succession of distichs (v.[15-17]), falls outside the scope of Balaam's farewell oracle (v.[14]), and is apparently the first of a number of brief prophecies (directed against various peoples) which at some time or other have been attached to Balaam's last words. The general sense of the v. is: the Edomites, the enemies of Israel, will become the subjects of the Israelites, while the latter pursue their victorious career. This is very awkwardly expressed, and Reuss may be right in thinking that "his enemies" (איביו) is the remnant of an otherwise lost line; see also von Gall (38 f.).—*Seʿir*] is here parallel to Edom, as in Jud. 5[4]; S 𝔊 read *Esau*, cp. Ob. v.[8], Mal. 1[2-4].

> [19] And may dominion be exercised out of Jacob,
> And survivors be destroyed out of cities.

The verbs of MT. are transitive (וְיֵרְדְּ and וְהֶאֱבִיד); the subjects must be indefinite, for the last-mentioned subject (*Israel*, v.[18]), in view of the clause *out of Jacob*, is unsuitable, and *Edom-Seir* is manifestly out of the question; nor is it natural to pass back * over v.[18] to the ruler alluded to in v.[17], even supposing that the ruler and not the people is the main subject of that v., and that v.[19] formed originally part of the same poem as v.[17]. The verse appears to be a general expression of such Messianic hope as is met with especially in the later prophecies: it contemplates the world-wide dominion of Israel and the violent destruction of all who oppose it (cp. *e.g.* Mic. 5[8], Is. 60, especially v.[12], Zech. 12[6]). The details are naturally obscure: of line *b* two interpretations alone need be mentioned: (1) may those who have escaped or fled from the open country before the conqueror to the cities (עיר collective, as perhaps in Ps. 72[16], Job 24[12]) for refuge (cp. Jos. 10[20]) be destroyed; or (2) עיר is the city of the ruler, viz. Zion (cp. Kön. iii. 294*b*): then מעיר is strictly parallel to מיעקב in line *a*. Ewald is so confident that this second is the right interpretation as to find in the verse a proof of Judæan origin of the oracle (*Jahrb. f. Bibl. Wissensch.* xi. 202). If v.[19] be closely connected with v.[18] עיר may be the chief city of Edom, or collectively all the cities of Edom.

* With Keil.

18 f. Von Gall reconstructs these verses thus—

והיה ארום ירשה
ואבד שריד משעיר
וישראל עשה חיל
ירד יעקב איביו.

This is preferable at least to the similar but less complete reconstruction in *SBOT*.—**18.** יְרֵשָׁה] so pointed here only, and here S has ירושה; in 𝔐 the more frequent יְרֻשָּׁה is indistinguishable.—**19.** וְיֵרְדְּ] apoc. impf. from רדה (as Ps. 72^{8}). This is preferable to וְיֵרֵד, (one) *shall come down* (𝔖 𝔗^O and ? 𝔊).

20–24. Fifth, sixth, and seventh utterances.—These pronounce the fate of ʿAmaleḳ (v.^{20}), Ḳain (v.$^{21f.}$), and some other people or peoples (v.$^{23f.}$). They are distinguished from the four preceding by their great brevity, so far as the fifth and sixth are concerned by an additional introductory phrase (. . . וירא *and he saw* . . .: yet cp. v.^{2} 22^{41} 23^{13}), and by containing no reference whatever to Moab or anything but at the most an implicit reference to Israel. Their position here is strange in view of the terms of v.^{14}. Partly on these grounds, partly on the ground of specific references, a different origin has been attributed to these final oracles by almost all modern scholars.

So Di., Reuss (*Gesch. der HS.*^{2} p. 214), Kön. (*Einl.* 208), Corn. (*Einl.*^{3} 63), We. (*Comp.*^{2} 113; cp. 361), De Wette-Schrader (*Einl.*^{8} p. 293), Kue., Bacon, Che., Addis (*EBi.* 464), Kalisch, van Hoonacker, CH. Oort maintained the unity (p. 82 ff.); but in *Het Oude Test. opnieuw overgezet* (ed. Oort) the verses are regarded as an addition.

The interpretation of these brief oracles, therefore, must not be governed by the assumption that they originated at the same time or under the same circumstances as the longer ones which precede. Unfortunately their brevity, combined with several strange and suspicious features in the text, renders anything approaching certainty in the interpretation out of the question. The present text is in some places unintelligible. Some alternatives might be ruled out if the date could be independently established, but it cannot.

20. *And he saw ʿAmaleḳ*] hardly in vision (cp. v.^{17}),* but rather as he had previously seen † in whole or in part the hosts of Israel (22^{41} 23^{13} 24^{2}); so in v.^{21}. But the phrase,

* Hengst., Ew., Keil. † Di.

unlike the following, *and he took up his discourse and said*, forms no part of the regular introductory formula prefixed to the preceding oracles ($23^{7.\ 18}$ $24^{3.\ 15}$). On the resumption of the shorter formula in v.[23], see below. It is scarcely necessary to infer that the writer or editor thought of the ʿAmaleḳites as resident or wandering E. of Jordan, for views of the Negeb, to which other references refer the ʿAmaleḳites (13^{29} $14^{43.\ 45}$, 1 S. 30), were supposed to be obtainable from points on the Pisgah (Dt. 34^{3}).

First of the nations is (was) ʿAmaleḳ;
But his last shall be (is) unto destruction.

There are no verbs, and, consequently, not even the slightest indication of tense. *First of the nations* (ראשית גוים, also Am. 6^{1} †) means *most choice* (cp. 1 S. 15^{21}, Am. 6^{6}, Job 40^{19}), and here apparently *most powerful of the nations*: such ʿAmaleḳ never was nor, so far as is known, was it ever, while it existed, so accounted; but later legendary or fictitious narratives of ancient Arabic authors described the ʿAmaleḳites as a mighty race.* The expression is partly due to poetic exaggeration, partly to the desire for a verbal antithesis to the ominous parallel (אחריתו). The implicit allusion to the power of ʿAmaleḳ in v.[7] is textually uncertain. The alternative rendering, *the beginning*, i.e. *the most ancient*, *of the nations*, is against the analogy of Am. 6^{1}, conflicts with Hebrew theory (Gn. 36^{12}), and is certainly not to be supported by the corrupt passage 1 S. 27^{8} (where read מטלם for מעלם). Assuming the Mosaic authorship of the verse, some (*e.g.* Keil) have explained the phrase to mean the first nation who fought against Israel (Ex. $17^{8\text{ff.}}$).—*His last*] אחריתו; see 23^{10} n.; *the future* of ʿAmaleḳ in contrast with Israel's future (23^{10}) will be *destruction*: the Hebrew expression is very strange (cp. phil. n.), though perhaps in these harshly expressed and obscure verses not impossible. Cheyne proposes, *But its last man Edom shall destroy* (אֱדֹם יְאַבֵּד). ʿAmaleḳ suffered severely at the hands of both Saul (1 S. 15) and David (1 S. 30), and, according to the Chronicler's evidence, was exterminated in the time of Hezekiah (1 Ch. $4^{42\text{f.}}$, as generally interpreted;

* Nöldeke, *Die Amoriter*; also *EBi.* 128 f.

yet see *HPN.* 237). Dt. $25^{17ff.}$ scarcely proves that ʿAmaleḳ was still a power of importance at the end of the 7th cent.; in a much later passage (Ps. 83^{7}, note *Gebal* as defining the date) ʿAmaleḳ is presumably used for contemporary enemies of Israel, as Greek authors of the 6th century A.D. used Scythians for the Goths (Nöld.).—Judged by itself, the oracle, then, may be a prophecy of ʿAmaleḳ's destruction while as yet its power was unbroken (*i.e.* before the time of Saul), or during its decline (from the time of Saul onwards), or a retrospect (? suggested by Ex. 17^{14}) after ʿAmaleḳ's destruction.

21. With line *a*, cp. v.^{20a}.—The *Ḳenites* at times ranked as a branch of the ʿAmaleḳites (1 S. 15^{6}; and see Moore on Jud. 1^{16}); at times they appear most closely associated and on friendly terms with Israel, and especially Judah (1 S. 27^{10} 30^{29}, Jud. 1^{16} 5^{24}). They are generally associated with the Negeb, though some at least, separating from the main stock, found a home in the districts of the Northern Israelitish tribes (Jud. 4^{17} 5^{24}); in the rhetorical list of Gn. $15^{19f.}$ they figure among the peoples of Canaan to be dispossessed by Israel. The gentilic form *the Ḳenite* (הַקֵּינִי) is here used collectively as in 1 S. 15^{6} 30^{29}; but in the poem itself, as in Jud. 4^{11}, the national name Ḳain (קַיִן) is used. In Hebrew Ḳain is identical in form with Cain, Adam's son. On this identity Stade has largely based a number of interesting speculations concerning the Ḳenites.*—Of the four lines of the oracle the first two are sufficiently straightforward. The third is the same, but that the opening conjunction is used in an extremely rare and somewhat suspicious sense; out of the fourth no reasonable meaning has ever yet been legitimately extracted.

21a Ever-during is thy habitation,
b And placed among the crags thy nest:
c But yet Ḳain must be destroyed;
d How long? Ashshur shall carry thee captive.

a, *b* describe the Ḳenites as having in the rocks their habitations, which, being inaccessible to enemies, are *ever-during*;

* *ZATW.* 1894, pp. 250–318; cp. Cheyne's art. "Cain" in *EBi.*

cp. Obadiah's description of Edom (v.[3f.]). In Obad. the term *nest* is suggested by the previous figure of the vulture: here it is used to gain a paronomasia (*ḳinneka* = *thy nest*: *Ḳêni* = *Ḳenite*). The word *ever-during* (איתן) is used especially of *perennial* water (see Am. 5^{24}, Dt. 21^4 with Driver's note there): the rendering of the Versions (𝔊 𝔖, EV.), *strong*, is not precise. With the present, cp. the similar phrase in Jer. 49^{19}. Lines *c d* should, in accordance with the general tenor of these oracles of doom, contain a transition similar to that in Ob. v.[3f.]: the Ḳenites think themselves unassailable, nevertheless they cannot escape the destined destruction. Either, therefore, כי אם is an error, or the conjunction is used here, although no negative has preceded, as a strong adversative (BDB. 475*a*); or we must regard line *b* as a virtual negative, *placed in the rock is thy nest, and therefore not to be taken; but nevertheless* . . . (Kön. iii. 372*g*). The text of *d* can only be translated as above; עד מה means quite regularly (Ps. 4^3 74^9 79^5 89^{47} †) *Until when? How long?*; consequently renderings such as *when once*, *until* are illegitimate. But the text really yields no sense: Di., following others, interprets *How long? sc.* will it last? *Ashshur will* finally *carry thee captive*, and so make of thee an utter end? But though to us Assyria may define a period in Hebrew history, would a Hebrew writer define a future period in a prophetic saying by a mere reference to Assyria? The truth is the last clause is no reply to the question, *How long?* The text must be more or less corrupt; but the corruptions are ancient, for the Versions indicate no real variations.

Cheyne by a radical, purely conjectural and, therefore, quite uncertain emendation gains good sense: he renders the last line, *Edom shall beat in pieces his dwelling* (ארם ירשש מושבו). Hommel also emends though less radically, with the result that his translation labours under some of the difficulties presented by the traditional text: he renders the last two lines thus: *and yet Ḳain shall belong to ʿEber* (לעבר for לבער); and *how long will it last? Ashshur will carry thee* (the Ḳenite) *captive*. Hommel understands Ashshur to mean Shur in South Palestine (an equation that cannot at present be regarded as more than a hypothesis). Following up a suggestion of Wellhausen's (*Comp.*[3] 351) that Ḳenite may here mean Nabatæan, von Gall (42f.) explains the poem with reference to attempts of the Seleucid empire at the beginning of the 3rd cent. B.C. to subdue

Se'ir; then עבר (so read for בער in v.[22a]) and אשור (=Syria) are terms for the two halves of the Seleucid empire separated by the Euphrates.

20. עדי אבר] v.[24]. עדי is a form of עד used mainly, or exclusively, in later poetry (Is. 26[4] 65[18], Ps. 83[18] 92[8] 104[23] 132[12. 14] 147[6], Job 7[4] 20[5]); it also occurs in the compound בלעדי. אֹבֵד has been regarded as a collective (cp. שריד in v.[19]), or an abstract (Barth, *NB.* § 98*a*: against this, see Kön. iii. 243*g*); then the phrase means literally *unto the perishing ones*, or *unto destruction.* The absence of a vb. in this line is almost intolerable. This was felt by the Versions, which seem to have had the consonants of the present text before them, but to have read them differently. 𝔊 (ἀπολεῖται, v.[24] ἀπολοῦνται) paraphrases; S reads עד יאבד; 𝔖 ܠܥܠܡ ܠܐܒܕܘܢ (v.[24] ܢܐܒܕܘܢ) and similarly 𝔗°.—**21.** שים) Part. pass.; G.-K. 73*f*.—**22.** עד מה אשור] S עד מאשור; 𝔊 (πανουργίας) read עד מה as ערמה.—תשבך] fem. with the name of a people; cp. *e.g.* Ex. 12[33], and see G.-K. 122*h*.

23. *And he took up*, etc.] 𝔊 assimilates this introductory formula to those of v.[20] and v.[21] by prefixing, *and he saw Og* ($𝔊^L$ *Gog*; cp. 24[7] 𝔊). The insertion probably depends on 21[33–35], itself a late editorial interpolation. Cheyne and Strack suggest that the whole introductory formula here is an interpolation, and that originally v.[21–24] formed a single poem.

The short poem contained in v.[23f.] can be translated word for word, but read as a whole it is most awkwardly and unnaturally expressed, and there is little probability that any interpretation of the text as it stands, or as it has been variously emended, reaches the original meaning. The present text scarcely appears to be satisfied by circumstances earlier than the Greek period; as emended by Cheyne, it can hardly be later than the Assyrian period, while Hommel so emends as to make it, in his judgment, a suitable product of the age of Moses.

The existing text may be translated as follows:—

> Alas! who shall live after God hath appointed him?
> But ships from the side of Kittim
> Shall afflict Ashshur, and shall afflict 'Eber;
> And he also (shall be) unto destruction.

This is commonly understood to mean: How terrible will Assyria be! none will expect to escape her power! yet she will perish at the hands of the Kittim. *After God hath appointed him?*] for the use of שים *to appoint*, see Is. 44[7], Hab. 1[12]; and for the use of מן (in משמו), which is "chiefly late" (BDB. 583*b*), see Lev. 9^{22}, Is. 44^{7}, Ps. 73^{20}, Dan. 11^{23}. The suffix *him* is generally understood to refer to Ashshur and 'Eber mentioned in the next v. and regarded here as a single idea (cp. v.[24] last line). The suffix might be treated as a neuter, *it* (𝔊 ταῦτα), *i.e.* who shall survive when God appoints what is to follow.—24. *Ships*] צים is used in this sense in Is. 33^{21}, Ezek. 30^{9}, Dan. 11^{30}†. For וצים S reads יוצאים (cp. 𝔊 ἐξελεύσεται) = *they* (*shall*) *come out*; 𝔖 𝔙 𝔗° give both *ships* or *troops* and a vb.—*From the side of*] *coast* (AV.) is an archaism (= *côte*). With יד = *side*, cp. כל יד נחל יבק "all the *side* of the Wady Jabbok" (Dt. 2^{37}), and ארץ רחבת ידים = "a land wide in *both directions*": see, further, BDB. 390*b*.—*Kittim*] the Heb. כִּתִּים or כִּתִּיִּים is derived from כתי, the name of a town (in Gr. *Kition*) in Cyprus which is frequently mentioned in the Phœnician inscriptions.* With the Hebrews the Kittim ranked as a son of Javan, *i.e.* Greece (cp. Ἰάονες = ἸάϜονες = Ionians); see Gn. 10^{4}. It agrees with this, that in Is. $23^{1.12}$ Kittim appears to mean the inhabitants of Cyprus. In Jer. 2^{10}, Ezek. 27^{6}, Kittim is used more widely of the Western maritime nations ("the isles of Kittim," איי כתים).† Later it is used with specific reference to one or other of these Western nations; Dan. 11^{30} refers to the Romans, as 𝔊 rightly perceived, and 1 Mac. 1^{1} 8^{5} to the Greeks. Both Dan. 11^{30} and 1 Mac. 1^{1} appear to allude to the present poem, and thus show how it was understood in the 2nd cent. B.C. Cp. the rendering of the phrase here in 𝔙, *venient in trieribus de Italia*. If the poem be as old as the 7th or 8th cent. B.C. "ships from Kittim" may mean ships bearing Cypriot mariners.—As the text stands, the first two lines of v.[24] must (as in the above translation) form one sentence (not, as in RV., two). But this, though grammatically possible (Driver, *Tenses*, § 123*a*), is extremely awkward; possibly, unless the text be even more corrupt, a vb. such as

* See, *e.g.*, *CIS.* 10^{2} (other references in Lidzbarski, *Nordsem. Epigr.* 299 f.). W. Max Müller (*Asien u. Europa*, 345) suggests another origin of the name, כתים = Hittites.

† Cp. Jos. *Ant.* i. 6^{1} (on Gn. 10) Χέθιμος δὲ Χεθιμὰ τὴν νῆσον εἶχεν· Κύπρος αὕτη νῦν καλεῖται· καὶ ἀπ' αὐτῆς νῆσοί τε πᾶσαι, καὶ τὰ πλείω τῶν παρὰ θάλασσαν Χεθιμ ὑπὸ Ἑβραίων ὀνομάζεται.

יבאו (*shall come*) has dropped out. The words are understood to mean: the Kittim shall overthrow the Assyrian empire. No overthrow of the Assyrian empire by the Western maritime peoples is known. Various unsatisfactory solutions of the difficulty have been offered (see Di.). The most interesting is that which has satisfied alike some of those who hold the poem to be a prophecy of far distant events,* and some † who see in it a reflection of historical events. According to this interpretation, the poem refers to the overthrow of the Persian empire by Alexander the Great (cp. 1 Mac. 1^1); in that case Ashshur here as in Ezr. 6^{22} means the Persian empire. It is impossible to determine the precise sense of ʿEber in this obscure poem; it is, however, altogether unlikely that it means *the Hebrews* (𝔊); rather than this the country *across* the Euphrates (𝔗°; cp. Jos. 24^3).—*And he also*] as in the first line, Ashshur and ʿEber are regarded as a single idea.

The obscurity and improbability of the text are sufficiently great to invite emendation; unfortunately the corruption of the text is more ancient than the Versions, and emendations must be conjectural and, consequently, uncertain. Among the most interesting is that of D. H. Müller (*Die Propheten in ihrer ürsprünglichen Form*, i. 215 f.; cp. Cheyne, *Exp.* (1896) iii. 77 ff.). He would read משמאל for משמו אל, and point עַנּוֹ instead of עַנּוּ; thus the first line becomes, *Alas! who can survive of Sham'al*, and v.[24] foretells the destruction of Sham'al at the hands of the Kittim, Assyria and 'Eber. Sham'al is a State in N.W. Syria mentioned in the Assyrian inscriptions. Sayce in criticism (*Early Hist.* p. 231 n.) points out that Samalla was only the Assyrian name for the district, the native names being Ya'di and Gurgum. The proposed interpretation of v.[24] is altogether improbable.

Cheyne's emendation (*Exp. Times*, x. 399) is far too hypothetical to be probable, though a Hebrew towards the end of the 8th cent. might possibly have written it. Hommel (*Anc. Heb. Trad.* 245ff.) reads איים (*jackals*) for אוי מי, משמאול (*from the north*) for משמו אל, and points צִיִּים (*wild cats*) instead of צים. The poem then becomes a prophecy of the invasion of Southern Palestine (Ashshur=Shur) by wild cats and jackals, *i.e.* wild hordes from the North or from the sea). Whether the probability of this suggestion is as great as its ingenuity, the reader may judge for himself.

25. Balak̟ and Balaam both leave the spot where they had stood together, and Balaam returns to his country (cp. v.[11] n.); ct. $31^{8.16}$. For the phraseology, cp. Gn. 18^{33} 32^1.

* Delitzsch (p. 121 f.) and Leibnitz (as cited by him).

† *E.g.* Corn.

XXV. The chapter divides into four sections of which the last three are closely connected with one another. (1) The Israelites provoke Yahweh's anger by their immoral intercourse with Moabite women and by their worship of Baʿal-Peʿor, v.$^{1-5}$. (2) During the progress of a "plague" (v.$^{8b.\,9}$; cp. v.^{6b}), an Israelite brings home a Midianite woman; they are taken in the act and slain by Phineḥas, v.$^{6-9}$ (cp. v.$^{14f.}$). (3) For his zeal, Phineḥas is promised through his seed eternal possession of the priesthood, v.$^{10-13}$; (4) for their wiles, the Midianites (cp. v.^{6}) are to be smitten by the Israelites, v.$^{16-18}$ (cp. c. 31).

Section (1) is a fragment; the carrying out of the judicial executions commanded in v.$^{4f.}$ is not recorded. Section (2) is also a fragment lacking the commencement, which must have related the outbreak of the plague and the assembling of the people at the tent of meeting (v.^{6b}). The editor may have been led to unite these really heterogeneous stories by the fact that both referred to Israelitish connections with foreign women.

V.$^{1-5}$ is derived from JE; v.$^{6-18}$ from P (though not entirely from P^g). The motive of v.$^{1-5}$ is characteristic of JE; here Yahweh is provoked by the worship of other gods (cp. Ex. 34^{14-16} 20^{3}), and the crime is punished by the judges (Ex. $18^{21ff.}$). The motive of v.$^{6-18}$ points to the age of P; the sin is intercourse with foreign women (cp. Ezr. 10); it is punished by the priest. The same motive appears elsewhere in P (Gn. $26^{34f.}$ 28^{1-9}).

The style of v.$^{6-18}$ clearly points to P; note, *inter alia*, עדה v.$^{6f.}$ (cp. 1^{2} n.); נשיא v.$^{14.\,18}$; וידבר . . . לאמר v.$^{10.\,16}$ (CH. 185); מגפה v.$^{8f.\,18}$ (cp. 14^{37} n.). In v.$^{1-5}$, as particular indications of JE, note ויחר אף יהוה v.^{3} (cp. 11^{1} phil. n.) and חרון אף יהוה in v.^{4}.

1–5 (JE). The Israelites are seduced into the worship of another god.—It is probable that the editor of JE has here combined elements from two similar stories in J and E; for v.^{4} and v.^{5} appear to contemplate different modes of death (see notes), and in v.^{1} clauses *a* and *b* have the synonymous subjects (*Israel*, *the people*) which appear elsewhere as a result of compilation (14^{1} 20^{1} n.).

Analysis in detail cannot be carried through with certainty. V.[3a] and v.[5] obviously go together, and *the judges* of v.[5] may point to E (cp. Ex. 18). Then v.[4] came (presumably) from J: with v.[2] cp. Ex. 34^{15} (J). CH. refer v.[1a. 3a. 5] to E, and v.[1b. 2. 3b. 4] to J.

In one account (J) the Israelites are led into idolatry by their immoral intercourse with the Moabite women, but the scene and the name of the Moabite god are undefined; in the other (E), the scene is Shiṭṭim, the god is Ba'al Pe'or; but the circumstances leading up to the idolatry are not given.

1. *And Israel abode*] 20^1 $21^{25. 31}$. *Israel* also occurs in v.[3a. 4b. 5]: ct. *the people*, v.[1b. 2. 4a], and *the children of Israel* which occurs 5 times in v.[6–18] (P).—*In Shiṭṭim*] the name (in Hebrew with the art.) means *the acacia trees.* From Shiṭṭim Joshua subsequently despatched the spies (Jos. 2^1 3^1 JE). In 33^{49} the place is mentioned, under its fuller name Abel-Shiṭṭim, as the last station of the Israelites, and as situated in the steppes of Moab. Hence 25^{1a} is the parallel in JE to 22^1 in P. The exact site of Shiṭṭim is uncertain; but it appears to be identical with Abila, which derived its name from the first part of the full name, and, according to Josephus (*Ant.* iv. 8^1, v. 1^1), was situated 60 stadia from the Jordan. Some have suggested the identification of Abila with Kefrēn.* But in any case Shiṭṭim lay in the country which, according to E's narrative, was, at the time of the Hebrew invasion, occupied by the Amorites, who had wrested it from the Moabites. Consequently, either the intercourse of the Israelites with the Moabite women was located, in the source whence v.[1b. 2] is drawn, far south of Shiṭṭim, or this source represented the Moabites as living at the time, whether in full occupation of the country or as a subject people, N. of the Arnon.—2. *And they called the people to the sacrificial feasts of their god*] Participation in the sacrificial feasts is the sequel to the intimacy with the women, not the cause of it, as the incorrect rendering of ותקראן in RV. ("for they called") suggests. The women not unnaturally summon their paramours to their feasts, which, according to ancient custom, were sacrificial occasions; in partaking of the feast

* Buhl, *Geog.* 116, 265.

the Israelites honoured the god (cp. *e.g.* Dt. $12^{5\ 7.\ 17-19}$, Ex. 24^{11}, Jud. 9^{27}). The god thus honoured is, presumably, Kemosh, the national god of Moab (21^{29}); the plural (אלהיהן), which could be rendered *their gods* (RV.), is used of Kemosh in Jud. 11^{24}, 1 K. 11^{33}; a single deity is clearly intended in v.$^{3.\ 5}$, where it is named Baʿal Peʿor. It would have been quite in accord with the sentiment even of the Israelites at an early period to worship Kemosh on his own territory (cp. *e.g.* 1 S. 26^{19}). The worship is here condemned, because the writer either considered that the territory in question had already become Yahweh's by right of conquest, or had discarded the doctrine that Yahweh might only be worshipped in his own land. The recollection of their nomadic life may have served to keep alive and develop a larger view of Yahweh's activity; in the ark or His angel Yahweh accompanied the people from place to place and, being in their midst, demanded that they should worship no other god (Ex. 24^{14} 20^{3}).—3. *The Baʿal of Peʿor*] the title resembles a number of divine titles found in Phœnician inscriptions and in the OT., some of which have become by abbreviation names of places; thus Baʿal Meʿon, originally a divine title, is also used as the name of a place, being in that case an abbreviation from Beth Baʿal Meʿon. The second element in these divine titles is commonly, though not exclusively, a geographical term; examples are the Baʿal of Meʿon, the Baʿal of Judah, the Baʿal of Lebanon (*CIS.* i. 1), the Baʿal of Mt. Ḥermon. Since, then, Peʿor (פעור = Φογωρ) occurs by itself as the name of places (23^{28}, Jos. $15^{59f.}$ 𝔊, Gn. 36^{39} 𝔊, Lagarde, *Onom. Sacra*, 300^{4}), it, too, was probably in the first instance a geographical name, and its meaning, even if it were clearer than it is, could cast no light on the nature of the cult of Baʿal Peʿor. The nature of that cult must be inferred from the known character of the cults of the local Baʿals who were worshipped as the beneficent sources of fertility, with agricultural festivals and often with immoral rites: see especially Hos. c. 2. As the Israelites identified the various local Baʿals with Yahweh, so the Moabites may have identified Baʿal Peʿor, whose cult was probably enough more ancient than their settlement in the country, with their national god Kemosh. See, further, Driver on Dt. 4^3; W. R. Smith, *Religion of the Semites*,[2] 94 ff.; Gray, *Hebrew Proper Names*, 124–136. The illegitimate worship of Baʿal Peʿor is frequently alluded to; see 31^{16}, Hos. 9^{10}, Dt. 4^3, Jos. 22^{17}, Ps. 106^{28}; cp. 1 Cor. 10^8.—4. *Take all the heads of the people and execute* (?) *them for Yahweh before the sun*] S *Command that they slay all the men that joined themselves unto the Baʿal of Peʿor.* S is a violent attempt to get rid of a difficulty rather than a genuine variant of the original text. As 𝔐 now runs, it can only mean that all the chiefs of the people are to be executed; S recasts this so that the actual offenders suffer. It is possible, however, that fusion of sources has accidentally caused the pronoun *them* (אתם) to refer to the chiefs, whereas in the original source it referred to the actual offenders (Di.), or possibly to selected representatives. Early Hebrew morality did not require the actual offender to expiate a crime (2 S. 21^{1-4}). The exact mode of execution intended is uncertain. But it is scarcely hanging (RV.), for which the Hebrews used another word (תלה). 𝔊 renders the word here used (הוקע) by *παραδειγμάτισον*; similarly 𝔖; and Di. argues for the meaning *expose, make an example*; but it is not satisfactorily derivable from the established usages of the root. W. R. Smith (*Rel. of the Semites*,[1] 398) suggested *cast them down*; cp. Ar. *waḳaʿa, to fall down*, and *auḳaʿa, to cause to fall down*. The verb is used of an execution in only one other OT. passage; according to that the execution takes place on a hill; as a result of it the executed persons fall down (ויפלו), and subsequently their bones are collected (2 S. $21^{6.\,9.\,13}$). It is some objection to this explanation that in the only passage where execution by casting people down a rock is clearly referred to (2 Ch. 25^{12}), the verb הוקע is not used.—*For Yahweh*] ליהוה: so 2 S. 21^6, Dt. 13^{17}, Jos. 6^{17}: cp. *before* (לפני) *Yahweh*, 2 S. 21^9.—*Before the sun*] *i.e.* openly, publicly: 2 S. 12^{12}.—5. The judges (Ex. 18^{12-27} E) are to *slay* (הרג) the offenders: in a parallel story (Ex. $32^{27f.}$ J) the Levites do this.—*Every man his men*] the men belonging to the companies over which the judges were severally appointed (Ex. $18^{25f.}$).

1. ויחל] 𝕲 καὶ ἐβεβηλώθη = ויחל.—לזנות] S להזנות: cp. Hos $4^{10.18}$ 5^{3}.—לזנות אל] a pregnant cstr. of a common type (Ezek. $16^{26.28}$). It certainly need not mean, as Kue. (*Th. Tijd.* xviii. 527 f.) wished to make it, that the Israelites needed to *search out* the Moabite women in the country districts of the conquered land.—ויאכל] 𝕲 correctly interprets καὶ ἔφαγεν τῶν θυσιῶν αὐτῶν.

6–15 (P). Phineḥas slays an offending Simeonite and the Midianite woman, and for his zeal the priesthood is secured to his descendants for all time.—The original introduction to this story, suppressed by the editor in favour of v.$^{1-5}$ (see above, p. 380), may have related that Balaam, a soothsayer resident among the Midianites, suggested to the Midianites that they should seduce the Hebrews into intermarrying with them, and thus involve Yahweh's destructive anger on their enemies; and that the stratagem so far succeeded that Yahweh plagued Israel (v.^{8}).* But this, of course, is not certain: it is by no means clear that this Midrash about Balaam (cp. p. 320) had arisen as early as P^{g}; c. 31, which connects Balaam with Baʿal Peʿor, is P^{s}.

The substance of the present section seems to be derived from P^{g}: it is entirely in his manner to connect the origin of an institution with an event. Hence v.$^{6-13}$ seems to be best referred to P^{g} in spite of the presence of expressions, not common in that writer, which led Di. to assign v.$^{10-13}$ to P^{s}. In these verses (v.$^{10-13}$) note חמה, השיב חמה, ברית שלום, קנאה (of God), תחת אשר, and כהנת עולם. On the other hand, v.$^{14f.}$ may well be a later addition; the position in which the additional information contained in it is placed is unnatural. V.$^{16-18}$ presuppose c. 31 (P^{s}).

6. *And behold, one of the Israelites came and brought home to his brethren* (ויקרב אל אחיו), *i.e.* introduced to his family, *the Midianite woman* of his choice *in the sight of Moses and all the congregation*] in the absence of the introduction, it remains uncertain how far this conduct is an aggravation of the offence that had caused the plague, or an offence different in kind. The former alternative seems the more probable. Possibly, as in JE's story (v.$^{1-5}$), the Israelites had previously consorted with foreign women in their own homes, but had not actually taken them to wife, and so, by bringing them home, defiled the camp. In any case, it must have been an

* So Di., Kit., Bacon, Dr., We.

aggravation of the offence that it was committed while the rest of the congregation were assembled before the tabernacle bemoaning the plague (v.[6b]).—7 f. Phineḥas the priest follows the offenders to their tent and pierces them to death. His zeal, which became an example to later ages (1 Mac. 2[26], 4 Mac. 18[12]), appeases Yahweh (v.[11]), and the plague, from which 24,000 died, ceases. Apart from a genealogical reference (Ex. 6[25]), this is the first allusion to Phineḥas: subsequent references are 31[6], Jos. 22[13. 30–32] (P) 24[33] (E), Jud. 20[28], Ecclus. 45[23]. Aaron, being now dead, and Eleʿazar high priest (20[22–29]), Phineḥas is free to distinguish himself in a deed for which his father was rendered unfit by his office; see 17[2] n. —8. *Into the tent*] the precise meaning of קֻבָּה, which occurs here only in OT., is uncertain; *alcove* (RV. marg.) is derived from the corresponding word in Arabic; see phil. note.—*And the plague was stayed*] 17[13. 15] n., 14[37] n.—9a. Cp. 17[14a] (P).

6. 'בא ויקרב אל אחיו את־הם] The variants in the Versions are not preferable, nor is Geiger's emendation based on them ('בא בקרב אחיו אל הם: *Urschrift*, 395 f.).—**7.** רמח] an alternative for חנית; it is rare in the early (Jud. 5[8], 1 K. 18[28]), but was popular in the later literature: in Joel 4[10] it replaces the חנית of Is. 2[4], Mic. 4[3]: see *Exp.* 1893 (Sept.), 214 f. The present is the only instance of רמח in the Hex.—**8.** איש־ישראל] on the indefinite איש see Dav. 20, R. 2; G.-K. 127*e*.—הַקֻּבָּה] 𝔙 *lupanar*; the word occurs with this meaning in New Hebrew (see Levy), but the context does not favour the adoption of it here, nor even of the meaning *the hinder* (*i.e.* the women's) *apartment of a tent.* قُبَّة and ܩܘܒܬܐ mean (1) *a vault* or *arch*; (2) *a vaulted tent, a tent of honour*; cf. Ges. *Thes. s.v.*—קֳבָתָהּ] from קֵבָה Dt. 18[3] (cp. قِبَة = *ventriculus*): for the *ḥateph-ḥameṣ* and various views of the origin of the form, see Kön. ii. 185; Olsh. § 160*c*.

10. *Phineḥas . . . hath turned back My wrath from* pouring itself out *upon* (מעל) *the children of Israel*] for the phrase השיב חמה *to turn back wrath*, cp. Jer. 18[20], Ps. 106[23].—*In that he was jealous with My jealousy*] *i.e.* resented, as deeply as Yahweh Himself, the dishonour inflicted on Yahweh by the people's sin.—12. *I give him My covenant, peace*] *i.e.* I assure him of My friendly attitude towards him; cp. Is. 54[10], Ezek. 34[25] 37[26], Mal. 2[4ff.].—*The covenant of an everlasting priesthood*] the passage appears to regard the priesthood as per-

petually limited to the family of Phineḥas. If this be so, it most probably reflects the theory of a time between Ezekiel and Ezra, and is on this ground best referred to P^g. The earlier historical books (Samuel, Kings) speak of the two great priestly houses of ʿEli and Ṣadoḳ, but attribute to neither descent from Phineḥas, nor even from Aaron. On the other hand, Ṣadoḳ was promoted to the priesthood by the king; and as late as the end of the 7th century the theory appears to have prevailed that ʿEli and Ṣadoḳ were not of the same descent (1 S. 2^{29-36}, especially v.^{31}—a Deuteronomic passage). Ezekiel confined the priesthood to the descendants of Ṣadoḳ, but did not connect them with Phineḥas. Later the connection of Ṣadoḳ and Phineḥas was genealogically established (Ezr. 7^{1-6}, 1 Ch. $5^{30ff.}$ $6^{35ff.}$ ($6^{4ff.\ 50ff.}$)). The present passage thus presents substantially the theory of Ezekiel, but gives to the exclusively Ṣadoḳite (Jerusalem) priesthood a more ancient origin. Other passages in the secondary strata of P or in the Chronicler (Lev. $10^{6.\ 12.\ 16}$, Nu. 3^{1-4}, 1 Ch. 24^{1-6}, Ezr. 8^2; cp. Neh. 10^{6-8}) extend the priesthood to the family of Phineḥas' uncle, Ithamar. Possibly the Ithamarites are the descendants of the local priests who succeeded in making good their claim to share with the Ṣadoḳites (= Phineḥas) the right to officiate in Jerusalem.*—13b β. Cp. 17^{12}.

12. אמר] 𝔖 אמרתי.—בריתי שלום] The cstr. is appositional, unless, as in the passages cited above, ברית שלום should be read: cp. 𝔊 διαθήκην εἰρήνης. On the broken ו in שלום, see Kön. *Einleitung*, 34, 84.

14 f. The offending Israelite was a *prince* (7^2 n.) of a Simeonite family, or *father's house* (1^2 n.). His name was *Zimrî*, his father's *Sālû*. Zimri (cp. 1 K 16^9, 1 Ch. 8^{36}) is derived from the name of an animal (Dt. 14^5), and is consequently a name of an early type (*HPN*. c. ii. § 2); the instances of names resembling *Sālû* (סָלוּא) are late: see 1 Ch. 9^7 (סַלּוּא), Neh. 11^7 (סַלָּא), 12^7 (סַלּוּ): cp. also the Aramaic אבסלי (*CIS*. ii. 122). *Cozbî* is from a root meaning *to deceive*; on the name *Ṣûr*, see p. 6. Here and in v.^{18} and Jos. 13^{21}

* See, further, We. *Proleg*. c. iv., especially pp. 122 ff., 138 ff.; Baudissin, *Priesterthum*, 54, 110 f., 133, 139, 198, 201; Nowack, *Arch*. ii. 105.

Cozbi's father is represented as prince (נשיא), in 31^8 as one of the five kings (מלכים), of Midian.—16–18. The verses are the note of a priestly editor familiar with the preceding composite story, and are intended to prepare the way for c. 31 (P^s).—16 f. *Attack the Midianites . . . for they did attack you with their crafty plans, which they craftily planned against you*] by means of their women, at the suggestion of Balaam (31^{16}). The allusion to the Midianites connects the note with v.[6-15] (P).—*In the matter of Peʿor*] this connects the note with v.[1-5] (JE). The annotator may have taken Peʿor itself to be a divine name; or he may have used the abbreviation as a mere reference to v.[1-5], without clearly distinguishing the place and the god.

15. אמות] Gn. 25^{16} † (of Ishmaelites); cp. אֻמָּה *people*, in Bibl. Aram. (with *masc.* pl. אֻמַּיָּא; cp. הָאֻמִּים in Ps. 117^1, unless לְאֻמִּים should be read there), Syr. and Pal. Targ.; and ܐܘܡܬܐ, *gens*, *familia*. If the present be the original text, trans. "a head of *the clans of* a father's house"; then אמה is a subdivision of בית אב (cp. 1^2 n.). בית אב, however, is possibly a gloss; we must then, it seems, read the sing. (cp. S 𝔊 𝔖), "a head of *a clan* [a father's house] in Midian."—**16.** 𝔊 + דבר אל בני יש' לאמר.—**18.** על דבר פער (1)] *in the matter of*; so על ד' כזבי and 31^{16}. In the last clause of the v. (cp. 17^{14}) על ד'=*on account of* (rather than *because of*, BDB. 184*a*).

XXVI. *The Second Census.*

(1) Moses and Eleʿazar are bidden to take a (second) census, v.[1-4]; (2) the families and numbers of the twelve secular tribes, v.[5-51]; (3) Moses is instructed that the land (of Canaan) is to be divided among the tribes in proportion to their size, v.[52-56]; (4) the families and numbers of the Levites, v.[57-62]; (5) a subscription and statement that Caleb and Joshua alone were alive at both the first and second census, v.[63-65]. The connection between the several sections is obvious, though (5) might more naturally have stood after (2).

The chapter is closely related to c. 1 and 3 (the first census), which are presupposed, and to Gn. c. 46, which contains the great majority of names of the Hebrew clans here given. In enumerating the tribes (v.[5-50]) ℌ follows the order of 1[20-43] (except that Ephraim and Manasseh change places with one another); 𝔊 keeps the order of Gn. 46. On the numbers given in the chapter, see pp. 10–15; and for fuller details regarding the clans and their names, see the commentaries on Gn. 46, and cp. 1 Ch. 2. 4. 5. 7. 8, Jubilees 44.

In v.[5-50] the names and numbers are given in recurring formulæ after the manner of P (cp. *e.g.* c. 1); but the scheme is once or twice interrupted by the introduction of matter which is, strictly speaking, irrelevant. Under each tribe there is given (1) the names of its subdivisions, which are generally identified with those of the sons of the tribal ancestor, but in the case of Judah, Manasseh, Ephraim, Benjamin, and Asher, with those of more distant descendants also, and in the case of Asher, in one instance, with that of a daughter; (2) the numbers of males over twenty years old (v.[4]) belonging to the tribe. The formula for the first information is:

The sons of A. according to their families: of X., the family of the Xites, of Y., the family of the Yites,

where A. is a tribal ancestor and X., Y. . . . sons (or other descendants).

The formula for the second statement is:

These are the families of A. according to them that were numbered of them, x y z,

where A. is as above, x thousands, y hundreds, z tens.

The first formula runs in a particular instance בני שמעון למשפחתם לנמואל משפחת הנמואלי . . ., and so without variation of the formula in v.[12f. 15ff. 20] (in v.[21] ויהיו is prefixed), [26. 38f. 44. 48f.]. Slight variations occur as follows: (1) אלה is prefixed in [35. 42], possibly under the influence of the second formula; cp. also v.[36]; (2) ל is omitted before חנוך (v.[5]) and תולע (v.[23]); (3) למשפחתם is omitted in v.[5. 29]. The variations are as early as 𝔊, but it is probable that they are due to early transcriptional error rather than to the intention of the original writer. The second formula runs in a particular instance אלה משפחות יהודה לפקדיהם . . .. In this formula instead of the simple tribal name (v.[22. 25. 34. 42. 50]) the gentilic form appears in v.[7. 14. 27], and the phrase *the sons of* . . . in v.[18. 37. 41. 47]. Some of these variations may be original, though they are less numerous in 𝔊 than in ℌ. Other variations are as follows: (1) for לפקדיהם (7 times; 𝔊 ἐκ τῆς (or ἐξ) ἐπισκέψεως αὐτῶν) ℌ, though not 𝔊, thrice has ופקדיהם (v.[34. 41. 50]) and once nothing (v.[14]), and in the first section ויהיו פקדיהם (v.[7]; and so 𝔊); (2) for אלה משפחתם there occurs in v.[41] אלה בני בנימין למשפחתם; and (3) between

ד and לפקדיהם there is inserted למשפחתם כל משפחת השוחמי. All these, though (2) and (3) already appear in 𝔊, are probably due to transcriptional causes, except that ויהיו פ' in v.[7] may well be original. Remoter descendants and the families named after them are introduced with ויהיו (v.[21]), ואלה (v.[36]), לבני (v.[45]): the text of v.[40] seems corrupt; see below.

The matter in v.[5–50] which does not accommodate itself to the formulæ is found in v.[8–11] and v.[30 (29)–33] Possibly both of these passages are interpolations.

V.[8] does not follow the general scheme (which would require לאליאב מש' האליאבי), and the remoter descendants of Reuben are inserted *after* the numbers of the tribe (v.[7]); ct. v.[21. 36. 40. 46]. In v.[30-33], while the regular formula occurs once (לחלק מש' החלקי), in the remaining five cases it is abandoned (*e.g.* איעזר מש' האיעזרי).

Strictly speaking, v.[19] and v.[28] are also irrelevant to the present section; but there is no independent reason for suspecting their present position not to be original.

The formulæ and the connections of the c. with other parts of P are sufficient evidence that it is the product of the priestly school (P). But it cannot be entirely the work of P^g; for v.[8-11] presuppose the existence of c. 16 (JE P) in its present form. Either an account of a second census in P^g has been annotated and perhaps recast by a later writer, or the entire chapter is the work of P^s. In addition to other matters CH. note that "the introduction of the division of the land (v.[52-56]) seems premature; the name of the land, even, is not mentioned, much less its conquest, or even the passage of the Jordan; ct. $33^{51ff.}$ $34^{2ff.}$: moreover, according to $27^{12ff.}$, Dt. $32^{49ff.}$, Moses was not permitted to cross the Jordan and could not be the instrument of the distribution."

1–4. Directions to take the census.—1. Aaron being dead, Eleᶜazar is associated with Moses in the taking of the second census.—**2.** The command is briefer, but otherwise couched in the same phraseology as in $1^{2f.}$.—**3 f.** The text is manifestly corrupt, though not easily emended: see phil. n. The scene of this census is the steppes of Moab; cp. 22^{1} (P).—**4.** *As Yahweh commanded Moses*] a frequently recurring phrase, especially in P^s (CH. 189*c*).—*And the children of Israel who came out of the land of Egypt*] to make this clause a second object to *commanded* (RV.) is to go against all analogy in the use of the formula *as Yahweh commanded Moses*; note further that את, which is prefixed to *Moses*, is absent from this clause. The words might better be taken as the subject of v.[5ff.]; cp.

Gn. 46^{8}. Rather less probable is Paterson's suggestion to read לבני for ובני, and to render *with regard to the children of Israel*, etc.

1. בן אהרן] 𝔊 om.—**3 f.** וידבר . . . אֹתָם] MT. reads wrongly אֹתָם; דבר את occurs often enough (*e.g.* 3^{1} 7^{89}), but in recording a communication of Moses to the Israelites the phrase here used is an unusual variant of וי׳ד אליהם. The beginning of the speech (v.^{4}) that followed לאמר (v.^{3}) is lost; at present it consists merely of a clause and a subordinate sentence: *from twenty years old and upwards, as Yahweh commanded Moses.* The corruptions lie behind 𝔊. 𝔖 indeed omits לאמר and inserts, *And Moses numbered them*; but this may be merely a makeshift of the same order as that adopted in RV. For a criticism of various unsuitable and insufficient emendations, see Di. The least unsuitable is that adopted by Paterson (in *SBOT.*), who reads ויפקד for וידבר and omits לאמר; then render, *And Moses and Ele'azar the priest numbered them . . . from twenty years old and upwards.*

5–51. The families and numbers of the Israelites.—5–7. Of Reuben.—*Reuben, the firstborn of Israel*] 1^{20}, Ex. 6^{14}; cp. Gn. 46^{8} (P). The *sons of Reuben, i.e.* Reubenite clans, are *Ḥanôch*, *Pallû'*, *Ḥeṣrôn* and *Carmî*; the same names are given in Gn. 46^{9}, Ex. 6^{14}, 1 Ch. 5^{3}.—**8–11.** An appendix to the section on Reuben, perhaps interpolated; see above.—**8.** *And the sons of . . .*] the pl. is used, though only one name follows: so often in the genealogies (*e.g.* v.^{36}, Gn. 46^{23}, 1 Ch. 1^{41}).—*Elî'āb*] 16^{1} n.—**9.** *The sons of Eliab*] are *Dāthān* and *'Abîrām* (16^{1} JE), and an otherwise unknown *Nemû'ēl*; for the last name, cp. v.^{12}.—*Elect of the congregation*] 1^{16} n.; cp. 16^{2} (P).—*The congregation of Ḳoraḥ*] the phrase betrays the hand of P^{s}; see 16^{5} n.—**10.** Citations from and verbal reminiscences of $16^{32.\ 35}$ (JE P).—*And they became a wonder*] or *warning*. The word נֵס regularly means *a standard*; nowhere else in OT. does it bear its present meaning; but it is often so used in post-biblical Hebrew; see Levy, *s.v.*—**11.** *But the sons of Ḳoraḥ died not*] Ḳoraḥ himself (v.^{10}) and the men that belonged to his company (16^{32}) perished; but not "the sons of Ḳoraḥ" themselves, for "a family of Ḳoraḥ" still exists (v.^{58}; cp. "the sons of Ḳoraḥ" of the Psalm-titles). Arguing thus, as it would seem, an annotator added the present note to the text.—**12–14.** The Simeonite clans (Gn. 46^{10}, Ex. 6^{15}, 1 Ch. 4^{24}) are *Nemû'ēl*, perhaps the correct form of *Jemû'ēl* (Gn., Ex.; see *HPN.* 307), *Jāmîn*,

Jāchîn (Ch. 𝔐, incorrectly, *Jārîb*), *Zeraḥ* (זרח; Gn., Ex. צחר), and *Shāûl*. A sixth clan, Ohad, mentioned between Jamin and Jachin in Gn., Ex., and Jubil., is here and in Ch. omitted. 15–18. The Gadite clans (Gn. 46^{16}) are *Sephôn*, which is incorrectly given as Ṣiphiôn in Gn. (𝔐 not 𝔊) and Jubil. 44^{20}, *Ḥaggî*, *Shûnî*, and *Oznî*, or rather Eṣbôn (Gn.; cp. Jubil. 44^{20}, 1 Ch. 7^{7}), *'Ērî*, *Arôd* (Gn. *Arodi*), and *Ar'ēlî*.—19. Gn. 46^{12}.—20. The clans of Judah (Gn. 46^{12}, 1 Ch. $2^{3f.}$, cp. Gn. 38 J) described as his *sons* are *Shēlah*, *Pereṣ*, and *Zeraḥ*, and (21) those described as his grandsons by Pereṣ are *Ḥesrôn* and *Ḥāmûl*.—23–25. The clans of Issachar (Gn. 46^{13}, 1 Ch. 7^{1}) are *Tôlā'*, *Puah* (*Puwwāh*), *Jāshûb* (in Gn., incorrectly, *Job*), and *Shimrôn*.—26 f. The clans of Zebulon (Gn. 46^{14}) are *Sered*, *Elôn*, and *Jaḥle'ēl*.—28. Cp. Gn. 46^{20}.—29–32. The Manassite clans, which for obvious reasons are not mentioned in Gn., consist of *Māchîr* described as a son, *Gile'ad* as a grandson of Manasseh, and six others (v.[30]) described as sons of Gile'ad. Translated out of genealogical language the meaning of the writer appears to be that the Manassite clan Machir came, whether by conquest or otherwise (cp. $32^{39f.}$ (JE), Dt. 3^{15}, Jos. 13^{31} (P)), into possession of Gile'ad (*i.e.* Manasseh's possession E. of Jordan), whence subsequently Manassite clans (*e.g.* Gile'ad's "sons" Shechem and I'ezer) separated and settled W. of Jordan. Machir is an ancient clan or tribal name (Jud. 5^{14}) which was early connected with Manasseh (Gn. 50^{23} (JE)). A clan might be described as the father of the district where it dwelt; cp. *e.g.* "Ḥamor the father of Shechem" (Gn. 34^{6}), "Ashḥur the father of Tekoa'," "Mareshah, the father of Ḥebron," etc. (1 Ch. $2^{24.\,42}$). There is nothing surprising in a late genealogist supposing that W. Manasseh was of later origin than E. Manasseh, and so representing Manassite towns or clans on the W. (Shechem, I'ezer) as sons of Gile'ad, even though, as earlier sources report (Jud. $12^{3f.}$; and see on 32^{39-42}), E. Manasseh was in reality an offshoot from the W. Other references agreeing with the present genealogical scheme are 27^{1} 36^{1}, Jos. 17^{3} (P). A different scheme is found in Jos. $17^{1b.\,2}$ (? JE); there Machir still appears as father of Gile'ad, but the six clans here classed as sons of Gile'ad are there sons of Manasseh and brothers of Machir. Yet a third scheme is found in 1 Ch. 7^{14-19}, and a fourth underlies 1 Ch. 2^{21-23}; for further discussion and genealogical tables, see Driver's art. "Manasseh" in Hastings' *DB.*; Kue. *Th. Tijd.* xi. 483 ff.—**30–32.** The six clans here, though not always (see preceding note), described as *sons of Gileʿad* are also mentioned in Jos. 17^{2} and in part in 1 Ch. $7^{18f.}$. *Iʿezer* is an abbreviation for Abîʿezer (Jos., Ch.; 𝔊 reads here, wrongly, Ἀχιέζερ); it was the clan whence Gideon sprang (Jud. $6^{11. 24. 34}$ $8^{2. 32}$), and was resident, in part at least, in his days at ʿOphrah, which, probably, lay not far from Shechem (cp. Jud. 9), and certainly west of Jordan (Jud. 8 in the light of 6^{34}). *Shechem*, though vocalised (שֶׁכֶם; but 𝔊 Συχεμ) in MT. (here, Jos. 17^{2}, 1 Ch. 7^{19}) differently from Shechem the well-known town (שְׁכֶם), must yet be closely connected with it. *Ḥēlĕk* and *Asrî'ēl* are mentioned only here and in Jos. 17^{2}; the names are absent from 1 Ch. 7^{14} (see Kit.); *Ḥēphĕr* is also mentioned in v.[33] 27^{1}, Jos. $17^{2f.}$; *Shemîdaʿ* in Jos. 17^{2}, 1 Ch. 7^{19}.—**33.** An irrelevant anticipation of 27^{1}. *Ṣelophehad's daughters* (27^{1} 36^{11}, Jos. 17^{3}) are towns or clans:* *Maḥlah* is parallel to the clan name Abîʿezer in 1 Ch. 7^{18}; *Tirṣah* is the name of one of the capitals of the northern kingdom (1 K. 15^{21}, Jos. 12^{24}); with *Ḥoglah*, cp. Beth-Ḥoglah (Jos. 15^{6}); *Milcah* is, strictly speaking, a divine name, but may, like the last, be an abbreviation, and stand for Beth-Milcah; *Noʿah* (נֹעָה; 𝔊 Νουα) is distinguished from the Zebulonite town of Neʿah (הַנֵּעָה Jos. 19^{13}; 𝔊[A] Αννουα, [L] Νουα) merely by the absence of the article and the vocalisation; it probably appears in a corrupt form (Aniʿam, אניעם) in 1 Ch. 7^{19} as a "son" of Shemidaʿ and "brother" of Shechem. Note that Gath-Ḥepher is mentioned just before Neʿah in Jos.—**35 f.** The clans of Ephraim which are described as his sons are *Shûthelaḥ* [*Becher*] and *Taḥan* (S *Taḥam*; 𝔊 Ταναχ); as his grandson by Shuthelaḥ, *ʿErān.* These, like the Manassite clans, and for the same reason, are not mentioned in Gn. 46; but cp. and ct. 1 Ch. 7^{20-29}. 𝔊 omits *Becher*, which is probably out of place here and should be transferred to v.[38] (*EBi.* 508), though it is, of course, possible

* Kue. *Th. Tijd.* xi. 488; cp. Gray, *Hebrew Proper Names*, 116.

that the clan at one time was counted to Ephraim, at another to Benjamin (2 S. 20^1). Possibly *Becher* has replaced *Bered*, which in 1 Ch. 7^{20} stands between *Shuthelaḥ* and *Taḥath*. *Shuthelaḥ* is mentioned only here and in 1 Ch. $7^{20\,(21)}$; with *Taḥan*, cp. *Taḥath*, 1 Ch. 7^{20}, rather than *Taḥan*, *ib.* v.[25]. *ʿEran*, or rather *ʿEdan* (S), is probably represented by Elʿadah or Elʿad in 1 Ch. $7^{20f.}$, and Laʿdan in 1 Ch. 7^{26}; see *EBi.* 1329.—**38–41.** The clans of Benjamin (Gn. 46^{21}, 1 Ch. 7^{6-12} $8^{1ff.}$) which are described as his sons are *Belaʿ* (*Becher*; see preceding note), *Ashbēl*, *Aḥîrām*, *Shephûphām*, *Ḥûphām*, and as his grandsons by Belaʿ, *Ard* and *Naʿamān*; in S and Gn. the last two also rank as sons of Benjamin; with the view of MT. here, cp. 1 Ch. 8^3 (ct. 7^7). Becher in Gn. stands between Belaʿ and Ashbel, and may lie concealed in בכרו *his firstborn* in 1 Ch. 8^3; see H. W. Hogg in *JQR*. xi. 109. "Eḥi and Rosh, Muppim" in Gn., are not genuine names; they are the result of a faulty reading of the consonantal text (שפופם, אחירם), which contained the names *Aḥîrām*, *Shephûphām*, correctly read here; Jubil. 44^{25} seems slightly less corrupt than Gn.; see *HPN*. p. 35 n. 1. On the other hand, Gera (Gn., also 1 Ch. 8^3) is a genuine name; but whether its omission here is accidental or intentional must remain uncertain. Ch. mentions a large number of Benjamite clans mentioned neither here nor in Gn.—**42 f.** Of Dan only a single clan is named, *Shûḥām*, called in Gn. 46^{23} Ḥûshîm.—**44–47.** The clans of Asher (Gn. 46^{17}, 1 Ch. $7^{30f.}$) described as his sons are *Imnah*, *Ishvah* (so read with Gn., Ch.; in Gn., Ch. "*and Ishvi*" is dittographic), *Berîʿah*; as his grandsons by Berîʿah, *Ḥēbĕr* and *Malchîʾēl*, and as his daughter *Seraḥ*. —**48–50.** The clans of Naphtali (Gn. 46^{24}, 1 Ch. 7^{13}) are *Jaḥṣeʾēl*, *Gûnî*, *Jēṣĕr*, and *Shillēm* (S, Ch. *Shallûm*).

9. הצו . . . בהצתם] S הועדו . . . בהועדתם. The Hiphil of נצה occurs elsewhere only in Ps. 60 title, and is there perhaps a corruption of הִכָּתוֹ.—**10.** ואת קרח] S הארץ.—באכל אש] S+ אֶת קרח.—**40.** ויהיו בני בלע ארד ונעמן] S omits this clause and has in its place simply לארד: see above. If the clause in 𝔐 be original לארד before משפחת הארדי has dropped out, for it is required by the scheme of the chapter. But it is likely enough that S is original (note also variations in 𝔊), and that the additional clause in 𝔐 has been added in thought of the theory underlying 1 Ch. $8^{3f.}$.—**44.** הימנה לישוי] the eye of a copyist confused the endings of the two words: read הימני לישוה. In Gn. 46^{17} וישוי is dittographic of וישוה; but, like the incorrect reading אחי וראש מפים (see p. 393), the error may be older than the compilation of the 70 names in Gn. There is thus no evidence that the name ישוי had any real existence; in 1 S. 14^{49} it is an intentional mutilation of another name (see, *e.g.*, We. on the passage).

52–56. The manner in which the land is to be divided among the tribes.—The meaning is not quite clear. Two principles of division are enjoined; on the one hand, the land is to be divided among the several tribes in proportion to their respective numbers; on the other hand, it is to be assigned by lot. How these two in themselves irreconcilable principles are both to be respected in the division is not said. The explanation commonly offered is that the districts in which the several tribes were to settle were determined by lot (cp. 33^{54}), and that then the size of the district was determined by the size of the tribe. It was an old tradition that the country was apportioned to the several tribes by lot, the older view being that the allotment was made *before* the conquest (Jud. 1^{1-3}, Jos. 17^{14-18} J), the later that the allotment was made *after* the conquest (*e.g.* Jos. 14^{1-5} 13^{15-23} P). If the fact may be pressed that the command is here (v.$^{52.\,54}$) given to Moses, the present passage takes the former view. For other references in OT. to the allotment of land, see Mic. $2^{4f.}$; for the custom among other peoples, Herod. v. 77 and other references in Di.; and for the historical probability of allotment before conquest, Kit. *Gesch. d. Hebr.* i. 245 ff.

The fact that the division is to be made according to number, accounts for the present section being placed after the account of the census; and the theory that Levi had no landed possession (v.^{62}), for its being placed before the census of Levi (v.$^{57-62}$).

53. *To these* tribes *shall the land be apportioned as an inheritance* (cp. 18^{26}) *according to the number of names*, *i.e.* of persons (cp. 1^2 n.), in the several tribes.—54. *For that* tribe *which is large, thou shalt make its inheritance* proportionately *large*; and *for that which is small thou shalt make its inheritance* proportionately *small*: for other antitheses of רב, מעט (המעיט, הרבה), *large* and *small* (especially with reference to numbers), see 35^8,

Ex. 16^{17}, Jer. 29^{6}, Gn. 30^{30}, Dt. 7^{7}.—According *to* (the number of) *those that were numbered of each tribe shall its inheritance be given.*—**55.** *According to the names of their fathers' tribes shall they inherit*] with מטות אבותם, cp. Nu. $1^{16.\ 47}$ 13^{2} 33^{54} 36^{4} †. The meaning is rather obscure; perhaps Di. interprets correctly: the land is first divided by lot to the twelve tribes; individuals gain their portion through their tribe and in the portion allotted to it.—**56.** *According to the lot shall its*, viz. Israel's (or, preferably, reading with 𝔊 (followed by RV. without acknowledgment) נחלתם *their*) *inheritance, i.e.* Canaan, *be divided between the more numerous and the less numerous* (tribes).

54. איש לפי פקדיו] G.-K. 139*c*.—יֻתַּן נחלתו] נחלתו is best regarded as an acc. after the Pass.; cp. with the same vb. 32^{5}, 1 K. 2^{21}; G.-K. 121.—**55.** לשמות מטות] 𝔊 *τοῖς ὀνόμασιν, κατὰ φυλάς* (=למטות): the effect of this is to make v.^{55} extend the apportionment by lot to the case of individuals: this is not directly enjoined in 𝔐.

57–62. The families and numbers of the Levites.—As at the first census ($1^{47\text{ff.}}$), the Levites are numbered apart from the other tribes; and on this occasion because the other tribes are numbered with a view to the distribution of the land among them (v.$^{53\text{f.}}$), whereas Levi is to receive no land (v.^{62}). This section may originally have consisted of v.$^{57.\ 62}$ only.

Even in 𝔐, and still more in 𝔊, which reads בני לוי for פקודי הלוי (𝔐), or פ' הלוים (S), v.^{57} follows closely the first formula for the secular tribes (see above). On the contrary, v.^{58a} is cast in a different mould: further, though making a fresh start, v.^{58} is in respect of its contents entirely parallel to v.^{57}; both give a list of Levitical families—v.^{57}, the three families which appear elsewhere as the main divisions of Levi (Gn. 46^{11}, Ex. 6^{16}, Nu. c. 3 f. 7^{7-9}, Jos. c. 21, 1 Ch. 5^{27} 6^{1} ($6^{1.\ 16}$) $15^{4\text{ff.}}$ 23^{6}); v.^{58a}, families named after persons appearing in the genealogies as grandsons or yet more remote descendants of Levi, *i.e.* families which were regarded as subdivisions. So far as the present chapter is concerned v.^{57} is primary and v.^{58a} secondary; but this by no means precludes the possibility, or indeed the probability, that v.^{58} contains an older theory of the Levitical families. V.$^{58b-61}$ is, like v.$^{8-10.\ 30-33}$, irrelevant, and, like v.$^{8-10}$, based on different sources.

57. The Levitical clans are given as in 3^{17} and frequently elsewhere (see preceding n.): *Gērshôn, Ḳŏhāth*, and *Merārî*.—**58.** A different list of Levitical families, in which only the gentilic forms of the names are used; ct. v.^{57}. Corresponding to the gentilics *Ḥebrôni* and *Ḳorḥî* are the names Ḥebrôn and Ḳoraḥ (3^{19} 16^{1}); the three remaining gentilics *Mûshî Maḥlî* and *Libnî* are themselves used as names in the priestly genealogies ($3^{20. 18}$); but the names from which they were originally derived are respectively Moses (Môsheh), Maḥlah, and Libnah; Libnah, like Ḥebron, is a town in the S. of Judah. As applied to Levites, it is probable that in some of these cases the gentilic form is the earlier, and that Ḥebroni and Libni, for example, did not figure as descendants of Levi till some time after various bodies of Levites had been known as the Libnite Levites, the Hebronite Levites, and so forth.* Maḥlah is identical with the Ephraimite clan name which appears (v.[33]) as one of Ṣelopheḥad's "daughters." In the scheme (v.[57]) which made Gershon, Ḳohath, and Merari the "sons," *i.e.* the main divisions of Levi, the eponyms of the five Levitical clans here mentioned occupy different positions; Ḳoraḥ is a "great-grandson" of Levi, a "grandson" of Ḳohath (16^{1}); the remaining four are always "grandsons" of Levi, but Libni is sometimes a son of Gershon (3^{18}, 1 Ch. $6^{2\,(17)}$), sometimes of Merari (1 Ch. $6^{14\,(29)}$); Maḥlî and Mûshî are always sons of Merari, Ḥebrôn of Ḳohath.—*And Ḳohath begat ʿAmram*] Ex. 6^{18}.—59. Cp. Ex. 6^{20} (P) 2^{1} (E). Miriam is mentioned nowhere else in P.—60. Cp. 3^{2}, Ex. 6^{23}.—61 = 3^{4}.—62. The Levites number 23,000 against 22,000 at the earlier census, 3^{39}.—62b. Cp. $1^{49f.}$ 18^{20}.—64 f. Apparently a subsequent addition to the chapter,† or an ill-placed section; see above, p. 387.—65. Cp. $14^{29f.}$; ct. v.[4f.] above.

59. אשר יָלְדָה אתה ללוי במצרים] this appears to be corrupt or out of place. יָלְדָה has generally been explained as a case of the indef. or unexpressed subj. (*sc.* אִמּוֹ or הַיּוֹלֶדֶת); cp. 1 K. 1^{6}. But cases of the indef. subj. with the 3rd sing. *fem.* are extremely rare (Kön. iii. 324*f*, 109). Read rather יָלַד; G.-K. 121*b*.—**62.** התפקדו] 1^{47} n. (p. 10).

XXVII. 1–11. The law of succession to landed property.— A particular instance, the death of Ṣelopheḥad without male issue, leads to the promulgation of a law providing that if a man die without male issue, his daughter shall succeed to his

* We. *Comp.* 185; S. A. Cook in *EBi.* 1662, 1665 f.
† We. *Comp.* 185 f.; Di.

(landed) property, if he die without any issue his brothers, failing these his paternal uncles, failing these his nearest of kin on his father's side. In c. 36 a general law proceeding from the same particular instance provides, by way of corollary, that daughters thus inheriting must marry within their own tribe. The carrying out of the law in the particular instance is recorded in Jos. $17^{3f.}$ (P).

Both the law and its corollary are designed to secure the effective working of a deep-rooted principle of Hebrew society, viz. that land must not be permanently alienated from the society (whether of the tribe or the family) to which it has belonged. The hold which this principle had on the Hebrews may be seen in the resentment evoked by violations of it (1 K. 21, Is. 5^{8}, Mic. $2^{1f.}$); and by the right and duty of purchase within the family (Jer. $32^{6ff.}$), or generally by the practice of redemption which culminated in the theory, if not in the practice, of the year of Jubilee (Lev. $25^{8ff.}$). According to the Levitical law this principle is based on the religious theory that all the land was Yahweh's, granted by Him to the various families merely for use, and therefore inalienable by them (Lev. 25^{23}).

The law occupies a suitable position; it immediately follows the census which had been taken with a view to the apportionment of the land (26^{52-56}).

The section is clearly derived from P: note the point of contact in v.[3] with 16^{2-7} (P^{g}) and stylistically *inter alia* אחזה, פתח אהל מועד, נשיאים. The only question is whether it belongs to the primary (We. *Comp.*[2] 114 f.) or the secondary (CH. n. on v.[1]) strata of P. See Introd. § 12.

The present law itself and the manner in which it is introduced indicate that the right of daughters to inherit was not an immemorial custom in the time of the writer (P). There is no trace of the existence of such a right in the pre-exilic period; and from the fact that Dt. ($21^{15ff.}$ 25^{5-10}) recognises only sons as heirs, and regulates the ancient custom of the levirate marriage in order to gain the same end as is here reached by extending the right of inheritance to daughters, it may be reasonably inferred that as late as the end of the 7th cent. B.C. the right of daughters to inherit was still unknown. But the custom of the levirate marriage cannot have been unknown to the author of this law; the fact, therefore, that he makes no allowance for it (v.[8]), is possibly an indication that he disapproved of marriages of the type (cp. Lev. 18[16] 20[21]). Be this as it may, the levirate marriage long continued to be practised (Mt. 22[24]). Job (42[15]) goes beyond the present law; for it represents daughters as coheirs with sons. But whether this represents the actual practice, or even a prevalent theory of the time, is doubtful.

1. On Ṣelopheḥad's genealogy see 26[30] n. The names of his daughters (26[33] n.) are names of clans or places, a fact which in itself is sufficient to show that this story is not a historical account of certain individuals, but a mode of raising a legal point.—2. Eleʿazar is associated with Moses as in 26[1]; in 36[1] he is not mentioned.—3 f. Ṣelopheḥad's daughters plead that there was no moral reason why Ṣelopheḥad's name should perish; he had sinned, it was true, with the rest of the people, and, sharing their punishment, had died during the forty years' wandering (14[28-35]); but he had committed no exceptional sin, such as participation in the revolt of Ḳoraḥ (c. 16), so as to merit the exceptional punishment of the destruction of his name. The passage is important as showing that originally Ḳoraḥ's company was not exclusively composed of Levites; it is assumed here that the Manassite Ṣelopheḥad might have been a member of it.—4. *Why should our father's name be withdrawn* (נגרע 9[7] n.) *from among his clan*, as it must needs be if he left no issue who could perpetuate it. According to early custom a son was requisite to perpetuate a man's name (Dt. 25[6f.]). The terms of the question imply that if this earlier custom be so far modified as to allow daughters to inherit, the land will not only continue in the possession of Ṣelopheḥad's descendants, but also in his clan (משפחה); and the same implication is present in the request *give us a possession in the midst of our father's brothers, i.e.* in the midst of our fellow-clansman. The case raised in 36[3] is at present ignored. —*Give unto us*] in 𝔐 (תנה) the subj. of the vb. is Moses; in S (תנו) 𝔊 𝔙 Moses and Eleʿazar.—*A possession*] the term אחזה is regularly used of *landed* possession; see also 36[2ff.].—

5–8a. Moses refers the case to Yahweh (cp. 9^{8} 15^{34} P, Ex. 18^{19} E); Yahweh approves the plea, and commands Moses to grant the request of Ṣelophehad's daughters and to promulgate a general law.—8b–11. The terms of the law: these have been summarised above, p. 396 f.

1. צְלָפְחָד] the name must be a compound. Nöld. (*Untersuchungen*, 89) proposed צַל פַּחַד; cp. 𝔊 Σαλπααδ; then for the use of צל, cp. 14^{9} n. and the names of Ṣilbel, king of Gaza (Schrader, *COT.* 162), Ṣili-Istar (Hommel, *Anc. Heb. Trad.* 302). פחד in this case refers to a deity: cp. Gn. 31^{42}.—**2.** וכל] 𝔊 𝔖 + ולפני.—**3.** מת (2)] S + אבינו.—**7.** כן . . . דברת] 36^{5}, Ex. 10^{29}.—להם . . . אביהם] S and some Heb. MSS. להן . . . אביהן; the forms at the end of the v. in 𝔐 are fem. For the masc. forms see Dav. 1 R. 3.—והעברת . . . ל] with a secular reference only here and in v.[8]; העביר ל is used several times of religious devotion (*e.g.* Ex. 13^{12}, Jer. 32^{35}). **8.** איש כי ימות] 5^{6} n.—**9.** לְאֶחָיו] 𝔊 לְאָחִיו; so in v.[10] 𝔊 reads לְאָחִי for לְאַחֵי (𝔐): cp. בתו, בת in v.[8f.] (𝔐); but אחים v.[10f.] justifies the plurals of MT. here and in v.[10].—**11.** והיתה] see second phil. n. on 15^{24}.—חקת משפט] 35^{29}.—כאשר צוה יהוה את משה] 1^{19} n.

12–23 (P). Moses, bidden to prepare for death, obtains the appointment of his successor, Joshua.

The priestly origin of the section is clear: note the parallelism and connection with 20^{22b-29} (P), the allusion to Ele'azar and numerous points of style, *e.g.* the formulæ in v.[15. 22a], עֵדָה (1^{2} n.), העמיד (v.[19. 22]; 3^{6} n.), נאסף אל עמיו. The parallels are in D, Dt. 3^{23-28} 31^{1-7}; in JE, Dt. $31^{14f. 23}$. On the relation of these to one another and to the present passage, see Driver, *Deut.* pp. 61, 337–339.

The death of Moses, unlike that of Aaron (20^{27b-29}), is not recorded immediately after the divine command to prepare for it; on the other hand, between the command and the record of the death (Dt. c. 34) there now intervene the last nine chapters of Nu. and the whole of Dt. The insertion of Dt. and much of Nu. c. 28–36 is due to the compiler of the Hexateuch (Introd. § 12). Consequently, in P^{g} the record of the death was separated from the present narrative by little more than some instructions given by Moses to Joshua. This being the case, it is improbable that the command of v.[12–14] was repeated in an expanded form by the original writer; and, therefore, either v.[12–14] or Dt. 32^{48-52} (the amplified command) was inserted by an editor.

The originality of the repetition becomes more defensible in proportion to the amount of matter admitted to have intervened: cp. We. *Comp.*[2]

115; Dr. *Deut.* 383. Whether the present passage is an abbreviation of Dt. 32^{48-52} which originally stood here (Di., CH.), or the latter an expansion of the former (*e.g.* Bacon), is uncertain. See, further, Driver as just cited.

12 f. The extent to which these verses have been verbally incorporated in, or derived from, the longer account in Dt. 32^{48-50} may be seen from the following translation in which the words reappearing in Dt. are italicised, "*And Yahweh* said *unto Moses, Go up into this mountain of the* ʿ*Abārim, and see the land which I* have *give*n *to the children of Israel*; and thou shalt see it, *and* thou also shalt *be gathered to thy kinsmen, as Aaron thy brother was gathered.*" On the ʿ*Abārim*, see 21^{11} n.; the particular peak intended is Mt. Nebo (𝔊; Dt. 32^{49} 34^{1}); with *be gathered to thy kinsmen*, cp. 20^{24} n. See, further, on the matter common to these verses and Dt., Driver, *Deut.* 383 f.—**14.** The sin of Moses and Aaron at Ḳadesh (20^{8-13}), here described as rebellion, is the reason why both alike had to die before the land of promise was reached. In substance the v. agrees with Dt. 32^{51}, but the verbal agreement is less than in the preceding verses. On the various descriptions of the sin of Moses and Aaron, see above, pp. 261 f., 263.—*In the strife*] *bim'rîbath*, a play on the first part of the name *Meribath-Ḳadesh* = *the strife of Ḳadesh.* See, further, the notes on Dt. 32^{51}.

12. ויאמר י״י אל משה] S וידבר י״י אל משה לאמר; cp. Dt. 32^{48}. But a divine command is also introduced as here in 𝔐 by the simple אמר אל even in Pg: see Gn. 17^{1}, Ex. 7^{19} 8^{16} 9^{8} 12^{43} 14^{26}.—לבני ישראל] 𝔊 + לאחוה: cp. Dt. 32^{49}.—**13.** אחיך] 𝔊 + בהר ההר; cp. Dt. 32^{50}.—**14.** פי . . . להקדישני] the words must be closely connected (*My commandment to sanctify Me*) though the intervening clauses make this awkward. ולא הקדשתני would be simpler; but it is precarious to infer from 𝔊 𝔖 𝔙 that they had such a reading before them.

15–17. Moses asks Yahweh to appoint his successor, that the community may not be left leaderless at his death.—**16.** *God of the spirits of all flesh*] 16^{22} n.—**17.** *Who may go out . . . and come in before them*] man *goes out* to business (Ps. 104^{23}): *to go out and come in* is an idiomatic way of expressing activity in general by reference to its commencement and conclusion (cp. Dt. 28^{6}, Zech. 8^{10}, Ps. 121^{8}), and is a *usus loquendi* similar in character to the frequent Semitic periphrases for *all* which consist of two terms for opposed classes: for example, *the* *fettered and the free, the dry and the thirsty, the binder and the bound* (see Driver, *Deut.* 376). Moses, therefore, begs that his successor may initiate all the undertakings of the people and see them through. The phrase *to go in and go out* may have a specific reference, as, for example, to military duties (1 S. $18^{13. 16}$; cp. 1 S. 29^{6}) or to others (2 K. 11^{9}, 1 Ch. 27^{1}); but nothing in the present context suggests any such limitation; cp. rather Jos. 14^{11}, Dt. $31^{2f.}$, 1 K. 3^{7}, 2 Ch. 1^{10}.—*As sheep that have no shepherd*] 1 K. 22^{17}.—**18–21.** Moses is bidden solemnly to appoint Joshua as his successor. Joshua has been previously mentioned in P's narrative only in connection with the spying out of Canaan, $13^{8. 16}$ $14^{6. 30. 38}$ 26^{65}.—*A man in whom is spirit*] *i.e.* a man already possessed of spirit (רוח); the term is not used specifically of the spirit of prophecy, but rather of capacity; cp. Gn. 41^{38}. Dt. 34^{9} is rather more explicit: Joshua is described as "full of the spirit of wisdom."—*And rest thine hand upon him*] The custom of placing the hand on a person at solemn moments was ancient (Gn. 48^{14} J); but the phrase used here is peculiar to P and 2 Ch. 29^{23}. A fuller form of the phrase, *to rest* (סמך) *the hand* (יד), or *hands, upon the head of*, is invariably used in P in the frequent cases in which the subject is a sacrificial animal; once also where the object is personal (Lev. 24^{14}); but in every other case where the object is personal, the abbreviated phrase *to rest the hand*(*s*) *upon* is employed (Nu. 8^{10} (ct. v.^{12}) $27^{18. 23}$, Dt. 34^{9}); and this also occurs once where the object is a sacrificial animal (2 Ch. 29^{23}). Whether one or two hands was used in the rite s uncertain: see phil. n. The significance of the rite is also difficult to determine: possibly it was not the same in all the very different cases in which it was employed—in the sacrifice of animal victims, before a blessing (Gn. 48^{14}), accompanying a solemn protestation against a person (Lev. 24^{14}, Susanna v.^{34}), or in the transference of power on admission to office. In the present and similar cases the action seems an obviously appropriate symbol of the transference of office, whether or not magical efficacy was originally attributed to the act on such occasions. Later the action was regularly employed in the admission of men to an order; cp. in NT. Ac. 6^{6}, and the use of סמך or סְמִיכָה in the Mishnah for the act of admitting to the position of Rabbi (Levy, *Neu.-hebr. Wörterbuch*, iii. 542, 545). For discussions of the significance of the act, see Bähr, *Symbolik*, ii. 306 f., 338–343.—**19.** *Commission him*] cp. Dt. 3^{28} (D). —**20.** *And thou shalt put some of thy majesty upon him*] by publicly declaring (v.^{19}) Joshua his successor (cp. v.$^{16f.}$) Moses is to confer on him some (מִן, cp. 11^{25}) of the majesty with which he has himself been clothed in virtue of his authority, so that Joshua, being also magnified in the people's sight (cp. 1 Ch. 29^{25}), may receive their obedience. הוד, which is used of the majesty of the king (Ps. 21^{6} 45^{4}, Jer. 22^{18}), occurs here only in the Hexateuch.—**21.** The position of Joshua is to be less exalted than had been that of Moses: Moses received instructions from Yahweh direct (*e.g.* v.$^{12. 15}$ and *passim* in P), Joshua is to obtain them through the priest, and the priest in his turn by use of the *Urim*, or sacred lot (Ex. 28^{30}, Lev. 8^{8}). Once, however, in the subsequent narrative of P, Yahweh speaks to Joshua direct (Jos. 20^{1}).—*At his command*] the pronoun refers to Eleʿazar; Joshua is actually to lead the people, but the priest is to instruct him when and how.—**23.** At the end of the v. S adds, *And He said unto him, Thine eyes are those that saw what Yahweh did*, and so forth, as Dt. $3^{21f.}$; cp. Introd. § 14*a*.

18. וסמכת את־ידך] as against the sing. here (in 𝔐 S; 𝔊 has pl.), see v.^{23}, Dt. 34^{9} where the pl. is used in 𝔐 and 𝔊, the sing. in S. In blessing Ephraim and Manasseh Jacob laid one hand on each (Gn. 48^{14}). With this conflict of evidence the question of the use of one or two hands in the rite as applied to persons must remain an open one, unless it be assumed that it must have been the same as in the sacrificial rite. In allusions to the sacrificial rite, the pl. *hands* is naturally used where the subj. is pl. (Ex. $29^{10. 15. 19}$, Lev. 4^{15} $8^{14. 18. 22}$ 24^{14}, Nu. $8^{10. 12}$), but where the subj. is sing. (Lev. 1^{4} $3^{2. 8. 13}$ $4^{4. 24. 29. 33}$ 16^{21}) the sing. *hand* is always used except in Lev. 16^{21} (Ḳ're שתי ידיו; 𝔊^{ABL} om. שתי), and even there the K'tib has the sing. (ידו). The evidence thus points strongly to the use of the single hand in the sacrificial rite.—**21.** שאל לו] cp. 1 S. $22^{10. 13. 15}$; with the following ב, cp. Ezek. 21^{26}.

XXVIII.–XXX. 1.—*A Scale of Public Offerings.*

The purpose of the present section is to define the quantities of the periodical (28^{2} 29^{39}) *public* offerings; incidentally it also, and of necessity, contains a list of the Jewish fixed feasts or sacred seasons.

The section is clearly derived from P, yet scarcely from P^g, for it stands in no organic connection with the Priestly narrative. It is not improbably post-Ezran in origin (P^s).

The connection with Lev. 23 (P), the allusions to 15^{1-16} (P) in $29^{18. 21. 24. 27. 30. 37}$, the fixed quantities and fixed dates, the definition of the months throughout by *number* (Dr. *L.O.T.* 156), and the constant use of מנחה with the meaning of *meal-offering* (16^{15} n.), all point to P. On the other hand, the attempts to connect the section with the preceding or following narrative have been unsuccessful. Rosenmüller, for example, suggested that the section is placed here because the people, enriched by the cattle of the vanquished, would soon be in a position to carry out the requirements of these laws. There are stylistic peculiarities in the chapters (see note on $28^{2. 26}$ 29^1 and the last n. on 28^7), but these do not *necessarily* point to P^s; nor does 28^6, which has every appearance of having been interpolated in the completed section (see n.). So also some of the other arguments adduced by Nöld. (89 f.), Kue. (*Hex.* 98, 299), and CH. in favour of posteriority appear to the present writer to point only to *difference* of origin. Indications of posteriority are to be found in the historical presuppositions, rather than in the literary characteristics and relations of the chapters.

As a *systematic* table of quantities of the *public* offerings required at *regularly-recurring periods* the present section has no parallel in the Hexateuch. Ezek. 45^{18}–46^{15} contains something similar, though there it is required that the prince should provide the offerings (45^{17}) and offer them on behalf of the people.

There are *scattered* allusions to *some* of the quantities here required (15^{1-16}, Ex. 29^{38-42}, Lev. $23^{13. 18-20}$); and other quantities are frequently prescribed; but these are either of the offerings of individuals (Lev. c. 1–7), or of public offerings not made on a fixed occasion (Lev. 4^{13-21}). The *scattered* allusions to the quantities of the fixed public offerings may be derived from this section; for this section is scarcely even in part (for it cannot be wholly) based on them. In the main the present table must either be based on lost documents, or contain the original statement of the actual praxis of the author's time, or of his theory of what that praxis should be.

But the framework of the section, consisting of the definitions of the sacred seasons, is to a large extent identical with parts of Lev. 23. Lev. 23 now consists of a combination of H and P with some subsequent additions (P^s). It is by no means clear that 28^{26a} is based on Lev. $23^{16. 20}$ (H); if it is not, there is nothing common to Nu. 28 f. and the parts of Lev. 23

derived from H, and it is improbable that Nu. 28 f. is based on Lev. 23. The presence of the common matter might be explained as due to Lev. 23 being based on Nu. 28 f., or more probably by both Lev. 23 and Nu. 28 f. being based on a now lost festal calendar. Note that 28^{16} is, strictly speaking, out of place here, since no quantity is prescribed for passover.

The corresponding parts of the two sections are as follow :—

Lev. 23^{5-8}	=	Nu. $28^{16-19a. 25}$.
,, 23^{21}	=	,, 28^{26b}.
,, $23^{24f.}$	=	,, 29^{1}.
,, $23^{27f.}$	=	,, $29^{7f.}$.
,, 23^{34-36}	=	,, $29^{12. 35f.}$.

The agreement is for the most part close and verbal, though the clauses in some cases are differently arranged. The variations are mainly due to the greater brevity of Nu.: thus the names of the feasts are absent from 28^{17} 29^{12}, *towards evening* from 28^{16}, *it is the Day of Atonement*, and Lev. 23^{28b} from $29^{7f.}$. The only noticeable addition in Nu. is that of עולה to אשה in 28^{19} $29^{8. 12}$. The resemblance of Nu. 28^{26a} to Lev. $23^{16. 20}$ (H) is comparatively slight; but it must be noticed that 28^{26} is the sole exception in the section to the definition of the season by the number of the day and the month.

So far as the occasions are concerned, the 8th day of the autumn festival (29^{35}, ct. Dt. $16^{13. 15}$) and the Day of Atonement (29^{7-10}) point to a post-exilic date for this section, and the latter possibly to the post-Ezran period, since it is not clear that the celebration of the Day of Atonement on the 10th day of the 7th month (ct. Neh. 9^{1}) is as ancient as Ezra. The remaining occasions, apart from the fact that they are fixed for definite days (see below, p. 407), do not point to even a relatively late date. A daily offering of some kind was offered before the Exile (see below), and "the beginnings of the month," or "days of new moon," were from a very early period regarded as sacred (see on 28^{11}). The other occasions mentioned here are also mentioned in Lev. 23; and for a fuller discussion of them, as also of the 8th day of the autumn festival and the Day of Atonement, the reader is referred to the commentary on Leviticus.

But the quantities required in the table point as a whole to the later development of Jewish religion.

The simple fact that quantities are *fixed* distinguishes this law from the earlier codes; see the remarks following the table below. The first specification of quantities for public sacrifices is found in Ezekiel, who fixes the quantities for the daily, sabbatical, and monthly sacrifices, and also for the offerings made at the spring and autumn festivals. These quantities are not the same as those here given (see table below); a mere comparison of the two tables scarcely proves P's posterior to Ezekiel's, but that it is so may be assumed in view of the wider arguments for the posteriority of P to Ezekiel.*

Only in the case of the daily offering can the history of the determination of the quantity be somewhat more closely followed. And unfortunately even in this case the most crucial passage (Neh. $10^{34\,(33)}$) is not entirely free from obscurity. But if, as seems to the present writer most probable, it implies that the daily offering included only *one* burnt-offering, the present law originated at some time between Ezra and the Chronicler, or the date of 𝔊, and probably, therefore, at some time in the 4th cent. B.C.

Before the Exile the daily offering consisted of a עולה in the morning and a מנחה in the evening (2 K. 16^{15}: cp. 1 K. $18^{29.\,36}$). Ezekiel also requires *one* עולה and *one* מנחה (clearly a *meal-offering*) to be offered every day, but requires both to be offered in the morning. Neh. $10^{34\,(33)}$ still speaks of a daily מנחה and a daily עולה; it does not specify the time of offering, and it is therefore uncertain whether in this respect it agreed with 2 K. 16^{15} or Ezek.; but in common with both of these it *co-ordinates* the עולה and מנחה. The present law (Nu. 28^{3-8}) requires *two* עולה daily, one in the morning and one in the evening, and also *two* מנחה; but the מנחה is in each case *subordinated* to the עולה. In the time of the Chronicler (1 Ch. 16^{40}, 2 Ch. 13^{11} 31^{3}) and later (*Tamid* iv. 1) *two* burnt-offerings, one in the morning and one in the evening, were actually offered.

Some have thought that the singular עולה in Neh. 10^{34} may cover the double offering of this law, and as a matter of fact the singular is used even here in allusion to the daily offering (28^{10} and often, עלת התמיד). But the difference between the co-ordination and subordination of the מנחה remains. Ezr. $9^{4f.}$, however, is quite inconclusive; the practice of offering a מנחה in the evening was the cause of "the time of the מנחה" becoming a term for the latter part of the day, but the phrase continued in use long after the מנחה had ceased to be characteristic of the evening; see Dan. 9^{21}, and cp. the antithesis in the Mishnah between תפלת שחר (=*morning-prayer*) and ת' המנחה (=*evening-prayer*); see Ber. iv. 1; Pes. x. 1, and Levy, *Neu.-hebr. Wörterbuch*, *s.v.* מנחה.

* Driver, *L.O.T.* 139 ff.

The numbers of the animals required by this law for the several public offerings, with the occasions on which they were offered, are given in the subjoined table, in which the bracketed figures are those required by Ezekiel ($46^{13-15. 4f. 6f.}$ 45^{21-25}).

Occasion.	Lambs.	Rams.	Bullocks.	Goats.
Each day (28^{3-8})	2 (1)	...	...	...
Each sabbath ($28^{9f.}$)	2 (6)	0 (1)	...	...
1st of each month (28^{11-15}) . .	7 (6)	1 (1)	2 (1)	1
Each day from 15th to 21st of 1st month (28^{16-25})	7 (0)	1 (7)	2 (7)	1 (1)
Day of first-fruits (18^{26-31}) . .	7	1	2	1
1st of 7th month (29^{1-6}) . . .	7	1	1	1
10th ,, ,, (29^{7-11}) . .	7	1	1	1
15th ,, ,, ...	14 (0)	2 (7)	13 (7)	1
16th ,, ,, ...	14 (0)	2 (7)	12 (7)	1
17th ,, ,, ...	14 (0)	2 (7)	11 (7)	1
18th ,, ,, ...	14 (0)	2 (7)	10 (7)	1
19th ,, ,, ...	14 (0)	2 (7)	9 (7)	1
20th ,, ,, ...	14 (0)	2 (7)	8 (7)	1
21st ,, ,, ...	14 (0)	2 (7)	7 (7)	1
22nd ,, ,, ...	7	1	1	1

Wine, oil, and meal are required with each of these animals, according to the scale of 15^{1-16}.

The offerings are cumulative: for example, the sabbath offering is *in addition* to the daily offering (28^{10}), the special offering on the 1st of the 7th month additional both to the daily offering and to that required for the first of each month (29^{6}).

The animals required are in all cases males. The lambs, rams, and bullocks are offered as burnt-offerings, the goats as sin-offerings.

The sacred number 7 (23^{1} n.) is very prominent. In addition to what is obvious in the above table, note the accumulation of special occasions in the 7th month, and the special character (implied by the special offerings) of the 1st day of that month, the seven-day duration of each of the two great festivals in the 1st and 7th month respectively (28^{17} 29^{12}); and, further, that the descending numerical series of bullocks required for the autumn (7th month) feast yields the total 70, and that thus the total number of victims offered on the seven days of this feast is 7 × 7 × 2 lambs, 7 × 7 rams, 7 × 10 bullocks, 7 goats.

These fixed quantities, and this fixing of the festivals on fixed days in particular months, separate these regulations from the practice in early Israel, which was preserved in the main as late as Dt. Earlier practice fixed the festivals with reference to agricultural operations, which, from the nature of the case, varied to the extent of some days in different years (Dt. 16^{9}, Ex. 23^{16} 34^{22}). The quantity offered at these feasts was left to individual discretion, with the exhortation that it should be "according to the blessing of Yahweh . . . which He hath given" (Dt. $16^{10.\,17}$). A further marked difference in character between the earlier festivals and those here regulated appears in the nature of the sacrifices. The sacrifices here required, alike for the old festivals and for the great fast-day, the "Day of Atonement," are exclusively *burnt-offerings* and *sin-offerings*; individuals, if they liked, might offer "vows and freewill offerings" (29^{39}), but the obligatory offerings are those which were made over entirely to the deity, and in which the laity had no share. On the other hand, the earlier codes never mention offerings of this kind in connection with the festivals, and the offerings which actually give their joyous character to the occasions are peace-offerings—offerings which formed the material for sacrificial meals in which all, priests and laity alike, partook (see Dt. 16^{1-17}, with Driver's notes). At the earlier festivals the laity *participate* in the fullest measure in the celebrations; on the occasions here regulated they are mere *onlookers*; they are required to abstain from work and generally to form a sacred gathering, but the actual celebrations are confined to the priests.

XXVIII. 1 f. Introductory command.—The offerings are to be offered at the times fixed.

2. *My oblation*] קרבן is confined to P (78 times) and Ezek. 20^{28} 40^{43} (CH. 118). The addition in the present instance of an objective suffix (*my*) referring to God is peculiar; yet see $9^{7.\,13}$ 31^{50} (P^{s}), Lev. 23^{14} (H); ct. Lev. 17^{4} $27^{9.\,11}$. Generally the suffix is subjective, and refers to the person who makes the offering.—*My food*] Ezek. 44^{7} (Ezek. 16^{19} is different).

Cp. *the food of thy God* (Lev. $21^{6.\,8.\,17.\,21f.}$ 22^{25} (H)): also v.[24], Lev. $3^{11.\,16}$, Mal. 1^{7}. The description of the sacrifices as the food of God is a survival "in the ancient technical language of the priestly ritual"* of the primitive conception that the gods ate and drank (Jud. 9^{13}). RV. (marg.) "my bread" is a doubtful limitation; לחם, it is true, means *bread*, sometimes even in contradistinction to other foods (*e.g.* 1 S. 25^{11}, 1 K 17^{6}); but it is also used in the wider sense of *food* (1 S. 14^{24}, Jud. 13^{16}, 1 K. 5^{2}); this sense is probably original; subsequently the word acquired mostly the specific sense of *bread* in Hebrew, of *flesh* in Arabic (لَحْم).—*My fire-offerings*] see 15^{10} n. and phil. n. on 15^{3}. For the suffix (*my*), cp. Lev. $6^{10\,(17)}$ (𝔐, not S 𝔊).—*My odour of rest*] 15^{3} n. The suffix here also is most unusual; in the other instances in which a suffix is used with this phrase (Ezek. 20^{28}, Lev. 26^{31}), it refers to those who make the odour.—*Ye shall observe to present*] peculiar in P; cp. the frequently recurring Deuteronomic expression *observe to do* (CH. 82^{D}; Driver, *Deut.* p. lxxxiii).

3–8. The daily- (or perpetual-) offering.—Cp. Ex. 29^{38-42}: on the relation between the two passages and on the history of the daily-offering, see above. The daily-offering consists of an offering made *in the morning* and another made *between the evenings*, *i.e.* in the afternoon or evening. Each consists of a yearling he-lamb presented as a burnt-offering, together with $\frac{1}{10}$ ephah of fine meal, $\frac{1}{4}$ hin of oil, and $\frac{1}{4}$ hin of wine: cp. $15^{4f.}$. The daily-offering formed the central and most important part of the Jewish cultus: its cessation was most deeply felt (Dan. 8^{11-13} 11^{31} 12^{11}), and counted as one of the five great calamities that happened on the 17th of Tammuz. The circumstances attending the offering in later times are fully described in *Tamid*, of which a summary is given by Schürer (*GJV.*[3] ii. 294–298; Eng. tr. II. i. 292–297).—**3.** *This is the fire-offering which ye shall present*] the Israelites as a community raised the money required for the offering: Neh. $10^{32f.}$; Jos. *Ant.* iii. 10^{1}.—*A continual burnt-offering*] The abbreviated form for the offering, *the continual* (התמיד), occurs in the late book of

* W. R. Smith, *Religion of the Semites*,[1] 207, [2]224; cp. *KAT*,[3] 594 f.

Daniel ($8^{11.12.13}$ 11^{31} 12^{11}; cp. Sir. 45^{14}), and gives its title to the tractate of the Mishnah which deals with the daily-offering.—4. *Between the evenings*] 9^3 n.—5. 7a. Cp. $15^{4f.}$—6. An allusion back to Ex. 29^{38-42}; but between v.[5] and v.[7], which are really continuous, v.[6] is out of place, and in all probability a gloss.—*In Mount Sinai*] 3^1 n.—7b. Not found in Ex. 29, and perhaps even here a gloss.—*The sanctuary*] 18^5 n. Here the court where the altar stood may be intended (cp. Ezek. 44^{27}, Ex. 28^{43}); for the wine of the libation, according to Ecclus. 50^{15}, was poured out at the base of the altar; cp. Jos. *Ant.* iii. 9^4. Str. thinks that the outer chamber of the tent, where the vessels used in libations were kept (Ex. 25^{29}), is intended.—*Strong drink*] 6^3 n. Since in all other cases *wine* is required for libations, *strong drink* may here be used exceptionally with reference to wine; cp., however, *KAT*,[3] 600 (*šikaru* used in Babylonian libations).

2. צו . . . ואמרת אליהם] 34^2; cp. notes on $5^{2.6}$.—אליהם] 𝔊 + לאמר.—לאשי] S לאשה.—במועדו] S במועדיו; cp. 𝔖 𝔙, also 29^{39} and 9^2 n. 𝔊 ἐν ταῖς ἑορταῖς μου = במועדי.—3. עלה תמיד] S עלת תמיד; cp. עלת התמיד in v.[10. 15] etc. 𝔐.—4. אחד] see 16^{22} n. But האחד (S; cp. v.[7] 𝔐 and Ex. 29^{39}) was probably the original reading, since השני stands in the next clause.—5. עשירית האיפה] elsewhere throughout the section (as in c. 15, Ex. 29) עשרון is used.—כתית] 𝔊 S om.—6. עלת תמיד הע׳] Driver, *Tenses*, 209 (2). The form of sentence is uncommon in Pg (see Di.); cp. Ex. 38^{24} (Ps).—אשה] 𝔊 omits this word here and in v.[8]; 𝔖 omits it in v.[13].—7. נסכו] the suffix refers to כבש: so in v.[8]: but in Ex. the fem. suffix refers to עולה.—ההין] 𝔖 and some MSS. of 𝔊 + יין; so Paterson.

9–XXIX. 38. The additional offerings to be made on special days over and above the daily offerings.—These offerings were in later Hebrew termed מוסף *additional*. The *Mûsāph* was offered between the two daily-offerings (*Siphrê* on v.[10]); the terms of 28^{23} suggest that it was to be offered *immediately* after the daily morning offering.

9 f. The sabbath-offering.—This is equal in amount to the daily-offering. The present is the only allusion in the Pentateuch to a special and regularly repeated public offering on the sabbath. Whether in theory or practice such an offering was earlier in date than Ezekiel ($46^{4f.}$), and, if so, how much, cannot be determined. In the time of Isaiah the sabbath was frequently chosen for presenting sacrifices; but, to judge from the allusions (Is. 1^{13}, Hos. 2^{11}), these offerings were not specially appointed, and the circumstances attending them were very different from those contemplated in this law. Evidence of the actual practice of this law is confined to post-exilic times (Neh. 10^{33}, 2 Ch. 8^{13} 31^{3}; Jos. *Ant.* iii. 10^{1}).

11–15. The offerings on the first day of each month.—This law, in requiring for these occasions as much as for each day of the great spring festival, demands more than Ezekiel had done: see table.

Not only is the quantity of this offering nowhere else defined in the Pent. (nor at all in the OT. except in Ezek. $46^{6f.}$), but the celebration of the new moon is never mentioned in JE, D, or H, nor elsewhere in P except in 10^{10}. From references outside the Pent., however, it is clear that the new moon was in early times an important festival and occasion of sacrifice (Is. 1^{13}, Hos. 2^{13}, Am. 8^{5}, 1 S. $20^{4ff.}$, 2 K. 4^{23}). Possibly as a popular festival it was associated with heathen practices, and, therefore, intentionally ignored by the early lawgivers (JE, D). It may have regained its place in this later law partly on account of the importance of the new moon in fixing the calendar and the due succession of festivals, and partly in accordance with the tendency to preserve but transform, customs that had a great hold on the people (see p. 47 f.). But be this as it may, though the sacred character of the days of new moon is ancient, the specific regulations of this law need not be. Definite allusions to these belong to the post-exilic literature (1 Ch. 23^{31}, 2 Ch. $2^{3\,(4)}$ 8^{13} 31^{3}, Ezr. $3^{4f.}$, Neh. 10^{32}). A survival of what was probably the chief celebration of the days in ancient times is incidentally referred to in 10^{10}, where it is implied that peace-offerings (of the flesh of which the offerer partook at the sacrificial meal) were also offered on these days. Later allusions to the celebration of the new moons are Judith 8^{6}, Col. 2^{16}; see, further, Nowack, *Arch.* ii. 138–140; We. *Proleg.*[4] 110 f.; Di. *Ex. Lev.* p. 579 ff.; "New Moon" in *EBi.*

12–14a. Cp. 15^{2-12}.—**15.** The sin-offering required at the new moons and on other occasions (v.$^{22.\,30}$, $29^{5.\,11.\,15ff.}$) is unknown to Ezekiel, and is not referred to in the subscription in Lev. 23^{37}.—**16.** = Lev. 23^{5}.

17–25. The special offerings on the 15th to 21st of the 1st month, *i.e.* on each day of the Feast of Unleavened Bread. **17–19a.** = Lev. 23^{6-8}.—**19b–24.** The offerings are to be of the same kind and amount as on days of new moon (v.$^{11-15}$). Ezekiel (45^{23}) requires a different but more valuable offering daily during the feast (see table): but it has been questioned by Corn. whether the text of Ezek. may not be corrupt.—25. = Lev. 23^{8}.

26–31. The special offering at the Feast of Weeks.—The quantity (v.$^{27-31}$) is the same as in the two preceding cases. It is given over again in Lev. $23^{18.19a}$; but the common matter is probably inserted there from this passage. The original law of H appears to have required only two he-lambs as *peace-offerings* (Lev. 23^{19b}) and two loaves (v.^{17}). See, further, on Dt. 16^{9-12} and Lev. 23. Ezekiel omits this feast altogether from his calendar.—**26.** On the relation of clause *a* to Lev. $23^{16.20}$ (H), see above; clause *b* = Lev. 23^{21} (P).—*The day of firstfruits*] the term יום הבכורים is not used elsewhere. It is the day on which the firstfruits (בכורים, *e.g.* Lev. 23^{17}) or "bread of firstfruits" (לחם הבכורים Lev. 23^{20}) was "brought to Yahweh" (18^{13} n.). The festival is called in other codes the "feast of harvest" (Ex. 23^{16} (E)), or "the feast of weeks" (Ex. 34^{22} (J), Dt. 16^{10}); the latter term is here abbreviated into *at your weeks* (בשבעתיכם).—**26b.** = Lev. 23^{21}.—**27.** See next n.—**31.** *Perfect shall they be unto you*] the clause has been accidentally transposed from the end of v.^{27}, where analogy (cp. *e.g.* v.^{19}) requires it. S (cp. 𝔊) has the words both in v.^{27} and v.^{31}.

XXIX. 1–6. The special offering of the 1st day of the 7th month.—**1.** = Lev. $23^{24f.}$.—*The day of trumpet-blowing*] the phrase (יום התרועה) is peculiar to Nu., though Lev. 23^{20} also refers to the תרועה ($10^{5ff.}$). The offering required on the seventh new moon is additional to, and almost of the same amount as, the offering for an ordinary new moon. Thus the seventh new moon stands to ordinary new moons much as the seventh day to ordinary days. For the special significance and celebration of the seventh new moon, see on Lev. 23^{24}.

7–11. The special offering of the 10th day of the 7th month, *i.e.* the Day of Atonement (Lev. 23^{27}). Irrespective of the offerings required by the rites described in Lev. 16, which may be in part referred to here in the phrase *the sin-offering of atonement* (v.^{11}, cp. Ex. 30^{10}), the special offering is the same in kind and character as the special offering on the first day of this month.—**7.** = Lev. $23^{27f.}$.

12–34. The special offerings of the 15th to 21st of the 7th month, *i.e.* during the Feast of Booths (Lev. 23^{34}). On the seven days of the autumn festival five times as many bullocks and twice as many rams and lambs were offered as on the corresponding days (15th–21st of the 1st month) of the spring feast (28^{17-25}). In this respect, again, the law differs from Ezekiel, who requires precisely the same offerings at the autumn as at the spring festival (Ezek. 45^{25}). See, further, the table above and the appended notes.

12. = Lev. $23^{34f.}$.—**14 f.** It is probably merely an accident that all allusion to the libations is omitted (in 𝔐, but cp. S at end of v.[15]) in this section. In subsequent sections (*e.g.* v.[18]) the libations are mentioned.

35–38. Special offering of the 8th day, *i.e.* the 22nd of the 7th month. The quantity required is different from that of the special offerings made on the first seven days of the feast, and the same as that required on the 1st and 10th days of this month.

39. Subscription.—The foregoing offerings presented by, and on behalf of, the community are additional to any private offerings of any kind that may be offered on the same days.

XXX. 1 (XXIX. 40). Conclusion, corresponding to $28^{1.\,2a}$.

XXVIII. 9. השבת] 𝔊 + προσάξετε = תקריבו: cp. v.[11] 𝔐.—**10.** עלת שבת בשבתו] *Siphrê* interprets thus: שאם עבר היום בטל קרבנו, *i.e.* if for any reason the sabbath-offering has not been made on the day, it cannot be made on another: similarly Rashi, Str., and, apparently, König, iii. p. 293 n. 1. Cp. דבר יום ביומו Ex. 5^{13}. Marti (on Is. 66^{23}) explains rather differently, giving to שבת two different senses: then translate, *the weekly-offering on its sabbath*, and below (v.[14]) *the monthly-offering on its new moon.* This is certainly favoured by the parallel usage in Is. 66^{23}, and satisfactorily explains the masc. suffix (שבת, חרש being masc., but עלה fem.). Otherwise the masc. suffix must be explained on the analogy of the agreement of the pred. with the gen. of a compound expression (Dav. 116, R. 2); cp. Kön. iii. 349*h*. For the cstr. form שַׁבַּת, cp. 1 Ch. 9^{32}; Kön. iii. 337*t*; also, in general, G.-K. § 130.—על] *in addition to*; so v.[15. 24] and frequently in P (*e.g.* 6^{20}, Gn. 28^{9}, Lev. 7^{12}). In v.[31] $29^{6.\,11}$ etc., על is replaced by מלבד.—**14.** יין] Paterson transposes this, and places it after the first הין; S reads the word in both places.—**17.** מצות יאכל] so Ex. 13^{7}; cp. G.-K. 121*b*. S 𝔊 read מצות תאכלו in agreement with Lev. 23^{6}.—**18.** קרש] 𝔊 + יהיה לכם; so Lev. 23^{7}: and in this c. in v.[25] 29^{1} etc. 𝔐.—**22.** שעיר חטאת אחר] What the original variations in the description of the sin-offering throughout these chapters may have been, it seems impossible to say; at present there are six in 𝔐 alone. The following statement may serve as an illustration of variations in 𝔐 (a few variant readings may be found in De Rossi), and between 𝔐 S and 𝔊. The variations are—

1. שעיר עזים אחד לחטאת : 𝔐 28^{15}, S 29^{11}, 𝔊 and S $29^{16.\ 19.\ 22.\ 25.\ 28.\ 31.\ 34.\ 38}$.
2. שעיר עזים אחד חטאת : 𝔐 $29^{11.\ 16.\ 19.\ 25}$.
3. שעיר חטאת אחד לכפר עליכם : 𝔐 28^{22}.
4. שעיר עזים אחד לכפר עליכם : 𝔐 28^{30}.
5. שעיר עזים אחד חטאת לכפר עליכם : 𝔐 29^{5}.
6. שעיר עזים אחד לחטאת לכפר עליכם : 𝔊 29^{11}, 𝔊 and S $28^{22.\ 30}$ 29^{5}.
7. שעיר חטאת אחד : 𝔐 $29^{22.\ 28.\ 31.\ 34.\ 38}$.

XXIX. 9. האחד] Paterson omits ; see his note.—**13.** תמימים יהיו] an intermediate form between the full ת' יהיו לכם (*e.g.* v.[8]) and תמימים in v.[17. 20] etc. ; see Paterson.—**15.** S rightly adds at the end of the v. ונסכיהם.—**19.** ונסכיהם] for this as also for ונסכיה of v.[31] restore וְנִסְכָּהּ **as in v.**[17] **and other allusions to the sin-offering.**

XXX. 2–17 (1–16). *Conditions of the validity of a Vow.*

Various regulations regarding vows are found elsewhere (see especially Dt. $23^{19.\ 22f.}$, Lev. $5^{4f.}$ and c. 27 (P), Nu. 6 (P)); but the conditions of the validity of a woman's vow, with which this law is almost entirely occupied, are treated nowhere else.

Points of style like איש כי (v.[2] ; cp. 5^{6} n.), מטות (v.[1] ; cp. 1^{4} n.), לענת נפש (v.[14] ; CH. 20) connect the section with P. But the isolation of the law and some stylistic peculiarities such as אִסָּר, הֵחֵל דְּבָר, מבטא (see notes below on v.[3. 7]), render it unlikely that it is the work of P^{g}. The date cannot be accurately determined, but the law may, with some probability, be referred to P^{s} on account of its approximation in style and treatment to the later Rabbinic discussions.

The Law provides that a man, having once uttered a vow, is unconditionally bound by it (v.[3]); that a woman widowed or divorced is similarly bound (v.[10]); but that the vow of an unmarried woman living in her father's house (v.[4–6]), or of a married woman (v.[7–9. 11–15]), is subject to the tacit approval of her father or husband, as the case may be. In either case the vow is valid unless objection is raised on first hearing of it. If the husband, after hearing of the vow and raising no objection, subsequently annuls it, the guilt is his (v.[16]).

Rabbinic discussions on the regulations of this c. will be found in *Nedarim*, c. 10 f.

2. The Introductory formula is doubly peculiar. (1) In form. A law is usually introduced by the direct statement that Yahweh delivered it to Moses (or Aaron); here this statement forms part of Moses' speech; the nearest parallels are Ex. $16^{16.32}$ 35^{4}, Lev. 8^{5} 9^{6} 17^{2}. (2) In being addressed to *the heads of the tribes* (ראשי המטות): this phrase occurs again only in 1 K 8^{1} ‖ 2 Ch. 5^{2}; cp. ראשי אבת המטות 32^{28}, Jos. 14^{1} 21^{1}.—3. If a man utters a vow, he must keep it. This is obvious. An absolute command would have been more suitable, but the form of sentence is probably chosen for the sake of symmetry with the following conditional sentences which are required by the nature of the case. The use of the conditional in the more specific regulation of Dt. 23^{22} ("If thou makest a vow . . . thou shalt not delay to pay it") is quite natural. Dt., too, adds expressly that the making of vows is in no sense a requirement of religion. Vows were of two kinds: (1) a vow might consist in a promise to give something to God; the classical example of this is Jephthaḥ's vow: cp. also Gn. $28^{20ff.}$: or (2) the vow might take the form of an undertaking to practise, for a longer or shorter period, some form or forms of abstinence, such as from wine, as in the case of the Nazirite (c. 6), or from food (1 S. 14^{24}; cp. also Ps. $132^{3f.}$). Both kinds are elsewhere covered by the single term נֶדֶר: here for the second kind a special term (אִסָּר) is employed, while the wider term נדר is limited to the first kind. The use of the noun אִסָּר in the OT. is confined to this chapter, but the vb. (אסר) is frequent with the sense *to bind*. In the Mishnic Heb. אסר is regularly used with the sense *to prohibit*; and in Bibl. Aram. the noun אֱסָר means *a prohibition* or *interdict* (Dan. $6^{8f.}$ etc.); the Syr. ܐܶܣܳܪ includes the meanings of *interdict* and *penance*, though it also means *vow* (Payne Smith, *s.v.*). Render: *If any man makes a vow to Yahweh, or subjects himself to some pledge of abstinence, he shall not profane*, *i.e.* break, *his word*; the Hiph. of the vb. (יַחֵל) occurs again with this sense only in Ezek. 39^{7}; the Piel is commoner; cp. Ps. 55^{21}, Mal. 2^{10}, and, especially in view of the context there and here, Ps. $89^{35\,(34)}$.—*He must do according to all that goeth forth*

from his mouth] with כל היצא מפיו, cp. מוצא שפתיך (Dt. $23^{24\,(23)}$). An intention only becomes binding when it has been embodied in speech, and so gained an independent existence; consequently stress is frequently laid, as here, on the *utterance* of the vow (*e.g.* 32^{24}, Jud. $11^{35f.}$, Ps. $66^{13f.}$, Jer. 44^{17}). And indeed, originally, so much stress was laid on the *utterance*, that it was held binding even when, as in the case of Isaac's blessing of Jacob, it did not express the intention of the speaker (cp. notes on 5^{17-23} 6^{22-27} 22^{6}). This is expressly corrected, so far as vows are concerned, in the Mishnah (*Tᵉrûmoth* iii. 8), where, after citing various illustrations, such as of a man intending to say "burnt-offering," but actually saying "peace-offerings," the general rule is given that nothing is binding unless intention and expression agree (לא אמר כלום עד שיהיו פיו ולבו שוין).—4. *In her father's house in her youth*] *i.e.* while she is young and unmarried. Women for purposes of this law are divided into three classes (1) young unmarried women, (2) married women, (3) widows or divorced women. The classification is not exhaustive, no account being taken of old unmarried women: but in Israel, where marriage was a religious duty, this class must have been a negligible quantity. The term *youth* (נערים) is vague: it may include infancy (Job 31^{18}: cp. נער Ex. 2^{6}, 1 S. 1^{22} 4^{21}), and need not include virginity (cp. נערה in Jud. 19^{3}, Am. 2^{7}); but here childhood is scarcely contemplated, the child, whether male or female, probably being assumed to be incapable under any circumstances of making a vow. The class contemplated in this v. would thus consist of young marriageable but (since still in the father's house) unmarried women. Many of the Rabbis * distinguished between *youth* (נערות), the time of and immediately after the first appearance of the signs of puberty, and the age of *puberty* (בגרות) itself; and they limited the class in this verse to those in the earlier stage (which lasted but a few months) in accordance with the dictum, "When a woman has attained puberty, her father has no longer authority over her" (*Nedarim* 47*b*). But this can hardly be the intention of the biblical passage; for youth (נערים) in biblical Hebrew covers a much later period

* *Siphrê*; Rashi on this passage; also Levy, ii. 191*a*, iii. 417*a*.

of life (see above).—5. *And her father comes to hear* (שמע) *of her vow*] that שמע is to be so translated is clear from v.[8]. It is not necessary that her husband or father should actually hear the vow uttered; but they must exercise their veto, if at all, when first made aware that the vow has been made.—*Her vows shall stand*] for קום, meaning *to be valid*, cp. Gn. $23^{17.20}$ ("The cave became Abraham's *valid* possession"); also Dt. 19^{15}.—6. *But if her father expresses his disapproval of her*] *i.e.* of her conduct in making the vow. The sense of הניא is sufficiently clear from the context here and in v.[9. 12]; it is an antithesis to giving tacit approval to, and its effect (v.[9]) is to annul (הפר) the vow. (Successful) *opposition* appears to be the fundamental sense in Hebrew; cp. the remaining uses of the vb. ($32^{7.9}$, Ps. 33^{10}, and, if the text be correct, Ps. 141^{5}). The only derivative is תנואה (14^{34}, Job 33^{10} †).—7–9. The case considered here is that of a woman who is married while under a vow which her father has not vetoed before marriage.—7. *The rash utterance*] this noun (מבטא) occurs again only in v.[9]; the sense is clear from the use of the vb. in Lev. 5^{4}, Ps. 106^{33} †; cp. בטה (Pr. 12^{18} †). To judge from some biblical references (Pr. 20^{25}, Eccles. $5^{1.\,3-5\,(2.\,4-6)}$, Ecclus. 18^{23}), and still more from the Mishnic tracts *Nazir* and *Nedarim*, vows were frequently taken very rashly. But rashness did not relieve a man of his obligation (cp. Lev. 5^{4}).—9. *If on the day that* (or, perhaps, simply *when*) *her husband comes to hear* of it *he expresses his disapproval of her, then he renders her vow invalid*] הפר is the antithesis of הקים (v.[14b]), הקים the causative of קום (v.[5] n.).—10. *Shall stand against her*] *i.e.* shall be valid, and she shall be responsible for discharging the vow.—14. *Every oath* taken pledging the woman to some form *of abstinence with a view to afflict the soul*] the last phrase (לענת נפש) is commonly used in connection with fasting, Ps. 35^{13}, Is. $58^{3.5}$; cp. Lev. 16^{29} (Day of Atonement) $23^{27-29.\,32}$, Nu. 29^{7}, and the post-biblical term תַּעֲנִית *fast*.—*Her husband can render valid, or her husband can render invalid*] see notes on v.[5. 9].—15. But by merely keeping silence the husband *renders all her vows valid* (והקים); in the parallel case (v.[5b]) the vb. is neuter, here causative.—16. In this verse the vb. הפר must be rendered rather differently;

if after coming to hear of the woman's vow and tacitly approving it, he forcibly *prevents the fulfilment of* the vow, guilt is incurred, but it rests on him and not on his wife.—*He shall bear* the consequences of *her* (𝔊 S *his*) *iniquity*; for the phrase, see Lev. 5^1, Ezek. 44^{10}, and the note on Nu. 18^{23}.

2. 'לבני יש] G.-K. 129*d*.—**3.** איש כי] 5^6 n. 𝔊 reads איש איש כי.—**3.** אִסָּר] but with suffix אֱסָרָהּ, see Stade, 208*a b*; Kön. ii. 141: Barth, *NB.* 62; Lagarde, *BN.* 175; Ryssel, *De El. Pent. Sermone*, p. 40. Both the form and the meaning (see above) suggest a late stage of the language.—או הִשָּׁבַע] The inf. abs. is used in a similar sentence in Lev. 25^{14}; Dav. 88, R. 1.—**5.** כל נדריה וכל אסר] Whether the interchange of singulars and plurals in these words throughout the chapter was intended by the author cannot be determined. S and 𝔊 generally have plurals; so here S reads אסרים. In 𝔐 it should be observed that the suffixes vary; in v.[13. 15. 16] אֹתָם, ־ָם, but in v.[14] ־ֶנּוּ.—**6.** יקום ויהוה] if the reading be correct, the vb. agrees exceptionally with the sing. כל instead of the plural genitives that follow (G.-K. 146*c*); but S reads יקומו יהוה; cp. וקמו in v.[8].—**9.** 𝔊, while giving the same sense, suggests a very different text.—יניא] S הניא].—נְדָרֶהָ] S נדריה; cp. 𝔊.

XXXI. *The Extermination of Midian.*

In view of the near approach of death (v.[2b]), Moses, at Yahweh's command, prepares to avenge Israel (v.[2]) and Yahweh (v.[3]) on the Midianites, who at the instigation of Balaam had led the Israelites to sin against Yahweh, and incur in consequence a plague from Yahweh (v.[16]). Moses commands each tribe to equip 1000 men, and despatches them, 12,000 in all, together with Phineḥas, who carries the sacred "objects" and the trumpets with him (v.[4-6]). Without losing a man themselves (v.[49]), the Israelites slay "every male" (*i.e.* every fighting man) of the Midianites (v.[7]), including the five kings of Midian ('Ĕvi, Reḳem, Ṣur, Ḥur, and Rebaʿ) and also Balaam (v.[8]), and burn all the Midianite cities and encampments (v.[10]). They return to Moses, Eleʿazar, and the rest of Israel in the steppes of Moab (v.[12]) with the Midianite women and children, of whom the virgins numbered 32,000 (v.[9. 35]), and the spoil consisting of 675,000 small cattle, 72,000 large cattle, 61,000 asses (v.[32-34]), and golden ornaments of which the portion falling to the officers was worth 16,750 shekels (v.[48-52]). Moses, Eleʿazar, and "the princes of the congregation" go to meet the returning army outside the camp. Moses, seeing that the women are brought back alive, is angry with the officers, inasmuch as it was the Midianite women who had caused Israel to sin; he therefore commands every male child and all women not virgin to be slain, leaving only the virgins alive; he further commands that both the warriors and the captives shall remain seven days outside the camp to purify themselves and their garments and all objects made of skin, goats' hair, or wood, from contamination (v.[13-20]). At this point Eleʿazar strikes in (as Rashi will have it, because Moses in his anger had forgotten to be particular enough), and explains that all objects that can bear it (viz. those of metal), must be cleansed by being passed through fire, and everybody else by "the water of impurity" (v.[21-24]). Yahweh now commands Moses to count the captured men and cattle, and to divide them into two equal parts, and to give one-half to those who had fought, the other half to those who had remained behind. Of the half that falls to the warriors $\frac{1}{500}$th is to be paid as a tax to the priests; of the other half $\frac{1}{50}$th to the Levites (v.[25-30]). The carrying out of this instruction is described at length (v.[31-47]). Thereafter the officers present to Moses, as an offering for Yahweh, the spoil in gold which they had captured for themselves; Moses and Eleʿazar place it in the tent of meeting as a memorial (v.[48-54]).

This is not history, but *Midrash.** The purpose of the story is to illustrate certain legal and religious themes, and especially the law of the distribution of booty (v.[25-30]) and of the removal of uncleanness from the dead (v.[19-24]; cp. c. 19). This explains why the writer is so indifferent to the actual war that he says nothing of the line of march, nor of the place and manner of battle, and dismisses the slain with a word, while he waxes prolix over the booty and the measures taken for purifying the returned warriors.

The unhistorical character of the narrative is so obvious that it need not be proved at length. It may, however, be pointed out that if it were historical, then, since *every* male Midianite was slain, Midian must have disappeared from

* On the term, see Driver, *L.O.T.* 529.

history in the time of Moses; and this conclusion would conflict with the prominent part played by Midian in the Book of Judges (c. 6–8), not to speak of later references (1 K. 11^{18}, Is. 60^{6}).

But though as a whole unhistorical, the narrative may and doubtless does contain some traditional elements, such as the names of the five kings. But it is impossible to determine the historical value of these traditions; the names need not even be Midianite names, still less Midianite names of the Mosaic period.

But the greater part of the chapter cannot have even a traditional basis. V.$^{19-24}$ merely describes the application of the law of c. 19; the law of the division of the booty (v.$^{25-30}$) is an inference from ancient Hebrew custom (1 S. $30^{24f.}$). Whence or how the primary numbers (v.$^{32-35}$) were obtained cannot be determined, but v.$^{31-47}$ merely records the results of certain simple arithmetical operations with these figures. Further, the part played by Phineḥas may have been suggested by c. 25; that the Israelites, while slaughtering a multitude never lose a single man, is similar to the flight of fancy of a kindred writer, who makes 25,700 Benjamites slay in two days, without losing a man themselves, 40,000 out of 400,000 Israelites opposed to them (Jud. c. 20); and the munificent present of the leaders (v.$^{48-54}$) has a parallel in c. 7.

The story belongs to the age which saw the rise of Midrashic literature; it clearly belongs to the secondary strata of the Priestly Code (P^s),* for it presupposes, without belonging to, P^g.

The style and vocabulary in general connect the c. with P (note, *e.g.*, עדה several times, and see notes and margins in CH.), and the chapter presupposes much of the preceding narrative of P^g; as, for example, that Aaron is dead and Ele'azar is priest (20^{22-29}), that the people are in the steppes of Moab (22^{1}), that Moses' death is imminent (27^{12-23}). On the other hand, the chapter itself clearly formed no part of P^g, for (1) the general Midrashic character is unlike that writer; (2) the preceding narrative of P^g does not prepare for this incident: 27^{12-23} does not anticipate a war with Midian before Moses' death, and still less that in such a war Joshua should have nothing to do; (3) the vocabulary of the chapter,

* Kue., We., Corn., Kit., Addis, CH.; cp. Di. and Str.

though it contains many of the characteristic words and expressions of P^g, contains also striking peculiarities. Among the most noticeable departures from the style and vocabulary of P^g are (1) עבדיך as a periphrasis for the pronoun (v.^{49}), טף (v.^{9}), and לקראת (v.^{13}), all of which are common in JE, but never used by P^g (cp. v.$^{13f.}$ n.; also 16^8 n.); and (2) the following words or phrases entirely peculiar to this c. or used here in a peculiar sense—מסר (v.^{5}), תפשי המלחמה (v.^{27}), מכם (v.^{28} and 5 times besides), עם הצבא (v.^{32}), מחצה (v.$^{36.\,43}$). Note also מלקח (v.^{11}), אחז (v.$^{30.\,47}$), נקמת י״י (v.^{3}). For details, see the notes below; but note that some of the expressions are most nearly paralleled in Ch.

1–8. The Israelites under Phineḥas are sent out to fight the Midianites.—**2a.** Resumptive of $25^{17f.}$.—**2b.** Cp. 27^{13}.—**3.** *Equip for yourselves men from among you*] a doubtful rendering of a certainly peculiar phrase (see phil. n.).—**5.** *And there were delivered*] presumably to Moses; on the unusual verb, see below.—**6.** The choice of Phineḥas rather than Eleʿazar to accompany (or, to lead?) the host was dictated by considerations similar to those that dictated the choice of Eleʿazar in 17^2 (see note there).—*The sacred objects*] What is intended is uncertain; the phrase כלי הקדש refers elsewhere to various appointments of the tabernacle or temple (3^{31} 4^{15} 18^3, 1 K. 8^4, 1 Ch. 9^{29}, 2 Ch. 5^5 †; cp. Neh. 10^{40}, 1 Ch. 22^{19}). Di. (after Del.) would interpret it here of the sacred garments; a unique sense of the phrase, such as this would be, is by no means impossible in this ch. For כלי = *garment*, cp. Dt. 22^5.—*The trumpets for the blast*] חצצרות התרועה 2 Ch. 13^{12} †, cp. Nu. 10^9 (והרעתם בחצצרת). On these trumpets, see 10^{1-10} (P).—**7.** *Every male*] the expression is very characteristic of P, including P^g; CH. 107.—**8.** The five kings are mentioned again by name and in the same order in Jos. 13^{21}; but they are there described as *princes* (נשיאי) *of Midian* and *chiefs* (נסיכי) *of Siḥon*, and are said to have been smitten by the Israelites in the same battle with Siḥon, king of the Amorites. Balaam there, as here, is associated with them, but receives the additional description of *the soothsayer* (הקסם). Neither passage seems to be based directly on the other; they are rather both based on a tradition anterior to either, which was already somewhat fixed in form, since the five kings seem to have attained to a fixed order of mention, and was yet told with such differences as are represented in the two written forms of the story. One of the kings (Ṣur) is also mentioned in 25^{15}, and is there described as head of a Midianite family—a description chosen, perhaps, in view of the description of Zimri as head of a Simeonite family. Of the names little is to be said, except that they have no appearance of being either artificial or late. On *Ṣur*, see 25^{15}. *Evi* and *Reba'* are otherwise unknown. *Ḥur* (which may possibly be the Egyptian Horus) is in E's account of the Exodus the name of an Israelite (Ex. 17^{10-12}; see *EBi.*). *Reḳem* appears elsewhere in the genealogies of Ch. (1 Ch. $2^{43f.}$ 7^{16}), and as the name of a Benjamite town in Jos. 18^{27}; in 𝔖, Reḳem is the equivalent of Ḳadesh.—*With their slain*] *i.e.* those slain in battle, not those afterwards slain as prisoners (v.[17]).

1. P's formula: CH. 185.—**3.** החלצו מאתכם אנשים] The Niphal of חלץ occurs again only in $32^{17. 20}$: there the word is a direct reflexive. Here, if correctly pointed, it must be an indirect reflexive, since מאתכם אנשים is clearly the direct object. Possibly החלצו should be pointed as Hiphil; but for the Hiphil there is only one, and that a doubtful parallel (Is. 58^{11}).—ויהיו על] rather peculiar: but cp. 2 S. 11^{23} with We.'s note (cited by Dr.). For לצבא ויהיו, 𝔊 possibly read לִצְבֹא לפני י״.—נקמת יהוה] Jer. $50^{15. 28}$ 51^{11}; cp. Jer. 11^{20} 20^{12}, Ezek. $25^{14. 17}$ †; so CH. marg.—**5.** וימסרו] v.[16] †. In v.[16] the reading is very doubtful, and some here follow 𝔊 and correct to וַיִּסָּפְרוּ. The root מסר is otherwise unknown in biblical Hebrew, though very common in post-biblical Hebrew and Aram., with the meaning *to deliver*. It also occurs in Sabæan = *to get taken away* (Hommel in *ZDMG.* xlvi. 530).—חלוצי צבא] 1 Ch. 12^{24}, 2 Ch. 17^{18} †; cp. חלוצי הצבא Jos. 4^{13} (R) †; כל חלוץ צבא 32^{27}; החלוץ לצבא 1 Ch. 12^{23} †.

9–12. The Israelites return victorious.—**9.** *Their little ones*] The word (טפם) is exceeding uncommon, if indeed ever found, in P^g; it occurs thrice in this c. (v.[17. 18]), 4 times in the next (v.[16f. 24. 26]), and in Gn. 34^{29}; otherwise 12 or 13 times in J, and 9 times in D; CH. 52^J.—**10.** *Their cities*] 13^{19} n.—*In their dwelling-places*] the places where they were *now* settled as distinguished from their original settlements: this is the usual interpretation, but whether the writer meant anything so definite may be doubted.—*And all their enclosures*] not the usual word (מחנה) for an encampment, but that (טירה) which is used specifically of the encampments of nomads (Gn. 25^{16}, Ezek. 25^4) and then more loosely (Ps. 69^{26}, 1 Ch. 6^{29}).—**11.** *All the spoil* (שלל) *and all that was taken* (מלקוח; also v.[12. 27. 32], Is.

49^{24} †); in the next v. these terms are repeated with a third, *the captives* (שבי), prefixed. The three terms are used rather loosely; but the first may exclude and the last particularly refer to human beings; the second certainly includes men in v.[27. 32]; but in v.[12], as in Is. $49^{24f.}$, these are sufficiently covered by שְׁבִי. The second and third are combined in v.[26].—**12b.** Cp. 22^1.

13–20. The reception of the warriors, and Moses' instructions to them.—13 f. *Ele'azar the priest* ($20^{26ff.}$) *and the princes of the congregation* (Ex. 16^{22} and often) are derived from P^g; *the captains of thousands* and *the captains of hundreds* (v.[14]), from elsewhere (*e.g.* Ex. 18^{25} E). For *the officers of the host* (פקודי החיל), cp. 2 K. 11^{15}; and note that פְּקֻדִים, though very frequent in P, has generally quite another sense (see, *e.g.*, 1^{45}; and CH. $115b^{P}$).—Moses and the rest go to meet the warriors *without the camp* (CH. $120a^{P}$), where they were required by law (c. 19 and below) to stay till purified from contamination by the dead.—**15.** Cp. 1 S. c. 15.—*Every female*] cp. v.[7] n.—**16.** Cp. 25^{18}. The Heb. cstr. is extraordinary, and the text in one respect corrupt (see below): the paraphrase of RV. gives the general sense. The women on account of their seduction of the Israelites, the male children (v.[17]) in order to secure the extinction of Midian, are to be slain; the virgins to be preserved alive (v.[18]).—**19 f.** Moses commands the warriors with their captives to stay without the camp till they have become ceremonially clean by "unsinning" (8^{21} n.) themselves on the third and seventh day (cp. 5^2 19^{16-19}), and by "unsinning" also their garments and everything with them that is made of skin (cp. Lev. $13^{49ff.}$), *goats' hair* (עזים 1 S. $19^{13.16}$, Ex. 25^4), or wood; these would be unclean on the principle of $19^{14f.}$. This purification of victorious warriors and their weapons is a very primitive custom. An instance of the custom among a modern savage people has been cited above (p. 243); see, further, Frazer, *Golden Bough*, i. 331–339.

21–24. Ele'azar adds some more explicit directions.—Everything that can stand it is to be purified by being passed through fire, and then *unsinned by means of the water of impurity* (19^9): everything else must be washed *with water*; not, as RV. ("the water") might suggest, with "the water of impurity."

The article with בַּמַּיִם, like that with בָּאֵשׁ, is generic (G.-K. 126*m*).—**21.** *The statute of the law*] 19^2 †.

9. בני יש׳] 𝔊 𝔙 om.—**12.** אל עדת בני יש׳] 𝔊 אל כל בני יש׳; 𝔖 S אל כל עדת בני יש׳. —**14.** צבא המלחמה = *the service of war*; this is rather peculiar; cp. 1 Ch. 7^4 12^{37} where the sense is perhaps different, and Is. 13^4 where it certainly is different.—**13.** לקראתם] לקראת is used in the Hexateuch 28 times in JE, 6 in D, never in P^g: but it is used in Gn. 14^{17}, a chapter which, like the present, is Midrashic in character and stylistically dependent on P^g; CH. 183^JE.—**16.** The whole of clause *a* is clumsily constructed; but למסר appears to be a textual error: even the post-biblical meaning of מסר (v.^{5} n.) is unsuitable here; the suggestion made by Ges. (*Thes.*) to read למעל has been generally accepted; then cp. especially 5^6, also 2 Ch. 36^{14}, Ezek. 14^{13}. 𝔊 𝔖 read למסר למעל as two infinitives; cp. Haupt in *SBOT.*—**17.** אשה ידעת איש למשכב זכר] similarly v.^{18} and v.^{35}; the only strict parallels are in Jud. $21^{11f.}$.—**19.** התחטאו] 8^{21} n. —**20.** תתחטאו] the alternatives are to regard the vb. as used in an unusual "indirect middle" sense (cp. החלצו v.^{3}), or to regard the whole of the preceding part of the v. as an unusual instance of the indirect acc. If the first be adopted, התחטא is used in three different senses in immediate succession; for in v.^{23} it must be passive (cp. Kön. iii. 101).—**21.** הבאים למלחמה] 32^6, 1 Ch. 19^7 †. Haupt, however, proposes to read here either היצאים לכל׳, or (after 𝔊) הבאים מצבא מלחמה.

25–47. The division of the booty.—**26.** Moses is assisted in estimating the booty by Ele'azar and the heads of families, as at the taking of the census he had been assisted by Aaron and "the princes of Israel" (1^{44}).—**27.** The equal division of the booty here enjoined between those *who had* actually *taken part in the battle* and *all the* rest of the *congregation*, *i.e.* those who had kept in camp, accords with early Hebrew custom, the establishment of which is attributed to David (1 S. $30^{24f.}$). Cp. also Jos. 22^8. On the Arabic and Mohammedan custom, which shows some points of similarity, see Ḳor. $8^{1.42}$; Sprenger, *Moḥammad*, iii. 126–128; Muir, *Mahomet*,[3] 221 f.—**28.** After the division of the spoil as between the two sections of the people and before its distribution to individuals, a tax is deducted for religious purposes. No such tax is mentioned in 1 S. $30^{24f.}$, but some such practice may be ancient; Mohammed required $\frac{1}{5}$th ("Know that whenever ye seize anything as a spoil, to God belongs a fifth thereof, and to His apostle, and to kindred and orphans, and the poor and the wayfarer," Ḳor. 8^{42}). —**28 f.** From the portion of the men who fought, $\frac{1}{500}$th is set apart as *a contribution* (5^9 n.) *to Yahweh* for the use of the priests.—**30.** From the half assigned to the rest of the congregation, $\frac{1}{50}$th is set apart for the use of the Levites. The whole body of Levites thus receive 10 times as much as the priests; this recalls the regulations as to tithe ($18^{25ff.}$), though the result of the distribution is rather different; in the case of tithe, the Levites retain for their own use only 9 times as much as is given to the priests.—**32.** *Now what was taken* ($v.^{11}$ n.), all *that remained over of the booty which the men who had fought* (עם הצבא, here only) *had made*, *i.e.* all that was left after the command of $v.^{17}$ had been carried out, or possibly, as Str. takes it to mean, all that had not been used up or worn to death (Gn. 33^{13}) on the homeward march.—**33–47.** See the summary of the chapter, above.

48–54. The report and present of the officers of the host.—**48 f.** The officers report to Moses that the army has returned from the war without the loss of a man.—**49.** *Thy servants*] This periphrasis for the personal pronoun occurs 6 times in this chapter and the next ($32^{4f. 25. 27. 31}$, P^s), 32 times in JE, and 2 times in D; CH. 73^{JE}.—*The men . . . who were under our authority*] with בידינו, cp. 2 S. 18^2.—**50.** The officers bring as an offering to Yahweh the various ornaments of precious metal, rifled from the bodies of the slain (cp. Jud. $8^{22ff.}$), which had fallen to their lot but had formed no part of the booty distributed as described in $v.^{25-27}$. The precise sense of many of the terms in $v.^{50b}$ is uncertain. כְּלִי זָהָב, *objects of gold* (not, as RV., "jewels of gold"), appears to be generic, the following terms being specific; cp. in the next v., *the gold . . . all the wrought objects* (את הזהב . . . כל כלי מעשה); אצעדה (2 S. 1^{10} and צעדה Is. 3^{20} †) is probably *an ornament for the arm*; cp. 2 S. 1^{10} and عَضُد, *the upper part of the arm* (Barth, *NB.* 151*d*). Some (*e.g.* RV.) prefer the meaning *anklet*, assuming that the word is from the root צעד *to march*, or *step*. The next term צמיד (Gn. $24^{22. 30. 47}$, Ezek. 16^{11} 23^{42} †) is clearly *an ornament for the hand* or *wrist*. The next two terms denote *rings*; טבעת is *the signet ring* which was worn on the hand (Est. 3^{12}, Gn. 41^{42}), and עגיל *the ear-ring* (Ezek. 16^{12} †). But כּוּמָז, also mentioned in Ex. 35^{22} †, though perhaps etymologically connected with كمز = *to roll something with the hands into a round form*, is of quite uncertain meaning.—*To make propitiation for ourselves before Yahweh*] cp. Ex. $30^{15f.}$.—52. The total weight of *the gold of the contribution which they contributed* was 16,750 shekels (= just over 600 pounds avoirdupois); ct. the smaller figures in Jud. 8^{26}.—53. The private soldiers had also secured similar plunder of gold and silver objects for themselves. Possibly the verse is a gloss.*—54a repeats v.[51].—54b. Cp. Ex. 30^{16b}.

26. ראשׁי אבות] confined to P (perhaps P^s; 32^{28} 36^{1} (cp. 17^{18}), Ex. 6^{25} (Jos. 14^{1} 19^{51} 21^{1}), Ch. and Neh.: CH. 84.—27. תפשׂי המלחמה] the phrase occurs nowhere else: cp. תפשׂי התורה Jer. 2^{8}; and for the vb. see also Am. 2^{15}, Gn. 4^{21}.—28. והֲרֵמֹת] G.-K. 72*i*.—מֶכֶס] the word is used only in this chapter (v.[37-41], 5 times); in post-biblical Hebrew and in Aram. it means *tax*; and in post-biblical Hebrew מוכס means *a tax-gatherer*. מכסה in Ex. 12^{4}, Lev. 27^{23} (P) has a different sense.—אחד נפשׁ] נפשׁ = *man* is masc. as in Gn. $46^{25b.27a}$. On the exceptional prefixing of the numeral אחד, see Kön. iii. 310*b*. But נפשׁ may be, as Paterson suggests, a gloss to show that the levy is to be made only on live spoil.—30. אחד אחז] cp. האחז אחד v.[47]: אחז *to take out* (of a number) occurs elsewhere only in 1 Ch. 24^{6}.—36. מחצה] v.[43] †.—53. אנשׁי הצבא] ct. אנשׁי המלחמה v.[28]; עם הצבא v.[32], and האנשׁים הצבאים v.[42].—54. שׂרי האלפים והמאות] an abbreviation (found also in 1 Ch. 13^{1}) of שׂ׳ האל׳ ושׂ׳, המאות v.[48].

XXXII. *The settlement of Reuben, Gad, and Manasseh on the East of Jordan.*

Being rich in flocks, Reuben and Gad seek to have allotted to them the rich pasture land of Gileʿad instead of territory on the W. of Jordan (v.[1-5]). Moses expresses his anger at the apparent selfish indifference of these two tribes to the common interests of the whole people (v.[6-15]). Reuben and Gad explain that they are willing before settling down themselves to assist the other tribes in the conquest of W. Palestine (v.[16-19]). Moses instructs Eleʿazar, Joshua, and the heads of the people to allot Gileʿad to Reuben and Gad if they fulfil their promise, and, if they do not, to punish them by making them settle W. of Jordan (v.[20-30]). Reuben and Gad rebuild certain cities (v.[34-38]) in which they had proposed to leave their women and

* Di., CH., Paterson.

children while they should be away fighting with the other tribes (v.$^{16ff.}$). Manassite clans make conquests E. of Jordan (v.$^{39-42}$).

The closing section of the chapter, apart from v.^{40}, consists of fragments from an ancient source: see on v.$^{39-42}$. The remainder (v.$^{1-38}$) appears to have been freely composed by a late writer working on materials derived from JE and P, and having some of the previous narrative, such as that of the spies (c. 13 f.), before him (cp. v.$^{6-15}$) in its present composite form (JE P). The chapter takes no account of c. 31, but (in v.$^{28ff.}$) it presupposes 27$^{15-23}$ (P), and is itself presupposed by 34$^{14f.}$ (cp. Jos. 13$^{15ff.}$ (P)). Consequently it was written, or recast, to occupy some place between c. 27 and 34. A strict analysis of the chapter as between JE and P cannot be satisfactorily carried through.

Driver assigns v.$^{1-17. 20-27}$ (in the main) $^{34-38}$ to JE, v.$^{18f. 24-32}$ to P; and certainly the indications of P, though some of them are sufficiently marked, are less numerous in the former than in the latter series of verses. Other analyses may be found in Bacon, *Triple Tradition*; Addis, *Documents of the Hex.*; Paterson, *SBOT.*; see also Holzinger's *Tabellen*. For the view taken above as to the whole of v.$^{1-38}$, see CH.; cp. Kue. in *Th. Tijd.* xi. 478 ff.

The mixed character of the narrative is illustrated in the notes that follow, but it will be convenient to group together the chief points here. (1) In common with JE this narrative speaks of the spies starting from Ḳadesh and going as far as the Wady Eshcol; and it contains such characteristic words and phrases as טף, ויחר אף יהוה, חרון אף, בלתי (=*except*), מקנה. (2) In common with P, the chapter makes Joshua as well as Caleb a spy, and speaks of Ele'azar the priest; in the vocabulary note העדה נשיאים, אחוזה, מבן עשרים שנה ומעלה. (3) As in D, Ḳadesh is here called Ḳadesh-Barnea'. Note the Deuteronomic phrases in v.$^{7-13}$ (see notes there). (4) For some linguistic peculiarities of the chapter see notes on הניא (v.$^{7. 9}$) and תרבות (v.^{14}). The presence of linguistic peculiarities and Deuteronomic characteristics, and the fact that some of the most marked peculiarities of P are embedded in sections that in other respects most closely resemble JE, render it more probable that the whole narrative has been recast than that it is the result of simple compilation from JE and P, such as is generally found elsewhere.

Proof that the substance of the story was as old as, and indeed older than, JE may be found in Dt. 33^{21}, which appears to allude to Gad assisting the other tribes after choosing his own portion. Like others, the story was told with variations in detail: according to Dt. 3^{12-21} Moses *unrequested* distributes the land to Reuben, Gad, and half Manasseh, and the condition that these tribes must assist the others is not suggested by themselves, but imposed on them by Moses.

1–5. Gad and Reuben make their request.—Rich in cattle, these tribes wish to settle in Gileʿad.—**1.** The cattle owned by the Israelites in the wilderness are frequently mentioned elsewhere (11^{4} n.), but neither here nor elsewhere is it explained how Gad and Reuben came to be richer in cattle than the remaining tribes. As a matter of fact, the pre-eminently pastoral (cp. Jud. $5^{16.\ 17a}$) character of the tribes which remained E. of Jordan must have been the result and not the cause of their settlement in this district.—*Reuben . . . Gad*] ct. *Gad . . . Reuben* in v.$^{2.\ 6.\ 25.\ 29.\ 31.\ 33}$; cp. v.$^{34-37}$. 𝕲 (except in v.$^{6.\ 33}$), S (except in v.^{2}), and 𝕾 keep *Reuben . . . Gad* throughout v.$^{1-33}$. The order *Reuben, Gad* is found in all the parallel passages and allusions in the Hexateuch (*e.g.* Dt. 3, Jos. 22) except in Jos. 18^{7}: it also occurs in 1 Ch. 5^{18} $6^{48.\ 63-65\ (63.\ 78-80)}$ 12^{37} 26^{32}. But in the present chapter the unusual order *Gad, Reuben* (cp. 2 K. 10^{33}) is probably original (cp. v.$^{34-37}$), and due to the pre-eminence of Gad (cp. Dt. $33^{20f.\ 6}$) in the period to which the story lying at the base of the present narrative belongs. If this be so, the text of 𝕳 in v.^{1} has been altered out of regard for the genealogical scheme which makes Reuben the firstborn of Jacob, and this alteration has been more consistently carried through in S 𝕲 𝕾.—*The land of Jaʿzer* (†ארץ יעזר) *and the land of Gileʿad*] the Gadite and Reubenite country is differently defined, or described, in different parts of the chapter. It is called "the land of Gileʿad" simply (v.^{29}), or defined by a series of towns (v.$^{3.\ 34-37}$: cp. v.^{26}), or described as the already conquered country (v.$^{4.\ 33}$; c. 21). The differences may be in part due to the combination of different sources.—On the site of *Jaʿzer*, see 21^{24} n. *Gileʿad* used in its widest sense would include Jaʿzer; cp. "Jaʿzer of Gileʿad," 1 Ch. 26^{31}. Jaʿzer may be particularly mentioned with a view to suggesting the eastward limit of the land described (cp. Jos. 13^{25}); for Gileʿad is a very elastic term. Sometimes (*e.g.* Jos. $22^{9.\ 13}$) it covers the whole land of Israel E. of Jordan in antithesis to Canaan, the land of Israel W. of Jordan. Gileʽad used in this widest sense generally consisted of the land between the Wady Ḥesbân (or even the Arnon) on the S. and the Yarmuk on the N.: the eastern border was indefinite; and the northern and southern were subject to expansion and contraction according to the power of the Aramæans and Moabites respectively. The country is cut by the Jabboḳ (mod. Nahr ez-Zerḳā) into what some biblical writers looked upon as the two halves of Gileʽad (Jos. 12[2. 5] 13[31], Dt. 3[12f.]); and the terms "land of Gileʽad," "mountains of Gileʽad," are often used when the writer has mainly, or exclusively, in mind either one of these two halves; so Gileʽad refers to the land N. of Jabboḳ in Jos. 17[1. 5f.], to the land S. of Jabboḳ in Jos. 13[25]. In the present chapter it is used in both of these limited senses. Here and in v.[29] (cp. Dt. 3[12f.]) it refers to the land S. of Jabboḳ; for the towns mentioned in v.[3. 34-37] and the territory elsewhere assigned to Gad and Reuben lay entirely south of that river. But in v.[39] Gileʽad means the country N. of the Jabboḳ.* The ancient name is now confined to the Jebel Jilʽād S. of the Nahr ez-Zerḳā and near es-Salṭ.—*The district was a district for cattle*] Gileʽad, especially southern Gileʽad, like Moab still further south, was celebrated in ancient as it is in modern times for its cattle; see Cant. 4[1] 6[5], Mic. 7[14], 1 Ch. 5[9]. A modern Arab saying runs, "Thou canst not find a country like the Belkaʽ" (*i.e.* the country between Jabboḳ and Arnon) for cattle and sheep.†

N. and S. Gileʽad differ somewhat in character. The following sentences from G. A. Smith's *Hist. Geog.* (p. 522 ff.) illustrate this, and vividly depict the present character of the country desired by Reuben and Gad. "Gilead, between the Yarmuk and the Jabbok, has its ridges covered by forests. . . . The valleys hold orchards of pomegranates, apricot, and olive; there are many vineyards, on the open plains are fields of wheat and maize, and the few moors are rich in fragrant herbs. . . . South of the Jabbok, the forests gradually cease, and Ammon and Moab are mostly high, bare moors. . . . More famous than the tilth of Eastern

* G. A. Smith, *Hist. Geog.* 534 f., 548 f.; Buhl, *Geog.* 45-48, 119-122; Cheyne, art. "Gilead" in *EBi.*

† G. A. Smith, *Hist. Geog.* 524, cited from Burckhardt, *Travels in Syria*, 369.

Palestine is her pasture. We passed through at the height of the shepherd's year. From the Arabian deserts the Bedouin were swarming to the fresh summer herbage of these uplands. We should never have believed the amount of their flocks had we not seen, and attempted to count them. . . . The Bedouin had also many sheep and goats. The herds of the settled inhabitants were still more numerous. In Moab the dust of the roads bears almost no marks but those of the feet of sheep. The scenes which throng most our memory of Eastern Palestine are . . . the streams of Gilead in the heat of the day with the cattle standing in them, or the evenings when we sat at the door of our tent near the village well, and would hear the shepherd's pipe far away, and the sheep and goats, and cows with the heavy bells, would break over the edge of the hill, and come down the slope to wait their turn at the troughs. Over Jordan we were never long out of the sound of the lowing of cattle or of the shepherd's pipe."

2b. Cp. $31^{12a.\,13a}$ (P^s).—3. The nine towns here enumerated are all again mentioned in v.$^{34-38}$, where the first four are assigned to Gad, the last five to Reuben. Five additional towns are there mentioned (four Gadite and one Reubenite). The order in which the names common to the two passages are mentioned is the same, except that Dibon there precedes ʿAṭaroth and Sibmah follows instead of preceding Nebo and (Baʿal) Meʿon. The forms of two or three of the names vary. Some of these places certainly lay S. of the Wady Ḥesbân, and all, apparently, S. of the Jabboḳ. See, further, on v.$^{34-38}$.—*Beʿon*] a transcriptional error for Meʿon.—4. The land already conquered, which included the places specified in v.^{3}, is suitable for cattle.—*The land which Yahweh smote*] the allusion is to the conquests recorded in c. 21 (JE). The mixed style of this c. is illustrated in this v.: *before the congregation* (1^2 n.) *of Israel* is reminiscent of P, *thy servants* (31^{49} n.) of JE, and *smite* (הִכָּה) is nowhere else used of the divine action in conquest. So v.^{5} *thy servants* is immediately followed by the characteristic priestly phrase לאחזה *for a possession* (*L.O.T.* 133, no. 22): מצא חן *to find favour*, occurs 21 times in JE, once in D, never in P^g (CH. 31).

6–15. Moses upbraids Gad and Reuben with selfish disregard of the common interests of Israel.—6. Moses understands the proposal of Gad and Reuben to imply a disregard for the unity of Israel similar to that with which the trans-Jordanic tribes, Reuben and Gileʿad (= Gad), are upbraided in the song of Deborah, Jud. 5^{17}.—7. *Wherefore do ye discourage the heart*] On the vb. הניא, see 30^{6} n. The phrase הניא לב is repeated in v.^{9}, but is peculiar to this chapter. The context, especially in v.^{9}, somewhat favours the translation just given. But the literal meaning of the phrase may rather be *to oppose the heart* or *determination*.—8. *Thus did your fathers*] The spies by their evil report discouraged the people from going forward to Canaan, and so provoked Yahweh's wrath: the Reubenites and Gadites, if they succeed in turning the people from their present purpose to cross Jordan, would call down on them a further period of wandering (v.$^{14f.}$).—8–13 summarises c. 13 f.—*When I sent them from Ḳadesh-Barneaʿ*] 13^{26b} (JE). The form Ḳadesh-Barneaʿ is chiefly used by writers of the Deuteronomic school (Dt. 1^{19} 2^{14} 9^{23}, Jos. 10^{41} $14^{6f.}$); and also in 34^{4} = Jos. 15^{3}†.—*To see the land*] v.^{9}; cp. 13^{18a} (JE); ct. 13^{2} (P), Dt. 1^{22}.—9. *And they went up unto the Wady Eshcol*] $13^{21a.\ 23a}$, Dt. 1^{24}.—10. *And He sware, saying*] Dt. 1^{34}; for the oath, see $14^{21ff.\ 23}$.—11. *From twenty years old and upward*] 14^{29} (P).—*The land* (האדמה) *which Thou swearest unto Abraham, unto Isaac, and unto Jacob*] Cp. 11^{12} n.; in the parallels (14^{23}, Dt. 1^{35}) ארץ, and the summarizing "(their) fathers" are used.—*Because they followed not fully after Me*] 14^{24} (phil. note).—12a. Cp. 14^{30}; ct. 14^{24}, Dt. 1^{36}.—*Caleb the son of Jephunneh the Ḳenizzite*] Jos. $14^{6.\ 14}$ † (D). In P (13^{6} 34^{19}) Caleb is a Judahite. The connection of Caleb-Ḳenaz is expressed in the earliest reference to Caleb (Jud. 1^{13}).—13. Summary of 14^{33-35}.—*And caused them to wander*] for the vb. וַיְנִעֵם cp. 2 S. 15^{20}, and the use of the Kal part. (נע) in Gn. 4^{12} of Cain; see also $14^{32f.}$ n.—13. *Which did that which was evil in the eyes of Yahweh*] a phrase which "gained currency through Dt." and is "rare, except in passages written under its influence" (Driver, *Deut.* p. lxxxii, no. 49).—14. *A brood of sinful men*] תרבות occurs here only; like מרבית (1 S. 2^{33}) it is a derivative from רבה, which frequently occurs in the phrase "Be fruitful and multiply."—15. *If*, like your fathers, *ye turn back from following Him* (השובן מאחריו, as 14^{43}), *and He again* as before *leaves them in the wilderness, then ye will destroy this whole people.*

1. עצום מאד] awkwardly removed from מקנה רב, and *possibly* derived from a different source (Di.). עצם *to be mighty*, *numerous*, is not infrequent in J and D, but never occurs in P^g: CH. 59^{JE}.—מקום מקנה] = ארץ מקנה v.[4]: cp. 24^{11} n.—**3.** שבם] 𝔊 Σεβαμα, S שבמה, and so elsewhere in 𝔐.—**4.** לעבדיך] cp. 31^{49} n.—לפני עדת יש׳] 𝔊 𝔖 לפני בני יש׳.—**10.** ויחר אף] v.[13]; JE's phrase (11^1 n.); ct. ויקצף Dt. 1^{34}.—ביום ההוא] Jos. 14^9.—**11.** מבן . . . ומעלה] 𝔊 + οἱ ἐπιστάμενοι τὸ κακὸν καὶ τὸ ἀγαθόν: cp. Dt. 1^{39} 𝔐.—**14.** לספות] rather לְסְפַּת, since ספה *to add*, is badly supported: G.-K. footnote to 69*h*.

16–19. The Gadites and Reubenites explain.—Having made their households and their cattle secure in the country of their choice, they are ready to assist the other tribes on the W. of Jordan till the conquest is complete.—**16.** *And they drew near to him*] the phrase is used in Gn. 44^{18} of an action in the middle of a conversation: cp. Gn. $27^{21f.}$ 45^4.—*Sheepfolds*] were probably built as to-day more frequently of stones piled up without mortar than of wooden stakes: Nowack, *Heb. Arch.* i. 226.—**17.** If the questionable text of 𝔐 be retained, the first words should be rendered, *We will equip ourselves hastening before the children of Israel.*

20–32. Moses accepts the explanation.—**20.** *Before Yahweh to the battle*] v.[27. 29], Jos. 4^{13}; cp. *before Yahweh*, v.[21f. 32]; and for the ancient conception of Yahweh as a God of battles, see 21^{14} n.—**21.** *Until He* (Yahweh) *dispossess His enemies* (cp. Jud. 5^{31}) *before Him*] the vb. הוריש *to cause* (others) *to possess*, *to dispossess*, occurs very frequently in D with Yahweh as subj. and the Canaanites as obj. (*e.g.* Dt. 4^{38} $9^{4f.}$ 11^{23}); see Driver, *Deut.* p. lxxix, n. 10).—**22.** *Then afterwards ye may return*] to your homes E. of Jordan; cp. v.[18].—*And be quit of obligation at the hands of Yahweh and Israel*] for נקי = *quit of obligation*, see Dt. 24^5; and for מן with the rare sense of *at the hands of*, *in the judgment of*, see Job 4^{17}: BDB. 579*b* (bottom).—**23.** *Know that your sin shall find you*] there is, as we should say, no escaping the consequences. But like the curse, another cause of calamity (see on 22^6), sin is here represented as possessing an independent existence and able to exact its own due; cp. Gn. 4^7.—**24.** *That which has gone forth from your mouth ye shall perform*] 30^3 n.—**25.** *My lord*] the form (אדני) with the sing. suffix, though more than one are speaking; so often, *e.g.* Gn. 23^6 (Kön. iii. 344*i k*).

17. נחלין] 31^{8} n.—חֻשִׁים] is explained as part. pass. (cp. G.-K. 72*p*), or act. (Barth, *NB.* 124*c*) of חוש *to hasten.* Others (after Kn.) emend to חמשים; cp. Jos. 1^{14} 4^{12}.—עד אשר אם] Gn. 28^{15}, Is. 6^{11} † (always with pf.).—18. התנחל] cp. $33^{54\,bis}$ 34^{13} (P), Is. 14^{2} and (rather differently) Lev. 25^{46} (P), Ezek. 47^{13} †.—19. לא ננחל] this absolute use of נחל is not found in JE; in P it occurs in 18^{20} 26^{55}, Jos. 16^{4} 19^{9}.—23b. G.-K. 117*h*: אשר is used thus after vbs. like ידע and ראה occasionally in early (Ex. 11^{7}), but "with growing frequency in late Hebrew" (BDB. 83*b*, top).—24. צנאכם] probably a mere *lapsus calami* for צאנכם (S); but see Kön. ii. 47.—25. ויאמר] S ויאמרו.—27. חלוץ צבא] 31^{5} n.—30. ונאחזו] On the form, see G.-K. 68*i*. The Niph. in this sense (ct. Gn. 22^{13}) is peculiar to P; see Gn. 34^{10} 47^{27}, Jos. $22^{9.\,19}$ †. Before ונאחזו 𝔊 inserts διαβιβάσετε τὴν ἀποσκευὴν αὐτῶν καὶ τὰς γυναῖκας αὐτῶν καὶ τὰ κτήνη αὐτῶν πρότερα ὑμῶν εἰς γῆν Χανάαν.—32. נחנו] S, as in the three other passages in the Pent. where 𝔐 has this abbreviated form, reads אנחנו.—אתנו] for את used of what is in one's possession, see Gn. 27^{15}, 1 S. 9^{7}.

33. This v. appears to be a late interpolation. For the half-tribe of Manasseh suddenly appears alongside of Gad and Reuben; and Moses, after promising the country under conditions to Gad and Reuben, and charging Joshua and Eleʿazar, subject to these conditions, to give it, here appears to give it himself without conditions. The story on which the main part of the present chapter appears to have been based presumably regarded only the Gadites and Reubenites as originally settled E. of Jordan, and the Manassites as later settlers in the district (cp. on v.[39]). Similar attempts have been made elsewhere to correct this older view by the insertion of the phrase "the half-tribe of Manasseh"; see especially Jos. 22; and, on the subject generally, Kue. *Th. Tijd.* xi. 478–496. The later view, that Moses determined the distribution of the E. territory to the Manassites as well as to the Gadites and Reubenites, appears far more frequently in the OT.; see Dt. $3^{12f.}$ 4^{43} $29^{7f.}$, Jos. 12^{6} $13^{29.\,31}$ 14^{3} 18^{7}.—*The kingdom of Siḥon*] 21^{21-31}.—*The kingdom of ʿOg*] 21^{33-35}. The inelegant close of the v. may, perhaps, be rendered *the land, according to its cities, with* (*their*) *districts, even the cities throughout the country.*

33. לבני גד . . . להם] for the occasional occurrence of this otiose use of the pron., which is so characteristic of Aramaic, see Kön. iii. 340 *n.*; Dr. *Deut.* 55. Kue. considers להם original and the clause לבני גד . . . בן־יוסף an interpolation.—33. שבט] not P's word for tribe; 4^{18} n.

34–38. The Gadite and Reubenite cities.—The fourteen cities here named lie within the territory bounded on the N. by the

Jabboḳ, on the S. by the Arnon, and on the W. by the Jordan and the Dead Sea. The most southerly are ʿAroʿer, which is 1 mile, and Dîbôn, which is 4 miles N. of Arnon; furthest north and also furthest east are Jogbehah (el-Jubeihāt) and (if identified with Yājūz) Jaʿzer, which lie between 10 and 15 miles S. of the Jabboḳ and nearly as far E. as ʿAmmân (= Rabbath-ʿAmmôn); in the Jordan valley, some miles E. of the stream, lie Beth-nimrah and Beth-haram.

Much of this territory frequently changed hands; and after the time of David, who subdued Moab (2 S. 8^{2}), it belonged now to Moab, now to Israel; see 21^{13} n.

There is direct evidence that 10 at least of these towns were at times in Moabite possession (MI. = Meshaʿ's inscription): Dîbôn (Nu 21^{30}, MI. $^{1. 21. 28}$, Is. 15^{2}, Jer. $48^{18. 22}$), ʿAṭaroth (MI. $^{10f.}$), ʿAroʿer (MI. ^{26}, Jer. 48^{19}), Jaʿzer (Is. $16^{8f.}$, Jer. 48^{32}), Ḥeshbon (Nu. 21^{25-29}, Is. 15^{4} 16^{8}, Jer. $48^{2. 34. 45}$), Eleʿaleh (Is. 15^{4} 16^{9}, Jer. 48^{34}), Ḳiryathaim (MI. ^{10}, Jer. $48^{1. 23}$, Ezek. 25^{9}), Nebo (MI. ^{14}, Is. 15^{2}, Jer. $48^{1. 22}$), Baʿal-meʿon (MI. $^{9. 30}$, Jer. 48^{23}, Ezek. 25^{9}), and Sibmah (Is. $16^{8f.}$, Jer. 48^{32}).

Even during the time that the territory was held by the Israelites, the ownership of individual cities changed; such at least is the Hebrew theory, and there is in it nothing intrinsically improbable. Dîbôn, for example, is here Gadite, in Jos. 13^{17} Reubenite; the same is true of ʿAroʿer (v.^{34}, Jos. 13^{16}, 1 Ch. 5^{8}), unless two different towns are intended. Ḥeshbon is here Reubenite, but in Jos. 21^{39} Gadite.* There is little to control the biblical data on these matters. Meshaʿ (l. 10) refers to the "men of Gad" as ancient inhabitants of the land of ʿAṭaroth (ואש גד ישב בארץ עטרת מעלם), but does not mention Reuben.

According to the theory of P (Jos. 13^{15-38}), the territory of Reuben lay S., that of Gad N., of a line drawn eastwards from the northern end of the Dead Sea; and this is the representation of the conventional maps of Canaan divided among the twelve tribes. But the point of view of the present chapter is entirely different; no line running east and west separates the

* See, further, W. H. Bennett's tables in Hastings' *DB.* ("Gad," "Reuben"), and H. W. Hogg's discussions in *EBi.* ("Gad," § 12; "Reuben," § 2. 14).

two tribes, for the two towns that lie furthest south (ʿAroʿer and Dibon) and the two lying furthest north (Jogbehah and Jaʿzer) are alike Gadite.

The several towns are mentioned in no exact geographical order, though the Gadite towns fall into groups (S., N.E., W.). Starting in the far S. with Dibon, the list goes N. to ʿAṭaroth, then furthest south to ʿAroʿer; it then mentions the north-eastern towns Jaʿzer and Jogbehah, then those lying W. in the Jordan valley. Again from Ḥeshbon (v.^{37}) it is N.E. to Eleʿaleh, but (probably) S. to Ḳiryathaim: Baʿal-meʿon, though it stands between Nebo and Sibmah, lay S. of both. A similar disregard of geographical order may be found in Jer. $48^{21ff.}$. It renders exact identification difficult.

34. *And the children of Gad built*] *i.e.* rebuilt, or repaired the cities which had suffered in the process of conquest: this is a frequent meaning of בנה; cp. "And they shall build up (ובנו) the ancient ruins," Is. 58^{12} 61^{4}; "I, Yahweh, have rebuilt (בניתי) that which was pulled down," Ezek. 36^{36}; see also, *e.g.*, 1 K. 16^{34}, Am. 9^{14}. So in Moabite, Mesha says (l. 9), "I rebuilt (ואבן) Baʿal-meʿon," and (l. 27) "I rebuilt Beth-bamoth, for it had been pulled down." The building here intended may be different from that of v.$^{16.\,24}$; the writers are different, and have different processes in mind.—*Dîbôn*] is the modern *Dhîbân*, 4 miles N. of Arnon (21^{30} n.). In $33^{45f.}$ the form Dîbôn-gad occurs; the fuller name is evidence of the Gadite possession of the town.—*ʿAṭārōth*] v.^{3} †; MI.$^{10f.}$. The name means *crowns*, and was given to several places; another on the E. of Jordan is mentioned in the next v.; and three, at least, on the W. of Jordan existed—two in or on the borders of Ephraim (Jos. $16^{2.\,7}$) and one (ʿAṭroth-beth-Joab) in Judah (1 Ch. 2^{54}). The name survives in the modern ʿAṭṭârûs which lies about 8 miles N.W. of Dhîbân. "On Jebel (Mt.) ʿAttârûs are to be found the considerable ruins of a former town ʿAṭṭârûs, whence the mountain received its present name."* Here and in v.^{3} ʿAṭārōth is mentioned with Dîbôn, in MI. directly after Baʿal-meʿon and Ḳiryathaim; and, therefore, it may well have occupied the site of ʿAṭṭârûs.—

* Seetzen, *Reisen*, ii. 342, cp. iv. 383; Tristram, *Moab*, 271–276.

'Arô'ēr] in addition to one 'Aro'er on the W. (1 S. 30^{28}), there were two 'Aro'ers E. of Jordan; one of these, described as "'Aro'er, which is on the edge of the Wady Arnon," stood on the site of the ruins of 'Arâ'ir,* which lie on the N. bank of the Arnon; the other 'Aro'er lay "before (*i.e.* E. of) Rabbah," and therefore, very much further N. The actual site has not been identified. In Jos. $13^{16.25}$ the southern 'Aro'er is described as Reubenite (cp. 1 Ch. 5^{8}), and the northern as Gadite; but, for reasons stated above, this is no argument for identifying the 'Aro'er of this v. with the more northerly (Jos. 13^{25}, Jud. 11^{33} †); on the other hand, the fact that it immediately follows Dîbôn and 'Aṭaroth does not prove it the more southerly. The southern 'Aro'er is much the more frequently mentioned, and serves to define Israel's southern border (Dt. 3^{12} 4^{48}, 2 K. 10^{33}, and, as read by We. and Dr., 2 S. 24^{5}).—*'Aṭrôth-shôphān*] site unknown, though in speaking of 'Aṭṭârûs (see above) Tristram says: "On the spot we find two places of the same name two miles apart" (*Moab*, 276). *Shôphān* (שופן; S שפים), like Addar in 'Aṭroth-addar, is probably enough a tribal name.—*Ja'zer*] various identifications have been proposed: see 21^{24} n. It certainly seems to have lain much further N. than the two first-mentioned towns; Beit Zerah, the most southerly identification, lies a few miles N.E. of Ḥeshbon; Yājūz, the most northerly, some miles N. of 'Ammân.—*Jogbehah*] Jud. 8^{11} †. "Jogbehah is surely echoed in the present Jubeihah, Gubeihah, or 'Ajbêhât, on the road from Salt to Ammân" (G. A. Smith, *Hist. Geog.* 585). 'Ajbêhât is about 6 miles N.N.W. from 'Ammân.—*Beth-nimrah*] lay in the Jordan valley (Jos. 13^{27}), where the modern Nimrin, some 8 or 10 miles N. of the Dead Sea and 13 E. of Jordan, preserves the name; in v.[3] the abbreviated form Nimrah is used, and in the Talm. Beth-nimrin (Neubauer, *Geog. du Talmud*, 248).—*Beth-haran*] lay in the same district; see Jos. 13^{27}, where the name appears in the softened form Beth-haram, and is mentioned immediately before Beth-nimrah. It is identified by some with Tel er-Rāmeh, a few miles S. of Nimrin in the Wady Ḥesbân; † by

* Tristram, *Moab*, 129–131.
† Cheyne in *EBi.*; cp. Buhl, *Geog.* 264.

others * with Beit-harran further down the same wady.—37 f. The Reubenite towns.—*Ḥeshbôn*] described as Gadite in Jos. 21^{39}, is the modern Ḥesbân (21^{25} n.), which lies about half-way between the most southern (Dîbôn, ʿAṭārōth) and the most northern (Jaʿzer, Jogbehah) Gadite towns mentioned in the preceding verses.—*Eleʿaleh*] also mentioned, and always in connection with Ḥeshbon, in v.[3], Is. 15^4 16^9, Jer. 48^{34} †. The modern El ʿAl lies ½ hr. N.E. of Ḥesbân.† —*Ḳiryathaim*] is, together with Baʿal-meʿon and Beth-jeshimoth, described by Ezek. (25^9) as "the glory of the country." The identification with Ḳureiyat, about 3 miles S.E. of ʿAṭṭârûs and a long way S. of Ḥesbân and El ʿAl, though very generally accepted,‡ ought to be considered quite uncertain. For Ḳureiyat may quite as well be Ḳerioth.§ In any case, the name is of too common a character (see *EBi.* "Names," § 105) to be a sufficient ground of identification. None of the biblical references *require* a place so far to the S.; and the fact that it is elsewhere associated with places further N. is, though not conclusive, rather in favour of a more northern site: here it stands between Eleʿaleh and Nebo; it is coupled with Nebo in Jer. 48^1, and stands between Baʿal-meʿon and ʿAṭāroth in MI.; see also Jos. 13^{19}, Jer. 48^{23}, Ezek. 25^9.—38. *Nebo*] the Moabite town of Nebo (also v.[3] 33^{47}, Is. 15^2, Jer. $48^{1.\,22}$, 1 Ch. 5^8 †; MI. l. 14) probably lay on, or near, Mt. Nebo (Dt. 32^{49} 34^1 †), which is identified with the modern Mt. Nebâ, 5 miles S.W. of Ḥesbân.‖ In this case Nebo lay S.W. of the two first-mentioned Reubenite towns, N. of that which immediately precedes, if Ḳureiyat = Ḳiryathaim, and N. also of that which follows, Baʿal-meʿon. The name Nebo is probably a survival of the worship in the district of the Babylonian god Nebo (Is.

* Tristram, *Moab*, 348; Di.

† *Survey of Eastern Pal.*, i. 16–19; Tristram, *Moab*, 339 f.; *EBi.*

‡ Smith, *Hist. Geog.* 567 n. 1; Buhl, *Geog.* 267; cp. Tristram, *Moab*, 275 f.; Di.

§ Cp. Seetzen, *Reisen*, ii. 342, iv. 384; Nöld. *Die Inschrift des Königs Mesa*, 25 f.

‖ Tristram, *Moab*, 325 ff.; Merrill, *E. of Jordan*, 242 ff.; *Survey of E. Pal.* i. 198 f.; Driver, *Deut.* 418 f.

46^{1}),* though an alternative explanation is offered by the Arabic النَّبَاوَة, *the height.*† In any case the evidence is insufficient to establish *Moabite* worship of Nebo; the name may go back beyond the Moabite occupation.—*Ba'al-me'on*] 1 Ch. 5^{8}, Ezek. 25^{9}†; MI. ^{9}; other forms of the name occur, viz. Beth-ba'al-me'on (Jos. 13^{17}†; MI. ^{30}), Beth-me'on (Jer. 48^{23}), Be'on (v.^{3}†), the last being probably a mere transcriptional error for Me'on. The name indicates that the place was a religious centre: on this and the variant forms see *HPN.* 126 ff. It was known to Jerome as Baal-maus (*OS.* 102^{7}), and in its simplest form the name has survived in the modern Ma'īn,‡ which lies some 5 miles S. of Nebâ and some 8 N. of Ḳureiyat.—*To be changed in name*] the words appear to be a gloss directing the reader to substitute something for the two preceding names, and so avoid the necessity for pronouncing the names of foreign deities. The dislike of the later scribes to the retention of Ba'al in proper names is well known, and has left its mark on the text of the books of Samuel, as, *e.g.*, in the corruptions Ishbosheth and Mephibosheth for Eshba'al and Meri-ba'al; see *HPN.* 121 ff.—*Sibmah*] Jos. 13^{19}, Is. $16^{8f.}$, Jer. 48^{32}†; cp. Sebam, v.^{3}†; the site is unknown.—*And they called with names the names of the cities that they had built*] this is generally interpreted to mean: they gave new (EV. "other") names to the cities.

35. ויגבהה] the את before יגבהה is anomalously omitted.—**37.** קריתים] it is disputed whether the ending is that of the dual (*two*, or *twin cities*), or a local ending; see *EBi.* "Names," § 107.—**38.** מוסבת שם] the part. can quite as well be read as a sing. מוּסַבַּת, so that the clause would refer to בעל מעון only. On the gerundial force of the part., especially in the Niphal, see Dav. 97, R. 1. For the word, of a change of *name*, cp. 2 K. 23^{34} (וַיַּסֵּב את שמו יהויקים) 24^{17}.

39–42. Manassite incursions E. of Jordan.—This passage is a fragment. Nothing that precedes indicates a starting-point from whence Machir, Jair, and Nobaḥ set out. It should also be observed that the separate action of these clans is

* Baethgen, *Beiträge*, 15. 89; Baudissin, *Studien*, 233; *KAT.*^{3} 407.
† So Nöld. *ZDMG.* xlii. 470.
‡ *Survey of E. Pal.* i. 176; Tristram, *Moab*, 303 f.

entirely unlike the common action of all Israel presupposed throughout the rest of the chapter.

Both in its historical standpoint and in its style this fragment closely resembles Jud. 1. The same kind of independent action here attributed to the clans of Manasseh is there attributed to the tribes of Israel. Both here and there the Hebrews occupy bits of country within a larger district, but not the whole country, whether as here E., or there W., of Jordan.

Phraseologically note וילכו v.^{39}, הלך v.$^{41f.}$, and cp. Jud. $1^{8b. 10f. 17}$; וילכדהו v.^{39}, וילכד v.$^{41f.}$, and cp. Jud. 1, *passim*. לכד, frequent especially in earlier sources, is never used by P (BDB. *s.v.*). Note also ובנתיה (v.^{42}) of towns dependent on another: cp. Jud. 1^{27}.

Probably, then, this fragment is altogether misplaced. It originally formed part of an account of the conquest after Moses' death; and v.^{40} (an interpolation which destroys the connection between v.^{39} and v.^{41}) is an editorial attempt to antedate Manasseh's occupation of country E. of Jordan, and to accommodate the fragment to its present position; cp. the similar editorial comment in Dt. 3^{15} (see Driver's note there).

Other considerations favour the substantial correctness of this view. Ja'ir, who gave his name to the Ḥavvoth-ja'ir (v.^{41}), lived, according to Jud. $10^{3f.}$, in an age subsequent to Moses. According to an early statement (Jos. 17^{14-18} J), Joseph (*i.e.* Ephraim and Manasseh) at first received only one lot in the distribution of the country. This could hardly have been asserted or admitted by one who held with the author of v.^{40} that Moses had given Gile'ad to Manasseh, for the one lot of Joseph certainly lay W. of Jordan. It is probable that the present fragment is derived from a fuller narrative, which described how several clans of Manasseh separated from their fellow tribesmen on the *west* of Jordan, and acquired settlements on the *east*. Thus the earliest Hebrew traditions appear to make the settlement of Manasseh W. of Jordan more ancient than the settlement of a part of this tribe E. of Jordan.

Budde (*Richter u. Samuel*, 32–39, 59f., 87; and later, with some counter criticisms of his critics, in his commentary on *Judges* (1897),

p. 12 f.) thinks the original home of the fragment was in J's account of the conquests of the house of Joseph, other fragments of which are preserved in Jos. 17^{14-18} 13^{13}: from the three fragments he reconstructs as follows: "Then the house of Joseph spoke with Joshua, and said, Why hast thou given me but one lot, seeing I am a great people, forasmuch as hitherto Yahweh hath blessed me? The hill-country is not enough for us: and the Canaanites that dwell in the land of the valley can I not drive out, because they are too strong for me. For they have chariots of iron, both they who are in Beth-shean and her towns, and they who are in the valley of Jezreel. And Joshua spoke unto the house of Joseph, Thou art a great people, and hast great power: thou shalt not have one lot only. But let the hill-country of Gile'ad be thine; get thee up into the forest, and cut down for thee there, since the hill-country of Ephraim is too narrow for thee; and the goings out thereof shall be thine. Then went Machir, the son of Manasseh, to Gile'ad, and took it, and drove out the 'Amorites who dwelt there. And Ja'ir, the son of Manasseh, went and took their tent-villages, and called them the tent-villages of Ja'ir. And Nobaḥ . . . went and took Ḳenath and the villages thereof, and called them Nobaḥ after his own name. But the children of Israel could not drive out the Geshurites and the Maachathites, and so Geshur and Maacha dwelt in the midst of Israel unto this day."

Whether the statement of the fragment, even if thus correctly restored to its original context and interpreted, corresponds to actual history or is merely an early theory, must be left doubtful. "The arguments to prove the invasion of Northern Gile'ad from W. Palestine . . . are inconclusive" (G. A. Smith, *Hist. Geog.* 577 n.). This may be so; but the arguments for the converse order in Manasseh's movements are still less conclusive. The statements of $26^{29f.}$ (P) and Jos. 17^{2} (not safely to be referred to JE) are a precarious support for the conclusion that Gile'ad is *actually* "older in Manasseh's history" than Abi'ezer and Shechem, though it is certainly P's theory that this was the case; see on 26^{29-32}.

39. *The children of Machir*] *i.e.* the members of the Manassite clan Machir (26^{29} n.); so Jos. 13^{31}: but the original text perhaps read, as in the interpolated v.^{40} and Dt. 3^{15}, simply *Machir*; cp. *Ja'ir*, *Nobaḥ* in v.$^{41f.}$ and *Machir* in Jud. 5^{14}.—*Went to Gile'ad*] they probably started from W. Palestine; see above. Northern Gile'ad is intended: see on v.^{1}.—*The Amorite*] cp. 13^{29} n.—40. An interpolation, which interrupts the connection between v.^{39} and v.^{41} by depriving the pronoun ("*their* tent-villages") in the next v. of any immediate antecedent; see also above.—41. *Ja'ir the son of Manasseh*] *i.e.* the Manassite clan Ja'ir; the relation of this clan to the tribe is differently expressed in different places: in 1 Ch. $2^{23f.}$ Ja'ir is the great-grandson of Machir. On the different genealogical schemes of Manasseh, see Kue. in the *Th. Tijd.* xi. 483 ff., and

Driver in Hastings' *DB.* ("Manasseh"). Ja'ir may have been subordinated, even in this passage, to Machir as well as to Manasseh, if the Ḥavvoth-Ja'ir be placed in Gileʿad (see next note); for Machir would be credited with the conquest of the whole, the subdivision Ja'ir with but part of the Manassite territory E. of Jordan. The judge Ja'ir (Jud. 10[3f.]) appears to be merely an individualisation of the clan; see Moore, *Judges*, 271.—*Their tent-villages*] the pronoun (suffix) refers to the collective term "the Amorite" in v.[39]; it can refer to nothing in v.[40], which is thus shown to be out of place. The word *ḥavvoth* is elsewhere in Hebrew confined to the compound phrase *Ḥavvoth-ja'ir.* Judging from the Arabic *ḥiwā'* and *ḥayy* (= Heb. חיי 1 S. 18[18]), the *ḥavvoth* were encampments or groups of tents.* But the name determines the character of the places only at the time when it was given. It may have clung to them long after the tents had given way to more permanent buildings or had even become fortified cities; just as Ḥaṣor, though the name means simply *an enclosure*, was already, in the 14th century B.C., a royal city mentioned along with Ṣidon.† Probably the Ḥavvoth-ja'ir were already more than mere tent-villages when Jud. 10[3f.] was written, although the term (עירים) there used is not conclusive proof of this (see 13[19] n.). The Ḥavvoth-ja'ir are also mentioned in Dt. 3[14], Jos. 13[30], Jud. 10[4], 1 K. 4[13], and 1 Ch. 2[23]. It need cause no difficulty that though generally described, in accordance with the present passage, as Manassite, they are exceptionally represented in Ch. as being in the possession of a mixed Judæo-Manassite population: for the tribal character of a population may vary in the course of centuries. Nor is the difference in number in Jud. (30) and in Ch. (23) serious. Much more difficulty is caused by the conflicting evidence as to the district in which these places lay—in Gileʿad according to Jud., 1 K., 1 Ch., in Bashan according to Dt. and Jos. The present passage would exclude Gileʿad if it means that Machir took Gileʿad, Ja'ir a district outside Gileʿad: but another interpretation is possible (last note). Different ways

* W. R. Smith, *Rel. Sem.*[1] 256; Moore, *Judges*, 83 f., 274 f.
† Tel el-Amarna Tablets, 154[41]; see *EBi.* "Names," § 105.

out of the difficulty have been suggested: (1) Gileʿad in its widest sense (cp. on v.[1]) includes Bashan: even if this be admitted, it does not appear, in view of 1 K. 4^{13}, to solve the difficulties of the Ḥavvoth-ja'ir (see Driver, *Deut.* 56 f.). (2) The reference of these places to Bashan originated with an attempt to harmonise Dt. 3^{14} with Nu. $22^{39.\ 40}$ (Driver, *ib.*). (3) Gileʿad is a textual corruption of Ṣalḥad (= Salchah, a border town between Bashan and Gileʿad); Cheyne in *EBi.* ("Havvoth-Jair," "Jair," "Jephthah," "Gilead"). If (3) be right the Ḥavvoth-ja'ir lay far to the N.E., near Boṣra and Ṣalḥad; if (2), S., if (1) N., of the Jarmuk. The name has not survived, and nearer localisation is in any case impossible.—**42.** *Nobaḥ* was presumably, like Machir and Ja'ir, a Manassite clan: "son of Manasseh" may have dropped out. Nobaḥ conquers *Ḳenâth and the dependent towns thereof.* Ḳenath is called Nobaḥ after the name of the conquering clan: cp. Jud. 18^{29}. The new name given in other cases to old towns is of a different character; see, *e.g.*, Gn. 28^{19}, 2 K. 14^{7}. In 1 Ch. 2^{23} the old name Ḳenath is used; possibly in the present instance the new name failed to establish itself; for it cannot be assumed with any certainty that this city is the Nobaḥ of Jud. 8^{11}† which lay near Jogbehah. If we are not bound by Jud. 8^{11}, nothing prevents identifying Ḳenath with the modern Ḳanawât, which "was on the western slopes of the Hauran mountains, in a beautiful neighbourhood, rich in water and trees," and was in Roman times a place of importance.* The identification, depending as it does on identity of name, is not certain; but, if correct, Ḳenath marks the extreme N.E. limit of Manasseh's territory.† Ḳenath and Ḥavvoth-ja'ir both lay in districts that suffered, at an unknown but possibly early date, capture by the Aramæans (1 Ch. 2^{23}, cp. Jos. 13^{13}).

39. וילכו בני מכיר . . . וילכדהו ויורש] If the original text, as suggested above, read מכיר instead of בני מ׳, the vbs. read originally וילך . . . וילכדהו ויורש. The singular ויורש in the present text is capricious, and may be, as Di. suggests, a (Massoretic) preparation for the sing. מכיר of v.[40].

---

* Buhl, *Geog.* 252; Schürer, *GJV.*[3] ii. 131 ff. (Eng. tr. II. i. 108 ff.).
† Buhl, *Geog.* 80.

XXXIII. 1–49. *The Itinerary.*

The Itinerary enumerates 41 stages, or 40 stations, between Raʿamses, the starting-point at the Exodus, and the final encampment of the Israelites by the Jordan.

It contains two dates: the date of the start, which is given as the 15th day of the 1st month (of the 1st year), and the date of Aaron's death, which took place on the 1st day of the 5th month of the 40th year (v.[38]), and at the 33rd station.

Clearly, then, the 40 stations are not intended to be 40 places at each of which the Israelites spent one of the 40 years of wandering. On the other hand, if the compiler shared the belief that the people left Sinai within about a year of the Exodus (10[11] n.), and were waiting to pass over Jordan at the end of the 40th year, then he refers 11 stations to the first year, 9 to the last, and assigns but 21 to the remaining 38 years.

Nor do the stages represent a day's march; for ʿEṣion-geber and Ḳadesh, though consecutive stations, are 70 miles apart. See also v.[8].

Very few of the sites are accurately identified. Many are altogether unknown. Apart from Punon, 16 are mentioned nowhere outside the itinerary.

The places most clearly identified are ʿEṣion-geber, Ḳadesh, Dibon-gad, Nebo, and the steppes of Moab. With these and the Egyptian starting-point to work upon, it is possible to discover certain general conceptions underlying the itinerary.

The itinerary may be divided into four sections (names peculiar to it being italicised), thus:—

1. Raʿamses to the wilderness of Sinai, v.[5–15].

   11 stages: Succoth, Etham, Pî-haḥîroth, Marah, Elim, Red Sea, wilderness of Sin, *Dophḳah*, *Alush*, Rephidim, wilderness of Sinai.

2. Wilderness of Sinai to ʿEṣion-geber, v.[16–35].

   20 stages: Ḳibroth-hatta'avah, Ḥaṣeroth, *Rithmah*, *Rimmon-Pereṣ*, *Libnah*, *Rissah*, *Ḳehelathah*, *Mt. Shepher*, *Ḥaradah*, *Maḳheloth*, *Taḥath*, *Teraḥ*, *Mithḳah*, *Ḥashmonah*, Moseroth, Bene-jaʿaḳan, Ḥor-hag-gidgad, Joṭbathah, ʿ*Abronah*, ʿEṣion-geber.

3. ʽEṣion-geber to the wilderness of Ṣin = Ḳadesh, v.[36].
 1 stage.

4. Ḳadesh to the steppes of Moab, v.[37–49].
 9 stages: Mt. Hor, *Ṣalmonah*, Punon, Oboth, ʽIyye-ʽAbarim, Dibon-gad, ʽAlmon-diblathaim, Mts. of the ʽAbarim before Nebo, steppes of Moab

Section 1 may, for aught that appears to the contrary, presuppose a simple direct line of march from Egypt to Sinai. Sections 3 and 4 imply the following successive movements: first a movement N.W. from the top of the Gulf of ʽAḳabah (ʽEṣion-geber) to ʽAin-Ḳadîs (Ḳadesh), then a movement which is in its total effect N.E. (across the northern part of Edom and through the south of Moab to Dibon-gad), then one N. through the north of Moab, and finally a descent into the Jordan valley E. of the river. Thus, like P^g (21^{10} n.), the itinerary recognises no *southern* movement from Ḳadesh.

Section 2 gives 20 stations between the wilderness of Sinai and ʽEsion-geber. Yet even if the traditional site of Sinai be correct, the distance between Sinai and ʽEṣion-geber is but little greater than that between ʽEṣion-geber and Ḳadesh; it is considerably less if Sinai lay near the top of the Gulf of ʽAḳabah (10^{30} n.). The stations in this section can therefore scarcely be given as points on a route; they are rather points scattered over a district of which ʽEṣion-geber and Ḳadesh may be taken as being respectively the southern and northern points. Thus section 2 probably gives the places visited during the period of wandering; they correspond in the itinerary to the wilderness of Paran in P^g.

The literary features of the itinerary are these: in the main it closely resembles P, alike in style and matter; here and there it resembles JE in both respects; it also contains matter peculiar to itself.

1. The resemblances to P are as follows: (*a*) In matter. All stations mentioned in P are incorporated in the itinerary except the wilderness of Paran. These include many stations mentioned *only* in P's narrative (Pî-haḥîroth, Sin, Sinai, Ṣin, Mt. Ḥor, Oboth, ʽIyye-ʽAbarim, Mts. of the ʽAbarim, steppes of Moab). Note, further, that the age of Aaron (v.[39]) is

in agreement with matter peculiar to P (Ex. 7^7); with v.^{4b} cp. Ex. 12^{12} (P); with v.^{7b} cp. Ex. $14^{2\,(9)}$ (P); with v.^{38} cp. 20^{22-29} (P); see also notes on v.$^{6.\,8.\,14b.\,48b}$. (*b*) In style. Note ... ויסעו מן ... ויחנו ב throughout, and cp. 21^4 n.; also the superscription (v.^{1}), the dates (v.$^{3.\,38}$), לצבאתם (v.^{1}) etc.

2. The resemblances to JE consist of: (*a*) Certain places mentioned by JE but not by P (Marah, Ḳibroth-hatta'avah, Ḥaṣeroth, Moseroth, Bene-ja'aḳan, Ḥor-hag-gidgad, Joṭbathah, 'Eṣion-geber, Shiṭṭim). On the other hand, several places (such as Shur, Tab'erah, Ḥormah, and the seven places given in $21^{11-13.\,16-19}$) which are mentioned in JE do not occur in the itinerary; and whereas in JE Ḥaṣeroth and Ḳadesh are successive places, the itinerary places eighteen between them. (*b*) Notes embodying matter peculiar to, or expressed in language practically identical with that of, JE; see v.$^{8b.\,9.\,40}$.

3. Entirely peculiar to the chapter are the sixteen places italicised above, and the statements of v.$^{2.\,4a.\,38b}$.

These facts seem best accounted for by assuming that the itinerary was compiled at a late date from P and JE and some other source, oral or written, no longer extant. If, as some think, the incident at Rephidim is misplaced in Ex. 17, and in the original source *followed* the stay at Ḥoreb, the position of Rephidim here would indicate that the itinerary was compiled from the *combined* work PJE: in any case this is perhaps most probable: for note also v.^{40} = 21^1 (JE) following v.$^{37-39}$ = 20^{22-29} (P).

Others (*e.g.* Di.) are of opinion that the itinerary is in substance older than P^g and was used by him, but that it was subsequently interpolated with glosses, some of which were drawn from JE.

1 f. The style is awkward and redundant, and may be represented in translation as follows: *These are the stages* ($10^{6.\,21}$ notes) *of the children of Israel by which they made their exodus from the land of Egypt by their hosts under the authority* (בְּיַד cp. 2 S. 18^2) *of Moses and Aaron. And Moses wrote down their starting-places on their several stages, according to Yahweh's commandment* (CH. 19^P): *and these are their stages,* (*defined*) *by their several starting-places.* The other references to the Mosaic authorship of, or authority for, parts of the Hexateuch are in JE (Ex. 17^{14} 24^4 $34^{27f.}$: cp. Jos. 24^{26}) and D (Dt. $31^{9.\,24}$). Some (*e.g.* Di.) infer that the compiler must in these cases, including the present, have had before him an ancient written source which he believed to have been written by Moses.—

3. *Ra'amses* is mentioned both in P (Gn. 47^{11} and, probably, Ex. 12^{37}) and in JE (Ex. 1^{11}). See the commentaries on these passages.—*On the morrow after the passover*] the same phrase (ממחרת הפסח) occurs in Jos. 5^{11} (P): cp. ממחרת השבת Lev. $23^{11.\,15f.}$. Passover was eaten in the afternoon or evening (בין הערבים 9^3 n.) of the 14th day of the 1st month (Ex. $12^{2.\,6}$). —*With a high hand*] 15^{30} n.—*In the sight of all the Egyptians*] cp. Ex. 12^{33} (JE).—4. The Egyptians were already engaged in burying their dead when the Hebrews departed. This is not stated in Ex. With v.^{4b} cp. Ex. 12^{12} (P).—5. Ex. 12^{37a} (? P).—6. Ex. 13^{20} (P).—7. Ex. $14^{2.\,9}$ (P).—8. *From before* (מפני) *Haḥîroth* is an obvious error for *from Pi-ha-ḥiroth* (מפי החירת), which was read, or restored, by S 𝔗^O 𝔖 𝔙.—*In the midst of the sea*] Ex. 14^{22} (P): ct. 14^{21b} (J).—*And they went three days' journey* (10^{33} n.) *into the wilderness*] cp. Ex. 3^{18} 15^{22} (J).—*Of Etham*] the wilderness is here defined by Etham (v.$^{6f.}$), in Ex. 15^{22} by Shur.—*Marah*] v.^{9}, Ex. 15^{23} † (J).— 9. *And they came . . . and encamped there*] but for two slight verbal variations this is identical with Ex. 15^{27} (JE); *Elim* also appears in Ex. 16^1 (P).—10a, 11b. Ex. 16^1 (P): the station *by Yam Suph* (v.$^{10b.\,11a}$) is unknown to Ex.—12 f. *Dophḳah* and *Alush* are unidentified places, mentioned only here; for some guesses, depending on particular theories of the routes of the Exodus, see Di. on Ex. 17^1. For *Dophḳah*, 𝔊 reads *Raphaka*. —14. *Rephidim*] Ex. 17^8 (E), 17^1 19^2 (P or R).—14b recalls the phraseology both of 20^2 (P) and Ex. 17^{1b} (JE).—15. Ex. 19^{2a} (P). —16. *Ḳibroth-hatta'avah*] $11^{34f.}$ (JE), Dt. 9^{22} †.—17. *Ḥaṣeroth*] 11^{35} 12^{16} (JE), Dt. 1^1; see 11^{35} n.—18b–29. None of the twelve places here mentioned (unless *Libnah* (v.^{20}) = Laban, Dt. 1^1) is mentioned anywhere else, and for none of them has even a probable identification been suggested, though many guesses have been put forward. From the position which these places occupy in the itinerary, it is probable that the compiler thought them to be situated in the wilderness of Paran (see above).—18. *Rithmah*] appears to be one of the class of place-names derived from plants, etc. (*EBi.* "Names," § 103). The Heb. *rōthĕm* (Ar. *ratam*, Aram. *rithmā*) is the name of a broom-plant, which grew in the deserts (1 K. $19^{4f.}$,

Job 30[4]), and, according to a modern traveller,* is "the largest and most conspicuous shrub of these deserts [S. of Palestine], growing in the water-courses and valleys." It is chosen by the Arabs on account of its shelter when encamping. The modern name Abu Retemât is attached to "a wide plain with shrubs and retem" on the route between ʿAḳabah and Jerusalem (Robinson). Rithmah is thus "a not unnatural name for a station on the desert's verge"; † but for this very reason the identification of Rithmah, merely on the ground of the name, with Abu Retemât is most hazardous. The names, v.[20] *Rimmon-pereṣ* and v.[21] *Libnah* (*poplar*), may be of the same character, though both are ambiguous: on Rimmon, see 13[23] n. (p. 143); and Libnah may owe its name to moon-worship (*EBi.* "Names," § 95). Pereṣ forms parts of other names (Pereṣ-ʿuzzah; Baʿal-peraṣim). *Libnah* is also the name of a town in Judah (Jos. 10[29]). With *Ḳehēlāthah* (v.[22]) and *Maḳhēloth* (v.[25]), cp. the Sabæan place-names קהלם, קהלן; ‡ with *Ḥarādah* (v.[24]), Ḥarod, itself, however, a rather questionable name (Jud. 7[1]); with *Ḥashmonah* (v.[30]), Ḥeshmon (Jos. 15[27]). *Teraḥ* and *Taḥath* occur elsewhere in the OT. as personal names. With *Rissah* (v.[22]; 𝔊[B] *Δεσσα*), cp. the Rasa of the Peutinger Tables. Some resemblances may be detected in modern names.§ There is no reason to question that these otherwise unknown names are genuine names of places, though some of them are very possibly more or less corrupt. The remarks of Doughty (*Ar. Des.* i. 49) on the subject of "the camping grounds of Moses" are worth citing: "All their names we may never find again in these countries,—and wherefore? Because they were in good part passengers' names, and without land-right they could not remain in the desert, in the room of the old herdsmen's names. There is yet another kind of names, not rightly of the country, not known to the Beduins, which are *caravaners' names.* The caravaners passing in haste, with fear of the nomads, know

* Robinson, *Biblical Researches*, i. 299, 279.

† Clay Trumbull, *Ḳadesh-Barnea*, 151.

‡ Ges.-Buhl, *s.vv.*

§ Palmer, *Desert of the Exodus*, 508 f.

not the wide wilderness without their landmarks; nor even in the way, have they a right knowledge of the land names. What wonder if we find not again some which are certainly caravaners' names in the old itineraries."—**30–34.** The four names, *Mosēroth*, *Bene-ja'aḳan*, *Ḥor-hag-gidgad*, and *Joṭbathah*, are, in spite of some variations of order and form, identical with the four names, Be'eroth-bene-ja'aḳan, Mosērah, Gudgodah, and Joṭbathah, which occur in a fragment of an itinerary (Dt. $10^{6f.}$) generally referred to E. The fragment in Dt. differs from the present itinerary in placing Aaron's death at Mosērah instead of Mt. Hor (below, v.^{38}). Direct literary dependence of either passage on the other is therefore improbable; and these places must have been firmly associated with the traditions of the wanderings at an early date. For attempts to harmonise the discrepancies, see Driver, *Deut.* 119 ff.—*Bene-ja'aḳan*] is an abbreviation of the fuller form of the name which is preserved in Dt., Be'eroth- (the wells of) bene-ja'aḳan. The result of the abbreviation is that the tribal denomination has become a place-name; cp. *EBi.* "Names," § 92. If, as is likely (cp. 1 Ch. 1^{42}, Gn. 36^{27}), the Bene-ja'aḳan were a Ḥorite tribe, the place named after them probably lay in, or on the confines of, Edom (Gn. $36^{20f.}$).—**36.** *'Eṣion-geber* (Dt. 2^{8}, 1 K. 9^{26} 22^{49}, 2 Ch. 8^{17} 20^{36}†) must have lain on the Red Sea, but, allowing for physical changes, may be identical with the modern 'Ain el-Ġuḍyan, which lies about 15 miles N. of the Gulf of 'Aḳabah.*—*The wilderness of Ṣin*] is mentioned frequently, but only in P (13^{21} 20^{1} 27^{14} 34^{3}, Dt. 32^{51}, Jos. 15^{1}). It lay N. of the wilderness of Paran (see on 13^{21}). Before the words *the same is Ḳadesh* (cp. 20^{1} n.), 𝔊 inserts, *And they journeyed from the wilderness of Ṣin and encamped in the wilderness of Paran.* 𝔊 thus identifies Ḳadesh and the wilderness of Paran; such an identification is made nowhere else.—**37 f.** = $20^{22ff.}$.—**38.** The date of Aaron's death (the 1st day of the 5th month of the 40th year of the Exodus) is not given elsewhere; but cp. 20^{1} (P) n. His age at death also is given only here, but it is a mere inference from the date and the statement of Ex. 7^{7} (P).—**40.** = 21^{1} (with slight verbal

* Robinson, *Bibl. Researches*,[1] 250 f.; Driver, *Deut.* 35 f.

variations), a fragment of JE which now stands immediately after P's account of Aaron's death.—41. *Ṣalmonah*] with this name cp. Ṣalmon, the name of (probably) two different mountains; Jud. 9^{48}, Ps. 68^{15}.—42. *Punon*] instead of this form (פונן) S 𝔖 𝔊 read *Pinon* (פינן). The place may be identical with the Edomite Pinon (Gn. 36^{41}, 1 Ch. 1^{52}†); Jerome speaks of Faenon as "nunc viculus in deserto, ubi æris metalla damnatorum suppliciis effodiuntur inter civitatem Petram et Zoaram" (*OS.* 123^{10-12}; cp. 299^{85-87}); the name may survive in that of a ruin (Ḳalʿat Phenan) which was visited by Seetzen (*Reisen*, iii. 17). In this case Pinon lay in the northern part of Edom. This would agree with the view suggested in 21^{10} n. that the itinerary, in common with P^g, represents Israel as passing straight across northern Edom from Mt. Ḥor to the borders of Moab.—43–45. *Oboth* and *Iyye-haʿabarim*] $21^{10f.}$ (P).—45. *Dibon-gad*] 21^{30} 32^{34} notes; the present form, of course, presupposes the Gadite conquest, or occupation of the country. —46 f. *ʿAlmon-diblathaim*] since this comes between Dibon and "the Mt. of the ʿAbarim before Nebo," it must lie between Arnon and the Wady Ḥesbân, and may well be the same as Beth-diblathaim (Jer. 48^{22}†; בת דבלתן in Meshaʿ's Inscr. (l. 30)). The exact site is uncertain. The first part of the name occurs by itself as the name of a place in Benjamin, Jos. 21^{18}.—47. *The mountains of the ʿAbarim*] 27^{12} (P).—*Nebo*] 32^{38} n. —48b. 22^{1} (P).—49. *Beth-jeshîmoth* (Jos. 12^{3} 13^{20}, Ezek. 25^{9}) may be the modern Suwême (Buhl, *Geog.* p. 265). Abel-shiṭṭim is not mentioned in P^g. In 25^{1} (JE) the abbreviated form Shiṭṭim is used; it is there mentioned as the place where the Israelites abode. If Beth-jeshîmoth and Abel-shiṭṭim be correctly identified with Suwême and Kefrên (25^{1} n.) respectively, they lay about 5 miles apart, and both of them a few miles from the river.

7. וַיֵּשְׁבוּ] rather וַיֵּשְׁבוּ; so S.—ויחנו לפני מגדל] except here and in v.[9] (cp. v.[36f.]) ויחנו is always followed by the name of the next starting-point: Paterson, therefore, suspects some corruption here; see his note in *SBOT*. —9. ויחנו שם] The compiler has abandoned his usual formula (see last n.) in favour of direct citation from Ex. 15^{27}.

XXXIII. 50–XXXVI.—*Various Laws relating to the Conquest and Settlement of Canaan.*

(1) Destruction of the idolatrous objects of the Canaanites and the distribution of Canaan by lot, 33^{50-56}; (2) the boundaries of Canaan, 34^{1-15}; (3) the names of the tribal princes who with Ele'azar and Joshua are to superintend the allotment of Canaan, 34^{16-29}; (4) Levitical cities, 35^{1-8}; (5) cities of refuge, v.$^{9-34}$; (6) heiresses required to marry within their own clan, c. 36.

All these laws except the last, which is an appendix to 27^{1-11} (P), and is placed in its present position for no very obvious reason, are introduced by P's usual formula, and are, both in style and in other respects, clearly connected with P; the scene of the communication of the laws as given in 33^{50} 35^{1} 36^{13} is that of 22^{1} (P^{g}); with 34^{16-29} cp. 1^{5-15} 13^{4-15} (P), and see, further, the notes that follow. The laws are much less miscellaneous in character than those of c. 5 f. and 15, and far more related to the implied circumstances than those of c. 5 f., or of c. 15, or of c. 19; as concerned with the occupation of the country W. of Jordan, they stand very naturally after the conquest of the country E. of the Jordan, but before the people actually cross the river (cp. Jos. 1). At the same time none of the laws seem essential to P^{g}'s scheme, and they may all be, as some of them certainly seem to be, the work of P^{s} rather than P^{g}.

Though differently described, the scene and circumstances of these laws are practically the same as of the laws of Dt. (cp. Dt. 1^{5}): the subjects also of two of them are the same, though the treatment in one case is very different. With 35^{9-34} cp. Dt. 19^{1-13} (cities of refuge), and with 33^{50-56} cp. Dt. $12^{2f.}$ (destruction of idolatrous objects).

XXXIII. 50–56. Yahweh commands the Israelites to destroy all idolatrous objects in the country which they occupy W. of Jordan, and to divide the land among themselves by lot.

The two subjects here combined are expressed in different styles: v.^{54} (the allotment of the land), like the introductory formulæ v.$^{50.\ 51a}$, is in the style of P; v.$^{52f.\ 55f.}$ (the destruction of idolatrous objects) recalls H and

D. Note especially במה and משכית (v.[52]), which occur nowhere else in the Pent. except in Lev. 26[1. 30] (H); see, further, the notes that follow. The combination of the two laws is best attributed to an editor (P^s). V.[54] points forward to c. 34.

50, 51a. Cp. 5[11. 12a] (P): see note there and also phil. n. on 5[6].—*In the plains of Moab*, etc.] 22[1] n. 26[3] 35[1] (P).—**51b.** Cp. 35[10], Dt. 11[31]; see also 15[2] n. and phil. n. below.—**52.** Having crossed Jordan and entered Canaan, the Israelites are to drive out the inhabitants and to destroy the remnants of their religion: cp. Ex. 23[24. 31–33] 34[11–16] (JE), Dt. 7[1–6] 12[2f.] Such commands are not found elsewhere in P.—*Ye shall dispossess*] this use of הוריש is characteristic of D, but is not found in P^g; see 32[21] n.—*Ye shall cause to perish*] the Piel of אבד, which is found twice in this v., occurs elsewhere in the Hex. only in Dt. 11[4] 12[2].—*Their figure(d stone)s*] *i.e.* stones with idolatrous symbols carved or otherwise represented on them. This meaning of משכיות is probable, though not absolutely certain (see phil. n.). The only other passage which refers to such objects is Lev. 26[1]; those mentioned there are certainly of stone (אבן משכית).—*Their molten images*] the image (צלם) was probably of the same figure as the god was conceived to possess; for צלם is used of the cast figures of mice (1 S. 6[5. 11]) and graven figures of men (Ezek. 23[14]); also in the phrase "images of males" (Ezek. 16[17]). The present phrase is the equivalent of "molten gods," which is used in the similar prohibitions of Ex. 34[17] (JE), Lev. 19[4] (H). Moore (*EBi.* 2148) points out that the molten image is the only kind prohibited in the oldest legislation (Ex. 34[17]); and considers it probable that both name and thing were borrowed from the Canaanites.—*And demolish all their bāmōth*] cp. Lev. 26[30] (H), "And I (Yahweh) will demolish all your high places." This is the only other passage in the Hex. in which the term *bāmāh*, commonly rendered *high place*, is used with a religious reference. The term appears to be derived from an otherwise unknown root *būm*. In certain poetical passages in the OT. it is used of *heights*, whether of the land (hills) or of the sea (waves); see, *e.g.*, 21[28], Is. 58[14], Dt. 32[13], Job 9[8], and cp. the Assyr. *ḫur re ù ba-ma-a-te šal͏a šadi-i* = *the ravines and heights of the moun-*

tains (Delitzsch, *Handwörterbuch*, 177*b*). Far more commonly in the OT. the *bāmāh* is a place of worship (cp. especially the parallelism with *miḳdāsh* in Am. 7^{9}, Is. 16^{12}); it is similarly used in the Inscription of Meshaʿ (l. 3). In certain early passages the *bāmāh* is represented as an altogether suitable place for the worship of Yahweh, and as consisting of, or situated on, a height; it is necessary to *ascend* to the *bāmāh* of Ramah, though the city itself lay on a hill: 1 S. 9^{12-25}; in Mic. 3^{12} *hill* (הר) and *bāmōth* are virtually equivalents. Later, the term underwent modifications: (1) it came to connote a place of worship that was illegitimate either as offered to other deities than Yahweh (1 K. 11^{7}, 2 K. 23^{8}, Jer. 19^{5}), or as offered outside Jerusalem (1 K. 14^{23} 15^{14} and often); (2) it implied something artificial: the *bāmāh* needed to be built (בנה), and could be pulled down (נתץ) or removed (סור); see references under (1) and (3); and (3) it lost any necessary connection with actual hill-tops; places of worship in valleys could be called *bāmōth* (Jer. 7^{31}); *bāmōth* were situated in the gates of Jerusalem (2 K. 23^{8}). Whether these *bāmōth* of later times consisted, as many have suggested, of artificial mounds is uncertain. Probably we should understand the word in this passage in the later sense, and the command as a command to destroy all the sanctuaries of the Canaanites; otherwise to *demolish the high places* must mean to destroy the appurtenances of Canaanite worship at these spots, such as the altars (Hos. 10^{8}) and, in some cases, sacred trees (1 S. 22^{6}) and feasting halls (1 S. 9^{22}) and the like.*—**53b.** Cp. Lev. 20^{24} 25^{46} (H), Gn. 15^{7} (JE); further, with *to possess it* (לרשת אתה) cp. the constantly recurring לְרִשְׁתָּהּ of D (*e.g.* Dt. 3^{18}; CH. 88), and ct. P's phrase לאחזה (32^{5} n.).—**54.** *And ye shall possess yourselves of*] 32^{18} phil. n. The clause might equally well follow immediately on v.[51]: then render *then ye shall*, etc.—*By lot*] 26^{55}.—*To that which is large*, etc.] 26^{54}.—*Whithersoever the lot falleth for any family, it shall have* (*its possession*)] it is impossible to render the Hebrew both literally and intelligibly; but the *any man* of RV. is rather misleading. לו here rendered *any family* refers back to למעט and לרב into which למשפחתיכם

* See more fully Moore's art. "High Place" in *EBi.*

(*your families*) is grammatically divided.—**55 f.** If not driven out of the land, the Canaanites will in future distress the Israelites, and ultimately Yahweh will treat the Israelites as He had intended to treat the Canaanites, *i.e.* He will remove them from their country; the writer has the Exile in view.—*Pricks in your eyes and thorns* (?) *in your sides*] similar figures are used in Jos. 23^{13}, Ezek. 28^{24}, and perhaps in the original text of Jud. 2^{3}. Elsewhere it is frequently represented that the Canaanites left in the land will be a *snare*: see Ex. 23^{33}, $34^{11ff.}$, Dt. 7^{16}.

51. כי אתם עברים] the part. after כי (=*when*) is unusual (BDB. 473*a*): it occurs twice elsewhere in this last section of Nu. (34^{2} 35^{10}); see also Dt. 11^{31} 18^{9}.—**52.** משכיתם] that the objects so termed were connected with the native cults is clear from the context here and in Lev. 26^{1} where אבן משכית is a fourth term following מצבה, פסל, and אלילים. סכא in Aram. means *to look out* (=צפה; so צִפָּה=סְכָוָאָה), *look for*, *expect*; in Heb. the root appears only in שכיה and משכית; these may perhaps mean *an object to look at*, a representation of something drawn or in relief; but it cannot be said that the precise sense of either term is established. The שכיות חמדה of Is. 2^{16}, the תפוחי זהב במשכיות כסף (? *silver carving*) of Pr. 25^{11}, the חדרי משכית (? *chambers of imagery*) of Ezek. 8^{12} are all uncertain. In Ps. 73^{7}, Pr. 18^{11}, משכית is used metaphorically. The Versions do not recognise the meaning *figured stones* either here or in Lev.; 𝔊 has λιθόσκοπος or λίθος σκοπός in Lev. and here σκοπιαί; 𝔗 and 𝔖 give משכית the sense of *cult*, *worship* (סגידא, ܣܓܕܬܐ).—**53.** והורשתם את כל הארץ] before הארץ 𝔊 inserts ישבי, thus assimilating the present phrase to that found in v.[52. 55] and restoring the normal construction of הוריש (=to dispossess) with a personal obj. If 𝔐 is correct, the Hiphil is here used with the sense of the Kal, *to acquire possession of*; cp. 14^{24}, Jos. 8^{7} 17^{12}, Jud. 1^{19} (וַיִּרַשׁ); Jos. 8^{7} seems conclusive proof that the Hiphil had this sense; for the context there does not allow of rendering *dispossess the city* (viz. of its inhabitants). But see BDB.—**55.** לשכים בעיניכם ולצנינים בצדיכם] the variant of this phrase in Jos. 23^{13} seems less correct. On Jud. 2^{3} see Moore. שִׂכִּים occurs here only; but the meaning of something *sharp*, or *pointed*, is well secured by سِكَّة *a sharp weapon*; ܣܟܬܐ *a nail*; Assyr. *šikkatu*, *a point*; cp. also the Heb. שֻׂכָּה (Job 40^{31}) and מְשׂוּכָּה *a thorn hedge* (Is. 5^{5}). A similar sense for צנינים (here and Jos. 23^{13} only) is less certain; the best support for it is צנות (Am. 4^{5}), which may mean *the hook* or *barb* (of a fishing spear). Another similar word צנים, commonly rendered *thorns*, occurs in two passages only (Job 5^{5}, Pr. 22^{5}), both of which may be corrupt.—**56.** דמיתי the vb. דִּמָּה occurs nowhere else in the Pent.

XXXIV. 1–15. The boundaries of the land to be occupied by the nine-and-a-half tribes.—The boundaries here given are certainly to some extent ideal; the country included within them was never in its entirety in the actual occupation of the Hebrews. This is clearest and indisputable in the case of the western boundary (v.[6]). The western boundary of the Hebrews always lay some distance back from the coast; not a single spot on the coast was ever in Hebrew occupation till, in the second half of the 2nd cent. B.C., Simon captured Joppa (1 Mac. 14[5]). It is possible that the northern and eastern boundaries here described also presuppose a much larger extent of territory than the largest ever held by the Hebrews. The southern border corresponds more closely to what incidental references to places belonging to Judah would suggest.

The certain existence of an ideal element in the present description renders it peculiarly difficult to determine what lines are intended by the present description of the northern and (north-) eastern boundaries. For it is precarious to allow the identifications of the places concerned to be determined by the consideration that they must not lie beyond, or at all events remote from, the line that may be established by taking account of incidental allusions to the furthest points *actually* held by the Hebrews. Yet apart from such a controlling consideration, it is impossible to identify the sites even approximately with any certainty. Some of the places in question are mentioned only here and in the parallel description in Ezek.; and with the exception of the "Entrance of Ḥamath," none of them are mentioned with any frequency, or in such a way as to give even much clue to the site.

The boundaries here given for the nine-and-a-half tribes are substantially, if not precisely, the same as those which Ezekiel gives for the land which is to be occupied by the *twelve* tribes after the restoration from Exile (Ezek. 47[13–20]). The variations in the two descriptions are certainly in part due to textual corruption. Here, as in other things, what Ezekiel embodies in his description of the ideal future, P embodies in his account of the idealised past; cp. above, pp. 18, 24.

3–5. The southern boundary is indicated summarily in v.[3a], and then by a series of points in v.[3b–5]. This boundary is defined twice elsewhere (Jos. 15^{1-4}, Ezek. 47^{19}), for the southern boundary of Judah (Jos.) is also the southern boundary of the whole country. The points given in the three passages are as follow:—

Nu.	Jos.	Ezek.
Dead Sea (S.E.).	Dead Sea (S.E.).	Tamar = (Dead Sea (S.E.)).
Ascent of 'Aḳrabbim.	Ascent of 'Aḳrabbim.	
Ṣin.	Ṣin.	
Ḳadesh-barnea'.	Ḳadesh-barnea'.	Meriboth-ḳadesh.
Ḥaṣar-addar.	Heṣron.	
	Addar.	
	Ḳarḳa'.	
'Aṣmon.	'Aṣmon.	
Wady Miṣraim.	Wady Miṣraim	(the) Wady (Miṣraim).
The sea.	The sea.	The great sea.

The eastern and western extremities of this boundary are known points; the western extremity, the outflow of the Wady Miṣraim (mod. Wady el-'Arīsh), is at a point on the coast of the Mediterranean about half-way between Gaza and Pelusium. Considerably *south* of a straight line between these two extremities lies the third known point, Ḳadesh (13^{26} n.). Be'er-sheba', which is frequently mentioned * as the southern limit of the land of Israel, and which is situated on the verge of the wilderness, or Negeb, which also sometimes ranks as the southern boundary (Dt. 11^{24}, Jos. 1^{4}; cp. Nu. 13^{21}), lies a very few miles *north* of the same straight line. The most natural boundary † in this region consists of the Wadys el-Fiḳreh, Marra, el-Abyaḍ, and el-'Arīsh, which together form an almost straight line from the S. end of the Dead Sea to the outflow of the Wady el-'Arīsh. The exact course of the boundary line from Ḳadesh to the coast is quite uncertain; for Ḥaṣar-addar (Ḥeṣron, Addar, and Ḳarḳa') and 'Asmon and the point at which the junction with the Wady el-'Arīsh was reached are unknown. From the Dead Sea the line indicated probably

* Jud. 20^{1}, 1 S. 3^{20}, 2 S. 3^{10} 17^{11} $24^{2.15}$, 1 K. 4^{25}, 2 K. 23^{8}, 2 Ch. 19^{4}, Neh. 11^{30}; cp. Am. 8^{14}; see H. W. Hogg, "Dan to Beersheba" (*Exp.*[5] (1898) viii. 411–421.

† Buhl, *Geog.* p. 11.

ran at first S.W. through the Wady el-Fiḳreh, which is a natural boundary, and then, turning round the Jebel Madurah (20^{22} n.), much more directly south to Ḳadesh. The ascent of ʿAḳrabbim may be sought in one of the passes on the N. side of the Wady el-Fiḳreh, and perhaps in particular in the Naḳb el-Yemen, which starts just opposite the Jebel Madurah, or in the Naḳb eṣ-Ṣafâ.

The northern side of the Wady el-Fiḳreh is a "bare and bald rampart of rock" about 1000 ft. high, precipitous in character, and without vegetation. "To one looking from the southern end of the Dead Sea, the open mouth of the Wady Feqreh shows itself prominently. . . . A southern boundary line . . . would therefore properly be supposed to enter this great dividing wady." "It is just southward of that Pass el-Yemen that a turn would naturally be made in a boundary line that had followed the border of Edom and was to hinge for a yet more southerly stretch in its onward sweep; for standing out all by itself in the wady which is being followed as the boundary line, or rather at the confluence of two other wadies with that one, there is a notable mountain, Jebel Madurah, around the north-western side of which the boundary line would turn to move on to its southernmost point" (Clay Trumbull, *Kadesh-Barnea*, 110, 113). Older discussions of the southern boundary are mostly vitiated by starting from Robinson's erroneous identification of Ḳadesh with ʿAin-el-Weibeh. Of recent discussions, see especially Clay Trumbull, *Kadesh-Barnea*, 106–124 (the philological suggestions and arguments are often untrustworthy); also Buhl, *Gesch. der Edomiter*, 23–26 (cp. 16 f.); G. A. Smith, *Hist. Geog.* 278–286.

3. *Your southern side*] RV. renders פאה here by "quarter"; but where פאה is defined by a point of the compass, it is used of a line rather than a space: so quite clearly in 35^{5}, Ezek. $48^{16. 18. 32ff.}$; cp. Ezek. $47^{17ff.}$.—*From the wilderness of Ṣin along the side(s) of Edom*] In Jos. 15^{1} Judah's territory is described as extending "unto the border of Edom, to the wilderness of Ṣin southwards" (אל גבול אדם מדבר צן נגבה). This implies that Edom formed part of Israel's southern border W. of Jordan (20^{16} n.). So here *along the side(s) of Edom* is best taken as describing the eastern end of the southern line. The prepositional phrase על ידי does not necessarily mean "along the sides of": for in Jud. 11^{26} it must refer to one, viz. the northern, side of Arnon only: cp. also 1 Ch. 6^{16}.—For the wilderness of Ṣin as a boundary, cp. 13^{21} (P).—*Your southern boundary shall be*, or extend, *from the* southern *extremity of the Salt Sea on the east*] Jos. 15^{2} states it more precisely "from the extremity of the Salt Sea, from the bay that turneth (or bendeth) south." *The Salt Sea* is the commonest designation of the Dead Sea in OT.; for others, see Dt. 3[17], Ezek. 47[18].— 4. *And your boundary line shall take a turn south of the pass of 'Aḳrabbim*] the pass of 'Aḳrabbim (Scorpions) is probably one of those leading N.W. out of the Wady el-Fiḳreh (see above). —*Ṣin*] is also mentioned in Jos. 15[3]. The site is unknown; but the place gave its name to the wilderness of Ṣin (13[21] n.). —*And its extremity* in this direction *shall be south of Ḳadesh-barnea'*] on the form Ḳadesh-barnea', see 32[8] n.—*And it shall make a (fresh) start to Ḥaṣar-addar and continue to 'Aṣmon: and at 'Aṣmon the boundary line shall turn to the Wady Miṣraim, and its* (western) *extremity shall be at the* (Mediterranean) *sea*] Turning N.W. at Ḳadesh the boundary strikes the north-westerly running Wady el-'Arîsh at this unidentified 'Aṣmon and follows its course to the Mediterranean. With this Jos. 15[3f.] is in general agreement, but it places the turning-point (ונסב) between Addar and Ḳarḳa', which is not mentioned here. Instead of Ḥaṣar-addar, Jos. gives two distinct places, Ḥeṣron and Addar. Neither this Ḥeṣron, nor Addar, nor Ḥaṣar-addar is mentioned again, and the sites are quite unknown. On names of the same type as Ḥaṣar, Ḥeṣron, see 11[35] n. Whether a single name (Ḥaṣar-addar) has in the course of textual transcription become two (Ḥeṣron, Addar), or two names one, is uncertain. Addar (cp. 1 Ch. 8[3] = Ard, Nu 26[40]) looks like a tribal name; but even so, it may have stood by itself as the name of a place (33[31] n.). Ḥeṣron is related philologically to Ḥaṣar in the same way that 'Aṣmon is to 'Eṣem, the name of a town sometimes assigned to Simeon, sometimes to Judah (Jos. 15[29] 19[3]); but the philological connection does not, of course, prove geographical identity. Clay Trumbull (*Kadesh-Barnea*, 117, 289 ff.) identifies 'Aṣmon with Ḳasaymeh; this receives a precarious support from the fact that the *later* Targums (𝔗[Jer Jon]) give קסם or קיסם for 'Aṣmon. —*The Wady of Miṣr(a)im* (נחל מצרים: RV. "the Brook of Egypt") is frequently mentioned as a boundary line, and generally as the southern boundary of the land of Israel (Jos. 15[4. 47], 1 K. 8[65], 2 K. 24[7], 2 Ch. 7[8], Is. 27[12] †; and originally, it may be, in Am. 6^{14}). The identification of the Wady of Miṣraim with the Wady el-ʿArîsh is now generally accepted.* The Wady el-ʿArîsh runs N. and N.W. from the middle of the Sinaitic peninsula and flows into the Mediterranean at a point on the coast of the Mediterranean about half-way between Pelusium and Gaza, where the ancient Rhinocolura (cp. Is. 27^{12} 𝔊) stood. It is a long and deep watercourse, but is only full after heavy rain. It has been commonly supposed that the wady was called the Wady of Egypt (Miṣraim) because it separated Canaan from Egypt. Recently another suggestion has been made: it has been argued† that Muṣur in the Assyrian inscriptions and Miṣr(a)im in the OT. are frequently the name of a north Arabian district including the country through which the Wady of Miṣraim flowed; and that the wady derived its name from this country. If the identification of Muṣur with the north Arabian country were established, this would be the most probable explanation of the name of the wady.

2. הארץ כנען] Driver, *Tenses*, § 190.—**4.** מנגב ל] ***on the south of***; BDB. *s.v.* מן 1. *c* (p. 578*b*).—צנה] Lagarde (*Bildung d. Nomina*, 46 f.) proposed חצן.—והיה תוצאתיו] Ḳ'rê והיו ת׳. The same variant occurs in Jos. 15^4 $18^{12. 14. 19}$. The cstr. of the K'tib can be explained by G.-K. 145*o*. But the sing. vb. in these cases may be a survival of an original text in which the noun also was sing.; S reads all through this c. והיה תוצאת(ו). Since the noun means "***the point*** at which a boundary terminates," the use of the plural would be very hard to explain; see *Journ. of Theol. Studies*, iv. 124 f.—**5.** At the end of the v. זה יהיה לכם גבול נגב appears to have dropped out; cp. v.$^{6. 9. 12}$ and also Jos. 15^4.

6. The western boundary is to be the Mediterranean; cp. Jos. 15^{12}, Ezek. 47^{20}. This never was the actual boundary of the land of Israel; see above, p. 453.—*The Great Sea* is one

* Palmer, *Desert of the Exodus*, 286 f.; Buhl, *Geog.* 66; Di.; *EBi.* 1249; Hastings' *DB. s.v.* "Egypt, River of."

† Winckler, *Altorientalische Forschungen* (1893), i. 24–41 (especially p. 26), and *Muṣri, Meluḫḫa, and Maʿîn*, i. ii. (1898); Hommel, *Vier neue arabische Landschaftsnamen*, 296 f., 303 ff.; *EBi.* "Egypt, River of," § 2, cp. "Mizraim," § 2*b*. In criticism of Muṣur = north Arabia, see Budge, *History of Egypt*, vi. pp. vii–xxx; König, *Fünf neue arabische Landschaftsnamen*, 19 ff. (especially on the Wady of Miṣraim, p. 21 f.); in counter-criticism, H. W. Hogg in *EBi.* "Simeon," § 6 n.

of the names for the Mediterranean (cp. Jos. 15^{47}, Ezek. 48^{28}), but it is more frequently called simply "the sea" (*e.g.* 13^{29}).

וגבול (2)] the use of ו (apparently = *also, at the same time*) is peculiar, but occurs several times in similar contexts; see, *e.g.*, Dt. 3^{16}, Jos. 13^{23}, and BDB. *s.v.* ו 1. *c.* Haupt (in *SBOT.*) proposes to read here and in similar cases וגבולו *and the district thereof*; Kön. (iii. p. 283 n. 1) argues that the force of the art. in הים הגדול is carried over to גבול, *and the* (*adjacent*) *district*; but this is really contrary to analogy.

7–9. The northern boundary is to extend from a site on the Mediterranean that cannot be identified to Ḥaṣar-ʿênān on the border of the territory of Damascus (Ezek. 47^{18} 48^{1}). Ḥaṣar-ʿênān may have stood on the site of the modern Bâniâs; but the exact position is uncertain, though it evidently (v.$^{10f.}$) lay well to the N. or N.E. of the Sea of Galilee.

In Ezek. 47^{15-17} (cp. 48^{1}) the description of the future northern boundary begins as here with the words "from the great sea," and contains, in common with the present description, the intermediate point Ṣedad and the eastern extremity Ḥaṣar-ʿênān (or -ʿênôn). In both passages, but especially in Ezek., the text has suffered corruption; still it is clear that both must have described the same, or almost the same, boundary line. But it is no longer possible to determine what that line was; for, with the exception of the Entrance of Ḥamath, mentioned here and, probably, in the original text of Ezek.,* none of the places are mentioned except in one or both of these passages; and none, not even the Entrance of Ḥamath, can be fixed with certainty. The main point at issue between those who have discussed the question of this boundary line is whether it ran south of, and so excluded, the Lebanon, or whether it included at least a large part of it; if the southern site suggested for the Entrance of Ḥamath (13^{21} n.) be adopted, the boundary excluded, if the northern site be adopted, it included, this region. The *actual* boundaries certainly did not include the Lebanon; for Dan, the proverbial northern town, lay south of the mountains (cp. also 1 K. $5^{20\,(6)}$); but this does not determine the *ideal* boundary.

* In Ezek. $47^{15f.}$ for לבא צדדה חמת read לבא חמת צדדה; see Bertholet on the passage, and Toy (in *SBOT.*); Corn. omits צדדה as a gloss from Nu.

Furrer (*Zeitschr. d. deutschen Palästina-Vereins*, viii. 27–29) has argued for the northern line. According to him the boundary almost immediately after leaving the Mediterranean passed Ḥethlon (mod. Heitela), distant nearly two hours from the coast, and situated between the Nahr el-Kebîr and the Nahr ʿAḳḳar. From Ḥethlon the boundary passed to Mt. Hor, "obviously the northern spur of Lebanon," and next reached the plateau of the Orontes. Here it took a N.E. direction to the Entrance of Ḥamath, the modern Restan, the ancient Arethusa, formerly the boundary of Syria Secunda, later of the principality of Antioch, and now the border town between the districts of Ḥöms and Ḥamath. Crossing the Orontes at this point the boundary struck S.E. to Ziphrôn (mod. Safrâne), thence S.S.E. to Ṣedad (mod. Ṣadad), thence E.N.E. to Ḥauran, the Ḥaurina of the Assyrian inscriptions and the mod. Ḥawarîn. About 10 miles due E. of the last point Furrer places the termination of the boundary, identifying Ḥaṣar-ʿênān with Ḳaryatēn, the last oasis in the Syrian desert towards Palmyra, which is 24 hours distant.

Van Kasteren (*Revue Biblique*, 1895, 23 ff.) has attempted to trace a more southern line. This starts at the mouth of the Nahr el-Ḳâsimîyeh (about 100 miles S. of Furrer's starting-point), a few miles N. of Tyre; Ḥethlon is ʿAdlûn; Mt. Ḥor, the mountain at the sharp turn of the Nahr el-Ḳâsimîyeh, a few miles N.W. of Tel el-Ḳâḍi (? Dan); the entrance of Ḥamath is the Merj ʿAyûn; Ṣedad (S 𝔊 Ṣerad) is Serâdâ, S. of Ḥermon, and close to the Merj ʿAyûn; Sibraim (Ezek. 47^{16}) is Senbarîye; and, finally, Ḥaṣar-ʿênān is el-Ḥaḍr, E. of Bâniâs.

Buhl (*Geog*. 10. 66 f.) criticises Furrer, and, though without accepting all the particular identifications, holds that Van Kasteren's line is approximately correct—in particular as to its starting-point.

7 f. *Ye shall mark out* (*the line*) *for yourselves unto Hor the mountain . . . ye shall mark out* (*the line*) *unto the Entrance of Hamath*] on the vb. see phil. n. The exact meaning is somewhat uncertain, but the change of cstr. in RV. is not correct. This Mount Hor is not mentioned elsewhere; for another, see 20^{22}; and for the *Entrance of Ḥamath*, see above and on 13^{21}.—*The termination of the boundary shall be at Ṣedād*] like the southern, the northern boundary is not a straight line: it makes an angle, or, as the Hebrew expresses it, has an "extremity" in the middle, and (v.[9]) *makes a* (*fresh*) *start*.—*Ṣedād*] S 𝔊 Ṣerād; for proposed identifications of this place and *Ziphron* (v.[9]), see above.—**9.** *Hăṣar-ʿênān*] v.[10], Ezek. 48^{1}† = Ḥaṣar-ʿênôn (Ezek. 47^{17}† 𝔐; 𝔊 *Αἰναν*). Some* consider that this place is also mentioned under a corrupt form in Ezek. 47^{16} (Ḥāṣēr hat-tîcôn). The name means *the enclosure of the spring*; the form *ʿênān* is more Aramaic, the form *ʿênōn*

* Smend, Corn., Cheyne (*EBi.*).

specifically Hebrew. Ḥaṣar-ʿênān is the point at which both the northern and eastern boundaries terminate. It is described in Ezek. as "on the border of Damascus," and is defined more closely, according to Cornill's reconstructed text of Ezek. 47^{18}, thus, "And the east side: from Ḥaṣar-ʿênān, which lies on the border between Ḥauran and Damascus, the Jordan forms the border between Gileʿad and the land of Israel." If this be accepted, Ḥaṣar-ʿênān lay actually on, or quite near to, the Jordan. In that case Furrer's identification with Ḳaryatēn is impossible; and the identification with Bâniâs, to which some scholars * incline, could not be far wrong; Bâniâs is situated at one of the sources of the Jordan—at a "spring," therefore, which may have given the place its ancient name.

7. הֹר הָהָר] 20^{22} n.—תְּתָאוּ] so v.^{8}: in v.^{10} וְהִתְאַוִּיתֶם. MT. thus distinguishes two verbs—תאה and אוה. Most modern scholars, like 𝔊 (always *καταμετρήσετε*), agree that the verbs in the three verses are from the same root. But (*a*) some (*e.g.* Di.) point here and in v.^{8} תְּתָאֲוּוּ, keeping v.^{10} unchanged; (*b*) some (*e.g.* Paterson, Ges.-Buhl, *s.v.* אוה) retain the punctuation in v.$^{7f.}$, and read וְהִתְאַיּתֶם in v.^{10}; (*c*) Cheyne (*EBi.* 2109) corrects in v.$^{7f.}$ to תְּתָאֲרוּ and in v.^{10} to וְתֵאַרְתֶּם; cp. the use of this same vb. (in the Kal) in Jos. $15^{9.\,11}$ (a very similar context) and (in the Piel) in Is. 44^{13}. As to the roots אוה and תאה, assumed in (*a*) and (*b*) respectively: אוה regularly means *to desire*; so Di., somewhat Rabbinically, sees in the use of the vb. an indication that the boundaries are to be ideal, and renders, *ye shall desire for yourselves.* Others assume for the vb. אוה a unique sense, *to mark out*: cp. the noun אות, آيَة, and see especially Fried. Delitzsch, *Prolegomena*, 116 f.; but his argument is very hypothetical, and the sense *mark out* there claimed for the Assyr. אוה ii. 2, does not appear to be given in his more recent *Assyr. Handwörterbuch.* The root תאה *might be* a by-form of תוה (Ezek. 9^{4}). Any interpretation of the text as it stands seems not less hazardous than the supposition that it is corrupt. Cheyne's entire restoration of v.$^{7b.\,8a}$ is worth giving: מן הים הגדל תתארו לכם עד חדרך ומחדרך תתארו עד לבא חמת. It is suggested by Halévy's emendation of חדרך for the strange הדרך in Ezek. 47^{15} and דרך in 48^{1} (*EBi.* 2046). הר ההר and לבא חמת are best taken as accusatives of direction, but עד (with Cheyne) or אל (cp. Jos. 15^{11}) prefixed to the names would have given a more usual cstr.

10–12. The eastern boundary starts from Ḥaṣar-ʿênān (v.^{9} n.), passes to Shephām (site unknown), "descends" to the Riblah (?) (site unknown), and then runs along the (eastern) shore of the Lake of Galilee, the Jordan, and the Dead Sea,

* Buhl, *Geog.* 67, 240; Cheyne (*EBi.*).

terminating at the S.E. end of the last (v.^{8} n.). The mention of intermediate points between Ḥaṣar-ʿênān and the Lake of Galilee shows that the former was some distance away from (N. or N.E. of) the latter. In Ezek. 47^{18} the eastern boundary is defined by the Jordan and Dead Sea only, and the same line is intended here, if Ḥaṣar-ʿênān was situated at one of the sources of the Jordan (*e.g.* Bâniâs; see above). On the other hand, if Ḥaṣar-ʿênān be placed with Furrer at Ḳaryatēn, the northern extremity of the eastern boundary lay a long way N.E. of any source of the Jordan, and consequently the northern strip of the boundary was not marked by the course of the river.

11. *The Riblah* (?)] Riblah on the Orontes, which is always, unlike the present name, written without the article (רבלה), cannot be intended; Riblah on the Orontes, had it been mentioned at all, must have been given as a place on the northern boundary after the Entrance of Ḥamath. As a matter of fact the punctuation of MT. is more than questionable; 𝔐 can equally well be read (cp. 𝔊) *to Harbel* (הַרְבֵּלָה), the final ה being the ה locale, used as in v.$^{4.\ 5.\ 8.\ 9.\ 10.\ 12}$ etc. The name then means "the mountain of Bel,"* and has been identified by some with Harmel, at the source of the Orontes, by others with Arbin (cp. Bethel, mod. Beitin), 3 or 4 miles N.E. of Damascus. Both places are, however, rather remote from the Sea of Galilee which is next mentioned, and inconsistent with the view of Ezek. that the Jordan formed the eastern boundary.—*On the east of ʿAin*] this definition of the site of the Riblah or Harbel is itself obscure; for ʿAin (= *the spring*) cannot be identified. Cheyne (*EBi.* 106) considers it to be most probably the source of the Nahr Ḥâṣbâny; for "from this fountain to the east shoulder of the Lake of Gennesaret a straight line of water flows, forming the clearest of boundaries." But if this be accepted, the identification of Ḥaṣar-ʿênān with Bâniâs, which lies considerably S. of the source of the Nahr Ḥâṣbâny, must be given up. Another possibility is that ʿAin is a mispronounced ʿIyyon (עִיּוֹן) which is mentioned in 1 K. 15^{20} and

* See the letters of T. K. Cheyne and the present writer in *Acad.* of June 21 and 28, 1896; also *HPN.* 123 f. Cp. Dr. in *DB.* "Riblah," 2.

2 K 15^{29}, survives in the modern Merj ʿAyûn, and is perhaps to be identified with Tel Dibbîn N.W. of Bâniâs (*EBi.* 2160).—*And it shall stretch along* (?) *by the* (*hills that*) *flank the sea of Kinnereth*] the meaning of the vb. is quite uncertain. כָּתֵף (RV., inadequately, *side*) means primarily *shoulder*; but it is used metaphorically of a line of hills (Jos. $15^{8.\,10.\,11}$ $18^{12f.\,16.\,18f.}$), here in particular oı the hills that rise from the eastern shore of the Lake of Galilee.—*The sea of Kinnereth*] cp. Jos. 13^{27}; also Jos. 12^{3} ("the sea of Kinneroth"). In Dt. 33^{23} the Lake of Galilee is called briefly "the sea." The name here given to it was more probably derived from the ancient town of Kinnereth (Jos. 19^{35}, Dt. 3^{17}), which is mentioned in the list of places conquered by Thothmes III.* (15th or 16th cent. B.C.), than from its resemblance in shape to a harp or lyre (*kinnôr*).

13. Moses obeys Yahweh's command given in v.$^{1f.}$.—**14 f.** The land of Canaan, the land of promise proper, the boundaries of which have just been described, is to be divided among nine-and-a-half tribes only, since two-and-a-half, viz. Gad and Reuben (c. 32 *passim*) and half-Manasseh (32^{33}), have already received portions E. of Jordan.—**15.** *Across the Jordan at Jericho*] "at Jericho" is an unsuitable limitation in describing the frontier line of two or two-and-a-half tribes: the phrase has perhaps been mechanically written or added under the influence of 22^{1} and other passages where the limitation is suitably used. For another instance of its unsuitable use, see Jos. 20^{8}, where 𝕲 omits it.

11. מחה] if the text be sound, מחה must be used here with a meaning which it possesses nowhere else in Hebrew. The prep. על and the connection are both satisfied by the meaning *stretcheth along*; but *to stretch along* or even *to rub past* is not satisfactorily derived from מחה=*to efface, erase.* Some, therefore, disconnect מחה here from מחה *to efface*, and assume that it is=Aram. מחא, a weakened form of מחע=مخض=מחץ, *to strike*, and so metaphorically (as we sometimes use *strike* of a path, or a traveller) *to strike down upon* (see BDB. *s.v.* מחה ii. and references there).—**14.** בני הראובני and בני הגדי, but מנשה; cp. 4^{28} n.—**15.** קדמה מורחה] 2^{3} n.

16–29. Yahweh gives Moses the names of twelve persons who are to superintend the allotment of Canaan.—The persons

* W. Max Müller, *Asien u. Europa*, 84 n. 1.

are chosen on the same principle which governed the selection of the persons who superintended the census (1$^{1-15}$ (P)); but since Aaron is now dead (20$^{22-29}$) and Moses is to die before the entrance into Canaan (27$^{12-14}$ (P)), Eleʿazar and Joshua (cp. 27$^{18-23}$ (P)) take the place of superintendents-in-chief, corresponding to the part played by Moses and Aaron at the census. Since only ten tribes are to share in the land W. of Jordan (v.$^{13-15}$), only ten tribal princes, as against twelve who were employed at the census, are to assist Eleʿazar and Joshua, one being chosen from each of the ten tribes concerned.

Not one of the twelve tribal princes who acted at the census is mentioned here, nor any of the twelve spies except Joshua and Caleb. This is in accordance with the theory of 14$^{26-30. 36-38}$ (P). With the exception of Joshua, Caleb, and Eleʿazar, none of the persons mentioned here are mentioned anywhere else, unless Elidad (v.^{21}) be identical with Eldad (11^{26} n.). Among the names of these otherwise unknown persons are some such as Aḥihud, Elidad, which are certainly ancient; but the list as a whole is hardly more ancient than that of c. 1, though the evidence in the present case is less varied and conclusive: see note on p. 6 f., and, further, *HPN.* 193 ff.

The order in which the tribes are here mentioned appears to be governed by their (subsequent) positions in Canaan; thus the four southern tribes come first (v.$^{19-22}$), then the two central tribes (v.$^{23f.}$), and, finally, the four northern tribes (v.$^{25-28}$).

16. Cp. 1^{1} n.—**17.** אלה שמות] 1^{5} 13^{4} (P); see, further, CH. 188^{P}.—יִנְחֲלוּ] cp. לִנְחֹל v.^{18} and Jos. 19^{49}; but in all three passages the Piel may have been intended; cp. לְנַחֵל v.^{29}, and see also Jos. 13^{32} 14^{1} 19^{51}.—**20.** שמואל] a well-known early name. 𝔊 has Σαλαμιηλ = שלמיאל; cp. 1^{6} n.—עמיהוד] 1^{10} n. —**21.** אלידד] S 𝔊 𝔖 אלדד; 11^{26} n.—כִּסְלוֹן] 𝔊^{B} gives both for this and the place-name כְּסָלוֹן, Χασλων. S here reads כסלן, which might, like שִׁפְטָן (v.^{24}) and עַזָּן (v.^{26}), be a noun in *-ān*.—**22.** נשיא] so v.$^{23-28}$; ct. v.$^{19-21}$; S 𝔊 = 𝔏; 𝔖 omits throughout.—בֻּקִּי] 1 Ch. 5^{31}; cp. בֻּקִּיָּהוּ (1 Ch. 25$^{4. 13}$ †); see *HPN.* 205 and *EBi. s.v.* "Bakbukiah." Like שלמי and the numerous names in ־ִי in c. 13 (see p. 136), it may be an abbreviation.—יגלי] this hardly means *led into exile*; if it did, it would be a late name; see *HPN.* 203.—**23.** חניאל] S חנאל. Cp. 2 Ch. 7^{39} †. חנאל is a Nabatæan proper name (de Vogüé, *Syrie Centrale*, No. 10); cp. the Phœn. names חנבעל (Hannibal), חנמלקרת

(Hamilcar)—the former common. An early Hebrew compound with the same root is אלחנן. 𝔖 has ܢܚܠܐܝܠ = נחליאל; this is otherwise unknown, for as a personal name it would not be the same as the נחליאל of 21^{19}, but equivalent in meaning to זבדיאל; cp. نحل *a gift*, and Heb. נחלה *a possession.*—אפד] here only as a proper name.—**24.** קמואל] also Gn. 22^{21} (J) and 1 Ch. 27^{17}.—שִׁפְטָן] here only.—**25.** אליצפן] cp. 3^{30} phil. n.—פרנך] Possibly the Persian Φαρνάκης (Herod. viii. 126); but not necessarily. It could be from the Semitic root *fnk*, which is found in Arabic, with inserted *r*; cp. G.-K. 30*q*. A district called Barnaki or Parnak is mentioned by Esarhaddon; cp. Hommel, *Anc. Heb. Trad.* 301.—**26.** פלטיאל] cp. פלטיאל 2 S 3^{15} (variant פלטי); פַּלְטִי Nu. 13^{9}, and פִּלְטַי Neh. 12^{17}.—עזן] 𝔊 Ὀζα (al. Ὀξα) = עזה, or עזא (*e.g.* 2 S. 6^{3}); 𝔖 עזור (cp. Jer. 28^{1}).—**27.** אחיהוד] here only, but probably to be read in 1 Ch. 8^{7}. The name is doubtless ancient; cp. אביהוד, עמיהוד, and see *HPN.* 205, 38 ff., and note on 1^{12}. $𝔊^{BFL}$ read Ἀχιωρ; cp. Judith 6^{5}; if original, this represents אחיאר (cp. אריה); G^{A} Ἀχιωβ, possibly representing אחיאב *the* (*my*) *brother is a spirit*)—שלמי] cp. v.[20] n.—**28.** פדהאל] cp. פדהצור (1^{10} n.) and see small-print note on 1^{5-15}. Cp. Phœn. בעלפדא.—עמיהוד] 1^{10} n. and v.[20] above.

XXXV. 1–8 (P^{s})—The Levitical cities.

The language of the section is that of P. With v.[1] cp. 33^{50}; with v.[2a], 34^{2}; with v.[8], 33^{54}; and note אחזה (32^{5} n.), מגרש (CH. 156), רכש (CH. 155); ערי המקלט, ct. Dt. $19^{2ff.}$; כפי (CH. 19). Peculiarities such as the unique combination of חיה, רכש, and בהמה in v.[3], and the use of קיר, with the meaning *wall of a city*, may be due to the fact (see below) that the section is P^{s}.

The secular tribes, each according to its size (v.[8]), are to contribute portions of their landed possession to the Levites—in all 48 square plots of land, each consisting of about 207 acres, and containing a town and pasture-ground.

The carrying out of the law is recorded in Jos. 21 (P^{s}), and the law is referred to in Lev. $25^{32.34}$ (P^{s}), Jos. 14^{4} (P^{s}), 1 Ch. 13^{2}, 2 Ch. 11^{14} $31^{15.19}$, and also, as some think, in Ezr. 2^{70} = Neh. 7^{73}; Neh. $11^{3.20.36}$.

According to these passages, the Levites duly received their cities and pasture-grounds in the days of Joshua. The priests received 13 from Judah, Simeon, and Benjamin; the non-priestly Ḳohathites, 10 from Ephraim, Dan, and W. Manasseh; the Gershonites, 13 from Issachar, Asher, Naphtali, and E. Manasseh: the Merarites, 12 from Reuben, Gad, and Zebulun. In the days of David the Levites still dwelt in their own cities; but at the time of the disruption of the monarchy the

Levites of the Northern kingdom, being disowned by Jeroboam, left their cities and settled in Judah. In Judah these cities survived at least as late as Hezekiah, and, if the passages in Ezr. and Neh. be interpreted as referring to these cities, were revived after the Exile.

But this history is fictitious. Levitical cities in the meaning of the law never existed; they were merely the objects of desire in certain circles. Like the strip of country across the centre of Canaan which Ezekiel (48$^{8-14}$) designed for the priests and Levites, these cities never passed out of the realm of theory into that of fact.

In pre-exilic times priests lived in different parts of the country, some in places (such as ʿAnathoth, Jer. 1^{1}) that appear in the list of Levitical cities (Jos. 21) and some in places that do not appear in that list, such as Nob (1 S. 21^{1}), Shiloh (1 S. 1–4), Bethel (Am. 7^{10}); so at a much later period Mattathias lived at Modin (1 Mac. 2^{1}), which is also not included in the list. In the time of Saul the priests at Nob were so numerous that the place passed by the name of "the city of priests" (1 S. 22^{19}); but to what extent these priests owned the land in and about the city, and whether they owned it as individuals or as a priestly community, is not stated. From other statements, however, it is clear that certain individual priests were landowners; Abiathar, after the massacre of the rest of his family at Nob, owned land at ʿAnathoth (1 K. 2^{26}), and centuries later the priestly family to which Jeremiah belonged owned land in the same city (Jer. 32$^{6ff.}$); but in neither of these cases is there any suggestion that the land belonged to the tribe of Levi, or to the individuals in virtue of their being priests or Levites. On the other hand, the Levites as a class are described as "divided and scattered in Israel" (Gn. 49^{7}); and in Dt. (7th century B.C.) they are distinguished from the rest of the tribes by the very fact that they possess no tribal portion of land, but enjoy instead the offerings made to Yahweh (Dt. 18$^{1-5}$). They live scattered over the country in various cities, which they dwell in as *gêrim* (15^{13} n.), but which belonged to others (Dt. 18^{6} 12^{18} etc.). Individual Levites may, like the priests mentioned above, have owned land; but the passage which may imply this is obscure (Dt. 18^{8b}). As a class the Levites in Dt. rank with the widow, the orphan, and the *gêr*, and are commended, on the ground that they have no landed property, to the charity of the people ($12^{12.\ 18f.}$ $14^{27.\ 29}$ $16^{11.\ 14}$ $26^{11ff.}$).

Not only is the unreality of the Levitical cities proved by the contradictory evidence of the earlier literature, but also by the impracticability of the law. As Graf has well observed, it would be possible to mark out 48 exact squares of ground in a South Russian steppe, or in the open and yet unoccupied tracts of western North America, but not in a mountainous country like Palestine. This geometrical treatment, impossible in the actual land, has its parallel in Ezekiel's *ideal* division of W. Palestine into a series of exact parallelograms (Ezek. 48). Further contradictions and impossibilities appear when we take account of the cities actually named in Jos. 21; for these, reference must be made to the commentary on that chapter.

The amount of land required by Ezekiel for the priests and Levites (25,000 × 20,000 cubits = about 40 square miles) considerably exceeds that required by the present law (2000 × 2000 cubits × 48 = about $15\frac{1}{2}$ square miles), and might on that ground be regarded as the later claim. On the other hand, the demand for Levitical land in Ezekiel is organically connected with his fundamental scheme,—the maintenance of a holy cordon round the temple, situated in the centre of the land,—whereas the priestly theory is so far governed by the actualities of the situation that it contemplates, instead of a single district, cities distributed over the country (cp. We. *Proleg.* 162). There seems no reason therefore to question that, here as in other matters, the ideals of Ezekiel were adopted with modifications from P. In this particular matter of grants and dues made to the priests and Levites two stages may be marked within P: the law contained in c. 18 (P^g), which was shown to be later than Ezekiel (see p. 236 ff.), provides (v.$^{20.\ 24}$, cp. 26^{62}) that the priests and Levites shall receive dues and tithes *instead of* landed property; the present law that the Levites (including the priests, cp. Jos. 21) shall have "cities to dwell in" (see n. on v.[2]). These cities and the surrounding land are elsewhere clearly asserted to be the inalienable possession of the Levites (Lev. 25^{32-34}). The most natural conclusion is that the present law and the connected passages are later than the theory of P^g, as stated in c. 18.

1. 33^{50}.—2. *Cities to dwell in* (ערים לשבת)] this has often been explained to mean "cities to dwell in, but not to own"; and so in Jos. 14^4 21^2. But the phrase does not necessarily mean this; for see Dt. 13^{13}, and especially Jud. 18^1. The distinction, if admitted, would be verbal rather than real. In Lev. 25^{32-34} the cities and pasture-land of the Levites are clearly inalienable.—*Pasture-ground*] such may have been the original meaning of מגרש (the place of driving (cattle); cp. מדבר); and if so, the original sense may be still retained in 1 Ch. 5^{16}. But in most of the passages in the OT. (Lev., Nu., Ezek., Ch. only) in which the word *migrāsh* is used, it has acquired a more technical sense, and means, apparently, the land round a town in which the community has common rights (cp. Ezek. $48^{15.17}$). In Jos. $21^{11f.}$, 1 Ch. $6^{40f.(55)}$ the *migrāsh* and *sādeh* (*field*; cp. on 22^{23} n.) are distinguished. Fenton (*Early Hebrew Life*, 38) has suggested that the *migrāsh* corresponded to the arable mark of a German community, *i.e.* the cultivated tract which lay immediately round a town, and was divided among the body of communists; whereas the *sādeh* corresponded to the pasture-mark or more distant land left in undivided commonalty. It is not clear that the present writer has so sharp a distinction between *migrāsh* and *sādeh* in mind; the only use of the *migrāsh* to which he refers is the use of them for pasture (v.[3]).—3. *For their cattle, and for their possessions, and for all their beasts*] between two words for living things, רכוש probably has the same meaning: cp. for such a use Gn. 13^6 and, perhaps, 31^{18}. The terms seem to be combined for effect, without thought of exact distinctions.—4. The pasture-ground or *migrāsh* is to extend 1000 cubits, *i.e.* about 500 yards from the wall of the town.—5. Each side (פאה) of the *migrāsh* is to measure 2000 cubits, *i.e.* about 1000 yards; thus the *migrāsh* is to be an exact square. Some (*e.g.* Di.), it is true, understand v.[4] and v.[5] taken together to

mean that the *migrāsh* shall consist of four plots of ground, each adjoining the side of the town, but not necessarily connected with one another, and each consisting of 2000 × 1000 *square* cubits. But this is certainly not the meaning of the text. Nothing could more exactly describe a square than v.[5]; and from this, interpretation must start. V.[4] implies, as Keil recognised, that each side of the *migrāsh* is 2000 + x cubits (x being the length of the city wall); v.[5] distinctly states that each side is 2000 cubits precisely; these two statements are only compatible with one another if $x = 0$, *i.e.* if the city be reduced to a point. If the text be correct (but see phil. n. on v.[4]), it necessarily follows that the writer in v.[5] forgot to allow for the dimensions of the city. That v.[5] really means, as Keil suggests, that each side of the *migrāsh* is not 2000 cubits, but 2000 cubits + the dimension of the city, is impossible. A remarkable attempt to harmonise v.[4] and v.[5] was made by Saalschütz (*Das Mosäische Recht*, 100 ff.), who took סביב in v.[4] to imply that the city was a circle, the 1000 cubits of v.[4] to be a line from this circle to an outer circle, the 2000 cubits of v.[5] this + a prolongation of 1000 cubits beyond the outer circle in four directions to four *corners* (פאה); the whole plan (of which Saalschütz gives a diagram) is a geometrical star, consisting of four triangles inscribed on a circle.—6 f. The cities are to number in all 48, and are to include the six cities of refuge which are described at length in the next section, v.[9ff.].—8. The tribes are to find cities for the Levites in proportion to their size; cp. 26[54] 33[54]. This is not very accurately observed in the narrative of Jos. 21; for Naphtali gives only three cities, though at the second census (c. 26) it was larger than either Ephraim or Gad, each of which gives four; and though Issachar and Dan are each twice as large as Ephraim, all three tribes give the same number of cities.

2. צו . . . ונתנו] unusual. For a slightly different and also rare formula, cp. 5[2] n.—נחלת אחזתם] the two words are thus combined here only; note the reverse combination אחזת נחלה 27[7].—תתנו] 𝕲 𝕾 יתנו.—מגרש] 𝕲 has no less than four renderings of this word in these 8 verses—*προάστια*, *ἀφορίσματα*, *ὅμορα*, and *συγκυροῦντα*; yet another, *περισπόρια*, appears in Jos. and Ch. The term מגרש was possibly also used in Phœn.: Hoffmann, *Ueber einige Phœn. Inschriften*, p. 6.—**4.** אלף] 𝕲 *δισχιλίους*.—קיר] the word regularly used elsewhere for the wall of a city is חומה: so, *e.g.*, Jos. 2^{15} $6^{5.20}$ (JE), Dt. 3^{5}, Lev. $25^{29.31}$ (H), Am. 1^{7}, 1 S. 31^{10}, Neh. 1^{3}. On the other hand, קיר, frequently used of the walls of a house (*e.g.* Lev. $14^{37.39}$ (P), 1 S. 18^{11} 20^{25}), also of a vineyard, 22^{25} (JE), and of the sides of the altar (Ex. 30^{3} 37^{26}, Lev. 1^{15} 5^{9}—all P), is quite exceptionally used of the wall of a city; Jos. 2^{15} is hardly parallel. This being the case it would be better to question the text (? read מהעיר for מקיר העיר) than to adopt any of the hazardous exegetical devices for harmonising the measurements in v.$^{4f.}$.—**5.** להם] 𝕲 𝕾 S לכם.—**6a.** The cstr. is faulty but possibly original; 𝕲 omits the first אשר, Paterson the second. The meaning of the whole is clear.—**7.** אתהן] cp. Jud. $20^{44b.46b}$, and see G.-K. 117*m*.—**8.** ינחלו] S ינחל.

XXXV. 9–24 (P).—The cities of refuge and the law of homicide.—V.$^{9-15}$, a command to appoint six cities for the reception of persons who accidentally commit homicide; v.$^{16-23}$, illustrations of the difference between manslaughter and murder; v.$^{24-28.30.32}$ (cp. v.$^{19.21b.}$), legal procedure in case of homicide; v.^{29}, a subscription; v.$^{33f.}$, the religious motive of the law. Grammatically, v.$^{22f.}$ and v.$^{24f.}$ are connected.

9 f. Introductory formulæ; with v.^{9} cp. 1^{1} n. (P); with v.^{10} cp. 33^{51} (P).—**10–15.** After Israel has crossed Jordan, six cities, three on the E. and three on the W. of Jordan, are to be appointed as places where all homicides, whether native Israelites, *gêr*, or *tôshāb*, may find an asylum from the kinsmen of the slain person till it can be legally determined whether death was inflicted wilfully or accidentally, and where the person who has accidentally committed homicide may find a permanent asylum (cp. v.$^{24f.}$). The appointment of six cities in accordance with this law is recorded in Jos. 20 (P). Both the present passage and Jos. 20 are at variance with Dt. 4^{41-43}, which refers the appointment of the three cities E. of Jordan to *Moses* himself *before* Israel crossed Jordan. On the relation of Dt. 4^{41-43} to the law of Dt. 19^{1-13}, and of both these passages to the present, see Driver, *Deut.* 78, 230 ff.—**11.** *Then shall ye select as suitable for yourselves cities*] הקרה means "to bring the *right*, or *fit*, thing before one" (cp. Gn. 24^{12} 27^{20}); if the text is right, the vb. has here acquired some such sense as "to select as *fit*, *suitable*"; but unless ויקרו should be read for ויקדשו in Jos. 20^{7},* there is no other instance of such a sense. 𝕲's διαστέλλω (cp. RV. *appoint*) appears to be a

* Kue. *Th. Tijd.* xi. 478.

mere paraphrase both here and in Dt. $19^{2.7}$, where it renders הבדיל. — *Cities of Refuge*] the exact meaning of מקלט is uncertain, but it may mean *place of reception* rather than *place of refuge*. The only other derivative from the root used in the OT. is קלוט (Lev. 22^{23} †), a word of obscure meaning. In Rabbinic the root is chiefly used in speaking of the cities of refuge; but it is also used more widely, as, for example, of the *collection* or *reception* of rain-water (see Levy). If the literal sense be "cities of reception," cp. Jos. 20^{4} "they (the elders of the city) shall receive (יאספו) him into the city." The technical term "cities of refuge" (ערי (ה)מקלט) occurs outside this chapter in Jos. $20^{2f.}$, 1 Ch. $6^{42.52\,(57.67)}$: the fuller phrase עיר מקלט הרצח occurs five times in Jos. 21. D uses no technical term.—*The manslayer*] by itself הרצח rather suggests a wilful murderer (cp. v.$^{16f.}$); it therefore requires here the addition of *the smiter of anyone* (נפש; 5^{6} n.) *unintentionally* (בשגגה; 15^{24} phil. n.).—12. *From a gō'ēl*] read rather with 𝔊, *from the gō'ēl had-dām*; cp. v.$^{19.21}$ (E) "avenger of blood." There is no satisfactory English equivalent for *gō'ēl*, *gō'ēl had-dām*. The primary meaning of the root *g'l* is uncertain; but apart from its secondary metaphorical use with reference to the divine deliverance of Israel, it most commonly means *to discharge the duties resting on one as next of kin*,* whether those duties be to contract a levirate marriage (Ru. 3^{13}), or to exact payment due to the deceased (5^{8}), or to buy a kinsman out of slavery into which poverty has compelled him to sell himself (Lev. 25^{48}), or to buy back a field sold under similar circumstances (Lev. 25^{25}), or to buy property to prevent its passing out of the family (Jer. $32^{7ff.}$). The duty of the *gō'ēl had-dām* must be interpreted in the light of these other duties. "In the event of the depletion of the family life by the loss of blood—the loss of a life—the goel had a responsibility of securing to the family an equivalent of that loss, by other blood, or by an agreed payment for its value. His mission was not vengeance, but equity. He was not an avenger, but a redeemer, a

* Cp. the Arabic *wâlî*, which corresponds to the Heb. *gō'ēl had-dām*, but means primarily *the one who stands near*, *the friend*: Goldziher, *Muham. Studien*, ii. 286.

restorer, a balancer" (Clay Trumbull, *Blood Covenant*, 260). The *gō'ēl had-dām* belongs properly to a period of family organisation; and the part played by him is only one instance of survivals from an earlier and simpler organisation in the more complex social life which the Hebrews subsequently developed. In three important respects the present law modifies the ancient custom: (1) It insists that life is to be forfeited only in case of wilful murder; in primitive custom it makes no difference whether loss of life was due to malice or accident; in either case loss had been inflicted on one family by another, and it was the duty of the *gō'ēl* to see that that loss was made good. (2) The law tacitly insists that the life of the actual murderer only can become forfeit. In primitive custom it was a matter of indifference whether the loss inflicted on a family was made good by shedding the blood of the actual homicide or another member of his family; cp. the case of the seven members of Saul's family slain for his offence (2 S. $21^{1ff.}$), and the still existing custom in Arabia according to which, when homicide is paid off in money, the money is exacted from all male members of the tribe.* (3) The law forbids the acceptance of a money equivalent for a forfeited life. But in spite of these important modifications the law is transitional; it still leaves the exaction of the forfeited life to the *gō'ēl had-dām*, the representative of the family, instead of making it the duty of a representative of the whole community; and thus it does not abolish the ancient family institution, but simply modifies and regulates it in the larger interests of the State. In the case of accidental homicide the community or State prevents the *gō'ēl* discharging his duty to his family; in the case of murder, it insists that he shall discharge that duty in a particular way, viz. by taking the life of the murderer. But though it thus remains to the last transitional, Hebrew law marks a very distinct advance by so modifying primitive custom as to secure an *adequate* punishment for the *individual* guilty of murder, and a clear distinction between accidental and wilful homicide.†—*The congregation*]

* W. R. Smith, *Kinship and Marriage in Arabia*, 262 f.

† See, further, on various points alluded to, Driver, *Deut.* 234, and

1[2] n. and phil. n. In what way, or by what representative body, the community acted in determining the guilt or innocence of one accused of murder is not stated either here or in v.[25f.]; the same vagueness marks other passages where judicial decision or execution is referred to the whole people; see 15[32-36], Lev. 24[14-16]. To limit *the congregation* here to the community of the place to which the homicide belonged (Di.) would make the procedure prescribed somewhat similar to that required in Dt. 19[12], but it would involve giving the phrase a meaning different from that with which it is constantly used by P.—**14.** *Beyond Jordan*] *i.e.* east of Jordan: the term is used anachronistically, for the people are represented as being E. of Jordan at the time this law is given (cp. v.[10] 22[1] 36[13]).—**15.** *The gêr*] 15[13] n.—*The tôshāb*] the term is confined to P (Gn. 23[4], Ex. 12[45], Lev. 22[10] 25[6. 23. 35. 40. 45. 47]) and Ps. 39[13], 1 Ch. 29[15]; it did not occur in the original text of 1 K. 17[1] (see 𝔊). The exact meaning of the term is not clear; possibly the *tôshāb*, or *settler*, was a person not of Hebrew birth, who was attached to a Hebrew family in some more permanent way than the day-labourer (שׂכיר); see n. on Lev. 25[6] in *SBOT.*, and cp. Ex. 12[45] with Baentsch's note.

16–23. The distinction between murder and manslaughter exemplified. — Cp. and ct. Ex. 21[12-14], Dt. 19[4f. 11f.]. The fundamental distinction is one of intention. Evidence of intention is to be sought in (*a*) the character of the instrument, v.[16-18]; (*b*) the previous feelings, or the feelings at the time of the homicide, whether friendly or the reverse, v.[20-23]. Obviously (*a*) and (*b*) may clash; apparently, if death resulted from the blow of a murderous instrument, the burden of proving lack of intention and absence of previous unfriendly relations with the slain man lay on the homicide; cp. v.[23] and v.[16-18].—**16–18.** Of the three classes of instruments or objects here mentioned, the two latter are distinctly described as calculated or likely to be the cause of death (אשר ימות בו). Failing evidence to the contrary (cp. v.[23]), the use of any of these

literature there cited, and also his art. "Goel" in *EBi.*; Clay Trumbull, *Blood Covenant*, 259–263; Otto Procksch, *Ueber die Blutrache bei den vorislamischen Arabern und Mohammeds Stellung zu ihr* (Leipzig, 1899).

must be taken as proof of intention to murder, and if death results the user must be adjudged a murderer and die. The case of less serious results from the use of such instruments is considered in Ex. $21^{18f.}$.—16. *An instrument of iron*] cp. Dt. 19^{5}.—17. *A stone in the hand*] *i.e.* a stone that can be grasped or thrown with the hand; cp. מקל יד *a staff carried in the hand*, Ezek. 39^{9}; and similarly 18 *a wooden instrument* such as can be held *in the hand*: so rather than *a stone large enough to fill the hand* (Rashi).—19, like v.^{21b}, anticipates the fuller discussion of procedure in v.$^{24ff.}$.—20 f. But death may be caused by a push or the like (v.^{20a}; cp. v.^{22a}), or by instruments of a type different from those just described (v.^{20b}; cp. v.^{22b}), or by a blow of the hand: in these cases, if previous enmity (איבה, or שנאה) can be proved, or it can be shown that the particular act was premeditated (בצדיה v.^{20b}), the man is a murderer, and to be left to destruction at the hands of the *gō'ēl*. The push, or the use of an instrument not in itself murderous, is, unless proof to the contrary be forthcoming, to be judged unintentional; a fatal blow with the hand cannot be unintentional, but may have been given in the heat of sudden (v.^{22}) anger, and without any intention of inflicting serious damage. —20. *If he push him*] the kind of action implied by הדף may be gathered from Ezek. 34^{21} ("because ye push with the side and the shoulder") and 2 K. 4^{27} (of Geḥazi's attempt to remove the Shunamitess from Elisha's feet).—*Or cast on him*] supply with 𝔊 and v.^{22} *any object* (כל כלי), *i.e.* any object not of the kind contemplated in v.$^{16-18}$, anything which would not ordinarily be employed with intent to kill.—22. Reverse of v.^{20}.—23. Continuation of v.^{22}: even if death has resulted from a murderous implement, the charge of murder can be repulsed by showing that the homicide did not see the slain man when he allowed the implement to fall, and that he had no previous enmity towards the deceased, nor any unsatisfied grudge. This case is the closest parallel to the only instance cited in Dt. 19, though even this case is very differently described in the two laws. The logical and symmetrical conclusion to this v. would have been: the manslayer is no murderer; the *gō'ēl* shall not put him to death. And again, logically and actually, v.^{24} belongs quite as much to v.$^{20f.}$ as to v.$^{22f.}$: the question of previous enmity and intent is precisely what the judges have to determine.

18. או] read ואם with 𝕲 S; cp. v.$^{16f.}$ 𝕳; in v.$^{20b. 21. 22b. 23}$ the use of או (=*or if*) is different; it introduces an alternative protasis; and there is but one—a common—apodosis which follows (v.^{22} and v.^{24}) the three alternative protases.—**20.** צדיה] also v.^{22} בלא צדיה †; cp. the use of the verb in Ex. 21^{13}, 1 S. 24^{12} †. The phrase need scarcely be rendered too literally (RV.); rather *insidiously*, or even *intentionally*.—**21.** רצח הוא] 𝕲 + מות יומת הרצח; cp. in 𝕳 v.^{18b} before v.^{19}.—**22.** בפתע] 6^{9} n. †.—**23.** בכל אבן . . . ויפל. The cstr. is irregular; ויפל after the objective clause could be explained by Driver, *Tenses*, § 127, but הפיל takes a direct acc.; the sentence seems to have been begun under the influence of other clauses introduced with the ב of the instrument. The negation of the part. מבקש by לא is also anomalous; Driver, § 162 (p. 205 n. 2).—On בְּלֹא, cp. BDB. 520*a*.

24–32. Legal procedure.—At some place, not the city of refuge itself (והשיבו v.^{25}), the community (cp. v.^{12} n.) is to adjudicate in accordance with the foregoing (v.$^{16-23}$) rules (v.^{24}), and on the evidence of at least two witnesses (v.^{30}); if the infliction of death is found to have been wilful, the *gō'ēl* must slay the homicide (v.$^{19. 21b}$); but if accidental or unpremeditated (v.$^{22f.}$), the homicide is sent back to the city of refuge and there detained till the death of the high priest, after which he may return to his own home (v.$^{25. 28}$); but if he leave the city during the high priest's lifetime, the *gō'ēl* has the right to slay him. In no case may a money payment be accepted either in lieu of the capital punishment for wilful murder, or of detention in the city of refuge for accidental homicide (v.$^{31f.}$).

In the parallel laws (Ex. 21$^{12-14}$, Dt. 19$^{1-13}$) neither the judicial authority nor the term of detention is defined; the elders of the homicide's city, who are mentioned in Dt. 19^{12}, are not the judicial authority; but, in a case otherwise determined to be one of wilful murder, they become intermediaries in the execution of justice. Read by itself, Dt. suggests that the detention was lifelong. While the mere altar was the asylum (Ex. 21$^{13f.}$), detention beside it can hardly have been prolonged; an instance of actual practice in the case of a refugee at the altar is to be found in 1 K. 1$^{50f.}$: the homicide leaves the altar under the protection of a solemn oath. In Jos. 20^{4} (v.$^{4-6}$ omitted by 𝕲) the homicide states his case to the elders of the city of refuge *before admission*, and, subsequently, according to the scarcely self-consistent v.[6], to the whole community.

24. *According to these judgments*] or legal rules; a similar set of legal rules stating what is to be done under given conditions, appear under the same title of משפטים in Ex. 21^1. *These* (אלה) refers to what precedes (in v.[16–23]) as often; see, *e.g.*, Gn. 9^{19}, Lev. 21^{14}, Ps. 15^5.—**25.** *The congregation shall send him back* (והשיבו) *to his city of refuge*, which, it must be inferred, he had left to take his trial.—*The high priest who has been anointed with the holy oil*] for similar redundant definitions, see Lev. 21^{10} 16^{32}. Most frequently in P, Aaron or Eleʿazar (as the case may be) is merely termed "the priest"; occasionally, and chiefly, as here, when no reference has been made by name to the person intended, more distinctive terms or descriptions are used; these most frequently refer to the distinctive anointing of Aaron and his successors (Ex. $29^{7.\,29}$, Lev. 8^{12}); see Lev. $4^{3.\,5.\,16}$ $6^{15\,(22)}$ 16^{32} $21^{10.\,12}$. For the term "high priest" (הכהן הגדל) see v.[28], Lev. 21^{10}, Jos. 20^6 (the only occurrences in the Hexateuch), 2 K. 12^{11} 22^4, Hag. $1^{1.\,12}$, Zech. 3^1, Neh. 3^1.—The determination of the detention of the homicide by the life of the high priest may be a complete novelty in this post-exilic law. It is also possible, as Di. suggests, that it is a modified survival of an earlier practice; it may be that at some of the asyla of ancient Israel, homicides were detained till the death of the chief priest who had charge of the sanctuary.—**27.** *He*, the *gōʾēl*, *has no blood*] viz. to answer for (cp. Ex. 22^1). The *gōʾēl* is free from blame, because the homicide, by leaving his asylum, falls again under the ancient custom that required the *gōʾēl* to kill; the blood shed is therefore not innocent, and does not call for vengeance (cp. Dt. 19^{13}).—**29.** A subscription which, presumably, once stood at the conclusion of a law. The regulations in v.[30–32] may have been drawn from some other law of manslaughter and asylum.—*A statute of judgment*] 27^{11} †.—*Throughout your generations* (10^8 n.) *in all your dwellings* (Ex. 12^{20}, Lev. 3^{17} etc.; CH. 55^{P}). *i.e.* perpetually over the whole country the law is to be valid.—**30.** Two witnesses are required before a capital sentence can be passed; cp. Dt. 17^{6}; Dt. 19^{15} requires at least two witnesses on any charge.—**31.** The wilful murderer is not to be allowed to buy off the death penalty by a money payment. The money equivalent for a life, which the Hebrews called כפר (cp. especially Ex. $21^{29f.}$), was widely prevalent; cp. the Greek ποινή, the Germanic *wergild* (for references, see Driver, *Deut.* p. 234). It seems to have been prohibited at an early period in Israel, though this is the earliest explicit prohibition; see Ex. 21^{12}, Dt. 19^{1-11} (note especially v.^{13}), Lev. 24^{17} (H), Gn. $9^{5f.}$ (P). But in a particular case of loss of life not due to wilful murder, the early code expressly provides for the payment of a כפר (Ex. $21^{29f.}$). Mohammed suffered the ancient practice of making a money payment to continue even in the case of wilful murder (Ḳor. $2^{173f.}$).—**32.** The prohibition of quit-money in lieu of detention at the asylum is peculiar to this law; it serves to bring out the punitive character of the detention.—*For him that is fled*] so RV.; it is a highly questionable rendering of MT. (לנוס), but rightly represents the original text; see below.—**33 f.** The law concludes with a religious motive for carrying it out, or, rather, for the careful distinction between murder and manslaughter, and for the infliction of the death penalty for murder. The land in the midst of which Yahweh dwells must be kept free from pollution (cp. 5^{3} n.); the defilement of Canaan even before Yahweh took up His dwelling there had brought destruction on the former inhabitants (Lev. 18^{25}; cp. Is. $24^{4f.}$). A grievous cause of pollution or profanation, and, consequently, of danger (cp. Dt. 21^{1-9}), is the shedding of blood, especially the blood of the innocent (Ps. 106^{38}; cp. Driver, *Deut.* p. 241); and such pollution can only be expiated by the shedding of the blood of the man who caused it (cp. Gn. $9^{5f.}$).—**34b.** Cp. Ex. 29^{45}.

32. לנוס] 𝔊 already found this reading; **but read** לָנָס. See Paterson's note in *SBOT.*—הכהן] S 𝔊 𝔖 +הגדול; cp. v.$^{25. 28}$ 𝔥. Di. suggests that הגדול may be in all cases a gloss.—**33.** תחניפו] This vb. only occurs in the Hexateuch in this v.—אשר אתם בה] 𝔊 𝔖 S insert ישבים before בה; cp. v.^{34} (𝔥).—**34.** תטמא] read תטמאו with S 𝔊 𝔖 𝔗°.

XXXVI. (P^s). A law regulating the marriage of heiresses.

Ṣelopheḥad's daughters marry their uncles.—This chapter is a supplement to 27^{1-11}. The case of Ṣelopheḥad's daughters there led to the promulgation of a law permitting the daughters of a man dying without male issue to inherit his (landed) estate. The object of that law was to prevent the estate passing away from the man's descendants; as a consequence, so it seemed to be there assumed (27^{4} n.), it would remain a part of the possession of his clan, and, therefore, of his tribe. This supplemental law explicitly enforces that consequence by forbidding women so inheriting to marry men of another tribe.

It thus seems likely that the present passage is a supplement by a later hand. Certain variations in style and expression are then at once explained; note ממשפחת בני יוסף (v.[1]) as against למשפחת מנשה בן־יוסף (27^{1}); וידברו לפני . . . ויאמרו (v.[1f.]) as against ותעמדנה לפני . . . לאמר (27^{2}); the persons approached here are Moses and the princes, "the heads of the fathers' houses" (הנשיאים ראשי אבות); but in 27^{2} they are Moses, Ele'azar, the princes, and all the congregation. This contrast is not removed even if the addition of Ele'azar here (𝔊 𝔖) is not, as it most probably is, merely an insertion from 27^{2}. Ct. also the introduction of the law here (v.[5]) and in 27^{6-8}. The supplementer is mainly influenced in style by P (cp. *e.g.* מטה), but not exclusively; note, *e.g.*, אדני (v.[2]), and, once, שבט (v.[8]).

1–4. The representatives of Gile'ad draw the attention of Moses and the representatives of Israel to the danger that the land allotted to Manasseh will be diminished if Ṣelopheḥad's daughters, who have inherited their father's land (27^{1-11}), marry men of other tribes.—**1.** *The heads of the fathers' houses*] cp. 1^{2} n. $17^{18\,(3)}$ 31^{26} n.—*Of the family of the children of Gile'ad*] Since the sons of Gile'ad (26^{30}) constituted many families (מִשְׁפְּחֹת), the word should perhaps be punctuated as a pl. here and rendered *of the families.*—**1b.** Cp. and ct. 27^{2}.—**2a.** 26^{52-56}.—**2b.** Cp. 27^{7}.—*My lord*] The periphrastic use of *my lord* for *you* never occurs in P^{g}, is common in JE (24 times), and occurs twice elsewhere in P^{s} ($32^{25.\,27}$): CH. 56^{JE}.—*Yahweh commanded my lord . . . and my lord was commanded by Yahweh*] (את אדני צִוָּה יהוה . . . ואדני צֻוָּה ביהוה) the prefixing of the obj. in the first clause and the change to the passive in the second are both strange. Geiger (*Urschr.* 330) surmised that the original form in each case was, *My lord* (*i.e.* Moses) *commanded,* and that the present text originated in a desire to avoid the appearance that Moses gave commands on his own account. In itself the passive of צֻוָּה is not open to objection; for even if Geiger is right in explaining away the punctuation in other Pentateuchal passages, the instances in Ezek. remain. Apart from the doubtful instance in Gn. 45^{19}, צֻוָּה is confined to P and Ezek. (Ex. 34^{34}, Lev. 8^{35} 10^{13}, Nu. 3^{16}, Ezek. 12^{7} 24^{18} 37^{7} †). For ב in ביהוה after the passive, cp. Gn. 9^{6}, Dt. 33^{29}.—**3.** *Their inheritance shall be withdrawn*] 27^{4} n.—**4.** Since the land would pass out of the tribe, not by sale, but by inheritance, it would not be affected by the law of jubilee (Lev. $25^{13ff.}$); it would remain, it is true, in the hands of the descendants (by the female line) of Ṣelopheḥad, but would be permanently withdrawn from the tribe of Manasseh. — **5–9.** The divine decision in the particular case is that Ṣelopheḥad's daughters must marry Manassites (v.[6]), and, generally (v.[8]), that all heiresses must marry within their father's tribe, the motive for the particular decision (v.[7]) and the general law (v.[9]) being the same, viz. to prevent the inheritance of the various tribes from being either diminished or increased by the transference of the portion of an individual family from one tribe to another. The theory frequently failed in practice (see on 32^{34-38}).—**5b.** Cp. 27^{7}.—**11 f.** In accordance with the decision, the daughters of Ṣelopheḥad marry Manassites (v.[12]), and, indeed (v.[11]), the sons of their paternal uncles (דודיהם). — **13.** A subscription, similar to that in Lev. 27^{34}, covering the laws between 22^{1} and 36^{12}. Though the position of this subscription is suitable, that of Lev. 27^{34} is not, since further Sinaitic laws follow in Nu. 1 ff. Addis has therefore surmised that both subscriptions were, as a matter of fact, added when the Pentateuch was divided into five books.

1. משה] 𝔊 𝔖 + ולפני אלעזר הכהן; cp. 27^{2} and see above.—**3.** ויהיו . . . ונוסף] For this hypothetical cstr., see Dr. § 149.—ונוסף] S ונוספה (cp. v.[4] 𝔐); the cstr. in MT. as with יגרע below is impersonal, *an addition shall be made.* In v.[4] יגרע is masc. *before* the fem. subj.; Dav. 113*b*, G.-K. 144*b*.—**4.** אם = *when*, is rare, especially with the impf.; BDB. 50*a b*.—**11.** The order of the names in 𝔐 differs from that in 26^{33} 27^{1}, Jos. 17^{3}; the order in these passages is preserved or restored by S here. $𝔊^{B}$ has here yet another order.

INDEX.

I. ENGLISH.

(See also the Tables of Contents, pp. xi f. and xxvi–xxix.)

II. HEBREW.

(Supplemental to Index I.)

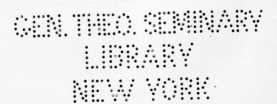

"*A decided advance on all other commentaries.*" — The Outlook.

DEUTERONOMY.

By the Rev. S. R. DRIVER, D.D., D.Litt.,
Regius Professor of Hebrew, and Canon of Christ Church, Oxford.

Crown 8vo. Net, $3.00.

"No one could be better qualified than Professor Driver to write a critical and exegetical commentary on Deuteronomy. His previous works are authorities in all the departments involved; the grammar and lexicon of the Hebrew language, the lower and higher criticism, as well as exegesis and Biblical theology; . . . the interpretation in this commentary is careful and sober in the main. A wealth of historical, geographical, and philological information illustrates and elucidates both the narrative and the discourses. Valuable, though concise, excursuses are often given." — *The Congregationalist.*

"It is a pleasure to see at last a really critical Old Testament commentary in English upon a portion of the Pentateuch, and especially one of such merit. This I find superior to any other Commentary in any language upon Deuteronomy." — Professor E. L. Curtis, of Yale University.

"This volume of Professor Driver's is marked by his well-known care and accuracy, and it will be a great boon to every one who wishes to acquire a thorough knowledge, either of the Hebrew language, or of the contents of the Book of Deuteronomy, and their significance for the development of Old Testament thought. The author finds scope for displaying his well-known wide and accurate knowledge, and delicate appreciation of the genius of the Hebrew language, and his readers are supplied with many carefully constructed lists of words and expressions. He is at his best in the detailed examination of the text." — *London Athenæum.*

"It must be said that this work is bound to take rank among the best commentaries in any language on the important book with which it deals. On every page there is abundant evidence of a scholarly knowledge of the literature, and of the most painstaking care to make the book useful to thorough students." — *The Lutheran Churchman.*

"The deep and difficult questions raised by Deuteronomy are, in every instance, considered with care, insight, and critical acumen. The student who wishes for solid information, or a knowledge of method and temper of the new criticism, will find advantage in consulting the pages of Dr. Driver." — *Zion's Herald.*

"We believe this series to be of epoch-making importance."
—The N. Y. EVANGELIST.

JUDGES.

By Dr. GEORGE FOOT MOORE, D.D.,
Professor of Theology, Harvard University.

Crown 8vo. Net, $3.00.

"The typographical execution of this handsome volume is worthy of the scholarly character of the contents, and higher praise could not be given it." — Professor C. H. TOY, *of Harvard University.*

"This work represents the latest results of 'Scientific Biblical Scholarship,' and as such has the greatest value for the purely critical student, especially on the side of textual and literary criticism." — *The Church Standard.*

"Professor Moore has more than sustained his scholarly reputation in this work, which gives us for the first time in English a commentary on Judges not excelled, if indeed equalled, in any language of the world." — Professor L. W. BATTEN, *of P. E. Divinity School, Philadelphia.*

"Although a critical commentary, this work has its practical uses, and by its divisions, headlines, etc., it is admirably adapted to the wants of all thoughtful students of the Scriptures. Indeed, with the other books of the series, it is sure to find its way into the hands of pastors and scholarly laymen." — *Portland Zion's Herald.*

"Like its predecessors, this volume will be warmly welcomed — whilst to those whose means of securing up-to-date information on the subject of which it treats are limited, it is simply invaluable." — *Edinburgh Scotsman.*

"The work is done in an atmosphere of scholarly interest and indifference to dogmatism and controversy, which is at least refreshing. . . . It is a noble introduction to the moral forces, ideas, and influences that controlled the period of the Judges, and a model of what a historical commentary, with a practical end in view should be." — *The Independent.*

"The work is marked by a clear and forcible style, by scholarly research, by critical acumen, by extensive reading, and by evident familiarity with the Hebrew. Many of the comments and suggestions are valuable, while the index at the close is serviceable and satisfactory." — *Philadelphia Presbyterian.*

"This volume sustains the reputation of the series for accurate and wide scholarship given in clear and strong English, . . . the scholarly reader will find delight in the perusal of this admirable commentary." — *Zion's Herald.*

"*We deem it as needful for the studious pastor to possess himself of these volumes as to obtain the best dictionary and encyclopedia.*"
—THE CONGREGATIONALIST.

ST. MARK.

By the Rev. E. P. GOULD, D.D.,

Late Professor of New Testament Exegesis, P. E. Divinity School, Philadelphia.

Crown 8vo. Net, $2.50.

"In point of scholarship, of accuracy, of originality, this last addition to the series is worthy of its predecessors, while for terseness and keenness of exegesis, we should put it first of them all." — *The Congregationalist.*

"The whole make-up is that of a thoroughly helpful, instructive critical study of the Word, surpassing anything of the kind ever attempted in the English language, and to students and clergymen knowing the proper use of a commentary it will prove an invaluable aid." — *The Lutheran Quarterly.*

"Professor Gould has done his work well and thoroughly. . . . The commentary is an admirable example of the critical method at its best. . . . The Word study . . . shows not only familiarity with all the literature of the subject, but patient, faithful, and independent investigation. . . . It will rank among the best, as it is the latest commentary on this basal Gospel." — *The Christian Intelligencer.*

"It will give the student the vigorously expressed thought of a very thoughtful scholar." — *The Church Standard.*

"Dr. Gould's commentary on Mark is a large success, . . . and a credit to American scholarship. . . . He has undoubtedly given us a commentary on Mark which surpasses all others, a thing we have reason to expect will be true in the case of every volume of the series to which it belongs." — *The Biblical World.*

"The volume is characterized by extensive learning, patient attention to details and a fair degree of caution." — *Bibliotheca Sacra.*

"The exegetical portion of the book is simple in arrangement, admirable in form and condensed in statement. . . . Dr. Gould does not slavishly follow any authority, but expresses his own opinions in language both concise and clear." — *The Chicago Standard.*

"In clear, forcible and elegant language the author furnishes the results of the best investigations on the second Gospel, both early and late. He treats these various subjects with the hand of a master." — *Boston Zion's Herald.*

"The author gives abundant evidence of thorough acquaintance with the facts and history in the case. . . . His treatment of them is always fresh and scholarly, and oftentimes helpful." — *The New York Observer.*

The International Critical Commentary.

"*It is hardly necessary to say that this series will stand first among all English serial commentaries on the Bible.*"

— THE BIBLICAL WORLD.

ST. LUKE.

By the Rev. ALFRED PLUMMER, D.D.,

Master of University College, Durham. Formerly Fellow and Senior Tutor of Trinity College, Oxford.

Crown 8vo. Net, $3.00.

In the author's Critical Introduction to the Commentary is contained a full treatment of a large number of important topics connected with the study of the Gospel, among which are the following: The Author of the Book — The Sources of the Gospel — Object and Plan of the Gospel — Characteristics, Style and Language — The Integrity of the Gospel — The Text — Literary History.

FROM THE AUTHOR'S PREFACE.

If this Commentary has any special features, they will perhaps be found in the illustrations from Jewish writings, in the abundance of references to the Septuagint, and to the Acts and other books of the New Testament, in the frequent quotations of renderings in the Latin versions, and in the attention which has been paid, both in the Introduction and throughout the Notes, to the marks of St. Luke's style.

"It is distinguished throughout by learning, sobriety of judgment, and sound exegesis. It is a weighty contribution to the interpretation of the Third Gospel, and will take an honorable place in the series of which it forms a part." — Prof. D. D. SALMOND, in the *Critical Review.*

"We are pleased with the thoroughness and scientific accuracy of the interpretations. . . . It seems to us that the prevailing characteristic of the book is common sense, fortified by learning and piety." — *The Herald and Presbyter.*

"An important work, which no student of the Word of God can safely neglect." — *The Church Standard.*

"The author has both the scholar's knowledge and the scholar's spirit necessary for the preparation of such a commentary. . . . We know of nothing on the Third Gospel which more thoroughly meets the wants of the Biblical scholar." — *The Outlook.*

"The author is not only a profound scholar, but a chastened and reverent Christian, who undertakes to interpret a Gospel of Christ, so as to show Christ in his grandeur and loveliness of character." — *The Southern Churchman.*

"It is a valuable and welcome addition to our somewhat scanty stock of first-class commentaries on the Third Gospel. By its scholarly thoroughness it well sustains the reputation which the INTERNATIONAL SERIES has already won." — Prof. J. H. THAYER, of Harvard University.

This volume having been so recently published, further notices are not yet available.

"*This admirable series.*"—THE LONDON ACADEMY.

EPHESIANS AND COLOSSIANS.

By the Rev. T. K. ABBOTT, B.D., D. Litt.

Formerly Professor of Biblical Greek, now of Hebrew, Trinity College, Dublin.

Crown 8vo. Net, $2.50.

"The latest volume of this admirable series is informed with the very best spirit in which such work can be carried out—a spirit of absolute fidelity to the demonstrable truths of critical science. . . . This summary of the results of modern criticism applied to these two Pauline letters is, for the use of scholarly students, not likely to be superseded."—*The London Academy.*

"An able and independent piece of exegesis, and one that none of us can afford to be without. It is the work of a man who has made himself master of his theme. His linguistic ability is manifest. His style is usually clear. His exegetical perceptions are keen, and we are especially grateful for his strong defence of the integrity and apostolicity of these two great monuments of Pauline teaching."—*The Expositor.*

"It displays every mark of conscientious judgment, wide reading, and grammatical insight."—*Literature.*

"In discrimination, learning, and candor, it is the peer of the other volumes of the series. The elaborate introductions are of special value."—Professor GEORGE B. STEVENS, of Yale University.

"It is rich in philological material, clearly arranged, and judiciously handled. The studies of words are uncommonly good. . . . In the balancing of opinions, in the distinguishing between fine shades of meaning, it is both acute and sound."—*The Church.*

"The exegesis based so solidly on the rock foundation of philology is argumentatively and convincingly strong. A spiritual and evangelical tenor pervades the interpretation from first to last. . . . These elements, together with the author's full-orbed vision of the truth, with his discriminative judgment and his felicity of expression, make this the peer of any commentary on these important letters."—*The Standard.*

"An exceedingly careful and painstaking piece of work. The introductory discussions of questions bearing on the authenticity and integrity (of the epistles) are clear and candid, and the exposition of the text displays a fine scholarship and insight."—*Northwestern Christian Advocate.*

"The book is from first to last exegetical and critical. Every phrase in the two Epistles is searched as with lighted candles. The authorities for variant readings are canvassed but weighed, rather than counted. The multiform ancient and modern interpretations are investigated with the exhaustiveness of a German lecture-room, and the judicial spirit of an English court-room. Special discussions are numerous and thorough."—*The Congregationalist.*

The International Critical Commentary.

"I have already expressed my conviction that the International Critical Commentary is the best critical commentary on the whole Bible, in existence."—DR. LYMAN ABBOTT.

Philippians and Philemon

BY

REV. MARVIN R. VINCENT, D.D.

Professor of Biblical Literature in Union Theological Seminary, New York.

Crown 8vo, Net $2.00.

"It is, in short, in every way worthy of the series."—*The Scotsman.*

"Professor Vincent's Commentary on Philippians and Philemon appears to me not less admirable for its literary merit than for its scholarship and its clear and discriminating discussions of the contents of these Epistles."—DR. GEORGE P. FISHER.

"The book contains many examples of independent and judicial weighing of evidence. We have been delighted with the portion devoted to Philemon. Unlike most commentaries, this may wisely be read as a whole."—*The Congregationalist*

"Of the merits of the work it is enough to say that it is worthy of its place in the noble undertaking to which it belongs. It is full of just such information as the Bible student, lay or clerical, needs; and while giving an abundance of the truths of erudition to aid the critical student of the text, it abounds also in that more popular information which enables the attentive reader almost to put himself in St. Paul's place, to see with the eyes and feel with the heart of the Apostle to the Gentiles."—*Boston Advertiser.*

"If it is possible in these days to produce a commentary which will be free from polemical and ecclesiastical bias, the feat will be accomplished in the International Critical Commentary. . . . It is evident that the writer has given an immense amount of scholarly research and original thought to the subject. . . . The author's introduction to the Epistle to Philemon is an admirable piece of literature, calculated to arouse in the student's mind an intense interest in the circumstances which produced this short letter from the inspired Apostle."—*Commercial Advertiser.*

"His discussion of Philemon is marked by sympathy and appreciation, and his full discussion of the relations of Pauline Christianity to slavery are interesting, both historically and sociologically."—*The Dial.*

"Throughout the work scholarly research is evident. It commends itself by its clear elucidation, its keen exegesis which marks the word study on every page, its compactness of statement and its simplicity of arrangement." —*Lutheran World.*

"The scholarship of the author seems to be fully equal to his undertaking, and he has given to us a fine piece of work. One cannot but see that if the entire series shall be executed upon a par with this portion, there can be little left to be desired."—*Philadelphia Presbyterian Journal.*

"*A decided advance on all other commentaries.*"—THE OUTLOOK.

PROVERBS

By the Rev. CRAWFORD H. TOY, D.D., LL.D.

Professor of Hebrew in Harvard University.

Crown 8vo. Net, $3.00.

"In careful scholarship this volume leaves nothing to be desired. Its interpretation is free from theological prejudice. It will be indispensable to the careful student, whether lay or clerical."—*The Outlook.*

"Professor Toy's 'Commentary' will for many years to come remain a handbook for both teachers and learners, and its details will be studied with critical care and general appreciation."—*The Athenæum.*

"The commentary itself is a most thorough treatment of each verse in detail, in which the light of the fullest scholarship is thrown upon the meaning. The learning displayed throughout the work is enormous. Here is a commentary at last that does not skip the hard places, but grapples with every problem and point, and says the best that can be said."—*Presbyterian Banner.*

"Professor Toy's commentary on Proverbs maintains the highest standard of the International Critical Commentaries. We can give no higher praise. Proverbs presents comparatively few problems in criticism, but offers large opportunities to the expositor and exegete. Professor Toy's work is thorough and complete."—*The Congregationalist.*

"This addition to 'The International Critical Commentary' has the same characteristics of thoroughness and painstaking scholarship as the preceding issues of the series. In the critical treatment of the text, in noting the various readings and the force of the words in the original Hebrew, it leaves nothing to be desired."—*The Christian Intelligencer.*

"A first-class, up-to-date, critical and exegetical commentary on the Book of Proverbs in the English language was one of the crying needs of Biblical scholarship. Accordingly, we may not be yielding to the latest addition to the International Critical Series the tribute it deserves, when we say that it at once takes the first place in its class. That place it undoubtedly deserves, however, and would have secured even against much more formidable competitors than it happens to have. It is altogether a well-arranged, lucid exposition of this unique book in the Bible, based on a careful study of the text and the linguistic and historical background of every part of it."—*The Interior.*

"While this commentary is called 'critical' and is such, it is not one in which the apparatus is spread out in detail; it is one which any intelligent English reader can readily use and thoroughly understand"—*The Evangelist.*

The International Theological Library.

EDITORS' PREFACE.

THEOLOGY has made great and rapid advances in recent years. New lines of investigation have been opened up, fresh light has been cast upon many subjects of the deepest interest, and the historical method has been applied with important results. This has prepared the way for a Library of Theological Science, and has created the demand for it. It has also made it at once opportune and practicable now to secure the services of specialists in the different departments of Theology, and to associate them in an enterprise which will furnish a record of Theological inquiry up to date.

This Library is designed to cover the whole field of Christian Theology. Each volume is to be complete in itself, while, at the same time, it will form part of a carefully planned whole. One of the Editors is to prepare a volume of Theological Encyclopædia which will give the history and literature of each department, as well as of Theology as a whole.

The Library is intended to form a series of Text-Books for Students of Theology.

The Authors, therefore, aim at conciseness and compactness of statement. At the same time, they have in view that large and increasing class of students, in other departments of inquiry, who desire to have a systematic and thorough exposition of Theological Science. Technical matters will therefore be thrown into the form of notes, and the text will be made as readable and attractive as possible.

The Library is international and interconfessional. It will be conducted in a catholic spirit, and in the interests of Theology as a science.

Its aim will be to give full and impartial statements both of the results of Theological Science and of the questions which are still at issue in the different departments.

The Authors will be scholars of recognized reputation in the several branches of study assigned to them. They will be associated with each other and with the Editors in the effort to provide a series of volumes which may adequately represent the present condition of investigation, and indicate the way for further progress.

CHARLES A. BRIGGS.
STEWART D. F. SALMOND.

Theological Encyclopædia.	By CHARLES A. BRIGGS, D.D., D.Litt., Professor of Biblical Theology, Union Theological Seminary, New York.
An Introduction to the Literature of the Old Testament.	By S. R. DRIVER, D.D., D.Litt., Regius Professor of Hebrew, and Canon of Christ Church, Oxford. (*Revised and enlarged edition.*)
The Study of the Old Testament.	By the Right Rev. HERBERT EDWARD RYLE, D.D., Lord Bishop of Winchester.
Old Testament History.	By HENRY PRESERVED SMITH, D.D., Professor of Biblical History, Amherst College, Mass. [*In Press.*
Contemporary History of the Old Testament.	By FRANCIS BROWN, D.D., LL.D., D.Litt., Professor of Hebrew, Union Theological Seminary, New York.
Theology of the Old Testament.	By the late A. B. DAVIDSON, D.D., LL.D., Professor of Hebrew, New College, Edinburgh. [*In Press.*

The International Theological Library.

An Introduction to the Literature of the New Testament.	By S. D. F. SALMOND, D.D., Principal of the Free Church College, Aberdeen.
Canon and Text of the New Testament.	By CASPAR RENÉ GREGORY, D.D., LL.D., Professor of New Testament Exegesis in the University of Leipzig.
The Life of Christ.	By WILLIAM SANDAY, D.D., LL.D., Lady Margaret Professor of Divinity, and Canon of Christ Church, Oxford.
A History of Christianity in the Apostolic Age.	By ARTHUR C. MCGIFFERT, D.D., Professor of Church History, Union Theological Seminary, New York. (*Now ready.*)
Contemporary History of the New Testament.	By FRANK C. PORTER, Ph.D., Professor of Biblical Theology, Yale University, New Haven, Conn.
Theology of the New Testament.	By GEORGE B. STEVENS, D.D., Professor of Systematic Theology, Yale University, New Haven, Conn. (*Now ready.*)
The Ancient Catholic Church.	By ROBERT RAINY, D.D., LL.D., Principal of the New College, Edinburgh. (*Now ready.*)
The Later Catholic Church.	By ROBERT RAINY, D.D., LL.D., Principal of the New College, Edinburgh.
The Latin Church.	By the Right Rev. ARCHIBALD ROBERTSON, D.D., Lord Bishop of Exeter.
History of Christian Doctrine.	By G. P. FISHER, D.D., LL.D., Professor of Ecclesiastical History, Yale University, New Haven, Conn. (*Revised and enlarged edition.*)
Christian Institutions.	By A. V. G. ALLEN, D.D., Professor of Ecclesiastical History, P. E. Divinity School, Cambridge, Mass. (*Now ready.*)
Philosophy of Religion.	By ROBERT FLINT, D.D., LL.D., Professor of Divinity in the University of Edinburgh.
Apologetics.	By the late A. B. BRUCE, D.D., sometime Professor of New Testament Exegesis, Free Church College, Glasgow. (*Revised and enlarged edition.*)
The Doctrine of God.	By WILLIAM N. CLARKE, D.D., Professor of Systematic Theology, Hamilton Theological Seminary.
The Doctrine of Salvation.	By GEORGE B. STEVENS, D.D., Professor of Systematic Theology, Yale University.
Christian Ethics.	By NEWMAN SMYTH, D.D., Pastor of Congregational Church, New Haven. (*Revised and enlarged edition.*)
The Christian Pastor and the Working Church.	By WASHINGTON GLADDEN, D.D., Pastor of Congregational Church, Columbus, Ohio. (*Now ready.*)
Rabbinical Literature.	By S. SCHECHTER, M.A., President of the Jewish Theological Seminary, New York City.

AN INTRODUCTION TO

The Literature of the Old Testament

By Prof. S. R. DRIVER, D.D., D.Litt.

Canon of Christ Church, Oxford

New Edition Revised

Crown 8vo, 558 pages, $2.50 net

"It is the most scholarly and critical work in the English language on the literature of the Old Testament, and fully up to the present state of research in Germany."—Prof. PHILIP SCHAFF, D.D.

"Canon Driver has arranged his material excellently, is succinct without being hurried or unclear, and treats the various critical problems involved with admirable fairness and good judgment."
—Prof. C. H. TOY.

"His judgment is singularly fair, calm, unbiassed, and independent. It is also thoroughly reverential. . . . The service, which his book will render in the present confusion of mind on this great subject, can scarcely be overestimated."—*The London Times.*

"As a whole, there is probably no book in the English language equal to this 'Introduction to the Literature of the Old Testament' for the student who desires to understand what the modern criticism *thinks* about the Bible."—Dr. LYMAN ABBOTT, *in the Outlook.*

"The book is one worthy of its subject, thorough in its treatment, reverent in its tone, sympathetic in its estimate, frank in its recognition of difficulties, conservative (in the best sense of the word) in its statement of results."
—Prof. HENRY P. SMITH, *in the Magazine of Christian Literature.*

"In working out his method our author takes up each book in order and goes through it with marvelous and microscopic care. Every verse, every clause, word by word, is sifted and weighed, and its place in the literary organism decided upon."
—*The Presbyterian Quarterly.*

"It contains just that presentation of the results of Old Testament criticism for which English readers in this department have been waiting. . . . The whole book is excellent; it will be found helpful, characterized as it is all through by that scholarly poise of mind, which, when it does not know, is not ashamed to present degrees of probability."—*New World.*

" . . . Canon Driver's book is characterized throughout by thorough Christian scholarship, faithful research, caution in the expression of mere opinions, candor in the statement of facts and of the necessary inferences from them, and the devout recognition of the divine inworking in the religious life of the Hebrews, and of the tokens of divine inspiration in the literature which records and embodies it."—Dr. A. P. PEABODY, *in the Cambridge Tribune.*

The International Theological Library.

A HISTORY OF

CHRISTIANITY IN THE APOSTOLIC AGE

BY

ARTHUR CUSHMAN McGIFFERT, Ph.D., D.D.

Washburn Professor of Church History in the Union Theological Seminary, New York.

Crown 8vo, 681 Pages, $2.50 Net.

"The author's work is ably done. . . . This volume is worthy of its place in the series."—*The Congregationalist.*

"Invaluable as a résumé of the latest critical work upon the great formative period of the Christian Church."—*The Christian World* (London).

"There can be no doubt that this is a remarkable work, both on account of the thoroughness of its criticism and the boldness of its views."

—*The Scotsman.*

"The ability and learning of Professor McGiffert's work on the Apostolic Age, and, whatever dissent there may be from its critical opinion, its manifest sincerity, candid scholars will not fail to appreciate."

—DR. GEORGE P. FISHER, of Yale University.

"Pre-eminently a clergyman's book; but there are many reasons why it should be in the library of every thoughtful Christian person. The style is vivid and at times picturesque. The results rather than the processes of learning are exhibited. It is full of local color, of striking narrative, and of keen, often brilliant, character analysis. It is an admirable book for the Sunday-school teacher."—*Boston Advertiser.*

"For a work of such wide learning and critical accuracy, and which deals with so many difficult and abstruse problems of Christian history, this is remarkably readable."—*The Independent.*

"It is certain that Professor McGiffert's work has set the mark for future effort in the obscure fields of research into Christian origin."

—*New York Tribune.*

"Dr. McGiffert has produced an able, scholarly, suggestive, and constructive work. He is in thorough and easy possession of his sources and materials, so that his positive construction is seldom interrupted by citations, the demolition of opposing views, or the irrelevant discussion of subordinate questions."—*The Methodist Review.*

"The clearness, self-consistency, and force of the whole impression of Apostolic Christianity with which we leave this book, goes far to guarantee its permanent value and success."—*The Expositor.*